LOSS OF CONTROL AND DIMINISHED RESPONSIBILITY

Loss of Control and Diminished Responsibility
Domestic, Comparative and International Perspectives

Edited by

ALAN REED
Sunderland University, UK

MICHAEL BOHLANDER
Durham University, UK

Routledge
Taylor & Francis Group

LONDON AND NEW YORK

First published 2011 by Ashgate Publishing

2 Park Square, Milton Park, Abingdon, Oxfordshire OX14 4RN
52 Vanderbilt Avenue, New York, NY 10017

Routledge is an imprint of the Taylor & Francis Group, an informa business

First issued in paperback 2020

Copyright © Alan Reed and Michael Bohlander 2011

Alan Reed and Michael Bohlander have asserted their right under the Copyright, Designs and Patents Act, 1988, to be identified as the editors of this work.

All rights reserved. No part of this book may be reprinted or reproduced or utilised in any form or by any electronic, mechanical, or other means, now known or hereafter invented, including photocopying and recording, or in any information storage or retrieval system, without permission in writing from the publishers.

Notice:
Product or corporate names may be trademarks or registered trademarks, and are used only for identification and explanation without intent to infringe.

British Library Cataloguing in Publication Data
Loss of control and diminished responsibility : domestic,
   comparative and international perspectives.
   1. Criminal liability of juristic persons. 2. Criminal
   liability of juristic persons--Great Britain. 3. Capacity
   and disability. 4. Capacity and disability--Great Britain.
   5. Provocation (Criminal law) 6. Provocation (Criminal
   law)--Great Britain. 7. Defense (Criminal procedure)
   8. Defense (Criminal procedure)--Great Britain.
   I. Reed, Alan (Matthew Alan) II. Bohlander, Michael, 1962-
   345'.04-dc22

Library of Congress Cataloging-in-Publication Data
Loss of control and diminished responsibility : domestic, comparative and international perspectives / by Alan Reed and Michael Bohlander.
      p. cm.
   Includes bibliographical references and index.
   ISBN 978-1-4094-3175-6 (hardback) -- ISBN 978-1-4094-3176-3
(ebook) 1. Insanity defense. 2. Homicide--Psychological aspects I. Reed, Alan (Matthew Alan) II. Bohlander, Michael, 1962-
   K5077.L67 2011
   345.'05044--dc23
                                                                      2011021124

ISBN-13: 978-1-4094-3175-6 (hbk)
ISBN-13: 978-0-367-60210-9 (pbk)

Contents

Notes on Contributors		*vii*
Preface		*xiii*
	Introduction *Alan Reed and Michael Bohlander*	1
1	The New Diminished Responsibility Plea: More than Mere Modernisation? *Ronnie Mackay*	9
2	The Modern Partial Defence of Diminished Responsibility *Rudi Fortson QC*	21
3	Loss of Self-Control under the Coroners and Justice Act 2009: Oh No! *Barry Mitchell*	39
4	The Model of Tolerance and Self-Restraint *Richard Taylor*	51
5	The Serious Wrong of Domestic Abuse and the Loss of Control Defence *Jonathan Herring*	65
6	Loss of Self-Control: When His Anger is Worth More than Her Fear *Susan S.M. Edwards*	79
7	Feminism, 'Typical' Women, and Losing Control *Neil Cobb and Anna Gausden*	97
8	Sexual Infidelity Killings: Contemporary Standardisations and Comparative Stereotypes *Alan Reed and Nicola Wake*	115
9	Killing in Response to 'Circumstances of an Extremely Grave Character': Improving the Law on Homicide? *Jesse Elvin*	135
10	The View from Ireland *John E. Stannard*	151

11	Partial Defences to Murder in Scotland: An Unlikely Tranquillity *James Chalmers*	167
12	Anglo-American Perspectives on Partial Defences: Something Old, Something Borrowed, and Something New *Alan Reed and Nicola Wake*	183
13	Provoking a Range of Responses: The Provocation Defence in British Overseas Territories and Crown Dependencies *Claire de Than*	207
14	A Comparative Analysis of English and French Defences to Demonstrate the Limitations of the Concept of Loss of Control *Catherine Elliott*	231
15	*When the Bough Breaks* – Defences and Sentencing Options Available in Battered Women and Similar Scenarios under German Criminal Law *Michael Bohlander*	247
16	Partial Defences to Murder in New Zealand *Warren Brookbanks*	271
17	Abnormal Mental State Mitigations of Murder: The US Perspective *Paul H. Robinson*	291
18	The Conflation of Provocation and Justification: An Analysis of Partial Defences to Murder in Islamic Law *Mohammad M. Hedayati-Kakhki*	311
19	Provocation and Diminished Responsibility in Dutch Homicide Law *Hein D. Wolswijk*	325
20	Partial Defences Due to Loss of Control and Diminished Responsibility under Spanish Criminal Law *Manuel Cancio Meliá*	341
21	Between Lack of Responsibility and Dangerousness: Determinism and the Specificity of the French Criminal Law on Lack of Intellectual Insight and Loss of Control *Caroline Fournet*	353
22	Diminished Responsibility and Loss of Control: The Perspective of International Criminal Law *John Cubbon*	367

Index 385

Notes on Contributors

Michael Bohlander is Professor of Law, Durham University. Before joining Durham Law School in 2004, he had been a member of the German judiciary since 1991. From 1999 until 2001 he served as the Senior Legal Officer of a Trial Chamber at the International Criminal Tribunal for the former Yugoslavia in the Hague. In 2010, Professor Bohlander was appointed to the Visiting Chair in Criminal Law at the Rijksuniversiteit Groningen.

He has published ten books and over 110 articles, essays, chapters, etc. His publications have been cited widely by and before courts in several domestic and international jurisdictions.

Warren Brookbanks (LL.B, LL.M, BD) is Professor of Law at Auckland University Law School where he has taught since 1983. He currently teaches in the areas of criminal law, mental health law and therapeutic jurisprudence. He has co-authored Simester and Brookbanks, *Principles of Criminal Law* (3rd edn, Wellington, Thomson/Brookers, 2007) and Bell and Brookbanks, *Mental Health in New Zealand* (2nd edn, Wellington, Thomson/Brookers, 2005). He has co-edited, *Psychiatry and the Law* (Wellington, LexisNexis, 2007) and *Criminal Justice in New Zealand* (Wellington, LexisNexis, 2007). He is also a contributing author and an update author for *Adams on Criminal Law* and *Brooker's Family Law – Incapacity*. Warren was a founding trustee of the Odyssey House Trust (NZ) and is a former president of the Australia and New Zealand Association of Psychiatry, Psychology and Law (ANZAPPL).

James Chalmers is Senior Lecturer in Law at the University of Edinburgh. He is the author of *The New Law of Sexual Offences in Scotland* (Edinburgh, W. Green/Scottish Universities Law Institute, 2010), *Legal Responses to HIV and AIDS* (Oxford, Hart Publishing, 2008) and *Criminal Defences and Pleas in Bar of Trial* (Edinburgh, W. Green/Scottish Universities Law Institute, 2006, with Fiona Leverick). He is currently Editor of the *Edinburgh Law Review*.

Neil Cobb is Lecturer in Law in the School of Law, Durham University, where he co-convenes the research cluster Gender and Law at Durham (GLAD). His principal research interests are feminist and LGBT/queer legal theory, and criminal law and criminology. Neil has published widely in these and other areas, including articles in *Cambrian Law Review*, *Journal of Law and Society*, *Legal Studies*, *Modern Law Review* and *Social and Legal Studies*. Neil is currently independent legal advisor to the North-East CPS Homophobic/Transphobic Hate Crime Scrutiny Panel.

John Cubbon is currently Senior Legal Officer in Chambers at the International Criminal Tribunal for the former Yugoslavia. Previous posts include: Legal Officer, Office of the Legal Adviser, UNMIK (2001–2006); Officer in Charge, Prosecution Services and Court Administration Section, UNMIK (1999–2001); Officer in Charge/Tuzla Team Coordinator/Associate Deputy Head, Judicial System Assessment Programme, UNMIBH (1998–1999); Legal Officer, UNMIBH (1996–1998); Legal and Liaison Officer, UN Office of the Special Coordinator for Sarajevo (1995–1996). He was called to the Bar of England and Wales in 1993.

Susan S.M. Edwards is Professor of Law and former Dean of Law of Buckingham Law School. She is currently University Dean of Research and is a practising barrister and a Door Tenant at Clarendon Chambers, London. She has acted as an expert witness in both civil and criminal cases of domestic violence and also acted in a consultancy capacity with regard to domestic violence in Europe and elsewhere. Her work on domestic violence and homicide spans several decades during which time she has advised the police, the CPS and also trained police forces in Denmark, Spain and Germany. Her work explores the interface of gender and culture, ethnicity and identity as these concepts impose themselves on the construction and interpretation of criminal and human rights law.

Catherine Elliott, LL.B, DEA, Barrister, is a Senior Lecturer at City University London. She has written extensively on both English and French criminal law. Her publications include a successful text book entitled *Criminal Law* published by Pearson and now in its eighth edition; a monograph entitled *French Criminal Law* (Cullompton, Willan, 2001) and a chapter on French criminal law in *The Handbook of Comparative Criminal Law* (Stanford, Stanford University Press, 2011).

Jesse Elvin graduated with a PhD in Law from the LSE in 2005. He is a Senior Lecturer in Law at City University London, where criminal law is one of his specialist fields. He has published in a number of leading journals, including the *Modern Law Review*, the *Cambridge Law Journal*, the *Law Quarterly Review*, the *King's Law Journal* (formerly known as the *King's College Law Journal*), and *Feminist Legal Studies*.

Caroline Fournet (LL.M Lund, DEA Strasbourg, PhD Leicester) was a Senior Lecturer at Exeter University until August 2011 and now holds a Rosalind Franklin Fellowship at the University of Groningen in the Netherlands. Her research interests lie in public international law and human rights law as well as international criminal law and criminal justice. She is the author of two monographs: *International Crimes – Theories, Practice and Evolution* (London, Cameron May, 2006) and *The Crime of Destruction and the Law of Genocide: Their Impact on Collective Memory* (Aldershot, Ashgate, 2007).

Rudi Fortson QC, LL.B (Lond), Barrister, has been a criminal law practitioner for over 30 years at 25 Bedford Row, London, and a visiting professor of law at Queen Mary, University of London. He has written and lectured extensively on criminal law issues. He was a member of the 'Police Foundation Independent Inquiry into the Misuse of Drugs Act 1971', and a member of the 'Criminal Justice Forum' for the Institute of Public Policy Research (IPPR). He is a member of the Criminal Bar Association of England and Wales, the Proceeds of Crime Lawyers Association, the Forensic Science Society, and the British Academy of Forensic Science.

Anna Gausden is a Master of Jurisprudence (MJur) candidate in the School of Law, Durham University, and a member of the research cluster Gender & Law at Durham (GLAD). Her research explores the role of gender in domestic violence and intimate partner homicide, with a view to developing a woman-centred approach to the defences to murder for abused women who kill.

Mohammad M. Hedayati-Kakhki graduated from Durham University in 2008 with a PhD in Middle Eastern Politics and Law. He qualified from Shahid Beheshti University in Tehran in 1990 with a law degree, and subsequently completed a Masters in International Law at the University of Shiraz (Iran) in 1999. He practised in both civil and criminal law as a First Class Attorney within the

Islamic legal system of Iran. Alongside teaching LL.M modules including Islamic law at Durham Law School, he continues his involvement in legal practice by acting as an expert in human rights and asylum cases. He is frequently appointed to conduct research and provide commentary into varying aspects Islamic law. He is also a Special Advisor to the Centre for Criminal Law and Criminal Justice at Durham University.

Jonathan Herring is a Fellow in Law at Exeter College, Oxford University and University Lecturer in Law at the Law Faculty, Oxford University. He has written on family law, medical law, criminal law and legal issues surrounding old age. His books include: *Older People in Law and Society* (Oxford, Oxford University Press, 2009); *European Human Rights and Family Law* (Oxford, Hart, 2010) (with Shazia Choudhry); *Medical Law and Ethics* (Oxford, Oxford University Press, 2010); *Criminal Law* (4th edn, Oxford, Oxford University Press 2010); *Family Law* (4th edn, Harlow, Pearson, 2009); and *The Woman Who Tickled Too Much* (Harlow, Pearson, 2009).

Ronnie Mackay is Professor of Criminal Policy and Mental Health at Leicester De Montfort Law School and has written and researched on mentally abnormal offenders for many years. He is the author of *Mental Condition Defences in the Criminal Law* published by Oxford University Press together with numerous other scholarly publications. He was a member of the Parole Board of England and Wales from 1995 to 2001. He has acted as a consultant to the Law Commission for England and Wales for whom he has conducted empirical studies on unfitness to plead, the insanity defence, diminished responsibility, provocation and infanticide.

Manuel Cancio Meliá: Licenciado en Derecho, 1991; Doctor en Derecho, 1997; Alexander-von-Humboldt Research Fellow, 2002–2009; Doctor *honoris causa*, 2008; Professor of Criminal Law at the Universidad Autónoma de Madrid (since 2008). His publications, regarding criminal law principles, criminal law legal dogmatics, comparative criminal law studies, European criminal law and several single offences, have been published in Spain, most countries of Latin America, Germany, the United States, Italy, Portugal, Great Britain, Turkey, Taiwan and China. He is a member of the advisory boards of several Spanish, Latin American and German journals on criminal law.

Barry Mitchell is Professor of Criminal Law and Criminal Justice at Coventry University. One of his principal research interests is homicide law on which he has published widely. Barry's research has been both theoretical and empirical, and he has worked with various government departments including the Law Commission, the Ministry of Justice, the Home Office and the Crown Prosecution Service. He has conducted public opinion surveys on homicide and the law and recently, in collaboration with Julian Roberts (Professor of Criminology at Oxford University) carried out the first survey of attitudes towards the mandatory life sentence for murder.

Alan Reed graduated from Trinity College, Cambridge University with a First Class Honours Degree in Law, and was awarded the Herbert Smith Prize for Conflict of Laws and the Dr Lancey Prize. Cambridge University awarded him a full Holland Scholarship to facilitate study in the United States and he obtained an LL.M Masters of Law (Comparative Law) at the University of Virginia. After completion of the Law Society Finals Examinations he spent three years in practice in London at Addleshaw Goddard, and also acted as a tutor in Criminal Law at Trinity College, Cambridge. He spent seven years as a lecturer in law at Leeds University, and from

September 2001 has been engaged as Professor of Criminal and Private International Law at Sunderland University.

Alan has published significant monographs, textbooks and articles in the substantive arena in leading journals in England, Australia, New York, Florida and Los Angeles. For the last ten years he has been editor of the *Journal of Criminal Law*.

Paul H. Robinson is one of the world's leading criminal law scholars as well as a former federal prosecutor and counsel for the US Senate Subcommittee on Criminal Laws and Procedures. Among his books are the standard lawyer's reference on criminal law defences, two monographs on criminal law theory, a highly regarded criminal law treatise, and an innovative case studies course book. He was the lead editor of *Criminal Law Conversations* (Oxford, Oxford University Press, 2009), and is author of *Distributive Principles of Criminal Law* (Oxford, Oxford University Press, 2008; also appearing in Spanish and Chinese). Robinson recently completed two criminal code reform projects in the United States and the first modern Islamic penal code under the auspices of the UN Development Programme.

John E. Stannard is a graduate of Oxford University, and has been on the staff of the Queen's University of Belfast since 1977. He has written widely on criminal law topics in a variety of journals including the *Irish Jurist*, *Legal Studies* and the *Law Quarterly Review*, and is the author of a textbook on Northern Ireland Criminal Procedure. He is a member of the Society of Legal Scholars, of the Irish Legal History Society and a fellow of the Institute of Teaching and Learning. He is also a past president of the Irish Association of Law Teachers.

Richard Taylor is Professor of English Law at the University of Central Lancashire. A member of the Law Panel for the 1996 and 2001 Research Assessment Exercises, he has written widely on criminal law and justice. He is a founding author of *Blackstone's Criminal Practice* (published annually since 1991) contributing, inter alia, the 'Homicide' chapter. Recent publications include 'The Nature of Partial Excuses and the Coherence of Second Degree Murder' (2007 Crim LR 345); 'Procuring, Causation, Innocent Agency and the Law Commission' (2008 Crim LR 32–49) and 'Complicity, Legal Scholarship and the Law of Unintended Consequences' (2009 (29) *Legal Studies*, 1–18).

Claire de Than, BA (Hons) LL.B, LL.M is a Senior Lecturer in Law at City University London, having previously held appointments at two London University colleges. A graduate of Queen Mary, University of London, she is the author or co-author of more than 15 books, including Heaton and de Than, *Criminal Law* (Oxford, Oxford University Press, 2010), and de Than and Shorts, *International Criminal Law and Human Rights* (London, Sweet & Maxwell, 2004). She has also published articles in a variety of national and international journals, including the *Modern Law Review*. Her research fields include human rights law, media law and criminal law. She has advised several governments and many organisations on human rights and law reform issues, with a specialism in the law of British Overseas Territories and Crown Dependencies.

Nicola Wake is a Lecturer in Law at the University of Sunderland. Nicola's research interests lie in the complex inter-relationship between intoxication and the partial defences to murder. She is a regular contributor to the *Journal of Criminal Law* in this particular arena, and she co-chaired the first UK conference on the 2009 governmental reforms to the concessionary defences; 'Coroners and Justice Act 2009 – Panacea or Pandora's Box for Partial Defences?'

Hein D. Wolswijk is a Senior Lecturer in criminal law at the University of Groningen. He studied law at the University of Utrecht and graduated in 1991, with special focus on criminal law and legal theory. He obtained his doctorate in 1998 cum laude with a thesis on 'Locus Delicti and Criminal Jurisdiction'. From 1996 until 2000 he was a lecturer in environmental law and criminal law at the University of Amsterdam. Since 2001 he has worked at the Department of Criminal Law and Criminology at the University of Groningen.

Preface

The genesis for the monograph was a conference held on 4th October 2010 at Durham University, jointly hosted by the Centre for Criminal Law and Criminal Justice at Durham and the Criminal Law and Justice Research Cluster at Sunderland University. The conference title was: 'The Coroners and Justice Act 2009 – Panacea or Pandora's Box for Partial Defences', with introductory remarks kindly provided by His Honour Judge Prince, Honorary Recorder of Durham, and Mr Chris Enzor of the Crown Prosecution Service acting as a panel convenor. Serendipitously, the event was held on the very day that the reform provisions in England and Wales, *vis-à-vis* loss of control and diminished responsibility as partial defences for murder, became effective in law. The conference, with world-class presentations in the substantive arena, from academia and practice, engendered stimulating and enervating debates centred around the controversial reform agenda. As such, it operated as a catalyst to extend consideration of this important subject, and to provide an overview and analysis from the UK perspective and beyond on the new law, its relation to previous practice, and potential problems that lie ahead.

Individual chapters within the monograph concentrate on particularised concerns: subjective and objective characterisations; revenge and mixed motive killings; sexual infidelity; conceptualisation of loss of self-control and diminished responsibility aligned with other defences; mistaken beliefs and self-defence; theoretical underpinnings of the reform as excusatory or justificatory in nature; partial defences and legal feminism; and the Law Commission reformulations. The comparative and international chapters provide a wider framework in relation to how other legal systems treat issues of human frailty short of full insanity (loss of control and diminished responsibility) in the context of the criminal law. The aim is production of an edited collection monograph which serves as a leading point of reference in the field of partial defences to murder and with respect to the mental condition defences of loss of control and diminished responsibility in general. In order to operate effectively, domestic laws depend on information about foreign legal systems and at least sometimes, also on comparative interpretation of their roles. It is submitted that this allows a refined application or reconsideration of home law via comparative interpretation and promotes an evaluation and perhaps improvement of our domestic regimes through learning from other countries' approaches. It will aid impacted parties applying their rules in a refined fashion through a comparative interpretation of key terms and optimal policy solutions. It is important, as Yntema highlights, that the focus is not simply on domestic issues and to treat international problems as an exotic sideshow:

> While legal science in each country will and should continue to cultivate first its peculiar institutions and traditions, these can no longer be accepted as the horizon of legal knowledge. The practical, specialized study of indigenous techniques, legislative, judicial and administrative, must be complemented by scientific comparison with other legal systems – to ascertain their manifold bearings on domestic interests; to prepare the reforms that may be desired from time to time to bring the municipal laws into harmony with advancing conceptions of justice and the requirements of the international community; to share in efforts to provide appropriate uniform legislation for the commerce of the world; in fine, to establish a more objective scientific basis

for the consideration of legal problems. To attain these ends, indeed even to appreciate the special genius of each legal system, the comparative method, necessarily supposing intensive historical and functional investigation of particular institutions, is indicated. Without this perspective, as Ihering pointed out long ago, there is no legal science worthy of the name. Blind without history, jurisprudence without comparative understanding can scarcely rise above the level of provincial casuistry and empirical craft.[1]

The debate in the UK is not over in this controversial arena, and the Coroners and Justice Act 2009 has arguably raised more interpretive questions than answers. Moreover, the wider context of overall reform of homicide offences still prevails and may in fact reach towards a more general approach to mental condition defences. Expert descriptions of the wider issues surrounding potential defences and of other legal systems' approaches will serve to stimulate and inform future developments.

We should like to acknowledge the help we have received from many people in the preparation of this book. Our work has been supported by a team of consummate professionals at Ashgate. They have displayed tolerance beyond the call of duty and have shepherded the text to production. A huge debt of gratitude is owed to our colleague Nicola Wake for her marvellous help in all aspects of the editorial process.

---

[1] Hessel E. Yntema, 'Foreword' in Ernst Rabel, *The Conflict of Laws: A Comparative Study* (2nd edition, University of Michigan Press, 1958).

Introduction

Alan Reed and Michael Bohlander

For a long time, the issues of provocation and diminished responsibility have plagued the legal system of England and Wales. The desire to treat people in circumstances at the borders of human endurance or capacity in a compassionate manner conflicted with the high moral threshold against condoning acts of homicide, even if only by reducing the available sentencing framework from the mandatory life sentence for murder. One needs to remember that cases of manslaughter because of loss of control and diminished responsibility are in fact nothing but instances of murder where the application of the mandatory life sentence appears too draconic in comparison to the blameworthiness of the defendant's act. Add to that the scintillation in the case law between the subjective and objective interpretation of the prongs of provocation, as well as the 'benign conspiracy' between prosecution, courts and medical experts in diminished responsibility scenarios and the ensuing high acceptance rate for plea bargains. Reform was thus eagerly awaited.

This volume is mainly concerned with the question of whether the Coroners and Justice Act 2009 delivers that reform. Assuming that the discussion will go on, and this collection is indeed testimony to the correctness of that assumption, we also thought it would be beneficial for the UK debate to have some input from foreign and international jurisdictions, which is the second focus of the book. The first part thus deals with the question from a (wider) domestic point of view which already includes some comparative aspects. The second part then proceeds to outline the major issues of some foreign jurisdictions.

In Chapter 1 entitled *The New Diminished Responsibility Plea: More than Mere Modernisation?*, Ronnie Mackay starts off by exploring the new diminished responsibility plea contained in s. 52 of the Coroners and Justice Act 2009. He questions whether the new plea, in the words of the then Minister, 'is really just a clarification of the way in which that defence works'. By exploring the reasons which prompted the reform of s. 2 of the Homicide Act 1957, he draws on the work of the Law Commission whose original reformulation was developed from a definition proposed by the Law Reform Commission of New South Wales, later implemented in the Crimes Amendment (Diminished Responsibility) Act 1997. The reasons which led to reform in New South Wales are compared together with the way in which the new plea has been implemented in that jurisdiction leading to a reduction in its use. The chapter asks the question whether that is also likely to be the result of s. 52.

Rudi Fortson, in Chapter 2, *The Modern Partial Defence of Diminished Responsibility*, suggests that, contrary to the government's view that revised s. 2 of the Homicide Act 1957 merely 'clarifies' the way in which the partial defence of diminished responsibility works, substantial changes have actually been made to the structure of the partial defence and this chapter considers the practical and theoretical implications of those changes. The revised rules of diminished responsibility are explained in the context of Parliament's decisions not to modify the structure of homicide offences nor to abolish the mandatory sentence of life imprisonment for murder. Whether and to what extent there is incoherence between revised diminished responsibility, the new partial defence of 'loss of self-control', insanity, and 'unfitness to plead', is also discussed.

In Chapter 3, *Loss of Self-Control under the Coroners and Justice Act 2009: Oh No!*, Barry Mitchell recalls that the concept of loss of self-control which is replacing the partial defence of provocation has been heavily criticised for its uncertainty of meaning and its propensity to lead to undesirable convictions for murder. The previous government retained it in order to exclude considered revenge homicides and cases where the killer was 'in full possession of his or her senses'. This chapter argues that these aims are misguided. There are mixed-motive cases in which considered revenge is at least understandable and possibly beneficial. The desire to exclude those 'in possession of their full senses' reveals a failure to understand the rationale of a provocation plea. The overt nature of the killer's physical reaction may give a significantly misleading picture of his state of mind. The loss of self-control defence should be abandoned and replaced by a plea which focuses on the killer's mental state.

Chapter 4, *The Model of Tolerance and Self-Restraint*, by Richard Taylor, looks at s. 54(1)(c) of the 2009 Act which addresses the question usually characterised in the common law as the objective question, although it is in truth a mixture of subjective and objective considerations. It is similarly subjective to the former *Camplin/Holley* test in that it concerns how a person of the age and sex of the accused would react and is similarly objective in so far as it assumes the 'normal degree of tolerance and restraint' of a person of that age and sex. Like the *Camplin/Holley* test it also recognises a further limited subjective aspect but it is formulated quite differently. Instead of asking whether the accused's characteristics would affect the gravity of the trigger for the loss of self-control (formerly the gravity of the provocation question), the statute now directs attention specifically to how a person (of normal tolerance and self-restraint) 'in the circumstances of D' might have reacted. This may open up a broader range of subjective considerations than under the *Camplin/Holley* test, notwithstanding that, rather like the old law, s. 54(3) effectively excludes circumstances 'whose only relevance to D's conduct is that they bear on D's general capacity for tolerance or self-restraint'. The difference is, however, that, whilst roughly the same sorts of things are excluded, there is now no positive requirement that, to be included, D's individual circumstances have to affect the gravity of the triggering conduct. Instead, all D's circumstances are included, provided only that they do not bear on his capacity for tolerance and self-restraint and they can be considered directly in terms of how he might have reacted rather than in relation to what was effectively the subsidiary question of whether they affected the gravity of the provocation/triggering conduct. The chapter asks the important questions to what extent does the tolerance and self-restraint test as enacted represent the best response to the lessons learned from the *Camplin/Smith/Holley* saga and whether the nature of the resultant defence will facilitate or hinder legitimate aims sought to be achieved by the abolition of provocation or by any coherent project of homicide reform, with or without degrees.

Jonathan Herring in Chapter 5, *The Serious Wrong of Domestic Abuse and the Loss of Control Defence*, considers the role played by domestic violence when considering whether conduct will be a 'qualifying trigger' for the purposes of the new loss of control defence. This involves an analysis of the literature on the meaning of domestic violence and identifying the wrong of domestic violence. This will assist in determining when a domestic violence background can render an apparently minor act something 'extremely grave' and generate a 'justifiable sense of being seriously wronged'. Moreover, other acts that might appear to be serious should not be regarded as a qualifying trigger, bearing in mind the domestic violence background of the relationship.

Chapter 6, *Loss of Self-Control: When His Anger is Worth More than Her Fear*, by Susan Edwards, points out that the Coroners and Justice Act 2009, s. 56, abolishes the common law defence of provocation, which relied on a sudden and temporary loss of self-control, and was criticised for privileging male violence but excluding from its ambit battered women who killed out of self-defence and fear. In its place is substituted a statutory defence of loss of self-control. For the first time fear qualifies as a new ground for loss of self-control (s. 55(3)) which will then potentially bring women who kill violent husbands within its ambit and so correct a historical injustice. However, the qualifying trigger to this loss of self-control must be based on a 'justifiable sense of being seriously wronged'. This will undoubtedly leave the question of what is justifiable to the jury, whose sense of justifiable may still be founded on masculinist notions of what is and what is not a justifiable cause of lethal anger. The chapter explores the new legislation and some of the inequities it resolves and some of the habituated thinking it may still perpetuate. The evaluation of the new legislation explores efforts by other jurisdictions to deal with the masculinism within the law and draws on a study of Ministry of Justice cases in provocation/loss of self-control in considering these questions.

Chapter 7 by Neil Cobb and Anna Gausden, *Feminism, 'Typical' Women, and Losing Control*, posits that the new partial defence to murder of 'loss of control' was created in response to compelling feminist concerns that its antecedent – provocation – was profoundly gender biased. The injustice that provocation created for women was demonstrated most clearly by its applicability to intimate partner homicide and domestic violence. The new defence is designed specifically to better protect abused women who kill, and those women killed by their partners. This chapter evaluates the requirement under the new defence that a person of normal tolerance and self-restraint would have reacted in the same or a similar way as the defendant. When judge and jury appraise normal tolerance and self-restraint, the defence directs them to consider the reaction of a person of D's sex (and inevitably, in turn, D's gender). It is argued that neither the Law Commission nor the Ministry of Justice considered carefully enough whether incorporation of sex into the evaluative standard will help or hinder women, and specifically abused women who kill. This chapter draws on a wealth of feminist scholarship which engages with this very question and explores why, while a sexed standard has the potential to ameliorate the structural impact of gender disadvantage, it also creates its own pitfalls for women. It concludes that the legislative schema overstates the role of sex and gender in explaining D's reaction, advocating instead that a reformed defence should abandon explicit reference to sex, so that sex and gender are only considered by judge and jury as part of the wider 'circumstances' of D.

Chapter 8, *Sexual Infidelity Killings: Contemporary Standardisations and Comparative Stereotypes*, by Alan Reed and Nicola Wake, addresses whether the controversial exclusion of sexual infidelity as a qualifying trigger for loss of self-control, contained now in s. 55(6)(c) of the Coroners and Justice Act 2009, fully accords with appropriate contemporary standards and societal mores of the day. The authors evaluate the interpretational difficulties created by the new wording, and focus on the tautological and imprecise nature of this final stage legislative amendment. The discussion embraces the putative search for a rationale to the heat of passion defence, with consequential iteration of the theoretical underpinnings to allow loss of self-control to operate in partially exculpatory fashion. In this regard the US experience in traditional and reform Model Penal Code (hereinafter MPC) states and extant Scottish law provide an important source of comparative extirpation, towards legitimate identification of the defence as grounded in either excusatory or justificatory concepts, or a combination of the two. It is submitted that there needs to be a more compartmentalised and prioritised approach to this sensitive area than simply a blanket exclusion of things said or done which constitute sexual infidelity. Different gradations of culpability may be demarcated, and illustrations are provided, that reflect more directly attitudinal behaviours to loss of self-control and societal concerns *vis-à-vis* appropriate levels of mitigation. Killings prompted by male proprietorialness, sexual jealousy, envy, and premeditation by a cuckolded partner should be excluded from the ambit of this concessionary defence, but in equal measure cases of 'gross provocation' regarding sexual infidelity embracing excessive taunting, sexual humiliation, and extreme breaches of trust ought in appropriate cases to be allowed for consideration by fact-finders. The tension between these parameters may be satisfied through invocation of the power of the trial judge to withdraw the matter of loss of self-control in sexual infidelity killings when there is no predicate on which a reasonable jury properly directed could conclude that it might apply. This is considered in terms of pre- and post-Coroners and Justice Act 2009 reforms, and a *via media* perspective is articulated as an optimal counterpoise.

Jesse Elvin in Chapter 9, *Killing in Response to 'Circumstances of an Extremely Grave Character': Improving the Law on Homicide?*, critically analyses ss. 55(4) and 55(6) of the Coroners and Justice Act 2009. Section 55(4) stipulates that the loss of self-control had a qualifying trigger if 'D's loss of self-control was attributable to a thing or things done or said (or both) which – (a) constituted circumstances of an extremely grave character, and (b) caused D to have a justifiable sense of being seriously wronged'. Section 55(6) explicitly limits the scope of the loss of control defence, providing restrictions in relation to sexual fidelity and preventing it from applying where 'D incited the thing to be done or said for the purpose of providing an excuse to use violence'. The author critically explores four important issues raised by s. 55(4) and s. 55(6). First, the chapter considers precisely what factors the jury can and should take into account in applying s. 55(4). Secondly, it examines whether the thing or things said or done have to be directed against D. Thirdly, it considers to what extent, if at all, D should be judged on the facts as he or she believed them to be where he or she made a mistake about them. Fourthly, it considers the extent of the restriction regarding sexual infidelity and whether this restriction improves the law. The chapter also considers relevant law from other common law jurisdictions, including Australia and Canada.

Chapter 10 by John Stannard gives *The View from Ireland* by explaining, for those readers who are not familiar with Irish law, the constitutional position regarding criminal law both in the north and the south, including the status of the English common law in Ireland following independence, and the way legislative powers in Northern Ireland in relation to criminal law were transferred to the Northern Ireland Parliament in 1921, removed in 1972, and restored in 2011. The chapter sets out the law relating to diminished responsibility, provocation and other partial defences as it has evolved both north and south of the border and also covers insanity, as the content of this defence differs substantially in both parts of Ireland from that seen in England and Wales, thus impacting on the scope of the diminished responsibility defence in both jurisdictions. Finally, it assesses what lessons can be learned from the Irish experience.

Chapter 11, *Partial Defences to Murder in Scotland: An Unlikely Tranquillity*, by James Chalmers, emphasises the striking fact that partial defences to murder in Scots law have been surprisingly uncontroversial compared to the experience of other jurisdictions, something which is perhaps the result of the inevitable lack of case law in a small jurisdiction combined with the benign exercise of prosecutorial discretion. However, both provocation and diminished responsibility have been reformulated significantly by the courts within the last decade (with the latter's formulation being put on a statutory footing earlier this year), while the Scottish Law Commission is about to embark on a major review of the law of homicide. This provides a timely opportunity to consider whether, and to what extent, these defences can survive in their present form.

Alan Reed and Nicola Wake in Chapter 12, *Anglo-American Perspectives on Partial Defences: Something Old, Something Borrowed, and Something New*, address the treatment of the severely intoxicated and mentally abnormal killer in the context of the partial defences to murder. The chapter focuses on extant law prior to the Coroners and Justice Act 2009 legislative reforms, and reflects on the novel classificatory system adopted therein as applied to this discrete category of offenders. How should we reconcile or align conditions of depression with alcohol dependency syndrome in terms of potentially explanatory behavioural patterns towards partial exculpation? Can appropriate delineations be made between chronic/harmful/acute intoxication as relevant factors in the context of diminished responsibility? In respect of individual loss of self-control, how relevant are voluntary intoxication or mental frailties to 'personification' or 'characterisation' of a societal expectation standard of 'reasonable' conduct? A comparative extirpation is briefly provided in this regard by reviewing the position adopted in traditional states in the US, set against the liberalised regime prevailing in the few states that have adopted a version of the MPC. The latter iteration focuses on the standard template of 'extreme mental or emotional disturbance'. It is submitted that extant law ought to reflect contemporary standardisations of attitudinal behaviour. There needs to be an appraisal, in effect as a moral and social barometer, of legitimate and appropriate rectitude and culpability of the chronic alcoholic or mentally abnormal killer.

Chapter 13, *Provoking a Range of Responses: The Provocation Defence in British Overseas Territories and Crown Dependencies*, by Claire de Than, is a comparative examination of the scope and interrelationship of defences to homicide offences, with a particular focus on the relevant laws of Crown Dependencies and British Overseas Territories. There is great variance in the relevant law of these British jurisdictions; some have fully modern written constitutions, some are based on early English common law principles, some have been influenced heavily by civil law principles, and some are yet to incorporate any human rights standards. No such review of this field of law has yet been conducted, and this a particularly opportune time since England and Wales are not the only British jurisdictions undergoing fundamental legal change; human rights, codification and constitutional reform are having an impact on criminal law across many British jurisdictions.

The second part of the collection starts with Chapter 14 by Catherine Elliott, *A Comparative Analysis of English and French Defences to Demonstrate the Limitations of the Concept of Loss of Control*. This chapter looks at the new branch of the loss of control defence: that the defendant killed due to a fear of serious violence. It considers the overlap between this form of the defence and self-defence. The assumption must be that Parliament intended the partial defence of loss of control to be available where the full defence of self-defence would fail. This chapter identifies where the differences lie between the two defences, noting the importance of timing and proportionality for the full defence, and evaluating the relevance of these issues for the partial defence in the light of both the wording of the 2009 Act and accompanying explanatory notes on the timing issue and how the objective test in the Act might be interpreted. The Conservative Party favours an extension of the availability of the defence of self-defence and the implications of this will be considered for the future role of the 'fear of serious violence' branch of the loss of control defence. A comparison is drawn with the availability of these two defences in English criminal law and the absence of a provocation/ loss of control defence in France. Where the defendant feared serious violence the only defence available in France is self-defence and the benefits and weaknesses of this approach will be considered.

Chapter 15, When the Bough Breaks – *Defences and Sentencing Options Available in Battered Women and Similar Scenarios under German Criminal Law*, by Michael Bohlander, takes the discussion to another continental jurisdiction: German criminal law does not know of a separate partial defence of provocation or loss of control, and the general defence of diminished responsibility under §21 of the Criminal Code has application across the board. Depending on the degree of loss of control, the two concepts can actually overlap. There are other instances in German law that allow for human frailty and uncontrollable emotion to be taken into account. The underlying law of the General Part of the Criminal Code and of the individual relevant homicide offences is first outlined and then applied to several Battered Women Scenarios.

Partial Defences to Murder in New Zealand are explained in Chapter 16 by Warren Brookbanks. This chapter examines the history of the provocation defence in New Zealand and offers a critique of factors leading to its recent demise. The abolition of provocation, which has not been replaced with any other partial defence, and the recent introduction of a three strikes sentencing regime has meant that serious violent offenders in New Zealand are significantly exposed to the risk of unfair treatment by the law, but with little corresponding gain in deterrence and public protection. The unwillingness to further investigate partial defences of diminished responsibility and excessive self-defence is discussed, with particular reference to the likely impact of the three strikes sentencing regime on the trial and disposition of serious violent offenders. The chapter concludes with the observation that official opposition to partial defences and the successful removal of provocation from the statute books has left major gaps in New Zealand criminal legislation. Populist punitiveness has made significant gains in New Zealand penal policy and it is likely to remain in the ascendency for the foreseeable future.

Chapter 17, *Abnormal Mental State Mitigations of Murder: The US Perspective*, by Paul Robinson, reviews those US doctrines that allow an offender's abnormal mental state to reduce murder to manslaughter. First, the modern doctrine of 'extreme emotional disturbance', as in the Model Penal Code §210.3(1)(b), mitigates to manslaughter what would otherwise be murder when the killing 'is committed under the influence of extreme mental or emotional disturbance for which there is no reasonable explanation or excuse'. While most American jurisdictions are based upon the Model Code, this is an area in which many states chose to retain their more narrow 'provocation' mitigation, based roughly on common law formulation. Second, the modern doctrine of 'mental illness negating an offense element', as in the Model Penal Code §4.02, allows a killing to be mitigated to manslaughter (or less) upon a showing that a mental disease or defect negated the culpable state of mind required for murder. This Model Code provision too has met with some resistance among the states, many of whom limit the use of such evidence to negate an offense element, although few impose such severe limits as to prevent it from negating the culpable state of mind required for murder.

Mohammad M. Hedayati-Kakhki in Chapter 18, *The Conflation of Provocation and Justification: An Analysis of Partial Defences to Murder in Islamic Law*, provides a rare and critical glimpse into a legal system that is in many ways fundamentally different from the secular European jurisdictions. The Coroners and Justice Act 2009 seeks to redress the imbalance in homicide law stemming from the radically different social circumstances that prevailed at the time of the law's last review over 50 years ago. By targeting the partial defence of provocation – long suspected of being discriminatory toward women – the Act pushes the law of homicide into the era of legislated equality. As the social zeitgeist is a clear determinant of the partial defences' implementation in homicide, this chapter seeks to examine how Islamic countries' substantially different gender interactions impact the law on partial defences of provocation and diminished responsibility. The chapter examines the general Islamic law and the particular countries' statutory equivalents of the 'qualifying trigger' concept found in the Coroners and Justice Act 2009, in particular the type and gravity of provocation necessary to activate the defence. It considers whether these triggers are discriminatory toward women, by examining cases and provisions in countries such as Iran, where the 'trigger' is often satisfied through showing a slight to family honour or an act of infidelity, potentially even serving as a complete defence. The chapter also compares the test of 'diminished responsibility' under the Coroners and Justice Act 2009 with the equivalent criteria, including understanding and self-control, in Islamic jurisprudence.

Chapter 19, *Provocation and Diminished Responsibility in Dutch Homicide Law*, by Hein D. Wolswijk, asks how Dutch homicide law accounts for the phenomena of provocation and diminished responsibility. Dutch law seems to differ fundamentally from English law. First of all, Dutch law recognises neither provocation nor diminished responsibility as independent legal concepts (statutory or otherwise). Secondly, the context in which these phenomena can be accounted for differs from English law: the way homicide is penalised, the sentencing system and defences. With regard to provocation or loss of control and diminished responsibility, several defences may be of relevance. Apart from (justificatory) *self-defence*, there is also *excessive force in self-defence*, which is again a full defence: a person who loses control and goes beyond what is necessary to defend himself (or another person) is, under the circumstances, exculpated (and therefore not liable). The same goes for the defence of *duress*, which is also applicable to murder. With respect to mental disorders, Dutch law recognises only a full defence: a person is not criminally responsible for an act if it cannot be attributed to him because he lacks the necessary mental capacity. In light of the above the chapter asks how the Dutch judiciary deals with provocation and diminished responsibility and whether differences with the English system also lead to different outcomes.

The jurisdiction of Spain, which has been strongly influenced by German doctrine, is addressed by Manuel Cancio Meliá in Chapter 20, entitled *Partial Defences Due to Loss of Control and Diminished Responsibility under Spanish Criminal Law*. As in most other commonwealth countries that derive their principles from a legislative code, Spanish criminal law does not possess a specific regulation of partial defences for murder or homicide. Cases related to these offences are treated according to general legal provisions. Therefore, 'loss of control' and 'diminished responsibility' are treated as cases of partial culpability. In coherence with many continental European legal systems, culpability is defined under the paradigm of whether the offender is capable first of *understanding* the wrongfulness of his act or omission, and secondly, that he is in a position to *behave according* to this understanding. Specific cases – the archaic male honour protection dispositions for husbands cuckolded by an unfaithful wife were removed as early as 1963 – are mainly temporal mental disorder, which can lead to a complete lack of responsibility or its reduction as a partial exoneration ground, and the possibility of mitigation that is provided for cases of violent passionate emotion.

The exposition returns to France with a more domestically oriented analysis by Caroline Fournet in Chapter 21, *Between Lack of Responsibility and Dangerousness: Determinism and the Specificity of the French Criminal Law on Lack of Intellectual Insight and Loss of Control*. Albeit codified in the Code Pénal, grounds for excluding or mitigating individual criminal responsibility for murder under French law are nonetheless rather vaguely defined and arguably open to judicial interpretation on a case-by-case basis. While similarly to the Coroners and Justice Act 2009, French law does provide for diminished responsibility as a partial defence to murder, it fails to consider loss of control and instead concentrates on self-defence and *force majeure*. This chapter proposes to critically review and comparatively assess the dispositions of the Code Pénal in order to consider whether the Coroners and Justice Act 2009 should be considered as a model to follow.

The collection ends with an outlook into the developing field of international criminal law in Chapter 22, *Diminished Responsibility and Loss of Control: The Perspective of International Criminal Law*, by John Cubbon. Diminished responsibility in international criminal law and practice operates within its own framework. The approaches that have been manifested so far in international criminal law, their basis and pointers to their future development are identified. It is suggested that diminished responsibility is more appropriately addressed as a ground for mitigation in international criminal law. The states of mind that give rise to the partial defence of loss of control in English law have been even less frequently considered in international criminal law and practice than those relating to diminished responsibility. The reasons for this are explored. Basic principles relating to loss of control in domestic legal systems are compared with relevant trends discernible at the international level.

The editors and authors hope to have contributed to the ongoing debate about the ambit of the partial defences and to have given incentives to think outside the box. It is not difficult to see that the entire problem in English law is caused by the reluctance of the legislator to remove the mandatory life sentence for murder, and the de facto decision to tie the sentence to the terminology rather than to the substance: both partial defences are nothing but sentencing considerations which due to the historical development and the traditional aversion in English law to any idea of codification or *ex ante* doctrinal approach led the judiciary and the rest of the legal community to invent a stopgap safety valve to avoid the ultimate penalty for murder by simply calling a murder committed under provocation and diminished responsibility manslaughter, in order to arrive at a more lenient sentencing frame. This is blatantly obvious from the fact that both partial defences as such do not apply to attempted murder. Why? Because the sentencing frame for attempted murder does not have a mandatory life sentence, so the partial defences are not needed to arrive at the desired result – possibly they are taken into account as general mitigating factors by the judge. Doctrinally speaking, that does, however, make little sense: a battered woman who attempts to kill her abuser but fails to reach the desired result will still be stigmatised in public and on her record by the label of the word 'murder' whereas the one who actually succeeds will be guilty of mere 'voluntary manslaughter' – the latter being merely another expression for intentional homicide, i.e. what is usually called murder. The perception by the wider public of the term 'manslaughter' is of a much less serious nature than that of 'murder'. The stigma for the failed killer is thus more severe but just as little or maybe even less deserved under current law than when the death of the victim ensues. Of course, the idea of an 'attempted manslaughter offence' is doctrinally difficult – although on policy grounds not impossible – to conceive if there is an intent to kill, but that is not necessary, either: might it not be an idea to solve the conceptual mess by opening the sentencing law up by a general clause based on the ideas underlying both partial defences and allowing for any mandatory minimum sentence to be reduced to a lesser scale without tampering with the substantive characterisation of the offence? In that case, a battered woman would still be called a murderer, but she would get around the life sentence and be treated in exactly the same way as her sister who fails to kill her abuser. Clearly, there are various ways of addressing this thorny issue, yet chances are that some of the issues which led to the reform efforts in the 2009 Act will refuse to go away until a more radical approach is taken.

Chapter 1
The New Diminished Responsibility Plea: More than Mere Modernisation?

Ronnie Mackay

Introduction

A new diminished responsibility plea was introduced into English law by s. 52 of the Coroners and Justice Act 2009. It received Royal Assent on 12 November 2009. The reformed plea was the culmination of work done by both the Law Commission and the Ministry of Justice. What is important, however, is to assess the potential impact of the new plea and, in particular, whether it merely modernises the old s. 2 or goes further than this. Certainly, the former has been the consistent view of the government and the Ministry of Justice. Most recently in the circular dealing with the new plea issued by the Criminal Policy Unit of the Ministry of Justice it is stated that 'It replaces the existing definition of the partial defence with a new, more modern one.'[1] A similar view was expressed by Maria Eagle MP, the Parliamentary Under Secretary of State saying 'it is really just a clarification of the way in which that defence works'.[2] In essence, therefore, the official view has been that the old s. 2 was in need of clarification and modernisation. Clarification, as the old plea did not explain what was involved in the substantial impairment of the defendant's mental responsibility; modernisation because the defence was not drafted with the needs and practices of medical experts in mind, so was out of step with current psychiatric thinking. However, rather than merely update the old s. 2, the new plea introduces a number of new concepts and as such could be regarded as a radical departure from its former self. It is important then to understand why such an approach was adopted.

The New Plea

The new plea for England and Wales[3] is contained in s. 52 of the Coroners and Justice Act 2009 which provides as follows:

---

[1] Ministry of Justice, *Partial defences to murder: loss of control and diminished responsibility; and infanticide: Implementation of Sections 52, and 54 to 57 of the Coroners and Justice Act 2009* (MoJ Circ. No 13, 2010).
[2] Coroners and Justice Bill, Public Bill Committee, 3 February 2009.
[3] Section 52 was implemented on 4 October 2010. Section 53 makes identical provision for Northern Ireland.

52 Persons suffering from diminished responsibility (England and Wales)

(1) In section 2 of the Homicide Act 1957 (c. 11) (persons suffering from diminished responsibility), for subsection (1) substitute—

(1) A person ("D") who kills or is a party to the killing of another is not to be convicted of murder if D was suffering from an abnormality of mental functioning which—

>	(a) arose from a recognised medical condition;
>	(b) substantially impaired D's ability to do one or more of the things mentioned in subsection (1A); and
>	(c) provides an explanation for D's acts and omissions in doing or being a party to the killing.

(1A) Those things are—

>	(a) to understand the nature of D's conduct;
>	(b) to form a rational judgement;
>	(c) to exercise self-control.

(1B) For the purposes of subsection (1)(c), an abnormality of mental functioning provides an explanation for D's conduct if it causes, or is a significant contributory factor in causing, D to carry out that conduct.

It is interesting to compare this with the old plea which provided:

> Where a person kills or is a party to the killing of another, he shall not be convicted of murder if he was suffering from such abnormality of mind (whether arising from a condition of arrested or retarded development of mind or any inherent causes or induced by disease or injury) as substantially impaired his mental responsibility in doing or being a party to the killing.

What is immediately apparent is that other than the words 'abnormality' and 'substantially impaired', very little of the old plea remains and gone is any reference to the term 'responsibility'. Contrast this with the new plea in Scotland contained in s. 168[4] of the Criminal Justice and Licensing (Scotland) Act 2010 which provides:

> A person who would otherwise be convicted of murder is instead to be convicted of culpable homicide on grounds of diminished responsibility if the person's ability to determine or control conduct for which the person would otherwise be convicted of murder was, at the time of the conduct, substantially impaired by reason of abnormality of mind.[5]

From a cursory glance at all three provisions the following tentative conclusion might be drawn, namely that the Scottish provision bears more likeness to the old s. 2 than to its newly reformed counterpart and in that respect seems more akin to an update or clarification than the new s. 2. What

---

4   New s. 51B of the Criminal Procedure (Scotland) Act 1995 as inserted by the Criminal Justice and Licensing (Scotland) Act 2010, s. 168.

5   Royal Assent was received on 6 August 2010 but the provision has yet to be implemented.

then influenced the shape of our new diminished responsibility plea? To answer this we need to consider the role of the Law Commission.

The Role of the Law Commission

Prior to the enactment of the new s. 2 the Law Commission gave full consideration to the question of reforming diminished responsibility first in relation to its work on partial defences to murder[6] and finally in connection with its work on murder.[7] In the former the Commission described past reform proposals which again did not seem to represent any radical departure from the original plea. More importantly, the Commission, drawing on the results of the empirical research it had commissioned, concluded:

> Our view is that for the time being, and pending any full consideration of murder, s2 should remain unreformed. There appears to be no great dissatisfaction with the operation of the defence and this is consistent with our consideration of the results of Professor Mackay's investigation of the defence in practice.[8]

Despite this clear conclusion that no reform was required the Commission under the heading 'A signpost for the future' stated:

> That said, we should not be shy about putting forward our thinking as to how a partial defence of diminished responsibility might be framed, were it to continue to be a defence under a reformed law of murder. We put forward our tentative suggestion as a "stalking horse" against which the wisdom of having any such defence may be judged.[9]

In making this suggestion the following remark is significant in terms of what reform proposal in particular seems to have influenced the Commission: 'We see some attraction in the part of the version proposed by the New South Wales Law Reform Commission.'[10] The Commission continued its consideration of diminished responsibility as part of its work on murder with the result that its 'tentative suggestion', after further consultation, was reformulated into the following recommended definition:

> (a) a person who would otherwise be guilty of first degree murder is guilty of second degree murder if, at the time he or she played his or her part in the killing, his or her capacity to:
>
> (i) understand the nature of his or her conduct; or
> (ii) form a rational judgement; or
> (iii) control him or herself,

---

6   Law Commission, *Partial Defences to Murder* (Law Com. CP No 173, 2003); and Law Commission, *Partial Defences to Murder* (Law Com. No 290, 2004).
7   Law Commission, *Murder, Manslaughter and Infanticide* (Law Com. No 304, 2006) paras 5.83–5.142.
8   Law Com. No 290, 2004 (n. 6) para. 5.86. My empirical study can be found at App. B of that Report.
9   Ibid., para. 5.93.
10 Ibid., para. 5.76.

was substantially impaired by an abnormality of mental functioning arising from a recognised medical condition, developmental immaturity in a defendant under the age of eighteen, or a combination of both; and (b) the abnormality, the developmental immaturity, or the combination of both provides an explanation for the defendant's conduct in carrying out or taking part in the killing.[11]

This proposal was then considered by the Ministry of Justice. In doing so the Ministry of Justice concluded that it was an appropriate vehicle for reform, with the result that, after parliamentary scrutiny, we now have a new diminished responsibility plea modelled on the Law Commission's proposal, subject to the exclusion of 'developmental immaturity'. As mentioned above, however, it seems clear that the work of the New South Wales Law Commission was an important factor in the overall thinking behind our new plea. Accordingly, it seems pertinent to consider this work together with why reform was felt necessary in that jurisdiction and what impact the reformed plea has had.

The Development of Diminished Responsibility in New South Wales

The defence of diminished responsibility exists in four Australian jurisdictions. They are New South Wales, Queensland,[12] the Australian Capital Territory,[13] and the Northern Territory.[14] The

---

11 Law Com. No 304, 2006 (n. 7) para. 5.112.

12 Criminal Code 1899 QLd s. 304A: 'When a person who unlawfully kills another under circumstances which, but for the provisions of this section, would constitute murder, is at the time of doing the act or making the omission which causes death in such a state of abnormality of mind (whether arising from a condition of arrested or retarded development of mind or inherent causes or induced by disease or injury) as substantially to impair the person's capacity to understand what the person is doing, or the person's capacity to control the person's actions, or the person's capacity to know that the person ought not to do the act or make the omission, the person is guilty of manslaughter only.'

13 Crimes Act 1900 s. 14: (1) A person on trial for murder shall not be convicted of murder if, when the act or omission causing death occurred, the accused was suffering from an abnormality of mind (whether arising from a condition of arrested or retarded development of mind or any inherent cause or whether it was induced by disease or injury) that substantially impaired his or her mental responsibility for the act or omission.

14 Criminal Code – NT, s. 159:

159. Trial for murder – partial defence of diminished responsibility

(1) A person (the *defendant*) who would, apart from this section, be guilty of murder must not be convicted of murder if:

(a) the defendant's mental capacity was substantially impaired at the time of the conduct causing death; and
(b) the impairment arose wholly or partly from an underlying condition; and
(c) the defendant should not, given the extent of the impairment, be convicted of murder.

(2) Expert and other evidence may be admissible to enable or assist the tribunal of fact to determine the extent of the defendant's impairment at the time of the conduct causing death.

(3) If the defendant's impairment is attributable in part to an underlying condition and in part to self-induced intoxication, then, for deciding whether a defence of diminished responsibility has been established, the impairment must be ignored so far as it was attributable to self-induced intoxication.

defence was first introduced into New South Wales in 1974 under s. 23A of the Crimes Act 1900. It was then identical to our original s. 2 of the Homicide Act 1957. However in 1993, in the case of *R v. Chayna*, Gleeson CJ expressed dissatisfaction with the plea and called for its possible reform saying:

> The fact that, as the present case shows, there can be such conflicting expert opinion about the application to a given case of the legal principles of diminished responsibility is a matter of concern ... it appears to me that the place in the criminal law of s 23A is a subject that is ripe for reconsideration. ((1993) 66 A Crim R 178 at 189 and 191)

Later in 1997 concerns were expressed about the scope of the plea following the conviction of Graham Cassel for diminished responsibility manslaughter, a plea which the Crown accepted. Although the case attracted considerable adverse publicity, the New South Wales Law Commission considered that such criticism was misplaced.[15]

On 17 March 1993, the Attorney General of New South Wales invited the New South Wales Law Reform Commission to review, inter alia, the partial defence of diminished responsibility with a view to developing proposals for reform and clarification of the substantive elements of the defence. As a result the New South Wales Law Reform Commission issued a discussion paper[16] and in May 1997 published a report which recommended retaining diminished responsibility but with a reformulated test which was as follows:

S23A of the *Crimes Act 1900* (NSW) should be amended as follows:

(1) A person, who would otherwise be guilty of murder, is not guilty of murder if, at the time of the act or omission causing death, that person's capacity to:

(a) understand events; or
(b) judge whether that person's actions were right or wrong; or
(c) control himself or herself,

was so substantially impaired by an abnormality of mental functioning arising from an underlying condition as to warrant reducing murder to manslaughter. "Underlying condition" in this subsection means a pre-existing mental or physiological condition other than of a transitory kind.[17]

---

(4) The burden of establishing a defence of diminished responsibility is a legal burden and lies on the defence.
(5) A defendant who would, apart from this section, be liable to be convicted of murder must be convicted of manslaughter instead.
(6) In this section: *mental capacity*, of a defendant, means the defendant's capacity to:

(a) understand events; or
(b) judge whether his or her actions are right or wrong; or
(c) exercise self-control.

underlying condition means a pre-existing mental or physiological condition other than of a transitory kind.

15   Law Reform Commission of New South Wales, *Partial Defences to Murder: Diminished Responsibility* (Law Reform Com. of NSW No 82, 1997) paras 3.17–3.18.
16   Law Reform Commission of New South Wales, *Provocation, Diminished Responsibility and Infanticide* (Law Reform Com. of NSW DP 31, 1993).
17   Law Reform Com. of NSW No 82, 1997 (n. 15) para. 3.43.

It is this reformulation which clearly influenced our Law Commission when it made its first 'tentative suggestion' for reform in 2003 which was as follows:[18]

> A person, who would otherwise be guilty of murder, is not guilty of murder but of manslaughter if, at the time of the act or omission causing death,
>
> (1) that person's capacity to:
>
> > (a) understand events; or
> > (b) judge whether his actions were right or wrong; or
> > (c) control himself,
>
> was substantially impaired by an abnormality of mental functioning arising from an underlying condition and (2) the abnormality was a significant cause of the defendant's conduct in carrying out or taking part in the killing. "Underlying condition" means a pre-existing mental or physiological condition other than of a transitory kind.

The similarities are marked, although even at this early stage our Commission introduced a causal provision in sub-paragraph (2). However, in much the same way as the Ministry of Justice and the government in England and Wales made changes to the Law Commission's final proposal, so did the New South Wales government. As a result the Crimes Amendment (Diminished Responsibility) Act 1997 (NSW) reformulated the test in similar but not identical terms to the New South Wales Commission's recommendation. In particular, it rejected 'abnormality of mental functioning' in favour of retaining 'abnormality of mind'. In addition it placed the need for the impairment to be substantial enough to warrant murder being reduced to manslaughter in a separate subsection and made it clear in another separate subsection that no evidence as to this factor is admissible. The final reformed New South Wales plea is as follows:

> 23A Substantial impairment by abnormality of mind
>
> (1) A person who would otherwise be guilty of murder is not to be convicted of murder if:
>
> > (a) at the time of the acts or omissions causing the death concerned, the person's capacity to understand events, or to judge whether the person's actions were right or wrong, or to control himself or herself, was substantially impaired by an abnormality of mind arising from an underlying condition, and
> > (b) the impairment was so substantial as to warrant liability for murder being reduced to manslaughter.
>
> (2) For the purposes of subsection (1)(b), evidence of an opinion that an impairment was so substantial as to warrant liability for murder being reduced to manslaughter is not admissible.
>
> (8) In this section "underlying condition" means a pre-existing mental or physiological condition other than a condition of a transitory kind.

---

18 See n. 8 above, para. 5.97.

There are two important points to be noted here about what motivated the reform of diminished responsibility in New South Wales. The first referred to above was judicial concern and some adverse publicity about the difficulties created by the original plea. The second was that such problems could be best dealt with by a reformulation which would make the plea tighter and more difficult to plead successfully. It is clear from the New South Wales parliamentary debates that this latter view was instrumental in the New South Wales government's reform agenda. For example, during debate on the bill the Attorney General for New South Wales stated:

> The bill repeals existing s23A of the Crimes Act 1900 and the defence of diminished responsibility. The bill introduces in its place the new and stricter defence of substantial impairment by abnormality of mind.[19]

I will return to these points in my assessment of the influence of the New South Wales provision on our own new plea but before doing so it seems pertinent to assess in turn whether or not the New South Wales government's attempt to narrow the plea's scope has been successful.

The Operation of the New Plea in New South Wales

In 2006 the Judicial Commission of New South Wales published a monograph which provided a comprehensive empirical study of partial defences in that jurisdiction for the period 1 January 1990 to 21 September 2004. As a result the study was able to compare the operation of the original diminished responsibility plea with the new 'substantial impairment' plea. In doing so the study reached the following conclusions:

- The reform of s. 23A in 1997 appears to have achieved its stated aim. The introduction of the notion of community standards has resulted in a stricter test. We found that, since the reforms, fewer offenders are raising the defence and fewer offenders are succeeding than under the previous diminished responsibility regime.
- Although the numbers are relatively small, success rates in jury trials are lower for the defence of substantial impairment than for diminished responsibility.
- Jury involvement did not change with the introduction of substantial impairment but plea rates increased by around 13 per cent to account for 55 per cent of such. (Partial Defences to Murder in New South Wales 1990–2004, Summary of Findings at pages 9 and 10.)

These results are interesting. They show that while the new plea is being used less frequently and successfully, the majority of successful pleas are not the result of jury involvement despite the clear emphasis on community values in ss. (1)(b). From this emphasis one might have supposed that all, or at least the vast majority, of substantial impairment pleas would come before a jury. But this is not the case. Indeed it is clear from the amended prosecution guidelines that the prosecutor must take into account the jury's role in deciding whether or not to accept such a plea. The Prosecution Guidelines of the Office of the Director of Public Prosecutions for New South Wales states as follows:

> If a prosecutor is contemplating accepting a plea of guilty to manslaughter on the basis of substantial impairment by an abnormality of mind arising from an underlying condition pursuant

---

[19] New South Wales Legislative Council Hansard, Crimes Amendment (Diminished Responsibility) Bill, Second Reading, 25 June 1997, 11064.

to s23A of the *Crimes Act* 1900, the community values inherent in the requirement of s23A(1)(b) are to be taken into consideration.[20]

What is not clear, however, is how the prosecutor goes about making an assessment of relevant community values. Nevertheless it seems clear from the figures referred to above that apparently such difficulties as there may be in taking account of community values are not preventing or hindering the prosecution when considering whether to accept a substantial impairment plea. One wonders, therefore, whether it is in fact the introduction of the notion of community standards which has resulted in a stricter test or whether other elements of the new substantial impairment plea may have had this effect. In short, the confident assertion by the Judicial Commission of New South Wales that the former is the case may be open to question.

A Stricter Plea in England?

A comparison of our new plea with that of New South Wales could lead one to conclude that ours is more rigorous in its requirements. Of course we do not have the community values provision or the exclusion of evidence in respect of that requirement in s. 2, but as was mentioned above, these requirements do not seem to have acted as a barrier to guilty pleas being accepted by the prosecution. But we do now have a number of different/additional requirements to be satisfied in s. 52 which are not present in the New South Wales plea. These will now be explored further.

The 'abnormality' requirement

Both provisions have an 'abnormality' requirement. However, the New South Wales legislature decided to retain 'abnormality of mind' in preference to 'abnormality of mental functioning' which had been preferred by the New South Wales Law Commission. There is no real discussion of this change other than the Attorney General for New South Wales remarking that the term 'has a restricted meaning in the context of this amendment'[21] in that to qualify for the plea the abnormality of mind must be shown to have substantially impaired D's capacity in one or more of the three specified ways. In much the same way here there was little discussion of 'abnormality of mental functioning' other than its being a term preferred by psychiatrists. It also seems a term which is wider than 'abnormality of mind'. However, both are subject to a qualification. The New South Wales provision requires the abnormality of mind to arise from 'an underlying condition' which means 'a pre-existing mental or physiological condition other than a condition of a transitory kind'[22] while s. 52 requires the abnormality of mental functioning to arise from 'a recognised medical condition'. The latter was regarded as desirable in order 'to accommodate future developments in diagnostic practice and encourage defences to be grounded in a valid medical diagnosis linked to the accepted classificatory systems which together encompass the recognised physical, psychiatric and psychological conditions'.[23] While it is difficult to know whether these differing 'abnormality' requirements will exclude any conditions which might formerly have qualified for a diminished responsibility plea, there is a concern that because 'recognised medical condition' focuses exclusively on the need for a defined and demonstrable clinical condition which is medically recognised, it may fail to include those 'mercy killing' cases which in the past qualified for a s. 2 plea. This concern stems from the fact that in such cases the wording of the old plea was so obscure

---

20 Guideline 20, 39.
21 See n. 19 above, 11065 (Attorney General).
22 New South Wales Crimes Act 1900, s. 23A(8), above.
23 Ministry of Justice, *Murder, Manslaughter and Infanticide* (MoJ CP No 19, 2008) para. 49.

that it permitted the psychiatric evidence to be stretched beyond 'recognised medical conditions' so as 'to produce a greater range of exemption from liability for murder than its terms really justify'.[24]

The 'capacity' and 'ability' requirements
Both provisions require that D's ability/capacity must have been substantially impaired in one or more of three ways. One of these ways, namely the reference to 'control', seems essentially the same[25] but the other two are different. First, the New South Wales provision's reference to 'understand events' seems less clear than 'understand the nature of D's conduct' in s. 52, while the former's reference to 'judge whether the person's actions were right or wrong' compared to 'form a rational judgement' is more like the M'Naghten Rules. In short, although it is difficult to predict whether these differences will lead to one plea being more strict than the other, it does seem clear that by focusing on the need for specific abilities/capacities to be impaired before either plea can succeed, the scope of the both will be more limited than that of their predecessors. However, the final requirement which s. 52 alone contains may make this even more likely. It is the causal requirement.

The causal requirement
The New South Wales provision contains no such requirement and as far as is known nor does any other diminished responsibility plea. It will be recalled that in order to plead s. 52 successfully D must prove that the abnormality of mental functioning 'provides an explanation for D's acts and omissions in doing or being a party to the killing' and that such an explanation can only be successfully given if D also proves that the abnormality of mental functioning 'causes, or is a significant contributory factor in causing, D to carry out that conduct'. The first mention of any such causal requirement is in the Law Commission's Consultation Paper on Partial Defences to Murder where it states:

> A possible avenue would be to reformulate the test in terms of causation. The focus would no longer be on whether there was "substantial impairment of mental responsibility" but rather on whether the defendant's "abnormality of mind" *was a significant cause* of his acts or omissions in doing or being a party to the killing.[26]

It did so because of concern about the lack of precision as to what was required for a substantial impairment of mental responsibility. However, at that stage this causal requirement was contained in only one of six alternative formulae put forward for a reworked plea and read:

> (6) an amended version which would provide:

> Where a person kills or is a party to the killing of another, he shall not be convicted of murder if he was suffering from an abnormality of mind (whether arising from a condition of arrested or retarded development of mind or any inherent causes or induced by disease or injury) and that abnormality of mind was a significant cause of his acts or omissions in doing or being a party to the killing.[27]

---

24 Edward Griew, 'The Future of Diminished Responsibility' [1988] Criminal Law Review 75, 84.
25 The New South Wales plea refers to capacity to 'control him or herself' while ours refers to ability 'to exercise self-control'.
26 Law Com. CP No 173, 2003 (n. 6) para. 7.92.
27 Ibid., para. 12.74.

What is at once apparent is that this alternative is identical to the original s. 2 but with the omission of 'substantial impairment of mental responsibility'. In short, there is no reference to three specified abilities which the new plea now contains. In addition, the Law Commission after considerable consultation eventually decided to reduce the strictness of the causal requirement to the one specified in s. 52 (1)(c) of the 2009 Act and no more. However, this did not satisfy the government and the Ministry of Justice, both of whom repeatedly demanded a stronger causal requirement with the result that ss. (1B) now states:

> For the purposes of subsection (1)(c), an abnormality of mental functioning provides an explanation for D's conduct if it causes, or is a significant contributory factor in causing, D to carry out that conduct.

In its circular dealing with the implementation of the new diminished responsibility provisions, the Ministry of Justice explains and defends this causal requirement as follows:

> The aim is that the defence should not be able to succeed where the defendant's mental condition made no difference to their behaviour i.e. when they would have killed regardless of their medical condition.[28]

> This contrasts with the position under the current definition of diminished responsibility which requires that a person's mental responsibility must be substantially impaired but does not specify in what respects this must be so.[29]

It is difficult to understand the purpose behind this new causal requirement other than to ensure that, much like in New South Wales, the new plea should be stricter. Unlike New South Wales, however, if this is indeed the case, it has been achieved covertly rather than overtly. Indeed, as was mentioned in the introduction to this chapter, any tightening up of our original diminished responsibility plea requirements runs counter to the government's clear view that the new plea is merely an updating and modernising exercise and no more. It is also difficult to understand the logic behind this new causal provision. Clearly the criticism of the original plea in the words of the circular was that the old plea merely 'requires that a person's mental responsibility must be substantially impaired but does not specify in what respects this must be so'. But this is no longer the case as the new plea clearly specifies the three abilities, one or more of which must be substantially impaired. In which case what more is needed – once this is proved to have arisen from a recognised medical condition – to satisfy the new causal requirement and how could such a person have 'killed regardless of their medical condition'? Let us consider a hypothetical case where the psychiatric evidence is as follows. D suffers from schizophrenia and killed V while experiencing delusions to the effect that God ordered him to kill. Schizophrenia is a recognised medical condition which led to D's experiencing an abnormality of mental functioning. This in turn is likely to have impaired D's ability to form a rational judgement and so clearly provides an explanation for the killing. The prosecution psychiatrist concurs with all this but unlike the psychiatrist for the defence expresses doubts as to whether the abnormality of mental functioning was the cause or a significant contributory factor in causing D to carry out the killing. One can only hope that this sort of dispute will be rare. But there is nothing to prevent it. A sensible way forward

---

28 HC Deb., 3 March 2009, Col. 410 (citing the Minister in Hansard).
29 MoJ Circ. No 13, 2010 (n. 1) paras 7 and 8.

might be for the courts to interpret this provision so that once it is proved that the 'abnormality of mental functioning' substantially impaired D's ability to (a) understand the nature of D's conduct; (b) to form a rational judgement; (c) to exercise self-control, then this of itself should be a sufficient explanation so that unless there is evidence to the contrary it will be assumed that the abnormality caused, or was a significant contributory factor in causing, D to carry out that conduct. In short, proof of all the other elements of the new plea would mean that in giving his opinion the psychiatrist is entitled, without more, to reach a conclusion that the causal requirement is satisfied. Such an approach would help to avoid the type of conflict referred to above where experts could disagree only on the issue of the causal requirement. However, while this might be a useful practical approach, there is nothing in the drafting of s. 52 to prevent an expert if he/she feels strongly enough about the issue from concluding that a diminished responsibility plea must fail, as the causal provision alone is not satisfied. In essence, therefore, although it remains to be seen how this provision will operate in practice, it does seem hard to avoid the conclusion that its inclusion as a new requirement for a diminished responsibility defence will make proof of the plea more difficult for the accused.

Conclusion

The diminished responsibility plea in New South Wales changed because of clear concerns about its scope and application. The policy was to try and ensure that the reformulated plea would be stricter and, as discussed above, this result has apparently been achieved. The position in England and Wales has, however, been different. When our Law Commission reviewed the diminished responsibility plea there were no similar public concerns about its scope. Indeed the Commission is on record as stating that there was 'no great dissatisfaction with the operation of the defence'.[30] Instead the motivation throughout was, on the face of it, more modest. It was to update and modernise. This may be contrasted with the position of the provocation plea in England and Wales where there were genuine political and policy concerns about its application. In short, therefore, by adopting a revised version of the New South Wales reformulated plea, it is legitimate to ask whether by doing so we have, through the back door, not just updated but also made our new plea stricter and whether this has not been made more likely by the inclusion of an explicit causal provision. It is possible then that what we have achieved in our new s. 2 is a diminished responsibility plea which will be even stricter than its New South Wales counterpart, but only time will tell.

---

30 See n. 8 above.

Chapter 2
The Modern Partial Defence of Diminished Responsibility[1]

Rudi Fortson QC

General Principles and Overview

Introduction

Lord Bingham articulated (extrajudicially) one of the most powerful reasons for the existence of the partial defences to murder, namely, that defendants must be 'neither over convicted nor under convicted' and must be punished appropriately.[2] The purpose of this chapter is to discuss the concept of diminished responsibility as a partial defence to murder, having regard to its origins and development, and to consider the legal issues that now arise under s. 2 of the Homicide Act 1957 as amended and revised by s. 52(1) of the Coroners and Justice Act 2009.

The concept of 'diminished responsibility' has a long history in Scotland, helpfully summarised by the Lord Justice-General (Rodger) in *Galbraith* v. *HM Advocate*.[3] The concept can be traced back to 1873,[4] which has been variously described by Scottish judges as 'diminished responsibility',[5] 'full responsibility to partial responsibility',[6] 'partial responsibility',[7] 'lessened responsibility',[8]

---

1 The author expresses his thanks to Professor David Ormerod (Queen Mary University, London) and to Nicola Wake (Sunderland University) for their comments in the preparation of this chapter. The usual caveats apply.
2 Law Commission, *Murder, Manslaughter and Infanticide* (Law Com. No 304, 2006) para. 1.64.
3 [2001] Scot HC 45; and see *HM Advocate* v. *Gareth Kerr* [2011] HCJAC 17. In *Kerr*, the Appeal Court, High Court of Justiciary held that 'in cases of attempted murder where the question of diminished responsibility of the accused is in issue, it is incumbent upon the jury to take into account any evidence in support of the accused's diminished responsibility in assessing whether he had the necessary wicked intention or wicked recklessness required for murder. If he did not, the accused cannot be convicted of attempted murder but only of a lesser charge of assault, with or without aggravations, by reason of diminished responsibility' [10] (Lord Hardie). This is not the position in English law. See also; Scottish Law Commission, *Report on Insanity and Diminished Responsibility* (Scot Law Com. No 195, 2004) 80–81.
4 In the preface to the third edition of Francis Wharton's *Treatise on Mental Unsoundness Embracing a General View of Psychological Law* (Kay and Brother, 1873) xiv: *Galbraith* [24].
5 *Kirkwood* v. *HM Advocate* 1939 SLT, 210 [37] (Lord Justice-General Normand); and see Transcript of the proceedings in Edinburgh High Court on 8 November 1938, 58, 1939 Justiciary Papers No 5, Advocates Library; and similarly by Lord Justice Clerk Cooper in *HM Advocate* v. *Braithwaite*, at 1945 JC, 57; 1945 SLT, 210, but, a year later, he referred to 'reduced responsibility': *Russell* v. *HM Advocate*, 1946 JC 37; 1946 SLT 93. Similarly, Lord Russell at trial, and Lord Normand on appeal, used the expression 'diminished responsibility': *Carraher* v. *HM Advocate*,1946 JC 108; 1946 SLT 225. Lord Normand used that expression again in *Caldwell* v. *HM Advocate* 1946 SLT (Notes) 9.
6 *HM Advocate* v. *Edmonstone*, 1909 2 SLT, 223, 224 (Lord Guthrie).
7 *HM Advocate* v. *Savage*, 1923 JC 49; 1923 SLT 659 (Lord Alness).
8 *Muir* v. *HM Advocate*, at 1933 JC, 47; 1933 SLT, 404 (Lord Justice-General Clyde).

and 'partial insanity'.[9] In *Galbraith*, the court said that, following *Caldwell* v. *HM Advocate*,[10] the expression 'diminished responsibility' seems to have taken root and it observed that '[even] in England the phrase "diminished responsibility" does not actually appear in the body of s2 of the Homicide Act 1957 but finds a toe-hold in the side-note'.[11] But whereas the body of the original s. 2(1) of the Homicide Act 1957 does at least refer to 'responsibility', the revised s. 2(1) does not. In Scotland, from a date to be appointed, s. 51B of the Criminal Procedure (Scotland) Act 1995 makes explicit reference to 'diminished responsibility'.[12] The history of diminished responsibility in England is short. In 1956, the then Home Secretary introduced a clause in the Homicide Bill, which was to become s. 2 of the Homicide Act 1957, to provide a new defence to those who 'although not insane in [the] legal sense, are regarded in the light of modern knowledge as insane in the medical sense and those who, not insane in either sense, are seriously abnormal, whether through mental deficiency, inherent causes, disease or injury'.[13] The original wording of s. 2 of the Homicide Act 1957 defined diminished responsibility as:

> such abnormality of mind (whether arising from a condition of arrested or retarded development of mind or any inherent causes or induced by disease or injury) as substantially impaired [D's] mental responsibility for his acts and omissions in doing or being a party to the killing.

Given that the House of Lords has considered the original s. 2(1) of the Homicide Act 1957 once in over 50 years[14] and that it appears to have worked largely as Parliament had intended,[15] one may wonder whether any revision of s. 2 of the Homicide Act 1957 was required. On the whole, psychiatrists did not 'have difficulty in forming and explaining to the jury their reasons for an opinion whether the defendant was suffering from an abnormality of mind within section 2'.[16] In its final report on the partial defences, the Law Commission proposed the retention of s. 2 of the Homicide Act 1957 as originally worded 'pending any full consideration of murder'.[17] More recently, the Law Commission and the government concluded that the partial defence of diminished responsibility needed to 'spell out more clearly what aspects of an offender's functioning must be affected in order for the partial defence to succeed'[18] having regard to the four aetiologies specified in the original s. 2 of the Homicide Act 1957. Furthermore, the common law partial defence of provocation was capable of producing hard cases because a key ingredient of that

---

9   Lord Justice Clerk, Dumfries High Court, 13 April 1933, 200, 1933 Justiciary Papers No 8, Advocates Library; and Lord Sands, P 50 (405).

10   1946 SLT (Notes) 9.

11   *Galbraith* v. *HM Advocate*, 2002 JC 1 [26].

12   Section 51B was inserted into the 1995 Act by s. 168 of the Criminal Justice and Licensing (Scotland) Act 2010. At the time of writing, ss. 168–71 of the Criminal Justice and Licensing (Scotland) Act 2010 have not come into force. Note that by s. 171 of the 2010 Act, 'any rule of law providing for (a) the special defence of insanity; (b) the plea of diminished responsibility; or (c) insanity in bar of trial, ceases to have effect'.

13   HC Deb., 15 November 1956, vol. 560, col. 1154; and, see Law Commission, *Partial Defences to Murder* (Law Com. CP No 173, 2003) paras 7.1–7.9.

14   Ibid., Law Com. CP No 173, 2003, para. 7.91; and Law Commission, *Partial Defences to Murder* (Law Com. No 290, 2004) para. 5.84.

15   Ibid., Law Com. CP No 173, 2003, para. 7.91. About half of those who responded to Law Com. CP No 173 addressed the partial defence of diminished responsibility; Law Com. No 290, 2004, ibid., para. 5.3.

16   Law Com. No 290, 2004 ibid., para. 5.50.

17   Ibid., para. 5.86.

18   Ministry of Justice, *Murder, Manslaughter and Infanticide* (MoJ CP No 19, 2008) para. 50.

defence is that the defendant lost his/her self-control.[19] Not only might persons who killed, as a slow-burn response to long-term physical and/or psychological abuse, find that provocation was not available to them, but they might also have struggled to bring themselves within the ambit of diminished responsibility and, thus, they were at risk of being convicted of murder. This risk, exemplified by cases such as *Ahluwalia*[20] and *Thornton (No 2)*,[21] might have been minimised had Parliament modernised the partial defence of 'provocation' in the language proposed by the Law Commission[22] rather than replacing common law provocation with the partial defence of 'loss of self-control'.[23] Consequently, such persons may now be driven to seek to explain their conduct in the language of the revised s. 2 of the 1957 Act. Accordingly, law reform in this area would only constitute an improvement if the partial defences were more effective at distinguishing between cases that justify the imposition of a mandatory life term of imprisonment and those cases that do not. It is respectfully submitted that in the enactment of the two partial defences, under ss. 52–6 of the Coroners and Justice Act 2009, Parliament has introduced a degree of incoherence between them that may prove problematic for the courts.

It is often said that problems associated with diminished responsibility (and other partial defences to murder) could be avoided were the mandatory life sentence to be abolished, but there is no realistic prospect of such a radical reform being implemented. In any event, a 'considerable body of informed opinion' favoured the retention of the defence of diminished responsibility even if the mandatory life sentence were to be removed.[24] Saddled with that reality, the Law Commission, in 2006, proposed a new 'offence structure for homicide',[25] namely, murder in the first and second degree, as well as an offence of manslaughter (and other related offences). Whereas first degree murder would carry a mandatory penalty of life imprisonment, second degree murder would not. The Commission's proposals for the revised partial defences of diminished responsibility and provocation, and participation in a suicide pact, would reduce first degree murder to second degree murder.[26] The Law Commission was guided by the 'ladder principle' by which individual offences of homicide 'should exist within a graduated system or hierarchy of offences' that 'reflect the offence's seriousness without too much overlap between [them]'.[27] Central to the Commission's proposals for revising the defence of provocation was the removal of the common law requirement that the defendant must have lost his/her self-control.[28] It is therefore important that the Commission's revised structure of homicide offences should be seen in the context of *all* of their recommendations and not just part of them.

---

19   Homicide Act 1957, s. 3. See *Duffy* [1949] 1 ALL ER (Devlin J).
20   (1993) 96 Cr App R 133 (CA).
21   [1996] 2 Cr App R 108 (CA).
22   Law Com. No 304, 2006 (n. 2) para. 5.11.
23   See Coroners and Justice Act 2009, ss. 54–6.
24   Law Com. No 290, 2004 (n. 14) paras 5.12–5.14.
25   MoJ CP No 19, 2008 (n. 18) para. 7 referring to Law Com. No 304, 2006 (n. 2); and see Law Com. CP No 173, 2003 (n. 13); Law Com. No 290, 2004 (n. 14) (2004); Law Commission, *A New Homicide Act for England and Wales?* (Law Com. CP No 177, 2005).
26   Law Com. No 304, 2006 (n. 2) para. 1.67. Central to the Law Commission's reforms of provocation was the removal of the element of 'loss of self-control' but not only is this element at the heart of the new partial defence of 'Loss of Self-Control' (Coroners and Justice Act 2009, ss. 54–6), the 2009 Act has also abolished the word 'provocation' from the legal lexicon.
27   Law Com. No 304, 2006 (n. 2) para. 1.64.
28   Ibid., paras 5.11 and 5.20.

In its consultation paper, *Murder, Manslaughter and Infanticide*,[29] the government largely accepted the Law Commission's analysis that a partial defence of diminished responsibility was warranted but, contrary to the latter's recommendations, the government was not prepared to reform the structure of offences for homicide or to abolish the mandatory sentence of life imprisonment for murder. Moreover, the government has put the element of loss of self-control at the heart of the new partial defence of 'loss of self-control'.[30] It is conceivable that unless the courts are prepared to give the expression 'loss of self-control' a non-literal interpretation and, unless the defendant's conduct comes within the rubric of 'diminished responsibility', battered women and other vulnerable persons who deliberately kill as a considered response to their plight, may find that they are at risk of falling outside the revised partial defences, convicted as 'murderers', and sentenced accordingly.

The revised definition[31] of diminished responsibility under s. 2 of the Homicide Act 1957 now includes the following requirements:

a. That the defendant suffered from an 'abnormality of mental functioning' (new s. 2(1) of the 1957 Act);
b. That the abnormality arose from a 'recognised medical condition' (s. 2(1)(a));
c. That the abnormality 'substantially impaired D's ability' (s. 2(1)(a)) to:
   (i) 'understand the nature of D's conduct' (s. 2(1A)(a)); and/or
   (ii) 'form a rational judgement' (s. 2(1A)(b)); and/or
   (iii) 'exercise self-control' (s. 2(1A)(c).[32]
d. That the abnormality of mental functioning 'provides an explanation for D's acts and omissions in doing or being a party to the killing' (s. 2(1)(c)) but 'only if it causes, or is a significant contributory factor in causing D to carry out that conduct' (new s. 2(1B)).

The revised definition of diminished responsibility may prove to be a great deal more profound than a quick reading of s. 52 of the 2009 Act and the accompanying Explanatory Notes, suggest. As Mackay has pointed out[33] little of the original s. 2 of the Homicide Act 1957 has been retained save for the expressions 'substantially impaired'[34] and 'abnormality'. Accordingly, it is difficult

---

29 See MoJ CP No 19, 2008 (n. 18).
30 See Coroners and Justice Act 2009, ss. 54–6.
31 That is to say, s. 2(1), (1A) and (1B) of the Homicide Act 1957, inserted by s. 52(1), Coroners and Justice Act 2009, and which came into force on 4 October 2010: see article 5 of the Coroners and Justice Act 2009 (Commencement No 4, Transitional and Saving Provisions) Order 2010 (SI 2010 No 816).
32 See *Byrne* [1960] 2 QB 396; and *Khan* [2009] EWCA Crim 1569.
33 Conference at Durham Castle, 30 September 2010, *The Coroners and Justice Act 2009: Panacea or Pandora's Box for Partial Defences?*: a collaboration of the University of Durham and the University of Sunderland; and see Ronnie Mackay, 'Coroners and Justice Act 2009 – The New Diminished Responsibility Plea' [2010] Criminal Law Review 290.
34 See *Egan* (1992) 95 Cr App R 278, where it was said in the context of original s. 2 of the Homicide Act 1957: 'Guidance as to the meaning of "substantial" should be explicitly provided for the jury by using one or other of the two meanings in *Lloyd* (1966) 50 Cr App R. 61, [1967] 1 QB 175, i.e. (1) the jury should approach the word in a broad commonsense way, or (2) that the word meant "more than some trivial degree of impairment which does not make any appreciable difference to a person's ability to control himself, but it means less than total impairment".'

to accept that the revised s. 2 of the Homicide Act 1957 merely clarifies the pre-existing law[35] concerning diminished responsibility and, therefore, care must be taken when seeking to draw upon case law decided in relation to the original s. 2 of the Homicide Act 1957.

The organisation 'Dignity in Dying' has argued that the new definition of diminished responsibility will create unjust outcomes for those who 'have acted rationally in response to persistent requests from a seriously ill loved one'.[36] However, for the purposes of the original s. 2 of the Homicide Act 1957, the courts appear to have treated irrationality as a feature of *all* cases of diminished responsibility,[37] whereas, for the purposes of the revised s. 2 of the Homicide Act 1957, irrationality is an aspect of the defendant's ability to do the thing mentioned in s. 2(1A)(b) of the Homicide Act 1957 but irrationality is not a requirement of the remaining two capabilities mentioned in s. 2(1A)(a) and (c). Accordingly, the new definition of diminished responsibility may embrace cases where a person has become clinically depressed as a result of long-term care for a partner who has become increasingly ill.[38]

Diminished Responsibility No Longer Involves a Moral Question[39]

Although the 2009 Act is headed 'persons suffering from diminished responsibility' the key word – 'responsibility' – is absent from the new ss. 2(1)–(1B) of the 1957 Act. This is in marked contrast to s. 51B of the Criminal Procedure (Scotland) Act 1995.[40] The focus of the original s. 2(1) of the Homicide Act 1957 was on whether D's 'mental *responsibility*' for his acts was substantially impaired by reason of his/her abnormality of mind. By contrast, the focus of the revised s. 2(1) of the Homicide Act 1957 is on whether, at the time of the killing, *D's ability to do any of the things mentioned in the new s. 2(1A)* was 'substantially impaired' by reason of D's 'abnormality of mental functioning'.

The impairment of D's mental responsibility had been 'a moral question of degree and essentially one for the jury'.[41] Arguably, it was logical that the ultimate issue should have been framed in terms of 'moral responsibility' because the partial defence of diminished responsibility was (and remains) structured on the premise that the defendant had performed the conduct element of the *actus reus* of murder (for example, killing another person using a knife or a gun) with the *mens rea* required for that offence. However, Griew regarded the wording of the original s. 2 of the Homicide Act 1957 as 'improperly elliptical' and that the word 'responsibility' served a 'double

---

35 'We do not believe that the changes we are proposing to diminished responsibility will change the numbers enormously; it is really just a clarification of the way in which that defence works'; HC Deb., 3 February 2009, cols 8– 9. (Parliamentary Under Secretary of State for Justice, Maria Eagle).

36 Joint Committee on Human Rights, *8th Report* (2008–2009), para. 1.150; evidence 44–5.

37 Consider *Byrne* (n. 32).

38 Public Bill Committee, 3 February 2009, written evidence (CJ/01); Joint Committee on Human Rights (n. 36) para. 1.151.

39 There has been much discussion about this aspect of the original s. 2 of the Homicide Act 1957: see, for example, Susanne Dell, 'Diminished Responsibility Reconsidered' [1982] Criminal Law Review 809; Home Office, *Report of the Committee on Mentally Abnormal Offenders* (Cmnd 5698, 1975); Glanville Williams, *Textbook of Criminal Law* (Stevens, 1978) 624.

40 See n. 12 above.

41 David Ormerod, *Criminal Law* (12th edn, Oxford University Press, 2008) 511. In Scotland, what must be 'substantially impaired' is D's ability 'as compared with a normal person, to determine or control his acts': *Galbraith* (n. 11); and see *Caldwell* v. *HM Advocate* (n. 5), and see Criminal Procedure (Scotland) Act 1995, s. 51B.

function' that was suggestive of the defendant's capacity to comprehend and to conform to the requirements of the law as well as an assessment of culpability for the killing that flowed from his condition.[42] But, as Lord Goddard CJ remarked in *Matheson*,[43] 'an abnormal mind is as capable of forming an intention and desire to kill as one that is normal: it is just what an abnormal mind might do'. By contrast, a 'defect of reason', for the purpose of the defence of insanity under the M'Naghten Rules,[44] concerns the defendant's intellectual ability to perceive that his/her physical acts were legally wrong.[45]

Unsurprisingly, the courts sought a less abstract, less elliptical, basis for determining whether the defendant lacked 'mental responsibility' for the killing. Some members of the judiciary had expressed their dislike of directions to the jury which 'give an undue normative role to their decisions' (Pitchers J), and Mr Justice Stanley Burnton (as he then was) stated that he dislikes a definition that 'involves the jury in a value judgment'.[46] Accordingly, juries were often not directed in terms that required them to act as moral barometers of a defendant's responsibility for the killing to which he/she was a party but to approach diminished responsibility from the perspective of 'essentially seeking to ascertain ... whether at the time of the killing the accused was suffering from a state of mind bordering on but not amounting to insanity. That task is to be approached in a broad common sense way'.[47] That approach was pragmatic and it had the virtue that juries were required to make an objective assessment of the defendant's mental condition notwithstanding that it sidesteps what is at the heart of the original s. 2 of the Homicide Act 1957, namely, the normative issue of D's moral responsibility for the killing. It is submitted that the removal of the term "responsibility" from s. 52 was logical and desirable (by contrast, see L. Kennefick, 'Introducing a New Diminished Responsibility Defence for England and Wales' (MLR (2011) 74(5) 750, at 764).

Inevitably, pleas of diminished responsibility have come to require the assistance of expert medical evidence. However, expressions such as 'abnormality of mind' and 'impairment of mental responsibility' are not recognised medical terms that have a settled meaning.[48] A forensic psychiatrist might be able to 'diagnose' a defendant as suffering from one or more of the four aetiologies specified in the original s. 2 of the Homicide Act 1957, but struggle on the issue of whether 'mental responsibility' had been 'substantially impaired', and the expert may decline to express an opinion on the ultimate issue. However, in practice, forensic psychiatrists frequently have been encouraged to express an opinion on matters that include the ultimate issue.[49] This state of affairs is unlikely to change.

---

42   Edward Griew, 'The Future of Diminished Responsibility' [1998] Criminal Law Review 75.
43   [1958] 1 WLR 474.
44   *M'Naghten* (1843) 8 ER 718; (1843) 10 Cl & F 200, 210.
45   Law Com. CP No 173, 2003 (n. 13) para. 7.26; see also *Byrne* (n. 32); and Ronnie Mackay, 'The Abnormality of Mind Factor in Diminished Responsibility' [1999] Criminal Law Review 117.
46   Law Com. No 290, 2004 (n. 14) para. 5.55 (fn. 61).
47   *Byrne* (n. 32) 404; and *Walton v. R* (1978) 66 Cr App R 25; [1978] 1 All ER 542.
48   Law Com. No 304, 2006 (n. 2) para. 5.111.
49   The Law Commission stated that it was 'apparent from Professor Mackay's study that although a minority of psychiatrists restrict themselves to the first limb of [the original s. 2 of the Homicide Act 1957], almost 70 per cent express an opinion on that 'ultimate question'; Law Com. No 290, 2004 (n. 14) para. 5.51.

Diminished Responsibility and the 'Benign Conspiracy'

Given the importance of psychiatric evidence when diminished responsibility is in issue, a 'benign conspiracy'[50] emerged between the parties to the proceedings and their advising psychiatrists, for the purpose of identifying cases where a plea of guilty to manslaughter on the grounds of diminished responsibility was appropriate and other cases where the issue of diminished responsibility should be determined by the jury. This practice has not enjoyed universal judicial approval but, in this instance, theoretical ideals may appropriately yield to pragmatism.[51] The Law Commission referred to cases where a conviction for murder could only be avoided by a 'benign conspiracy' between the parties to bring cases within the limits of diminished responsibility.[52] Where there is no dispute about the defendant's mental condition and where there is no reason to doubt the defendant's history in relation to it, then a plea of manslaughter on the grounds of diminished responsibility may be justified. Such pleas can only be accepted by the Crown with the approval of the court. It may not be in the public interest to require a jury to determine the issue of diminished responsibility when it would probably be proved by the defendant and where a Mental Health Act disposal is merited.

Concern has been expressed that the revised, tighter, definition of diminished responsibility might reduce the potential usefulness of the defence as a means of giving judges discretion when sentencing persons who have killed but who ought not to be stigmatised as 'murderers'.[53] Given that the existing construction of the offences of murder and manslaughter remains untouched by the 2009 Act, and that the legislator has not excepted killings which have occurred in extenuating circumstances from the mandatory requirement to impose a sentence of life imprisonment for murder, it is unlikely that the revised definition of diminished responsibility will see the end of a practice that has (it is submitted) worked satisfactorily. The burden of proving the partial defence of diminished responsibility remains on the accused,[54] and decisions by prosecutors to accept such a plea are not taken lightly. The existence and exercise of discretion within the criminal justice process has much to commend it,[55] being apt to deal with borderline cases, for example, some 'mercy killing' cases, or the battered spouse who was suffering from post-traumatic stress

---

50 See Ronnie Mackay, 'Diminished Responsibility and Mentally Disordered Killers' in Andrew Ashworth and Barry Mitchell (eds), *Rethinking English Homicide Law* (Oxford University Press, 2000) 79; and see Law Com. No 290 (2004) para. 2.34; see also Tenney Cotton, 'The Mandatory Life Sentence for Murder: Is It Time for Discretion?' (2008) 72 Journal of Criminal Law 288.

51 Consider, for example, *Matheson* [1958] 1 WLR 474; *Cox* [1968] 1 WLR 308; and *Vinagre* (1979) 69 Cr App R 104. See also Law Com. No 173, 2003 (n. 13) paras 7.62–7.66; and Griew (n. 42).

52 Law Com. No 290, 2004 (n. 14) para. 2.34.

53 See, for example, Jo Miles, 'The Coroners and Justice Act 2009: A "Dog's Breakfast" of Homicide Reform' (2009) 10 Archbold News, 6; and see L. Kennefick, 'Introducing a New Diminished Responsibility Defence for England and Wales' (MLR (2011) 74(5) 750, at 758)..

54 See Homicide Act 1957, s. 2(2).

55 See the debate of David Howarth MP, HC Deb., March 3 2009, col. 412.

disorder,[56] or depression.[57] It is submitted that the simplest way to contain the 'benign conspiracy' is to end the mandatory sentence of life imprisonment in cases of murder.[58]

Abnormality of Mental Functioning

The Law Commission recommended replacing 'abnormality of mind' with an 'abnormality of mental functioning' that arose from 'a *recognised* medical condition'[59] and this has been given statutory effect in the revised s. 2 of the Homicide Act 1957. The revised wording constitutes a significant shift from what had been proposed in CP 177, namely, that the source of the abnormality should be an '*underlying ... pre-existing mental* or *physiological* condition'[60] – which is broader than a 'medical condition' because 'a mental condition ... will include cases in which the origins of the condition itself lie in *adverse circumstances* with which the offender has had to cope'.[61] The Royal College of Psychiatrists supported the narrower formulation because the restriction would 'ensure that any such defence was grounded in *valid medical diagnosis*'.[62]

The proposal in CP 177 might have overlapped with the partial defence of provocation (now 'loss of self-control')[63] in cases where, for example, a battered spouse killed her/his cohabitee after years of abuse and depression.[64] Depending on the breadth of the expression 'a recognised medical condition', practitioners may need to consider whether, and to what extent, such an overlap exists between the partial defence of diminished responsibility and the new partial defence of loss of self-control.[65] This is because Parliament has enacted that a loss of self-control need not be 'sudden',[66] that the test to be applied is whether a person of the defendant's sex and age with a normal degree of tolerance and self-restraint and, *in the circumstances of the defendant*, might have reacted in the same or in a similar way.[67] If one circumstance is that D killed whilst suffering from a 'recognised medical condition' then that circumstance may be relevant for the purposes of both the partial

---

56 See WHO ICD-10, 'Classification of Mental and Behavioural Disorders', F43.1, 120; and see *Ahluwalia* [1992] 4 All ER 889.

57 The WHO ICD-10, 92, refers to depressive episodes ranging from mild to severe. In this regard, the comments of Professor John Spencer QC are noteworthy: 'I think the vagueness of the present section 2 is in truth a merit, rather than a defect. Personally I share the view, once expressed by the Scottish Law Commission [quoted in Law Commission, No 290 (Report on Partial Defences), §5.16] that diminished responsibility is really "a device to enable the courts to take account of a special category of mitigating circumstances in cases of murder". The more tightly the statute that provides for it is drafted, the less effective it is as vehicle for enabling the mandatory life sentence to be avoided in cases where mitigating circumstances exist': Ministry of Justice, *Murder, Manslaughter and Infanticide* (MoJ CP(R) No 19, 2008) para. 28.

58 During the passage of the Coroners and Justice Bill in the House of Lords, an amendment was moved (but defeated) to make provision where the killing occurred in 'extenuating circumstances', HL Deb., October 26 2009, cols 1008, and 1026–7; and see John Spencer QC, 'Lifting the Life Sentence?' (2009) Archbold News, 5.

59 Law Com. No 304, 2006 (n. 2) para. 5.112 (emphasis added).
60 Law Com. CP No 177, 2005 (n. 25) para. 10.21 (emphasis added).
61 Ibid., para. 6.54 (emphasis added).
62 Law Com. No 304, 2006 (n. 2) para. 5.114 (emphasis added).
63 More accurately: 'Loss of self-control manslaughter'. See Coroners and Justice Act, ss. 55–6.
64 Consider Law Com. CP No 177, 2005 (n. 25) para. 6.55.
65 Coroners and Justice Act 2009, ss. 54–6.
66 Ibid., s. 54(2).
67 Ibid., s. 54(1)(c).

defence of loss of self-control[68] and the partial defence of diminished responsibility. However, whereas the burden is on the prosecution to rebut a defence of 'loss of self-control',[69] the burden of establishing diminished responsibility rests on the defendant.[70]

Recognised Medical Condition

By ensuring that the defence of diminished responsibility is founded on valid medical diagnoses, the Royal College of Psychiatrists believe that it will 'encourage reference within expert evidence to diagnosis in terms of one or two of the accepted internationally classificatory systems of mental conditions',[71] that is to say, the World Health Organization: International Classification of Diseases (ICD-10); and the American Psychiatric Association: Diagnostic and Statistical Manual of Mental Disorders (DSM-IV),[72] 'without explicitly writing those systems into the legislation'.[73]

The revised definition of diminished responsibility is intended to prevent 'idiosyncratic diagnosis' being advanced as a basis for a plea of diminished responsibility.[74] The government recognised that the revised s. 2 of the Homicide Act 1957 should be sufficiently flexible to cater for emerging medical conditions, stating that it is open to the defence to call a 'recognized specialist who has had their work peer-reviewed, although it has not quite got on the list'. Although the jury must decide whether the statutory requirements are met, it is submitted that it is a question of law whether a condition is medically recognised for the purposes of revised s.2 HA 1957.[75]

Familiar psychotic disorders and neurotic disorders (such as post-traumatic stress) are likely to meet this condition. Presumably, a 'recognised medical condition' will include disabilities of cognition, perception, mood (for example, bipolar affective disorder,[76] or manic episodes[77]), or of volition (for example, impulsive violent reactions). The condition need not be permanent. Although it is true that the revised s. 2 of the Homicide Act 1957 does not expressly contain words of limitation concerning the duration of the condition, it cannot (it is submitted) be taken as a foregone conclusion that the courts will not exclude conditions that are merely temporary or transient. An abnormality of mental functioning, which arose from a recognised medical condition, must *substantially* impair D's ability to do one or more of the things mentioned in s. 2(1A).[78] Given that the defendant's condition must be medically based (for example chronic depression) and not merely due to circumstances, for example, physical abuse (unless the abuse has resulted in, for example, depression) it is submitted

---

68 Ibid., s. 54.
69 Ibid., s. 54(5).
70 Homicide Act 1957, s. 2(2).
71 Law Com. No 304, 2006 (n. 2) para. 5.114.
72 See MoJ CP No 19, 2008 (n. 18) (fn. 13).
73 Ibid.
74 Ibid., para. 49.
75 HC Deb., 3 March 2009, col. 414. See also Ministry of Justice, *Partial Defences to Murder: Loss of Control and Diminished Responsibility; and Infanticide: Implementation of Sections 52, and 54 to 57 of the Coroners and Justice Act 2009* (MoJ Circ. No 13, 2010) para. 12; see also, Law Commission, *Expert Evidence in Criminal Proceedings in England and Wales* (Law Com. No 325, 2011).
76 See WHO ICD-10, *Manual of Mental and Behavioural Disorders*, F31, 97.
77 Ibid., F30, 94.
78 It is well established that impairment, for the purposes of the original s. 2 of the Homicide Act 1957, need not be total but must be more than trivial or minimal: see *Lloyd* [1967] 1 QB 175; and see R [2010] EWCA Crim 194; David Ormerod, *Criminal Law* (13th edn, Oxford University Press, 2011) 533; and see Nicola Wake, 'Substantial Confusion within Diminished Responsibility?' (2011) 75(1) Journal of Criminal Law, 12–16.

that the existence of a recognised medical condition is best determined by looking for *symptoms of a disability* rather than a mere diagnosis of a specific condition.

'Arrested and Retarded Development' Contrasted with 'Developmental Immaturity'

'Arrested or retarded development of mind' is one of four aetiologies specified in the original s. 2(1) of the Homicide Act 1957. The history of that condition is detailed in Law Com. CP 173.[79] In summary, persons who were mentally deficient 'from birth or from an early age' came within the scope of the Mental Deficiency Act 1913. Such persons were characterised as having never possessed a normal degree of intellectual capacity. However, the Mental Deficiency Act 1913 did not contain a legal concept to describe this characteristic. It was in the Mental Deficiency Act 1927 that the phrase 'arrested or *incomplete* development of mind' first appeared; its purpose was to define 'mental defectiveness'. The 1957 Act substituted 'retarded' for 'incomplete' and hence the expression 'arrested or retarded development of mind'.[80] It is against that background that the Law Commission observed that this aetiology does not include 'immaturity and the effect of traumatic events other than those involving injury'.[81] There was criticism from Dr Eileen Vizard (and others) that the original definition of diminished responsibility was defective in relation to children and young people because it omitted reference to 'developmental immaturity'.[82] It is important to note that 'developmental immaturity' is not an abnormal condition but a naturally occurring stage or process of mental development that has not yet finished.

Developmental Immaturity: Proposals for Reform

The Commission found that there had been 'very little systematic analysis of the aetiological components by the English courts'.[83] The circumstances in which a person, whose mental age fell far below his/her chronological age, was able to plead diminished responsibility successfully, was unclear.

The Commission had proposed that developmental immaturity in a defendant *under the age of 18 years* should be a discrete ground of diminished responsibility that could be raised alongside or combined with an abnormality of mental functioning.[84] But this would have meant that a defendant, who was *aged 18 or over* at the time of the killing, could not plead diminished responsibility on the grounds of his *developmental immaturity*.[85] The age limit was set at 18 years given the representations made by some consultees to CP No 177 that developmental immaturity as a ground of diminished responsibility was 'too generous to those who had killed with the fault element for

---

79 See WHO ICD-10, F70–79, 174. The opening paragraph to the introduction to F70 reads, 'Mental retardation is a condition of arrested or incomplete development of the mind, which is especially characterized by impairment of skills manifested during the developmental period, which contribute to the overall level of intelligence, i.e. cognitive, language, motor, and social abilities' (176).

80 Law Com. CP No 173, 2003 (n. 13) para. 7.49–52, and fn. 65.

81 Law Com. CP No 177, 2005 (n. 25) para. 6.34 (fn. 27).

82 Law Com. No 290, 2004 (n. 14) para. 5.102.

83 Law Com. CP No 173, 2003 (n. 13) para. 7.45.

84 Law Com. CP No 177, 2005 (n. 25) para. 6.84.

85 Consider *Raven* [1982] Crim LR 51; albeit a case of provocation.

first degree murder'.[86] The Royal College of Psychiatrists had recommended an age limit of 21 years.[87] The Criminal Bar Association of England and Wales (responding to Law Com. CP No 177) supported the inclusion of 'developmental immaturity' as a possible source of diminished responsibility, irrespective of whether the accused's development was 'arrested or retarded', but that it could see no reason why developmental immaturity should be restricted by physical age.[88] The Law Commission made the important point that experts might find it impossible to distinguish between the impact of *developmental immaturity* and *mental abnormality* on D's functioning process and thus it concluded that it was 'wholly unrealistic and unfair' to expect medical experts to assess the impact of mental abnormality whilst disregarding developmental immaturity.[89] However, the government was not convinced that the issue of developmental immaturity created significant problems in practice. It feared that the inclusion of developmental immaturity would catch inappropriate cases.[90]

Developmental Immaturity under the New Section 2 of the Homicide Act 1957

The revised s. 2 of the Homicide Act 1957 says nothing about either 'developmental immaturity' or 'arrested or retarded development'. Notwithstanding the government's stance on this issue, the question remains whether developmental immaturity constitutes a 'recognised medical condition' for the purposes of s. 2 of the Homicide Act 1957. If the developmental immaturity is merely the result of social and/or environmental influences, then it seems unlikely that the defendant would satisfy the requirements of s. 2(1)(a) of the Homicide Act 1957.

In his powerful paper, 'Response to Ministry of Justice Consultation Paper "Murder, Manslaughter and Infanticide": Proposals for Reform',[91] Professor John Spencer QC accepted that the government was right in so far as the expression 'developmental immaturity' means 'the defendant's mental age was significantly below his physical age'. But Professor Spencer described as 'grossly unfair' rules that allow a man aged 40, with a mental age of ten, a partial defence of diminished responsibility on the grounds that his 'developmental immaturity'[92] amounts to a 'recognized medical condition' whereas a child who is actually aged ten will not be able to avail himself of this defence unless (apart from his age) he has some other recognized medical condition that brings him within the scope of the new s. 2(1) of the Homicide Act 1957. Interestingly, Professor John Spencer QC has reported that a psychiatrist and a psychologist stated at a stakeholders' meeting that a person who is 'developmentally immature', in the sense that the defendant's mental age was significantly below his physical age, would be seen as suffering from a 'recognized medical condition'.[93] However, what might actually have been described at the meeting was not 'developmental immaturity', but 'arrested or retarded development' (i.e. the pre-existing language of s. 2 of the Homicide Act 1957).

---

86 Law Com. 304, 2006 (n. 2) para. 5.129.
87 Law Com. No 177, 2005 (n. 25) paras 5.125; and 5.129 (fn. 90).
88 *CBA News*, Issue 3, September 2006, 6.
89 Law Com. No 304, 2006 (n. 2) para. 5.128.
90 MoJ CP No 19, 2008 (n. 18) para. 53.
91 Ibid.
92 It is not entirely clear whether Professor Spencer was actually referring to developmental immaturity, or arrested or retarded development. The author has assumed that Professor Spencer meant the latter condition.
93 MoJ CP (R) No 19, 2008 (n. 57) para 34.

Given the abolition of the *doli incapax* defence for children aged between 10 and 14 years,[94] it is unclear whether it will be harder to contend that the new s. 2 of the 1957 Act permits the separation of the psychological cause of a killing carried out by D, from his/her legal responsibility for the killing notwithstanding D's retarded development with a mental age of between 10 and 14 years.[95]

The Three Bases for Establishing Diminished Responsibility

Defendant's Ability to Understand the 'Nature of D's Conduct': Section 2(1A)(a)

Section 2(1A)(a) of the Homicide Act 1957 is confined to D's understanding of his own conduct and not that of (for example) the victim.[96] If D's impairment at the time of the killing was such that he/she lacked the ability to form a rational judgement with regard to the victim's conduct (that is to say, that D misjudged it, for example, on a deluded basis) then – arguably – his/her case may fall within s. 2(1A)(b) of the Homicide Act 1957. It is doubtful that, in practice, defendants will be prejudiced merely because s. 2(1A)(a) is confined to their own conduct.

Defining the expression 'nature of D's conduct' may prove to be a judicial nightmare. It will be incumbent on a trial judge to explain to a jury what that expression means. It is submitted that it will be for the courts to identify, as a matter of law, those aspects of the defendant's conduct that bear on the 'nature' of it. Unfortunately, the amended Homicide Act offers no guidance on this issue. Law Com. No 304 states[97] that the wording (as it now appears in s. 2(1A)(a)) was preferred to 'understand events' (at the suggestion of the Criminal Cases Review Commission and Professor Mackay) in order to ensure that the accused's lack of understanding of, say, global political events, is not relevant to his or her plea. With respect, it is not entirely easy to see why a lack of such an understanding might not be relevant to D's understanding of the nature of his own conduct. For example, if D (with substantial perception impairment) killed V to prove his belief that people do not die but are reincarnated, would that come within s. 2(1A)(a) or not? The example given by the Law Commission is that of a ten-year-old boy who, having played very violent video games, killed the victim believing that he would be able to revive the victim as had happened in the games that he had been playing continually.[98] Beyond that example there is little else by way of guidance.

It is arguable that the language of s. 2(1A)(a) is wide enough to include a normative element akin to the outdated definition of insanity that either (a) D by reason of his own disability did not appreciate the nature or quality of his act (for example its lethality), or (b) D did not understand that the act was 'wrong'. For example, if D knew that his/her conduct could kill and acted 'rationally' for the purposes of s. 2(1A)(b), but he did not know that the act of killing was 'wrong', is that sufficient for the purposes of s. 2(1A)(a)? In *Byrne*,[99] Lord Parker CJ contrasted 'abnormality of

---

94 *R* v. *T* [2009] UKHL 20.

95 G.R. Sullivan, 'Intoxicants and Diminished Responsibility' [1994] Crim LR 156.

96 The wording of s. 2(1A)(a) closely follows the wording proposed by the Law Commission: see Law Com. No 304, 2006 (n. 2) para. 5.112. See Robert Sullivan, 'Intoxicants and Diminished Responsibility' [1994] Criminal Law Review 156.

97 Ibid., para. 5.112 (fn.84); Law Com, C.P. No.177 had proposed that D should 'understand events' (para.10.21).

98 Ibid., 5.121.

99 *Byrne* (n. 32).

mind' with the expression 'defect of reason' for the purposes of the M'Naghten Rules[100] and held that an 'abnormality of mind' was wide enough to cover 'the mind's activities in all its aspects, not only the perception of physical acts and matters, and the ability to form a rational judgement *whether an act is right or wrong*, but also the ability to exercise willpower to control physical acts in accordance with that rational judgement'.[101] As stated above, rational decision making is an aspect of s. 2(1A)(b) but not of (a) or (c). It is stressed that the relevant aspect of the decision in *Byrne* to this discussion is the reference to D's ability to judge whether an act is right or wrong – an ability that has been a recognised basis for a plea of diminished responsibility under Scottish law.[102] However, in English criminal law, this basis for a plea of diminished responsibility has not featured prominently in appellate decisions.[103] It is tentatively submitted that a defendant who genuinely does not appreciate that his/her act is 'wrong' by reason of an 'abnormality of mental functioning', falls within s. 2(1A)(a). Although it is possible to confine that provision to D's understanding of circumstances and consequences, it would not unduly strain the language of that provision to hold that it encompasses D's *normative* understanding of his own conduct. If a defendant's inability to understand that his/her conduct is 'wrong' has no place in the modern s. 2 of the Homicide Act 1957 then where does it have a place? There is clear authority for the proposition that the partial defence of diminished responsibility is not available to a defendant who is 'unfit to plead' within the meaning of s. 4 of the Criminal Procedure (Insanity and Unfitness to Plead) Act 1964.[104] If the defendant, by reason of an abnormality of mental functioning, does not understand that his conduct was 'wrong', should this be a sufficient basis to protect D mental functioning, such that he is from being convicted of murder on the grounds that he is unfit to plead? Professor Duff suggests that the answer ought to be in the affirmative because 'since the trial aims to determine whether the defendant is guilty of wrongdoing she must be able to understand this normative dimension to the trial'.[105] However, this is not the position in English law.[106]

---

100 *M'Naghten* (1843) 8 ER 718; (1843) 10 Cl & F 200, 210.

101 Emphasis added.

102 *Galbraith* (n. 11) [51], 'The abnormality may mean, for example, that the individual perceives physical acts and matters differently from a normal person. In some cases he may suffer from delusions. Or else it may affect his ability to form a rational judgment as to whether a particular act is right or wrong or to decide whether to perform it. In a given case any or all of these effects may be operating and may impair the accused's ability to determine and control his acts and omissions. The cases of diminished responsibility recognised by the law in the past do indeed involve abnormality of mind of this kind and, therefore, fall within this general description.' However, s. 51B of the Criminal Procedure (Scotland) Act 1995, inserted by s. 168 of the Criminal Justice and Licensing (Scotland) Act 2010 (in force on a date to be appointed), may significantly modify the scope for a plea of diminished responsibility in Scotland. Section 51B(1) reads, '(1) A person who would otherwise be convicted of murder is instead to be convicted of culpable homicide on grounds of diminished responsibility if the person's ability to determine or control conduct for which the person would otherwise be convicted of murder was, at the time of the conduct, substantially impaired by reason of abnormality of mind. (2) For the avoidance of doubt, the reference in subsection (1) to abnormality of mind includes mental disorder.'

103 Consider *Khan* [2009] EWCA Crim 1569; and, of less relevance, see *Walker* [2009] EWCA Crim 1829.

104 See also, *Antoine* [2001] 1 AC 340.

105 R.A. Duff, 'Fitness to Plead and Fair Trials: Part I: A Challenge' [1994] Criminal Law Review 419; and see R.A. Duff, *Trials and Punishment* (Cambridge University Press, 1986).

106 See, for example, *Pritchard* (1836) 7 C & P 303; *Padola* [1996] 1 QB 325; and, *Walls* [2011] EWCA Crim 443.

If the defendant is fit to plead, notwithstanding his abnormality of mental functioning, such that he is unable to understand that his conduct was 'wrong', we are taken back to the question of whether D's inability in that regard brings him within s. 2(1A)(a)–(c). If the answer is in the negative then, unless D is 'insane' within the meaning of the M'Naghten Rules, he falls to be convicted of murder.

The tension that exists between the partial defence of diminished responsibility and unfitness to plead is discussed in Law Com. CP No 197,[107] as well as in the joint response of the Bar Council, and the Criminal Bar Association of England and Wales,[108] that discuss the cases of *Erskine*,[109] *Diamond*,[110] and *Murray*,[111] where the issue was whether D killed at a time when his responsibility was diminished by an abnormality of mind notwithstanding that in each case the defendant was fit to plead (or at least where no point had been taken on the latter issue).

Defendant's Ability to Form a Rational Judgement: Section 2(1A)(b)

If the defendant's inability to understand that his conduct was wrong is not capable of falling within s. 2(1A)(a) of the Homicide Act 1957, it is not evident that his condition falls within s. 2(1A)(b) either. The Law Commission preferred the wording of what is now s. 2(1A)(b) to the words 'to judge whether his or her actions were right or wrong'.[112] The example given by the Law Commission to illustrate the application of this provision is where D believes himself to be the reincarnation of Napoleon, and although he might realise that it is morally and legally wrong to take the law into his own hands by killing V, he does so by reason of his substantially impaired capacity to form a rational judgement.[113] But what if D has no such delusion but his ability to distinguish between right and wrong is substantially impaired? The Act affords no easy answer (it is submitted).

Impaired Ability to Exercise Self-Control: Section 2(1A)(c)

For the purposes of the original s. 2 of the Homicide Act 1957, the Court of Criminal Appeal held, in *Byrne*, that the provision was wide enough to cover the defendant's ability to exercise will power to control physical acts 'in accordance with … rational judgement'.[114] One might question whether a loss of self-control can ever be 'rational' but the modern s. 2 of the Homicide Act 1957 does not expressly link a defendant's inability to exercise self-control with irrational judgements or irrational thought processes. The Law Commission has given the example of the person who believes that he is possessed by the devil and implants in him a desire to kill.[115] But rather more commonplace scenarios may also bring the defendant within s. 2(1A)(c) of the Homicide Act 1957, for example, where organic brain damage causes the defendant to lash out violently. The problem for fact-finders will be distinguishing between cases of actual impairment of a defendant's ability to exercise self-control and cases where the defendant *chooses* not to control his or her conduct.

---

107 Law Commission, *Unfitness to Plead* (Law Com. CP No 197, 2010).
108 <http://www.criminalbar.com/281/> (accessed 26 January 2011).
109 [2009] EWCA Crim 1425; [2009] 2 Cr App R 29.
110 [2008] EWCA Crim 923.
111 [2008] EWCA Crim 1792.
112 Law Com. No 304, 2006 (n. 2) para. 5.112 (fn. 85).
113 Ibid.
114 *Byrne* (n. 32.)
115 Law Com. No 304, 2006 (n. 2) para. 5.121.

However, in practice, this problem weighs more heavily on the shoulders of the accused than on the prosecution because it is the former who, by s. 2(2) of the Homicide Act 1957, carries the burden of proving the partial defence of diminished responsibility (to the civil standard of proof).

Proving that the Defendant's Abnormality was a Cause of the Killing

In the majority of cases, the causal link between D's abnormality of mental functioning and his act of killing, or being a party to the killing, will be self-evident. Clearly, there may be cases where proving a causal connection is problematic.

The Law Commission was particularly concerned about the second limb of s. 2(1) of the 1957 Ac, as originally worded (i.e. substantial impairment of D's *mental responsibility* for the killing) and that a 'possible avenue would be to reformulate the test in terms of causation. The focus would no longer be on whether there was 'substantial impairment of mental responsibility' but whether the defendant's 'abnormality of mind' was a significant cause of his acts or omissions in doing or being a party to the killing.[116] But, almost a year later, the Commission recommended that s. 2 of the 1957 Act ought to remain unreformed pending any full consideration of murder,[117] noting that there was no substantial support of any of the alternative formulations which had been canvassed in the consultation paper.[118]

The Commission reported that leading experts such as Professor Mackay advised against the introduction of a strict causation requirement. Although the Royal College of Psychiatrists did not object to the requirement, it cautioned against creating a situation in which experts might be called on to 'demonstrate' causation on a scientific basis, rather than indicating from an assessment of the nature of the abnormality, what its likely impact would be on thinking, emotion, volition, and so forth.[119] The Law Commission acknowledged that although the final choice of words was a matter for the legislator, it was of the view that an abnormality of mental functioning that was shown to be 'an explanation' for D's conduct, ensures that there is an 'appropriate connection' with the killing. It would leave open the possibility that other causes or explanations (e.g. provocation/loss of self-control) may have operated 'without prejudicing the case for mitigation'.[120] The government agreed with the Law Commission that it would be 'impracticable to require abnormality to be the sole explanation [for D's acts]' and that there must be 'some connection between the condition and the killing in order for the partial defence to be justified'.[121] No further elaboration of the government's thinking appears in its consultation paper or in the Explanatory Notes to the 2009 Act.

Whether the Problem of Causation is More Apparent than Real

It is submitted that there are three reasons why concerns about the existence of the causation requirement in s. 2(1)(c) ought not to be overstated:

1. Regard must be paid to the combined effect of s. 2(1)(c) and (1B) of the 1957 Act. It is plain that it is sufficient that the abnormality provides *an* explanation for the defendant's

---

116 Law Com. No 173, 2003 (n. 13) para. 7.92.
117 Law Com. No 290, 2004 (n. 14) para. 5.86.
118 Ibid., para. 5.87.
119 Law Com. No 304, 2006 (n. 2) para. 5.123.
120 Ibid., para. 5.124.
121 MoJ CP No 19, 2008 (n. 18) para. 51; and see HC Deb., 3 March 2009 (Maria Eagle).

conduct, or that it was a 'significant factor in causing [D] to carry out that conduct'. Thus, the abnormality need not be the sole cause/explanation for the defendant's conduct.

2. It is at least arguable that the causation requirement does no more than give legislative effect to the decision and reasoning of the House of Lords in *Dietschmann*,[122] in which their Lordships held that the original s. 2(1) of the 1957 Act *did not require the existence of an abnormality of mind to be the sole cause of the defendant killing or being a party to the killing*.[123] The issue has frequently arisen in cases where a defendant (D) killed at a time when D had suffered from an abnormality of mind, and D had taken alcohol before the killing. Lord Hutton opined that 'even if the defendant would not have killed if he had not taken drink, the causative effect of the drink does not necessarily prevent an abnormality of mind suffered by the defendant from substantially impairing his mental responsibility for his fatal acts'.[124] It is submitted there is some support for this argument in HO Circular 2010/13, which states that 'The aim is that the defence should not be able to succeed where the defendant's mental condition made no difference to their behaviour i.e. when they would have killed regardless of their medical condition.'[125] Similarly, in Scotland, s. 51B(3)(b) of the Criminal Procedure (Scotland) Act 1995 provides[126] that the fact that a person was 'under the influence of alcohol, drugs or any other substance at the time of the conduct in question does not of itself prevent an abnormality of mind from being established' for the purpose of mounting a partial defence of diminished responsibility within the meaning of s. 51B.

Each case will therefore turn on its own facts. As Lord Hutton remarked in *Dietschmann*, 'no doubt in many cases (as in *Fenton*)[127] if the jury concluded that the defendant would not have killed if he had not taken drink they will also find that his abnormality of mind had not substantially impaired his mental responsibility for his fatal acts'.[128] *Dietschmann* was not a case that involved 'alcohol dependence syndrome', and the distinction between the aetiology of the abnormality of the mind (or an abnormality of mental functioning arising from a recognised medical condition), and a transient state of intoxication, needs to be kept in mind.[129]

Although, in Report No 304, the Law Commission makes no reference to *Dietschmann*,[130] it seems likely that the inclusion of the words 'an explanation' in the Law Commission's recommended definition of diminished responsibility,[131] and in the new s. 2(1B) of the 1957 Act, was intended to produce results consistent with that decision.[132]

3. The Advice of the Judicial Committee, given by Lord Keith of Kinkel in *Walton v. The Queen*,[133] remains relevant, namely, that 'upon an issue of diminished responsibility the jury

---

122 [2003] UKHL 10; and see *Hendy* [2006] Cr App R 33.
123 Ibid., [18].
124 Ibid.
125 MoJ Circ. No 13, 2010 (n. 75) [8]. See also, HC Deb., 3 March 2009, 410.
126 If or when ss. 168 and 171 of the Criminal Justice and Licensing Act 2010 come into force (s. 168 of that Act inserts s. 51B into the Criminal Procedure (Scotland) Act 1995.
127 (1975) 61 Cr App R 261.
128 *Dietschmann* (n. 122) [34] (Lord Hutton).
129 See, for example, *Tandy* [1989] 1 All ER 267; *Wood* [2008] EWCA Crim 1305; *Stewart* [2009] EWCA Crim 593; and Robert Sullivan, 'Intoxicants and Diminished Responsibility' [1994] Criminal Law Review 156.
130 The case is discussed in Law Com. CP No 173, 2003 (n. 13) and Law Com. No 290, 2004 (n. 14).
131 Law Com. No 304, 2006 (n. 2) para. 5.112.
132 See *Fenton* (n. 127) and *Gittens* [1984] QB 698.
133 [1978] AC 788, 793 [F].

are entitled and indeed bound to consider not only the medical evidence but the evidence upon the whole facts and circumstances of the case' (and see *Khan*,[134] noting, in particular, the observations of the court at para. 18 of the judgment).

Diminished Responsibility and the Role of Experts

The courts will continue to be guided by the opinions of experienced forensic psychiatrists on the issue of whether, at the time of the killing, the defendant lacked the ability to do one or more of the things mentioned in s. 2(1A) of the Homicide Act 1957.[135] The *extent* to which experts will express an opinion on the elements of the revised s. 2 of the Homicide Act 1957 is unclear. The Royal College of Psychiatry suggested to the Law Commission that the court's acceptance or encouragement of psychiatric experts to comment upon whether the defendant's impairment was substantial was one that 'should be resisted',[136] presumably for the reasons given by Professor Nigel Eastman to the Law Commission, namely, that to do so means that the expert takes a view about matters of fact and 'opens up enormously the lines of cross examination'.[137] However, whilst 'trial by expert' is to be avoided,[138] the issue of 'substantial impairment' under the revised s. 2 of the Homicide Act 1957 no longer involves a value judgement of a defendant's moral responsibility for the killing but a qualitative assessment of his/her ability to do one or more of the things mentioned in s. 2(1A) of the Homicide Act 1957. The psychiatric expert is the person usually best placed to assess the extent of the defendant's impairment. It is submitted that test results (and the methodology for testing) of a defendant's cognitive and other abilities (relevant to s. 2 of the Homicide Act 1957) coupled with an explanation of the possible significance of that data, is receivable evidence that ought to be given unless there is good reason for not doing so.

Concluding Remarks

At the time of writing this chapter, no cases had reached the Court of Appeal (Criminal Division) concerning the proper construction of the revised s. 2 of the Homicide Act 1957. Such appeals are inevitable. Even if the repeal of the mandatory life sentence comes to pass, it is unlikely that the partial defences to murder will cease to exist. One can point to theoretical incoherence between rules relating to diminished responsibility, insanity, and unfitness to plead, but – in practice –

---

134   [2009] EWCA Crim 1569.
135   See Law Com. No 304, 2006 (n. 2) paras 5.117–5.118.
136   Ibid., para. 5.118.
137   Ibid., para. 5.120.
138   A jury is not bound to accept the opinion of medical experts even if the experts are agreed provided that there is some proper evidential basis for departing from a consensus of medical opinion: consider *Kiszko* (1979) 68 Cr App R 62, applying *Walton*. The law was stated by Lord Goddard CJ in *Matheson* (1958) 42 Cr App R 145, 151; [1958] 1 WLR 474, 478: 'What then were the facts or circumstances which would justify a jury in coming to a conclusion contrary to the unchallenged evidence of' the doctors? 'While it has often been emphasised, and we would repeat, that the decision in these cases, as in those in which insanity is pleaded, is for the jury and not for the doctors, the verdict must be founded on evidence. If there are facts which would entitle a jury to reject or differ from the opinions of the medical men, then this Court would not, and indeed could not, disturb their verdict, but if the doctors' evidence is unchallenged and there is no other on this issue, a verdict contrary to their opinion would not be "a true verdict in accordance with the evidence"'; and see *Vernege* (1982) 74 Cr App R 232; and *Sanders* [1991] Crim LR 781.

imperfections are likely to be resolved by a combination of the exercise of discretion, the so-called 'benign conspiracy', judicial interpretation and guidance, and the common sense of juries and practitioners.

Chapter 3
Loss of Self-Control under the Coroners and Justice Act 2009: Oh No!

Barry Mitchell

Introduction

On 4 October 2010 sections 54 to 56 of the Coroners and Justice Act 2009 came into force, replacing the partial defence of provocation with loss of self-control.[1] Where it is pleaded successfully the defendant's liability is reduced from murder to voluntary manslaughter.

The old common law plea of provocation had been subjected to considerable criticism over many years. It was reviewed by the Law Commission between 2003 and 2004, at the end of which the Commission recommended that it be 'reformed' so that it would arise where 'the defendant acted in response to (a) gross provocation (meaning words or conduct or a combination of words and conduct which caused the defendant to have a justifiable sense of being seriously wronged); or (b) fear of serious violence towards the defendant or another; or a combination of (a) and (b); and a person of the defendant's age and of ordinary temperament, i.e. ordinary tolerance and self-restraint, in the circumstances of the defendant might have reacted in the same or similar way'.[2]

The Commission then undertook a wider review of the homicide law between 2005 and 2006, and reiterated its reformed definition of provocation, the effect of which should reduce murder in the first degree to murder in the second degree.[3]

The then New Labour government's response to the Law Commission's recommendations was very limited. It ignored those more fundamental proposals which referred to the structure of the substantive law, but through the Coroners and Justice Act 2009 it has effectively revised the provocation plea and renamed it 'loss of self-control'. Under s. 54(1) the accused has a defence to murder if his acts or omissions resulted from a loss of self-control which itself had a 'qualifying trigger', and (adopting some of the Law Commission's wording) 'a person of D's sex and age, with a normal degree of tolerance and self-restraint and in the circumstances of D, might have reacted in the same or similar way to D'. By virtue of s. 55 a qualifying trigger must be either 'D's fear of serious violence from V against D or another identified person', and/or 'a thing or things done or said (or both) which (a) constituted circumstances of an extremely grave character, and (b) caused D to have justifiable sense of being seriously wronged'. A plea of loss of self-control will fail if the trigger had been incited by the defendant,[4] and – somewhat controversially – sexual infidelity is expressly excluded as a sufficient basis for the defence.[5]

---

1 The plea is labelled 'loss of control' in s. 54, but contents of the section clearly refer to 'loss of self-control'.
2 Law Commission, *Partial Defences to Murder* (Law Com. No 290, 2004) para. 3.168.
3 Law Commission, *Murder, Manslaughter and Infanticide* (Law Com. No 304, 2006) paras 9.16 and 9.17.
4 Coroners and Justice Act 2009, s. 55(6)(a) and (b).
5 Ibid., s. 55 (6)(c).

The defence must be left for the jury to decide if 'sufficient evidence is adduced to raise an issue with respect to the defence ... on which, in the opinion of the trial judge', they could, properly directed, 'reasonably conclude that the defence might apply'.[6] If the matter is left to the jury, they 'must assume that the defence is satisfied unless the prosecution proves beyond reasonable doubt that it is not'.[7]

The new loss of self-control plea is similar to the old common law which it replaces in that it requires defendants to comply with both subjective (viz. a loss of self-control triggered by – in crude terms – fear or anger) and objective (the person of normal tolerance etc.) tests. The focus of this chapter, however, is very much on the concept of loss of self-control which clearly lies at the very heart of the plea.

Common Law Provocation – Especially the Loss of Self-Control Requirement

Unlike diminished responsibility, which is a relative newcomer to English criminal law,[8] the other plea which most commonly reduces murder to voluntary manslaughter,[9] provocation, had long been recognised, having emerged (albeit in a much narrower form) in the seventeenth century.[10] The basis of the law at the time it was repealed was set out in the judgment of Devlin J in *Duffy*[11]; the law called for 'some act, or series of acts, done by the dead man to the accused, which would cause in a reasonable person, and actually causes in the accused, a sudden and temporary loss of self-control, rendering the accused so subject to passion as to make him or her for the moment not master of his mind'. This common law concept was modified by s. 3 of the Homicide Act 1957 which stated that the provocation must be something done and/or said: in other words, the trigger had to be some form of human action. The *Duffy* definition was further expanded by case law – the provocation did not have to emanate from the victim,[12] and it did not have to be directed at the accused.[13]

But at its heart there had to be a sudden and temporary loss of self-control, and this requirement proved highly controversial. It should be acknowledged at the outset, however, that the law was not always thus. Over the years the courts adopted various epithets in an attempt to illustrate the nature of the law, and they often pointed not so much to the physical dimension of the defendant's reaction, but to his state of mind. For example, in *Hayward*, Tyndal CJ directed the jury to consider whether there had been time (between the provocation and the defendant's fatal assault) 'for reason to resume its seat'.[14] The ruling in *Duffy* clearly also refers to the impact on the accused's mental state – he must no longer be 'master of his mind' – as well as the physical dimension.

---

6   Ibid., s. 54(6).
7   Ibid., s. 54(5).
8   It was first recognised in s. 2 of the Homicide Act 1957.
9   It is extraordinarily difficult to quantify the number of cases in which a provocation defence succeeded because the government statistics did not quantify them as a separate category – they merely distinguished between diminished responsibility and 'other manslaughter'.
10 For interesting discussions of the historical evolution of provocation, see John Kaye, 'The Early History of Murder and Manslaughter' (1967) 83 Law Quarterly Review 365 and 569; Andrew Ashworth, 'The Doctrine of Provocation' (1976) 35 Cambridge Law Journal 292; and Jeremy Horder, *Provocation and Responsibility* (Oxford University Press, 1992).
11 [1949] 1 All ER 932 n.
12 Davies [1975] QB 691.
13 Pearson [1992] Crim LR 193.
14 (1833) 6 C&P 157, 159.

The loss of self-control requirement in common law provocation received enormous criticism. In *Richens*[15] the Court of Appeal held that it would be wrong to say that there must be a complete loss of control. Indeed, that would imply some sort of state of automatism, which would point towards a complete defence, not simply a partial reduction of liability. In simple terms, the law envisaged that the defendant should be so angry that he was unable to control his reaction, and the addition of the words 'sudden and temporary' implied that there should be a spontaneous reaction. Any evidence of premeditation or of a time interval between the provocation and the defendant's response would almost certainly undermine the defence. But there was always a conspicuous absence of any definition of loss of self-control, and it was unclear whether it meant that the accused simply failed to exercise self-control or whether it implied a basic incapacity to do so – though medical science almost certainly could not determine whether a defendant in fact suffered from such an incapacity. The fact that defendants not infrequently expressed themselves in a way which suggested they were unable to control their reactions was by no means convincing.[16]

The lack of legal definition of loss of self-control was perhaps graphically and tragically illustrated in *Cocker*,[17] a case which in many respects appeared to be one of mercy killing.[18] The defendant's wife suffered from Freidreich's ataxia, a disease which is both incurable and incapacitating. He had been caring for her for almost 11 years. She repeatedly begged him to kill her, and she became increasingly irritable. After keeping him awake for most of one night with regular pleas that he should kill her, the defendant finally gave in, put his hands around her throat and then smothered her with a pillow for about 30 seconds. He gave himself up to the police, saying it was 'the last straw'. At his trial for murder, he testified that what had prompted him to kill her was her final request for her life to be ended and that her persistent begging was simply too much for him. The trial judge and the Court of Appeal took the view that there was no evidence that he had been provoked to lose his self-control. Rather than lose his self-control, the defendant had acceded to his wife's entreaties. This seems to be based on an unfortunately narrow interpretation of loss of self-control – the defendant acted in an apparently calm and deliberate manner, rather than in an overtly uncontrolled fashion – and, especially in light of the mandatory life sentence for murder, it was a pity that the court did not feel able to bring him within Devlin J's definition on the basis that he had lost his self-restraint and that amounts to the same thing.[19]

Of course, the question of provocation only arose where there was a *prima facie* case of murder against the defendant; i.e. the defendant caused the victim's death either intending to kill or to cause serious injury. The law had long ago effectively rejected the expression used by Sir Edward Coke in the seventeenth century that murder required the accused to have killed 'with malice aforethought'. Neither malice nor forethought had to be proved: all that is necessary is that the

---

15 [1993] 4 All ER 877.

16 In 2004 the Law Commission reported that their discussions with psychiatrists revealed that those who do strike out – lose their self-control – in anger can usually afford to do so. 'An angry strong man is much less likely to "lose self-control" and attack another person in circumstances in which he or she is likely to come off worse by doing so'; see Law Com. No 290, 2004 (n. 2) para. 3.28.

17 [1989] Crim LR 740.

18 Paul Taylor, 'Provocation and Mercy Killing' [1991] Criminal Law Review, 111–14, where the case is discussed in the context of an argument that there is no insurmountable reason why provocation should not have been available in some cases of mercy killing. (In practice, where a case is regarded as a genuine instance of mercy killing, the plea of diminished responsibility is likely to be construed very generously so as to lead to a manslaughter conviction and thus the avoidance of a mandatory sentence of life imprisonment.)

19 Interestingly, the concept of loss of self-restraint is used in the new law (see s. 54) and appears to be synonymous with loss of self-control.

defendant was fleetingly aware that his actions would lead to death or serious harm. But as the Law Commission reminded us, there was degree of tension between the need for such an intent and the loss of self-control requirement. As Devlin J had stated, the defendant had to have reached the point at which he was 'no longer master of his mind', yet that meant that 'in one way, [he] lacked the full *mens rea*'.[20]

One of the most critical comments arising from the loss of self-control requirement was that it revealed a gender bias in the law, that it reflected a typically male reaction to provocation, but one which women were very unlikely to display. When men are provoked they become angry and lash out in the heat of the moment, but for the reasons indicated earlier (in footnote 16) women instinctively recognise that they cannot afford to react in the same way. They have to exercise self-control, and battered women, for example, choose to give vent to their reaction by attacking him at a later time when their abuser is off guard. As the Law Commission commented, 'Women's reactions to provocation are less likely to involve a "loss of self-control", as such, and more likely to be comprised of a combination of anger, fear, frustration and a sense of desperation. This can make it difficult or impossible for women to satisfy the loss of self-control requirement, even where they otherwise deserve at least a partial defence.'[21] A similar point was made by Professor Ormerod who wrote that the concept 'has the potential to operate in a discriminatory way, rendering the defence too readily available to those who are quick to temper (more commonly men), and less accommodating of those who endure the provoking circumstances before responding with lethal force (often women who kill abusive partners)'.[22]

In the face of this it was not particularly surprising that the courts decided to adopt a flexible approach in what came to be known as 'slow-burn' cases – i.e. there was a lengthy history of abuse against the defendant and the last incident of abuse which preceded the fatal assault was relatively modest. Seen only in that light there was a real danger that the court would reject a provocation plea and the defendant would be convicted of murder. So in cases such as *Ahluwalia*[23] the Court of Appeal held that evidence of the history of abuse, and not simply the last incident of it, was admissible – though at the same time the court reiterated that there must still be evidence that the defendant did lose her self-control.

To the extent that this enabled the defence to make the court aware of the full context in which the killing took place, this development was surely welcomed. But at the same time it proved problematic. One of the basic aims of the loss of self-control requirement was to distinguish deserving cases where the defendant had been seriously provoked and reacted spontaneously from those which were committed in considered revenge and thus undeserving of the courts' sympathy. The law's accommodation of slow-burn homicides clearly undermined this aim. The approach taken in slow-burn cases was not confined to battered spouse homicides and it effectively reduced the potential significance of any lapse of time between the provocation and the fatal assault. It surely led to some difficult situations in which juries were placed in the invidious position of having to reach a verdict where there was evidence of much provocation but also of planning and deliberation. Not only did this cause real concern for the parties to individual cases, but it also raised fears of a 'jury lottery' – the inevitable inconsistency that must have occurred through different juries reaching different verdicts. It is perhaps worth noting at this point that the author's own empirical research revealed occasions when it seems that the courts occasionally returned

---

20 Law Commission, *Partial Defences to Murder* (Law Com. CP No 173, 2003) para. 4.28.
21 Law Com. No 304, 2006 (n. 3) para. 5.18.
22 David Ormerod, *Smith and Hogan: Criminal Law* (12th edn, Oxford University Press, 2008) 492, 493.
23 [1992] 4 All ER 889.

verdicts of manslaughter based on provocation even though the evidence disclosed little or no sign of a loss of self-control.[24]

Furthermore, as the Law Commission acknowledged in their 2006 report, cases sometimes reveal a mixture of motives, of which revenge is only one. In *Baillie*,[25] for example, the victim was a drug dealer who had supplied drugs to the defendant's three sons. The defendant discovered that one son intended to get his drugs from a different dealer, that the victim had learned this, and that in consequence all three sons were 'going to get a slap'. One son told the defendant, in tears, that the victim had threatened him. So the defendant armed himself with a sawn-off shotgun and a cut-throat razor, confronted the victim, cut him and shot at him. On the one hand, this could be construed as a case of revenge, but on the other hand, the defendant's actions could be construed as preventing further crime by the victim drug-dealer. Making the considered-revenge-versus-bona-fide-provocation distinction is not necessarily as straightforward as it initially seems. Predictably, therefore, commentators have criticised the law's use of the loss of self-control requirement. 'It is an imperfect tool for distinguishing between revenge killings of a premeditated or calculated nature from killings committed in the heat of the moment.'[26] Similarly, the Law Commission described it as 'a judicially invented concept, lacking sharpness or a clear foundation in psychology. It was a valiant but flawed attempt to encapsulate a key limitation to the defence – that it should not be available to those who kill in considered revenge.'[27]

Aims of the New Law

The previous section of this chapter concentrated on criticisms of the loss of self-control requirement in provocation, but that was only part of the story. If anything, commentators were even more critical of the way in which the objective test – that the court must be satisfied that the defendant had done what any reasonable person would have done in the same circumstances – developed over the years. The year 1976 saw the publication in the *Cambridge Law Journal* of Professor Andrew Ashworth's seminal article in which he argued that when applying the objective test it was right that certain personal characteristics of the accused should be taken into account.[28] In other words, the objective test should be partially subjectivised. This was endorsed and given judicial support not long afterwards by the decision of the House of Lords in *Camplin*[29] where Lord Diplock stated that 'the reasonable [person] … is a person having the power of self-control to be expected of an ordinary person of the sex and age of the accused, but in other respects sharing such of the accused's characteristics as they think would affect the gravity of the provocation to him'.[30] Both Professor Ashworth and Lord Diplock sought to stress that the law should distinguish between characteristics which were the object of the provocation and those which simply relate to the defendant's ability to exercise self-control, and that only the former should be relevant to the objective test. In the event, however, there was a series of conflicting appellate court decisions in which this distinction was at times upheld and at other times ignored. By a majority of three to two the House of Lords held in

---

24 See Barry Mitchell, 'Distinguishing between Murder and Manslaughter in Practice' (2007) 71 Journal of Criminal Law 318–41.
25 [1995] Crim LR 739.
26 Ormerod (n. 22) 492.
27 Law Com. No 290, 2004 (n. 2) para. 3.30.
28 Andrew Ashworth, 'The Doctrine of Provocation' (1976) 35 Cambridge Law Journal 292.
29 [1978] AC 705.
30 Ibid., 718.

Smith (Morgan)[31] that the jury could take into account characteristics other than age and sex, whether or not they were relevant to the provocation in the case. But in another divided decision the Privy Council (six to three) in *AG for Jersey* v. *Holley*[32] held that *Smith* was wrongly decided and reiterated the distinction advocated by Professor Ashworth and Lord Diplock that only those characteristics relevant to the provocation should be considered when applying the objective test.[33]

Moreover, the situation became more confusing and unsatisfactory when the courts had to decide whether discreditable characteristics or characteristics which are repugnant to or inconsistent with the idea of the reasonable person might nevertheless be taken into account. In *Dryden*[34] the Court of Appeal held that obsessiveness and eccentric personality should have been taken into account. In *Humphreys*[35] the Court felt that abnormal immaturity and attention-seeking should have been left to the jury, and in *Morhall*[36] the House of Lords regarded the defendant's addiction to glue-sniffing in the same way. Quite how the jury were meant to apply these tests was never made clear!

Against this background it was not at all surprising that many commentators expressed their frustration and impatience with the law, and called for the abolition of the common law plea of provocation.[37] In their review of the law the Law Commission seemed to have two principal aims in mind – one positive and one negative. On the positive side there was a desire that the law should accommodate battered spouses who killed their abusers even though he/she acted with some degree of premeditation and there was no evidence of a loss of self-control.[38] Conversely, adopting a more negative approach, the Commission thought it right to exclude cases of considered revenge, such as honour killings.[39]

The New Loss of Self-Control

Notwithstanding the Law Commission's strong opposition to the retention of the loss of self-control requirement, the government was worried that without it there would be a real risk of undeserving cases – such as honour killings, gang-related homicides, and some battered spouse cases – continuing to benefit from the partial defence. In a consultation paper the government explained:

> there is ... a fundamental problem about providing a partial defence in situations where a defendant has killed while basically in full possession of his or her senses, even if he or she is frightened, other than in a situation which is complete self-defence.[40]

---

31 [2000] 4 All ER 289.

32 [2005] UKPC 23.

33 Although Privy Council decisions are clearly not binding on English courts, it seems that the majority view in *Holley* has been followed by the Court of Appeal. See *Mohammed (Faqir)* [2005] EWCA Crim 1880; *Van Dongen* [2005] EWCA Crim 1728; and *James and Karimi* [2006] EWCA Crim 14.

34 [1995] 4 All ER 987.

35 Ibid., 1008.

36 [1995] 3 All ER 659. See Alan Norrie, 'From Criminal Law to Legal Theory: The Mysterious Case of the Reasonable Glue Sniffer' (2002) 65 Modern Law Review 538.

37 See, for example, Celia Wells, 'Provocation: The Case for Abolition', Andrew Ashworth and Barry Mitchell (eds), *Rethinking English Homicide Law* (Oxford University Press, 2000) 85–106.

38 Law Com. No 290, 2004 (n. 2) paras 3.65–3.70.

39 Law Com. No 304, 2006 (n. 3) paras 5.11–5.32. This is now given legislative force through the Coroners and Justice Act 2009, s. 54(4).

40 Ministry of Justice, *Murder, Manslaughter and Infanticide* (MoJ CP No 19, 2008) para. 36.

The point was then reinforced at the end of the consultation process: removal of the loss of self-control requirement would quite simply create too great a risk that the partial defence would become available to 'cold-blooded killing'.[41]

In contrast to the former provocation plea, the loss of self-control under the Coroners and Justice Act 2009 need not be 'sudden and temporary'. The old common law deliberately sought to reflect the idea of an explosion of anger – during which the defendant lashes out with fatal violence – which then subsides. But the effect and significance of this was weakened by the courts' willingness to show sympathy in the 'slow-burn' cases. By allowing the admission of what might be a lengthy period of abuse/provocation – i.e. the historical context – and simultaneously accepting that the instance of provocation which immediately preceded the fatal assault might be relatively trivial, the courts provided an opening for what some regarded as dubious cases. In other words, the accommodation of slow-burn cases produced what were arguably undesirable side effects.

It is difficult to think of a situation in which a loss of self-control would not be temporary, though admittedly the adjective 'temporary' did not necessarily mean that it would be as brief as the paradigmatic explosion of anger might normally imply. Nevertheless, the more interesting issue arose from the requirement of suddenness. As Ashworth remarked, this requirement had no judicial authority before *Duffy*.[42] The removal of the suddenness requirement seems to reflect a desire to accommodate slow-burn cases, which characterises some battered spouse homicides, but the loss of self-control condition – assuming it is construed in at least broadly the same fashion as under the old law – clearly represents a significant restriction on the availability of the new defence. At the same time, one commentator has hinted that removal of the suddenness requirement from the wording of the new law may not bring about much of a change. Norrie writes 'it might be thought, a test for and constitutive feature of any loss of self-control in anger is that it have an element of suddenness. How else does one identify a loss of self-control, except as a moment of departure from being in control?'[43] It will, of course, be interesting to see whether the loss of self-control under the Coroners and Justice Act is construed by the courts any differently from the subjective test in the old common law.

It is also difficult to avoid the conclusion that retention of the loss of self-control requirement does not always sit comfortably with the government's declared aims in the Coroners and Justice Act. In its response to consultation, the government welcomed the support for the partial defence to murder in cases based on a fear of serious violence, and expressly made the point that it should be available even though the violence is not imminent.[44] The problem lies most clearly in conceiving of situations in which the accused was fearful of non-imminent serious violence and yet still lost his or her self-control. The loss of self-control requirement would surely still exclude a significant proportion of battered women who kill their abusers. Moreover, in its response to a concern of a number of respondents on this very point, the government stated that a loss of self-control is not necessarily 'inconsistent with situations where a person reacts to an *imminent* fear of serious violence',[45] but made no comment where the fear is not imminent.

---

41 Ministry of Justice, *Murder, Manslaughter and Infanticide* (MoJ CP (R) No 19, 2008) para. 62.
42 Andrew Ashworth, *Principles of Criminal Law* (6th edn, Oxford University Press, 2009) 253.
43 Alan Norrie, 'The Coroners and Justice Act 2009 – Partial Defences to Murder: (1) Loss of Control' [2010] Criminal Law Review 275, 288.
44 MoJ CP No 19, 2008 (n. 40) paras 26 and 29.
45 Ibid., para. 63 (emphasis added).

Back to First Principles

As the Introduction makes clear, the emphasis in this chapter is on the concept of loss of self-control that lies at the very heart of the new law. The reason for the government's persistence with the concept is well understood, but is it well founded? This latter question can only be addressed by going back to first principles and rehearsing what happens when someone is provoked. That in itself, of course, requires some consideration of what constitutes provocation. Both the old and the new law seem to restrict it to some form of human conduct – s. 3 of the Homicide Act 1957 referred to 'things done', 'things said' or 'both together'. Given that the courts have essentially envisaged a provoked defendant as one who lashes out in anger with fatal force, and he/she is then partially excused liability because the law recognises that it was reasonable for the defendant to have reacted as he/she did,[46] it is surprising that there has been relatively little querying of the source of the provocation. One of the very few commentators on this is Professor David Ormerod who correctly suggested that loss of self-control by, for example, a farmer when his crops are destroyed by a flood would not give rise to a provocation plea. 'If D may rely on the defence where the crops … were destroyed … why should it be different where no human agency was involved? The "provocation" is no more and no less.'[47] Historically, it is perhaps understandable that provocation should be limited in this manner because the law had a much narrower concept of the plea,[48] but over the years it had clearly expanded quite considerably.

What is important is that the defendant has been emotionally disturbed by something in circumstances that the law thinks merit some attenuation of culpability. Naturally, whatever it is that triggers the defendant's reaction must be of sufficient substance to justify the emotional disturbance, but there appears to be no good reason why it should be a form of human conduct. The law's sympathy originates from the defendant's reaction and the circumstances in which it occurred, not from the source of the trigger *per se*. Examination of the old case law and of the numerous critiques (including that of the Law Commission in 2003–04) reveals a conspicuous lack of any attempt to rationalise the limitation on the source of the provocation. Ironically, the insistence that the provocation stems from human conduct makes it resemble a kind of revenge, which is something that the courts have always been very keen to distinguish.

It is perhaps useful to think about how provocation impacts on people in a fairly crude but simple way. Whatever form it takes, it must surely impact initially on the individual's mind, through one of the senses – hearing, sight, or even touch, smell, etc. Assuming there is sufficient gravity in the provocation, the individual may react to it on an emotional level in one or more ways; he/she will become angry, frightened, desperate, frustrated, etc. It is important to recognise here that emotional reactions may well be not simply reasonable but in some instances positively desirable in the circumstances. Broadly following the Law Commission's (2006) recommendations, the new law focuses on just two kinds of emotional reaction – anger and fear – and that is presumably because (a) the law has traditionally conceived of provocation as an anger-based plea, and (b) numerous concerns have been raised very publicly about the way in which the old law (failed to) accommodate battered women who were frightened by their abusers. But there appears to be no valid reason for limiting the law's sympathy to these emotions; other forms of emotional disturbance in the face of provocation are just as understandable and reasonable, and indeed many battered women experience great desperation as well as fear.

---

46 English criminal lawyers in particular traditionally regarded provocation as partly justificatory.
47 Ormerod (n. 22) 49.
48 See the references in n. 10.

Loss of self-control is, of course, entirely consistent with anger, but is more difficult to reconcile with other emotional reactions. Those who are fearful may outwardly appear calm but their normal process of rational thinking is likely to be disrupted – the degree of disruption being in proportion to the extent of their fear. Such individuals are unlikely to be thinking in a calm and rational manner. (Others may, of course, be demonstrably panic-stricken.) Many people who act out of fear would not conform to the law's traditional interpretation of having lost their self-control, though it is possible that in future the courts might adopt a broader construction which would bring such individuals within the ambit of the new defence. Similar arguments apply to those who are, for example, desperate or frustrated. But whatever the nature of the individual's emotional reaction, what prompts our sympathy is the impact of the provocation/trigger on their mental processes. Referring to the loss of self-control requirement under the old provocation law, Lord Taylor (in *Ahluwalia*) explained that it 'encapsulates an essential ingredient of the defence of provocation in a clear and readily understandable phrase. It serves to underline that the defence is concerned with the actions of an individual who is not, at the moment when he or she acts violently, master of his or her own mind.'[49]

If the courts continue to construe loss of self-control in substantially the same way as they have done hitherto, then there must be serious doubt that the new law will bring about any significant reform. Significant reform could only be achieved by, at the very least, expanding the loss of self-control concept. The courts would have to recognise the importance of the mind's control over the physical action (or inaction), and the argument would be that the individual's normal thinking processes had been seriously disrupted by the provocation/trigger. In other words, the mind was not working normally and thus the physical actions were not being controlled in the usual way.[50]

The Search for a Rationale – for a 'Moral Plank'[51]

One of the constant features of commentaries on the old provocation law was the uncertainty of its rationale. The basic question, why should the law show sympathy to those who are provoked to kill, was uncomfortably difficult to answer with any great satisfaction or confidence. American commentators in particular tended to see it as essentially based on excuse. The fact that the accused had been provoked to lose his self-control justified our desire (instinct?) to show some compassion towards him, but it did not justify his act of killing another person. In this loose sense, provoked killers are in a broadly analogous position to the insane killer, though the latter's insanity has a more radical impact on his personal responsibility for killing since the verdict is 'not guilty by reason of insanity' – whereas the provoked killer's responsibility is only partially extinguished.

In contrast, some English commentators preferred to treat provocation as a mixture of excuse and justification. The loss of self-control provided grounds for excusing, but the fact that by definition the accused fulfilled the law's requirement that he had shown reasonable self-control in the circumstances evidenced an element of justification. Moral condemnation of the accused's reaction to the provocation should therefore be limited or qualified in some degree.

But the argument being made here is clearly that retention of the loss of self-control requirement is unlikely to bring about any significant reform of the law because it focuses attention on the

---

49 n. 23.
50 This would require a radical change from the approach adopted in cases such as *Ibrams* (1982) 74 Cr App R 154, where the Court of Appeal specifically rejected the idea that 'impairment of judgement' is synonymous with loss of self-control.
51 This was a phrase used by the Law Commission; Law Com. CP No 173, 2003 (n. 20) para. 4.28.

wrong issue. Even assuming that it is right to insist on some form of human activity as providing the trigger, the law should concentrate on the nature and extent to which that trigger has disturbed the accused's thinking, judgement and perceptions. Obviously, the killer's liability should only be affected if the trigger has had a serious or substantial impact on his mental processes. Throughout our lives we are frequently subjected to pressures and stresses that have some influence on our state of mind but these do not and should not lessen our personal responsibility for how we behave at the time. But where the provocation has substantially disturbed the individual's thinking, etc. – and where the individual's emotional reaction was reasonable – there must surely be good grounds for reflecting that in their criminal liability. There does not appear to be – at least to the author – any obvious or readily apparent means of determining whether there has been a sufficient mental disturbance, and it does not seem to be measurable in a purely objective manner. In cases where we are likely to be sympathetic, the accused's state of mind might well be described as 'abnormal', and this, in tandem with the very fact that the emphasis is on the impact on the accused's mental processes, undeniably raises the question of the relationship between provocation/loss of self-control and diminished responsibility.

Arguments about this relationship have been rehearsed elsewhere[52] and this is not the place to go over them again in detail. For the present purposes the essential points are that (i) there is no evidence in the law (e.g. the Homicide Act 1957) or in the debates which preceded it that provocation and diminished responsibility should be regarded as mutually exclusive; (ii) the relationship between normal and abnormal people should not be seen as a black or white one. Rather (psychiatrically) normal individuals may exhibit abnormal features in their thinking and/or behaviour, especially if they have been under stress or pressure, and (psychiatrically) abnormal people will show normal characteristics in their thoughts and conduct. Over a period of time all individuals show fluctuating levels of normality and abnormality, without being absolutely normal or abnormal; (iii) treating the relationship between provocation and diminished responsibility as mutually exclusive would breach the principle of fair labelling[53] because those suffering from a mental abnormality and who were provoked to kill would have to choose one or other of them to plead, so that (if the defence succeeded) the verdict would only partially reflect the reality. What matters for the present discussion is that we may call the accused's state of mind abnormal in two quite different ways. It may be abnormal in the sense that it is not that person's normal or usual state of mind (it is abnormal for him or her), or we may describe it as abnormal in the strict psychiatric sense. In either sense the accused's mental processes may have been so disturbed that he/she should not be regarded as wholly responsible for the killing. Thus, the basis on which liability is reduced is one of partial denial of responsibility.

---

52 See Ronnie Mackay and Barry Mitchell, 'Provoking Diminished Responsibility: Two Pleas Merging into One?' [2003] Criminal Law Review 745–59; James Chalmers, 'Merging Provocation and Diminished Responsibility: Some Reasons for Scepticism' [2004] Criminal Law Review 198–212; John Gardner and Timothy Macklem, 'No Provocation without Responsibility: A Reply to Mackay and Mitchell' [2004] Criminal Law Review 213–18; Ronnie Mackay and Barry Mitchell, 'Replacing Provocation: More on a Combined Plea' [2004] Criminal Law Review 219–23; and Barry Mitchell, Ronnie Mackay and Warren Brookbanks, 'Pleading for Provoked Killers: In Defence of *Morgan Smith*' (2008) 124 Law Quarterly Review 675–705.

53 According to the fair (or representative) labelling principle, offences should be defined and labelled so as to reflect the nature and severity of the wrongdoing. Partial defences such as loss of self-control and diminished responsibility are relevant here because they influence the category of the accused's crime. For general discussion of the principle, see for example, Andrew Ashworth, 'The Elasticity of Mens Rea', Tapper (ed.), *Crime, Proof and Punishment* (Butterworths, 1981); Glanville Williams, 'Convictions and Fair Labelling' [1983] Cambridge Law Journal 85; and James Chalmers and Fiona Leverick, 'Fair Labelling in Criminal Law' (2008) 71 Modern Law Review 217.

Practical Implications

Viewing provoked killings in the manner that is being contended in this chapter has certain practical implications. Of course, the fact that it is suggested that provocation and diminished responsibility should not be regarded as mutually exclusive pleas also makes us think of the concept, in the American Law Institute's Model Penal Code, of extreme mental or emotional disturbance:

> A homicide which would otherwise be murder [is manslaughter when it] is committed under the influence of extreme mental or emotional disturbance for which there is a reasonable explanation or excuse. The reasonableness of such explanation or excuse shall be determined from the viewpoint of a person in the actor's situation under the circumstances as he believes them to be.[54]

Deserving cases are determined by the adjective 'extreme' which, as commentators have quickly pointed out, is ambiguous and carries the risk that it would lead to inconsistent verdicts.[55] However, it is suggested that rather than simply rely on this kind of vague language – and note that another potentially elastic concept, of 'substantial' impairment is retained in the redefinition of diminished responsibility in s. 52(1) Coroners and Justice Act 2009 – it would be more appropriate for the law to permit expert evidence to be adduced as to the accused's thinking, judgement and perceptions so as to provide a clear and reliable picture of his state of mind. That would enable the jury to make an informed assessment of the impact of the provocation/trigger. Whilst this suggestion to adduce more expert evidence may initially be criticised, the fact is that the legal system has to make crucial judgements about serious matters, so that the factual basis on which such judgements are made is extremely important. Some jurors are likely to be able to imagine how they would have reacted in similar circumstances to those that confronted the accused; others quite simply will not. But the issue here is how the law should redefine the subjective requirement in what used to be called provocation. It is therefore absolutely vital that evidence is available of how the defendant reacted to it, evidence which is as accurate and reliable as possible. However much experience of life individual jurors may have had, it surely makes good sense to provide them with expert evidence. This would avoid the need to place total reliance on individual jurors drawing their own conclusions – making their own guesses – and it would thus reduce the danger that different juries would reach different verdicts about the same case.

Placing the emphasis on the reaction in the accused's mind rather than the physical manifestation of it has other potentially controversial implications. One sub-category of cases in which defendants have pleaded 'extreme mental or emotional disturbance' is often known as the 'brooder cases'. A conspicuous feature of these is that the defendant responded to the provocation/trigger in a manner which is the very antithesis of the old provocation plea: instead of a sudden eruption of violence through a visible loss of self-control, the defendant goes away and thinks about it, quite possibly for a matter of days, and carefully decides what to do. This obviously carries a strong implication of revenge, which is traditionally also viewed as the absolute antithesis of a deserving case. But it is implicit in the argument being made in this chapter that excluding undesirable cases of revenge cannot satisfactorily be achieved simply by imposing a time limitation between the trigger and the defendant's physical response to it. Nor can it be properly achieved by assuming that any evidence of premeditation should be fatal to the plea – that would, for example, clearly prejudice the interests

---

54 Model Penal Code and Commentaries, s.210(3)(1)(b).
55 See, for example, Law Com. No 304, 2006 (n. 3), para. 5.22. Note, however, that the Commission expressly acknowledged that 'the phrase has formed the basis for a provocation defence in at least some American state jurisdictions, and cannot therefore be dismissed as unworkable'.

of a significant proportion of battered women who kill their abusers, and there clearly seems to be a desire to show sympathy for their predicament. Thus, the partial defence of 'extreme mental or emotional disturbance' has been available in some brooder cases, because the law's attention is on the accused's state of mind more generally, rather than on the immediate object of his/her intent or on how quickly he/she responded to the trigger. (It is perhaps also worth remembering at this point that expert psychiatric or medical evidence is a feature of many 'extreme mental or emotional disturbance' cases.)

Conclusions

It is a statement of the obvious, but nevertheless worth stating, that the task facing law reformers here is a tough one. There clearly are some cases of vengeful killing or premeditated killing which are (almost) universally regarded as meriting no sympathy, but the law needs to adopt a sophisticated approach if it is not to exclude instances where our sympathy is appropriate. That in itself should persuade us to look elsewhere for a solution to the problem. The decision to retain the loss of self-control requirement and place it at the heart of the new law is likely to become regarded as a retrograde step – a lost opportunity at best. What may have happened is that attention was focused on cases which are regarded as unmeritorious and the view was that something had to be incorporated into the law in order to exclude them from the new defence, without at the same time looking carefully at similar situations which deserve less condemnation, and comparing the two. The nature and extent of the criticism of the concept under the old provocation law ought, as the Law Commission recommended, to have signalled its demise. If the label 'provocation' evoked so many bad memories that the new law had to be repackaged, then surely the loss of self-control concept should have gone with it or at least been given a radical rethink. But this is not to imply that it should simply have been relabelled or dressed up in a different guise.

The unavoidable conclusion must be that in the absence of a really significant reinterpretation of the loss of self-control concept, the new law will attract further criticism and be seen as achieving very little by way of genuine reform. Whilst it may well succeed in excluding many unmeritorious cases of considered revenge, it is likely to be of no use to many battered women for precisely the same reasons as the old provocation plea. The removal of the qualifying phrase 'sudden and temporary' is unlikely to have a major impact, certainly not enough to benefit battered women. What is necessary is a more radical rethink. Labelling the defence 'provocation' seems quite appropriate, but the disapprobation heaped on the old law – much of which was justifiable – indicates that decisions about how to define it in the early part of the twenty-first century should not be unduly influenced by its previous incarnations. Any proposed new definition of a defence should of course be tested to see if it would accommodate unmeritorious cases, but the process of reform should begin by thinking about the deserving cases and what it is about them that prompts our sympathy. Unfortunately, loss of self-control is not the answer.

Chapter 4
The Model of Tolerance and Self-Restraint

Richard Taylor

Introduction

The question which troubled the highest appellate courts most frequently under the law of provocation was the approach to be taken to the 'reasonable man' test and to what extent the personal characteristics and circumstances of the accused could or should be taken into account in assessing the question of whether a reasonable person would have responded in the way that the accused did. That question, as is now well known, was ultimately resolved for the law of provocation by reverting in *Holley*[1] to the *Camplin*[2] test of a person having the power of self-control of an ordinary person of the same sex and age as the accused but sharing such other characteristics as would affect the gravity of the provocation. This test crucially hinged on the distinction between the matters affecting the power of self-control and matters affecting the gravity of the provocation. The power of self-control was subject to an almost exclusively objective test, subject only to modification for the defendant's characteristics of age and sex, whereas the gravity of the provocation test was less prescriptive in that allowance could be made, in principle, for virtually any characteristic or circumstance of the defendant provided that it affected the gravity of the provocation. This reflected the consideration that, particularly in relation to verbal provocation, it is unrealistic and really quite meaningless to ask how grave is a taunt, e.g. about race or sexual capacity, to someone to whom it is inapplicable. The somewhat looser question, however, which for a time had been approved in *Smith (Morgan)*[3] of 'whether, having regard to all the circumstances, the jury consider the loss of self-control was sufficiently excusable' was rejected and with it the idea that a characteristic or circumstance such as depression or brain damage could be included in the jury's assessment if it merely affected the accused's ability to exercise self-control and did not actually affect the gravity of the provocation. Familiar as this history of the 'objective condition' may now seem, it should not be forgotten that at the time when the Law Commission was initially formulating its views on the reform of provocation, views which have ultimately led to the provisions in s. 54 and s. 55 of the Coroners and Justice Act 2009, it was the *Smith (Morgan)* doctrine which for most of that time held sway, the confusion emanating from its being one at least of the prime causes of the pressure for reform.

Against this background, it has been widely assumed that the test which is to be found in s. 54(1)(c) of whether

> a person of D's sex and age, with a normal degree of tolerance and self-restraint and in the circumstances of D, might have reacted in the same or in a similar way to D.

---

1 *Attorney General for Jersey* v. *Holley* [2005] 2 AC 580.
2 *DPP* v. *Camplin* [1978] AC 705.
3 *Smith (Morgan)* [2001] 1 AC 146.

was intended to be a more or less straight replacement for the objective condition referred to above and was simply designed to resolve the controversy between *Smith (Morgan)* and *Camplin*, in the same way as was ultimately done by the Privy Council in *Holley*, by preferring the *Camplin* approach. Whilst this is to some extent true, the thrust of this chapter will be to show how this analysis would be an oversimplification which would gloss over some important points of detail in the development, articulation and interpretation of s. 54(1)(c). The model of a person of a normal degree of tolerance and restraint should rather be seen as a more subtle and nuanced construction which could have important implications for how the new defence will operate in practice and in particular it will be argued that the introduction of the concept of 'tolerance' is highly significant. Furthermore, it will be shown how the new objective test in s. 54(1)(c) performs rather a different function in the new defence as compared to the function performed by the objective condition in the old defence of provocation. It will be seen that, at least in cases of 'things done or said', the objective test cannot be regarded as wholly to be found in s. 54(1)(c), but is also to be found in the meaning of the qualifying trigger in s. 55(4). The same is not necessarily true of cases of loss of control due to fear of serious violence, which is where the independent meaning of the new objective test may potentially have more impact, but where the analysis to be offered here is potentially most helpful in ensuring that the 'fear of serious violence' trigger is not unduly undermined. Before dealing with the differential impact of the new objective test in relation to the two qualifying triggers, the development of the two key components of the new objective test, 'a normal degree of tolerance and self-restraint' and 'in the circumstances of D' will be considered in the order in which they appear in the subsection.

The Development of the Test of 'a Normal Degree of Tolerance and Self-Restraint'

This test emerged between the initial Law Commission Consultation Paper on Partial Defences[4] (hereafter the 'consultation paper') in October 2003 (which did not make any specific recommendations or formulate any specific proposals on the reform of provocation) and the Report on Partial Defences[5] (hereafter the 'report') a year later in August 2004 in which the adoption of this test was recommended. The test as formulated in fact first publicly emerged in a document on the Law Commission website, entitled *Provisional Conclusions on Consultation Paper No 173*, dated May 2004, in which it was proposed at para. 40 that

> The defence should only be available if a person of ordinary temperament, i.e. ordinary tolerance and self-restraint, in the circumstances of the defendant might have reacted in the same or a similar way.

This new 'objective test', as it was called, was to replace the 'objective condition' governed at the time by *Smith (Morgan)* in which decision the phraseology of the 'reasonable man' had been heavily criticised as being anachronistic and best avoided notwithstanding its specific mention in s. 3 of the Homicide Act 1957. Not surprisingly, therefore, the Law Commission came up with a formulation which did not use the phrase 'reasonable man' (which it fully agreed was inappropriate and misleading) but instead used the phrase 'a person of ordinary temperament', which it then explained as a person of 'ordinary tolerance and self-restraint'. Whilst moving away from the

---

[4] Law Commission, *Partial Defences to Murder* (Law Com. CP No 173, 2003).
[5] Law Commission, *Partial Defences to Murder* (Law Com. No 290, 2004).

'reasonable man' wording, the Law Commission did not in other respects agree with the majority of the House of Lords in *Smith (Morgan)* but instead agreed with the *Camplin* approach as preferred by the minority in *Smith (Morgan)*, the approach which was later approved in *Holley*.

Although it is not difficult to understand why the Law Commission avoided references to the reasonable man, the question arises as to why did it refer to the person of ordinary temperament, rather than to a person with ordinary powers of self-control, and what was the significance of the introduction of 'ordinary tolerance and self-restraint' rather than an ordinary degree of self-control? Part of the answer may well be the fact that the Law Commission had decided to abandon the requirement of 'loss of self-control' which it considered to be lacking in clarity and which 'had proved very unsatisfactory'.[6] If the defence was not to be predicated essentially on loss of self-control, the requirement to have the objective test expressed as requiring at least a normal degree of self-control was not so obviously relevant, and given the Law Commission's reservations about the utility and coherence of the concept of loss of self-control, it is not surprising that they preferred the phrase 'self-restraint'.[7] But why go further and adopt a test of 'tolerance and self-restraint'? The answer to this part of the question may lie in the controversy surrounding *Smith (Morgan)* and the discussion by Lord Hoffmann in *Smith (Morgan)* of the Australian case of *Stingel*,[8] Lord Hoffmann's comments being discussed by the Law Commission both in its consultation paper[9] and then in its report[10] where the Commission first of all summarised the case of *Stingel* as follows:

> The defendant stalked a former girlfriend. She obtained a court order preventing him from approaching her, but he ignored it. After a party he found her (according to his account) in a car with another man having sex. He was sworn at and told where to go. He fetched a knife from his car and killed the man. The judge withdrew the defence of provocation from the jury and the High Court upheld his decision.

The Commission then went on to note that:

> In *Smith (Morgan)*, Lord Hoffmann, agreeing with the decision, said:

> "Male possessiveness and jealousy should not today be an acceptable reason for loss of self-control leading to homicide, whether inflicted upon the woman herself or her new lover."

In the consultation paper[11] the Law Commission noted that Lord Hoffmann also went on to suggest:

> a direction that characteristics such as jealousy and obsession should be ignored in relation to the objective element is the best way to ensure that people like Stingel cannot rely upon the defence.

---

6   Law Com. No 290, 2004 (n. 5) para. 3.115.
7   Law Com. CP No 173, 2003 (n. 4) para. 4.27. The Law Commission had noted that loss of self-restraint is not the same as loss of self-control and referred to *Cocker* [1989] Crim LR 740, in which the defendant in suffocating his incurably ill wife 'gave way to his wife's entreaties and far from losing his self-control acceded to what she wished to happen'.
8   *Stingel* (1990) 171 CLR 312.
9   Law Com. CP No 173, 2003 (n. 4) para. 4.83.
10 Law Com. No 290, 2004 (n. 5) para. 3.143.
11 Law Com. CP No 173, 2003 (n. 4) para. 4.83.

The introduction of the notion of tolerance can therefore be seen as a means of capturing this aspect of Lord Hoffmann's concerns in *Smith (Morgan)* (notwithstanding his generally more liberalising approach to the objective condition with which the Law Commission did not agree) about characteristics which should be excluded from consideration.

In a similar vein, and perhaps even more significantly, one of the cases discussed by the Law Commission as illustrating the 'evaluative free-for-all' resulting from *Smith (Morgan)* (unless one excludes certain characteristics as morally unacceptable as Lord Hoffmann was prepared to do) was the case of *Weller*[12] where the question was left open whether obsessive and jealous characteristics of the defendant husband should have been taken into account. The Law Commission's solution to this problem was explained as follows:[13]

> The test under our proposal is not whether the defendant's conduct was reasonable, but whether it was conduct which a person of ordinary temperament might have been driven to commit (*not a bigot or a person with an unusually short fuse*). We believe that a jury would be able to grasp and apply this idea in a common-sense way.

The italicised comments very clearly illustrate the thinking behind 'a normal degree of tolerance and self-restraint'. A test of a normal degree of self-restraint excludes those with an unusually short fuse, just as the previous ordinary powers of self-control test excluded them. But the new additional test of a normal degree of *tolerance* also excludes, inter alia, those who are bigoted or prejudiced against (or unacceptably intolerant towards) individuals from minority or vulnerable or protected groups in society or who are unacceptably intolerant in other ways, e.g. because of jealousy or male possessiveness or perhaps because of unacceptable attitudes such as those underpinning so-called 'honour killings'.[14]

Thus the introduction of a normal degree of 'tolerance' can be seen as a highly significant concept in its own right and not simply as part of the reformulation of the reasonable man test, simply referring to self-restraint rather than self-control. Tolerance and self-restraint may at first glance sound like, or be read as, a composite concept, but the words are clearly better read as incorporating two separate qualities and the new objective test requires a normal degree of each quality separately. That they should be considered as separate qualities rather than simply a composite concept is also supported by the concluding words of s. 54(3) which refers to D's general capacity for tolerance *or* self-restraint.[15] Tolerance is a different matter from either self-restraint or self-control, it is a matter of attitude and an aspect of respect for others as required in a modern liberal society. As will be seen, it is a concept that is also reflected in other aspects of the new defence, in particular in the notion of having a justifiable sense of being seriously wronged within s. 55(4). But before considering that matter we need to examine the second part of the objective test in s. 54(1)(c), the meaning of the phrase 'in the circumstances of D'.

---

12 *Weller* [2004] 1 Cr App R 1.
13 Law Com. No 290, 2004 (n. 5) para. 3.127 (emphasis added).
14 See the comments of the Home Office Minister, Maria Eagle, during the House of Commons Committee Debates on the Coroners and Justice Bill (HC Deb., 3 March 2009, col. 442): 'we all agree that we do not want to allow honour killings to sneak into the partial defence'. In support of this aim she quoted the text of the bill stating that the jury must be satisfied that 'a person ... with a normal degree of tolerance ... might have reacted in the same way or in a similar way'.
15 In this connection, what is notable about the quote from Maria Eagle in n. 14 is that the Minister herself chose to refer separately to a normal degree of *tolerance* as the relevant factor and chose to leave out the reference to self-restraint.

The Development of the Test of 'in the Circumstances of D'

The model person with a normal degree of tolerance and self-restraint has to be considered 'in the circumstances of D' and s. 54(3) of the Act defines 'the circumstances of D' as 'a reference to all of D's circumstances other than those whose only relevance to D's conduct is that they bear on D's general capacity for tolerance or self-restraint'.

Paragraph 41 of the Report on Partial Defences was quite explicit about how this aspect of the new objective test came to be formulated:

> In deciding whether a person of ordinary temperament in the circumstances of the defendant might have reacted in the same or similar way, the court should take into account all the characteristics of the defendant other than "matters that bear simply on [his or her] general capacity for self-control" (to adopt a succinct expression used by Professor Glanville Williams in his analysis of the decision in *Camplin*). The only qualification which we would make is that the court should have regard to the defendant's age, because capacity for self-control is a factor of maturity, and it would be unjust to expect the same level of a twelve-year-old and an adult (as was recognised in *Camplin*). In other words, we prefer the minority position in *Smith (Morgan)*, which also accords broadly with the law in Australia, Canada and New Zealand, and with the recent provisional recommendations of the Irish Law Reform Commission.

As can be seen, this formulation was adopted, almost as a matter of convenience, from the 'succinct' phrase that Glanville Williams had used to summarise the effect of *Camplin*. It is important however to note a little more precisely just what Glanville Williams had actually written[16] which was:

> "Characteristics" therefore do not *include* matters that bear simply on the general capacity for self control.

It was a statement therefore of what characteristics are not included rather than a positive definition of what characteristics are included. The Law Commission took this exclusionary phrase and then prefaced it with its own inclusionary words, 'the court should take into account all the characteristics of the defendant' without reference to the inclusionary test from *Camplin* that the characteristic should affect the gravity of the provocation. Although the Commission clearly regarded its formulation as being in line with the views of the minority in *Smith (Morgan)* and as re-establishing the *Camplin* test, it had created, whether or not deliberately, a potentially significant difference between the *Camplin* test and its own formulation, a formulation which is now effectively enshrined in the 2009 Act.[17] The point is that the *Camplin* test was a positive test of whether the characteristic or circumstance affected the gravity of the provocation. The new test is different in that it is essentially a negative test of not being things 'whose only relevance is that they bear on D's general capacity for tolerance or self-restraint'. This is not surprising since, as has already been pointed out, Glanville Williams was not, in the passage quoted from his textbook, giving a full or positive test for what was then regarded as a relevant 'characteristic' (something which affects the gravity of the provocation), he was merely explaining what was certainly not counted (something

---

16   Glanville Williams, *Textbook of Criminal Law* (2nd edn, Stevens, 1983) 540 (emphasis added).

17   The only difference being that the Act refers to D's general capacity for *tolerance or self-restraint* as opposed to D's general capacity for *self-control*.

which only affects self- control). The test enshrined in the 2009 Act, however, as a result of simply adopting the exclusionary partial definition from Glanville Williams, no longer positively requires that the circumstances should affect the gravity of the conduct triggering the loss of control; it is simply enough that the circumstances have some relevance to D's conduct other than bearing on D's capacity for tolerance and self-restraint.

The difference from the *Camplin/Holley* test can in fact be put in three separate ways. Firstly, that one no longer has to show positively that the circumstance affects the gravity of the triggering conduct (or, as it was formerly known, the gravity of the provocation). Secondly, that whilst some relevance to something (other than capacity for tolerance and self-restraint) has to be shown, the relevance of the circumstance is said to be to D's conduct rather than to the triggering conduct engaged in by V or some third person. Thirdly, that whilst a circumstance is still not relevant simply because it bears on the general capacity for tolerance and self-restraint, it can still be relevant provided that is not its only relevance to D's conduct.

These differences may raise some doubts about some of the assumptions that the Law Commission offered in its subsequent report on murder, manslaughter and infanticide.[18] For example, at paragraph 5.40 of that report the Law Commission said:

> Our provisions impose a duty on the judge to instruct the jury to ignore factors that affect D's general capacity for self-control. Alcoholism, for example, or another mental deficiency or disorder that is liable to affect temper and tolerance are obvious examples.

This reasoning is only strictly correct if the only relevance of the alcoholism or other mental deficiency or disorder to D's conduct is the effect it has on tolerance and self-restraint but if it has that relevance and also some other relevance in addition, it could yet be included in D's circumstances. This was true under the old law but only if it affected the gravity of the provocation, e.g. as in *Morhall*,[19] if the provocation was constituted partly by taunts about the addiction. The circumstance could still be relevant on this basis under the new law if the taunt about the addiction (or alcoholism) was relevant to D's conduct (which it arguably would be since the taunt striking home at the sensitive point contributed to him doing what he/she did). But the defence would not now be limited to showing the relevance of the circumstance due to being taunted about it (or due to its affecting the gravity in some other way). The circumstance could now theoretically be relevant in ways other than affecting the gravity of the triggering conduct (and other than the consequent additional impact on D's conduct due to that increased gravity). To provide an example of how this might be the case in a way that might affect a typical 'things done or said' case is not easy (although defendants or their legal advisers will doubtless not be slow to think of one) but a worked out example in relation to a defence triggered by fear of serious violence will be given at a later and more appropriate point of this chapter.[20] For the moment it may suffice to refer to a brain damaged person[21] who might argue that his brain damage was relevant to his conduct of killing, not because it affected the gravity of the triggering conduct or because it affected his tolerance and self-restraint (even if it did so) but rather because it influenced his conduct in some other way.

---

18 Law Commission, *Murder, Manslaughter and Infanticide* (Law Com. No 304, 2006).
19 *Morhall* [1996] AC 90.
20 Below at page 60.
21 For the position of such a person under the *Camplin* approach, see *Luc Thiet Thuan* v. *The Queen* [1997] AC 131.

Summary in Relation to the New Objective Test in Section 54(1)(c)

The new test is not primarily about powers of self-control but about normal temperament which includes the concept of self-restraint, which may be similar to self-control, but the new test is wider in including also the notion of tolerance. It is the inclusion of tolerance which enables it, in effect, to exclude unpalatable characteristics such as jealousy and racial, religious, sexual and other forms of intolerance, prejudice and bigotry and other unacceptable attitudes such as those underpinning so-called 'honour killings'. The definition of 'the circumstances of D' was developed as a response to the unduly wide and imprecise standard which the decision in *Smith (Morgan)* had approved and was intended in general terms to return the law to the *Camplin* approach which the Privy Council in any event subsequently reintroduced for the law of provocation in *Holley*. However, the new test is subtly different from the *Camplin/Holley* test, not only in the new (and potentially very significant) reference to tolerance as well as to self-restraint, but also in that all the circumstances of the accused are in principle brought in provided that they do not bear only on the capacity for tolerance or self-restraint but can be shown to have some other relevance to D's conduct, even if not necessarily to the gravity of the triggering conduct. There may not be many circumstances which neither bear on the gravity of the triggering conduct nor bear only on the capacity for tolerance and self-restraint, but defendants will no doubt seek to present their circumstances or highlight them in a manner which shows some relevance to D's conduct, other than to his/her capacity for tolerance and self-restraint, even if the circumstances do not directly affect the gravity of the triggering conduct.

The Potentially Reduced Importance of the New Objective Test in Section 54(1)(c) in Relation to 'Things Done or Said'

Having noted that the objective test is not quite as similar to the *Camplin/Holley* test as might at first sight have been assumed, further consideration of its role in the overall structure of the new defence might suggest that, in many cases at least, it will not have a major impact on whether the defence ultimately is made out. This is because, at least in relation to the 'things done or said' trigger in s. 55(4), there is a requirement that the trigger 'constituted circumstances of an extremely grave character' and 'caused D to have a justifiable sense of being seriously wronged'. These tests are sufficiently demanding that if they are satisfied by the triggering conduct, it is highly unlikely, or at least it will be relatively unusual, that such conduct might not also cause 'a person with a normal degree of tolerance and self-restraint, and in the circumstances of D, to react in the same or similar way to D'. Under the old law of provocation, where the subjective question was simply whether 'there was evidence on which a jury could find that the accused was provoked to lose his self-control',[22] the controlling effect of the objective condition was a critical aspect of any attempt (not always successful) to prevent the application of the defence of provocation to trivial or inappropriate cases. Now that the threshold for 'things done or said' has been raised so significantly in s. 55(4)(a) and (b), there will be much less need, in relation to this trigger, for the objective test to limit the much more serious, and limited number, of instances which will be likely to succeed in getting over the threshold and causing the s. 54(1)(c) question even to be asked.

This then raises the question of whether the restrictive nature of the qualifying trigger in s. 55(4) will render the law *too* restrictive. Could it mean that legitimate factors personal to the accused which might have increased the seriousness of the triggering conduct to the accused (and

---

22 Homicide Act 1957, s. 3.

thus would have been admissible even under the *Camplin/Holley* test) will no longer be of any relevance or of any help to the accused? This depends on to what extent the tests under s. 55(4)(a) and (b) are purely objective and to what extent they admit of subjective considerations. Under the Law Commission's proposals, the question would have primarily arisen in relation to what is now s. 55(4)(b) – the justifiable sense of being seriously wronged – since s. 55(4)(a) (circumstances of an extremely grave character) was not part of their proposals under which the provocation simply had to be 'gross', a concept which was explained purely in terms of the 'justifiable sense of being seriously wronged'. Of this latter phrase, the Law Commission had this to say:[23]

> In deciding whether there was gross provocation in the sense of words and/or conduct which caused the defendant to have a justifiable sense of being seriously wronged, we do not intend the test to be purely subjective, i.e. what the defendant thought. It is for the jury to decide whether there was gross provocation in the relevant sense. In making that judgement the jury must of course consider the situation in which the defendant found him or herself and take into account all the characteristics of the defendant which they consider to be relevant. Taking into account the circumstances and characteristics of the defendant does not mean that if the defendant considered it to be gross provocation, the jury must therefore accept that it was gross provocation. The jury may conclude that the defendant had no sufficient reason to regard it as gross provocation, or indeed that the defendant's attitude in regarding the conduct as provocation demonstrated an outlook (e.g. religious or racial bigotry) offensive to the standards of a civilised society. Dr Horder gives an example:
>
> Reconsider the imaginary case of Terreblanche, whose deep-rooted beliefs include the belief that it is the gravest of insults for a coloured person to speak to a white man unless spoken to first. If he became enraged and killed a coloured person for speaking to him in this way, is the jury to be directed to take his beliefs into account – qua characteristics – in judging the gravity of the provocation (assuming there is held to be a "real connection" between the provocation and those beliefs, or that the victim deliberately spoke to him as a challenge to those beliefs)? Would not such a direction be an outrageous compromise of society's commitment to racial tolerance?
>
> Our answer to the question posed in the last sentence is yes. No fair-minded jury, properly directed, could conclude that it was gross provocation for a person of one colour to speak to a person of a different colour. In such a case the proper course would therefore be for the judge to withdraw provocation from the jury.

Thus whilst the Terreblanche example[24] makes it clear that the test is not purely subjective (it is not satisfied purely by D's sense of being seriously wronged if that sense is not justifiable) neither is it completely objective since the circumstances and characteristics of D have to be taken into account in deciding what he sensed and whether it was justifiable, ignoring any unacceptable justifications he puts forward which would be inconsistent with the concept of a tolerant individual enshrined in s. 54(1)(c). One perhaps begins to see here the close interrelationship of the objective test in s. 54(1)(c) with the test for the qualifying trigger in s. 55(4). The notion of the tolerant individual introduced in s. 54(1)(c), whose significance has already been highlighted, is leaking back into the question of what is a justifiable sense of being

---

23 Law Com. No 290, 2004 (n. 5) para. 3.70.
24 Taken from Jeremy Horder, *Provocation and Responsibility* (Oxford University Press, 1992).

seriously wronged, and undesirable characteristics are also being excluded at this stage as not grounding a justifiable sense of being wronged.

However, an even more explicit connection between the expected content of the objective test and the demands of the qualifying trigger is to be found in s. 55(4)(a) which was the government's eventual resolution of its attempt to give a clearer articulation of the concept of gross provocation once it had determined that the word 'provocation' was itself best dropped completely. Initially, the replacement for the requirement of grossness was expressed in terms of the requirement of there being an 'exceptional happening'[25] but ultimately this was replaced[26] by the expression now to be found in the Act, 'circumstances of an extremely grave character'. Unlike the phrase, 'justifiable sense of being seriously wronged' there was no real discussion (no doubt due to its late inclusion in the proposals) of the extent to which this incorporates subjective considerations into what is, on the face of it, an objective test, but the use of the word gravity (whether intentionally or otherwise) sounds a clear echo of the *Camplin* question of factors 'which affect the gravity of the provocation'. Just as Lord Diplock in that case reasoned that one can hardly assess the gravity of verbal provocation without considering at least some of the characteristics and circumstances of the person to whom the provocation is addressed, similarly it is difficult to see how the question of whether things done or said constitute circumstances of an extremely grave character can be answered without considering relevant characteristics/circumstances of the person whose loss of control they are alleged to have triggered. The relevance of D's characteristics and circumstances to the gravity of the things done or said thus seems to have resurfaced under the definition of the trigger in s. 55(4)(a) even though it is not explicitly required in the objective test under s. 54(1)(c) (under which the question is simply one of whether the characteristics or circumstances bear only on D's general capacity for tolerance or self-restraint). Of course the question under s. 55(4)(a) is still a much more demanding one than the old *Camplin* test since the triggering conduct has to constitute circumstances of an extremely grave character, but the fact that the things done or said strike home at a particular circumstance or characteristic of the individual defendant will potentially assist in showing that the triggering conduct was not only grave but was 'extremely' grave.

The Relatively Greater Importance of the Objective Test in Section 54(1)(c) in Cases Triggered Primarily by Fear of Serious Violence

The limitation imposed by the objective test, of what a person with a normal degree of tolerance and self-restraint might have done in D's circumstances, is likely to be much more important in cases where the accused is relying on a fear of serious violence as the trigger for loss of control under s. 55(3). This is because there is no further express requirement in s. 55(3) relating to any requirement of extreme gravity or of any justifiable sense of being seriously wronged. Whereas the whole point of s. 55(4) is to restrict the availability of the defence so it is not inappropriately, or too readily, available to (typically male) unjustified violence in anger, the whole point of s. 55(3) is to extend the ambit of the defence so as to make it more amenable to victims of domestic abuse who lose control and kill their abusers due to fear (even though they may have gone beyond reasonable self-defence) and also to make it available to other analogous cases, such as domestic

---

25 Ministry of Justice, *Murder, Manslaughter and Infanticide: Proposals for Reform of the Law* (MoJ CP 19, 2008) Annex A, draft clause 1(6)(a).

26 Ministry of Justice, *Murder, Manslaughter and Infanticide: Proposals for Reform of the Law. Summary of Responses and Government Position* (MoJ CP (R) 19, 2009) para. 40.

occupiers who find they have overstepped the mark in using lethal force against unlawful intruders. There is no limiting factor within this qualifying trigger other than the fact that the fear must be of serious violence and there is no requirement even that there is, or has been, any actual serious violence (although often of course there will have been), provided there is the fear of it. In these circumstances, the objective test in s. 54(1)(c) may have more scope for application and, especially if not carefully thought through, for limiting (justly or otherwise) the success of the defence. This is where the subtle differences between the *Camplin/Holley* test and the test as now formulated in the statute may become much more significant, and indeed the differences may be helpful in ensuring that the objective test does not inappropriately limit the new fear of violence trigger.

To illustrate how the new objective test might operate differently from, and potentially more helpfully than, the *Camplin/Holley* test, take, for example, a brain damaged person who is the victim of long-term physical abuse from a member of his family. Let us say that the abuse has escalated recently and, although it has not yet reached the level of serious violence, he now fears (whether reasonably or not) serious violence for the future. Let us say also, in the light of this fear, he loses control and intentionally stabs his abuser several times and, as a result of the stab wounds, the abuser dies (but self-defence is not available because the force is considered to be unreasonable in the light of the nature, or lack of imminence, of the feared violence). Under *Camplin/Holley*, the fact that the brain damage may have affected his powers of self-control is not relevant (as was held in *Luc*[27]) and it would be difficult (though admittedly not impossible) to argue (and it was not argued in *Luc*) that the brain damage can be regarded as affecting the gravity of the provocation. Under s. 54(1)(c), again the fact that his brain damage may have affected his degree of tolerance and self-restraint does not make it relevant but it is now not necessarily irrelevant just because he cannot show it affects the gravity of the triggering conduct. It is now open to him to show that it is not a circumstance 'whose only relevance' to his conduct is its bearing on his general capacity for tolerance or self-restraint. Thus he might argue that his brain damage was relevant to his conduct, not because it affected the gravity of the triggering conduct or because it affected his tolerance and self-restraint (even if it did so) but rather because it influenced his conduct in some other way, e.g. because it affected his understanding of the risks involved in intentionally stabbing someone. So he might argue that it was not intolerant and lacking in normal self-restraint for him to stab his abuser (as opposed to, say, striking a blow) in the light of the fear of serious violence which he had, even though the normal person who lost control would not have done more than use blows or would have inflicted fewer or less serious stab wounds. The brain damage (or other mental disorder) prevented him from realising the lethal nature of the wounds he was inflicting (even though he did intend to inflict GBH) and should be included in the circumstances considered under s. 54(1)(c) because it does not bear only on his capacity for tolerance and self-restraint as it was relevant to his (understanding of) his conduct in another way (but did not deprive him of *mens rea*).

The example may be thought to be somewhat artificial and contrived (although experience teaches that life throws up situations more bizarre than our most fevered imaginations can dream of) but the point being made is of potentially wider application and importance than the particular example given in that it illustrates how the defendant does not have to point to, as was required under the old law, a connection between the characteristic/circumstance and the gravity of the provocation/triggering conduct. All circumstances are now included in D's circumstances except those whose only relevance is that they bear on the general capacity for tolerance and self-restraint. The starting point is therefore that circumstances are included, unless they are excluded as only bearing on tolerance and self-restraint, as opposed to a starting point of having to show that the

---

27 *Luc Thiet Thuan* v. *The Queen* [1997] AC 131.

circumstance affects the gravity of provocation. Of course, showing that the only relevance of a circumstance is not its bearing on tolerance and self-restraint does mean that the circumstance must in fact have some other relevance, but the change of starting point, and the almost limitless range of other potential relevancies which can be argued for, will no doubt be exploited advantageously by defendants and their advisers. They will be able to use this argument to limit the impact of the test in s. 54(1)(c) on fear of serious violence cases, where it is potentially a more serious limitation than in 'things done or said' cases, where it may add little to the high threshold in s. 55(4).

Conclusions

Tolerance and Self-Restraint

The test of a person with a normal degree of tolerance and self-restraint could be seen purely as the reasonable man test updated and put into a more modern vernacular, simply eschewing the outmoded language of the reasonable man and substituting a new expression, in place of the ordinary powers of self-control, but which would nevertheless mean much the same thing. This would be to read tolerance as merely referring to the ability to deal with a certain level of fear, or sense of being wronged, and thus to be merely another aspect of self-control or self-restraint to which it would add very little on this reading. However, the way in which the test was developed by the Law Commission, and the way in which tolerance in particular was (albeit relatively briefly) discussed by it, means that tolerance is much better seen as an independent quality or concept which is distinct from self-restraint (as is made clear by the concluding words of s. 54(3)). Tolerance, on this reading, adds a different moral dimension to the defence and brings a different kind of evaluative component to the objective condition, quite apart from the question of normal powers of self-control, and one which is essentially about a civilised and acceptable attitude to other individuals in a modern pluralistic society.

The requirement of a normal degree of tolerance in this sense is also quite logical given the introduction at the heart of the defence of the requirement, in the 'things done and said' trigger at least, of the justifiable sense of being seriously wronged (which in the Law Commission's formulation completely supplanted the need for loss of control). The normative requirement that a person with an ordinary degree of self-control might have acted in a similar way is the obvious requirement where loss of control is the gist of the defence as was the case with provocation. But where the essence of the defence is (or includes, as one must now put it, given that loss of control has been put back, nominally at least, in the centre stage) that one has a justifiable sense of being seriously wronged, a normative requirement that a person of ordinary tolerance (towards the behaviour of others) might also have felt seriously wronged by the other's conduct is an equally logical aspect of an objective test. Thus the nature of the objective test is rightly influenced by the nature of the justification (or at least a significant aspect of it) for giving the defence in the first place. This interrelationship between the nature of the objective test and the requirement of a justifiable sense of being seriously wronged was most clearly seen perhaps in the discussion by the Law Commission of the hypothetical racist, Terreblanche.

Whether one can point to a similar inter-relationship between the test of tolerance and the trigger of 'fear of serious violence' is not as easy to discern. Perhaps even here there is a de facto, if not de iure, element of being seriously wronged as a result of the fear of violence, whether it be at the hands of an abusive partner or of a frightening intruder, and perhaps this is the consideration that is most relevant in the loss of control defence as opposed to the imperative of personal safety or protection which would be the overriding consideration where the defence is one of self-defence. This would explain why force which is unreasonable from a point of view of self-protection, and thus not objectively justified as a matter of self-defence, might still be able to satisfy the different objective requirement of being such force that a person of ordinary tolerance and self-restraint might have used. The explanation is that D's sense of being wronged by the fear to which he/she is exposed is such that even the model person, with an ordinary degree of tolerance and self-restraint in D's circumstances would not be expected to tolerate continuing to be subjected to such fear. Although this is an aspect of tolerance with a rather different emphasis from that previously discussed, it is still a notion of tolerance which is bound up with what conduct in others we should be expected to tolerate (or not tolerate) as opposed to simply being an aspect of how much self-control or self-restraint we should be expected to be able to exercise. It has to be admitted, nevertheless, that the separate notion of tolerance, as distinguished from self-restraint, may be of less significance in cases based on the 'fear of serious violence' trigger than in relation to cases based on 'things done or said'.

In the Circumstances of D

This test again might be seen as simply an updated version of the *Camplin/Holley* test for characteristics affecting the gravity of the provocation, but the analysis undertaken has sought to demonstrate that, whilst there are similarities, there are also important differences, not least in that the starting point under the new law is that all circumstances are included, whether or not they affect the gravity of the triggering conduct, but that they are subject to exclusion if their only relevance to D's conduct is that they bear on his/her capacity for tolerance and self-restraint. Whilst this may seem to some like splitting hairs, it is a distinction which one can confidently expect to see defendants seeking to use. Arguments about how the defendant's circumstances were relevant to his/her conduct other than by reference to his/her capacity for tolerance and self-restraint can be expected to be a common feature of the early case law under the Act. An example of a possible argument along these lines has been given earlier, based on a brain damaged defendant, and the courts as a result of such cases may have to think again about the question of whether there is a dividing line or an overlap between diminished responsibility and loss of control.

The Impact on the Qualifying Triggers and their Interpretation

The test of a person with a normal degree of tolerance and self-restraint is more likely to become a live issue in cases based on the first qualifying trigger, 'fear of serious violence'. In this context, the additional values brought in by the separate notion of tolerance are less likely to be of significance than in relation to the second trigger of 'things done or said'. However, the fact that the test of 'in the circumstances of D' is somewhat more inclusive than the *Camplin/Holley* test may well be of some significance in such cases and will assist in making the new trigger more workable and less susceptible to the restrictive argument that if the force used was not reasonable self-defence, it also does not satisfy the objective test of the person of ordinary tolerance and self-restraint. In relation to the second trigger of 'things done or said', the restrictive nature of the criteria to be satisfied, in terms of extreme gravity and a justifiable sense of being seriously wronged, may mean that the objective test will be largely redundant in many cases. Nevertheless, the fact that tolerance, in the attitudinal sense argued for here, is an aspect of the objective test may be of some assistance in the interpretation of 'a justifiable sense of being seriously wronged'. If it helps to demonstrate that some objectionable claims to having a sense of being seriously wronged would not succeed anyway because they would fall foul of the notion of a person with a normal degree of tolerance, that may create the room for an otherwise more liberal or subjective interpretation of the word 'justifiable' in other, more appropriate, cases. In other words, the presence of a person with a normal degree of tolerance in the objective test may encourage a greater degree of tolerance by the courts in the interpretation of other aspects of the defence. If tolerance, or at least having the right degree of it, is a virtue, this might be described as a virtuous circle; but that might be to risk causing a loss of control even in the reader who can be assumed to be the very model of tolerance and self-restraint.

Chapter 5
The Serious Wrong of Domestic Abuse and the Loss of Control Defence

Jonathan Herring

Introduction

Five per cent of male victims of homicide were killed by their partner, ex-partner or lover in 2009–10.[1] In many of these cases the defendant claimed she had been abused by the victim. Much literature has been produced considering which defences are, or should be, available to defendants in such cases. This chapter will consider the circumstances in which the new defence of loss of self-control will be available where the defendant is relying on the 'serious wrong' qualifying trigger. There is not space to consider the many other defences that might be relied upon in such a case, such as self-defence, diminished responsibility, or loss of control relying on the violence qualifying trigger.[2] I believe that these defences, and in particular, self-defence, will be better suited in many cases where the defendant was in a violent relationship.[3] However, the central argument of this chapter is that the serious wrong loss of control defence should be available in many cases where victims of domestic violence kill their abusers.

This chapter will focus on the question: What is the wrong in cases of domestic abuse? This is a central question for two reasons. First it is essential in determining whether the qualifying trigger applies. Section 55(4) defines the serious wrong qualifying trigger:

> This subsection applies if D's loss of self-control was attributable to a thing or things done or said (or both) which –
>
> (a) constituted circumstances of an extremely grave character, and
> (b) caused D to have a justifiable sense of being seriously wronged.

An understanding of the wrong of domestic abuse will assist in determining whether the circumstances were of an extremely grave character and whether they caused D to have a justifiable sense of being seriously wronged. Second, the defence is only available if the defendant acted as

> a person of D's sex and age, with a normal degree of tolerance and self-restraint and in the circumstances of D, might have reacted in the same or in a similar way to D.[4]

---

[1] Home Office, *Homicides, Firearm Offences and Intimate Violence 2009/10* (Home Office, 2011). For a detailed discussion of the statistics see Catherine Itzen, Ann Taket and Sarah Barter-Godfrey, *Domestic and Sexual Violence and Abuse* (Routledge, 2010).

[2] Victoria Nourse, 'Self-Defense and Subjectivity' (2001) 68 University of Chicago Law Review 1235.

[3] Aileen McColgan, 'In Defence of Battered Women Who Kill' (1993) 13 Oxford Journal of Legal Studies 508.

[4] Coroners and Justice Act 2005, s. 54(1)(c).

That also requires a consideration of the wrongfulness of the domestic abuse, so that an assessment can be made of how the hypothetical woman would have reacted.[5]

The Background to the Reform

One of the arguments used to justify the reform of the law of provocation was that the law worked inadequately in the context of victims of domestic violence who kill their abusers.[6] Cases such as *Thornton*[7] and *Ahluwalia*[8] highlighted some of the difficulties. Much has been written on these inadequacies of the previous law of provocation and so there is no need for me to explore that further here.[9]

The early reaction of some commentators to the reforms has been to suggest that the serious wrong trigger will not be much used by defendants who killed their domestic abuser. Andrew Simester and Bob Sullivan in their excellent textbook suggest they will 'most likely' rely on the fear of serious violence trigger.[10] Susan Edwards argues also that they will 'do better' to develop an argument around the violence trigger, relying on the concept of cumulative fear.[11] Richard Card suggests the serious wrong trigger will only apply to a small number of cases, such as where 'a rape-victim loses self-control and kills the rapist who has taunted her'.[12] While not disagreeing that the violence trigger can be relied upon in many cases, this chapter is more optimistic than those commentators about the potential use of the serious wrong qualifying trigger in these cases. It will argue that properly understood domestic abuse should readily be regarded as a very serious wrong. Indeed, such a serious wrong that it can provide the partial justification necessary for the defence.

Before turning to that argument I want to outline the significance of the change in the emphasis of the new defence. It is important to stress that the reforms have abolished the old defence of provocation and replaced it with a new defence. The temptation may be to regard the new loss of control defence as merely an amended version of the old provocation law. However, the new defence has a significantly different philosophical underpinning and this, I suggest, will affect how the law will be interpreted. The new defence moves from a defence based on 'angry loss of self-control' to one based on righteous indignation or moral outrage.[13] Under the old law the focus was on whether the defendant lost self-control and then whether a reasonable person in their situation would have responded in the way they did.[14] This meant that for victims of domestic violence who killed their abusers the focus was often on seeking to show that they suffered

---

5   Alan Norrie, 'The Coroners and Justice Act 2009 – Partial Defences to Murder: (1) Loss of Control' [2010] Criminal Law Review 275.

6   Law Commission, *Partial Defences to Murder* (Law Com. No 290, 2004), para. 4.18; Ministry of Justice, *Murder, Manslaughter and Infanticide* (MoJ CP No 19, 2008).

7   *Thornton* [1992] 1 All ER 306.

8   *Ahluwalia* [1992] 4 All ER 889.

9   Jeremy Horder, *Provocation and Responsibility* (Oxford University Press, 1992).

10 Andrew Simester, John Spencer, Robert Sullivan and Graham Virgo, *Simester and Sullivan's Criminal Law* (4th edn, Hart, 2010) 400–401.

11 Susan Edwards, 'Anger and Fear as Justifiable Preludes for Loss of Self-Control' (2010) 74 Journal of Criminal Law 223.

12 Richard Card, *Criminal Law* (19th edn, Oxford University Press, 2010), 285.

13 Edwards (n. 11).

14 Homicide Act 1957, s. 3.

from the controversial 'battered women's syndrome'.[15] This played the dual role of enabling the defendant to claim that her psychological state was evidence of the loss of self-control and that it also made her response reasonable. While the new defence is yet to be expounded upon by the courts, I would argue that the focus of the loss of control defence will be on the wrongfulness of the conduct and whether it is regarded as being of an extremely grave character. Once the serious wrong qualifying trigger is satisfied, the requirements of loss of control and that the response reflected a normal degree of tolerance and self-restraint will readily be found. This is because any normal person facing circumstances of an extremely grave character which gave them a justifiable sense of being seriously wronged *might* lose control. This is particularly so given the removal of the requirement for immediacy in loss of control and the explicit requirement that the killing be not motivated by revenge.[16] For victims of domestic abuse, therefore, the focus may shift away from their psychological state and on to the wrongfulness of the abuse they are suffering.[17] The benefit of this approach is that they need not present themselves as suffering from a psychological disorder, but rather as responding in the way any ordinary person might when facing a most grave wrong.

It may be replied that such an approach overlooks the fact that the loss of self-control is still a central requirement of the defence and that indeed the government failed to adopt the proposals of the Law Commission to remove the loss of self-control requirement.[18] However, the explanation given by the government for rejecting the Law Commission's proposals is informative. The Law Commission, in arguing for a removal of the loss of control trigger, emphasised that in domestic abuse cases 'women's reactions are less likely to involve a "loss of self control", but more likely comprise a combination of anger, fear, frustration and a sense of desperation'.[19] The government, in deciding to retain the requirement for loss of self-control, expressed concern that otherwise the defence would be open to 'honour killings' or gang-related violence.[20] That reasoning may not be persuasive,[21] but it reveals that the role of loss of self-control is perceived as essentially exclusionary, rather than carrying moral weight as the basis of the defence. In other words, the government's perception of the role played by loss of self-control is to ensure that the defence should not be available to those acting out of revenge or in a cold-blooded way,[22] rather than regarding it as central to the philosophical basis for the defence.[23]

Even if that is a misreading of the Act and the loss of control is regarded as a central element, it would be wrong to assume that the notion of loss of control in the new defence is the same as that used under the previous law on provocation. First, the notion of loss of self-control as a form of 'partial insanity through anger' has been subject to considerable academic criticism from lawyers and psychologists.[24] It was partly as a result of the dissatisfaction with it, that the proposals for reform were developed. Second, the fact that fear of violence is one of the two qualifying triggers demonstrates that we have moved well beyond the notion of an angry outburst being the paradigm

---

15   Felicity Kaganas, 'Domestic Homicide, Gender and the Expert', in Andrew Bainham, Shelly Day Sclater and Martin Richards (eds), *Body Lore and Laws* (Hart Publishing, 2001).
16   Coroners and Justice Act 2009, s. 54(2).
17   Norrie (n. 5).
18   Law Com. No 290, 2004 (n. 6) para. 391.
19   Law Commission, *Murder, Manslaughter and Infanticide* (Law Com. No 304, 2006) para. 5.18.
20   MoJ CP No 19, 2008 (n. 6) para. 36.
21   Anna Carline, 'Reforming Provocation: Perspectives from the Law Commission and the Government' [2009] 2 Web Journal of Current Legal Issues.
22   MoJ CP No 19, 2008 (n. 6) 62.
23   Carline (n. 21).
24   Richard Holton and Stephen Shute, 'Self-Control in the Modern Provocation Defence' (2007) 27

for loss of control. Third, the removal of the requirement that the loss of control be sudden and temporary indicates a further departure from the traditional understanding. This opens the law up to a new understanding of loss of self-control. No longer are we considering only loss of control resulting from anger, but also other emotions such as fear, outrage or despair. Also it provides an opportunity to think again what loss of control means. Stephen Shute and Richard Holton in their sophisticated analysis of the concept argue:

> self-control consists in a particular kind of control over one's actions – in each case the obvious contrast is with actions that are driven purely by one's (first-order) desires. Accordingly, loss of self-control involves a loss of this particular kind of control. It does not require that the agent "goes berserk", loses control of her body, or fails to know what she is doing. The agent will still be an agent when self-control is lost, and her acts will still be intentional, driven by a desire for revenge, or whatever. What is lost when one loses self-control is control over which mental elements drive one's actions.[25]

This kind of understanding of loss of control means we are not looking for a defendant driven 'crazy' by anger, but a defendant battling conflicting emotions and where control is lost over which emotion is to determine her actions. I argue that it can readily be found, even assumed, once the jury have concluded that the defendant was facing exceptional circumstances causing the defendant to have a justifiable sense of being seriously wronged, that there will be a loss of control of the kind even a normal person might experience. Hence, the key question in cases using this qualifying trigger will be the wrongfulness of the things done or said to the defendant.

What is Domestic Abuse?

Academic criminal lawyers have a rather uneasy relationship with domestic violence. In the index of one leading textbook the topic is not even mentioned.[26] Given the significant percentage of assaults which are domestic violence cases, it is surprising that it has received relatively little attention from substantive criminal lawyers.

The questions of what is domestic abuse and what is wrong in domestic abuse are, of course, closely linked. Often definitions of domestic abuse tend to be shaped in such a way so that all conduct which falls in them is marked by the wrong of domestic abuse. Others will see this as putting the cart before the horse. Of course, all depends on the use to which the definition is being put. If it is being used as a description of the kind of behaviour for which a particular legal response is appropriate, then the definition will be driven by the policy discussions of which kinds of behaviour should give rise to the particular legal response. For the purposes of this chapter, my focus will be an explanation of the wrong that can arise in domestic abuse behaviour. In this chapter I do not need to be concerned with whether behaviour which does not contain the features discussed herein is correctly categorised as domestic violence.

Oxford Journal of Legal Studies 49; Jeremy Horder, 'Reshaping the Subjective Element in the Provocation Defence' (2005) 25 Oxford Journal of Legal Studies 123.
  25 Holton and Shute (n. 24) 50.
  26 Simester, Spencer, Sullivan and Virgo (n. 10). Contrast Nicola Lacey, Celia Wells and Oliver Quick, *Reconstructing Criminal Law* (4th edn, Cambridge University Press, 2010).

For now I shall adopt the analysis of the definition domestic abuse described by Michelle Madden Dempsey.[27] This provides a powerful way of describing and discussing abuse within the context of an intimate relationship. She describes three elements of domestic violence: violence, domesticity and patriarchy. Her claim is not that a case only involves domestic violence where all three elements are present, but rather we can determine whether a case involves domestic violence in a weaker or stronger sense depending upon the combination of elements a case involves. The benefit of this analysis is that it enables us to present a definition of what will be a central, strong case of domestic violence: an act which is violent, takes place within domesticity and sustains or perpetuates patriarchy. Other acts which involve only one or two of these elements will only be domestic violence in a weak sense or not be domestic violence at all. We do not need to go into all of the permutations (Michelle sets them out with considerable sophistication in her writings). The significance of her approach is that it emphasises that we do not need to treat all incidents of domestic violence as equally serious. Incidents which are not violent or not domestic may still constitute domestic violence, but only in a weak sense. The benefit of these categories is that they provide a way for recognising the extent of the wrong in different cases.

The Wrong of Domestic Abuse

Early feminist writing sought to establish that an act of violence in the home was as serious as an act of violence in the street by a stranger. The fact it was 'just a domestic' should not lead to its severity being diminished.[28] Now, a stronger claim can often be made that an act of violence or abuse in the home is a greater wrong than a similar act of violence in the street. I wish here to explain why that is so, by highlighting four specific wrongs connected with domestic violence.

Domestic Abuse as 'Coercive Control'

Criminal lawyers are familiar with assessing the severity of an attack by assessing the degree of physical injury that is caused by the defendant. We teach students to consider whether the injury caused is a battery, actual bodily harm or grievous bodily harm. The extent of bruising or breaking of the skin is the subject of many an ingenious problem question set by criminal law examiners. Yet, the assessment of the severity of the harm by focusing on the extent of bodily impact at the moment in time is a narrow construction of harm. This abstracting of the injury avoids an assessment of the severity of the attack in the overall context of the relationship between the parties and the life of the victim and of the broader social context within which the act is done.[29] Even where emotional harm is regarded as bodily harm, that is only if it can be medically recognised as a recognised condition. *Dhaliwal*[30] lays bare the law's inability to consider the broader context and impact of acts, rather than using a narrow focus on the extent of injury to the skin or body.[31] The definition of harm in that case is presented as a medical issue, rather than an attempt to assess the experience of the conduct

---

27 Michelle Madden Dempsey, 'What Counts as Domestic Violence' (2006) 13 William and Mary Journal of Women and the Law 301.
28 Michelle Madden Dempsey, *Prosecuting Domestic Violence* (Oxford University Press, 2009).
29 Deborah Tuerkheimer, 'Recognizing and Remedying the Harm of Battering' (2004) 94 Journal of Criminal Law and Criminology 959.
30 *Dhaliwal* [2006] EWCA Crim 1139.
31 Mandy Burton, 'R v. Dhaliwal Commentary' in Rosemary Hunter, Clare McGlynn and Erika Rackley (eds), *Feminist Judgments* (Hart, 2010).

for the individual.[32] To be fair, the criminal law is beginning to broaden its vision of the notion of harm. The Protection from Harassment Act 1997, for example, acknowledges that only by taking a broader perspective in time and range of conduct can the gravity of the incident be appreciated.

Considerable work has been done on the way that domestic abuse is best understood, not as simply a series of violent or abusive acts, but rather as a programme of 'coercive control' (to use Evan Stake's phrase)[33] or 'patriarchal terrorism' or 'intimate terrorism' (to use Michael Johnson's phrase). Michael Johnson distinguishes intimate terrorism from what he calls 'situational couple violence' or 'mutual violence'. Patriarchal terrorism is 'violence enacted in the service of taking general control over one's partner'.[34] By contrast, in the situational couple violence or mutual violence, there is violence but there is no attempt to control the relationship. Rather, an incident of violence that arises in a moment of conflict during an intimate relationship is not generally marked with inequality. It involves a lashing out in self-defence, anger or frustration, rather than an attempt to exercise control.

It is the coercive control form of domestic violence which is the focus of this chapter. Psychologist Mary Ann Dutton explains:

> Abusive behaviour does not occur as a series of discrete events. Although a set of discrete abusive incidents can typically be identified within an abusive relationship, an understanding of the dynamic of power and control within an intimate relationship goes beyond these discrete incidents. To negate the impact of the time period between discrete episodes of serious violence – a time period during which the woman may never know when the next incident will occur, and may continue to live with on-going psychological abuse – is to fail to recognize what some battered woman experience as a continuing "state of siege".[35]

Mary Ann Dutton and Lisa Goodman, examining the experiences of victims of domestic abuse, have explored the forms of coercion and see these as covering nine areas of control: 'personal activities/appearance', 'support/social life/family', 'household', 'work/economic/resources', 'health', 'intimate relationship', 'legal', 'immigration', and 'children'.[36] Evan Stark comments on the role of control in domestic abuse:

> Perpetrators commonly spy on or stalk partners even when they are living together and control their access to and means of transportation, monitor them at work, and use beepers, cell phones, or human proxies to monitor their activities.[37]

The behaviour of the abuser is designed to dominate the victim and diminish her sense of self-worth: control on going to work; isolation from friends; psychological manipulation, and so forth, are commonly used weapons to this end. Violence is a tool used in the relationship structure to

---

32 Ibid.
33 Evan Stark, *Coercive Control* (Oxford University Press, 2007).
34 Michael Johnson, 'Apples and Oranges in Child Custody Disputes: Intimate Terrorism vs. Situational Couple Violence' (2005) 2 Journal of Child Custody 43.
35 Mary Ann Dutton, 'Understanding Women's Response to Domestic Violence' (2003) 21 Hofstra Law Review 1191, 1204.
36 Mary Ann Dutton and Lisa Goodman, *Development and Validation of a Coercive Control Measure for Intimate Partner Violence* (US Dept of Justice, 2006).
37 Evan Stark, 'Commentary on Johnson's "Conflict and Control: Gender Symmetry and Asymmetry in Domestic Violence"' (2006) 12 Violence Against Women 1019.

keep one party inferior.[38] Not only does the violence itself enforce control, it reduces self-esteem and ensures future compliance. In one study of men arrested for domestic violence, 38 per cent admitted preventing partners freely coming and going in their daily routine and 59 per cent had denied partners access to money or resources.[39] In another study, in one-third of cases involving domestic violence, the man had sought to prevent the woman from working and in half, had taken steps to ensure she remained at home looking after children.[40]

The extent of control exercised can be extraordinary. Consider this case:

> Mark restricts Vanessa's access to money and employment. At home, Mark keeps all household supplies and toiletries under lock and key. If Vanessa or her three children need anything they must prove it is necessary; and only then will he unlock a cabinet and provide them with it. This includes tooth paste. Tampons. Laundry detergent. At dinner, Mark tells the children to ignore their mother because Vanessa is too stupid to be able to understand their conversations. Instead, Mark tells them she is there simply to make the food and serve it. Privately, Mark often tells Vanessa that if they ever separated, the children would never choose to live with her because they do not respect her.[41]

Or take a single incident from the case of *State* v. *Norman*:[42]

> John Norman asked Judy Norman to make him a sandwich; when Judy brought it to him, he threw it on the floor and told her to make him another. Judy made him a second sandwich and brought it to him; John again threw it on the floor, telling her to put something on her hands because he did not want her to touch the bread. Judy made a third sandwich using a paper towel to handle the bread. John took the third sandwich and smeared it in Judy's face.

The significance of this incident can only be understood when seen in its context of the ongoing relationship between the parties, one in which the victim was effectively detained in the home, yet her work in the home consistently undermined.

This control is used to obtain compliance with all the abuser's demands. To pursue this, attempts are often made to ensure the woman does not find external sources of value or support. Consider, for example, the comments of two women who had tried to start a course of study in the hope of pursuing a career:

> Things really started to go down hill when I went to university, there's no doubt about that. ... I don't think there'd been any need for him to be violent to me [to that point in the relationship] because he had me so much in his control in other ways, financially, at home with the children.[43]

---

38 Orly Rachmilovitz, 'Bringing Down the Bedroom Walls: Emphasizing Substance Over Form in Personalized Abuse' (2007) 14 William and Mary Journal of Women and Law 495.

39 E.S. Buzawa, G.T. Hotaling, A. Klein, and J. Byrne, *Response to Domestic Violence in a Pro-Active Court Setting*. Final Report Submitted to the National Institute of Justice (Lowell, University of Massachusetts Lowell, 1999).

40 Evan Stark, *Coercive Control* (n. 33).

41 Margaret Johnson, 'Redefining Harm, Reimagining Remedies and Reclaiming Domestic Violence Law' (2009) 42 UC Davis Law Review 1107.

42 *State* v. *Norman* 366 SE 2d 586, 588 (NC App 1988).

43 Liz Kelly, *Surviving Sexual Violence* (Polity Press, 1988), 129.

> He almost burnt my work one time – three years of research and writing. He had lots of my papers out in the garden and the incinerator was burning. I had to beg and plead and agree to various conditions to get it off him.[44]

One important point to emphasise at this stage is that control is not limited to violence. It can involve emotion and psychological abuse:

> He always found something wrong with what I did, even if I did what he asked. No matter what it was. It was never the way he wanted it. I was either too fat, didn't cook the food right. ... I think he wanted to hurt me. To hurt me in the sense ... to make me feel like I was a nothing.[45]

This helps explain why some victims fail to recognise domestic abuse for what it is, but also how others so readily fail to acknowledge it. Paula Nicolson quotes from Connie:

> At the time I didn't really know, I didn't recognise it for what it was because I mean it was things like not speaking to you, like nudging you and bumping into you and at one point he pulled my hair and pushed me over, things like that. I just thought that was sort of like a bit over zealous but I didn't really recognised it from the start off.[46]

As this quote shows, the abuse is difficult to prove or explain to an outside authority. The act of bumping into a person appears trivial when referred to in isolation. How easy to dismiss the concerns as paranoid. Yet as the control develops it creates the conditions in which escape from the controller becomes harder. As one social worker is reported as saying:

> Well it's such a power based-based relationship isn't it? They feel weak, they feel powerless, they feel vulnerable, they feel they can't exist without them [men], you know ... I think they don't know anything else, and haven't experienced it, or their self-esteem is very low for numerable reasons. That "something" is better than nothing and nothing is much too frightening you know to be without a partner is just unimaginable.[47]

The role of coercive control as part of domestic abuse can be seen also in the link between pregnancy and domestic abuse. Indeed domestic abuse is the leading cause of maternal mortality.[48] In his partner's pregnancy the abuser perceives a loss of control and that he is no longer the centre of attention. It explains also why attempts to leave the relationship are linked with the most serious violence.[49]

The study of women who kill their abusive partners summarises the research well:

---

44 Ibid.
45 Deborah Tuerkheimer, 'Recognizing and Remedying the Harm of Battering' (2004) 94 Journal of Criminal Law and Criminology 959.
46 Paula Nicolson, *Domestic Violence and Psychology* (Routledge, 2010) 35.
47 Ibid., 159.
48 Rebecca O'Reilly, Barbara Beale, and Donna Gillies, 'Screening and Intervention for Domestic Violence During Pregnancy Care: A Systematic Review' (2010) 11 Trauma Violence Abuse 190.
49 Joan Kelly and Michael Johnson, 'Differentiation Among Types of Intimate Partner Violence' (2008) 46 Family Court Review 467.

Women who killed their abusers were more likely to have experienced frequent attacks, severe injuries, sexual abuse, and death threats against themselves or others. They were caught in a web of abuse that seemed to be out of control. Seventy-six percent of Browne's homicide group reported having been raped, 40 percent often. Sixty-two percent reported being forced or urged to engage in other sexual acts that they found abusive or unnatural, one-fifth saying this was a frequent occurrence. For many of these women, the most severe incidents took place when they threatened or tried to leave their partner. Another major factor that distinguished the homicide group from women who had not killed their abusive partners is that many of them had either attempted or seriously considered suicide. These women felt that they could no longer survive in this relationship and that leaving safely was also impossible.[50]

To summarise, the importance of understanding domestic abuse as a form of coercive control is threefold.

First, it moves beyond simply examining the individual incident in isolation but considers the overall impact of the series of acts together.[51] It also shows that conduct which can appear trivial, changes its character once appreciated as part of a pattern of controlling behaviour.

Second, the control can be managed through acts which do not involve violence. It is the level of control which is more significant than the level of violence in this model. Third, it reflects the motivation for domestic abuse: as a means of exercising control over their partner.[52] The violence or abusive conduct is not used in its own right but as a means to an end: intimidation, isolation and control.[53] Domestic violence should not, therefore, be readily dismissed as merely the symptoms of a failing relationship or an 'anger management problem'.

Domestic Abuse as a Breach of Trust

In this section I shall argue that domestic abuse involves a serious breach of trust. First, I wish to develop an argument about the importance of the intimate sphere of life. Protection of intimacy is important because it enables people to flourish. John Eekelaar has argued that trust is at the heart of the intimacy, and that enables love and autonomy to develop.[54] It is in being able to be completely honest and vulnerable with a partner that relationships can deepen, an understanding of self can grow and sense can be made of life. But all of that depends on trust. In a case of domestic violence the abuse has misused the intimate sphere. There are three forms of that misuse I wish to bring out.

First, an intimate relationship involves 'thick interpersonal trust',[55] which is distinct from how we might simply trust an acquaintance. An intimate relationship involves the disclosing of parts of ourselves (both physical and emotional) that we wish to keep free from others. The kind of openness necessary for intimacy is so extensive that there are particularly strong bonds of trust. The trust involves not only imposing an obligation not to misuse information acquired during the relationship (something the law is generally ready to protect); but also that the relationship is not used to take advantage of the other person. Notably the law is more ready to protect confidential

---

50 Ibid.
51 Alasdair Burke, 'Domestic Violence as a Crime of Pattern and Intent' (2007) 75 George Washington Law Review 552.
52 Neil Jacobson and John Gottman, *When Men Batter Women: New Insights into Ending Abusive Relationships* (Simon & Schuster, 2007).
53 Evan Stark, *Coercive Control* (n. 33) 5.
54 Ibid., 4–47.
55 Dimitry Khodyakov, 'Trust as a Process: A Three Dimensional Approach' (2007) 41 Sociology 116.

information disclosed in a personal relationship than to control the misuse of the relationship to exercise power or control over the other party.

Second, the abuse of trust within an intimate relationship causes an especial harm. Intimate relationships are central to our identity and sense of self.[56] Within our intimate relationships we can be truly ourselves, free of pretence. Through them, we can there explore and discover ourselves. Domestic abuse strikes at the very conception of the self for the victim. As Evan Stark writes:

> In the romantic vernacular, love and intimacy compensate women for their devaluation in the wider world. Personal life does something more. It provides the state where women practice their basic rights, garner the support needed to resist devaluation, experiment with sexual identities, and imagine themselves through various life projects. Coercive control subverts this process, bringing discrimination home by reducing the discretion in everyday routines to near zero, freezing feeling and identity in time and space, the process victims experience as entrapment. Extended across the range of activities that define women as person, this foreshortening of subjective development compounds the particular liberty harms caused by coercive control.[57]

As it is through our relationships that we form our identities as to who we are and try and make sense of the world, domestic abuse turns what should be a tool for self-affirmation and self-identification into a tool for alienation and self-betrayal. The victim almost becomes used as a tool against herself.[58] It is not surprising therefore that domestic violence causes a wide range of mental health problems for victims, ranging from anxiety, depression, post-traumatic stress, substance abuse and suicidal tendencies.[59] A REFUGE report on the impact of domestic abuse[60] concludes 'there can be a persistent negative change to thoughts, feelings and behaviours, including a lack of trust in people, social isolation, self-medication using alcohol or drugs, a distorted appraisal of the abuse and one's reality, resulting guilt, self-blame, crippling low self-esteem and helplessness about the future.' In domestic abuse the intimacy that should make us whole is used to destroy us.

Thirdly, there is more to domestic abuse than simply depriving the victim of the benefits of an intimate life. Domestic abuse can involve the use of information gathered during the relationship so that the abuse can be personalised.[61] In *Attorney General's Reference (No 90 of 2009)*,[62] where a sentence of ten years was increased to 18 in a case of marital rape, the Court of Appeal explained:

> This is an extreme case of its kind: rape by a husband of his wife from whom he was separated. The facts that we have narrated demonstrate, and the conduct of his defence confirms, that the offender deliberately chose to use sexual intercourse with his wife without her consent as a weapon with which to dominate and humiliate her. This was the woman with whom he had once had a

---

56 Rachmilovitz (n. 38).

57 Evan Stark, *Coercive Control* (n. 33) 363.

58 Lynne Arnault, 'Cruelty, Horror, and the Will to Redemption' (2003) 18 Hypatia 155.

59 Itzen, Taket and Barker-Godfrey (n. 1) 61; Ximena Arriaga and Nicole Capezza, 'Targets of Partner Violence: The Importance of Understanding Coping Trajectories' (2005) 20 Journal of Interpersonal Violence 89.

60 Cited in Vanessa Munro and Sangeeta Shah, 'R v. Dhaliwal' in Rosemary Hunter, Clare McGlynn and Erika Rackley, *Feminist Judgments* (Hart, 2011), at para. 10.

61 Evan Stark, *Coercive Control* (n. 33) 376.

62 [2009] EWCA Crim 2610. For further discussion of marital rape see Jonathan Herring, 'No More Having and Holding: The Abolition of the Marital Rape Exemption', in Stephen Gilmore, Jonathan Herring and Rebecca Probert (eds), *Landmarks in Family Law* (Hart, 2011).

relationship of genuine affection and who had borne him two children. There was a grave breach of trust. The offender used the kind of knowledge that couples have of each other, which he would have acquired during their moments of warm intimacy, about a sexual practice that she found wholly unacceptable. With that knowledge he forced her to submit to it. Apart from the sheer humiliation and horror, she suffered physical pain. Having done that, he added to her degradation by raping her vaginally. The offender's actions were quite merciless.[63]

Domestic Violence and Children

There is ample evidence that domestic violence harms children.[64] This is so not only where the child has witnessed the incidents directly, but even where the child is living in the same house as the behaviour. Children raised in families characterised by domestic violence are 30–60 per cent more likely to suffer child abuse themselves.[65] The impact on children includes behavioural, cognitive and emotional problems, leading to depression, anxiety, truancy and low educational achievement. It also can lead to interpersonal problems and poor social skills. There are higher rates of sibling violence in cases of domestic violence. Marianne Hester found that children were present in 55 per cent of cases of domestic violence.[66] Ten per cent of children who witnessed domestic violence witnessed their mother being sexually assaulted.[67] All of this means that in cases where children are present in the house the domestic violence can correctly be regarded as a form of child abuse.[68]

The law generally recognises that crimes against children involve a greater wrong than crimes against others.[69] This recognises the particular obligation that adults owe to children, particularly those who are playing a parental role. It also recognises that children often lack the physical, emotional and social capabilities to respond to harmful incidents. All of these points emphasise the wrongfulness of domestic violence.

Domestic Violence and Patriarchy

Madden Dempsey's emphasis on the role played by patriarchy highlights the way that domestic violence can involve and build on coercive control exercised by one party over the other in a myriad ways. But it does more than this, she explains. It reinforces and relies upon power exercised by

---

63 Ibid., para. 21.
64 The research is summarised in Joan Kelly and Michael Johnson, 'Differentiation Among Types of Intimate Partner Violence' (2008) 46 Family Court Review 467 and Royal College of Psychiatrists, *Domestic Violence: Its Effect on Children* (RCP, 2010).
65 Itzen, Taket and Godfrey (n. 1) 4.
66 Marianne Hester, *Who Does What to Whom? Gender and Domestic Violence Perpetrators* (Northern Rock, 2009). According to a study by the charity Barnado's *Bitter Legacy* (Barnado's, 2004), in nine out of ten cases of domestic violence children are in the room of, or in the room next door to, the violence.
67 Audrey Mullender, *Tackling Domestic Violence: Providing Support for Children Who Have Witnessed Domestic Violence* (Home Office, 2005).
68 Todd Herrenkohl, Cynthia Sousa, Emiko Tajima, Roy Herrenkohl and Carrie Moylan, 'Intersection of Child Abuse and Children's Exposure to Domestic Violence' (2008) 9 Trauma Violence Abuse 84; Patricia Romito, *A Deafening Silence : Hidden Violence Against Women and Children* (Policy, 2008).
69 See, for example, the particular offences protecting children under the Sexual Offences Act 2003.

men over women in society more generally.[70] As the Parliamentary Assembly, Council of Europe, Committee on Equal Opportunities for Women and Men puts it:

> Violence against women is a question of power, of the need to dominate and control. This in turn is rooted in the organization of society, itself based on inequality between the sexes. The meaning of this violence is clear: it is an attempt to maintain the unequal relationship between men and women and to perpetuate the subordination of women.[71]

As this quote indicates, domestic violence not only reflects wider inequalities, it contributes to them. Michelle Madden Dempsey explains:

> the patriarchal character of individual relationships cannot subsist without those relationships being situated within a broader patriarchal social structure. Patriarchy is, by its nature, a social structure – and thus any particular instance of patriarchy takes its substance and meaning from that social context. If patriarchy were entirely eliminated from society, then patriarchy would not exist in domestic arrangements and thus domestic violence in its strong sense would not exist ... Moreover, if patriarchy were lessened in society generally then *ceteris paribus* patriarchy would be lessened in domestic relationships as well, thereby directly contributing to the project of ending domestic violence in its strong sense.[72]

Michelle Madden Dempsey describes patriarchy as 'wrongful structural inequality'. The wrongfulness she separates out into: sex discrimination, sexism, and misogyny. Structural inequalities she explains are functions of social structures, the 'set of rules and principles that govern activities in the different domains of social life. When social structures sustain or perpetuate the uneven distribution of social power, they can be understood as structural inequalities.'[73] Domestic abuse plays this role because it works to reinforce the other social structures that inhibits women's access to places of power. Further, it replicates the disadvantages in the outside world within the domestic. Of course it is not just sexist inequalities that domestic violence perpetuates. It can reflect and reinforce marginalisation of other groups.[74] For example, the attempts by the male perpetrators of abuse to prevent their female partners entering the workplace or public arena are but imitations of broader attempts to restrict women's access to the workplace.

Some may question the claims about the broader significance of domestic violence. But we must remember that domestic violence plays a major role in the lives of so many women. The latest

---

70   Evan Stark, *Coercive Control* (Oxford University Press, 2007).
71   Parliamentary Assembly, Council of Europe, Committee on Equal Opportunities for Women and Men, *Domestic Violence* (2002) para. 12.
72   Michelle Madden Dempsey, 'Towards a Feminist State' (2007) 70 Modern Law Review 908.
73   Ibid.
74   Leigh Goodmark, 'Reframing Domestic Violence Law and Policy: An Anti-Essentialist Proposal' (2009) Washington University Journal of Law and Policy 39. Julie Goldscheid, 'Elusive Equality in Domestic and Sexual Violence Law' (2007) Florida State University Law Review 731. T. Bryant-Davies, H.J. Chung and S. Tillman, 'From the Margins to the Center: Ethnic Minority Women and the Mental Health Effects of Sexual Assault' (2009) 10 Trauma Violence and Abuse 330; Aarati Kasturirangan, Sandhya Krishnan, and Stephanie Riger, 'The Impact of Culture and Minority Status on Women's Experience of Domestic Violence' (2004) 5 Trauma Violence Abuse 318. Joanna Bunker Rohrbaugh, 'Domestic Violence in Same-Gender Relationships' (2006) 44 Family Court Review 287.

statistics[75] indicate that 29 per cent of women have experienced domestic abuse since they were 16. Fifty-four per cent of serious sexual assaults were by a current or former partner. And it starts at a young age. A recent survey found that 16 per cent of teenage girls questioned (whose average age was 15) had been hit by their boyfriends. A further 15 per cent had been pushed and 6 per cent forced to have sex by their boyfriends.[76] The impact of a behaviour on such a large section of the population must have a significant social impact, even for those who do not accept the broader feminist account.

Women on Men Violence

One of the most controversial issues among writers on domestic violence is the extent to which this is a gendered issue. In response to the traditional feminist approach that domestic violence is predominantly a male activity practised by men against women, some researchers have responded that violence by women against men is in fact at a similar level as violence by men against women.[77] The issue has given rise to considerable debates over the statistics, which are muddied by the variety of definitions of domestic violence used.

The best view, it is suggested, is that women are violent to men, but that the nature of that violence is different from that used by men in two ways. First, Michael Johnson claims that while in cases of 'couple violence' there are equal numbers of men and women, this is not so in cases of 'intimate terrorism' cases. So, women's violence is very rarely part of a programme of coercive control of her partner. For women the violence is more often used in self-defence or where the couple are using similar levels of force against each other.[78]

Secondly, there is a difference in the degree of violence used. When men use violence the injury rates are much greater for women.[79] Dobash and Dobash explain:

> In those cases where women had used violence against their male partner, the findings reported here suggest that women's violence differs from that perpetrated by men in terms of nature, frequency, intention, intensity, physical injury and emotional impact. All of the women in this study had been the victims of repeated physical violence from their male partner, often over many years. Despite this, just over half had used any form of violence against their abuser, none had used sexual violence and only a few had used serious or injurious violence. Of the women who had used violence, the consequences in terms of emotional impact were usually inconsequential; the consequences in terms of injuries were usually, though not always, less severe; the violence often, though not always, occurred in the context of "self-defence" or "self-protection"; and women's violence was usually, although not always, rated by both partners as "not serious". In addition,

---

75 Home Office, *Homicides, Firearm Offences and Intimate Violence 2009/10* (Home Office, 2011).
76 NSPCC Teen Abuse Survey of Great Britain (NSPCC, 2005).
77 Linda Kelly, 'Disabusing the Definition of Domestic Abuse: How Women Batter Men and the Role of the Feminist State' (2003) 30 Florida State University Law Review 791.
78 Marianne Hester, *Who Does What to Whom? Gender and Domestic Violence Perpetrators* (Northern Rock, 2009).
79 Mary Silverzweig, 'Domestic Terrorism: The Debate and Gender Divides' (2010) 12 Journal of Law and Family Studies 251.

women did not use intimidating or coercive forms of controlling behaviour associated with the "constellation of abuse".[80]

So while a superficial look at some studies might suggest levels of domestic violence between men and women are similar, looking more carefully at the context of the violence, it is clear that domestic violence as a means of control is predominantly a male activity.

Conclusion

This chapter has sought to consider the availability of the serious wrong form of the loss of control defence for victims of domestic violence who kill their abusers. It has argued that the concept of being seriously wronged is at the heart of the new defence and that once that requirement has been proved it will be relatively easy for the other elements to be established.

This chapter has sought to highlight the ways in which domestic abuse is typically a serious wrong to the woman. The wrongs highlighted are not restricted to physical abuse. In doing this the chapter has highlighted four elements: the coercive effect of domestic abuse; the breach of trust involved; the impact of children; and its contribution to patriarchy.

In fact, the arguments presented in this chapter, if accepted, could form the basis for a range of other arguments: for a specific offence of domestic abuse; or for a specific defence that recognises the unique wrong that the abused women were facing. But those arguments are for another day.

---

[80] Rebecca Dobash and Russell Dobash, 'Women's Violence to Men in Intimate Relationships' (2004) 44 British Journal of Criminology 324–49.

Chapter 6
Loss of Self-Control:
When His Anger is Worth More than Her Fear

Susan S.M. Edwards

Introduction

The Coroners and Justice Act 2009, s. 56, abolishes the common law defence of provocation, which required a sudden and temporary loss of self-control. The former defence of provocation privileged male angered states but excluded from its ambit abused women who killed out of a state of fear or of self-preservation. In the place of provocation is now substituted a statutory defence of 'loss of self-control'. The range of excuses and justifications hitherto accepted for lethal violence are now restricted by expressly excluding the repugnant excuse of sexual infidelity and otherwise requiring the triggering act or fuse to include 'extremely grave' circumstances. The 'reasonable person', so called, is now defined in statute as an individual possessing 'tolerance and self-restraint', whilst the circumstances precipitating the 'loss of self-control' must amount to a 'justifiable sense of being seriously wronged'. The predicament of abused women and their erstwhile exclusion from law is partly addressed through removing the immediacy requirement from the defence. Significantly, and for the first time, fear qualifies in its own right as a new ground for loss of self-control (s. 55(3)). Recognition in law of the fearful state of mind is intended to bring women who kill violent partners within law's ambit and mercy and so correct a habituated historic injustice.[1] However, fear is not a sufficient prerequisite, qualifying only when it follows on from 'serious violence'. This chapter explores the limitations and laxity of the former law on provocation and the extent to which these limitations have been addressed and laxity curtailed in these new provisions. This author is of the view that habituated gendered thinking will continue to impress on the construction of what is a 'qualifying trigger', on what behaviour is deemed a 'loss of self-control', on what is fear, on what is 'serious violence', on the nature of the circumstances considered to meet the threshold of 'justifiable sense of being seriously wronged' and on the requirement of 'tolerance and self-restraint', such that the fearful woman facing or anticipating abuse may still find herself outwith the reach of law's protection. Her continued exclusion from the law is likely because on the face of it women will still be required to lose self-control in the conventional way and her fear will not be understood. Thus, the law continues by lending legitimacy to some conduct to sustain a gendered normative universe maintaining a world of lawful, unlawful, valid and void, in the arena of manslaughter.[2]

---

[1] In *Luc Thiet Thuan* v. *R* [1996] 2 All ER 1033, Lord Steyn (dissenting opinion) said this: 'But even more important than the promptings of legal logic is the dictates of justice.'

[2] Austin Sarat (ed.), *Law, Violence and the Possibility of Justice* (Princeton University Press, 2001) 5.

Extent of 'Domestic' Homicide

The preoccupation with the provocation/loss of self-control defence is the product of both a philosophical and a jurisprudential quest for a just and rational partial defence to murder, the need to manage involuntary manslaughter, especially with regard to domestic homicide, and the changes introduced to the sentencing regime for murder by the Criminal Justice Act 2003.[3] The legal outcomes of homicide offences are the product of the law on murder and manslaughter and its authorisation of excuses and justifications for human lethal conduct.[4] Official statistics for 2009/10 show 619 offences currently recorded as homicide.[5] In 2003/4, 606 defendants were convicted of homicide, 339 defendants were convicted of murder, 21 of (s. 2) diminished responsibility manslaughter and 246 defendants of (s. 3) 'other manslaughter'. In 2008/9, of 670 cases initially recorded as homicide (a court decision is still pending in 129 cases), 227 defendants were convicted of murder, 31 defendants of s. 2 diminished responsibility manslaughter, and 129 defendants of 'other manslaughter'.[6] The once coined 'husband–wife', 'spousal' homicide, now 'partner/ex-partner' homicide, has accounted for the deaths of approximately 100 women and 20 men annually for the past three decades,[7] which underscores the importance of law reform in this area. In 2004/5, 30 men were killed by a partner or ex-partner; 22 in 2005/6; 30 in 2006/7; 34 in 2007/8; 31 in 2008/9 (this figure includes male/female perpetrators in same-sex partnerships although a greater number of men than in previous years are being killed by same-sex partners). In 2010, 21 were killed (the apparent decline in number is due to proceedings still pending). This compares with the deaths of 105 female partners in 2004/5; 90 in 2005/6; 91 in 2006/7; 79 in 2007/8; 101 in 2008/9; and 95 in 2010.[8] Partner/ex-partner homicide clearly accounts for a very significant proportion of the overall homicide statistic, and law reform, particularly in recent years, has been quite properly concerned with this constituency. As killing has never been a woman's vice within or outside the family, her explanatory accounts have not been advanced in the courtroom and therefore have not become part of the voiced or received excusatory narratives which have informed and shaped the development of the law. Women facing murder convictions arising from circumstances of domestic violence also face a 'double jeopardy' in that the Criminal Justice Act 2003 set a minimum tariff for killings with weapons, which means that women who resort to weapons and kill violent abusive husbands in this their only means of defence from male violence, and where provocation, diminished responsibility and no intent manslaughter have failed, are doubly punished.[9]

---

3 See Susan Edwards, 'Descent into Murder: Provocation's Stricture – The Prognosis for Women Who Kill Men Who Abuse Them', 71 Journal of Criminal Law 342.

4 David Matza, *Delinquency and Drift* (John Wiley, 1964) argues that the criminal law invites the defendant to neutralise his normative attachment to it.

5 *Homicide, Firearm Offences and Intimate Violence*, Supplementary Volume 2 to Crime in England and Wales 2009/10, Kevin Smith, Kathryn Coleman, Simon Eder and Philip Hall (eds).

6 Ibid. The 'other' category needs to distinguish provocation – loss of self-control and fear – loss of self-control from 'no intent' manslaughter, 28.

7 Ibid.

8 Ibid. See 'Homicides currently recorded for all victims by relationship of victim to principal suspect' 1999/2000 to 2009/10, Table 1.05.

9 Criminal Justice Act 2003, Sch. 21, para. 5a, and 5(2)(b).

Tale as Old as Time – Male Violence against Women

What has prompted this more recent move towards law reform has been a specific concern with malecentric law which has historically privileged male anger as an adequate ground for provocation. The new law is the product of the struggle of women's organisations, including Southall Black Sisters, Women's Aid, Justice for Women, together with members of the Criminal Bar and defence solicitors who have played a significant role in crafting legal arguments around a battered woman defence.[10] The Coroners and Justice Act 2009, s. 55, displaces particular male excuses which had become calcified within the law, expressly ousting from the law the sexual infidelity excuse/ justification whilst destabilising trivial male excuses, requiring all excusatory rationales to satisfy the 'extremely grave' threshold. Male immunity from the murder of female partners has been the fulcrum of feminist criticism for at least two centuries.[11] Francis Power Cobbe in the nineteenth century explained: 'Should she be guilty of nagging or scolding, or of being slattern, or of getting intoxicated, she finds usually a short shrift and no favour – and even humane persons talk of her offence as constituting, if not a justification for her murder, yet an explanation of it.'[12] Sue Lees,[13] rather more recently, exposed the continued success such excuses have had in provocation defences.

From the 1980s, the legal academic community began to join themselves to the cause and acknowledged the historic gender basis of excuses for provocation which whilst often excluding domestic violence as an adequate ground for provocation when women killed men, frequently accepted trifling and petty excuses when men killed women. Domestic abuse was advanced by women as their reason for killing men, whereas men pleaded a wife's adultery or her behaviour. Ashworth[14] regarded 'really serious provocation', to include 'repeated beatings or flagrant adultery'. Horder[15] similarly considered as grave, 'the case of *Wright*, where a man killed his wife after years of her "flagrant adultery", and in *Ratcliffe* a wife killed her husband, who had hit her and tortured her'. In addition, the courts, when sentencing men for crimes of violence against female partners, began to treat domestic violence as seriously as violence in the street. Ormrod LJ in *Giboin*[16] (where a husband asked his wife to kiss him for the last time and while she was doing so he stabbed her in the chest and in the back) said: 'The view that this Court takes is that assaults on wives are to be regarded as very serious matters, and not to be lightly brushed aside as due to emotional upsets or

---

10 See Michael Mansfield QC and Edward Fitzgerald QC in *R v. Thornton* (No 2) [1996] 1 WLR 1174; [1996] 2 All ER 1023. See also Susan Edwards and Charlotte Walsh, 'The Justice of Retrial?' (1996) 146 New Law Journal 857. See Geoffrey Robertson QC in *R v. Ahluwalia* [1992] 4 All ER 889, Helena Kennedy QC in *R v. Hobson* (1997) Times, 25 June, *Crime – murder – 'battered woman's syndrome' – retrial ordered*. See Edward Fitzgerald QC in *R v. Criminal Cases Review Commission, ex parte Pearson* [1999] All ER (D) 503, and in *HKSAR Nancy Ann Kissel* HCCC 55 of 2010 (Hong Kong).

11 Jill Radford, 'Marriage Licence or Licence to Kill? Womanslaughter in the Criminal Law' (1982) *Feminist Review* 88–96; Adrian Howe, 'Provocation in Crisis – Law's Passion at the Crossroads – New Direction for Feminist Strategists' (2004) 21 Australian Feminist Legal Journal 53.

12 Frances Power Cobbe 'Wife-Torture in England', reprinted in Diana Russell and Jill Radford (eds) *Femicide: The Politics of Woman Killing* (Open University Press 1992) 47.

13 Sue Lees, 'Naggers, Whores and Libbers: Provoking Men to Kill', in Diana Russell and Jill Radford, ibid., 267–88.

14 Andrew Ashworth, 'Sentencing in Provocation Cases' [1975] Criminal Law Review 552.

15 Jeremy Horder, 'Sex, Violence, and Sentencing in Domestic Provocation Cases' [1989] Criminal Law Review 546–54. See also Martin Wasik, 'Cumulative Provocation and Domestic Killing' [1982] Criminal Law Review 29.

16 (1980) 2 Cr App R (S) 9.

jealousy or anything else ... there is no reason why a man should not be punished in the same way for assaulting his wife as he would be for assaulting any other person.' In more recent times, Lord Hoffmann, in *Smith*,[17] identified male proprietorialness as an excuse which should be expressly excluded from the defence of provocation. He said: 'A person who flies into a murderous rage when he is crossed' and 'male possessiveness and jealousy should not today be an acceptable reason for loss of self-control leading to homicide'.[18] Notwithstanding these opinions, such male motives or excuses have continued to be advanced in domestic homicides successfully reducing murder to manslaughter. Although manslaughter was not accepted in the case of *Ramchurn*,[19] undoubtedly the circumstances had an impact on setting the sentence to be served. Here the deceased and the appellant were cousins and the appellant offered his cousin a home, whereupon the deceased began a sexual relationship with the appellant's wife. When the affair was discovered the deceased moved out of the house, and the affair continued. Ramchurn told the court that the deceased had goaded him by saying 'You're not a man,' and 'Leave your wife, your wife doesn't want you.' In *R* v. *Entwistle* a plea of provocation failed where the appellant assaulted Claire Atkinson and, in April 2009, made several threats to kill her, subsequently persuading her to get into his car whereupon he stabbed her 13 times. The court said, 'this was a murder committed by a man who decided, out of sexual jealousy, that if his former partner could not live with him, she could not live at all'.[20] However, notwithstanding the exclusion of sexual jealousy from the new law, immunity from a murder conviction may still be realised through the defence of diminished responsibility manslaughter, provided that sexual jealousy falls within a recognised medical condition.[21]

The Coroners and Justice Act 2009 – Loss of Self-Control

The loss of self-control provisions in s. 54 provide '(1) Where a person ('D') kills or is a party to the killing of another ('V'), D is not to be convicted of murder if – (a) D's acts and omissions in doing or being a party to the killing resulted from D's loss of self-control; (b) the loss of self-control had a qualifying trigger; and (c) a person of D's sex and age, with a normal degree of tolerance and self-restraint and in the circumstances of D, might have reacted in the same or in a similar way to D.' This section replicates almost word for word the recommendations of the Law Commission (2006) which stated: '(1) Unlawful homicide that would otherwise be first degree murder should instead be second degree murder if: (a) the defendant acted in response to: (i) gross provocation (meaning words or conduct or a combination of words and conduct) which caused the defendant to have a justifiable sense of being seriously wronged; or (ii) fear of serious violence towards the defendant or another; or (iii) a combination of both (i) and (ii) and (b) a person of the defendant's age and of ordinary temperament, i.e., ordinary tolerance and self-restraint, in the circumstances of the defendant might have reacted in the same or similar way.'[22]

---

17   [2001] 1 AC 146, 169.
18   See also *Stingel v. R* (1990) 171 CLR 312.
19   [2010] EWCA Crim 194.
20   [2010] EWCA Crim 2828.
21   In accordance with the American Psychiatric Association's Diagnostic and Statistical Manual of Mental Disorders (DSM-IV).
22   Law Commission, *Partial Defences to Murder* (Law Com. No 2003); Law Commission, *Murder, Manslaughter and Infanticide* (Law Com. No 304, 2006). See also Anna Carline, 'Reforming Provocation: Perspectives from the Law Commission and the Government' [2009] 2 Web Journal of Criminal Law <http://

Objective Test – Objective Subjects

The former objective test of provocation which relied on how the reasonable man/reasonable person, possessed of the same characteristics of the defendant, would act given similar circumstances is now captured by defining in law the standard person as a person possessing, 'a normal degree of tolerance and self-restraint' (s. 54(c)). Interestingly, Lord Morris in *Camplin* stated, 'As Lord Goddard CJ said in *Reg.* v. *McCarthy* [1954] 2 Q.B. 105, 112: "No court has ever given, nor do we think ever can give, a definition of what constitutes a reasonable or an average man. That must be left to the collective good sense of the jury." ... In my view it would now be unreal to tell a jury that the notional "reasonable man" is someone without the characteristics of the accused: it would be to intrude into their province.'[23] The House of Lords in *Camplin* went on to articulate the difficulty of stripping the reasonable man of his characteristics for the purposes of self-control. 'But it is one thing to invoke the reasonable man for the standard of self-control which the law requires: it is quite another to substitute some hypothetical being from whom all mental and physical attributes (except perhaps sex) have been abstracted.'[24] In its former guise an assessment of provocation centred on circumstances since which, 'the jury shall take into account everything both done and said according to the effect which, in their opinion, it would have on a reasonable man'. However, Lord Diplock was also at pains to add that the 'reasonable man' test was a somewhat 'inapt expression', 'since powers of ratiocination bear no obvious relationship to powers of self control'.[25] The current law substitutes the reasonable man by requiring the jury to consider how a person with a 'normal degree of tolerance and self-restraint' might have reacted. The insertion here of 'normal degree' reinstates the objective requirement which was destabilised in *Smith*[26] when the House of Lords accepted that there could be circumstances when a man with an 'abnormal degree' of tolerance might still qualify for the defence of provocation.

Since *Camplin*, it is evident that the courts have developed two different approaches to the capacity issue. One trajectory remaining loyal to the notion that the capacity for self-control is normative and therefore fixed – what I shall call from this point forward 'the Ashworth position'. Ashworth's construction of the law on provocation, however, preceded the House of Lords decision in *Camplin*[27] when he said: 'The proper distinction ... is that individual peculiarities which bear on the gravity of the provocation should be taken into account, whereas individual peculiarities bearing on the accused's level of self-control should not.'[28] The other view, which embraces the possibility of a variable capacity for self-control, is represented by the majority judgment in *Smith*. Much discussion on the capacity for self-control followed the ruling in *Smith*, and anguished over the question under what circumstances a lowered capacity might be acceptable, as where a defendant suffered from a mental affliction (Smith suffered with clinical depression) or where, for

---

webjcli.ncl.ac.uk/2009/issue2/carline2.html> (accessed 4 April 2011); Jesse Elvin, 'The Doctrine of Precedent and the Provocation Defence: A Comment on R v. James' (2006) 69 Modern Law Review 819.

23   [1978] 2 All ER 168, 177.
24   [1978] AC 705, 725; [1978] 2 All ER 168; [1978] QB 254.
25   Ibid., 716.
26   [2001] 1 AC 146.
27   *Camplin* (n. 24).
28   Andrew Ashworth, 'The Doctrine of Provocation' [1976] Cambridge Law Journal 292, 300. On this point Lord Goff said in *Luc Thiet Thuan* v. *R*, PC [1997] AC 131, [1996] 2 All ER 1033, 'The similarity as between the approach recommended by Professor Ashworth, and that adopted by the House of Lords in *Camplin*, is so great that it is difficult to believe that his article did not, at least indirectly, influence the reasoning and the conclusion in that case.'

example, there was a history of violence and the defendant feared further violence from an abusive partner (as in *Thornton*,[29] and *Ahluwalia*[30]). In *Ahluwalia*, where a battered woman suffered from depression and killed a violent husband, it had been acceded that her capacity for 'tolerance and self-restraint' might be affected by her state of mind. The Court of Appeal said this: 'characteristics relating to the mental state or personality of an individual can also be taken into account by the jury, providing they have the necessary degree of permanence'.[31]

In my view, courts that had adopted a more liberal interpretation of the law in this regard were more likely to allow for a lesser capacity for tolerance and self-restraint in those cases where there was a causal connection or nexus between the reason for the provocation (the trigger) and the lowered capacity for self-control, as indeed had been the case in *Ahluwalia*. Indeed, such a nexus is blindingly obvious where a woman is being abused and the abuse has created in her a condition of fear, anxiety, anticipation and depression. In *Smith*, however, the defendant's severe clinical depression had no connection whatsoever with the circumstances of the provocation (trigger). Nevertheless, the House of Lords held that they could consider even those 'stand alone' (my phrase) characteristics which lowered the capacity for self-control notwithstanding that those characteristics might be different from those upon which the defendant relied for the gravity part of the test. *Smith* went a step further in liberalising the law and imported the concept or threshold of 'sufficiently excusable' as the yardstick or measure of mitigation of a defendant's conduct to be satisfied for the defence to operate, and held that, 'The jury must think that the circumstances were such as to make the loss of self-control sufficiently excusable to reduce the gravity of the offence from murder to manslaughter. This is entirely a question for the jury ... but ... not allowing someone to rely upon his own violent disposition.' The Judicial Studies Board which followed *Smith* drafted this direction, 'It is then for you to decide whether or not D's loss of self-control was sufficiently excusable to reduce the gravity of the offence from murder to manslaughter ...'.[32] Critics of *Smith*[33] considered this development to be overly subjective and such opposition paved the way for the judgment in *Attorney General* for *Jersey* v. *Holley*.[34] In *Holley*, a husband killed his wife and pleaded provocation claiming alcoholism as lowering his capacity for self-control. However, since the claimed reason for his lowered capacity for self-control was separate from the source of the provocation, the fact of this disjuncture was of relevance to whether it could be considered. In *Holley*, whilst it was decided that the characteristic of alcoholism could be a relevant factor, it was ruled that drunkenness could not. In addition, the court ruled that the relevant factor could only be considered where it was connected to the gravity of the provocation itself. *Holley* therefore reinserted the objective test insisting that the accused must be judged by the standard of a person possessing the ordinary powers of control. However, Lords Bingham and Hoffmann, in a joint dissenting judgment, considered this position to go against the grain of logic and said: 'the gravity of the provocation cannot rationally and fairly be divorced from consideration of the effect of the provocation on the particular defendant in relation to both limbs of the defence'.[35] This

---

29 [1992] 1 All ER 306.

30 [1992] 4 All ER 889.

31 Ibid., 898.

32 Judicial Studies Board Direction. April 2003, Archbold *Criminal Pleading, Evidence and Practice* 2003 para 19–50.

33 Sentencing Guidelines Council (guideline: manslaughter by reason of provocation) – [2005] All ER (D) 376 (Nov).

34 [2005] UKPC 23; [2005] 2 AC 580.

35 There is, however, nothing in the report, or argument, or the speeches to suggest that the House in DPP v. Camplin was referring to the article by Andrew Ashworth (n. 28), or his view that consideration of

position followed a line of authority from *Stingel*,[36] which held that in certain cases it was virtually impossible, illogical, and contrary to human experience to sever the personal characteristics from the second limb of the test. Significantly, the majority judgment in *Holley* did not expressly exclude mental afflictions, nor did they preclude the possibility of whether, where a mental affliction is both the subject of the gravity of the provocation (the trigger) and the capacity for self-control, then the degree of tolerance and self-restraint might indeed be variable.[37] Interestingly, the nomenclature of 'sufficiently excusable', so critiqued, continued to be applied even after the ruling in *Holley*.[38]

The new law, in my view, has the potential for embracing both these positions. On the one hand, it gives further weight to the 'Ashworth position', which was the intention. However, at the same time it allows for the variable capacity position, but in very specific circumstances only. Let me explain how I think this will work. Section 54(3) states 'In subsection (1)(c) the reference to "the circumstances of D" is a reference to all of D's circumstances other than those whose only relevance to D's conduct is that they bear on D's general capacity for "tolerance or self-restraint".' There are two observations to be made here. First, the new legislation refers to 'all of D's circumstances' and not to 'any characteristics'. Second, it rejects those stand alone characteristics or circumstances that affect the capacity but do not bear on the provocation.

Lord Hoffmann, who, in delivering the joint dissent in *Holley*, had begun to craft the possibility that circumstances forming part of both the gravity and the capacity might be considered and said this: 'Otherwise one is losing sight of the essential question whether, in all the circumstances …'.[39] The new law also embraces the thinking of Lord Taylor CJ in *Thornton* (No 2),[40] when he stated in relation to battered woman syndrome which formed the basis of both the gravity and the capacity: 'The severity of such a syndrome and the extent to which it may have affected a particular defendant will no doubt vary and it is for the jury to consider … it may form an important background to whatever triggered the *actus reus*.'[41] In my view s. 54(3) should, and indeed could, permit a consideration of circumstances that go to the capacity for self-control provided that they also go to the trigger. Under these specific circumstances a variable capacity for self-control is permitted, thus allowing a battered woman to plead a lowered capacity for self-control or indeed allowing a defendant with a mental affliction to plead a lowered capacity for self-control provided the factor of relevance to capacity is the very same factor that forms part of the qualifying trigger.

---

the gravity of the provocation cannot rationally and fairly be divorced from consideration of the effect of the provocation on the particular defendant in relation to both limbs of the defence.

36   *Stingel* (n. 18).

37   See Susan Edwards, 'Attorney-General for Jersey v. Holley Judgment', in Rosemary Hunter, Claire McGlynn and Erica Rackley (eds) *Feminist Judgments* (Hart 2010) 292.

38   See *Ramchurn* (n. 19). See also R (on the application of Farnell) v. Criminal Cases Review Commission [2003] EWHC 835 (Admin), [2003] All ER (D) 267 (Apr), (2003) Times, 2 June, UK DC, Attorney General's References (Nos 74, 95 and 118 of 2002) – [2002] All ER (D) 366 (Dec).

39   *Holley* (n. 34).

40   *Thornton* (n. 29).

41   Ibid., a retrial was ordered. The retrial was heard at Oxford Crown Court commencing on 30 May 1996.

Subjective Test – Subjective Subjects

Evidence of loss of self-control is often coined the subjective test in that it defines the reaction of the individual subject to the qualifying trigger. There are three aspects to consider here. The first revolves around the question of time and the meaning of its passing. In order to qualify, the law once required that loss of self-control follow immediately on the qualifying trigger such that any passage of time after the ruling in *R* v. *Duffy*[42] had been axiomatically considered to indicate a state of mind which negated a loss of self-control. However, it is no longer a requirement that the loss of self-control follow immediately in time after the qualifying trigger in order that murder (malice) be negatived, thereby overruling this part of the Duffy ruling. Section 54(2) states, 'for the purposes of ss (1) (a), it does not matter whether or not the loss of control was sudden'. Removing this requirement is intended to address what Horder termed 'the immediacy dilemma'[43] and therein to extend a manslaughter defence to abused women who kill where there had been a period of time elapsing between the last act of 'provocation', now called 'circumstances that cause the defendant to lose self-control', and the killing – Mrs Duffy's 'alleged' predicament.[44] It is Devlin J's formulation of the central importance of immediacy, endorsed by Lord Goddard CJ in the Court of Appeal,[45] that over 50 years later is overruled by the new law. Devlin J, in placing immediacy at the heart of the defence, had placed as a secondary consideration the state of mind of the defendant during the time lapse. He said this: 'In considering whether or not there has been provocation the law attaches importance to: (a) Whether there was what is sometimes called "time for cooling", that is, for passion to cool and for reason to regain dominion over the mind.' However, Park J in *Fisher*, a century before, held that 'whether the blood had time to cool or not, is rather a question of law'.[46] But the immediacy requirement is not abandoned altogether, the time lapse remaining of relevance as part of background circumstances, with the result that the ruling of Lord Taylor in *Ahluwalia* will continue to be persuasive. 'We accept that the subjective element in the defence of provocation would not as a matter of law be negatived simply because of the delayed reaction in such cases, provided that there was at the time of the killing a "sudden and temporary loss of self-control" caused by the alleged provocation. However, the longer the delay and the stronger the evidence of deliberation on the part of the defendant, the more likely it will be that the prosecution will negative provocation.' In order to discern the varying degrees of criminal responsibility that will be necessary following the abolition of immediacy, the new law imports a concept of 'considered desire for revenge' to mark out those cases where the passage of time will still subsist as an indicator of premeditation[47] from those cases involving battered women who deserve the law's protection and respect for their right to life.

---

42   [1949] 1 All ER 932.

43   Jeremy Horder, 'Reshaping the Subjective Element' (2005) 25 Oxford Journal of Legal Studies 127.

44   *Duffy* (n. 42). I say 'alleged' because my own reconstruction of this aspect of the case indicates there was very little time elapsing. See Susan Edwards, 'Mr Justice Devlin's Legacy: Duffy – A Battered Woman "Caught" in Time' [2009] Criminal Law Review 851.

45   Ibid., Edwards.

46   [1837] 8 C & P 182.

47   In *Ibrams and Gregory* [1982] 74 Cr App R 154, a five-day time lapse was too long and in addition the judge said that there was no evidence of loss of self-control and withdrew the defence from the jury. In *Brown* [1972], 56 Cr App R 564, although the judge did not withdraw the defence from the jury as the time lapse of 'a morning' was approved in principle, the defence of provocation was rejected by the jury.

Time – Out of Mind

The second consideration rests with the state of mind of the defendant prior to the killing, including any passage of time between the provocation and the lethal act. The common law, prior to *Duffy*, had focused on the state of mind, both where the lethal act was immediate and when it was not, as quintessential to an assessment of provocation. Sir James Fitzjames Stephen[48] said, 'In deciding the question [of provocation] whether this was or was not the case, regard must be had to the nature of the act by which the offender causes death, to the time which elapsed between the provocation and the act which caused death, to the offender's conduct during that interval, and to all other circumstances tending to show the state of his mind.' In the Stephen formulation these aspects presided equally and state of mind in the interval was a consideration. Devlin J's definition of provocation subordinated to time the altered state, such that time lapse defined and limited the possible states of mind, presuming a time to cool and subsequently a mind of intention. Indeed, as Mitchell, Mackay and Brookbanks argued prior to the introduction of the new law, 'Instead of retaining a requirement for "loss of self-control", as is currently construed in the rather unsophisticated sense of overtly physically out of control, the law should look at the extent of the defendant's emotional disturbance and how far that disrupted the individual's normal thinking, reasoning and judgment.'[49] Whilst the common law acknowledged the potential for cooling during a time lapse, the courts after *Duffy* presumed that a time lapse ensured the regaining of control.

Evidence of Loss of Self-Control

The third aspect of the subjective element turns on what (facts) the law has regarded as providing (evidence of) a state of mind in the Stephen sense. The authorised reasons for loss of self-control may have undergone some modification in that the qualifying trigger precipitating the loss must now be 'grave' but the particular externalities of loss of self-control remain intact and the law continues to infer a particular state of mind from an exclusive behavioural outward expression. Thus, loss of self-control continues to be fixed and anger is its signature.[50] The new law continues to endorse what Fisher in *The Vehement Passions* observed: 'It is in the details of anger that these features of the will can be grasped most easily. Anger has been subjected historically to the most detailed scrutiny because of the acts of violence to which anger leads. Anger is the necessary bridge between a purely internal account of the passions and an interest in action, because it is with anger that the aroused state in the soul or spirit has the most immediate links to the physical acts of our fists or our body in the outer world.'[51] In *Hayward*,[52] Tindal CJ expressed the state of mind as 'smarting under a provocation'. It is, of course, and always has been, a masculinist manifestation including,

---

48 *Digest of the Criminal Law* [1st edn, 1877] (3rd edn) (MacMillan and Co 1883) art. 317.

49 Barry Mitchell, Ronnie Mackay and William Brookbanks, 'Pleading for Provoked Killers: in Defence of Morgan Smith' (2008) 124 Law Quarterly Review 124, 675.

50 Law Commission, *Partial Defences to Murder* (Law Com. CP, 2003) para. 4.163, observes, 'The defence of provocation elevates the emotion of sudden anger above emotions of fear, despair, compassion and empathy.' See also Dan Kahan and Martha Nussbaum, 'Two Conceptions of Emotion in Criminal Law' (1996) 96 Columbia Law Review 269.

51 Philip Fisher, *The Vehement Passions* (Princeton University Press, 2002) 172.

52 (1833) 6 C & P 157.

'went berserk',[53] 'snap',[54] 'exploded',[55] 'spin round quickly',[56] 'black out',[57] and 'bellowing like a bull',[58] hardly accounting for women's anger or the 'other' expression(s) of women's loss of self-control at the moment of killing a violent man. Within the law of excuses it is the provoked state of anger that has become the core justification/excuse for a failure in exercising control over human conduct which because of its correspondent observable physical reaction, has been regarded as further evidence of the presence of an inner state and the absence of self-control.[59] In *Humes (Attorney General's Reference)*[60] where a wife said, 'I don't love you we are finished', the accused explained that he 'lost it completely' and said, 'you can see a red mist'. In *Wilkinson (Attorney General's Reference)*,[61] where the relationship had ended and she said 'I've got the kids ... I don't care if I've hurt you,' the accused told the jury that he 'just ... boiled over, red haze, gripped hold of her, adrenaline really going'. In *Philpot*,[62] an altercation about who should pay for the Christmas tree escalated, wherein the wife reproached her husband for an act of infidelity five years previously. He said 'something seemed to snap in my head, and I jumped up and caught her by the throat. I lost control of myself altogether. I was holding a very strong galvanic battery, and wanted to leave go, and could not.' Anger in the new statutory provision then, continues to be authorised in law and has been left unchallenged, remaining not only the dominant, but the exclusive, vehement template of loss of self-control giving permission to express lethal force through anger. Drawing on Ferdinand de Saussure,[63] loss of self-control itself can be read, and is being read as text. Thus anger is regarded as the sign. The signifier is the concept, construct or the idea which situates the meaning of the sign in its place and time. What is manifestly apparent is that loss of self-control for all legal purposes has been, is, and remains fixed in its meaning. Given this fixity, alternate realities of loss of self-control remain submerged and silenced. The difficulties and misfit for the battered woman trying to negotiate a provocation/loss of self-control defence remains. The battered abused woman in fear, it would appear, has to conform to an outward expression of loss of self-control predicated on the vehement passion of anger when her emotional state and her state of mind are intractably one of a state of fear as is her response to the violence which presents itself. Yet her state of mind and manifestation of behaviour at the time of the killing are not a loss of self-control in the traditionally masculinist sense at all. Nor is she in the period before the killing in a state of anger. She is in a state of fearful contemplation. Indeed, Lord Taylor comprehended for the battered woman an alternate state of mind that could lead to loss of self-control. He identified a state of 'brooding'. 'The appellant went to bed about midnight. She was unable to sleep and brooded upon the deceased's refusal to speak to her and his threat to beat her the next morning.'

---

53   *Richens* [1993] 4 All ER 877; the trial judges' direction on provocation included the phrase 'going berserk'. In *Campbell* [1997] 1 Cr App R 199, the fact that the defendant had 'gone berserk' provided the opportunity for retrial on grounds of provocation (where the defendant had hit a woman hitch-hiker with a hockey stick and strangled her).

54   Warner, *Guardian*, 1 May 1982; Wyatt, 22 November 1984, Manchester Crown Court.

55   Hinton, *Daily Telegraph*, 26 March 1988; see Horder (n. 43) 109.

56   *Phillips* [1969] 2 AC 130.

57   *Brown* (1972) 56 Cr App R 564.

58   *Attorney General's Reference* (Nos 74, 95 and 118) [2002] EWCA 3982 (para. 58) (*Humes, Wilkinson*).

59   Mitchell, Mackay and Brookbanks (n. 49).

60   *Humes* (n. 58).

61   Ibid., para. 73.

62   Cr App R [1912] 140, 141.

63   Ferdinand DeSaussure, *Course in General Linguistics* (Duckworth, 1995); see also Paul Thibault, *Re-Reading Saussure: The Dynamics of Signs in Social Life* (Routledge, 1996).

Even within the new law the cumulative and chronic state of mind of the battered woman will still need to be established as a loss of self-control shaped in anger's template. How exactly will this be legally accomplished, as it must be, if the new fear basis for the loss of self-control defence is to be realised? It is this inherent contradiction within the fear defence which threatens and undermines its very purpose and potential.

The time lapse abolition contains other problems of its own by extending the defence to men who kill and will need to exclude those male broodings which are clearly deliberated killings as in jealous broodings. Consider for example, the brooding of *George-Davies*, who committed arson on a family of six causing the death of one.[64] Or the separation, 'it's over' or sexual disloyalty broodings, as in *Phillips*,[65] where the husband drowned his wife because she wanted to leave him, or in *Regina* v. *Parimal Gondhia*,[66] where the defendant brooded over his wife leaving him and slashed her face and throat. Removing the immediacy requirement may resolve the problem said to have faced Mrs Duffy but it is also potentially removed for all deliberated and planned killings. It will be for the courts to ensure that revenge killings are not drawn within the ambit of loss of self-control manslaughter.[67] The subsection expressly precludes those cases where there is 'a considered desire for revenge' thus underscoring the need for the prosecution to find further evidence beyond time lapse before revenge and therefore malice can be established. Considered desire for revenge returns the standard here to one of premeditation rather than legal intention. The courts will need to discern between cases which are deliberate killings involving mixed inculpatory motives as in cases where battered women in statements or in giving evidence say 'I had to do it', 'He drove me to it', 'I couldn't stand his violence anymore', 'He deserved it', or 'I am glad I did it', and non-domestic cases where there was considerable planning.

'Extremely Grave' Circumstances

In limiting the circumstances which can be relied upon, in particular sexual infidelity and the petty and trivial excuses proffered in the past for lethal killing, the law historically authorises the behaviours it has conceded as extremely grave promising to provide a safeguard against the use of trite excuses. Ashworth[68] documented the pecking order of such behaviours in citing the early consideration of the question by Lord Holt CJ in *Mawgridge*.[69] Extremely grave behaviour, rebutting malice, included: angry words followed by assault, the sight of a relative or friend being beaten, a citizen being unlawfully deprived of liberty and a man in adultery. The law has also recognised that gravity is a social construct with the result that men are no longer permitted to claim

---

64 R v. *Stephen George-Davies* [2010] EWCA Crim 919, [2011] 1 Cr App R (S) 13. See also *Henry Larkin* (1944) 29 Cr App R 18, 'where brooding upon his wrongs ... "I pulled the razor out of my pocket and cut her throat. I ran out of the house and along the street after Nielsen, but I did not catch him".' See also *Weller* [2003] EWCA Crim 815; [2004] 1 Cr App R 1 as an example of 'separation homicide'.

65 *Regina* v. *Alun Charles Phillips*, Case No 2004/66/MTS [2006] EWHC 441 QB, where he was brooding about his grievances against Dennis Wills.

66 [2008] EWCA Crim 3268, 2008 WL 1867213. See also *Entwistle* (n. 20), in which a murder was committed because the defendant was not prepared to accept that his relationship with the deceased was over.

67 Law Commission, *Partial Defences to Murder* (Law Com. No 290, 2004), para. 1.51, had identified the problem of provocation post-*R* v. *Smith* [2000] 4 All ER 289 when stating, '... there is now no clear test for differentiating between a "provoked killing" and a "revenge killing"'.

68 Ashworth (n. 28) 1976, 293.

69 [1707] Kel 119.

'honour' or 'hubris' or more particularly 'sexual honour' or 'sexual hubris' as an adequate ground for killing another human being. The habituated sex and violence discourse of excuses, deployed in the courtroom and identified by Horder,[70] in the new law promise to eschew male hubris and to accommodate the very conditions that Devlin J had said 50 years previously were to be excluded. It now matters very much whether the dead man was cruel and violent. And this now goes towards establishing fear, although such a background may also be used, by the prosecution, to establish motive. One of the most significant developments in the new law is the limit placed on the male license to kill by, first, expressly excluding sexual infidelity as a qualifying trigger. Section 54(c) brings to an end the historical tyranny of sexual infidelity at least as a stand alone excuse and anger being a 'normal' reaction. 'Unwifelike carriage'[71] had provided adequate justification for killing or beating her, where jealousy and proprietorialness had presided: 'jealousy is the rage of man and adultery is the highest invasion of property'.[72] The second point to make is that the circumstances forming the qualifying trigger must be considered to be 'extremely grave' (s. 55(4)) and where there is a 'justifiable sense of being seriously wronged' (s. 55(4)). Lords Bingham and Hoffmann (dissenting) in *Smith* held that 'the defence of provocation must attain a certain degree or level of seriousness and gravity'. Trifling irritants will be excluded by this requirement. Consider for example, when women moved mustard pots.[73] 'Between Erika's place and mine there was a tube of mustard where I usually put the newspaper so that I could read it and we could do the crossword. Seeing the mustard, I picked it up and moved it from the centre of the table to the right of my glass. No sooner had I done it than Erika picked up the mustard and slammed it back on the mat. She started [flailing] her hands at me. Then, something seemed to snap and I seemed to be falling.'[74] Or drank alcohol,[75] as did Joseph McGrail's wife, or repeated themselves.[76] Or, the 'It's over' excuses, as in *R. v. Garrie Matthew Light*.[77] 'At about 5.45 a.m. the appellant said to police officers, "She wanted to leave me. She named Edgeler and he has become a friend of the family and now I know why." He said, "I grabbed her and just squeezed and squeezed and squeezed."' So what will the courts consider to be extremely grave? Threats to expose another's sexuality, denying a partner access to children, incessant taunting? As for what passes the 'justifiable sense of being seriously wronged' rubicon will rely on habituated excuses that have not been expressly excluded by the law. Of course this most recent formulation is no different from the 'sufficiently excusable' test coined by Lord Hoffmann in *Smith* that was so criticised because of its subjectivity!

What of Fear of Serious Violence? – The Colour Purple

Section 55(3) of the Coroners and Justice Act 2009 provides for the first time a defence for those who kill because, or out of, fear. Specifically drafted with the battered woman in mind, it overturns

---

70   Jeremy Horder, 'Sex, Violence, and Sentencing in Domestic Provocation Cases' (n. 15) 546–54. See also Jeremy Horder, *Provocation and Responsibility* (Clarendon Press, 1992).
71   See William Whately, *A Bride Bush* 1623; Elizabeth Forster, 'Male Honour, Social Control and Wife Beating in Late Stuart England', 1 Transactions of the Royal Historical Society (Sixth Series) (1996), 6, 215–24.
72   *Mawgridge* (n. 69).
73   Corlett case reported in *The Times* 10, 15 July 1987.
74   Ibid., *The Times*, 15 July 1987.
75   Joseph McGrail case, *The Guardian*, 1 August 1991.
76   Bisla Singh Rajinder case, unreported, Central Criminal Court, 29 January 1992.
77   (1995) 16 Cr App R (S) 824.

Devlin J's express exclusion of the kind of thinking when he said, 'severe nervous exasperation or a long course of conduct causing suffering and anxiety are not by themselves sufficient to constitute provocation in law'.[78] The emotional states of grief, despair, fear and terror have not been traditionally recognised as a 'loss of self-control', and have not been recognised in law, although it is certain that each of these states are not states of control of self and are certainly altered states of a troubled mind. Holton and Shute argue, 'We have seen already that states like stress and anxiety can destroy self-control.'[79] In 2009, there were an estimated 70 women in prison for killing a violent partner.[80] It is certainly the case that many of them killed because of a state of fear, having failed to satisfy the jury either that they were suffering from mental illness to qualify for a defence of diminished responsibility or to qualify for a defence of provocation. Consequently, Sharon Akers, who said, 'I will only get five years if he dies; he was so abusive and horrible he would not leave me alone. Is he dead? Did I kill him? I am sick and tired of the harassment. He was abusive. I had enough.'[81] Denise Lawrence (where the defendant's daughters made allegations that the deceased had sexually abused them),[82] Stephanie Williams (where the defendant was provoked in an argument),[83] are just some of the many women currently serving prison sentences who could benefit from this new defence, notwithstanding its shortcomings. The case of Tara May Fell[84] stands as an exception to the way battered women are traditionally treated in the law.

But the fear defence will be no guaranteed panacea. First, it does not provide an absolute defence. Fear is a qualifying (creditable) trigger, but is only a necessary condition, it is not a sufficient condition and is qualified not by 'extremely grave circumstances', as is the anger defence, but specifically by the fear of 'serious violence'. And so whilst the advent of the fear defence appears to have understood that fear drives women to kill violent men, the evidential requirement is more stringent and more specific than the anger qualifying trigger and suggests that there has been an incomplete understanding of the circumstances confronting an abused woman and the impact of living with a violent man on her risk assessment of future harm. Already, an inequity lies embedded in the two types of defences. The state of anger must follow on from extremely grave circumstances whilst the state of fear must flow from serious violence. In addition, extremely grave circumstances can include any circumstances, whilst there is one precondition to the fear defence, that of 'serious violence'. Courts will determine what passes for 'serious' violence, and may take a restrictive view of 'violence' such that, for example, a woman who is constantly humiliated by a partner, who is tied up and has water poured over her, or is made to sleep in the bath or outside, or is subjected to cruelty, may not satisfy the threshold of 'serious violence'.

The courts will also negotiate what amounts to 'fear'. Who is to judge? It will discern what passes for fear and what evidence is required. The annals of philosophy, psychology and psychiatry and behavioural science will all be drawn upon. And in so doing the experience and over-therapeutisation of the battered woman defence should stand as a warning.[85] From a practical and

---

78   *Duffy* (n. 42).

79   Richard Holton and Stephen Shute, 'Self Control in the Modern Provocation Defence' (2007) 27 Oxford Journal of Legal Studies 57.

80   *The Guardian*, 26 June 2009 (Julie Bindel).

81   [2007] EWCA 2066.

82   [2006] EWHC 140 (QB).

83   [2007] EWCA 2264.

84   Case No 99/06509/W4 2000 WL 571218; [2000] 2 Cr App R(S) 464.

85   See David Faigman, 'The Battered Woman Syndrome and Self Defence: A Legal and Empirical Dissent' (1986) 72 *Virginia Law Review* 619–47; Clare Dalton and Elizabeth Schneider, *Battered Women and the Law* (Foundation Press, 2001).

legal point of view, fear, of course, has cognitive consequences. As Burke noted, 'No passion so effectively robs the mind of all power of acting and reasoning as fear.'[86] It is true that fear reduces the capacity for rationality where the defendant has 'serious difficulty in thinking straight about behaviour'.[87] If this is true then in some cases the terrified woman may not be capable of reasoning. Beyond the cognitive processes, the behavioural response of a person in fear will almost certainly place the terrified woman outside the jurisdiction of anger's expression and its typological template of loss of self-control. For the battered woman who has endured many years of abuse before the fatal act of self-preservation is carried out, much of her life up until then may have been one not of action but of inaction. The inaction of fear is addressed in the tenth book of *The Iliad*, where the two Greek leaders aimed a spear at the head of a Trojan: 'He stood still and fell into a gibbering terror – his teeth began to chatter in his mouth and he went white with fear ... He burst into tears ... His body was trembling.'[88] This typifies the reaction of some women, especially those with no chance of escape. This was true of the defendant in *Entwistle* who had faced a long history of violence and withdrew allegations she made because of fear.[89] But neither is this behavioural response fixed and the problem for women pleading battered woman syndrome in the past was frequently, as the prosecution alleged, that she did not conform to its typology of helplessness. And so with the fear defence we face once again the danger of reductionism and essentialism, which had characterised the approach to battered woman syndrome (BWS).[90] The fear descriptors must be cast so as to reflect the multifacetedness of women's experience of, and reaction to, violent abuse and its threat. But certainly the outward manifestation of her fear is likely to be the antithesis of anger's externality. As Mitchell, Mackay and Brookbanks recognise, 'fear ... will probably result in what is overtly less frantic, more deliberate behaviour'.[91] This may drive women into the cul-de-sac of the classic portrayal of premeditation. In this regard there needs to be some discourse on the distinction between the 'considered desire for revenge' which is beyond mere deliberation, and the killing in self-preservation occasionally contemplated.

Anticipating Violence – The Case of the Keys in the Lock

The fear defence must be triggered by serious violence, or the anticipation of serious violence in the future. The fear of serious violence in the future is rather more problematic. That is because her fear of serious violence in the future depends on her risk assessment and anticipation. Weiss notes: 'Fear sears the expectations of many, often making them suffer in anticipation ...'.[92] Her anticipation holds fear of violence in the continuous present. Hilberman and Munson write on battered women, 'There was a chronic apprehension of imminent doom. They remained vigilant, unable to relax or sleep.'[93] It will be difficult for the battered woman in fear of serious violence to convey her psychological perception of the likelihood of her experiencing serious violence to the jury where his last act prior to her fatal act of survival does not in itself meet the standard of

---

86 Ibid., 115.
87 Mitchell, Mackay and Brookbanks (n. 49) 680.
88 Fisher, *The Vehement Passions* (n. 51) 15, 122.
89 *Entwistle* (n. 20).
90 See Susan Edwards, *Sex and Gender in the Legal Process* (Oxford University Press, 1996).
91 *Fisher* (n. 46) 683.
92 Paul Weiss, *Emphatics* (Vanderbilt University Press, 2000) 214.
93 Cited in Cynthia Gillespie, *Justifiable Homicide* (Ohio State University, 1989) 124.

serious violence. Is she to wait and see what happens? In the past this had been formulated as 'last straw' arguments in the context of cumulative provocation, and again it was Lord Taylor who allowed for cumulative provocation in developing case law principles. But that door of the last straw has been totally shut to battered women because now, whilst the history of abuse is a relevant feature of the circumstances, the bar has been set at fear of serious violence not last straw. So we have changed the nomenclature and concept reflecting the woman's state of mind from cumulative provocation to fear acknowledging a history of violence, but actually in reality may have made it harder for women to succeed with this defence because last straw 'frayed elastic' arguments may be excluded. The tale of the keys in the lock illustrates her predicament under the new law. For many women who are the victims of abuse and live in fear, the act immediately preceding the fatal act is the last straw, but may not be the most serious. Indeed, unless it is in self-defence and she is in the throes of being attacked, if she is to survive at all the last act will not be the most serious. Thus, the last act preceding the killing of the abusive partner may be the sound of keys turning in the lock, or a car parking in the driveway, hardly an act of violence, let alone serious violence. But when the keys in the lock are turned by a violent man and when a car is being parked by a violent man the reaction of an abused woman must be seen in this context. The abused woman reacts then to his imminent arrival as it is a forewarning of what is to come. And, if she is to survive, this is the only moment of survival. Heather Osland was convicted of murder after killing her husband who abused her over many years. She describes her anticipation of his behaviour: 'We waited at the front window to see him get out of the car, like we usually did, to see what mood he was going to be in. We always stood there watching we did that for months. If he was laughing more jovially with his mates then we knew we were in trouble when he got inside. If he was more solemn when he got out of the car he wouldn't be so bad when he got inside.'[94]

Fear's Own Reasoning

But killing upon anticipation has been regarded as overreaction. Norrie has coined her killing out of fear 'imperfect justification'.[95] But does she overreact? Or more accurately does she have a heightened perception of her future safety which is not comprehensible to the untrained juror who has not been in her situation. Schneider recognises, 'battered women have learned to be attentive to the signs of escalating violence ... subtle motions or threats that might not signify danger to an outsider or to a trier of fact acquire added meaning for the battered woman whose survival depends on an intimate knowledge of her assailant'.[96] But does her assessment of the likelihood of violence and her assessment of the degree of violence have to be reasonable? And who can be the judge of that? We have visited this debate before.[97] Reasonable to a battered woman or reasonable to a woman with no experience whatever of abuse. Consider, for example, that management of risk requires realistic risk assessment. So, for example, when the risk of child sexual abusers preying

---

94 Cited in Celia Wells, 'Provocation; The Case for Abolition', in Andrew Ashworth and Barry Mitchell (eds), *Rethinking English Homicide Law* (Oxford University Press, 2000) 97.
95 Alan Norrie, 'The Coroners and Justice Act 2009 – Partial Defences to Murder: (1) Loss of Control' [2010] Criminal Law Review 275, 269. See also Carol Withey, 'Loss of Control: Loss of Opportunity' [2011] Criminal Law Review 275, 278.
96 Edwards (n. 90) 232.
97 Ibid. Chapter 6, 'Unreasonable Women – Battered Woman Syndrome on Trial', 227.

on children,[98] or of nuclear leakages from nuclear power plants,[99] is assessed by experts, they are the reasonable men. So who are the experts with regard to the battered woman? Is *she* not the expert and in fact what she perceives is that not a real risk and not an overreaction? A fear killing following on from serious violence or anticipation of serious violence contains some of the characteristics of self-defence but without the requirement of immediacy. To what extent will the new fear defence manoeuvre itself into a position which is distinct from self-defence?

Considering self-defence the Criminal Justice and Immigration Act 2009 s. 76 provides: '(4) If D claims to have held a particular belief as regards the existence of any circumstances – (a) the reasonableness or otherwise of that belief is relevant to the question whether D genuinely held it; but (b) if it is determined that D did genuinely hold it, D is entitled to rely on it for the purposes of subsection (3), whether or not – (i) it was mistaken, or (ii) (if it was mistaken) the mistake was a reasonable one to have made. (5) But subsection (4)(b) does not enable D to rely on any mistaken belief attributable to intoxication that was voluntarily induced.'

To succeed with a defence of self-defence the defendants 'belief' has to be reasonable therefore has to be reasonable. Will her belief in the likelihood of his serious violence within the Coroners and Justice Act 2009 be required to be objectively reasonable under the fear defence? Surely it must be subjective based on her perception of the situation she finds herself in and based on the background of his prior violence. Furthermore, s. 76(6) of the Criminal Justice and Immigration Act states, 'The degree of force used by D is not to be regarded as having been reasonable in the circumstances as D believed them to be if it was disproportionate in those circumstances.' Again, the problem for women pleading self-defence has been that her fatal act frequently follows on from a lesser attack. That is why she survives! But how will she negotiate the loss of self-control defence? Surely her reaction cannot be expected to be objectively proportionate to his last act of violence. Indeed, the Law Commission struggled with this with regard to the loss of self-control defence and considered her fear to be an overreaction.[100] Section 76(7) of the Criminal Justice and Immigration Act states: 'In deciding the question mentioned in subsection (3) the following considerations are to be taken into account (so far as relevant in the circumstances of the case) – (a) that a person acting for a legitimate purpose may not be able to weigh to a nicety the exact measure of any necessary action.' Weighing to a legal nicety both the degree of his likely violence and the reaction necessary to repel it is also a problem for women pleading the fear/loss of self-control defence.

Misfits and Loss of Self-Control

The fear configuration in the new law has been inadequately constructed. There has been little attempt to understand the impact of fear on the human will, or on an abused woman's thinking or behaviour. There are at least three obstacles to realising this new defence for battered women. First, the loss of self-control template continues to authorise anger such that women's behaviour at the time of the killing under a fear defence and also under a combined anger and fear defence will simply fail to satisfy the traditional requirements of the outward manifestation of loss of self-control upon which the defence still relies. This will need to be challenged. Second, the fear defence is construed through a lens of proportionality whereby the only fear that is objectively legitimate is that which is the product, or perception, of serious violence. This too will need to be

---

98 *The Times*, 19 March 2011.
99 *The Guardian*, 16 March 2011.
100 See n. 22 (2006) para. 1.61; See also Norrie (n. 95) 'The Coroners and Justice Act 2009 – Partial Defences to Murder: (1) Loss of Control'.

challenged. The framing of the construct of reasonableness persists in the cognizance of a typified objective standard of what can be legitimately feared. This was a problem articulated in the *State of Washington* v. *Yvonne L. Wanrow*, where the Supreme Court said: '... [the] objective standard ... through the persistent use of the masculine gender leaves the jury with the impression that the objective standard to be applied is that applicable to an altercation between two men.'[101] In *R* v. *Lavellee*,[102] the Supreme Court of Canada said: 'I do not think it is an unwarranted generalization to say that due to their size, strength, socialization and lack of training, women are typically no match for men in hand-to-hand combat.'[103] Whilst this problem can be partly addressed by taking into consideration sex (gender) in the capacity/characteristic in addressing inequality in physical size and strength, it does not address the fear of someone who has lived with a violent partner for any length of time and experiences what I shall call anticipation 'syndrome'. Justice Wilson in *R* v. *Lavellee*,[104] went on to say this: 'I am skeptical whether the average fact-finder would be capable of appreciating why her subjective fear may have been reasonable in the context of the relationship. After all, the hypothetical "reasonable man" observing only the final incident may have been unlikely to recognise the batterer's threat as potentially lethal.' In the New South Wales case of *Hickey*,[105] a plea of self-defence succeeded where the defendant stabbed her husband after he headbutted and attempted to strangle her. The Supreme Court did not regard battered woman syndrome as evidence of abnormality of mind. Instead it treated the syndrome as shedding light on how normal women who are battered by their spouses might have viewed the need to take reasonable defensive action. These cases are both instructive and their judgements intuitive. As I have said elsewhere, 'A battered woman's reaction to her abuser's violence does not necessarily follow from the severity of the last act of violence, but flows from her perception of the severity of the threat he poses to her life.'[106] The approach of the Law Commission on this point has been to disavow the wisdom of Justice Wilson. This will need to be challenged. Third, in distinguishing fear killings from revenge killings the background evidence will be of crucial importance. However, in looking for evidence of a course of cruel conduct and violence, a fact-finding problem is presented, since she may have not spoken, she may have remained silent and endured. The fearful battered woman who kills remains somewhat a legal misfit and the law for its part continues to excuse his anger more than it excuses her fear.

---

101   See Edwards (n. 90) 233; see also Clare Dalton and Elizabeth Schneider, *Battered Women and the Law* (Foundation Press, 2001) ch. 10.

102   [1990] 1 SCR 152.

103   Ibid., [57]. See also Robbin Ogle and Susan Jacobs, *Self-Defence and Battered Women Who Kill: A New Framework* (Praeger, 2002) 73–4.

104   [1990] 1 SCR 15.

105   (1992) 16 Crim LJ 271.

106   Susan Edwards, 'Anger and Fear as Justifiable Preludes for Loss of Self Control' (2010) 74 Journal of Criminal Law 223–41, 233.

Chapter 7
Feminism, 'Typical' Women, and Losing Control

Neil Cobb and Anna Gausden

Introduction

Recent reformulations of the provocation defence, first in proposals issued by the Law Commission,[1] and then by the Ministry of Justice in the form of the new partial defence of loss of control,[2] were a response, in part at least, to compelling feminist legal scholarship and activism, which had demonstrated the defence's profound gender bias. This bias was evident especially when provocation was used as a defence to murder by battered women who killed their abusive male partners, and by violent men who killed their girlfriends or wives.[3] Attention was drawn by feminist legal scholars, taking a woman-centred approach to the defence,[4] to the gendered implications of the need for a defendant, D, to experience a sudden and temporary loss of control, which excluded women from the ambit of the defence. It was argued in particular that the actions of abused women are shaped typically in part by fear as well as anger, while the masculine assumptions underpinning the concept of loss of control unjustifiably sanctioned the fatal actions of abusive men. The new partial defence was designed to respond to these feminist concerns.[5] It does so, primarily, by recognising for the first time fear of serious violence as a relevant triggering event,[6] reducing the importance of the temporal requirement,[7] and tightening up the concept of provocation to limit the legitimation of male violence against women.[8] However, feminist concerns with the defence remain, especially the retained concept of loss of control, which fits uneasily with accounts of the reactions of abused women who kill.[9]

---

1 Law Commission, *Partial Defences to Murder* (Law Com. No 290, 2004).

2 Ministry of Justice, *Murder, Manslaughter and Infanticide* (MoJ CP (R) 19, 2008).

3 For excellent introductions see: Jeremy Horder, *Provocation and Responsibility* (Clarendon Press, 1993) ch. 9; Susan Edwards, *Sex and Gender in the Legal Process* (Clarendon Press, 1996) ch. 9.

4 A woman-centred approach to law is one that seeks to address 'the systemic failure of the legal order to recognize and to redress the injuries that women experience': Stephanie Wildman, 'Ending Male Privilege: Beyond the Reasonable Woman' (2000) 98 Michigan Law Review 1797.

5 Susan Edwards, 'Anger and Fear as Justifiable Preludes for Loss of Self-Control' (2010) 74 Journal of Criminal Law 223.

6 Coroners and Justice Act 2009, s. 55(3).

7 Ibid., s. 54(2).

8 Ibid., ss. 54(4) and 55(6)(c).

9 Jo Miles, 'The Coroners and Justice Act: A "Dog's Breakfast" of Homicide Reform' (2009) 10 Archbold News 6. Importantly, many feminist legal scholars have instead demanded abolition of provocation and the creation of a new partial defence of excessive force in self-defence: Susan Edwards, 'Abolishing Provocation and Reframing Self-Defence – The Law Commission's Options for Reform' [2004] Criminal Law Review 181. Others have noted that self-defence is a more appropriate defence for abused women, especially as it ensures complete exculpation: Aileen McColgan, 'In Defence of Battered Women Who Kill' (1993) 13 Oxford Journal of Legal Studies 508.

Feminist criticism of the old common law of provocation was directed also at the evaluative standard: that a 'reasonable person' would have reacted in the same or a similar way to D.[10] Specifically, the extent to which certain characteristics of D should be given to the reasonable person created its own feminist controversies, as we consider later in this chapter. However, the new partial defence of loss of control now relies on an almost identical codified approach to evaluating conduct as the common law of provocation after *Holley*.[11] One aspect of the evaluative standard retained by the 2009 Act is the incorporation of sex as a characteristic of the person of normal tolerance and self-restraint.[12] This requirement, introduced by the common law in the case of *Camplin* in the late 1970s,[13] again ensures that the effects of sex and, by implication, gender are considered by judge and jury when evaluating D's response to a particular triggering event. Intriguingly, the decision to retain this reference to sex was not, however, part of the Law Commission's own proposals.[14] Instead, the Commission originally argued that D's sex should no longer be allotted to the hypothetical person of normal tolerance and self-restraint,[15] but the Ministry of Justice simply rejected this part of the Commission's proposals.[16]

That both the Law Commission and Ministry of Justice aimed in their proposals to tackle the gender bias of the old law of provocation, but disagreed over whether to incorporate reference to sex into the evaluative standard, makes this aspect of the reform process especially intriguing for feminists. In this chapter, we explore how this conflict has parallels in recent feminist legal scholarship, which has debated the implications for women of sexed evaluative standards. The Law Commission argued for a de-sexed standard on formal equality grounds. However, sexed standards have also been proposed by feminist scholars to address the bias against women entailed by superficially gender neutral laws.[17] Explicit reference to sex (and so gender), they suggest, is needed to challenge the masculine norms embedded in otherwise neutral evaluative standards, by enabling lawyers to introduce evidence in court of the 'typical' reaction of women. Others though have criticised the use of sexed standards for opening up decision-making to the dual dangers of stereotyping and essentialism.[18] The aim of this chapter is to re-evaluate the implications for women, and abused women in particular, of the sexed standard now codified in the new defence of loss of control, in light of this sophisticated feminist legal scholarship.

In our view the Ministry of Justice's reincorporation of sex into the evaluative standard is a mistake. What we advocate instead is reform of the new defence to bring it into line with the Law Commission's original proposal to remove sex from the evaluative standard. This is not to suggest that sex and gender have no relevance at all; we recognise, as feminists have consistently and compellingly explained, that there is a need to explain to juries the particular response patterns of women qua women, especially those of abused women who kill. It is to argue instead that the sexed

---

10   Edwards (n. 3) 380–86.
11   *Attorney General of Jersey* v. *Holley* [2005] 2 AC 580.
12   Coroners and Justice Act 2009, s. 54(3).
13   *DPP* v. *Camplin* [1978] AC 705; see also *Morhall* [1995] 3 All ER 659 (HL).
14   Law Com. No 290, 2004 (n. 1) para. 3.110.
15   As we demonstrate later in this chapter, under the Law Commission's original proposals, it would still have been possible to introduce considerations of the sex and gender of D as part of the wider 'circumstances' of D.
16   MoJ CP (R) 19, 2008 (n. 2) 18.
17   Caroline Forell and Donna Matthews, *A Law of her Own: The Reasonable Woman as a Measure of Man* (New York University Press, 2000).
18   Naomi Cahn, 'The Looseness of Legal Language: The Reasonable Woman Standard in Theory and in Practice' (1991–92) 77 Cornell Law Review 1398.

evaluative standard as it is currently conceived in the 2009 Act *overstates* the relevance of sex and gender to D's reaction, by permitting consideration of sex when *solely* relevant to the capacity of D to exercise self-control. In turn, this unnecessarily refracts and reinforces stereotypes that men and women differ in their ability to control their behaviour, while also encouraging, to a greater extent than required to achieve protection for abused women, essential understandings of female reactions which obfuscate the complexities created at the intersection of gender with class, race, sexuality or disability.

We suggest instead that it would be both possible, and more appropriate, for D's sex and gender to be considered under the partial defence of loss of control as part of the positioning of the hypothetical person within the wider 'circumstances' of D.[19] This approach ensures that sex and gender become important only when they are deemed to affect more than merely the capacity of a hypothetical person to exercise tolerance and self-restraint, in relation to which being male or female is, we argue, entirely irrelevant. By doing so, the opportunity for stereotyping is reduced, while the essentialism encouraged by the pre-eminent significance given to sex and gender under the current schema is replaced by a system in which sex and gender are granted the same significance as other attributes that intersect with these characteristics to shape D's reaction. We accept, of course, that reform of the defence of loss of control which we propose will still create opportunities for stereotyping and essentialism under the evaluative standard. As such, we end the chapter by refocusing feminist attention toward the evidential difficulties still involved in addressing these dual dangers, especially the legal limits on the expert evidence that can be used to explain the 'typical' reactions of abused women qua women.

Loss of Control's Evaluative Standard

Defending a charge of murder on grounds of loss of control depends not only on an assessment that D actually lost self-control in response to a prescribed triggering event, but that 'a person ... with a normal degree of tolerance and self-restraint might have reacted in the same or in a similar way to D'.[20] This evaluation requires a trial judge and jury[21] to appraise the normative acceptability of D's actions,[22] in much the same way as under the old law of provocation.[23] Evaluative standards within

---

19 Coroners and Justice Act 2009, s. 54(1)(c).

20 Ibid.

21 Under the new defence the judge is granted much greater power to withdraw the defence from the jury, as the trial judge must now be persuaded that 'a jury, properly directed, could reasonably conclude that the defence might apply' before it can be put to jurors for consideration: Coroners and Justice Act 2009, ss. 54(5) and (6).

22 In the words of Cynthia Lee, 'The open-ended nature of the reasonableness requirement is designed to allow community input on matters involving difficult value judgements and provide greater flexibility and fairness in legal decision making than is permitted by strict rules': *Murder and the Reasonable Man: Passion and Fear in the Criminal Courtroom* (New York University Press, 2007) 3–4.

23 The new defence of loss of control changes the terminology of the normative requirement from a reasonable person to a person of normal tolerance and self-restraint. By moving the new standard away from ideas of reasonableness, the new defence appears to address the concern historically that the idea of a reasonable person killing in response to a loss of control was inconceivable: Victoria Nourse, 'Passion's Progress: Modern Law Reform and the Provocation Defense' (1997) 106 Yale Law Journal 1331. Instead, the ordinary person is a typical rather than a remarkable individual. Compare Lee, who suggests ordinariness in provocation is 'problematic because views that are popularly held do not always correlate with notions of equality and justice': Lee (n. 22) 4.

the criminal law tend in practice to develop into what Lee has described as a 'hybrid subjectivized-objective standard',[24] and the partial defence is no exception. The hypothetical person is drawn to some extent from the context of D. The legislation dictates that this hypothetical person must be given D's sex and age, and he or she must also be placed 'in the circumstances of D'.[25] Under this new legislative schema the liability of a woman who kills her abusive partner must now be evaluated according to a judge and jury's perception of a woman of her age's reaction, in the context of any other circumstances that apply to more than merely her capacity to exercise tolerance and self-restraint.[26]

The evaluative standard under the new partial defence parallels the approach of the common law following the decision of the Privy Council in *Holley*.[27] After *Holley*, Susan Edwards concluded that battered women would 'be back to finding themselves once again outside the law',[28] because unlike the position under *Smith (Morgan)*,[29] it seemed to prevent battered spouse syndrome from being considered as affecting the capacity of the reasonable person to exercise tolerance and self-restraint. However, the feminist credentials of the more subjectivised standard established in *Smith (Morgan)* were themselves challenged by scholars at the time.[30] The *Holley* approach ensured that abnormal characteristics which male Ds argued reduced their capacity for self-control when they killed their female partners were ignored.[31] What is more, and leaving aside for a moment the criticisms of battered spouse syndrome by feminists in recent years, it was claimed that the *Holley* approach did not necessarily mean that abused women would be shorn of contextual information relevant to their reaction. Lord Millett, dissenting in *Smith (Morgan)*,[32] argued that the *Holley* approach would still permit the hypothetical woman to be located within D's own experience of abuse, so that battered spouse syndrome could be considered as an effect of that abuse on an otherwise normal woman.[33]

Lord Millett's analysis of the effect of the *Holley* approach on abused women who kill their partners was enough to persuade the Law Commission that abused women would not be disadvantaged by the codification of the *Holley*-style standard in its own reformulation of provocation,[34] and the same conclusion seems to have been drawn by the Ministry of Justice when it put forward its plans for the new defence of loss of control. In the same way as under the old common law, the new partial defence introduced by the 2009 Act now provides that the evaluative hypothetical person should be located in the wider 'circumstances' of D.[35] This additional subjective consideration permits the hypothetical person to be positioned within the history of abuse experienced by D herself, which presumably will permit consideration of the effect of abuse

---

24 Lee (n. 22) 206.
25 Coroners and Justice Act 2009, s. 54(1)(c).
26 Ibid., s. 54(3).
27 [2005] 2 AC 580.
28 Susan Edwards, 'Descent into Murder – Provocation's Stricture – The Prognosis for Women Who Kill Men Who Abuse Them' (2007) 71 Journal of Criminal Law 342, 361.
29 [2001] 1 AC 146.
30 Mandy Burton, 'Intimate Homicide and the Provocation Defence – Endangering Women? *R* v. *Smith*' (2001) 9 Feminist Legal Studies 247.
31 For a well-known example of the anti-feminist impact of the *Smith* decision see: *Weller* [2003] Criminal Law Review 724.
32 [2001] 1 AC 146.
33 Ibid., 213.
34 Law Com. No 290, 2004 (n. 1) para. 3.11.
35 Coroners and Justice Act 2009, s. 54(1)(c).

on the capacity of an abused woman to exercise self-control – for example, through the admission of evidence of battered spouse syndrome – to inform the defence's evaluative standard, as explored by Lord Millett in his judgment in *Smith (Morgan)*.

More important to us, however, is the role played by consideration of sex and gender under the *Holley*-style evaluative standard. The introduction of a sexed evaluative standard in English law has been charted by Yeo.[36] The test first emerged in *Camplin*, when the House of Lords concluded the reasonable person had always been sexed (and gendered).[37] Their Lordships added that the justification for incorporation of a sexed reasonable person standard was that juries would be unable to comprehend an abstraction that did not include the sex and gender of the reasonable person.[38] Even as the appellate courts moved back and forth between primarily objective and primarily subjective interpretations of the reasonable person standard, after *Camplin* there was an apparent consensus that the evaluative standard should continue to be sexed. It would take the Law Commission's review of the provocation defence in 2003–4 before the issue was subjected to further critical scrutiny, and perhaps surprisingly the Commission formed rather different conclusions about the relevance of sex and gender.

The Law Commission was informed in its own approach to reform by a desire to address the gender bias at the heart of the defence. In particular, it had been instructed to address the effect of the partial defences, and provocation especially, in the specific context of domestic violence and intimate partner homicide.[39] It was from this perspective that it reached the conclusion that incorporation of a sexed evaluative standard was not a good idea. Instead, it was of the view that formal gender equality was required unless there were compelling reasons to depart from it,[40] and in the apparent absence of any reasons to do so it removed reference to sex from the evaluative standard. The Ministry of Justice was also motivated primarily by the interests of women, and especially abused women who kill.[41] However, when it embarked on its own assessment of the Commission's proposals, it reached an entirely different woman-centred position on the sexed evaluative standard. The Ministry of Justice ignored entirely this part of the Commission's proposals and, noting the importance it placed on the gender impact of the reformed defence (although providing little else by way of explanation for its decision), concluded instead that the sexed evaluative standard should and would be retained.[42]

This conflict between the Law Commission and the Ministry of Justice (one of a series of differences of approach, including their positions on the loss of control requirement) is an intriguing aspect of this area of law reform. It should be of particular interest to feminists, however, because while both organisations were motivated by gender equality, they each reached diametrically opposing conclusions about the role played by sex and gender. To what extent, then, was the Commission's adherence to formal gender equality a better theoretical and strategic objective for feminists than the Ministry of Justice's incorporation of sex and gender into the 'normal tolerance

---

36   Stanley Yeo, 'The Role of Gender in the Law of Provocation' (1997) 26 Anglo-American Law Rev 431.

37   [1978] AC 705, 716–17 (Lord Diplock), 724 (Lord Simon of Glaisdale).

38   Ibid.

39   Law Com. No 290, 2004 (n. 1) para. 1.2.

40   Ibid., para. 3.78.

41   Ministry of Justice, *Coroners and Justice Act 2009: Equality Impact Assessment – Homicide* (TSO 2008) <http://www.justice.gov.uk/publications/coroners-justice-bill.htm> (accessed 4 April 2010).

42   MoJ CP (R) 19, 2008 (n. 2) 18.

and self-restraint' standard?[43] A similar question has been asked many times before by feminist scholars, because it is tied ultimately to wider feminist concerns with questions of sameness and difference,[44] and the related debates between feminist lawyers over the potential and pitfalls of sexed evaluative standards in a wide range of legal fields including sexual harassment, sexual violence and defences to murder.[45] What becomes quickly apparent from a survey of this feminist literature, however, is that, in much the same way as the Law Commission and the Ministry of Justice, feminist scholars are polarised in their views on the benefit to women of evaluating behaviour in light of sex and gender.

The Role of Sex and Gender in the Evaluative Standard

The Law Commission reached its decision to abandon a sexed evaluative standard, as part of its own proposals to reform provocation, on the basis of the presumed importance of formal gender equality in the criminal law.[46] This adherence to formal equality, and the sameness between men and women that it appears to presume, while an important part of liberal feminist thinking, is problematic when applied to the operation of evaluative standards within the criminal law. As radical feminist scholars – none of which the Law Commission cites – have argued, evaluative standards are in practice invariably gender biased. These standards, operating as they do within a patriarchal culture, promote an 'essentially male viewpoint under the guise of universality'.[47] The hypothetical person is in practice gendered because that person is conceptualised within a gendered social context. What advocates of gender neutral evaluative standards fail to recognise is that sameness leads to substantive inequality in a system of criminal law that adheres to masculine standards because it reflects relations of power grounded in male privilege. Abused women who kill find it difficult to satisfy the expectations of the standard. They are rendered abnormal for not leaving the relationship; for the delay between provocation and killing; and for using weapons rather than their fists to kill.[48]

Feminist scholars adopting a woman-centred analysis of the defences to murder, and judges persuaded by this analysis, have helped to challenge the assumptions underpinning this gender bias by explaining the 'typical' response pattern of abused women who kill in light of the sexed and gendered realities of their embodied existence. As Justice Bertha Wilson of the Supreme Court of Canada noted in *Lavallee* v. *The Queen*, it is unlikely to be 'an unwarranted generalization to say that due to their size, strength, socialization and lack of training, women are typically no match for

---

43 We have assumed in this chapter, as others have, that when the evaluative standard refers to 'sex' it means not only the physical characteristics of men and women, but also their 'gender', or psychological and social characteristics: see Yeo (n. 36); Edwards (n. 5).

44 For an exploration of the sameness/difference debates see: Vanessa Munro, *Law and Politics at the Perimeter: Re-evaluating Key Debates in Feminist Theory* (Hart, 2007) ch. 1.

45 For consideration of feminist debates across these areas see: Mayo Moran, *Rethinking the Reasonable Person: An Egalitarian Reconstruction of the Objective Standard* (Oxford University Press, 2003) ch. 6.

46 This was also the approach adopted in a number of other jurisdictions, notably by the Australian High Court in *Stingel* v. *The Queen* (1990) 171 CLR 312, and the Supreme Court of Canada in *Hill* (1986) 25 CCC (3d) 322.

47 Kathleen Kenealy, 'Sexual Harassment and the Reasonable Woman Standard' (1992) 8 Labor Lawyer 203, 204.

48 Elizabeth Schneider, *Battered Women and Feminist Law-Making* (Yale University Press, 2000).

men in hand-to-hand combat'.[49] In response to the assertion that abused women should be expected to leave their abusers, rather than killing them, Chief Justice Wilentz of the New Jersey Supreme Court responded that 'external social and economic factors often make it difficult for some women to extricate themselves from battering relationships ... women typically make less money and hold less prestigious jobs than men, and are more responsible for child care. Thus, in a violent confrontation where the first reaction might be to flee, women realize soon that there may be no place to go'.[50] In short: 'one of the "circumstances" under which women kill is the circumstance of being female'.[51]

Given this recognition that abused women react differently qua women some feminist scholars have argued that the gender bias of the defences to murder can only be addressed meaningfully by introducing conceptions of sex and gender into the evaluative standards on which these defences rely, whether they employ conceptions of the 'reasonable', 'ordinary' or any other normative hypothetical person with whom D should be compared.[52] Sexed evaluative standards have been supported on this ground, in the context of defences to murder, by feminist legal scholars, and on occasion by progressive feminist judges.[53] As Justice L'Heureux-Dubé concluded, for example, in a decision of the Supreme Court of Canada on self-defence, 'the perspectives of women, which have historically been ignored, must now equally inform the "objective" standard of the reasonable person'.[54]

In much the same way, it would seem the continued recognition of women's difference enabled by the sexed evaluative standard now found in the defence of loss of control serves the interests of abused women who kill. Like feminist evaluations of the old common law of provocation, the role of sex and gender as explicit considerations under the new defence has either been overlooked entirely by feminist commentators or, where it has been considered, the retention of a sexed standard has been treated as a positive development. For instance, Carline recently concluded in her own analysis of the changes introduced by the 2009 Act that the government 'should be applauded' for retaining sex in loss of control's evaluative standard;[55] Susan Edwards has also sanctioned its approach.[56] To us, though, the progressive credentials of the evaluative test are not quite so clear-

---

49   [1990] 1 SCR 852, 883.

50   *United States* v. *Kelly* (1985) 478 A2d 364, 372. This failure to leave the relationship has been explained alternatively as an aspect of the 'learned helplessness' central to the now controversial 'battered women's syndrome' developed in Lenore Walker, *The Battered Woman* (Harper, 1979).

51   Laurie Taylor, 'Provoked Reason in Men and Women: Heat-of-Passion Manslaughter and Imperfect Self-Defence' (1986) 33 UC Los Angeles Law Review 1679, 1734.

52   Forell and Matthews (n. 17) (applying reasonable woman standard to both male and female defendants).

53   *State* v. *Wanrow* (1977) 559 P 2d 548 (Supreme Court of Washington State).

54   *R* v. *Mallott* [1998] 1 SCR 123, 140–41.

55   Anna Carline, 'Reforming Provocation: Perspectives from the Law Commission and the Government' (2009) 2 Web Journal of Current Legal Issues <http://webjcli.ncl.ac.uk/2009/issue2/carline2.html> (accessed 4 April 2011).

56   Edwards (n. 5) 235–8. Edwards supports her position partly on the basis that the purpose behind the sex criterion in the 2009 Act is to address gender bias, whereas the *Camplin* approach was grounded in the gender stereotyping endemic to the period (communication with the authors). We accept that the purpose behind the sex criterion has radically changed from its inception in *Camplin* to its reappearance in the 2009 Act. However, for us an explicitly 'feminist' purpose behind the retained sexed standard will not in itself preclude use of sex as a basis for gender stereotyping or essential conceptions of female reaction, as its operation depends on constructions of sex and gender formulated by lawyers, judges and juries in particular trials.

cut. What remains insufficiently analysed in these feminist appraisals, in our view, is the work of scholars who have argued that, rather than addressing male privilege, sexed evaluative standards may well create their own injustices for women, and abused women who kill in particular. These scholars have been, and remain, acutely aware of the oppressive consequences of including sex and gender in this way, warning in turn that 'arguments about gender characteristics have to be handled with care'.[57]

These scholars have identified two key problems with the introduction of sexed evaluative conceptions of the reasonable, ordinary or typical woman into criminal laws. The first of these concerns is that these sexed evaluative tests, in buying into claims of sex and gender difference to address the problems associated with sameness, threaten to exacerbate powerful gender stereotypes, because they are applied within patriarchal culture and relations of power.[58] Sexed evaluative standards fail to engage effectively with wider systems of male privilege within which defences to murder operate,[59] as 'femaleness still occupies a subordinate position in the prevalent gender hierarchy that privileges maleness'.[60] Female subordination rests upon widely held assumptions about women, or 'preexisting norms of womanhood as defined by men',[61] which are likely to be held by those same decision-makers – i.e. judges and juries – who are charged with evaluating the acceptability of D's conduct.[62] Put another way, as Cahn has pointed out, '[r]eifying a [sexed evaluative] standard does not get us away from the problem of who is interpreting that standard'.[63]

In relation to the loss of control defence specifically, sexed evaluative standards may be used by judge and jury to claim a typical woman would lose her control with much greater difficulty than a typical man, and in particular with much greater difficulty than the abused female D who responds to that abuse by killing.[64] Those abused women who are judged to have failed to meet the expectations of their sex can then be punished by decision-makers.[65] Marie Fox has observed that 'an angry woman who breaks the law commits a double transgression – she is seen as offending both the tenets of the criminal law and the dictates of nature'.[66] Even where contradictory gender constructions operate that appear to limit the criminal liability of female Ds, such as the view that regards women 'as highly strung, emotionally fragile, fickle, hysterical, and less able to control

---

57 Katherine O'Donovan, 'Defences for Battered Women Who Kill' (1991) 18 Journal of Law and Society 219, 229.

58 Wildman (n. 4).

59 Cahn (n. 18) 1809.

60 Ibid., 1810.

61 Kenealy (n. 47) 204.

62 Carline cites Glanville Williams' claim that women have higher levels of self-control than men: Carline (n. 55). Notions of female passivity have long shaped judicial attitudes: 'No matter how you may dispute and argue, you cannot alter the fact that women are quite different from men. The principal task in the life of women is to bear and rear children: ... He is physically stronger and she the weaker. He is temperamentally the more aggressive. It is he who takes the initiative and she who responds. These diversities of function and temperament lead to different outlooks which cannot be ignored. But they are, none of them, any reason for putting women under the subjugation of men': Lord Denning, *The Due Process of Law* (Butterworths, 1980) 194, quoted in Carol Smart *Feminism and the Power of Law* (Routledge, 1995) 13.

63 Cahn (n. 18) 1812.

64 Donald Nicholson, 'Telling Tales: Gender Discrimination, Gender Construction and Battered Women Who Kill' (1995) 3 Feminist Legal Studies 185; Anna Carline, 'Zoorah Shah: An Unusual Woman' (2005) 14 Social and Legal Studies 215.

65 Nicholson (n. 64); Carline (n. 64).

66 Marie Fox, 'Legal Responses to Battered Women Who Kill', in Susan Millns and Jo Bridgeman (eds), *Law and Body Politics: Regulating the Female Body* (Dartmouth, 1995) 176.

themselves in the ordinary sense of the word',[67] they do so at an obvious cost for D and women more generally. Women are produced as well as regulated by legal decision-making, ensuring these negative stereotypes are reflected and refracted from the structure and implementation of the defence back into wider social discourse.[68]

Of course, one might argue that to focus attention on explicitly sexed evaluative standards misses the point; gender stereotyping permeates every part of the criminal justice process irrespective of the existence of specific sexed evaluative standards in individual criminal defences. The embodied sex of D is always already present in the minds of judge or jury, and gendered expectations are therefore inevitably implicated in judicial directions and jury decision-making. As such, it seems gendered stereotyping would continue to operate whether or not sex was explicitly included in the standard. The problem with explicit reference to sex, however, is that attention is drawn formally by the law to these characteristics, and as such the potential for gender stereotyping by judge and jury is further exacerbated by the terms of the partial defence. Specific reference to sex in the evaluative standard *requires* judge and jury to consider the potential effects of sex and gender on D's reaction. Of even greater concern, however, is that, by formally nominating sex and gender as relevant characteristics, the legislation impliedly asserts that sex and gender make a difference, ensuring that law contributes to wider societal assumptions about sex and gender from which this social stereotyping derives.

Gender stereotypes can be addressed to an extent by the introduction of appropriate expert evidence;[69] and indeed, a sexed evaluative standard seems to be necessary to support the admissibility of expert opinion about 'typical' female responses which can help to counter stereotyping by judge and jury. As Kaganas has argued, though, and as we consider later in this chapter, rules of evidence can limit the admissibility of suitable evidence, and it is always open to a jury to ignore any evidence which is actually admitted.[70] As such, gender stereotyping can still be exacerbated wherever and whenever sexed evaluative standards operate. There is, however, an even more significant potential difficulty with the current adherence by some feminist legal scholars to sexed evaluative standards. The assertion that a 'typical' woman's response exists, even where this is grounded in feminist epistemologies rather than gender stereotypes, is problematic due to its essentialism. In short, sexed evaluative standards treat women as though they all share an identical embodied existence.[71] This post-structurally inflected argument has helped to draw attention to the inevitable generalisations about women (and men) that would still occur even if one were to avoid the gendered stereotypes derived from male privilege, and especially those differences that invariably exist at the axes of gender and, for example, class, race, disability and sexual orientation. In the absence of an intersectional understanding of identity,[72] abused women

---

67 Edwards (n. 5) 236.

68 Smart (n. 62).

69 Felicity Kaganas, 'Domestic Homicide, Gender and the Expert' in Andrew Bainham, Shelley Day Sclater and Martin Richards (eds) *Body Lore and Laws* (Hart, 2003).

70 Ibid., 124.

71 Of course, as Cynthia Lee observes, 'Essentialism is a problem that inheres anytime one utilizes a reasonableness requirement, even a hybrid subjectivized-objective standard of reasonableness': Lee (n. 22) 220. While we accept this is inevitable under a reasonableness standard, we also recognise that sex and gender remain deeply embedded social categories that lend themselves to particularly pernicious generalisations, and lead to more harmful implications for society than other assumptions about battering.

72 For consideration of intersectionality as a mode of analysis, but also criticisms of this method, see Joanne Conoghan, 'Intersectionality and the Feminist Project in Law', in Emily Grabham, Davina Cooper,

are over-generalised when they are evaluated against the standard of a typical woman, which can never fully account for the specificity of their experiences.

The upshot is that the sexed standard in the defence of loss of control raises serious concerns. In its explicit direction to judge and jury to consider D's sex and gender it has the potential to exacerbate gendered stereotyping of D, unless adequately addressed through expert evidence. However, irrespective of these gender stereotypes, in giving particular attention to the relevance of sex and age alone, the standard created by the new defence of loss of control implicitly prioritises these concepts in ways which render them potentially more significant to lawyers, judges and juries than other elements of D's embodied circumstances that might affect D's reaction, especially where D is an abused women.[73] As a result, this sexed system distorts the representation of the (female) D. It heightens the relevance of these characteristics at the expense of the intersection of class or race or sexual orientation or disability in ways that threaten to crystallise implicitly in the minds of judge and jury a typicality that is ultimately white, middle class, heterosexual and able-bodied. In doing so, we would argue that the priority given to sex and gender in the current evaluative schema of the loss of control defence encourages an analysis tied to questionable legal generalisations of womanhood.

Restricting the Sexed Evaluative Standard

Sexed evaluative standards, and the particular standard found in the loss of control defence, are clearly controversial for some feminist legal scholars. While they might help to challenge the otherwise unnoticed gender bias of the decision-making of judge and jury, they simultaneously bring with them the danger of distorted representations of women and men, either in the form of gender stereotypes, or simply through the claim of a typical female reaction, which is unrepresentative of all women. This has discursive and material implications for those judged according to these standards, not least the criminal liability of abused women who kill their partners, and abusive men who kill their wives or girlfriends. Feminists continue to navigate the inevitable tensions between attempts at representation of women's lives through a sexed evaluative concept and the stereotype/essentialism which invariably attends this agenda.[74] Further questions need to be answered, in turn, about the role of sex and gender within the evaluative processes of the defences to murder. How can feminists ensure that the difference that marks women's lives can be effectively incorporated into the new partial defence of loss of control, while avoiding, or at least reducing, stereotyping and essentialism?

One solution to this quandary offered by feminist legal scholars is to abandon altogether the use in law of evaluative standards.[75] Such a proposal effectively means that a judge and jury would no longer be directed to consider explicitly whether the reaction of D was the typical response of a hypothetical person, but rather attention would be drawn simply to whether the particular D lost control in the circumstances, and went on to kill. This approach appears to have much to

---

Julie Krishnadas and Didi Herman (eds), *Intersectionality and Beyond: Law, Power and the Politics of Location* (Glasshouse, 2009).

73 However, as we argue below, under certain conditions (i.e. when not related solely to capacity for control) the defence permits incorporation of attributes such as class or race as part of the wider 'circumstances' of D.

74 Carline (n. 55).

75 Dolores Donovan and Stephanie Wildman, 'Is the Reasonable Man Obsolete? A Critical Perspective on Self-Defense and Provocation' (1981) 14 Loyola of Los Angeles Law Rev 435.

commend it.[76] The experience of domestic violence by D would be explained without any attempt to render her reaction 'typical' or 'ordinary' or 'reasonable' in the circumstances. One consequence of this is that the minds of judge and jury would not be directed formally to whether D abided by their expectations of her sex. However, abandoning the evaluative standard creates new difficulties for feminists.[77] It would mean abandoning the justificatory element of loss of control, losing the sense that what D did was understandable according to common moral values.[78] Subjectivising the defence also opens it up to unacceptable use by men who claim abnormal predisposition to violence.[79] For these reasons we accept that some form of evaluative standard needs to be retained by the new partial defence.[80]

Another option is an entirely de-sexed evaluative standard, in which a formally gender neutral person is positioned instead in the context of D. For instance, Felicity Kaganas has argued (with respect to the old law of provocation) against a 'reasonable woman' standard, in favour of 'an expanded, context-sensitive version of the reasonable person'.[81] This approach refuses to jettison the objective standard entirely, but instead locates a de-sexed hypothetical person within at least certain circumstances of D herself, most importantly, perhaps, her experience of abuse at the hands of the deceased. While, as Kaganas herself accepts, drawing the line between a purely subjective and a hybrid subjectivised-objective standard is likely to pose its own problems,[82] this approach, in its rejection of all consideration of D's sex and gender, also reduces the potential for stereotype and essentialism. However, while it provides an apparent solution to the problems of a sexed standard, we remain unconvinced by this attempt to remove sex and gender entirely from the evaluative standard, primarily because we believe it is quite impossible to conceive how the contexts of women, especially abused women who kill, can be understood and expressed without any reference to sex and gender.

Neither abandoning the evaluative standard entirely, nor returning to a de-sexed standard, seems to us to provide a suitable feminist model for meaningful change to the operation of the loss of control defence. We are therefore more convinced by the approach taken by those feminist scholars who, while recognising the threat of essentialism and negative stereotype when sex and gender are incorporated into sexed evaluative standards, go on in any case to conclude that the benefits to women of a hypothetical woman standard outweigh the risks of stereotyping

---

76   Indeed, it was proposed by at least some respondents to the Ministry of Justice: (n. 2) para. 76.

77   Moran (n. 45) ch. 6.

78   This is also a problem with diminished responsibility, which renders D 'abnormal' through its psychiatric explanation of her violent reaction to the abuse she suffers at the hands of her partner: see Donald Nicholson and Rohit Sanghvi, 'Battered Women and Provocation – The Implications of *R* v. *Ahluwalia*' [1993] Criminal Law Review 728.

79   Although much has been done by the 2009 Act to preclude claims of loss of control by men who kill their partners, especially through the requirement that provocation must be of 'an extremely grave character and caused D to have a justifiable sense of being seriously wronged' (Coroners and Justice Act 2009, s. 55(4)) and the specific exclusion for killings in response to sexual infidelity (Coroners and Justice Act 2009, s. 55(6)(c)).

80   See further the debate between Nourse and Lee on whether to abandon evaluative standards entirely: Victoria Nourse, 'Upending Status: A Comment on Switching, Inequality, and the Idea of the Reasonable Person' (2004) 2 Ohio State Journal of Criminal Law 361; Cynthia Lee, '"Murder and the Reasonable Man" Revisited: A Response to Victoria Nourse' (2005) 3 Ohio State Journal of Criminal Law 301.

81   Kaganas (n. 69) 122.

82   Ibid.

and essentialism.[83] Carline provides an example of this approach. When appraising the sexed evaluative standard she notes:

> sex specific tests can be used in a problematic manner ... conceptions of "man" and "woman" are undoubtedly difficult and one could question why sexual difference is favoured over and above other relevant axes of identity, such as race or class.[84]

However, in the end Carline still accepts the sexed standard as an appropriate measure to address gender bias, implying that she has weighed up the strategic pros and cons for feminist politics and reached the conclusion it is better to include sex in the test with all its attendant risks than to remove it entirely as the Law Commission proposed. Are feminists right to adopt this mode of reasoning in respect of the defence of loss of control? Are the dangers involved in stereotyping and essentialising abused women who kill outweighed by the need to incorporate their difference when applying the partial defence, in order to address the masculine norms that invariably underpin its operation?

On Carline's analysis the sexed evaluative standard employed within the new partial defence of loss of control seems to be a necessary development. The decision of the Ministry of Justice to reintroduce sex into the evaluative standard should be welcomed, while the Law Commission's adherence to formal equality principles appears to form a simplistic feminist agenda that fails to recognise the intrinsic gender bias in the application by judge and jury of purportedly gender neutral legal tests. We accept that addressing gender bias in the law, and the risks of stereotyping and essentialism, lie inevitably in tension. However, while we acknowledge that a balance must be struck, we disagree with the view that the loss of control defence, at least, strikes this balance correctly. The assumption seems to be that there are only two possible approaches to the issue: either sex is included explicitly within the evaluative standard, or it becomes impossible to describe the experiences of abused women who kill to a judge and jury and address the gender bias of the defence. It appears to us, however, that a third option is possible within the terms of the new loss of control defence, whereby the role of sex and gender is narrowed further by considering them instead as part of the wider 'circumstances' of D.

Sex and Gender as 'Circumstances' of D

In our view, recognition of sexed and gendered difference must be restricted to the absolute minimum required to address adequately the gender bias of the evaluative standard in the partial defence of loss of control, given the role it can play in exacerbating stereotyping and essentialism. However, closer examination of the legislative schema created by the Coroners and Justice Act 2009 leads us to conclude that as it stands it *overstates* the significance of sex and gender. What is quite clear from the structure of the 2009 Act is that sex, like age, must be considered in relation to all aspects of the hypothetical person's reaction. However, under the schema, judge and jury are also directed to take into consideration the wider 'circumstances' of D, so long as they are not *solely* relevant to the capacity of a person of normal tolerance and self-restraint. Read together, these

---

83 For an example of an explicit attempt to balance the threats of essentialism and stereotyping with the benefits of a reasonable woman standard, though in the particular context of sexual harassment law, see: Caroline Forell, 'Essentialism, Empathy, and the Reasonable Woman' (1994) University of Illinois Law Review 769.

84 Carline (n. 55).

provisions dictate that explicit reference to sex (and age) when characterising the normal person enable these particular circumstances alone to be considered even when they are only relevant to D's capacity to control her behaviour.[85] As such we agree with Alan Norrie that 'presumably the idea is that sex [like age] generally affects capacity for self-control', irrespective of their relevance to other aspects of a normal person's reaction. The problem is that 'exactly how' sex is relevant to capacity 'is left unstated'.[86]

More importantly, how does a conception of sex and gender-specific capacity for self-control really contribute positively to the feminist project in law? At least to our knowledge, feminists have never argued that women should be understood as different from men with regard to their respective abilities to control their behaviour. According to the feminist accounts of the role of sex and gender in shaping the reaction of abused women who kill which we described above, the relevance of these concepts does not relate to capacity for self-control. Sex is irrelevant when considering whether the normal person would have lost control in the circumstances of D in the absence of any justification for the conclusion that women are more or less likely to lose their control than men.[87] Where a typical woman's reaction has proved significant to provocation in particular is where it explains the peculiarities of what Stanley Yeo terms an abused woman's 'response reaction', or whether a typical woman would go on to kill as a result of her loss of control and would kill in the same or a similar fashion to D.[88] However, the response reaction of the hypothetical person goes to an aspect of D's behaviour distinct from the question of the general capacity of that person to maintain self-control.[89]

In light of this, i.e. because feminist accounts of the role of sex and gender in shaping the reactions of abused women who kill are limited to her response reaction, rather than her capacity for self-control, we would suggest that the current evaluative standard under the new partial defence of loss of control is over-extensive in its explicit reference to a sexed hypothetical person. Comprehending the typical woman's response reaction does not require the explicit sexing of the evaluative standard. Instead, when judge and jury evaluate the response reaction of the hypothetical person they can take into consideration both sex and gender as part of the 'circumstances' of D, which will apply in any case to an evaluation of D's response reaction, because this aspect of D's

---

85 In relation to this proposal, we have assumed that the common law distinction drawn between 'circumstances' and 'characteristics' has been done away with by the new legislation, which seems to have been the intention in any case after *Camplin*, in which Lord Simon was of the view that 'in determining whether a person of reasonable self-control would lose it in the circumstances, the entire factual situation, which includes the characteristics of the accused, must be considered': *R v. Camplin* [1978] AC 705, 727.

86 Alan Norrie, 'The Coroners and Justice Act 2009 – Partial Defences to Murder: (1) Loss of Control [2010] Criminal Law Review 275, 281.

87 Yeo (n. 36) 450.

88 Ibid., 452.

89 In this respect, at least according to Yeo's own analysis, the 2009 Act may well have subtly altered the approach under the old common law. Yeo argues that the old 'power of self-control' standard under *Camplin* included both consideration of 'capacity for self-control' and the 'response reaction' of the reasonable person (ibid., 447–57). As such, circumstances other than age or sex could only be considered by judge and jury when evaluating D's response reaction if they also affected the gravity of the provocation. Under the new defence, however, the circumstances of D can always be considered when evaluating the response reaction, whether or not they are relevant to the gravity of the 'triggering events', because they relate to something other than 'capacity' for self-control. Thus, there appears to have been a further 'rolling back' of the stricter objective standard (i.e. age/sex only) in this area under the new legislation. For the argument that D's 'response reaction' (referred to as 'act reasonableness') should be subject to a strict objective standard see Lee (n. 22) ch. 10.

conduct involves an issue other than merely D's general capacity for tolerance and self-restraint.[90] Putting things another way, closer scrutiny of the structure of the evaluative standard demonstrates that explicit reference to sex *does too much work*, because it demands a sexed and gendered evaluation even where these aspects of an individual's identity are deemed relevant *solely* to the capacity of D to exercise self-control.

However, incorporation of sex and gender under the new defence is not simply unnecessary to support a suitably feminist account of the typical reaction of abused women. It is also dangerous, because it opens up sex and gender too far as grounds for questionable claims about the ability of women, and in particular abused women who kill, to control their behaviour: claims which lend themselves to the type of problematic stereotyping which supports common conceptions of women as either less able to control themselves or typically more self-restrained than men and therefore appropriately held to a higher standard of tolerance. What is more, this legal basis for gender-based assumptions about capacity for self-control extends beyond the role of abused women as Ds, as the defence operates as a partial exculpation not only for abused women, but also men who kill their female partners. While the new partial defence restricts the potential for abusive partners to mitigate a murder charge, it still permits judge and jury to reach the view that women and men share differing capacities for self-control, and more so than is strictly necessary to ensure the typical response reactions of abused women are understood by these decision-makers through the introduction of gender-specific evidence.

It also seems to us that the dangers posed by this over-extension amount to more than the increased opportunities for stereotyping of men and woman by judge and jury. By entitling them to consider only sex and age when their relevance is related solely to the capacity for tolerance and self-restraint, the legislation also works itself to further reinforce the widely held societal conception that a difference in capacity for control can indeed be found between men and women. In other words, in the process of selecting these characteristics, and no other, for special consideration, the law impliedly further condones this unfounded stereotype, and suggests to all those who engage with the partial defence – lawyers, judges, juries, the public – that a sexed capacity for self-control exists. Explicit reference to sex is *not only unnecessary* to achieve feminist goals, but *permits and reinforces* powerful stereotypes that women are subject to greater or lesser capacities for self-control. On this ground too we believe that explicit reference to sex in the evaluative standard should be abandoned, and considerations of sex and gender considered instead as part of the circumstances of D, ensuring that they are excluded from appraisal when solely relevant to capacity for tolerance and self-restraint.

Restricting consideration of sex and gender to the wider 'circumstances of D' imposes much more defensible limits on the potential for gender stereotyping that we have highlighted in this chapter. By ensuring these concepts are admissible only when their relevance goes beyond mere capacity for tolerance and self-restraint, the potential for negative gender stereotyping is narrowed, though not entirely removed. We further argue though that removal of the explicit sexed evaluative standard may help to address the problems of essentialism inherent in the claim of a 'typical' woman's reaction. Transfer of conceptions of sex and gender to the circumstances of D ensures the significance of a meaningful shared experience among women qua women is reduced, because sex and gender would no longer be put forward by the legislation as though they had some pre-

---

90 Edwards recognises this possibility: 'Of course, it can be argued that sex in this context would be relevant, in any event, under 'the circumstances of the defendant', but clearly providing for this characteristic in statute underscores its importance': n. 5, 237. We argue instead, however, that underscoring sex in this way is likely to create more harm than good due to the legitimacy it provides for gender stereotyping and essentialism.

eminent significance to the hypothetical person's reaction above and beyond attributes such as class, race or sexual orientation. Instead, sex and gender would be treated as one of numerous other aspects of D's identity that might influence the way in which she would react to particular triggering events, including domestic violence, encouraging, we would suggest, a more nuanced intersectional analysis of her experience.

For all these reasons we suggest that the Law Commission was correct in its decision to abandon the explicit reference to sex in the schema it proposed to govern evaluation of the reaction to be expected of a person of normal tolerance and self-restraint. The major problem for us is its reasoning: its simplistic adherence to a blanket policy of formal equality failed to engage sufficiently with the complex implications for women, and abused women in particular, of sexed evaluative standards explored by feminist legal scholars and which we have briefly described in this chapter. We recognise, though, that reform of the loss of control defence to remove reference to sex from the evaluative standard does not entirely solve the problems we have identified. Where sex and gender continue to be used to explain the 'typical' reactions of women qua women, which remains possible under our proposed reform (although in fewer situations than under the current legislative system), these conceptions of sex and gender can also support less acceptable judicial and jury decision-making derived either from negative stereotyping of Ds, or a failure to recognise the differences in reaction that might derive from the intersections between gender and other axes of subordination.

As such, while we propose that sex and gender should figure under loss of control's evaluative standard in the limited terms that we describe, we reiterate the pivotal role that can be played by expert evidence in dispelling the stereotypes to which this standard will still give rise.[91] Feminists have been equivocal about the role of expert evidence,[92] but in a context of male privilege we remain persuaded that it is a necessary evil to effectively represent abused women who kill.[93] Feminists must therefore continue to draw attention to those rules of evidence which prevent experts from presenting to judge and jury a sufficiently feminist epistemology of how sex and gender shape abused women's responses. In particular, it must be remembered that concerns remain about the difficulties posed for a woman-centred account of the effects of domestic violence by *Turner*.[94] Through its 'necessity' test, *Turner* seems to foreclose the opportunity to educate judge and jury in sexed and gendered reactions to abuse in a non-stereotypical or non-essentialist fashion, because it prioritises psychiatric testimony, especially evidence of the problematic battered spouse syndrome,[95] over non-medicalised, social scientific expert accounts of the gendered reactions of abused women who kill.[96]

---

91 Kaganas (n. 69) 124.

92 Elizabeth Schneider, 'Describing and Changing: Women's Self-Defense Work and the Problem of Expert Testimony on Battering' (1986) 9 Women's Rights Law Reporter 195.

93 As O'Donovan noted in light of the Canadian decision in *Lavellee*: 'Why can't women's experiences be accommodated by law without resort to experts? Canadian law provides answers on a number of levels. In summary, myths about, and stereotypes of battered women must first be displaced. Then the experiences of such women can be introduced. To accomplish both of these tasks experts are required': Katherine O'Donovan, 'Law's Knowledge: The Judge, the Expert, the Battered Woman, and her Syndrome' (1993) Journal of Law and Society 427, 430.

94 [1975] 1 QB 834, 841 (Lawton LJ).

95 Battered spouse syndrome has been described as 'profoundly anti-feminist': Anne Coughlin, 'Excusing Women' (1994) 82 California Law Review 1, 6.

96 Kaganas (n. 69) 118–22.

Perhaps only once this rule is further refined,[97] will it be possible for abused women's embodied experiences to be expressed in a form that adequately addresses stereotyping and essentialism.[98] Non-psychiatric expert evidence could then be used to explain the 'typical' response reactions of abused women who kill while avoiding the stereotyping of battered spouse syndrome. Thoughtfully prepared, social scientific evidence might also help to challenge the essentialism which subsists in any reference to 'typical' female behaviour, by ensuring that sufficient attention is paid to the inevitable differences that exist *between* women. Of course, the law can only do so much. Addressing the potential for stereotyping and essentialism is necessarily dependent on continued ethical reflection by feminist lawyers, who alone can ensure that evidence put forward in practice to explain the typicality of their client's reaction to abuse does justice to the reality of her embodied, gendered existence.[99] Nevertheless, reformulating the rules of expert evidence is perhaps the next step in enabling the experiences of abused women to be understood within a criminal justice system that continues to operate according to masculine assumptions about women, and their fatal reactions to abusive men.[100]

Conclusions

When defences to murder, like the partial defence of loss of control, are used to defend abused women who kill, 'the issue of how to represent the complexities of women's experiences ... is both complicated and frustrating'.[101] The use of a sexed evaluative standard is an understandable, and sometimes successful, way in which feminists have attempted to address the inevitable gender bias of reasonable or ordinary person standards in a legal system which continues to underwrite male privilege. Loss of control's sexed standard of a woman of normal tolerance and self-restraint seems to follow this mode of thinking, rather than the misguided 'sameness' advocated by the Law Commission, which reinforces the gender bias masked by ostensibly gender neutral criminal law. However, the sexed standard creates its own problems. In particular, it suffers from both the negative portrayal of gendered difference in a world of male privilege, which ensures that ordinary women are judged according to male standards and stereotypes, and essentialism, which erases the many and varied differences between women. The potential

---

97 Compare the approach in the Canadian Supreme Court decision in *Lavellee* v. *Queen* [1990] 1 SCR 852. Notably, the recent Law Commission Consultation Paper on admissibility of expert evidence failed to engage in a review of the 'necessity' criterion in *Turner*: see Law Commission, *The Admissibility of Expert Evidence in Criminal Proceedings in England and Wales* (Law Com. CP 190, 2009) and Editorial, 'Examining Expert Evidence' [2009] Criminal Law Review 387. See also Law Commission, *Expert Evidence in Criminal Proceedings in England and Wales* (Law Com. 325, 2011), and the Draft Criminal Evidence (Experts) Bill, which will leave the common law 'necessity' test largely untouched.

98 Of course, as Kaganas points out 'expert evidence is no guarantee of success. For one thing, juries might take the view that, despite what they may have been told about domestic violence, it is insufficient to provide a moral excuse or justification for killing an abuser': Kaganas (n. 69) 124.

99 Cahn (n. 18) 1446.

100 For a different approach, which proposed to refine *Turner* to support the admissibility of expert evidence designed to dispel rape myths, see: Office for Criminal Justice Reform, *Convicting Rapists and Protecting Victims – Justice for Victims of Rape: A Consultation Paper* (TSO 2006), ch. 4. The proposal was never taken forward. Thanks to Heather Keating for bringing this aspect of the consultation paper to our attention.

101 Cahn (n. 18) 1420.

dangers for women posed by a sexed evaluative standard require us to be sure that a standard of this kind is applied only when absolutely necessary.

Closer scrutiny of the loss of control defence has led us to conclude that the sexed evaluative standard, while potentially useful, is currently far too blunt an instrument to ensure justice for women, and for abused women who kill in particular. For this reason it requires reformulation. The implication behind the current schema, in which sex is explicitly referred to as a characteristic of the hypothetical person, is twofold. The legislation implicitly assumes, first, that sex and gender have some special significance when considering the capacity for control expected of the hypothetical person, and secondly that the special effects of sex and gender is justifiably incorporated into the standard to be expected of a particular D when judges and juries make moral judgements about the capacity for control she demonstrates. In light of the compelling concerns of feminists with stereotyping and essentialism, while conceptions of sex and gender difference remain necessary to tackle male privilege, this can be achieved more positively by considering these characteristics instead as part of the wider 'circumstances' of D. In this way, the law might better help to curtail stereotypes regarding the differing capacities of women and men for self-restraint, while also challenging essentialism by reducing the pre-eminence granted to sex and gender over other axes of identity which are likely to shape a woman's 'typical' reaction to lost control.

However, even if the partial defence is reformed to remove its current explicit reference to sex, as we propose here and as the Law Commission originally advocated, the problems of stereotyping and essentialism cannot be removed altogether. While conceptions of the 'typical' reaction of women to domestic violence may draw attention to the problematic assumptions of juries about appropriate behaviour shaped by a society of male privilege, this typicality can also, in its drift towards essentialism and stereotyping, constrain the understanding of judges, juries and lawyers, about women, and abused women who kill, in all their specificity. In this chapter we have considered some of the ways that feminists have proposed to move away entirely from sexed evaluative standards. In the end, however, we cannot accept that either abandoning an evaluative standard entirely, or imposing instead a wholly de-sexed, but contextualised, standard to govern the applicability of the defence, will adequately express the gendered differences of women's reactions. Instead, we add our voices to those feminist legal scholars who argue that what is still needed is scrutiny of the present system of expert evidence, so it can better challenge stereotyping and essentialism whenever judge and jury are asked to consider the role of sex and gender under loss of control's evaluative standard.

Chapter 8
Sexual Infidelity Killings: Contemporary Standardisations and Comparative Stereotypes

Alan Reed and Nicola Wake

We would make ourselves look extraordinarily foolish if we say that a jury cannot take account of what most people recognise as being the most dominant cause of violence by one individual against another. Every opera you go to, every novel you read has sexual infidelity at one point or another. Otherwise it is not worth listening to … It is an incredibly powerful voice. In every newspaper you read there is a case where somebody has killed or attempted to kill a spouse, lover, lost lover, or whatever. To rule this out as not being an area of activity where human passions are deeply engaged, leading to violent action, is absurd.[1]

The Putative Search for a Rationale to the Heat of Passion Defence

It is essential that the ambit and theoretical underpinnings of loss of self-control as a partial defence to murder reflect contemporary attitudinal standards and societal mores. In English law this 'appropriate' standardisation was controversially transplanted by the government of the day into the final stages of the parliamentary process (at bill stage) to exclude sexual infidelity as a qualifying trigger for fact-finder evaluation.[2] The schematic template promulgated advanced specific triggers centred around fear of violence and partially justifiable anger but not in all senses, and not as the Law Commission[3] had articulated. This was subsequently enacted in the Coroners and Justice Act 2009, and now 'the fact that a thing done or said constitutes sexual infidelity is to be disregarded'.[4] The need for a consistent moral basis to the newly constituted loss of self-control defence mandated, in the view of some commentators, 'that it is unacceptable for a defendant who has killed an unfaithful partner to rely on that unfaithfulness to try to escape a murder conviction',[5] and more broad criticism of sexual inequalities under extant law whereby, 'essentially what we have in this defence is moral culpability wrapped up in psychiatric nosology where instead anger, rage and jealousy are the sickness'.[6]

---

1 HL Deb., 26 October 2009, 1061 (Lord Neill of Bladen).
2 See generally, Jo Miles, 'A "Dog's Breakfast" of Homicide Reform' (2009) 10 Archbold News 6; and Leonard Leigh, 'Murder, Manslaughter and Infanticide: Proposals for Reform of the Law' (2008) 172 Justice of the Peace and Local Government Law, 700.
3 See Law Commission, *Partial Defences to Murder* (Law Com. No 290, 2004); Law Commission, *Murder, Manslaughter and Infanticide* (Law Com. No 304, 2006); and Ministry of Justice, *Murder, Manslaughter and Infanticide* (Law Com. CP No 19, 2008).
4 Coroners and Justice Act 2009, s. 55(6)(c).
5 HL Deb. (n. 1) 1062 (Lord Bach, Parliamentary Under Secretary of State).
6 Susan Edwards, *Sex and Gender in the Legal Process* (Blackstone Press, 1996) 402. See also Susan Edwards, 'Abolishing Provocation and Reframing Self-Defence – The Law Commission's Options for Reform' [2004] Criminal Law Review 181; and Susan Edwards, 'Anger and Fear as Justifiable Preludes for Loss of Self-Control' (2010) 74 Journal of Criminal Law 223.

The posited issue of whether the controversial exclusion of sexual infidelity fully accords with appropriate contemporary standards and societal mores of the day is considered further below. It is also appraised in the purview of the contextual ambit of the judge and jury in this perspective. The perceived need for change, however, reflected a view of heat of passion cases that deleteriously focused upon egregious precepts of male proprietorialness, jealousy and envy. The need to avoid these discreditable phemenological reflections and behaviours precipitated the straitened boundaries of the new legislative reforms. Lord Hoffmann in *Smith (Morgan)*,[7] had presaged the belief that for some aspects of personification of the characteristics of the reasonable man the jury's moral rigour should not be trusted. The partial defence, as in *Stingel*,[8] an Australian case involving an excessively jealous boyfriend, who stalked his former girlfriend and then killed her new paramour, ought objectively to be removed from jury consideration by the trial judge:

> Male possessiveness and jealousy should not today be an acceptable reason for loss of self-control leading to homicide, whether inflicted upon the woman herself or her new lover ... it is suggested, a direction that characteristics such as jealousy and obsession should be ignored in relation to the objective element is the best way to ensure that Stingel cannot rely upon the defence.[9]

Difficulties have prevailed in Anglo-American law *vis-à-vis* the conditions of the defence relating to a response of excessive anger to the initial provoking act. Is it possible to delineate 'appropriate' responses to provoking acts in terms of compartmentalisation and prioritisation between the parameters of jealousy/envy/proprietorialness (wholly inappropriate) set against partially legitimate excessive anger invoked by violations of 'sacred' intimacy, humiliation and extreme breaches of trust? This raises the further dilemmatic choice(s) of whether different expectation levels, or rather continuums of level of control, are nuanced both within and outside intimate relationships. It is oxymoronic to refer to the excessively angered and sexually jealous, but 'reasonable' killer of a partner. The focus, as such, is not reflective standards of how this individual 'should' respond to ocular or verbal identification of an intimate partner cheating on their relationship, since *cadit quaestio*, the response is that it is never legitimate to kill.[10] Rather, the lodestar of this heat of passion defence ought to be whether this mitigation can ever be appropriate in terms of the compartmentalised level of taunting producing consequential fatal action of a spontaneous nature which may in some limited circumstances be regarded as inappropriate but partially exculpatory conduct.[11] On one side of the divide Reilly,[12] and others,[13] have asserted that: 'There seems no good reason why a defence based on loss of self-control should not also be extended to actors who kill under conditions of intense fear, or sadness, or under other emotional

---

7   [2001] 1 AC 146.
8   (1990) 171 CLR 312.
9   *Smith (Morgan)* (n. 7) 169.
10 Clare McDiarmid, 'Don't Look Back in Anger: The Partial Defence of Provocation in Scots Criminal Law', in James Chalmers, Fiona Leverick and Lindsay Farmer (eds), *Essays in Criminal Law in Honour of Sir Gerald Gordon* (Edinburgh University Press, 2010) 201.
11 Ibid.
12 Alan Reilly, 'Loss of Self-Control in Provocation' [1977] 21 Criminal Law Journal 320.
13 See generally, Jeremy Blumenthal, 'Law and the Emotions: The Problems of Affective Forecasting' (2005) 80 Indiana Law Journal 155; and Ronnie Mackay and Barry Mitchell, 'Provoking Diminished Responsibility: Two Pleas Merging into One?' [2003] Criminal Law Review 745.

conditions such as compassion, depression or jealousy',[14] whilst Horder,[15] hugely influential in the context of recent English reforms, has presciently advocated a restricted provocative condition:

> I have defended this view, in so far as fear for one's (or for another's) safety is concerned. How plausible is this view, though, when applied to, say, extreme emotional disturbance produced by "sadness", or by "jealousy", whether or not the victim was in any plausible sense causally implicated in bringing about the violent reaction? Every stalker who feels that the object of his obsessive love should be reciprocating, even though she has never shown the slightest interest in him, would in principle be entitled to be acquitted of murder if he deliberately killed her when he was "overcome" by sadness or jealousy at her continuing rejection. He would be so entitled, moreover, even if he had forearmed himself for the final encounter, which took the form of slitting her throat as she slept.[16]

At a practical level, the constrained exclusion in the Coroners and Justice Act 2009 of things done or said that constitute sexual infidelity will create interpretational difficulties, and reveals drafting of a tautological and imprecise nature. It is difficult, if not impossible, to countenance how something 'verbal' is embodied as occurrence/action of constituents of sexual infidelity. It may be that a purposive meaning is attached whereby things said *relating* to the infidelity fall within the confines of the section, but it is unfortunate that this matter has been expressed opaquely.[17] Potentially, the section may not be as restrictive as purported. Infidelity is effected by the partner against the 'cuckolded' defendant; by parity of reason does the new provision consequently exclude from the parameters of restriction sexual acts or taunts by the new paramour of the victim in that they are not the actual progenitor of the 'infidelity'? Is 'infidelity' restricted to the confines of breach of marital relationships? Although unlikely as an intuitive response it remains a feasible argument until settled judicially. Moreover, the very pre-eminence attached to sexual infidelity as a primordial exclusionary basis, beyond other circumstances of 'appropriate' disenfranchisement such as honour killings, homophobic fatalities or gang-related violence, is regarded by many as illogical stereotyping.[18]

An unfortunate bifurcatory divide may be created by this 'micro-management of the defence'.[19] The separation, provides 'more harm than good'[20] in that the episodic nature of breaches of intimacy and ending of a relationship, beyond sexual infidelity, may be highly relevant and appropriate for jury consideration as part of all the circumstances appurtenant to a qualifying trigger of partially inculcated justifiable anger.[21] As such, it may be troublesome to disentangle the nature and import

---

14 Reilly (n. 12) 329

15 Jeremy Horder, 'Reshaping the Subjective Element in the Provocation Defence' (2005) 25 Oxford Journal of Legal Studies 123.

16 Ibid., 138–9.

17 For an excellent discussion of key reforms pertaining to sexual infidelity see Rudi Fortson QC, 'Homicide Reforms Under the CAJA 2009' (Criminal Bar Association of England and Wales Seminar, October 2010). <http://www.rudifortson4law.co.uk/legaltexts/Homicide%20Offences_CBA_handout_for_16thOct2010_R_Fortson_submitted_v.7.pdf> (accessed 27 March 2011).

18 See generally, Amanda Clough, 'Loss of Self-Control as a Defence: The Key to Replacing Provocation' (2010) 74 Journal of Criminal Law 118.

19 Miles (n. 2).

20 Ibid.

21 During Parliamentary debates, Lord Thomas of Gresford noted the problems with this approach: A 'woman who suffers neglect or violence at the hands of her husband over a period of years but who finally

of excessive taunts relating to cheating, inadequacy and disaffection. This resonates with confusion engendered at the very nub of this inclusionary/exclusionary argument with sexual jealousy or envy coalesced together and potentially transmogrified as the only embodiment of sexual infidelity *per se*. Shortly after the further liberalisation of the objectivised 'reasonable man' in *Morgan (Smith)*,[22] the Home Office noted its concern that the reinterpreted standard would make it easier for 'sexually jealous' defendants to claim provocation based on a spouse's 'sexual infidelity'.[23] Throughout the parliamentary debates these concerns were echoed[24] and it was suggested that the exclusion clause should preclude the defence to those who kill out of sexual jealousy/envy in response to sexual infidelity.[25] Sexual jealousy and sexual infidelity may constitute two very different conceptualisations in terms of emotion or act, and this led Horder to question which of the two the government really ought to exclude.[26] The search for a rationale to the heat of passion defence remains as confused as ever.

The American Experience: Reform and Traditional States

The English Law Commission in two detailed reports[27] prior to legislative reforms in the Coroners and Justice Act 2009, examined in detail the American jurisprudential landscape in the wider context of overall reforms to homicide with a new gradation of culpability template, and more specifically addressing partial defences to murder. At no point did a proposal materialise to unilaterally obfuscate sexual infidelity *per se* as a provoking circumstance. The debate more generally focused on the rationale for allowing loss of self-control to operate in partially exculpatory fashion.[28] In this regard the US experience provides an important source of comparative extirpation towards legitimate identification of the defence as grounded in either excusatory or justificatory concepts, or a combination of the two.[29] Although difficult to generalise about the US position, given divergence between reflective state practices, nonetheless a degree of bifurcation has emerged. This evaluation focuses on 'traditional' states which have followed a heat of passion defence reflective of an abridged and constrained English common law approach, which in many states

---

takes up the hammer or the meat knife when she sees him having sex with her best friend. That is the last trigger. She sees him being unfaithful, but she has had a terrible life up to that point ... must the jury ignore the proximate insult, the cause of her attack – namely, her seeing sexual infidelity in her husband – and simply consider provocation on the basis of the treatment of her over a period of years leading up to that point? How do you expect the jury to disentangle one set of circumstances from another?' HL Deb., 11 November 2009, 840.

22 *Smith (Morgan)* (n. 7).
23 Home Office, *Safety and Justice: The Government's Proposals on Domestic Violence* (Cmnd 5847, 2003) para. 64.
24 HL Deb. (n. 21) col. 835.
25 Ibid., col. 836.
26 Memorandum from Jeremy Horder to the House of Commons (Coroners and Justice Bill, Committee Stage, 3 February 2009, CJ 01).
27 Law Com. No 290, 2004 (n. 3); and Law Com. No 304, 2006 (n. 3).
28 See generally, Law Com. No 304 2006 (n. 3) paras 5.61–5.77; and Oliver Quick and Celia Wells, 'Getting Tough with Defences' [2006] Criminal Law Review 514, 524, who assert, 'Male killing is about power and control. Women killing abusers is about avoiding power and control ... women do not often kill from anger, while anger is what fuels many male killings.'
29 Law Com. No 290, 2004 (n. 3) para. 3.47–3.59, and App. F.

follows pre-1957 Homicide Act reform.[30] Alternatively, a number of 'reform' states, at least in part, have adopted a more liberalised 'subjectivised' perspective based upon Model Penal Code §210(3)(1)(b) which looks to a test of 'extreme mental and emotional disturbance', and precipitates far greater jury consideration.[31] This latter point, the divide between the role and province of the judge and jury as contemporary arbiters of sexual infidelity killings, is absolutely fundamental in different jurisdictions, and the comparative significance is important to detail.

Sexual infidelity killings may straddle the analytical divide in terms of conceptualisation of the partial defence as either justificatory or excuse in basis.[32] The 'justificatory' embodiment of a defence concentrates upon a recognition that the conduct was legitimate in the presented circumstances and that punishment should be mitigated since harm caused is outweighed by the need to avoid an even greater harm or to further a greater societal interest;[33] whereas an excuse, 'represents a legal conclusion that the conduct is wrong, undesirable, but that criminal liability is inappropriate because some characteristic of the actor vitiates society's desire to punish him'.[34] In the context of sexual infidelity, as stated, if the defence is articulated via the legal prism of partial justification, the primordial consideration is on the provoker's conduct, and whether it may be stigmatised as wrongful, untoward or egregious in the first place. The core of the justificatory defence is that a fatality ought to be standardised as 'morally less reprehensible' than murder where the victim abjures some responsibility for their impact on producing the provokee's rage and anger.[35] Intuitively the paradigm shift towards the provoker's conduct (the victim) seems inapposite, and obviously raises the hackles of their affronted and distressed family, in light of the genuflective role reversal. On the contrary if a sexual infidelity killing is viewed as partially excusatory in nature, then via this kaleidoscope the pre-eminent examination attaches to the provokee and whether the cuckolded or taunted defendant lacked personal culpability for some (at least partially) valid reason.[36]

---

30 See generally, Douglas Brown, 'Disentangling Concessions to Human Frailty: Making Sense of Anglo-American Provocation Doctrine through Comparative Study' (2007) 39 New York University Journal of International Law & Politics 675; and Paul Robinson, 'Abnormal Mental State Mitigations of Murder : The US Perspective', Chapter 17, *infra*.

31 See, generally, Kevin John Heller, 'Beyond the Reasonable Man? A Sympathetic but Critical Assessment of the Use of Subjective Standards of Reasonableness in Self-Defence and Provocation Cases' (1998) 26 American Journal of Criminal Law 1.

32 In terms of the dichotomy between justification and excuse note the succinct illustration provided by Kent Greenawalt, 'The Perplexing Borders of Justification and Excuse' (1984) 84 Columbia Law Review 1897–1927: 'If A's claim is that what he did was fully warranted – he shot B to stop B from killing other people – A offers a justification: if A acknowledges he acted wrongfully but claims he was not to blame – he was too disturbed mentally to be responsible for his behaviour – he offers an excuse.' See also Vera Bergelson, 'Victims and Perpetrators: An Argument for Comparative Liability in Criminal Law' (2005) 8 Buffalo Criminal Law Review 385, 414, who asserts, 'The fact that the law asks not only how badly the actor was distressed, but also *why* he was so badly distressed implies that the rationale for the defence lies in the *source* of provocation, not merely the actor's disturbed state of mind.'

33 Paul Robinson, *Criminal Law Defenses* (Thompson West, 1984) s. 24(a), 83. See also Paul Robinson, 'Criminal Law Defenses: A Systematic Analysis' (1982) 82 Columbia Law Review 199.

34 Ibid., s. 25(d). See, generally, Mitchell Berman, 'Justification and Excuse, Law and Morality' (2003) 53 Columbia Law Review 1–77.

35 Law Commission, *Partial Defences to Murder* (Law Com. No 137, 2003) paras 12.12–12.17.

36 Ibid., para. 12.15.

The partially valid reason (excuse) in heat of passion cases has been the focus of detailed and expert examination by a number of leading commentators in the US.[37] The killer, confronted by ocular or verbal taunts relating to a partner's infidelity, and subject thereby to excessive anger of an internalised nature, may be partially excused according to Dressler's analysis since, 'anger affects choice-capabilities, not mere opportunities'.[38] Anger may be an inculcated emotion which is embodied as 'a normal and expected human response to the situation',[39] and thereby the accused, is consequentially, 'less able to respond in a legally and morally appropriate fashion'.[40] Arguments, however, range across the divide as Nourse,[41] in an expert critique of intimacy killings within Model Penal Code (hereinafter MPC) states, has reflected in her conclusions that a fresh appraisal *de novo* is required whereby the defence should be severely constrained to individual cases in which the provoking act is itself a 'wrong' that the law would punish irrefragably by imprisonment.[42] The defence, although partially justificatory in ascription, viewed through the impact of the provoker's illegal conduct, would be severely curtailed in nature and delimited by the 'wrongfulness' of the provoker's conduct leading to potential incarceration.[43]

A number of US academicians,[44] although promoting a justificatory perspective leading to a deduction of liability in certain cases, have suggested a categorisation between 'act justification' and 'emotion justification'.[45] The sight of a partner committing adultery or other breaches of intimacy such as dancing provocatively with another, although potentially 'emotion-justified' could never in this perspective ever be 'act-justified'.[46] No deduction of concessionary/mitigatory liability would occur.[47]

In this brief articulation of potential heat of passion rationale(s), a subject upon which much ink has been spilt, there is an exposition of the difficulties presented in achieving a conceptual edifice for this controversial defence. This struggle is evident in the Law Commission's minute examination of the issue,[48] and consideration of disparate approaches. The result contained in the Coroners and Justice Act 2009 is a significant momentum shift, outwith the exclusion of sexual infidelity more generally, and reflects a movement away from 'compassionate excuse' as a juridical

---

37 See, for example, Joshua Dressler, 'Why Keep the Provocation Defense? Some Reflections on a Difficult Subject' (2002) 86 Minnesota Law Review 959; Emily Miller, '(Wo)manslaughter: Voluntary Manslaughter, Gender and the Model Penal Code' (2001) 50 Emory Law Journal 665; and Joshua Dressler, 'When "Heterosexual" Men Kill "Homosexual" Men: Reflections on Provocation Law, Sexual Advances and the "Reasonable Man" Standard' (1995) 85 Journal of Criminal Law & Criminology 726.
38 Joshua Dressler, 'Rethinking Heat of Passion: A Defense in Search of a Rationale' (1982) 73 Journal of Criminal Law & Criminology 421, 464.
39 Ibid.
40 Ibid.
41 Victoria Nourse, 'Passion's Progress: Modern Law Reform and the Provocation Defense' (1997) 106 Yale Law Journal 1331.
42 Ibid., 1396.
43 Ibid.
44 Susan Rozelle, 'Controlling Passion: Adultery and the Provocation Defense' (2005) 37 Rutgers Law Journal 197. See also Miller (n. 37) 29, and Robert Mison, 'Homophobia in Manslaughter: The Homosexual Advance as Insufficient Provocation' (1992) 80 California Law Review 133.
45 Rozelle, ibid., 228.
46 Ibid.
47 Ibid., 233.
48 Law Com. No 137, 2003 (n. 35) at para. 12.12–12.17; Law Com. No 290, 2004 (n. 3); and Law Com. No 304 (n. 3).

touchstone towards 'imperfect justification' as a qualifying trigger.[49] This partial justification reflects normative beliefs in fear and anger as partially appropriate responses to causally related behaviour of the provoker. If the government had not intervened at the last minute to exclude sexual infidelity as a circumstance then sight of adultery or taunts of infidelity would have been relevant to the qualifying trigger of partially justified inculcated anger. Justification would have provided partial exculpation, or might potentially have exculpatory effect in consideration by the jury of all the circumstances:

> we think that the moral blameworthiness of homicide may be significantly lessened where the defendant acts in response to gross provocation in the sense of words or conduct (or a combination) giving the defendant a justified sense of being severely wronged. We do not think that the same moral extenuation exists if the defendant's response was considered, unless it was brought about by a continuing state of fear. (There are also strong policy reasons for the law not to treat vendettas as partial excuses.) We do not suggest that these are the only circumstances which could significantly extenuate moral responsibility for homicide, but we do think that they fall into a distinct category.[50]

As previously stated, beyond the theoretical extrapolations of a rationale for the heat of passion defence, a significant divergence in approach applies at a practical level in the US.[51] This bifurcatory divide is between the traditional common law states whose principles reflect an austere orthodoxy reflective of pre-1957 English antediluvian tradition,[52] and by way of comparison, the number of states who have adopted a more 'subjectivist' MPC approach.[53] The different treatment of sexual infidelity and killings attendant to intimacy breakdown is significant and relevant. In the former case, despite varying nuances, the general proposition in the preponderance of jurisdictions has been that a provocation defence will be applicable (including for cases of sexual infidelity killings) which 'involves the intentional killing of another while under the influence of a reasonably-induced ["heat of passion"] causing a temporary loss of normal self-control'.[54] Similar to pre-existing English common law, US jurisprudential authorities have generally applied the defence only if the provocation, 'would render any ordinarily prudent person for the time being incapable of that cool reflection that otherwise makes it murder'.[55] Many state jurisdictions have

---

49 Alan Norrie, 'The Coroners and Justice Act 2009 – Partial Defences to Murder: (1) Loss of Control' [2010] Criminal Law Review 275, 284.

50 Law Com. No 290, 2004 (n. 3) para. 3.63, asserting the key rationale for the defence. Note also para. 3.38 considering excessive anger: 'anger can be an ethically appropriate emotion and that in some circumstances it may be a sign of moral weakness or human coldness not to feel strong anger. That does not legitimise a violent response, one of the functions of the legal system is to channel legitimate anger at wrongdoing in ways that are considered just and proportionate. Nevertheless, a killing in anger produced by serious wrongdoing is ethically less wicked, and therefore deserving of a lesser punishment, than, say a killing out of greed, lust, jealousy or for political reasons.'

51 Paul Robinson, 'Abnormal Mental State Mitigations of Murder: The US Perspective', Chapter 17, *infra*.

52 Dressler, 'Rethinking Heat of Passion: A Defense in Search of a Rationale' (n. 38) 429–31.

53 Dressler, 'Why Keep the Provocation Defense? Some Reflections on a Difficult Subject' (n. 37) 984–8.

54 Wayne LaFave, *Criminal Law* (4th edn, West, 2003) 776.

55 *Addington* v. *United States*, 165 US 184, 186 (1897). See also *Fields* v. *State*, 52 Ala 348, 354 (1975) (stating that in order to constitute a defence, the provocation must 'in the mind of a just and reasonable man stir resentment to violence endangering life …'), *People* v. *Webb*, 300 P 2d 130, 139 (Cal Dist Ct App 1956) (finding provocation as would 'naturally tend to arouse the passion of an ordinarily reasonable man').

adopted rigid deontological reasoning to the traditional heat of passion defence, notably in denying words of infidelity alone to be supererogatory, and through a straitened role for judge and jury.[56] A vignette of this constriction, indicative of many state practices, was reflected by the decision of the Supreme Court of Ohio in *State* v. *Shane*.[57]

In *Shane*, the defendant shared an apartment in Philadelphia with his fiancée and their infant son.[58] After she verbally confessed to sleeping with other men and stated that she no longer cared for the defendant, he lost control and strangled her to death.[59] Two important matters arose for consideration by the Supreme Court of Ohio: (i) the issue of the exact province of judge and jury over the ambit of a provocation plea;[60] and (ii) the issue whether 'mere words' of a victim were reasonably sufficient provocation to incite the use of deadly force.[61] Could verbal admission of infidelity and breach of intimacy constitute adequate provocation?

In terms of the former issue the court determined that even when some evidence of adequate provocation is presented, the trial judge should only grant a voluntary manslaughter instruction if the jury could reasonably find the defendant guilty of the lesser offence.[62] In essence, the trial judge in traditional common law states is granted discretion, and operational control of the exculpatory defence is within their purview, to decide whether to give a voluntary manslaughter instruction by applying an objectified standard to determine whether a reasonable person would be provoked to act out of passion rather than reason.[63] A circumscribed role for jury consideration of the loss of self-control defence has been mandated in the Coroners and Justice Act 2009 reforms (see below), replacing the liberalised test of jury adoption in s. 3(1) of the Homicide Act 1957:

> The Homicide Act, in allowing insults as provocation, inevitably alters the position, because an insult uttered in private is neither a crime nor even a tort. S3 contains no restriction to unlawful acts, and the courts seem to be ready to allow any provocative conduct to be taken into consideration, even though that conduct was itself provoked by the defendant. Consequently, there is no longer any reason why the defence should not be available (if the jury uphold it) to the jilted lover who kills the object of his affections or her new lover, or the man who kills his irritating neighbour, or the parent who kills a constantly crying baby.[64]

Could the verbal confessions of infidelity by the provoker (victim) in *Shane* constitute sufficient provocation to incite the use of deadly force, and consequently partially justify the provokee's fatal response? The court categorically rejected this proposition, and mechanistically drew a bright-line

---

56 Brown (n. 30); and Heller (n. 31).

57 590 NE 2d 272 (Ohio 1992); and Mark Biggerman, '*State* v. *Shane*: Confessions of Infidelity as Reasonable Provocation for Voluntary Manslaughter' (1993) 19 Ohio Northern University Law Review 977.

58 *Shane*, ibid., 273.

59 Ibid.

60 Ibid., 276.

61 Ibid., 277.

62 Ibid., 275.

63 Ibid., 278. Note that 'in each case the trial judge must determine whether evidence of reasonable sufficient provocation occasioned by the victim has been presented to warrant a voluntary manslaughter instruction', ibid., 276 (fn. 2). 'The judge furnishes the standard of what constitutes adequate provocation ... which would cause a reasonable person to act out of passion rather than reason', quoting *People* v. *Pouncey*, 471 NW 2d 346, 350 (Mich, 1991).

64 Glanville Williams, *Textbook of Criminal Law* (2nd edn, 1983) 534–5.

test for general adoption.[65] The majority of jurisdictions in the US have subsequently determined that mere words, no matter how inflammatory, are not sufficient provocation to allow the reduction of murder to voluntary manslaughter,[66] albeit some courts have permitted inclusion in a marital rather than unmarried relationship.[67] The synergistic effect of the twin issues reconciled in *Shane* has been to delimit the provocation plea in Ohio, and other traditional common law states. The trial judge remains empress as the gatekeeper for consideration of the defence at all, and verbal confessions of adultery are generally denied recognition.

A wholly different comparative outlook applies in the minority of states in the US that have passed legislation similar to the American Law Institute's Model Penal Code.[68] The result has been an extraordinary liberalisation of the provocation defence, in marked contrast to the austerity and rigidity of the traditional common law circumscription.[69] As such, the MPC template provides an illuminating counterpoise for evaluation as a contrast to the restrictive Coroners and Justice Act 2009 provisions, especially the bulwark presented to fact-finder engagement with ocular and verbal attachments to infidelity.[70] Under §210.3(1)(b) of the MPC, any intentional killing will be viewed as manslaughter when, 'committed under the influence of extreme mental or emotional disturbance for which there is no reasonable explanation or excuse'. Further, the MPC allows a heightened subjectivist appraisal of personified characteristics because it requires a jury to examine the reasonableness of the actor's conduct 'from the viewpoint of a person in the actor's situation under the circumstances as he believed them to be'.[71]

The consequential effect in MPC states has been to obviate the common law traditional requirement pertaining to 'adequate provocation'; draw a coach and horses through the bright-line

---

65 *Shane* (n. 57) 278.

66 See, for example, *Hambrick v. State*, 353 SE 2d 177, 179 (Ga 1987) ('provocation by words alone is inadequate to reduce murder to manslaughter'), *Perigo v. State*, 541 NE 2d 936, 939 (Ind 1989) (holding that victim's words alone, though highly emotional, were not sufficient provocation to reduce murder to manslaughter), *People v. Eagen*, 357 NW 2d 710, 711–12 (Mich Ct App 1984) (noting that defendant's claim of provocation based on former girlfriend's remark about sex was without merit).

67 See for example, *People v. Williams*, 576 NE 2d 68, 73 (Ill App Ct 1991) ('an admission of adultery is equivalent to a discovery of the act itself'), *Commonwealth v. Schnopps*, 417 NE 2d 1213, 1215–16 (Mass 1981) (holding that sufficient provocation may be found in information conveyed to a defendant by word alone when there is a marital relationship). Note Dressler's criticism, 'Rethinking Heat of Passion: A Defense in Search of a Rationale' (n. 38) 440, of this limitation to marriage in the cases where one unmarried lover discovers another being unfaithful: 'an unmarried individual who kills upon sight of unfaithfulness by one's lover or fiancée is [considered] a murderer. Only a highly unrealistic belief about passion can explain this rule in terms of excusing conduct. It is implausible to believe that when an actor observes his or her loved one in an act of sexual disloyalty, that actor will suffer from less anger simply because the disloyal partner is not the actor's spouse. Instead, this rule is really a judgment by courts that adultery is a form of injustice perpetrated upon the killer which merits a violent response, whereas "mere" sexual unfaithfulness out of wedlock does not. Thus, it has been said that adultery is the "highest invasion of [a husband's] property" whereas in the unmarried situation the defendant "has no such control" over his faithless lover.'

68 As Robinson comments in Chapter 17, *infra*, nn. 56–7, although 34 states adopted modern comprehensive codes promulgated around the MPC, only 11 of the 34 states actually embraced the MPC's 'extreme emotional disturbance formulation': Arkansas, Connecticut, Delaware, New York, Hawaii, Kentucky, Maine, Montana, North Dakota, Oregon and Utah. Further, only five states within the 11 adopted the proposal without 'significant' alterations or modifications.

69 Law Com. No 290, 2004 (n. 3) App. F, 271–2.

70 Ibid.

71 Model Penal Code, §210.3(1)(b) (hereinafter MPC).

mechanistic provision denying that words alone can never provide an exculpatory mitigation; and significantly enhances jury appraisal of provoking circumstances and individual characteristics of an accused tangentially invoking reduced powers of self-control (provocability).[72] Arguably, an evaluative free-for-all has been engendered, lacking reflection of contemporary attitudinal standardisation of fidelity/infidelity and expected powers of individual ratiocination or control. In many respects the impact has been to emasculate the role of the trial judge, and simply letting fact-finders decide in this regard reflects unfortunate judicial abstentionism, 'The very act of sending a case to a jury requires some kind of normative judgment, some choice about those cases in which a rational jury could find a "reasonable" explanation for rage.'[73] The impact of this liberalisation has, on occasions, proved extraordinary with *Dixon v. State*[74] a notorious cause célèbre illustration of the unfortunate consequences of unrestrained mitigatory principles devoid of effective distillation by the trial judge.

The defendant in *Dixon* violently beat his fiancée to death, the attacks occurring over an extended period, after the victim had the 'temerity' to dance with another man at her engagement party.[75] The consecutive assaults transpired directly at the party itself, at her sister's home when the defendant followed her, and the fatal violence took place in the early hours of the morning at their own home. In accordance with MPC §210(3) it was determined that a reasonable jury in Arkansas could decide, and the trial judge empowered them accordingly, whether totally outwith acts or taunts of sexual infidelity, merely dancing with another man at her engagement party provided a 'reasonable' excuse for the excessive anger of that affronted defendant.[76] A manslaughter verdict followed amazingly, on that predicate. It seems the truism that hard cases make bad law applies in equal measure to rather more straightforward determinations! The result has been to liberalise the provocation defence in reform states,[77] as Nourse has expertly reviewed in an in-depth study, way beyond the parameters of any appropriate 'concessionary' defence. Examination has revealed that in these reform states the fact-finders, without normative iteration by the trial judge of the legitimate constraints of the defence, have been presented with situations for consideration far beyond heat of passion infidelity, and within the different strictures of simple relationship breakdown, termination of intimacy, departures from shared accommodation and any kind of 'disrespectful' flirting with another:

> Reform has permitted juries to return a manslaughter verdict in cases where the defendant claims passion because the victim left, moved the furniture out, planned a divorce, or sought a protective order. Even infidelity has been transformed under reform's gaze into something quite different from the sexual betrayal we might expect – it is the infidelity of a fiancée who danced with another, of a girlfriend who decided to date someone else, and of the divorcée found pursuing a new relationship months after the final decree. In the end, reform has transformed passion from the classical adultery to the modern dating and moving and leaving. And because of that transformation, these killings, at least in reform states, may no longer carry the law's name of murder.[78]

---

72 See, generally, Dressler, 'Why Keep the Provocation Defense? Some Reflections on a Difficult Subject' (n. 37) 984–8.
73 Nourse (n. 41) 1372.
74 *Dixon v. State*, 597 SW 2d 77 (Ark 1980).
75 Ibid., 78. See generally, Rozelle (n. 44).
76 Ibid.
77 Nourse (n. 41).
78 Ibid., 1332–3. See, further, Nourse's expository rationale for the defence: 'To merit the reduction of verdict typically associated with manslaughter, the defendant's claim to our compassion must put him in a

The polemics in the US reveal a significant divide between reform and traditional states in their treatment of sexual infidelity killings, and other state adoption ranges along this continuum. This chasm is currently manifested in Anglo-Scottish law[79] with fundamental differences in operability and applicability. As with US comparative appraisal, an extirpation of the rationale behind this bifurcation between the Scylla and the Charybdis on concessionary defences, may enervate discussion and provide support for a *via media* approach.

Scottish Law and Contemporary Standardisation of Sexual Infidelity Cases

A remarkable anachronism has occurred in Anglo-Scots law in this arena. South of the border things done or said constituting sexual infidelity are disenfranchised from fact-finder evaluation on loss of self-control. The polar opposite applies north of the border and the very same behaviour in this context forms one of only two bases for consideration by fact-finders. In one jurisdiction sexual infidelity represents the very essence of mitigatory behaviour and of primordial importance, yet for a few miles of geographic separation it is pre-eminently excluded. A provoked defendant in Edinburgh who kills through ocular and verbal taunts of a partner's infidelity may, in certain circumstances, rely on the partial defence to reduce murder to manslaughter (culpable homicide).[80] On the very same facts in Berwick that defendant is precluded from jury consideration of the defence as sexual infidelity leading to excessive anger no longer forms a qualifying trigger within the Coroners and Justice Act 2009. The different jurisdictions have figuratively taken the high and low road in respect of the separate pathways to liability in their doctrinal perspectives. It mirrors the recent demarcation that has occurred between the House of Lords[81] and the High Court of Justiciary[82] in the substantive context of homicide liability of a drug supplier where a victim has ingested the drug themselves with full capacity. Radically different views now prevail in terms of issues related to causation, foreseeability and voluntariness in drug administration cases.[83]

The two qualifying conditions in terms of provoking behaviour in Scottish law, those of violence and the discovery of sexual infidelity, reflect the historical lineage of the provocation defence set out in this chapter. At the heart of the partial defence in Scotland lies excessive anger, poorly controlled, where the emotion is generated by unjustified actions by a provoker, and the accused's response may be partially vindicated as a concession to human frailty and weakness, and that it

---

position of normative equality *vis-à-vis* his victim. A strong measure of that equality can be found by asking whether the emotion reflects a wrong that the law would independently punish ... My proposal would also bar the defense in cases in which the defendant claimed rage inspired by infidelity. Society is no longer willing to punish adultery.'

79 For an excellent topical discussion of extant Scottish law, see McDiarmid (n. 10).

80 See, generally, *Drury* v. *HM Advocate* 2001 SLR 1013; *HM Advocate* v. *Hill* 1941 JC 59; and *Low and Reilley* v. *HM Advocate* 1994 SLT 277.

81 *Kennedy (No 2)* [2007] UKHL 38, [2007] 4 All ER 1083, 1090, where Lord Bingham determined that the victim's independent act operates as a bulwark against liability for unlawful act manslaughter in this scenario. See, generally, Alan Reed and Ben Fitzpatrick, *Criminal Law* (4th edn, Sweet & Maxwell, 2009) 49.

82 *Michael Kane* v. *HM Advocate*, *The Times*, 2009 SLT 137. The High Court of Justiciary, focusing upon issues of immediacy and directness of the ingestion allied to foreseeability of action (V's conduct) determined that Scots law in appropriate cases might attribute liability for ingestion and so for death to the reckless offender (culpable homicide). Reliance was placed on extant law in certain states in the US and in South Africa.

83 Reed and Fitzpatrick (n. 81) 46–50.

may be appropriate.[84] The embodiment, in policy terms, of this linkage between provoking conduct (sexual infidelity) and fatal violence is that, 'law recognises that when an accused discovers that his or her partner, who owes a *duty of sexual fidelity*, has been unfaithful, the accused may be swept with sudden and overwhelming *indignation* which may lead to a violent reaction resulting in death'.[85] The continued pre-eminence attached to a 'duty of fidelity' and righteous 'indignation' gives cause for disquiet, and we shall return to contemporary standardisation of the social mores attached to fidelity/infidelity subsequently. It is also provided in Scottish law that verbal taunts of infidelity may constitute provocative behaviour, the over-reaction to the infidelity must equate to that of an ordinary man and woman who has not been personified with individual characterisation, and aligned with this the loss of self-control must be immediate.[86] Experience reveals, unsurprisingly, that the defence has been male-dominated in application,[87] and indeed it was not until 1996 that it was acknowledged in Scotland that women could rely on this 'exceptionally' provocative nature as a defence;[88] a defence stigmatised in Anglo-Scottish antediluvian heritage as 'bound to encourage and exaggerate a view of human behaviour which [was] sexist, homophobic and racist'.[89]

The exceptionally provocative nature of sexual infidelity, consequently providing a partial defence, has arisen in Scotland across a widened ambit of behaviour patterns, as in reform states in the US, beyond catching your married partner in bed with a new paramour and responding instantaneously with violence. It applied in *HM Advocate* v. *Hill*,[90] where a returning army corporal killed his wife and new partner in the marital home with a service revolver. A demarcation applied from traditional heat of passion in that the accused had been informed previously about his wife's affair, and the killing had nuances of premeditation, planning and revenge. More recently, it applied in *Drury* v. *HM Advocate*,[91] in the context of an unmarried couple whose relationship may have ended, but they continued a sexual relationship. The accused was affronted by the non-exclusivity of this intimacy and in 'indignation' killed the victim with a claw hammer. Prior conduct engaged stalking the victim, and the defendant had five convictions for breach of the peace attendant to this behaviour. As previously stated, Lord Justice-General Rodger highlighted that the ambit of the sexual infidelity concessionary defence focused around sudden 'indignation' and controversially the emotional turbulence created by the casting aside of a 'duty of sexual fidelity'.[92]

In terms of contemporary standardisation of behaviour and values it seems completely anathema to current social mores of attitudinal behaviour to propagate any 'duty of sexual fidelity'. Views on fidelity or otherwise may differ widely at a societal level, and within the confines of marital/unmarried individual relationships. Whilst to some breach of relationship trust in an exclusive and intimate relationship, a relationship at the epicentre of their life, may prompt excessive anger and a violent emotional outburst, to others in a partnership it may be a matter of complete indifference.[93]

---

84 McDiarmid (n. 10) 201–3.
85 *Drury* v. *HM Advocate* 2001 SLT 1013 [75] (Lord Justice-General Rodger) (emphasis added).
86 Ibid., [25]–[32].
87 See generally, Edwards, 'Anger and Fear as Justifiable Preludes for Loss of Self-Control' (n. 6).
88 McDiarmid (n. 10) 207, who also asserts, 'The defence is now available to anyone in a situation in which sexual fidelity is expected including cohabitees, and those in same-sex relationships, and even following *Drury* v. *HM Advocate*, on/off relationships where the parties occasionally sleep together.'
89 Celia Wells, 'Provocation: The Case for Abolition', in Andrew Ashworth and Barry Mitchell (eds), *Rethinking English Homicide Law* (Oxford University Press, 2000) 85.
90 *Hill* (n. 80).
91 Above (n. 85).
92 Ibid., [25].
93 McDiarmid (n. 10) 208.

It is not that excessive taunting about another's infidelity, or witnessing the behaviour at first hand, is not exceptionally provocative (or may be to some), but rather whether it should be given the pre-eminent qualifying threshold attached in Scotland.[94] At the same time the exclusion of such provoking behaviour in English law – like many last minute government reforms[95] without proper reflection, consideration and thorough debate – seems counter-intuitive in some cases of excessive taunting prompting extreme 'uncontrolled' reactions through partially justified inculcated anger. A *via media* can beneficially be promulgated in both jurisdictions allowing a proper role for judge and jury. The following five illustrations are highlighted to demonstrate that different gradations may apply within 'things done or said that constitute sexual infidelity', and consequentially that on occasions a more nuanced approach than currently applies in Anglo-Scottish law needs to be deconstructed and adopted:

- A man was told by his wife that as soon as their children had left home she would leave him and live with another man whom she'd known for many years. He brooded on this for four weeks and then killed her by poisoning her tea. He said he couldn't bear the thought of her being with another man, and psychiatrists reported that he suffered from an extreme form of jealousy ('The Brooding Jealous Husband').[96]
- A man, whose wife had had a series of affairs with other men, decided to kill her if she had another affair. Soon afterwards, he discovered she was having a further affair and he strangled her to death. Psychiatrists reported that he was not mentally ill ('The Cuckolded Husband'). Suppose instead that when he discovered that she was having an affair he confronted her and she taunted him about his sexual inadequacy – whereupon he lost his temper and killed her ('The Taunted Husband').[97]
- D's marriage is broken up when his wife is seduced by a wealthy adventurer, V. D is distraught. One day D hears V boasting in a pub of his sexual victories, including with Mrs D. D gets up to leave. V notices him and taunts him. D sees red, picks up a bottle and brings it down on V's head, causing a fractured skull from which V dies. ('Taunting by New Paramour').[98]
- D is devastated when her husband, V, with whom she has been involved in a committed and devoted relationship for ten years, has embarked on an affair with her best friend (P). V, in order to humiliate D, has posted many intimate pictures of P and himself together on Facebook and other social networking sites with explicit references to D's sexual inadequacies. These pictures have also been disseminated to all of D's family and friends, and to all her work colleagues. Humiliated, she has felt compelled to leave her beloved job. She returns to the marital home to find all her possessions left in bin bags in the street. V

---

94   Ibid., 209.

95   University tuition fees may provide a moot point in this regard, allied with fluctuations regarding the 10p starting rate of income tax!

96   See Law Com. No 290, 2004 (n. 3) App. C, 'A Brief Empirical Study of Public Opinion Relating to Partial Defences to Murder presented by Mitchell'. A sample of 62 respondents were presented with a variety of homicide scenarios, with objectives to determine whether each particularised scenario was regarded as one of the more or less serious homicides, and to identify factors which influenced this assessment. Note scenario (i) in the text is repeated verbatim from Mitchell's scenario H ('The Brooding Jealous Husband').

97   Ibid., scenarios J1 and J2 presented by Mitchell.

98   This illustration was presented by the Law Commission who asserted that they did *not* believe that the general public would consider a sentence of life imprisonment to be appropriate; see Law Com. No 137, 2003 (n. 35) para. 12.25.

and P are present at the time with P in night apparel. V mocks her again over her sexual inadequacies, his new relationship and the intimate photographs. D picks up some broken glass off the pavement from a shattered wedding picture, and stabs V in the throat killing him instantly ('Excessive Taunting and Sexual Humiliation').
- D loses self-control and kills V when V (D's husband) admits having had long-standing affairs with (and made pregnant) each of D's three 16–18-year-old daughters by a previous marriage ('Extreme Breach of Trust').[99]

The first two illustrations above formed part of a survey of public opinion relating to partial defences to murder expertly conducted by Mitchell[100] as part of the Law Commission project. The responses in situation (i) and to the first part of (ii) revealed little sympathy for the defendant in light of premeditation, no adequate response, and suspicions centred around extreme jealousy.[101] A different picture was apparent where the accused responded to an immediate taunt of infidelity, with a proportion of respondents identifying this spontaneity as a rationale for a mitigatory sentence of less than ten years' imprisonment. Importantly, there was no significant difference between the replies of male and female respondents.[102] In terms of community standardisation and contemporary social rectitude it is interesting that scenario (iii) above was presented by the Law Commission in their consultation paper as a key example of a case where the 'general public' would not consider a sentence of life imprisonment to be appropriate.[103]

The postulation in (iv) is presented *de novo* to suggest that a *via media* needs to be adopted in Anglo-Scottish law. In general terms verbal taunts of infidelity will rarely be sufficient to allow a concessionary defence, but circumstances of 'a most extreme and exceptional character' may, on occasions, apply.[104]

Beyond excessive taunting, example (v), presented to the Commons by Horder during the committee stages of the Coroners and Justice Bill, is representative of sexual infidelity as provocative conduct in its most extreme form. The scenario expertly highlights that a loss of control in response to the actions of a faithless lover, in some cases, has much more to do with the breach of trust involved, and serious relationship violation, rather than proprietorial instinct.[105] Sexual infidelity should 'never be an excuse or justification for murder, but that is quite a different

---

99   Note that scenario (v) is repeated verbatim from Horder's memorandum submitted to the Commons at the committee stage of the Coroners and Justice Act 2009 (House of Commons, Coroners and Justice Bill Committee, Memorandum submitted by Jeremy Horder, 3 February 2009, CJ 01). Horder notes that the scenario gives rise to multifarious difficulties: 'May the jury take into account the girls' pregnancies that are the result of the infidelity, in that these mean offspring born are related to D? Further, suppose V started an affair with one of the daughters before meeting/marrying D. Would D be able to rely on evidence of that affair, given that there was no obligation of fidelity to D at that stage? How far into the question whether the affair started before V met D should the court be prepared to go?'
100   Law Com. No 204, 2004 (n. 3) App. C.
101   In scenario H, interestingly, only 20 per cent of respondents viewed sentences of between five and ten years as appropriate, 24 per cent looked to 10–20 years, 20 per cent supported 20 years' imprisonment or more, 20 per cent life imprisonment with release on licence, and 16 per cent 'natural life' imprisonment.
102   Significantly, 52 per cent of respondents supported a sentence of between five and ten years in this regard.
103   Above (n. 98).
104   See Law Com. No 290, 2004 (n. 3) para. 3.144; and *Holmes* v. *DPP* [1946] AC 588, 600.
105   HL Deb. (n. 1) 1060 (Lord Thomas of Gresford).

thing from saying ... that the impact of another's sexual infidelity on a person's thoughts, actions and emotions should be disregarded entirely'.[106]

These five examples serve to illustrate that the provocative nature of sexual infidelity may operate on a continuum of severity. There needs to be a more compartmentalised and prioritised approach to this sensitive area than simply a blanket inclusion or exclusion of things said or done which constitute sexual infidelity. As iterated previously, history demonstrates and modern justice demands, any review of loss of self-control as a partial defence necessarily involves the study of how levels of culpability can and should be judged according to contemporary social standards. Different gradations of culpability may be demarcated that reflect more directly attitudinal behaviours to loss of self-control and societal concerns *vis-à-vis* appropriate levels of mitigation. Killings prompted by male proprietorialness, 'sexual jealousy', 'envy', and premeditation by a cuckolded partner ought to be excluded from the ambit of this concessionary defence, but in equal measure cases of 'gross provocation' regarding sexual infidelity embracing excessive taunting, sexual humiliation, and a spontaneous fatal blow ought in appropriate cases to be allowed for consideration by fact-finders.[107] This will also mandate an inclusionary consideration of 'extreme' breaches of trust as identified by Horder in postulation (v). The tension between these parameters can be satisfied through invocation of the power of the trial judge to withdraw the matter of loss of self-control in sexual infidelity killings when there is no predicate on which a reasonable jury properly directed could conclude that it might apply. This is considered below in terms of pre- and post-Coroners and Justice Act 2009 reforms. Anglo-Scots law ought to operate a preliminary filter mechanism to cases engaging sexual infidelity where only circumstances of an extreme and exceptional character fall for jury consideration, and where a defendant can be partially exculpated in rare situations of excessive uncontrollable anger through 'gross' provocation:

> It is a sad commonplace that when relationships break up there are often arguments and mutual recriminations. We think that it would be seldom that words spoken in such a situation could legitimately make the other party feel severely wronged, to the extent that a person of ordinary tolerance and self-restraint in such a situation might have used lethal violence; but there may be cases where one party torments another with remarks of an exceptionally abusive kind ... there are bound to be borderline cases.[108]

The *Via Media*: Province of Judge and Jury in Sexual Infidelity Killings

The disparate treatment of heat of passion adjudications in reform and traditional states in the US reveals the importance of the province of judge and jury as arbiters of the partial defence. In traditional states the defence has steadily been precluded from fact-finder evaluation in respect of verbal taunts. The Coroners and Justice Act 2009 reveals significant changes in terms of 'objectification' of the defence of provocation, whereby s. 56(2)(a) abolishes s. 3 of the Homicide Act 1957, and s. 56(6) mandates, in effect, that the partial defence will only be left to the jury if sufficient evidence is adduced to raise an issue with respect to the defence on which, in the opinion of the trial judge, a jury, properly directed, could reasonably conclude that the defence might apply.

---

106 HL Deb. (n. 1) 1060 (Lord Henley).
107 Above (n. 104).
108 Ibid.

This seismic shift in role of the trial judge arguably reflects an optimally balanced position for sexual infidelity killings, and ought to be determinative in Anglo-Scottish law.

Before the passing of s. 3 of the Homicide Act 1957 the trial judge was entitled to withdraw the issue of provocation from the jury on the ground that, even if the accused had himself been provoked, no reasonable man would have reacted in the way he did to the provocation. In the early eighteenth century the 'reasonable man' received little consideration, rather the courts adjudged the defendant's response according to the prevailing code of honour existing at the time.[109] Of the limited categories of provocative conduct that the trial judge would leave to the jury, there was 'no greater form of provocation'[110] than a wife's adultery, whether the defendant was made aware orally or by catching his faithless spouse in flagrante delicto.[111] The wife was regarded *sub virga viri sui*,[112] and any act of infidelity was the 'highest invasion of property'.[113] As an affront to a man's personal honour, failure to retaliate was deemed a 'social disgrace'.[114] If a man were to respond by a sudden and fatal blow to his wife or her paramour, he was believed to be acting out of 'pure will' rather than immoral resolve.[115] The courts considered that the 'injustice'[116] of the wife's infidelity invoked the defendant's anger ('for jealousy is the rage of a man'[117]) and his retaliation 'restored the balance of justice'.[118] Notwithstanding the prevailing preoccupation with female fidelity in the early eighteenth century, by the beginning of the nineteenth century trial judges were unprepared to leave provocation to the jury where a man killed following his unfaithful inamorata's admission of illicit intercourse.[119] It was more difficult for an unmarried man to claim that his beau's clandestine encounter constituted an invasion of property. Similarly, the courts refused to allow the defence to the jealous man who killed following his lover's flippant remark that she was going to leave him for another man.[120] As emphasis on the 'reasonable man'[121] requirement became more prominent, Viscount Simon, in *DPP* v. *Holmes*, identified a shift in normative expectations of the marital relationship in the context of sexual perfidy:

> we have left behind us the age when the wife's subjection to her husband was regarded by the law as the basis of the marital relation ... Parliament has now conferred on the aggrieved wife the same right to divorce her husband for unfaithfulness alone as he holds against her, and neither, on hearing

---

109 Jeremy Horder, *Provocation and Responsibility* (Clarendon Press, 1992) 27.

110 *Mawgridge* [1707] Kel J 119; 84 ER 1107, 1114–15 (Lord Holt CJ).

111 Ibid.; and see *Rothwell* (1871) 12 Cox CC 145; and *R* v. *Jones* (1908) 72 JP 215.

112 The government contended that specifically excluding sexual infidelity under the new loss of control defence 'would send a message to the country at large that women are not the property of men'; HL Deb. (n. 21) 840 (per Lord Thomas of Gresford).

113 *Mawgridge* (n. 110).

114 Law Com. No 290, 2004 (n. 3) App. G, para. 76.

115 Horder, *Provocation and Responsibility* (n. 109) 8.

116 Aristotle, *Nicomachean Ethics*, Book V, 8, in Ashworth, 'The Doctrine of Provocation' (1976) 35 Cambridge Law Journal 292.

117 *Mawgridge* (n. 110).

118 Marc Ancel, 'Le Crime Passionnel' (1957) 73 Law Quarterly Review 36, 37.

119 *Palmer* [1913] 2 KB 29; 82 LJ KB 531; 29 T L R 349; 8 Cr App R 207.

120 The trial judge in *R* v. *Alexander* (1913) 9 Cr App R 139, 141, declined to leave provocation to the jury where the defendant killed his girlfriend after she made a flippant remark about leaving him for another man.

121 *Welch* (1869) 11 Cox CC 336.

an admission of adultery from the other, can use physical violence against the other which results in death and then urge that the provocation received reduces the crime to mere manslaughter.[122]

Trial judges began to consider that a reasonable man only lost his self-control when he found his wife in the act of adultery and not when he had been told of it; that a reasonable man who was provoked by fists did not retaliate with a knife but only with fists; that reasonable men would not lose their self-control when taunted about a peculiar characteristic, for example impotence, since reasonable men did not possess that characteristic; and reasonable men would cool off after a certain period of time and regain their self-control.[123]

In so far as trial judges before 1957 were entitled to withdraw the issue altogether from the jury on the basis of an objectified standardisation, s. 3 of the Homicide Act removed that power, and reflected an important shift in momentum. Post-1957 the judge had to leave the issue to the jury if evidence prevailed that the accused (subjectively) was provoked to lose his self-control. In *Doughty*,[124] for instance, the Court of Appeal determined that where evidence persisted that the accused had been provoked by the crying of his 17-day-old child, the trial judge was consequentially under an obligation to leave the defence of provocation to the jury. The changes effected by s. 3 were of fundamental importance because this section: (1) established that words alone may constitute sufficient provocation if the jury decided that they would have provoked a reasonable man;[125] (2) treated the 'mode of resentment' or proportionality rule only as a factor, not a prerequisite, in judging whether a reasonable man would have acted as the actor did;[126] (3) took away the power of the judge to withdraw the defence from the jury on the grounds that there was no evidence on which the jury could find that a reasonable man would have been provoked to do as the defendant had done;[127] (4) authorised the defence to be used if a third person, not the victim, was the provoker;[128] and (5) removed the power of the judge to dictate to the jury what were the characteristics of the reasonable man.[129] The role of the jury was integral to determining the availability of the provocation defence, and judicial recognition of the primacy of the jury pre-2009 reforms was provided in *Rossiter*[130] by Russell LJ, who opined:

> The emphasis in that section is very much on the function of the jury as opposed to the judge. We take the law to be that wherever there is material which is capable of amounting to provocation, however tenuous it may be, the jury must be given the privilege of ruling on it.[131]

The pre-existing law, following *Rossiter* and *Stewart*,[132] established that even where defence counsel in a sexual infidelity case did not raise the issue of provocation, and even if they preferred

---

122   *Holmes* (n. 104) 600.
123   See, generally, Martin Wasik, 'Cumulative Provocation and Domestic Killing' [1982] Criminal Law Review 29.
124   (1986) 83 Cr App R 319.
125   See *Phillips* v. *The Queen* [1969] 2 AC 130.
126   See *Brown* [1972] 2 QB 229; and see, generally, Reed and Fitzpatrick (n. 81).
127   *Baillie* [1995] 2 Cr App R 31.
128   *Davies* [1975] QB 691.
129   Reed and Fitzpatrick (n. 81).
130   (1992) 95 Cr App R 326; and see, further, *Van Donegen and Van Donegen* [2005] EWCA Crim 1728.
131   Ibid., 333.
132   [1995] 4 All ER 999.

not to because it inconsistently juxtaposed with and detracted from the primary defence, the judge had to leave the issue to the jury to decide if *any* material existed which suggested that the accused may have been provoked. This *prima facie* obligation accrued unless no evidence emerged from whatever source, suggesting a reasonable possibility that the defendant *might* have lost his self-control due to words or deeds of another, or a combination of the two.[133] This was affirmed by the House of Lords in *Acott*, where a 48-year-old defendant, financially dependent upon his mother and treated like a child, was charged with her murder, but claimed her injuries were sustained as a result of a fall and his unskilled efforts to resuscitate her. A loss of self-control caused by fear, panic, sheer bad temper or circumstances (for example, a slow-down of traffic due to snow) was not enough. There had to be some evidence, albeit slight, tending to show that the killing might have been an uncontrolled reaction to provoking conduct rather than an act of revenge. A frenzied attack was more likely to point to a sudden and temporary loss of self-control, than would evidence of a solitary wound. Lord Steyn concluded in *Acott*[134] that what was required was a *specific provoking event*; it was insufficient that the issue of loss of self-control may have simply been raised by the prosecution in cross-examination of the defendant. An accused who reacted with excessive anger to ocular or verbal identification of a partner cheating upon them easily met the threshold standard in terms of provoking events; the trial judge consequently was emasculated from removing inappropriate cases from jury consideration and outcomes were determinative on empathetic or sympathetic fact-finders.

A new *via media* applies in the Coroners and Justice Act 2009 that ought to have rendered nugatory the late insertion of a sexual infidelity exclusion provision. The trial judge has become emperor or empress of the qualifying threshold for jury consideration of loss of self-control. This new approach, an objectification of old law, strikes the perfect balance in that the decision to withdraw the issue from the jury is one for the judgment of the trial judge following determination from counsel. Their role is not straitened and constricted, as in Scotland and reform states in the US, by unduly liberal perspectives to infidelity and breach of intimacy whether or not appropriate and legitimate. As stated by the Law Commission in argument: 'Our approach has been to seek to set out broad principles, to rely on the judge to exercise a judgment whether a reasonable jury could regard the case as falling within those principles and then to rely on the jury to exercise its good sense and fairness in applying them.'[135]

In many respects the position adopted in s. 54(6) of the Coroners and Justice Act 2009 regarding the province of judge and jury, and taunts of a sexual nature, might have restored our law to the position existing back in 1946 when *Holmes* v. *DPP*[136] was determined. It will be recalled that the accused killed his wife after a confession of her adultery by a blow to the head with a blunt instrument and through strangulation. Viscount Simon in the House of Lords clearly stated that, 'a confession of adultery without more is never sufficient to reduce an offence which would otherwise be murder to manslaughter';[137] and more pithily he added, 'Even if Iago's insinuations against Desdemona's virtue had been true, Othello's crime was murder and nothing else.'[138] To this a caveat would be extended as Viscount Simon added (*obiter*) that in circumstances of gross provocation,

---

133 Ibid., 1007.
134 [1997] 1 All ER 706.
135 Law Com. No 290, 2004 (n. 3) para. 3.150.
136 *Holmes* (n. 104); and note discussion of this issue in a different context in Horder, 'Reshaping the Subjective Element in the Provocation Defence' (n. 15) 132. See consideration above of the historical development of provocation as a defence vis-à-vis sexual infidelity killings.
137 *Holmes* (n. 104) 599.
138 Ibid., 598.

'of a most extreme and exceptional character' the duty would rest upon the trial judge to direct the jury accordingly as to whether the partial defence was applicable.[139] Excessive taunting or extreme breaches of trust, even in sexual infidelity cases, as in scenario (iv) and (v) postulated above, should fit within this limited ambit with significant responsibilities on a trial judge whose decision whether or not to withdraw loss of self-control ought to be required to be supported by reasons. Unfortunately, the Law Commission's further proposition,[140] that consideration be given to the creation of an interlocutory appeal against a judge's ruling that the defence should not be put to the jury in circumstances of partially justifiable anger, fell on deaf ears, and is not within the Coroners and Justice Act 2009. This interlocutory appeal system in cases of sexual infidelity killings could have facilitated an optimal *via media* in exceptional cases of ocular or verbal taunts of infidelity. It would allow a contemporary standardisation of circumstances, albeit limited, for normative evaluation by fact-finders in a compartmentalised and objectified delineation.

The rejection of things done and said constituting sexual infidelity within the purview of the Coroners and Justice Act 2009 may, in any event, simply have closed one door and one partial defence for the accused. It is questionable what the government were really seeking to achieve with this specific exclusion. The breadth of this exclusion is also up for debate in terms of disentanglement of 'infidelity' from other circumstances of taunts regarding inadequacy and disaffection.

By sleight of defence hand the new model template may presciently be to utilise evidence of grossly provoking conduct to support a denial of the *mens rea* element for murder.[141] This may be predicated on the argument that because of the 'victim's' outrageously provocative behaviour in terms of excessive taunting of infidelity this caused the accused to act in spontaneous anger, with the outcome that she lacked any intention to kill or cause grievous bodily harm at the commission point of the fatal action. The whole history of provoking conduct may be put in evidence to this issue of fault, and an effort to persuade sympathetic or empathetic fact-finders.[142] It is disappointing that, rather than the piecemeal iterations of the 2009 reforms, a thorough review and legislative reform of all aspects of homicide liability has not been engendered. This root and branch reform needs to finely tune levels of criminal responsibility on a hierarchical structure addressing differential culpability, and on occasions, appropriately exculpating or mitigating defendant's liability when acting in demarcated emotional states of mind with reduced control expectations.[143]

---

139 Ibid., 600.

140 Law Com. No 304, 2006 (n. 3) para. 5.16 asserting: 'This appeal should be permitted only before the trial (the basis of the defence should be considered at a pre-trial hearing under modern case management procedures) so that the trial itself is not substantially delayed by the use of the interlocutory procedure. The Higher Court Judges' Homicide Working Party could see no special problems arising from the provision of such an appeal.'

141 Ibid., paras 5.71–5.72.

142 Ibid. Note that the Law Commission stressed: 'we believe that it is important to highlight what will be the continuing evidence of all kinds of provocation to murder cases, whether or not the formal defence of provocation is itself more severely restricted than we are already suggesting that it should be'.

143 Note the strident criticism presented by Lord Thomas of Gresford in this regard: 'The Government have not followed its [the Law Commission's] recommendations for wholesale reform of the law relating to homicide into a three-tier system ... they have totally undermined the coherence of the Law Commission's proposals in a way that can only bring further chaos and difficulty in this field'; HL Deb. (n. 21) 837.

Chapter 9
Killing in Response to 'Circumstances of an Extremely Grave Character': Improving the Law on Homicide?

Jesse Elvin

Introduction

This chapter critically analyses the loss of control partial defence to murder in so far as it relates to killing in response to 'circumstances of an extremely grave character'. This loss of control defence replaces the common law provocation defence.[1] Like the previous provocation defence, it potentially reduces what would otherwise have been murder to manslaughter. It was created by the Coroners and Justice Act 2009, s. 54(1) of which stipulates:

> Where a person ("D") kills or is a party to the killing of another ("V"), D is not to be convicted of murder if –
>
> (a) D's acts and omissions in doing or being a party to the killing resulted from D's loss of self-control;
> (b) the loss of self-control had a qualifying trigger; and
> (c) a person of D's sex and age, with a normal degree of tolerance and self-restraint and in the circumstances of D, might have reacted in the same or in a similar way to D.

There are two types of 'qualifying trigger' under the 2009 Act. Section 55(3) states that the loss of self-control had a qualifying trigger if it was 'attributable to D's fear of serious violence from V against D or another identified person'. Section 55(4) provides that the loss of self-control had a qualifying trigger if 'D's loss of self-control was attributable to a thing or things done or said (or both) which – (a) constituted circumstances of an extremely grave character, and (b) caused D to have a justifiable sense of being seriously wronged'. Section 55(6) explicitly limits the scope of the loss of control defence, providing restrictions in relation to sexual infidelity and two other specific matters. This chapter critically explores four important issues raised by ss. 55(4) and 55(6). First, it considers precisely what factors the jury can and should take into account in applying s. 55(4). Secondly, it examines whether the thing or things said or done have to be directed against D. Thirdly, it considers to what extent, if at all, D should be judged on the facts as he or she believed them to be where he or she made a mistake about them. Fourthly, it considers the extent of the restriction regarding sexual infidelity and whether this restriction regarding sexual infidelity improves the law. It will consider relevant law from other common law jurisdictions, including Australia.

---

[1] Abolished by the Coroners and Justice Act 2009, s. 56.

The remainder of this chapter is divided into three sections. The first section provides a brief overview of the background to the 2009 reforms so that readers can understand these reforms in their context. The second section analyses the four important issues identified above, considering not just how the courts are likely to approach these issues but how they should do so. The final section presents the conclusions.

The Background to the 2009 Reforms

The 2009 reforms relating to loss of control derive from a 2004 Law Commission report on partial defences to murder,[2] produced at the request of the government. The Law Commission made a number of recommendations in 2004, one of which was that they be asked to conduct a wider review of the law on homicide.[3] Agreeing with this recommendation, the Ministry of Justice asked the Law Commission to undertake a comprehensive review of the law on homicide in 2005, requesting that it make proposals that take account of four specified matters, including the need for the law to be 'fair and non-discriminatory in accordance with the European Convention of Human Rights and the Human Rights Act 1998'.[4] The Commission produced many reform proposals in a 2006 report, some of which formed the basis for the reforms introduced in the Coroners and Justice Act 2009.[5] However, as we shall see, it is important to bear in mind that the Ministry of Justice made certain amendments to the Commission's proposals as they relate to the loss of control defence.

Critical Analysis

What Factors Should the Jury Take into Account in Applying Section 55(4)?

Paragraph 346 of the Explanatory Notes to the 2009 Act states: 'Whether a defendant's sense of being seriously wronged is justifiable will be an objective question for a jury to determine (assuming that there is sufficient evidence for the defence to be left to the jury)'. However, as Carol Withey says, this merely begs the question of what is meant by an 'objective' test.[6] This important issue is related to the correct interpretation of the test of whether a 'normal' person might have reacted in the same or a similar way to D. As Russell Heaton and Claire de Than explain:

> Where the qualifying trigger is circumstances of an extremely grave character that caused D to have a justifiable sense of being seriously wronged, D may argue that the extremely grave wrongdoing almost by definition proves that a person of D's age and sex, with a normal degree of tolerance and self-restraint, might have reacted in the same or in a similar way.[7]

This is not to say that D will automatically satisfy the test of whether a normal person might have reacted in the same or a similar way to D where circumstances of an extremely grave

---

2 Law Commission, *Partial Defences to Murder* (Law Com. No 290, 2004).
3 Ibid., para. 1.12.
4 Law Commission, *Murder, Manslaughter and Infanticide* (Law Com. No 304, 2006) para. 1.1.
5 See Ministry of Justice, *Murder, Manslaughter and Infanticide* (MoJ CP (R) 19, 2008) paras 1–7 for a fuller summary of the background to the 2009 reforms.
6 Carol Withey, 'Loss of Control', Criminal Law and Justice Weekly, 3 April 2010.
7 Russell Heaton and Claire de Than, *Criminal Law* (3rd edn, Oxford University Press, 2010) 186.

character caused D to have a justifiable sense of being seriously wronged. There will be certain cases where the court will not accept that D might have responded in the same or in a similar way to such circumstances; 'where, for example, D tortured V in the process of killing'.[8] However, the qualifying trigger test may be the main hurdle for D in many cases where D claims that the qualifying trigger was circumstances of an extremely grave character that caused a justifiable feeling of being seriously wronged.

In considering what factors the jury should take into account in determining whether D's loss of self-control was in fact caused by such a qualifying trigger, it is important to bear in mind Alan Norrie's analysis of the philosophy underpinning the 2009 reforms. Norrie has pointed out that the Law Commission's proposals, upon which the 2009 Act is based, were inspired by a philosophy of what he calls 'imperfect justification'.[9] The rule about circumstances of an extremely grave character that caused D to have a justifiable sense of being seriously wronged, inspired by Law Commission proposals and implemented in the 2009 Act, requires that D had a justifiable sense of anger. While the Law Commission recognised that anger cannot justify a killing, they concluded that 'a killing in anger produced by serious wrongdoing is ethically less wicked, and therefore deserving of a lesser punishment, than, say, killing out of greed, lust, jealousy or for political reasons'.[10] Norrie contrasts this approach with the philosophy that underlaid the old law on provocation, which he calls 'compassionate excuse'. As Norrie explains,[11] the law on provocation operated as a concession to human frailty. The law took the view that losing one's control was always wrong but sometimes understandable, and that killings in anger were therefore sometimes to be partially excused even where D did not have a justifiable sense of being seriously wronged. Norrie rightly states that the law on provocation condemned 'the act both for the wrong done and the loss of control, but still ... [extended] a compassionate hand to the actor'.[12] There has been a major shift in philosophy, which has significant implications for the outcome of cases. As Norrie explains, 'Under the new law, the idea of a justifiable sense of being seriously wronged directs the jury to consider what is morally or politically acceptable, and, further, the judge has the power to remove cases from the jury's consideration.'[13]

Where does this leave the law? The requirement under the new law that D had a justifiable sense of being seriously wronged clearly rules out a repetition of cases like *Doughty*,[14] where the Court of Appeal stated that a baby's crying could amount to provocation: 'crying would not amount to circumstances of an extremely grave character, and D could never have a justifiable sense of being seriously wronged by it'.[15] Equally clearly, some characteristics of D must be taken into account in applying s. 55(4). As the majority of the Australian High Court put it in considering the related issue of the correct operation of the provocation defence in *Masciantonio* v. *The Queen*:

---

8   Ibid.
9   Alan Norrie, 'The Coroners and Justice Act 2009: Partial Defences to Murder: (1) Loss of Control' [2010] Criminal Law Review 275, 277.
10 Law Com. No 290, 2004 (n. 2) para. 3.38.
11 Norrie (n. 9) 278–9.
12 Ibid., 279.
13 Ibid., 280.
14 (1986) 83 Cr App R 319.
15 Heaton and de Than (n. 7) 183. Diminished responsibility might still be available as a partial defence in such cases, but only where D was suffering from an abnormality of mental functioning which arose from a recognised medical condition and where the other conditions of this defence are satisfied (see the Homicide Act 1957, s. 3, as amended by the Coroners and Justice Act 2009, s. 52).

Conduct which might not be insulting or hurtful to one person might be extremely so to another because of that person's age, sex, race, ethnicity, physical features, personal attributes, personal relationships or past history. The provocation must be put into context and it is only by having regard to the attributes or characteristics of the accused that this can be done.[16]

However, this does not mean that all of D's characteristics should be taken into account in D's favour in applying s. 54(4), particularly since the new law is underpinned by the idea of a justifiable sense of being seriously wronged. The issue of which of D's characteristics, if any, to take into account in his or her favour has been explored numerous times in provocation case law and law reform proposals, not just in England and Wales but also in related jurisdictions such as Australia and Canada. McHugh J held in *Masciantonio* that the law must take account of D's age, race, culture and background:

Without incorporating those characteristics, the law of provocation is likely to result in discrimination and injustice. In a multicultural society ... the notion of an ordinary person is pure fiction ... Worse still, its invocation in cases heard by juries of predominantly Anglo-Saxon-Celtic origin almost certainly results in the accused being judged by the standard ... attributed to a middle class [person] of Anglo-Saxon-Celtic heritage, that being the stereotype of the ordinary person with which the jurors are most familiar.[17]

It is easy to sympathise with this point about potential injustice in a multicultural society. However, McHugh J's reasoning is ultimately unpersuasive because it goes too far: 'it is obviously problematic if D's culture is itself open to criticism on the grounds that it is discriminatory'.[18] John McInnes and Christine Boyle rightly point out:

The trick is to determine what constitutes "legitimate" divergences [in cultural, social or gendered perceptions of reasonableness] ... in a manner that protects society from harm, especially the vulnerable in society, without unfairly or unequally imposing the dominant construction of reasonableness on everybody else.[19]

The correct approach for English law is alluded to in a recent Canadian provocation case: *R* v. *Tran*.[20] In this case, D entered his estranged wife's locked apartment, without her permission and without being expected. He then killed his wife's boyfriend, V, having discovered V in bed naked with her. The Supreme Court of Canada held that 'the requisite elements of the defence, taken together, make clear that the accused must have a *justifiable* sense of being wronged',[21] and that

---

16 (1995) 183 CLR 58, 66–7.
17 Ibid., 73.
18 Heaton and de Than (n. 7) 185.
19 John McInnes and Christine Boyle, 'Judging Sexual Assault Law against a Standard of Equality' (1995) 29 University of British Columbia Law Review 341, 380. For analysis of this issue in the context of 'homosexual sexual advance' cases, see Anthony Gray, 'Provocation and the Homosexual Advance Defense in Australia and the United States: Law Out of Step with Community Values' (2010) 3 The Crit 53.
20 2010 SCC 58. To say this is not to claim that there are no significant differences between Canadian and English law in this context or that the operation of this area of Canadian law is flawless: for critical analysis of relevant Canadian law, see Rosemary Cairns, 'Culture, Religion and the Ordinary Person: An Essay on *R* v. *Humaid*' (2009–10) 41 Ottawa Law Review 1.
21 Ibid., para. 22.

there was no evidence on the facts to support D's claim to have had a justifiable sense of being wronged. An important aspect of this decision for the purposes of this chapter is that the court stated that 'the ordinary person standard must be informed by contemporary norms of behaviour, including fundamental values such as the commitment to equality provided for in the Canadian Charter of Rights and Freedoms'.[22] A similarly explicit reference to fundamental values such as equality and human rights is lacking in the relevant provisions of the Coroners and Justice Act 2009. However, as Norrie says, it is implicit in the new English law: thus, the Law Commission wrote that the jury should be able to conclude 'that the defendant's attitude in regarding the conduct as provocation demonstrated an outlook (e.g. religious or racial bigotry) offensive to the standards of a civilised society'.[23] English law does not have a Charter of Rights and Freedoms. Nonetheless, it does have a commitment to equality, most obviously in the form of the Equality Act 2010, which prohibits certain discrimination on the grounds of protected characteristics such as race, sex and religion. Furthermore, it has a commitment to human rights in the form of the Human Rights Act 1998, the enjoyment of which 'shall be secured without discrimination on any ground'.[24] This commitment to equality and human rights should inform the correct interpretation of s. 54(4) of the Coroners and Justice Act 2009, just as the commitment to equality provided for in the Canadian Charter of Rights and Freedoms at least in principle informs the application of the Canadian law on provocation. Thus, the law must not enable the taking of life to be met with lesser punishment in some situations compared to others without justification for any such difference.

One can illustrate how the 2009 provisions should work in practice by considering *R* v. *Mohammad (Faqir)*, a 2005 English case on the operation of the provocation defence.[25] D, a devout Muslim, stabbed his 24-year-old daughter to death when he discovered a young man, with whom she had been having a sexual relationship, in her bedroom. When questioned about this, he said that what his daughter and the young man had done 'was not permitted by his religion'.[26] D argued that his loss of control had been excusable in the circumstances, given the provocation to which he had been subjected. The Court of Appeal upheld his conviction for murder, stating that the provocation defence could not apply on the facts at hand. A court should reach an equivalent conclusion under the new provisions in order to fulfil its commitment to fundamental values such as equality and human rights. As the Court of Appeal put it in *Mohammad (Faqir)*, the essence of D's defence was twofold: first, he argued 'that, as a Muslim of devote belief, he believed that his daughter should not have boyfriends but should enter an arranged marriage'.[27] Secondly, he claimed that he believed that 'sex outside marriage is a grave offence which, if discovered, brings shame on the families of the individuals involved'.[28] D should not be able to plead loss of control in relation to a case like this because his beliefs are premised upon the assumption that a daughter does not have the right to determine for herself with whom she forms a relationship and whether she has sex outside of marriage. D is entitled to hold these beliefs, but they are not justifiable because they do not sufficiently respect his daughter's right to autonomy, and thus V's contravention of them did not constitute circumstances of an extremely grave character that caused D to have a justifiable sense of being seriously wronged. D has rights to respect for private and family life and to freedom of thought, conscience and religion under Articles 8 and 9 of the European Convention on Human

---

22 Ibid., para. 34.
23 Law Com. No 290, 2004 (n. 2) para. 3.70.
24 European Convention on Human Rights, Art. 14.
25 [2005] EWCA Crim 1880.
26 Ibid., [14].
27 Ibid., [22].
28 Ibid.

Rights respectively. However, these rights are limited, and have to be construed in the light of the rights of D's daughter. Article 8(2) allows limitations to the right to respect for private and family life that are 'in accordance with the law and necessary in a democratic society in the interests of national security, public safety or the economic well-being of the country, for the protection of health or morals, or for the protection of the rights and freedoms of others'. Similarly, Article 9(2) stipulates that the right to freedom of thought, conscience and religion can be subject 'to such limitations as are prescribed by law and are necessary in a democratic society in the interests of public safety, for the protection of public order, health or morals, or for the protection of the rights and freedoms of others'.[29] Each of these grounds for potentially legitimate limitations to the Article 8(2) and Article 9(2) rights has a specific meaning under case law; it is the 'protection of the rights and freedoms of others' ground that is of most significance here. D's rights under Articles 8 and 9 should not assist him in the determination of the correct interpretation of s. 54(4) of the 2009 Act on the facts of a case like *Mohammad (Faqir)* because the law should attach priority to the fundamental rights and freedoms of D's daughter, and conclude that D did not have a justifiable sense of being seriously wronged.[30]

Does the Serious Wrongdoing Have to be Directed Against D?

It might seem that the thing or things done or said (or both) which constituted circumstances of an extremely grave character do indeed have to be directed against D, since the loss of control defence states that they must have caused D to have a justifiable sense of being seriously wronged. However, the Law Commission stated:

> We feel that a jury would be able to recognise that where there is a close personal connection between the defendant and the person directly wronged, the defendant may well have a feeling of suffering jointly from the wrongdoing so as to fall within the principle of the formula which we have proposed.[31]

In accordance with this, the Explanatory Notes to the 2009 Act indicate that the defence might apply where the wrongdoing was directed against someone close to D, since they state that the loss of control defence might apply 'where a person discovers their partner sexually abusing their young

---

29 On the 'prescribed by law' term, see *Hasan and Chaush* v. *Bulgaria* (2002) 34 EHRR 1339 and *Maestri* v. *Italy* (2004) 39 EHRR 38, making it clear that the provisions have to be accessible to those affected by them and allow them to foresee the likelihood of any possible offences they could have committed. On the 'necessary in a democratic society' term, see *Manoussakis* v. *Greece* (1997) 23 EHRR 387, making it clear that a restriction has to be proportionate to a legitimate aim pursued.

30 In this context, it is significant that the European Court of Human Rights has stated, for instance, that 'the guarantee afforded by Article 8 of the Convention is primarily intended to ensure the development, without outside interference, of the personality of each individual in his relations with other human beings' (*von Hannover* v. *Germany* (2005) 40 EHRR 1 [50]). This statement attaches priority to the right of each individual to develop his or her personality, which would include the right of a 24-year-old woman of sufficient mental capacity to determine for herself with whom she forms a relationship and whether she has sex outside marriage.

31 Law Com. No 290, 2004 (n. 2) para. 3.73.

child (an act that amounts to sexual infidelity) and loses self-control and kills'.[32] Furthermore, it is arguable that it should have an ever wider scope in principle.[33]

We must return here to the philosophy of 'imperfect justification' that underpins the new reforms: that is, the belief that 'a killing in anger produced by serious wrongdoing is ethically less wicked, and therefore deserving of a lesser punishment, than, say, killing out of greed, lust, jealousy or for political reasons'.[34] It is obvious that 'anger' and 'serious wrongdoing' are required for the killing to be ethically less wicked from the perspective of this philosophy, and it must be remembered that the defence only applies where 'a person of D's sex and age, with a normal degree of tolerance and self-restraint and in the circumstances of D, might have reacted in the same or in a similar way to D'.[35] However, there is nothing in the philosophy underpinning the 2009 Act that as a matter of principle requires that the wrongdoing be directed against D or indeed against someone close to D.

At the time at which the provocation defence was abolished, there was no stipulation under this defence that the things done or said had to be directed at D, and there is no reason why the serious wrongdoing limb of the new law should contain such a requirement. In *Pearson*, two brothers had been abused by their violent father.[36] The Court of Appeal held that acts directed at a third party could count as provocation and be taken into account in D's defence in determining whether a 'reasonable man' might have done what D did. The new law should take an equivalent approach: some people may retain self-control if personally wronged, but understandably lose it if they see V do serious wrong against a vulnerable person to whom they have a close personal connection.[37]

The more difficult question is whether the serious wrongdoing qualifying trigger should apply in cases where the wrongdoing was directed against somebody to whom D was not close. It is possible that the prosecution would draw an analogy with the criminal law duress defence here. Duress potentially applies where D's will was overborne by threats or circumstances, but it is subject to strict limitations. There are significant differences between the loss of control defence and duress: for instance, unlike loss of control, duress is a complete defence to all crimes, with the exception 'of murder ... attempted murder ... and, perhaps, some forms of treason'.[38] However, there are also meaningful similarities between these two defences. First, as Lord Bingham said in *Hasan*, 'The relevant tests pertaining to duress have been largely stated objectively, with reference to the reasonableness of the defendant's perceptions and conduct.'[39] This is similar to the law on loss of control, where there are important tests relating to reasonableness. Secondly, duress does not justify D's conduct: as Lord Bingham put it in *Hasan*, it 'is now properly to be regarded as a defence which, if established, excuses what would otherwise be criminal conduct'.[40] In this way, duress could be taken as similar to the loss of control defence, since nobody would claim that anger can justify a killing, even where it is in response to serious wrongdoing. Norrie rightly characterises the loss of control defence as an 'imperfect justification' in the limited sense that D

---

32 Coroners and Justice Act 2009, Explanatory Notes, 3.49.
33 It is notable that the 'fear of serious violence' limb of the loss of control defence is not limited to situations where the feared violence was directed against D or someone close to D.
34 Law Com. No 290, 2004 (n. 2) para. 3.38.
35 Coroners and Justice Act 2009, s 54(1)(c).
36 [1992] Crim LR 193.
37 See *Blackstone's Criminal Practice 2008* (Oxford University Press, 2007) 166, making a similar point about the law on provocation.
38 *Hasan* [2005] UKHL 22, [2005] 2 AC 467 [21] (Lord Bingham).
39 Ibid.
40 Ibid., [18].

must have a justifiable sense of being seriously wronged in order to use this defence; his use of the term 'imperfect justification' is part of an attempt to describe 'the layering of the moral argument so that the killing has an element of "rightfulness in an overall context of wrongfulness"'.[41] However, Norrie acknowledges that this characterisation 'may itself be "imperfect"'.[42] As he says, 'justification' and 'excuse' are terms that are 'notoriously difficult to use';[43] exactly how they should be understood is a matter of dispute, as is their application to defences in criminal law.[44] It is easy to imagine that the prosecution might argue that loss of control is a compassionate excuse that applies where circumstances drove D to act in a certain way, that it is thereby similar in nature to duress in this respect, and that the circumstances of an extremely grave character limb of the loss of control defence should therefore be limited by a rule that is equivalent to the one in duress that 'The threat must be directed against the defendant or his immediate family or someone close to him'.[45] Any such argument could be strengthened by reference to the requirement in s. 54(4) that D justifiably felt seriously wronged, since it is difficult to claim that D could justifiably feel seriously wronged by conduct that is not directed against D or someone close to him or her. However, a court should reject any argument that the serious wrongdoing must be directed against D or someone close to him or her. The philosophy underpinning the loss of control defence is that 'a killing in anger produced by serious wrongdoing is ethically less wicked'[46] where a person of D's sex and age, with a normal degree of tolerance and self-restraint and in the circumstances of D, might have reacted in the same or in a similar way to D. Thus, the focus should be on whether D had a justifiable sense of anger and whether a 'normal' person might have done the same or something similar to D in the circumstances. Whether the thing said or done was directed against D or somebody close to him or her should be relevant in considering these matters, but there should be no requirement that the wrongdoing was directed against D or somebody close to him or her. As the Law Commission put it in summarising their underlying approach in relation to these reforms, the law should 'set boundaries in a reasoned, sensitive and nuanced way' rather than adopt rigid rules that do not allow the judge and jury to make value judgements.[47]

To What Extent, if at all, Should D be Judged on the Facts as He or She Believed Them to be Where He or She Made a Mistake About Them?

The Law Commission's view on this issue is that D should be given the benefit of the mistake, and judged on the facts as he or she perceived them to be, where there is an 'intelligible basis' for D's belief.[48] The precise meaning of the phrase 'intelligible basis' is unclear, but it would appear that the test under this approach might be whether the mistake was capable of being honestly made by a person who was not suffering from paranoid delusions.[49] The Law Commission's view about mistakes in this context is similar to the equivalent approach under the law on provocation,

---

41 Norrie (n. 9) 289. Norrie acknowledges that the old law contained 'a vague justificatory element, concerning whether the loss of self-control was acceptable'.
42 Ibid.
43 Ibid.
44 On this issue in general, see Marcia Baron, 'Justifications and Excuses' 2 (2004–2005) Ohio State Journal of Criminal Law 388.
45 Ibid., 21.
46 Law Com. No 290, 2004 (n. 2) para. 3.38.
47 Ibid., para. 3.142.
48 Ibid., para. 3.157–3.158.
49 Ibid., para. 3.158 on the issue of paranoid delusions.

where D was judged on the facts as he or she believed them to be, whether or not this belief was reasonable.[50] It is also similar to the approach adopted by the American Law Institute. The Model Penal Code contains a partial defence to murder which applies where 'murder is committed under the influence of extreme mental or emotional disturbance for which there is reasonable explanation or excuse'.[51] Furthermore, it specifically states: 'The reasonableness of such explanation or excuse shall be determined from the viewpoint of a person in the actor's situation under the circumstances as he believes them to be'.[52] The Law Commission think that their approach to mistakes in this context is acceptable because they believe that this aspect of the law on provocation did not 'appear to have been problematical'.[53] However, the Explanatory Notes to the 2009 Act indicate that whether D's sense of being seriously wronged is justifiable will be an 'objective' question, and contrast it with the fear of violence qualifying trigger, which they characterise as a 'subjective test … [where the] defendant will need to show that he or she lost self-control because of a genuine fear of serious violence, *whether or not the fear was in fact reasonable*'.[54] The emphasised words, and the absence of equivalent words in the Explanatory Notes relating to the 'circumstances of an extremely grave character' qualifying trigger, suggest that there is a difference between the two types of qualifying triggers in relation to mistakes, and that D may need to show that any mistake was reasonable in order to use the 'circumstances of an extremely grave character' qualifying trigger. This can be seen as consistent with the wording used in the Act, which requires D to have a 'justifiable sense of being seriously wronged'. It is arguable that D cannot have had a justifiable sense of being seriously wronged where D made an unreasonable, and hence unjustifiable, mistake.

The one issue that is relatively clear in this context is that D should be judged on the facts as he or she perceived them to be where D made a reasonable mistake about the situation. Norrie's term 'imperfect justification' is useful to the extent that it highlights a shift in the philosophy underpinning the law. However, it is important not to be overly distracted by labels here. As Anthony Duff puts it, rather than beginning by trying to characterise each type of defensive plea as an 'excuse', a 'justification', or something else, 'we should [first] try to get clear about its character, content, grounds and implications, and about its similarities to and its differences from other kinds of defensive plea'.[55] The philosophy underpinning the circumstances of an extremely grave character aspect of the new defence is that 'a killing in anger produced by serious wrongdoing is ethically less wicked, and therefore deserving of a lesser punishment, than, say, killing out of greed, lust, jealousy or for political reasons'.[56] There can be no ethical distinction between a killing in anger produced by serious wrongdoing and the same killing produced by a reasonable mistake about the circumstances. Thus, D should be judged on the circumstances as he or she believed them to be where he or she made a reasonable mistake about them. However, it does not logically follow that D should be able to rely upon an unreasonable mistake. D must have had a 'justifiable sense of being seriously wronged'. This does not require that D must have actually been seriously wronged, but it arguably does require that D cannot always be judged on the circumstances as he or she believed them to be. Marcia Baron claims, 'Clearly, a belief may be justified without being true. When we say that a belief is justified, we mean that there are good grounds for it,

---

50 *Brown* (1776) 1 Leach 148, 168 ER 177; *Letenock* (1917) 12 Cr App R 221.
51 Model Penal Code §210.3(1)(b). This defence is wide enough to include cases that would be dealt with under the diminished responsibility defence in English law.
52 Ibid.
53 Law Com. No 290, 2004 (n. 2) para. 3.155.
54 Coroner and Justice Act 2009, Explanatory Notes, para. 345 (emphasis added).
55 Anthony Duff, 'Rethinking Justifications' (2003–2004) 39 Tulsa Law Review 829, 832.
56 Law Com. No 290, 2004 (n. 2) para. 3.38.

and we generally mean that the agent believed it on (some of) those grounds'.[57] On this basis, it is possible to argue that D cannot have had a justifiable sense of being seriously wronged where D made an unreasonable mistake about the facts, and that D should thus not be able to rely upon an unreasonable mistake about the facts in relation to the 'circumstances of an extremely grave character' qualifying trigger. Nonetheless, this is a controversial subject: it is equally possible to claim that a killing in anger produced by a genuine but unreasonable mistaken belief in serious wrongdoing is deserving of lesser punishment than murder, and that the crucial issue in establishing that there were 'circumstances of an extremely grave character' that caused D to have a justifiable sense of being seriously wronged is whether a 'normal' person would have become so angry as to lose control, given the facts as D perceived them to be. It is disappointing that the Law Commission did not take a principled approach to this issue, and that they simply proposed no changes to the law in this respect on the basis that the mistaken beliefs about provocation had caused no problems in practice. It is equally, if not more, disappointing that the Ministry of Justice did not explore this issue at all in the papers that they issued when considering reform in this area.[58]

What is the Extent of the Restriction Regarding Sexual Infidelity and Does this Restriction Improve the Law?

The 2009 Act specifically limits the scope of the loss of control defence in three respects. It is the sexual infidelity aspect of this provision which is contentious and therefore important for the purposes of this chapter. Section 55(6)(c) states that 'In determining whether a loss of self-control had a qualifying trigger ... the fact that a thing done or said constituted sexual infidelity is to be disregarded'. The Explanatory Notes clarify the significance of this provision:

> The effect is that, if a person kills another because they have been unfaithful, he or she will not be able to claim the partial defence. It is the fact of sexual infidelity that falls to be disregarded under the provision, so the thing done or said can still potentially amount to a qualifying trigger if (ignoring the sexual infidelity) it amounts nonetheless to circumstances of an extremely grave character causing the defendant to have a justifiable sense of being seriously wronged.[59]

The Ministry of Justice introduced s. 55(6)(c) because they thought that 'sexual infidelity on the part of the victim can never justify reducing a murder charge to manslaughter.'[60] They believed that 'It is quite unacceptable for a defendant who has killed an unfaithful partner to seek to blame the victim for what occurred.'[61] Before considering the validity of this reasoning, it is important to consider the scope of the restriction regarding sexual infidelity.

It is not clear how the s. 55(6)(c) bar would work with a case where the thing done or said constitutes a taunt about sexual infidelity. The thing would clearly not constitute sexual infidelity in itself; it would refer to a fact that is supposed to be disregarded, but D might legitimately be able to argue that taunts about sexual infidelity can in exceptional circumstances provide the basis for a successful loss of control defence. This would seem to be consistent with the view of the Law Commission, which did not propose a rigid formula to deal with cases of sexual infidelity.

---

57 Marcia Baron, 'The Provocation Defense and the Nature of Justification' (2009) 43 University of Michigan Journal of Law Reform 117, 128.
58 See Ministry of Justice, *Murder, Manslaughter and Infanticide* (MoJ CP 19, 2008) and (n. 5).
59 Coroners and Justice Act 2009, Explanatory Notes, para. 349.
60 MoJ CP 19, 2008 (n. 58) para. 32.
61 Ibid.

The Commission sympathised with Lord Hoffmann's view in *Smith (Morgan)* that male jealousy and possessiveness should not be an excuse lessening the gravity of the crime from murder to manslaughter;[62] it accordingly recommended that the judge should withdraw the provocation defence from the jury in cases of simple separation or sexual infidelity. However, the Law Commission rightly recommended a nuanced approach in this context, stating that this aspect of the law should not be reduced to a formula 'which removes any evaluative function from the judge and jury', and that 'there may be cases [involving additional taunts or insults] where one party torments another with remarks of an exceptionally abusive kind or where one party's behaviour puts quite exceptional emotional pressure on the other'.[63] As the Law Commission stated, it would be very harsh for the law to completely disregard the fact of sexual infidelity even if this sexual infidelity is the subject of exceptionally abusive taunts.[64] It would thus seem that taunts about sexual infidelity should amount to qualifying triggers in exceptional cases, although it is not clear that this is how the law will be interpreted.

A second concern relating to the exemption about sexual infidelity was raised in response to the Ministry of Justice's 2008 consultation preceding the reforms. As the Ministry of Justice put it: 'More than one women's group ... thought that the [sexual infidelity] exemption might exclude a woman who killed after years of abuse, in response to a final act of sexual infidelity.'[65] The Ministry of Justice dismissed these concerns, arguing: 'We believe that where sexual infidelity is one part in a set of circumstances which led to the defendant losing self-control, the partial defence should succeed or fail on the basis of those circumstances disregarding the element of sexual infidelity.'[66] How would the current provisions work in practice in a case where D killed V after years of abuse in response to a final act of sexual infidelity? D could argue that her loss of self-control was attributable to this abuse in the sense that it would not have occurred but for it, and that the abuse constituted circumstances of an extremely grave character that caused her to have a justifiable sense of being seriously wronged. However, while there is no requirement that the loss of control be an immediate or almost immediate response to the circumstances in question, it must be borne in mind that s. 54(4) of the 2009 Act prohibits use of the loss of control defence 'if, in doing or being a party to the killing, D acted in a considered desire for revenge'. It might seem that this prohibition about a considered desire for revenge would effectively undermine D's defence where D killed after years of abuse in response to a final act of sexual infidelity, since s. 55(6)(c) means that D could not use this final act of sexual infidelity to demonstrate that her loss of control had a qualifying trigger. Nonetheless, s. 55(6)(c) would not prevent D from using evidence of this final act to demonstrate that she did not act in a considered desire for revenge. Thus, D might rightly be able to use the loss of control defence where D killed V after years of abuse in response to a final act of sexual infidelity.

---

62 [2001] 1 AC 146 (HL) 169, approving of *Stingel* v. *The Queen* (1990) 171 CLR 312, where the Australian High Court held that no jury, acting reasonably, could have concluded that an ordinary person would lose self-control and kill in response to being told to 'piss off' when he found his former partner having sex with another man.

63 Law Com. No 290, 2004 (n. 2) para. 3.147. The Commission's final proposals in Law Commission, *Murder, Manslaughter and Infanticide* (Law Com. No 304, 2006) reflects this view.

64 There is evidence that this opinion is shared by approximately 50 per cent of members of the public, and that there is no significant difference between the attitudes of men and women in this respect: see Law Com. No 290, 2004 (n. 2) para. 3.146.

65 MoJ CP (R) 19, 2008 (n. 5) para. 49.

66 Ibid., para. 55.

A more fundamental issue here is whether the Ministry of Justice is right to claim that sexual infidelity on the part of V can never justify reducing a murder conviction to manslaughter. There is of course support in certain other jurisdictions, such as Canada, for the view that sexual infidelity on the part of V does not necessarily justify reducing a murder conviction to manslaughter. Provocation is a partial defence to murder in s. 232 of the Canadian Criminal Code. Section 232(1) of this Code states that 'Culpable homicide that otherwise would be murder may be reduced to manslaughter if the person who committed it did so in the heat of passion caused by sudden provocation'. Section 232(2) stipulates that 'A wrongful act or an insult that is of such a nature as to be sufficient to deprive an ordinary person of the power of self-control is provocation for the purposes of this section if the accused acted on it suddenly and before there was time for his passion to cool'. The Canadian Supreme Court dealt with the correct interpretation of s. 232 in *Tran*. The court stated that the facts did not support D's contention 'that, in the context of his relationship with ... [his wife], his discovery of her sexual involvement with ... [V] amounted to an insult at law'.[67] The court held that nothing done by D's wife or V came close to an 'insult', since their behaviour was lawful, discrete and private. However, *Tran* is not authority for the view that sexual infidelity or the ending of a relationship can *never* justify reducing a murder conviction to manslaughter. Having observed that 'the ordinary person standard must be informed by contemporary norms of behaviour, including fundamental values such as the commitment to equality provided for in the Canadian Charter of Rights and Freedoms',[68] the Supreme Court concluded that 'there can be no place in this objective standard for antiquated beliefs such as "adultery is the highest invasion of property" ... nor indeed for any form of killing based on such inappropriate conceptualizations of "honour"'.[69] Nonetheless, it added that whether sexual infidelity or the ending of a relationship could in principle make D have a justifiable sense of being wronged depends upon the context, stating:

> while one spouse undoubtedly has a legal right to leave his or her partner, in some circumstances the means by which that spouse communicates this decision may amount *in fact* to an "insult", within the ordinary meaning of the word. However, to be recognized *at law*, the insult must be of sufficient gravity to cause a loss of self-control, as objectively determined.[70]

It is notable that Scottish law takes a different approach to English law on this issue. In Scotland, it has been stated that provocation only applies as a defence where D has been assaulted or 'when an accused discovers that his or her partner, who owes a duty of sexual fidelity, has been unfaithful'.[71] Is English law right to specifically state that sexual infidelity *per se* cannot justify reducing what would otherwise be a murder conviction to manslaughter? This aspect of the new law was strongly disparaged in parliamentary debate when it was proposed. Lord Neill

---

67 *R* v. *Tran* (n. 20) [43]. D did not argue that he was provoked by a 'wrongful act'. For analysis of what counts as a 'wrongful act' or 'insult' in Canadian law on provocation, see Wayne Renke, 'Calm like a Bomb: An Assessment of the Partial Defence of Provocation' (2010) 47 Alberta Law Review 729, 755–8.

68 Ibid., [34].

69 Ibid.

70 Ibid. [29]. For a similar Australian authority, see *Arrowsmith* v. *The Queen* (1994) 55 FCR 130, 138, where the court stated: 'In Australia in the 1990s it would be entirely out of line with ... [the required] standard if the mere telling of a partner that a relationship is over, whether accompanied or not by an admission of infidelity, were taken as potentially sufficient to induce an ordinary person to so lose control as to deliberately or recklessly inflict fatal violence on the other.'

71 *Drury (Stuart)* v. *HM Advocate* 2001 SCCR 558 (High Court of Justiciary) [25].

characterised the sexual infidelity provisions as 'ridiculous and out of line with the way in which people think about human passions'.[72] Similarly, Lord Lloyd, a retired Law Lord, criticised the proposals for seeking to remove discretion from the jury.[73] Furthermore, Lord Phillips, then Senior Law Lord, questioned the law reform proposals in a public lecture in 2008, stating: 'I must confess to being uneasy about a law which so diminishes the significance of sexual infidelity as expressly to exclude it from even the possibility of amounting to provocation'.[74] The Ministry of Justice did not share this unease. Like certain women's rights organisations[75] and a number of academics who have analysed the provocation defence from a feminist perspective,[76] the Ministry of Justice clearly believed that there were inequalities between male and female defendants in this area, and they supported reform relating to sexual infidelity on the basis that it would reduce these inequalities. Welcoming the reforms, Harriet Harman, the Minister for Women, stated:

> For centuries the law has allowed men to escape a murder charge in domestic homicide cases by blaming the victim. Ending the provocation defence in cases of "infidelity" is an important law change and will end the culture of excuses.
>
> There is no excuse for domestic violence, let alone taking a life. Whatever happens in a relationship does not justify resorting to violence. So men who kill their wife will have to face a murder charge and will no longer be able to claim "it's her fault, she provoked me".[77]

In considering whether Harman is right, it is necessary to put to one side the fact that the law does actually rightly accept that what happens in a relationship can justify resorting to violence[78] and return to Alan Norrie's analysis of the philosophy underpinning the 2009 reforms. Norrie's view about s. 56(6)(c) is that 'As a general rule, one can see exactly why the Government should take this position [about sexual infidelity], especially on an approach to angry killing that seeks to identify those forms of killing that are imperfectly justified.'[79] It is easy to agree with Norrie. To say this is not to argue that sexual infidelity is acceptable: rather, it is to say that sexual infidelity *per se* does not generally constitute wrongdoing of an 'extremely grave character' that could cause D to have a justifiable sense of being 'seriously wronged', and thus to be deserving of a lesser

---

72 HL Deb., 7 July 2009, vol. 712, col. 576.
73 Ibid., 578.
74 Joshua Rozenberg, 'Homicide Reforms Would Be "Nightmare" for Juries, Says Top Law Lord', *The Telegraph*, 7 November 2008.
75 See Ministry of Justice (n. 5) para. 47.
76 See, for example, Celia Wells, 'Provocation: The Case for Abolition', in Andrew Ashworth and Barry Mitchell (eds), *Rethinking Homicide Law* (Oxford University Press, 2000); Mandy Burton, 'Intimate Homicide and the Provocation Defence – Endangering Women? *R* v. *Smith*' (2001) 9 Feminist Legal Studies 247; Mandy Burton, 'Sentencing Domestic Homicide upon Provocation: Still Getting Away with Murder' (2003) 11 Feminist Legal Studies 279; Oliver Quick and Celia Wells, 'Getting Tough with Defences' [2005] Criminal Law Review 514; Susan Edwards, 'Descent into Murder: Provocation's Stricture – The Prognosis for Women Who Kill Men Who Abused Them' (2007) 71 Journal of Criminal Law 342; Susan Edwards, 'Justice Devlin's Legacy: Duffy – A Battered Woman "Caught" in Time' [2009] Criminal Law Review 851; Anna Carline, 'Reforming Provocation: Perspectives from the Law Commission and the Government' [2009] Web Journal of Legal Issues 2.
77 'Anger no Longer an Excuse for Murder' (29 July 2008) <http://www.justice.gov.uk/news/newsrelease290708a.htm> (accessed 21 March 2011).
78 For example, where D acts reasonably in self-defence: see s. 3(1) of the Criminal Law Act 1967.
79 Norrie (n. 9) 288.

punishment. It must be remembered that the central issue here is not whether sexual infidelity is wrong: it is whether D deserves to be labelled as a murderer and punished accordingly. Once the issue is seen in this way, it is arguable that the reforms should have gone further: for example, specifically stating that if D kills V simply because V has ended a relationship between them, D will not be able to claim the partial defence. However, it is important to note the qualifying words in Norrie's argument: 'as a general rule'. Section 55(6)(c) introduces an absolute, rather than general, rule. In this sense, it goes too far. There is evidence 'that juries are less prone than is sometimes thought to return verdicts of manslaughter on grounds of provocation where the provocation alleged is simple separation or infidelity'.[80] This suggests that removing the restriction regarding sexual infidelity would not mean that D would be able to escape liability for murder by arguing that V committed a minor act of sexual infidelity, even if the judge were willing to allow the issue to go to the jury: D would still have to establish that the sexual infidelity constituted circumstances of an extremely grave character that caused D to have a justifiable sense of being seriously wronged, which would presumably not be possible in cases of minor sexual infidelity. The problem with the current restriction is that it introduces a rigid rule that does not cater for the fact that there might be cases 'where one party's behaviour puts quite exceptional emotional pressure on the other'.[81] Cases where D killed V because of V's sexual infidelity do not necessarily involve male possessiveness, or indeed possessiveness at all; as Lord Thomas pointed out in a parliamentary debate about this issue, they can involve serious betrayal of trust: 'there are cases in which there has been a deep bond of trust between the partners, or at least one of the partners has thought there was, and they have been betrayed. That betrayal gives rise to the deepest of emotions'.[82] Lord Thomas argued that 'this removal of sexual infidelity as a cause of loss of self-control is ... illogical' and reflects a failure to trust the common sense of the jury.[83] This is true, but the Ministry of Justice's failure to trust actually goes much further than this: the provisions about sexual infidelity also reflect a failure to trust the judge to remove the issue from the jury in cases where no properly directed jury could reasonably conclude that the loss of control defence should apply.

This absolute restriction relating to sexual infidelity does not exist in the context of the diminished responsibility defence, another partial defence to murder which also reduces the conviction to manslaughter where it is pleaded successfully. Thus, there is a significant anomaly in the law here.[84] The diminished responsibility defence was amended by the Coroners and Justice Act 2009, s. 52 of which states:

(1) A person ("D") who kills or is a party to the killing of another is not to be convicted of murder if D was suffering from an abnormality of mental functioning which –

(a) arose from a recognised mental condition;
(b) substantially impaired D's ability to do one or more of the things mentioned in subsection (1A); and
(c) provides an explanation for D's acts and omissions in doing or being a party to the killing.

(1A) Those things are –

---

80 Law Com. No 290, 2004 (n. 2) para. 3.145.
81 Ibid., para. 3.147.
82 HL Deb., 26 October 2009, vol. 713, col. 1060.
83 Ibid.
84 I am grateful to Claire de Than for making this point, and for providing the following hypothetical example used to illustrate it, in personal correspondence on the issue.

(a) to understand the nature of D's conduct;
(b) to form a rational judgment;
(c) to exercise self-control.

Let us imagine that D, a schizophrenic, hallucinates that V, his wife, has committed adultery.[85] D could argue that he was suffering from an abnormality of mental functioning, that this abnormality arose from a recognised mental condition, that it substantially impaired his ability to form a rational judgement, and that it provides an explanation for his carrying out the killing. The phrase 'to form a rational judgement' is ambiguous. However, as Ronnie Mackay has pointed out, there is no requirement in the amended diminished responsibility defence that the abnormality of mental functioning affects D's ability to form a rational judgement as to what is right or wrong.[86] Thus, D might be able to argue that his schizophrenia substantially impaired his ability to form a rational judgement by affecting his perception of reality. If this is the case, D will be able to successfully plead diminished responsibility, but he would not be able to plead loss of control. It might be argued that this is appropriate, since the loss of control and diminished responsibility defences are designed to deal with 'normal' and 'abnormal' defendants respectively. However, there is no reason why D should be able to escape a murder conviction in a domestic homicide case by proving that he hallucinated that his wife had committed adultery, if he cannot escape a murder conviction by arguing that she actually committed adultery and that this constituted serious wrongdoing.

Conclusions

One aspect of the killing in response to 'circumstances of an extremely grave character' reforms is admirable; the requirement under the new law that D had a justifiable sense of being seriously wronged rules out a repetition of cases like *Doughty*: the law now rightly recognises that killing a baby for crying is not ethically less wicked and therefore deserving of a lesser punishment than, for example, killing for lust or money. Other aspects of the reforms are more contentious. One problem is that certain aspects of the new law are unclear: for instance, as explored in this chapter, it is unclear precisely what factors the jury can take into account in applying s. 55(4). This lack of clarity means that the success of the rules relating to 'circumstances of a grave character' will to some extent turn on their precise interpretation by prosecutors, judges and juries. Perhaps the most deplorable aspect of the new provisions is the absolute restriction relating to sexual infidelity. Lord Judge LCJ has rightly stated that this restriction is not 'a sensible way for us to proceed'.[87] The problem is that it is absolute; it does not allow for cases where sexual infidelity *per se* caused D to have a justifiable sense of being seriously wronged. To say that sexual infidelity could cause D to have a justifiable sense of being seriously wronged is not to say that male possessiveness is acceptable or that men should have a right to kill women for disobedience.[88] Nor is it to say that men should be allowed to commit a form of 'honour killing' where a woman's adultery has brought

---

85 Ibid.
86 Ronnie Mackay, 'The Coroners and Justice Act 2009: Partial Defences to Murder: (2) –The New Diminished Responsibility Defence' [2010] Criminal Law Review 290, 296.
87 House of Lords, Select Committee on the Constitution, 9th Report of Session 2010–11: Meetings with the Lord Chief Justice and the Lord Chancellor (HL Paper 89) 7.
88 See Justice for Women, 'Coroners and Justice Bill: Justice for Women Briefing to Peers', at <http://www.justiceforwomen.org.uk/storage/coroners-justice-bill.pdf> (accessed 21 March 2011), arguing in favour of the sexual infidelity restriction: 'In this country in the 21st century no one owns anyone. No one has the

dishonour to them.[89] Rather, it is to agree with Lord Thomas that sexual infidelity can involve a serious betrayal of trust.

---

right to kill someone for disobedience. Many men control their wives by saying "don't you dare ever leave me – I don't mind doing 7 years for you".'

[89] See Anna Carline (n. 76), arguing: 'Mitigation due to an act of adultery is historically based on the notion of male honour … and thus retaining the defence in circumstances of sexual infidelity is to permit certain forms of "honour killings".'

Chapter 10
The View from Ireland

John E. Stannard

Introduction

The aim of this chapter is to examine the reforms to provocation and diminished responsibility in the Coroners and Justice Act 2009 in the light of the history and development of these defences in the two jurisdictions of Ireland, that is to say, the Republic of Ireland[1] and Northern Ireland. One of the advantages of this exercise is that the law of these two jurisdictions is sufficiently close to that of England and Wales to make the comparison worthwhile, whilst also sufficiently distinct to allow for different developments in the law to have taken place. As well as this, the law relating to insanity is considered, as the Irish law of diminished responsibility, both north and south, can only be understood in the context of the different formulations of the insanity defence in those jurisdictions. We shall be considering all of these matters at greater length in due course, but first it may be helpful to clarify, for those readers who are not familiar with it, the constitutional sources of the criminal law in the two jurisdictions.

The Constitutional Background

A convenient starting point for our purposes is the Union of 1800, which created the 'United Kingdom of Great Britain and Ireland' out of what had hitherto been two separate kingdoms, albeit with the same monarch.[2] At the same time the old Irish Parliament, which had existed since medieval times, was abolished and its powers effectively transferred to Westminster.[3] However, there continued to be a separate Irish Executive based in Dublin,[4] and also a separate system of courts, albeit one organised on similar lines to those of England and Wales.[5] There were some significant differences with regard to the administration of criminal justice, especially in relation

---

1   According to Art. 4 of the Irish Constitution, the official name of the state in the English language is 'Ireland', and this is the name that should be used in the official context: see *Ellis* v. *O'Dea* [1989] IR 530, 539–40 (Walsh J). However, s. 2 of the Republic of Ireland Act 1948 also sanctions the use of the term 'Republic of Ireland' and to avoid confusion with the geographical island of Ireland this term will be used throughout this chapter. See further Kelly, *The Irish Constitution* (3rd edn, edited by Gerard Hogan and Gerry White, Butterworths, 1994) 24.
2   James Casey, *Constitutional Law in Ireland* (2nd edn, Sweet & Maxwell, 1992) 2.
3   Ibid., 1.
4   Ibid., 2.
5   F.H. Newark, *Notes on Irish Legal History* (Scarlett & Son, 1966) 21–3; Brice Dickson, *The Legal System of Northern Ireland* (5th edn, SLS Legal Publications, 2005) 14–17.

to matters of policing, the prosecution of offences, and the magistracy,[6] but as far as the substantive criminal law was concerned the position was largely the same as in England.

However, the second half of the nineteenth century saw growing demands for the grant of Home Rule to Ireland.[7] Bills to this effect were introduced into Parliament in 1886, 1893 and 1912, but none of them made it into law, not least because of strong resistance from the strong Unionist faction in the province of Ulster.[8] Following the Irish War of Independence a further Home Rule Bill was introduced, which ultimately became the Government of Ireland Act 1920.[9] This provided for not one but two devolved administrations and legislatures, both of which were to be subject to the sovereignty of Westminster.[10] The first of these, based in Belfast, covered six counties of the old province of Ulster, namely Antrim, Down, Armagh, Fermanagh, Londonderry and Tyrone.[11] The second, based in Dublin, was to cover the remaining 26 counties.[12] However, this constitutional settlement was quickly superseded, at least in the case of the 26 counties, by the Anglo-Irish Treaty of 1921, which effectively partitioned the island of Ireland into the two jurisdictions we see today.[13]

Republic of Ireland

Following the Anglo-Irish Treaty, a new Constitution was drawn up for the 26 counties, which now became the Irish Free State. This had the status of a Dominion within the British Commonwealth, with an independent legislature, executive and judiciary.[14] This was superseded in 1937 by the present Irish Constitution, under which legislative powers are exercised by the Oireachtas, or Irish Parliament, which sits in Dublin.[15] As far as the courts are concerned, the Constitution itself only provides for 'Courts of First Instance' and a 'Court of Final Appeal',[16] but under the present statutory structure trials on indictment are heard in the Circuit Court and the Central Criminal Court,[17] with the possibility of an appeal to the Court of Criminal Appeal, and on to the Supreme Court in certain cases.[18] It should also be noted that under Article 50.1 of the Constitution laws in force prior to its coming into operation shall continue to have effect except in so far as they are either inconsistent with the Constitution or are later repealed. This meant the continuance of a good deal of the old criminal law in force prior to partition.[19] All in all, as far as the criminal law is concerned, the main sources of statute law are twofold: (1) Acts of the Oireachtas; and (2) Acts of

---

6   Ian Bridgeman, 'The Constabulary and the Criminal Justice System in Nineteenth-Century Ireland', in Ian O'Donnell and Finbarr McAuley (eds), *Criminal Justice History: Themes and Controversies from Pre-Independence Ireland* (Four Courts Press, 2004) 113.

7   Casey (n. 2) 3–4; Brigid Hadfield, *The Constitution of Northern Ireland* (SLS Legal Publications, 1989) ch. 1.

8   Hadfield (n. 7) 5, 17 and 23.

9   Ibid., 32.

10 Ibid.

11 Ibid.

12 Ibid.

13 Casey (n. 2) 6.

14 Constitution of the Irish Free State, Art. 12 (legislature), Arts 51–4 (executive), and Arts 64–72 (courts).

15 Constitution of Ireland, Art. 15.1.

16 Ibid., Art. 34.2.

17 This is the name given to the High Court when it hears criminal cases: Courts (Supplemental Provisions) Act 1961, s. 14.

18 Courts (Establishment and Constitution) Act 1961.

19 A similar provision appeared in Article 73 of the Free State Constitution.

the old Westminster Parliament prior to 1921, subject to the provisions of Article 50.1. The main sources of case law are again twofold: (1) decisions of the Supreme Court and Court of Criminal Appeal; and (2) decisions of the courts prior to 1921, again subject to the provisions or Article 50.1.

Northern Ireland

The constitutional history of Northern Ireland since 1921 is a long and convoluted one,[20] but as far as the criminal law is concerned a distinction can be drawn between the legislative and judicial functions. As far as legislation is concerned, criminal law was mainly dealt with between 1921 and 1972 by the old Northern Ireland Parliament at Stormont, set up under the Government of Ireland Act 1920.[21] Following the collapse and subsequent abolition of the old Stormont Parliament, its functions were effectively transferred to the Privy Council,[22] which continued to legislate for Northern Ireland in the fields of criminal law and justice until 2010, when most of these functions were transferred to the Northern Ireland Assembly,[23] again sitting at Stormont. The position with regard to judicial matters is more simple; following partition, a separate court system was set up for Northern Ireland,[24] including a Court of Criminal Appeal,[25] the functions of which were later transferred to the Court of Appeal.[26] The highest court in the Northern Ireland system is the Supreme Court (formerly the House of Lords), and though the decisions of that court are not strictly binding in Northern Ireland except in relation to Northern Ireland cases, its decisions have always been treated with the greatest respect.[27] A similar principle applies to decisions of the Court of Appeal in England and Wales – though clearly not binding on any of the courts in Northern Ireland, they will always be treated with respect, at least in so far as the law of the two jurisdictions is the same. The upshot of all this is that, as far as criminal law is concerned, the main sources of statute law are fourfold: (1) legislation of the Westminster Parliament; (2) legislation of the old Stormont Parliament from 1921 to 1972; (3) Northern Ireland Orders in Council from 1972 to 2010; and (4) Acts of the Northern Ireland Assembly since that date. The main sources of case law are threefold: (1) decisions of the English and Irish courts prior to 1921; (2) decisions of the Northern Ireland Court of Appeal, the former Court of Criminal Appeal, the House of Lords and the Supreme Court in Northern Ireland cases; and (3) decisions of the English Courts, including the Court of Appeal, and of the House of Lords and the Supreme Court in English cases.

The Defences

With this in mind, we can now look at the way in which the relevant defences have developed in the two jurisdictions, beginning with the Republic of Ireland and then going on to Northern Ireland.

---

20 Dickson (n. 5) 3–14; Hadfield (n. 7).
21 Dickson (n. 5) 5.
22 This was done by virtue of various provisions, including s. 1 of the Northern Ireland (Temporary Provisions) Act 1972, Schedule 1 para. 1(1) of the Northern Ireland Act 1974, and s. 85 of the Northern Ireland Act 1998.
23 By the Northern Ireland Act 1998 (Amendment of Schedule 3) Order 2010.
24 Dickson (n. 5) 12.
25 Criminal Appeal (NI) Act 1930.
26 Judicature (NI) Act 1978, Part III.
27 Dickson (n. 5) 90.

Republic of Ireland

The effect of Article 73 of the Free State Constitution, followed by Article 50.1 of the 1937 Constitution, was to preserve the existing law in so far as it did not conflict with the provisions of those constitutions. This meant that following independence the old criminal law continued in force for some time. However, over the years which followed the relevant provisions and doctrines began, as might have been expected, to diverge from their counterparts across the Irish Sea. This applied particularly in the case of insanity and the mitigating defences.

Insanity

After 1921 the Irish courts continued to apply the old M'Naghten Rules[28] in cases of insanity. However, they refused to apply them as strictly as was the practice in England, as can be seen from the 1935 case of *Attorney General* v. *O'Brien*,[29] decided in the Court of Criminal Appeal. This was a case of murder in which the defence argued that the accused was suffering from an insane blackout at the time of the act, and that the trial judge should have directed the jury that if, by reason of mental disease, the accused was unable to control his actions they should find him insane in point of law.[30] The appeal was dismissed on the grounds that there was no evidence of this being the case,[31] but in giving the judgment of the court Kennedy CJ gave his opinion that, the views of the English courts notwithstanding,[32] there might be room in Irish law for an insanity plea based on irresistible impulse.[33] *M'Naghten*'s case, he observed, was not a legal decision, but the answers to a series of questions put to the judges in the specific context of insane delusions, and the Rules should therefore be read in that light.[34]

Thirty years later, this was taken up by Henchy J in the unreported decision of *People (Attorney General)* v. *Hayes*,[35] where the accused was charged with murder following a fatal attack on his wife. He was agreed to be medically insane at the relevant time, and it was argued that as a result he could not exercise free volition. Whilst agreeing that legal insanity did not necessarily coincide with medical insanity, Henchy J observed that even if the accused understood the nature and quality of his act, and understood its wrongfulness both in moral and in legal terms, it was nevertheless open to the jury to find him not guilty on the ground of insanity if, due to a defect of reason, he was 'debarred from refraining from assaulting his wife'.[36]

This 'volitional' test of insanity[37] was later confirmed by the Supreme Court in *Doyle* v. *Wicklow County Council*,[38] a case involving a claim for criminal injury compensation by the owner of a slaughterhouse whose premises had been burnt down by an arsonist. The evidence established that the person responsible was suffering from a mental disorder at the relevant time, that he believed

---

28 (1843) 4 St Tr (NS) 847, 930.
29 [1936] IR 263.
30 Ibid., 266.
31 Ibid., 273.
32 *Jolly* 83 JP 296; *Holt* (1921) 15 Cr App R 10; *Kopsch* (1927) 19 Cr App R 50.
33 [1936] IR 263, 271.
34 Ibid., 269.
35 Central Criminal Court, 30 November 1967; O'Hanlon, 'Not Guilty Because of Insanity' 3 Irish Jurist (NS) 61.
36 *Doyle* v. *Wicklow County Council* [1974] 1 IR 55, 72 (quoted by Henchy J).
37 Finbarr McAuley and Paul McCutcheon, *Criminal Liability: A Grammar* (Round Hall, Sweet & Maxwell, 2000) 662.
38 [1974] 1 IR 55; *People (DPP)* v. *O'Mahony* [1985] IR 517.

that his love of animals entitled him to burn down the slaughterhouse, and was so determined to carry out the plan that nothing would have stopped him.[39] Giving the judgment of the court, Griffin J referred to some of the criticisms to which the M'Naghten Rules had been subject,[40] and reiterated the view that they did not provide an exhaustive test of insanity.[41] In the present case the key issue was whether, as a result of a defect of reason arising from his mental disorder, the arsonist was debarred from refraining from committing the damage in question, and the case was remitted to the lower court to decide on the evidence whether this was so.[42]

The result was an insanity defence much as stated by Stephen in his *Digest of Criminal Law*, including the bracketed passages:[43]

> No act is a crime if the person who does it is at the time when it is done prevented [either by defective mental power], or by any disease affecting his mind
>
> (a) from knowing the nature and quality of his act; or
> (b) from knowing that the act is wrong; [or
> (c) from controlling his own conduct, unless the absence of the power of control has been produced by his own default].

The reasoning of the courts in these cases has been subjected to criticism on the ground that the test of whether the defendant was 'debarred from refraining' from committing the act is a difficult one for juries to apply, and that it may not be as generous as it appears at first sight.[44] It was conceded, for instance, that if the arsonist in *Doyle* had found policemen present at the scene, he would have not gone ahead with his plan, but would have waited until they had gone before proceeding to set the fire.[45] If this is true, it would seem to negate any notion of *irresistible* impulse. Be that as it may, the volitional test has now been incorporated into the new statutory defence of insanity under s. 5 of the Criminal Law (Insanity) Act 2005, which reads as follows:

> Where an accused person is tried for an offence and ... the court ... or ... the jury finds that the accused person committed the act alleged against him or her and, having heard evidence relating to the mental condition of the accused given by a consultant psychiatrist, finds that –
>
> (a) the accused person was suffering at the time from a mental disorder; and
> (b) the mental disorder was such that the accused person ought not to be held responsible for the act alleged by reason of the fact that he or she –
>
> (i) did not know the nature and quality of the act, or
> (ii) did not know that what he or she was doing was wrong, or
> (iii) was unable to refrain from committing the act,

---

39 Ibid., 57.
40 Ibid., 69.
41 Ibid.
42 Ibid., 71.
43 Art. 28.
44 See the extensive discussion in McAuley and McCutcheon (n. 37) 662–80.
45 [1974] IR 55, 57.

the court or the jury, as the case may be, shall return a special verdict to the effect that the accused person is not guilty by reason of insanity.

We shall now see how all this has impacted on the availability of a defence of diminished responsibility in the Irish Republic.

Diminished responsibility
Prior to 2005, the Irish Republic did not have any defence of diminished responsibility; the fact that the defendant in a murder case may have been suffering from mental abnormality short of insanity did not affect his liability for the crime, though it might provide grounds for a reprieve by the Executive.[46] Thus in *AG v. O'Shea*,[47] the defendant was tried for murder following the brutal rape and killing of a young woman. Evidence was given that the killer had had sexual intercourse with the victim both before and after death, and it was suggested to the jury that the killing had been motivated by sadism and necrophilia. The jury found the accused guilty of murder but added a rider to their verdict indicating that in their opinion he was suffering from mental abnormality at the relevant time. However, it was held by the Court of Criminal Appeal that this did not affect the reliability of the verdict in any way; mental abnormality which did not amount to insanity could not relieve the individual of the consequences of his crime.[48]

This state of affairs was commented on unfavourably by the Henchy Committee in 1978.[49] As the law stood, for the purposes of determining guilt or innocence judges and juries were debarred from taking mental disorder into account unless it was sufficiently serious to amount to insanity in law.[50] The result was that many persons were being dealt with by the courts as normal offenders when they were clearly in need of psychiatric treatment.[51] The Committee therefore recommended that a new definition of insanity should be introduced, whereby the accused should have a defence if at the relevant time he was suffering from mental disorder (as defined) such that he should not be found guilty of the offence.[52] In tandem with this, the Committee recommended that a defence of diminished responsibility should be introduced, whereby the accused should be guilty of manslaughter rather than murder if at the relevant time he was suffering from mental disorder which, while not such as to justify a verdict of not guilty on the grounds of mental disorder, was such as to diminish substantially his responsibility for the act or omission charged.[53] While nothing came of these proposals at the time, they were, as we shall see, to have a significant influence on the defence provided in s. 6 of the Criminal Law (Insanity) Act 2005.

Following this, an attempt was made to get the defence recognised as part of the common law. In *People (DPP) v. O'Mahony*[54] the accused was charged with the murder of a neighbour during the course of a botched robbery, and evidence was given that he was a 'borderline mental

---

46 See generally Louise Kennefick, 'Diminished Responsibility in Ireland' (2011) 62 Northern Ireland Legal Quarterly (forthcoming).
47 [1931] IR 713.
48 Ibid., 729.
49 *Third Interim Report of the Interdepartmental Committee on Mentally Ill and Maladjusted Persons: Treatment and Care of Persons Suffering from Mental Disorder Who Appear Before the Courts on Criminal Charges* (Dublin, Stationery Office, 1978).
50 Ibid., para. 4.
51 Ibid.
52 Ibid., para. 7; Draft Criminal Justice (Mental Illness) Bill, cl. 17(1).
53 Ibid., para. 9; Draft Criminal Justice (Mental Illness) Bill, cl. 18(1).
54 [1985] IR 517.

defective', and that he suffered from a psychotic condition that prevented him from stopping or withdrawing from violent acts.[55] Arguing that the defence of diminished responsibility was part of Irish law, counsel sought to rely on a formula found in the English Butler Report of 1975.[56] This provided a defence to murder provided that the accused was suffering at the time from a form of mental disorder, and in the opinion of the jury this was such as to be an extenuating circumstance which ought to reduce the offence to manslaughter.[57] However, this attempt to introduce diminished responsibility into the law through the back door, as it were, was firmly rejected by the Supreme Court, on the grounds that it involved an unacceptable overlap between the proposed defence and insanity. If the accused had really been unable to control his actions, said Finlay CJ, he would have been entitled to an insanity verdict,[58] which involved no imputation of criminal liability and allowed for the accused to be detained only in so far and for so long as he continued to be a danger to the public.[59] A person found guilty of manslaughter, in contrast, was branded as a criminal and could be punished on that basis.[60] It was not possible that, having regard to these considerations, there could exist side by side with the law of insanity a defence of diminished responsibility which would in effect leave to an accused person and his advisers the choice as to whether to seek to have him branded as a criminal or whether to seek on the same facts the more humane and, in a sense, lenient decision, that he was not guilty of a crime by reason of insanity.[61]

Thirty years were to pass before the defence of diminished responsibility was finally introduced into Irish law. According to s. 6(1) of the Criminal Law (Insanity) Act 2005:

> Where a person is tried for murder and the jury or, as the case may be, the ... Court finds that the person –
>
> (a) did the act alleged;
> (b) was at the time suffering from a mental disorder; and
> (c) the mental disorder was not such as to justify finding him or her not guilty by reason of insanity, but was such as to diminish substantially his or her responsibility for the act, the jury or court, as the case may be, shall find the person not guilty of that offence but guilty of manslaughter on the ground of diminished responsibility.

This defence is more or less the same as that proposed by the Henchy Committee in 1978,[62] and differs from both the old and the new versions of its English counterpart in being closely aligned with the defence of insanity. Thus both defences require the trigger of a 'mental disorder' as defined by the Act.[63] Indeed, they are mutually exclusive, diminished responsibility being available only

---

55 Ibid.
56 Home Office, *Report of the Committee on Mentally Abnormal Offenders* (Cmnd 6244, 1975).
57 [1985] IR 517, 518–19.
58 Such a person would not, of course, fall under the M'Naghten Rules, but did come under the broad formulation given in *Doyle* v. *Wicklow County Council* (n. 38).
59 *Doyle* (n. 38) 522–3.
60 Ibid., 523.
61 Ibid.
62 Compare s. 6(1) with clause 18(1) of the Draft Criminal Justice (Mental Illness) Bill (n. 53).
63 This is defined in s. 1 of the Act as including mental illness, mental disability, dementia or any disease of the mind but not intoxication.

if the mental disorder is not such as to justify an insanity verdict.[64] It remains to be seen what problems this may cause to the courts in the Irish Republic,[65] but it will be argued below that the basic principle of dealing with the two defences in tandem was a sound one.

Provocation
The Irish Republic has no statutory provision corresponding to s. 3 of the Homicide Act 1957. It might therefore be supposed that the old law of provocation, with all its illogicalities and absurdities, would still apply in that jurisdiction. However, this is not the case. In 1978, shortly after the key decision of the House of Lords in *Camplin*,[66] the Irish Court of Criminal Appeal broke new ground of its own in *People (DPP)* v. *MacEoin*.[67] In this case, the trial judge had directed the jury that provocation was no defence to murder unless it was sufficient to deprive the accused of the capacity to form the necessary intention to kill or cause serious injury, as required by s. 4 of the Criminal Justice Act 1964.[68] This was held to be erroneous; provocation was not a factor negating the intention to kill or do serious injury, but something which gives the accused a defence notwithstanding the existence of such intent.[69] This would have been sufficient to dispose of the appeal, but bearing the possibility of a retrial in mind Kenny J also discussed the status of the objective 'reasonable man' test.[70] This, he admitted, was a well-established feature of the law in other jurisdictions, most notably England and Wales.[71] However, given that there was no Irish authority in point, and given the many criticisms that had been made of the objective test,[72] Kenny J concluded that it 'should be declared no longer part of our law'.[73] Somewhat confusingly, however, he added that the nature of the provocation had to be such as to justify the degree of force used, having regard to the state of mind of the accused at the relevant time.[74] If the prosecution could prove beyond reasonable doubt that the force used was excessive having regard to the provocation, the defence would fail.[75]

In the light of this case, it was not at all clear to what extent, if at all, the Irish defence of provocation included an objective element. For a while judges battled valiantly to make sense of the decision in *MacEoin*,[76] but at the end of the day the choice had to be made between abandoning either the 'reasonable retaliation' principle or the assertion of Kenny J that the objective test formed no part of the law. In a series of cases in the Court of Criminal Appeal following on from *MacEoin*,

---

64 This is no doubt due to the illogicality identified by Finlay CJ in *DPP* v. *O'Mahony*, namely allowing a defendant to choose whether to be innocent or to be branded a criminal.
65 Kennefick (n. 46).
66 [1978] AC 605.
67 [1978] IR 27; John Stannard, 'Towards a Normative Defence of Provocation' (2002) 66 Journal of Criminal Law 528.
68 [1978] IR 27, 30.
69 Ibid., 31. In this respect Kenny J followed the approach of Lord Goddard in *Attorney General for Ceylon* v. *Perera* [1953] AC 200, 206, and that of Lord Devlin in *Lee Chun-Chuen* v. *R* [1963] AC 220, 228 rather than that of Lord Simon in *Holmes* v. *DPP* [1946] AC 588, 598.
70 [1978] IR 27, 31; *Welsh* (1869) 11 Cox CC 336.
71 *Holmes* (n. 69) 32
72 Notably the dissenting judgment of Murphy J in *Moffa* v. *R* (1977) 13 ALR 225, 242.
73 [1978] IR 27, 34.
74 Ibid.
75 Ibid.,34–5.
76 John Stannard, 'Making Sense of *MacEoin*' (1998) 8 Irish Criminal Law Journal 20.

it was said that the question of proportionality merely went to the credibility of the defence case.[77] If the reaction of the accused was out of all proportion to the alleged provocation, that might very well lead the jury to disbelieve the evidence given by the accused, but at the end of the day the test to be applied was purely a subjective one.[78] The only issue for the judge is whether there is any evidence of provocation which, having regard to the accused's temperament, character and circumstances, might have caused him to lose control of himself at the time of the wrongful act.[79] If there is, the defence must be left to the jury.

Not all commentators in Ireland are entirely happy with this purely subjective test.[80] In particular, it has been argued that it fails to set any minimum standard of self-control,[81] and that it allows a defence to those whose loss of self-control is triggered by 'morally repugnant beliefs and values'.[82] This may be so, but at the end of the day there is no question of a complete acquittal in this kind of case; the accused will still be convicted of manslaughter, and there is nothing to stop the court passing a high sentence in unmeritorious cases. The only effect of ruling out a defence of provocation in cases of this sort is to eliminate the distinction between a person who kills in cold blood and one who does not.[83] In so far as it avoids the illogicalities inherent in the objective test, and the horrible morass into which it has led the courts across the Irish Sea, the subjective test in *MacEoin* would seem to have a lot to commend it.

Other partial defences
There are two other partial defences in the Irish Republic that are worth mentioning, not only for the sake of completeness but because they illustrate the general approach taken in that jurisdiction to this area of the law. The first of these is infanticide. This was provided for in the Infanticide Act 1949, which was in the same terms as provided for in the English Infanticide Act 1938, whereby a woman who caused the death of her child under the age of 12 months was to be punished for manslaughter rather than murder if at the relevant time the balance of her mind was disturbed either: (1) by reason of not having fully recovered from the effect of giving birth to the child, or (2) by reason of the effect of lactation consequent on the birth of the child.[84] When the defence of diminished responsibility was introduced in 2006,[85] a considerable overlap with infanticide was created, and this is recognised by s. 22 of the 2006 Act, which deleted the reference to lactation in s. 1 and substituted a reference to a 'mental disorder' within the meaning of the

---

77 See in particular *People (DPP)* v. *Mullane* (Unreported, Court of Criminal Appeal, 11 March 1997); *People (DPP)* v. *Bambrick* [1999] 2 ILRM 71; *People (DPP)* v. *Kelly* [2000] 2 IR 1; *People (DPP)* v. *Boyle* [2000] 2 IR 13; *People (DPP)* v. *Davis* [2001] IR 146; *People (DPP)* v. *McDonagh* [2001] 3 IR 201.
78 *People (DPP)* v. *Kelly* [2000] 2 IR 1, 5 (Barrington J).
79 *People (DPP)* v. *McDonagh* [2001] 3 IR 201, 208 (Murray J); *People (DPP)* v. *Sean Egan* [2010] IECCA 28.
80 McAuley and McCutcheon (n. 37) 872–7.
81 Ibid., 875.
82 Ibid., 877. In this context the authors give the example of the bigot who is outraged by the sight of a sexual relationship between two partners of a different race, loses his self-control and duly kills them both. But even here it can be argued that the law should distinguish between such a killing done in hot blood and one done in cold blood.
83 For a cogent criticism of the 'hot tempered man' argument, see John Smith and Brian Hogan, *Criminal Law* (4th edn, Butterworths, 1978) 305; Glanville Williams, 'Provocation and the Reasonable Man' [1954] Criminal Law Review 751.
84 Infanticide Act 1949, s. 1(3).
85 By s. 6 of the Criminal Law (Insanity) Act 2006 (n. 61).

2006 Act.[86] Moreover, the effect of a conviction for infanticide was amended to make it clear that the defendant could be dealt with in the same way as if she had been found guilty of manslaughter on the grounds of diminished responsibility.[87]

As well as this, there is the so-called doctrine of 'excessive defence', which was introduced by the Supreme Court in 1972 in *People (Attorney General)* v. *Dwyer*.[88] The accused in this case was charged with murder after killing the victim in a brawl outside a bar in Dublin. He raised the defence of self-defence, and the judge directed the jury that if he had used more force than was reasonably necessary in the circumstances, he should be convicted of murder.[89] However, his conviction for that crime was quashed by the Supreme Court on the ground that the jury had not been invited to consider whether, despite having used excessive force, he might have used no more force than he honestly believed to be necessary. In that event, he was entitled to be convicted of manslaughter only, the reasoning being that he would not have the necessary intention for murder as prescribed by the Criminal Justice Act 1964.[90] In the words of Butler J:

> A person is entitled to protect himself from unlawful attack. If he uses no more force than is reasonably necessary, he is acting lawfully and commits no crime even though he kills his assailant. If he uses more force than may objectively be considered necessary, his act is unlawful, and if he kills, the killing is unlawful. His intention, however, falls to be tested subjectively and it would appear logical to conclude that, if his intention in doing the unlawful act was primarily to defend himself, he should not be held to have the necessary intention to kill or cause serious injury. The result of this view would be that the killing, though unlawful, would be manslaughter only.[91]

In coming to this conclusion the court relied on the case of *Howe*, decided in the High Court of Australia.[92] Though this case had been disapproved by the English courts,[93] the effect of the Irish 1964 Act had not been to petrify the law and prevent its development on the lines of *Howe*; on the contrary, it pointed the way to that development by its insistence on the intention to kill or cause serious injury as an essential ingredient in the crime of murder, and by providing that the presumption that an accused person intended the natural and probable consequences of his act might be rebutted.[94] The doctrine of excessive defence was always doubtful in scope,[95] and was later abandoned in the place of its origin.[96] However, the defence is still alive and well in Irish law;[97] and what is of interest here is not the content of the defence as such, but the way in which the

---

86 Ibid., s. 22(a).
87 Ibid., s. 22(b).
88 [1972] 1 IR 416.
89 Ibid., 428.
90 Criminal Justice Act 1964, s. 4.
91 [1972] 1 IR 416, 431.
92 (1958) 100 CLR 448.
93 *Palmer* v. *R* [1971] AC 614; *McInnes* [1971] 1 WLR 1600.
94 [1972] 1 IR 416, 423–4 (Walsh J) and 432 (Butler J).
95 Sean Doran, 'The Doctrine of Excessive Defence' (1985) 36 Northern Ireland Legal Quarterly 341; Finbarr McAuley, 'Excessive Defence in Irish Law' in Stanley Yeo (ed.), *Partial Excuses to Murder* (Federation Press, 1992) 198; John E. Stannard, 'Excessive Defence in Northern Ireland' (1992) 43 Northern Ireland Legal Quarterly 147; D. Lanham, 'Death of a Doubtful Defence' (1988) 104 Law Quarterly Review 239.
96 *Zecevic* v. *DPP for Victoria* (1987) 61 ALJR 375.
97 *People (DPP)* v. *O'Carroll* [2004] 3 IR 521; *People (DPP)* v. *Barnes* [2007] 3 IR 130; *People (DPP)* v. *Nally* [2007] 4 IR 145.

Irish courts are willing to develop the law by admitting the existence of new mitigating defences as the need arises.

Northern Ireland

The position in Northern Ireland is somewhat different. Though the courts do not, as we have seen, regard themselves as bound by English decisions, the tendency has been to follow them fairly closely in matters where the law of the two jurisdictions is the same. This means that innovations of the type that we have just been discussing have not been replicated north of the border. The same is generally true of legislation; though criminal justice matters were devolved to Stormont from partition up to 1972, and have been again since 2010, a cautious approach was traditionally adopted in criminal law matters, with England being allowed to take the lead in matters of reform. Thus prior to the 1960s the only mitigating defences allowed were infanticide and provocation, and no attempt was made to introduce reforms on the lines of those in the Homicide Act 1957. One reason for this was that the murder rate was exceedingly low, and so the problems did not really arise.

Homicide and Criminal Responsibility Bill 1963
However, all of this was to change in the early 1960s. This saw a number of celebrated murder cases in Northern Ireland, including what remain two leading authorities on the law of insanity, *Bratty* v. *AG for Northern Ireland*,[98] and *AG for Northern Ireland* v. *Gallagher*.[99] As well as that, there was the case of Robert McGladdery, hanged in Belfast just before Christmas 1961 for the murder by strangulation of Pearl Gamble. This sort of murder would not have carried the death penalty in England, and following a campaign by the Northern Ireland Association for the Reform of the Law on Capital Punishment, a private member's bill was introduced into the Stormont Parliament by Sheelagh Murnaghan, a well-known member of the Bar and the Member for Queen's University.[100] The Homicide and Criminal Responsibility Bill contained a number of reforms, including the abolition of capital punishment,[101] the reform of the law of insanity,[102] and the introduction of measures similar to those found in the Homicide Act 1957.[103] At the end of the day it was the first of these that proved too much for the Members to stomach, and the bill was thrown out on Second Reading,[104] but William Craig, then Minister for Home Affairs, indicated that he was sympathetic to the other parts of the bill, and that measures for the reform of homicide law would be introduced in due course.[105]

Criminal Justice Act (NI) 1966
All of this came to pass in the Criminal Justice Act (NI) 1966. This Act was largely based on the 1963 Bill,[106] the main exception being that whereas the latter sought to abolish the death penalty in

---

98 [1963] AC 386.
99 [1963] AC 349.
100 W.N. Osborough, 'Homicide and Criminal Responsibility Bill (NI) 1963' (1965) 16 Northern Ireland Legal Quarterly 73.
101 Clause 12 of the Bill.
102 Ibid., clause 7.
103 Ibid., clauses 3, 4 and 8.
104 HC Deb. (NI), 55, 1012.
105 Ibid., 1003.
106 HC Deb. (NI), 62, 1314.

its entirety, the 1966 Act followed the Homicide Act 1957 in drawing a distinction between capital and non-capital murder. This particular aspect of the Act is now of purely historical significance.[107] Far more important are the provisions relating to insanity and the mitigating defences, to which we must now turn.

Insanity The defence of insanity is dealt with in ss. 1–3 of the Act. Section 3(1) gives a defence to any person found to be, at the time the offence is committed, an 'insane person' within the meaning of the Act. To find the meaning of 'insane person' we turn to s. 1 of the Act, which gives the following definition:

> "insane person" means a person who suffers from mental abnormality which prevents him –
>
> > (a) from appreciating what he is doing; or
> > (b) from appreciating that what he is doing is either wrong or contrary to law; or
> > (c) from controlling his own conduct ...

'Mental abnormality' is defined in turn as:

> an abnormality of mind which arises from a condition of arrested or retarded development of mind or any inherent causes or is induced by disease or injury ...

The effect of all this was to give Northern Ireland an insanity defence based largely on the broader version of the test in Stephen's Draft Code,[108] including the bracketed passages, but substituting for his tests of 'disease affecting ... [the] mind' and 'defective mental power' a test of 'mental abnormality' more or less identical to that provided for diminished responsibility in s. 2 of the Homicide Act 1957.

Impaired Mental Responsibility Section 5 of the 1966 Act introduced into Northern Ireland the defence of diminished responsibility, or 'impaired mental responsibility' as it was termed in the Act. According to s. 5:

> Where a person charged with murder has killed or was a party to the killing of another, and it appears to the jury that he was suffering from mental abnormality which substantially impaired his mental responsibility for his acts and omissions in doing or being a party to the killing, the jury shall find him not guilty of murder but shall find him guilty (whether as principal or accessory) of manslaughter.

This of course was more or less identical to s. 2 of the Homicide Act, the only difference being that there was no need for an exhaustive definition of 'mental abnormality', since this had already been defined in s. 1.

---

107 The death penalty was finally abolished in Northern Ireland by the Northern Ireland (Emergency Provisions) Act 1973, s. 1.
108 Above (n. 43).

Provocation Section 7 dealt with provocation. This was in the same terms as s. 3 of the Homicide Act, and read as follows:

> Where on a charge of murder there is evidence on which the jury can find that the person charged was provoked (whether by things done or by things said or both together) to lose his self-control the question whether the provocation was enough to make a reasonable man do as he did shall be left to be determined by the jury; and in determining that question the jury shall take into account everything both done and said according to the effect which, in their opinion, it would have on a reasonable man.

Other defences These were not the only defences provided for by the 1966 Act. There was also a defence provided in s. 6 of the Act for the case where a person charged with murder was found to be an insane person whose mental abnormality was of a temporary nature and caused solely by his own voluntary conduct in taking drink or drugs; such a person was to be convicted of manslaughter, though a murder conviction was to be brought in cases where the defendant was shown to have had the necessary intent to kill or do serious bodily harm immediately prior to taking such liquor or drugs.[109] As well as this, s. 14 provided for a defence of suicide pact, on the lines of s. 4 of the Homicide Act 1957. The overall effect was very pleasing; in essence, what the Act did was to provide for Northern Ireland a miniature code dealing with insanity and the mitigating defences (other than infanticide).

Coroners and Justice Act 2009
Unfortunately this elegant picture is spoiled somewhat by the Coroners and Justice Act 2009. Sections 54 to 56 of the Act, which replace provocation with the new defence of 'loss of control', extend to Northern Ireland,[110] so s. 7 of the 1966 Act is now repealed[111] and those who want to look up the law have now got to refer to the 2009 Act. Worse still, s. 53 of the 2009 Act replaces s. 5 of the 1966 Act with what is basically the new English definition of diminished responsibility found in s. 2 of the Homicide Act 1957, as substituted by s. 52 of the 2009 Act. The effect of this is to sever the connection between the defences of insanity and impaired mental responsibility in Northern Ireland; instead of the same test – that of 'mental abnormality' – applying to both defences, we now have a different test for diminished responsibility, namely that of 'abnormality of mental functioning' arising from a 'recognised mental condition'.[112] Whether and to what extent there is any difference between the two concepts remains to be seen; what is clear is that this is piecemeal legislation of the very worst sort.

---

109 This was obviously passed with the case of *AG for NI v. Gallagher* in mind (n. 99), but was also on the lines of a provision in the Japanese Penal Code: Osborough (n. 100) 75.

110 Coroners and Justice Act 2009, s. 181(3)(a). This was contrary to the usual practice in this area of the law of legislating separately for Northern Ireland by means of an Order in Council.

111 Ibid., s. 56(2)(b).

112 Criminal Justice Act (NI) 1966, s. 5(1)(a) as substituted. For some reason the reference in s. 53 is to a recognised *mental* condition, whereas that in s. 52 is to a recognised *medical* condition. Whether this is significant, or merely a typographical error, is not clear. (I am grateful to Dr Karen Brennan for pointing this out.)

The Wood and the Trees

The new provisions of the Coroners and Justice Act 2009 regarding mitigating defences are based on the recommendations of the Law Commission, but have been rightly criticised for having taken those recommendations completely out of the context in which they were made.[113] The recommendations in question were intended to form part of a broader reform of the law of homicide, including the abolition of the crude murder/manslaughter division, and its replacement with a more graduated ladder of offences consisting of first degree murder, second degree murder and manslaughter.[114] However, what the government then proceeded to do was to 'cherry pick' the proposals on mitigating defences and push them through Parliament in isolation.[115] In effect, the new provisions deal with the trees without giving any thought to the wood as a whole. To what extent can lessons be learned in this respect from the way the law has developed in Ireland?

First of all, there is the need to view the partial defences as a coherent system and not in isolation from each other. In this respect it helps to have the defences set out in the same statute. Both the Homicide Act 1957 and the Criminal Justice Act (NI) 1966 achieved this to some extent, but not entirely. In particular, neither statute dealt with infanticide, and only part of the law relating to provocation was set out; as well as this, there were unnecessary inconsistencies as between the different defences concerning the burden and standard of proof.[116] But the general approach was a good one. One undesirable result of the Coroners and Justice Act is that the law in England is now spread out over three separate statutes. The position in Northern Ireland is even worse, in that one of the statutes concerned (the Coroners and Justice Act 2009 itself, which sets out the defence of loss of control) is a UK statute, where one would not expect to find provisions relating to the criminal law of Northern Ireland.[117] This is not a helpful approach.

Second, there is the relationship between diminished responsibility and insanity. One of the most attractive features of the Criminal Justice Act (NI) 1966 was the neat way in which these two defences were dovetailed together, with a common test of 'mental abnormality' as defined by the Act.[118] As we have seen, the crude transplantation of the new English defence into the 1966 Act by the Coroners and Justice Act 2009 completely destroys this scheme, and creates new inconsistencies that did not exist before.[119] In the Republic of Ireland the Criminal Law (Insanity) Act 2005 still preserves a common test of 'mental disorder' for both defences; indeed, it goes even further than the Criminal Justice Act (NI) 1966 by making them mutually exclusive.[120] Whether this was either necessary or desirable is open to debate, but it is certainly better than the English

---

113   Jo Miles, 'The Coroners and Justice Act 2009: A "Dog's Breakfast" of Homicide Reform' [2009] 10 Archbold News 6.

114   Law Commission, *Murder, Manslaughter and Infanticide* (Law Com. No 304, 2006).

115   Miles (n. 113) 6.

116   This was particularly marked in Northern Ireland, where there were no less than three different standards of proof, with provocation requiring an evidential burden only (*Cocker* [1989] Crim LR 740), insanity and diminished responsibility requiring proof on the balance of probabilities (Criminal Justice Act (NI) 1966, ss. 2(1) (insanity) and 5(4) (impaired mental responsibility)), and suicide pact requiring proof beyond all reasonable doubt (1966 Act, s. 14(2)).

117   Criminal law provisions are normally to be found in the Acts of the old Stormont Parliament or in Orders in Council made under the direct rule provisions, both of which are found in the Northern Ireland Statutes. Provisions in UK statutes dealing with Northern Ireland law have to be looked up in the UK statutes, and are not replicated in the Northern Ireland series.

118   Above, page 163.

119   Ibid.

120   Above (n. 64).

approach which has two completely different tests for the two defences, one in the Homicide Act and the other in the antiquated M'Naghten Rules, which have somehow managed to survive for almost two centuries despite the criticisms to which they have been subjected from the start.

The third point concerns the theoretical basis for the defences. Most mitigating defences are excusatory in nature, but provocation has always been an exception to this, with its roots in the old doctrine of 'chance medley' and its close links to self-defence.[121] The tension between what has been termed 'imperfect justification' and 'compassionate excuse' has been apparent throughout the history of the defence,[122] but the tendency in English law since the Homicide Act had been towards the latter rationale. However, the new defence in the Coroners and Justice Act, with its requirement of a 'qualifying trigger', has moved strongly back towards a justificatory rationale.[123] This is in sharp contrast to the position in the Irish Republic, where as we have seen the subjective formulation adopted in *MacEoin* has more or less eliminated any justificatory requirement.[124] The reason why this approach was not favoured by the Law Commission is clear, namely the reluctance to make allowances for unmeritorious defendants such as those involved in road rage and honour killings.[125] However, drafting the defence so as to exclude these cases comes at the price of theoretical incoherence, not only as between different mitigating defences but also within the defence of loss of control itself.

During the debates on the Coroners and Justice Bill, Lord Lloyd of Hampstead described the new homicide provisions as a 'dog's breakfast'.[126] While the present author would not be so trenchant in his criticisms, it was certainly a missed opportunity. Back in 2004 the Law Commission warned against trying to deal with the partial defences in isolation without also addressing the offence of murder itself,[127] yet this is precisely what the Coroners and Justice Act 2009 went on to do. Worse still, it deals with those defences in a piecemeal way, without any reference either to the other mitigating defences or to the closely related topic of insanity. Though the law of Ireland is certainly not perfect in this respect, either north or south of the border, it does at least make some effort to look at the broader picture. What is really needed, in both parts of Ireland no less than in England and Wales, is a comprehensive review of the law of homicide as a whole. In England and Wales the Coroners and Justice Act 2009 may have made this less likely, but one is encouraged to hope that both the Oireachtas and the new Stormont Assembly will put this item rather higher on the agenda.

---

121 Andrew Simester and others, *Simester and Sullivan's Criminal Law* (4th edn, Hart Publishing, 2010), 394–6. The Irish doctrine of 'excessive defence' (nn. 88–97) also has significant justificatory elements.

122 Alan Norrie, 'The Coroners and Justice Act 2009 – Partial Defences to Murder: (1) Loss of Control' [2010] Criminal Law Review 275, 277–9.

123 Ibid., 288.

124 Above (n. 67).

125 Law Com. No 304, 2006 (n. 114), paras 5.27–5.32; Norrie (n. 122) 286.

126 Miles (n. 113) 7.

127 Law Commission, *Partial Defences to Murder* (Law Com. No 290, 2004) para. 2.8.

Chapter 11
Partial Defences to Murder in Scotland: An Unlikely Tranquillity

James Chalmers

Introduction

Given the debates on the appropriate scope of partial defences which have taken place in other jurisdictions – including, but by no means limited to, England and Wales – it is surprising that, north of the border, the issue has barely troubled law reformers or parliamentarians. The diminished responsibility defence has recently been put into statutory form,[1] but with only the most minor changes to the common law defence being made. More surprisingly, although provocation will form part of a review of the law of homicide by the Scottish Law Commission,[2] there is little impetus behind this exercise, which has been delayed for some years already in order to allow the Commission to carry out other projects.

This chapter aims to set out the current law of partial defences in Scotland and to offer some necessarily tentative hypotheses as to why they have been attended with little controversy. It does not offer a comprehensive critique of the current law, although some of the principal criticisms which may be made of it will be noted. Finally, it concludes by briefly assessing the likely future of partial defences in Scots law.

The Structure of Homicide and Partial Defences in Scots Law

Like its English counterpart (but without replicating English terminology), the Scottish law of homicide is bipartite in nature, distinguishing between murder and culpable homicide. As in England, murder carries a mandatory sentence of life imprisonment,[3] while sentencing for culpable homicide is at the discretion of the court.[4] Culpable homicide is, in the academic literature,[5] typically divided into 'voluntary' culpable homicide – cases which would be murder but for the presence of a partial defence – and 'involuntary' culpable homicide, which comprises cases either

---

[1] Criminal Justice and Licensing (Scotland) Act 2010, s. 168, inserting s. 51B into the Criminal Procedure (Scotland) Act 1995.

[2] Scottish Law Commission, *Eighth Programme of Law Reform* (Scot. Law Com. No 220, 2010) para. 2.13.

[3] Criminal Procedure (Scotland) Act 1995, s. 205.

[4] And so can range from admonition (see e.g. *HM Advocate* v. *Brady*, High Court of Justiciary, October 1996 (n. 21)) through to life imprisonment (*Kirkwood* v. *HM Advocate* 1939 JC 36).

[5] See Gerald Gordon, *The Criminal Law of Scotland* (3rd edn, W. Green, 2001), vol. 2 by Michael Christie, chs 25–6.

of an unlawful act resulting in death[6] or 'lawful act' culpable homicide where death is caused by recklessness on the part of the accused.[7]

Only two partial defences are formally recognised by Scots law: provocation and diminished responsibility.[8] Oddly, although provocation itself has given rise to little controversy in Scots law in recent years, the leading decision on the plea, *Drury* v. *HM Advocate*,[9] can fairly be regarded as the most controversial decision on Scots criminal law in recent memory. *Drury*, however, is controversial not for what it says about provocation, but for what it says about the structure of murder more generally. In that case, the appeal court attempted to define the offence of murder so as to set out conclusive conditions of liability, by arguing that defences (both full and partial) operated so as to negate *mens rea*.[10] On that basis, the court argued that it was wrong to speak of a partial defence 'reducing' murder to culpable homicide – even though it reverted to that terminology in the leading case on diminished responsibility, decided around the same time.[11]

This account of murder has been heavily criticised,[12] but it in fact has little relevance to the plea of provocation itself. The main objection which may be offered to it is that it threatened inexorably to undermine the general Scottish approach to mistake of fact in defences (particularly, but not exclusively, self-defence), which Scots law has consistently required to be based on reasonable grounds.[13] If defences operated because – as was said in *Drury* – the accused's motive served to negate *mens rea*, then that seemed to leave no room for a reasonableness requirement. Nevertheless, while not disowning the *Drury* analysis explicitly, the appeal court has since decided that this requirement remains unchanged.[14]

---

6   Exactly what qualifies as an 'unlawful act' for these purposes, beyond assault, is not entirely clear. See, most recently, *MacAngus* v. *HM Advocate; Kane* v. *HM Advocate* 2009 SLT 137.

7   This is not identical to gross negligence manslaughter in English law, as recklessness here is understood subjectively and requires an awareness of risk. The term 'lawful act' culpable homicide indicates only that the legality or otherwise of the act causing death *per se* is irrelevant. For both points, see *Transco plc* v. *HM Advocate* 2004 JC 29.

8   Cf. House of Lords Select Committee, *Report on Murder, Manslaughter and Life Imprisonment* (HL 1998–99, 78-I) para. 89. The Committee recommended that a partial defence of excessive self-defence should be recognised in English law, which (the Committee claimed) would bring English law into line with Scots law. This was news to Scots lawyers. See further James Chalmers, Christopher Gane and Fiona Leverick, 'Partial Defences to Homicide in the Law of Scotland: A Report to the Law Commission for England and Wales', in Law Commission, *Partial Defences to Murder: Overseas Studies* (Law Com. CP No 173 (Appendices), 2003) 151, 179–80.

9   2001 SLT 1013.

10   For criticism, see James Chalmers, 'Collapsing the Structure of Criminal Law' 2001 SLT (News) 241.

11   *Galbraith* v. *HM Advocate* 2002 JC 1. See also *HM Advocate* v. *Kerr* [2011] HCJAC 17.

12   For a full list of references, see James Chalmers and Fiona Leverick, 'Murder Through the Looking Glass' (2007) 11 Edinburgh Law Review 230, n. 2, where it is noted that 'Oddly, it appears that the only academic defence of *Drury* is be found in a paper on South African law written to assist the (English) Law Commission in its review of partial defences to murder.'

13   The leading case being *Owens* v. *HM Advocate* 1946 JC 119. See also *Jones* v. *HM Advocate* 1990 JC 160. The approach was different in rape and other sexual offences, where it was recognised in *Jamieson* v. *HM Advocate* 1994 JC 88 that an unreasonable mistake as to consent could negate *mens rea*, consent being an element of the offence and so distinct from a 'substantive defence'. That approach has now been abandoned by statute: see the Sexual Offences (Scotland) Act 2009, Part 1.

14   *Lieser* v. *HM Advocate* 2008 SLT 866. See Fiona Leverick, 'Unreasonable Mistake in Self-Defence' (2009) 13 Edinburgh Law Review 100.

It should be noted that at common law, it appears that partial defences in Scots law apply both to murder and attempted murder (the latter being reduced to assault).[15] In its recent review of diminished responsibility, however, the Scottish Law Commission concluded that this plea should not be available in respect of attempted murder.[16] That is unfortunate: it is illogical to label a person as having attempted to place himself within a class to which he could in fact never have been assigned,[17] and it makes little sense unless the sole rationale for recognising partial defences is thought to be the avoidance of the mandatory life sentence.[18]

Such is the formal structure of the law. Before turning in more detail to each of the two partial defences, it is necessary to explain how they fit within a wider context of broad prosecutorial discretion.

The 'Unofficial Categories' and the Role of Prosecutorial Discretion

The 'Unofficial Categories'

Although Scots law, as explained, gives formal recognition only to two partial defences, matters may in fact be rather more complex. Writing in 1978, Sir Gerald Gordon suggested that there are six 'unofficial categories', being 'certain circumstances in which as a matter of practice only culpable homicide is charged, although a charge of murder could properly be brought'.[19] These are infanticide, euthanasia, suicide pacts, necessity or coercion, killings 'in excess of duty' and homicide by omission.[20]

There is fairly clear evidence for the first three of these categories, although given that they involve the exercise of discretion they cannot be regarded as firm categories. In particular, it should not be assumed that all cases of euthanasia will necessarily result in the Crown accepting a plea of guilty to culpable homicide.[21] As regards the other two categories, they arise in part because

---

15 Brady v. HM Advocate 1986 JC 68; Salmond v. HM Advocate 1992 SLT 156 (provocation); HM Advocate v. Blake 1986 SLT 661; HM Advocate v. Kerr [2011] HCJAC 17 (diminished responsibility). The courts have not been required to consider what the appropriate verdict might be in respect of an attempt to kill not involving an assault. For discussion, see James Chalmers, 'Reforming the Pleas of Insanity and Diminished Responsibility: Some Aspects of the Scottish Law Commission's Discussion Paper' (2003) 8 Scottish Law and Practice Quarterly 79, 86–7.

16 This conclusion is given effect in s. 168 of the Criminal Justice and Licensing (Scotland) Act 2010, quoted below.

17 James Chalmers and Fiona Leverick, Criminal Defences and Pleas in Bar of Trial (W. Green, 2006) para. 11.18.

18 The Commission recognised the issue of fair labelling which arises here, but rejected this argument on the basis that reducing attempted murder to assault was not analogous to reducing murder to culpable homicide (Scottish Law Commission, Report on Insanity and Diminished Responsibility (Scot. Law Com. No 195, 2004) para. 3.49). That may be correct, but as an argument it is incomplete.

19 Gerald Gordon, The Criminal Law of Scotland (2nd edn, 1978) para. 25.02. In his third edition of Gordon's work, Michael Christie prefers the term 'unofficial factors' but retains Gordon's sixfold categorisation: Gordon, Criminal Law, 3rd edn (n. 5) vol. 2, para. 25.02. Given the Crown's approach to cases where a woman has killed an abusive partner (discussed below), it may be that this categorisation is now incomplete.

20 Gordon, Criminal Law, 2nd edn (n. 19) paras 25.02–25.07.

21 Indeed, while Gordon described this as an 'unofficial category', he noted that there were 'no reported cases of this' (ibid., para. 25.03). In HM Advocate v. Brady, High Court of Justiciary, October 1996, the Crown

of the absence of legislation analogous to that which exists south of the border: Scots law has no equivalent of the Suicide Act 1961[22] or the Infanticide Act 1938. Given Scots law's long-standing recognition of the defence of diminished responsibility (discussed below), there will be some cases of infanticide where the mother is entitled to that partial defence,[23] and the Scottish practice has been described as a presumption by the Crown that she is of diminished responsibility.[24]

The remaining categories are, however, open to more doubt. The Scottish courts have yet to decide whether necessity or coercion are available as either full or partial defences to murder,[25] and there is no evidence of the Crown regarding them as partial defences for practical purposes (although there is equally nothing to bar such a course). Killing 'in excess of duty' is also a speculative category, although it is consistent with Scots law's continued recognition of the defence of superior orders.[26] Most cases of killing by omission will in practice amount to culpable homicide and not murder, but this is a pattern seen also in English law and may be due solely to the difficulty of establishing the *mens rea* of murder where death has been brought about in this way.[27] Indeed, the Crown has more recently made an unsuccessful attempt to bring a prosecution for murder where a mother's alleged inaction in the face of a violent assault on her child was argued to have caused the child's death.[28]

Understanding the Significance of Prosecutorial Discretion

Even if the scope of the unofficial categories is less extensive than might seem to be the case at first glance, they illustrate a distinctive feature of the Scottish criminal justice system, which is the weight given to prosecutorial discretion. Of course, the significance of such discretion should not be overstated: it is an inevitable feature of any criminal justice system, even one which professes to disdain it, and it may conversely be exercised only to a limited extent even in systems which laud it.[29]

Nevertheless, the discretionary power of the Scottish prosecutor is significant. One clear demonstration of this is the fact that, while the English courts were prepared to declare that withdrawing artificial feeding and treatment from a patient in a permanent vegetative state was not

---

initially pursued a charge of murder in a case of a man who had killed his brother, who was suffering from a degenerative illness and had pleaded for his life to be ended. A plea of guilty to culpable homicide was accepted and the accused was admonished. See 'Brother in Mercy Killing Case Escapes Prison Sentence', *The Times*, 15 October 1996. See also Martyn McLaughlin, 'We'll Consider Suicide Law Guidance', *The Scotsman*, 24 October 2009, who notes a two-year prison sentence in a 1980 case where a 78-year-old man killed his senile wife.

22 For discussion, see James Chalmers, 'Assisted Suicide: Jurisdiction and Discretion' (2010) 14 Edinburgh Law Review 295. See also Gerald Gordon, 'Suicide Pacts' 1958 SLT (News) 209.

23 *HM Advocate* v. *Abercrombie* (1896) 2 Adam 163 is a case where the partial defence of diminished responsibility was left to the jury in such circumstances, although in the event they acquitted on the ground of insanity.

24 Gordon, *Criminal Law*, 2nd edn (n. 19) para. 25.02.

25 See, however, *Collins* v. *HM Advocate* 1991 SCCR 898, 902, where the trial judge (Lord Allanbridge) directed the jury that coercion was not available. In doing so, he appears to have adopted the language used by Lord Mackay of Clashfern in *R* v. *Howe* [1987] AC 417, 456.

26 See Chalmers and Leverick, *Criminal Defences* (n. 17) ch. 6.

27 Something which is not, of course, impossible: see e.g. *R* v. *Gibbins and Proctor* (1919) 13 Cr App R 134.

28 *Bone* v. *HM Advocate* 2006 SLT 164.

29 See H. Jung, 'Criminal Justice – A European Perspective' [1993] Criminal Law Review 237, 241–2.

a criminal offence,[30] the Scottish courts declined to rule on the matter and instead invited the Lord Advocate (the head of the Scottish prosecution service) to issue a policy statement on when such action could be taken without risking a criminal prosecution.[31] Such a statement was duly issued,[32] and the approach of the Scottish courts to such prosecutorial statements means that it remains binding on the Crown and could be pleaded as a bar to any prosecution of a doctor who acted in accordance with its terms.[33]

Perhaps the most striking example of the scope of the Scottish prosecutor's discretion is found in the diary of Lord Stott, who was a judge of the High Court of Justiciary from 1967 until 1984. Immediately prior to his elevation to the bench, he served as Lord Advocate. In his diary he records a 'most interesting murder case' which arose during his final months in that role:

> ... the case of a teacher's wife who had murdered her invalid father-in-law. The invalid was a cantankerous old man who was incapable of looking after himself and gave endless trouble in his son's household, where as there was nowhere else for him to go he had been dumped for the purpose of being looked after. The daughter-in-law was a diabetic, with a plentiful supply of insulin to inject herself; and one night when she got the old man to herself she injected sufficient of it into him to kill him.[34]

The death had initially been certified as due to natural causes, but suspicion had been aroused and the true facts determined by prolonged scientific testing. Lord Stott continued:

> It seemed obvious that the young woman had acted only when driven to distraction by the old man's tantrums; and I soon made up my mind to mark the papers "No Pro" [no proceedings] – after which Bowen and I set out finding sufficiently good grounds in law for this decision, which we had little difficulty in doing.[35]

Discretion and Partial Defences

As extreme as this case is, it hints at the role which discretion may play in mitigating the effects of restrictively defined partial defences. This is particularly significant given the extent to which the context of domestic violence has been influential in reviews of this area elsewhere.[36] Here, the definitions of provocation and diminished responsibility found in Scots law are such as to make them of only very limited applicability in cases where an individual kills an abusive partner.

---

30   *Airedale NHS Trust* v. *Bland* [1993] AC 789.

31   *Law Hospital NHS Trust* v. *Lord Advocate* 1996 SC 301.

32   See 1996 SLT 867.

33   See *Lockhart* v. *Deighan* 1985 SLT 549; and Chalmers and Leverick, Criminal Defences (n. 17) ch. 17.

34   George Gordon Stott, *Judge's Diary* (Mercat Press, 1995) 42–3. See also Peter Duff, 'The Prosecution Service: Independence and Accountability', in P. Duff and N. Hutton (eds), *Criminal Justice in Scotland* (Ashgate, 1999) 115.

35   Stott, *Judge's Diary* (n. 34) 43. Stanley Bowen was the Deputy Crown Agent at the time.

36   When the Home Secretary asked the Law Commission to review partial defences to murder in 2003, the Commission was 'asked to have particular regard to the impact of the partial defences in the context of domestic violence': Law Commission, *Partial Defences to Murder* (Law Com. No 290, 2004) 1. See also e.g. New Zealand Law Commission, *Some Criminal Defences with Particular Reference to Battered Defendants* (New Zealand Law Commission No 73, 2001); New Zealand Law Commission, *The Partial Defence of Provocation* (New Zealand Law Commission No 98, 2007).

Despite this, there appears to be no clear example, at least in recent memory, of a woman who killed an abusive partner being convicted of murder in Scotland. In the literature, the starting point is implicitly regarded as the 1979 case of *HM Advocate* v. *Greig*,[37] where the accused killed her abusive partner as he sat in a chair, probably dozing. The trial judge allowed the jury to consider the plea of provocation, while emphasising that it required violent or threatening conduct immediately prior to the killing – something which was clearly absent. Nevertheless, the jury returned a verdict of culpable homicide.

Since then, cases where women have killed violent partners seem almost invariably to have been dealt with by the Crown accepting a plea of guilty to culpable homicide.[38] There are two well-known instances where a murder prosecution was pursued, but in one of those the jury accepted a plea of self-defence (something which appears tenuous on the facts of the case).[39] The other is *Galbraith* v. *HM Advocate*,[40] which eventually led to the appeal court rewriting the Scottish defence of diminished responsibility, quashing the conviction and ordering a retrial. In that case, a murder charge appears to have been pressed primarily because the Crown did not accept Kim Galbraith's claims of abuse; at the retrial, a plea to culpable homicide was accepted.[41]

Diminished Responsibility

The doctrine of diminished responsibility is apt to fill Scots lawyers with a faint sense of nationalistic pride. It is generally regarded as having originated in this jurisdiction, with roots which are centuries old.[42] Since then, it has been adopted by English law in the Homicide Act 1957,[43] and discussion of the doctrine (and its Scottish origins) has spread as far as the unlikely venue of the International Criminal Tribunal for the Former Yugoslavia.[44]

The doctrine crystallised in a series of cases in the late nineteenth and early twentieth century, where individual judges – primarily one judge, Lord Deas – permitted juries to consider whether they might return a verdict of culpable homicide in cases of what might be called 'murder with

---

37 High Court of Justiciary, May 1979. See Christopher Gane, Charles Stoddart and James Chalmers, *A Casebook on Scottish Criminal Law* (4th edn, W. Green, 2009) 444.

38 See the cases cited by C. Connelly, 'Women Who Kill Violent Men' 1996 Juridical Review 215; Chalmers, Gane and Leverick (n. 8) 181–3.

39 *HM Advocate* v. *McNab*, High Court of Justiciary, August 1995. See Connelly (n. 38) 216.

40 2002 JC 1.

41 *The Scotsman*, 22 May 2002.

42 The foundational case is generally regarded as being *HM Advocate* v. *Dingwall* (1867) 5 Irv 466, although it can be traced back rather further: see George Mackenzie, *The Laws and Customs of Scotland in Matters Criminal* (2nd edn, Symson 1699) 9; *John Somerville* (1704) Hume i, 42 and 44. For discussion of the history, see Nigel Walker, *Crime and Insanity in England, Volume 1: The Historical Perspective* (Edinburgh University Press, 1968) ch. 8; Chalmers and Leverick, *Criminal Defences* (n. 17) paras 11.03–11.09.

43 Section 2 of which was, according to the Attorney General, designed to 'introduce into English law the Scottish doctrine of diminished responsibility'. See HC Deb., 27 November 1956, col. 318.

44 *Prosecutor* v. *Delalic and Others* (IT-96-21), International Criminal Tribunal for the Former Yugoslavia (Appeals Chamber), 20 February 2001. See also, in the United States, *US* v. *Pohlot*, 827 F.2d 889, 904 (3rd Cir 1987).

extenuating circumstances'.[45] Not all judges accepted this development,[46] but in the absence of a criminal appeal court at the time there was no opportunity for the matter to be authoritatively resolved. By the time that court was created (in 1926)[47] the doctrine appears to have been too firmly established to be dislodged.[48]

The Modern Law of Diminished Responsibility

The modern law of diminished responsibility is set out in the leading case of *Galbraith* v. *HM Advocate*.[49] Prior to *Galbraith*, juries had been directed on the basis of a set of criteria said to derive from the charge given to the jury by the Lord Justice-Clerk (the second most senior Scottish judge) in the case of *HM Advocate* v. *Savage*.[50] On the basis of *Savage*, it was said that diminished responsibility required aberration or weakness of mind; mental unsoundness; a state of mind bordering on insanity and some form of mental disease.[51]

As 'criteria' these are obviously unsatisfactory,[52] but their most important practical consequence was the requirement for 'mental disease', which led the courts to exclude pleas based on conditions such as personality disorders.[53] In *Galbraith*, where a woman killed her husband after (she alleged) he had abused her for some years, the trial judge therefore directed the jury that they could not find diminished responsibility established on the basis of evidence of a 'form of post-traumatic stress disorder' or 'learned helplessness'.[54] The defence accordingly failed.

On appeal, this was held to be a misdirection: the 'criteria' supposedly found in *Savage* had been a misreading of the directions given by the trial judge in that case, who was merely giving examples of the kind of cases which might amount to diminished responsibility rather than laying down cumulative criteria.[55] Accordingly, the court was required to reformulate the test, concluding that the question to be asked by the jury was as follows:

> [whether] at the relevant time, the accused was suffering from an abnormality of mind which substantially affected the ability of the accused, as compared with a normal person, to determine or control his acts.[56]

---

45 *HM Advocate* v. *Dingwall* (1867) 5 Irv 466 at 479. For the other cases, which run from *John Tierney* (1875) 4 Coup 152 to *HM Advocate* v. *Abercrombie* (1896) 2 Adam 163, see Chalmers and Leverick, *Criminal Defences* (n. 17) para. 11.06.

46 Dissenters were (somewhat tentatively) Lord Stormonth Darling in *HM Advocate* v. *Aitken* (1902) 4 Adam 88 and (very explicitly) Lord Johnston in *HM Advocate* v. *Higgins* (1913) 7 Adam 229.

47 Criminal Appeal (Scotland) Act 1926.

48 See, for example, *Muir* v. *HM Advocate* 1933 JC 46, the first case where the phrase 'diminished responsibility' was judicially used.

49 2002 JC 1.

50 1923 JC 49.

51 *Connelly* v. *HM Advocate* 1990 JC 349.

52 In *Lindsay* v. *HM Advocate* 1997 JC 19 they led to the odd result that the trial judge felt it necessary to give the jury directions on the defence of insanity (so that they could understand what might be meant by a state of mind bordering on insanity) even though insanity was not directly in issue.

53 *Williamson* v. *HM Advocate* 1994 JC 149.

54 *Galbraith* v. *HM Advocate* 2002 JC 1 [7].

55 As Lord Justice-General Rodger explained, having consulted newspaper reports of the case which provided more factual background than that available in the law reports, if they had been intended as cumulative criteria, there would have been no basis for leaving Savage's defence to the jury. See ibid. [34]–[39].

56 *Galbraith* [54].

This is worth comparing with s. 2 of the Homicide Act 1957 which (prior to s. 52 of the Coroners and Justice Act 2009 coming into force) defined the English plea of diminished responsibility in the following terms:[57]

> ... such abnormality of mind (whether arising from a condition of arrested or retarded development of mind or any inherent causes or induced by disease or injury) as substantially impaired his mental responsibility for his acts and omissions in doing or being a party to the killing.

Section 2 was referred to only very incidentally by the *Galbraith* court, but the similarities are obvious. There are only two real differences: first, the 'normal person' is invoked as a comparator, but such a comparison had been read into the 1957 Act from its inception.[58] Secondly, and more significantly, the *Galbraith* court's formulation does not restrict 'abnormality of mind' in the same way as the (much-criticised)[59] bracketed causes found in s. 2. Instead, the *Galbraith* court approached this issue by identifying two specific 'abnormalities' – voluntary intoxication and 'psychopathic personality disorder' – which fell to be excluded from the scope of the defence for 'sound policy reasons'.[60]

The Scottish Law Commission's Review: Statutory Restatement

Only a matter of months after the decision in *Galbraith*, the Scottish Law Commission was asked to undertake a review of the law of insanity and diminished responsibility.[61] The reference to the Commission was the result of a (pre-*Galbraith*) recognition that the defence was 'obscure, and difficult to apply in individual cases'.[62] The Commission noted that this point had been addressed by *Galbraith* and that various practitioners had expressed 'general satisfaction' with the newly formulated test.[63]

While recommending that the defence be set out in statute, the Commission therefore confined its proposals for change to the policy exclusions identified in *Galbraith*, concluding that personality disorders should not be excluded from the scope of the plea. On intoxication, the Commission was more circumspect, noting Scots law's general rejection of any defence (or denial of *mens rea*) based on voluntary intoxication.[64] While adhering to that rule, the Commission recommended that diminished responsibility should not be excluded where the accused was intoxicated but this intoxication co-existed with an underlying condition which provided a basis for the plea,[65] or where

---

57 See further James Chalmers, 'Abnormality and Anglicisation: First Thoughts on *Galbraith* v. *HM Advocate (No 2)*' (2002) 6 Edinburgh Law Review 108.

58 See *R* v. *Byrne* [1960] 2 QB 396, 403, where Lord Parker CJ defined 'abnormality of mind' as 'a state of mind so different from that of ordinary human beings that the reasonable man would term it abnormal'.

59 See, for example, Edward Griew, 'The Future of Diminished Responsibility' [1988] Criminal Law Review 75.

60 *Galbraith* [43]. For criticism, see James Chalmers, 'Reforming the Pleas of Insanity and Diminished Responsibility: Some Aspects of the Scottish Law Commission's Discussion Paper' (2003) 8 Scottish Law and Practice Quarterly 79, 88–94.

61 See Scottish Law Commission, *Report on Insanity and Diminished Responsibility* (n. 18) para. 1.1.

62 Millan Committee, *Review of the Mental Health (Scotland) Act 1984* (SE/2001/56, 2001) ch. 29 para. 55.

63 Scottish Law Commission, *Report on Insanity and Diminished Responsibility* (n. 18) para. 3.4.

64 The leading case being *Brennan* v. *HM Advocate* 1977 JC 38.

65 In this respect, the Commission referred approvingly to *R* v. *Dietschmann* [2003] UKHL 10, [2003] 1 AC 1209, but appears to have wrongly interpreted *Dietschmann* as laying down or at least supporting a causal

the intoxication was the consequence of this underlying condition. In due course, the Scottish Parliament passed the Criminal Justice and Licensing (Scotland) Act 2010, s. 168 of which defines the plea of diminished responsibility in the following terms:[66]

Diminished responsibility

(1) A person who would otherwise be convicted of murder is instead to be convicted of culpable homicide on grounds of diminished responsibility if the person's ability to determine or control conduct for which the person would otherwise be convicted of murder was, at the time of the conduct, substantially impaired by reason of abnormality of mind.

(2) For the avoidance of doubt, the reference in subsection (1) to abnormality of mind includes mental disorder.

(3) The fact that a person was under the influence of alcohol, drugs or any other substance at the time of the conduct in question does not of itself –

(a) constitute abnormality of mind for the purposes of subsection (1), or
(b) prevent such abnormality from being established for those purposes.

(4) It is for the person charged with murder to establish, on the balance of probabilities, that the condition set out in subsection (1) is satisfied.

(5) In this section, "conduct" includes acts and omissions.

The Difficulty of Evaluating the Scottish Approach

In the absence of either empirical research as to the operation of the diminished responsibility defence post-*Galbraith*,[67] or further cases having come before the appeal court, the most that can be said is that the defence *seems* to work, as the practitioners consulted by the Scottish Law Commission suggested. Whether it works because of or in spite of its legal formulation is another question. As Mackay has noted, an obscurely worded diminished responsibility plea means that 'the court and the experts are sometimes able to enter into a benevolent conspiracy', going beyond what the statutory language can really be said to justify.[68]

---

test (that is, asking whether the abnormality of mind was a substantial cause of the killing). *Dietschmann* does not in fact do this, and the legislation flowing from the Commission's proposals does not require it either. See, however, the trial judge's charge to the jury in *HM Advocate* v. *McLeod*, High Court of Justiciary, February 2002, noted by J. Casey, 'Intoxication and Diminished Responsibility' 2003 Juridical Review 331.

66 By inserting a new s. 51B into the Criminal Procedure (Scotland) Act 1995. Subject to some minor differences in drafting technique, this replicates exactly the formulation found in the Commission's draft bill: see Scottish Law Commission, *Report on Insanity and Diminished Responsibility* (n. 18) 80–81. Section 168 was still to be brought into force at the time of writing.

67 Details of some trial level cases post-*Galbraith* can be found in J.H.M. Crichton, R. Darjee and D. Chiswick, 'Diminished Responsibility in Scotland: New Case Law' (2004) 15 Journal of Forensic Psychiatry and Psychology 552.

68 Ronnie Mackay, 'The New Diminished Responsibility Plea' [2010] Criminal Law Review 290, 294.

It seems that Scottish practitioners are conscious of the framework set out by the court and ready to work within it. So, in *Galbraith*, Lord Rodger attempted to formulate the defence 'in colloquial terms' as meaning that 'there must, unfortunately, have been something far wrong with the accused, which affected the way he acted'.[69] This can hardly be taken as a formal medical test, but shortly afterwards a psychiatrist was quoted as having used exactly this form of words in giving evidence prior to sentencing in a case where the accused had pleaded guilty to culpable homicide under diminished responsibility.[70]

The statutory language of the 2010 Act is in some respects similar to that found in s. 52 of the Coroners and Justice Act 2009. The English legislation goes further in defining what is meant by 'abnormality of mental functioning' (the term now preferred in English law to 'abnormality of mind') and 'substantially impaired'.[71] The language of s. 52 is generally consistent with Scots law, save for the requirement that the abnormality of mental functioning must cause or be 'a significant contributory factor in causing' the defendant to carry out the conduct in question in order for the defence to succeed. A causal requirement such as this is deeply problematic,[72] and it is fortunate that it is not found in the Scottish legislation.[73]

Provocation

The foundations of the modern doctrine of provocation in Scots law can be found in David Hume's 'Commentaries on the Laws of Scotland, Respecting Crimes'. The continued use of this work (and other older Scottish texts) today reflects the particular status which Scots law gives to certain historical works as 'institutional writings'.[74] Works such as Hume's *Commentaries* are regarded as authoritative statements of the law at the time when they were written, and the relative lack of statutory – and, in some respects, even judicial – development of the law since then means that they remain of practical relevance even centuries later.[75]

For Hume, who traced provocation's history to the ancient distinction between murder and 'slaughter on suddenty, or *chaude melle*',[76] it was important to stress that the plea was restricted in nature compared to English law. English law (Hume believed) held that any assault by the victim on the killer meant that manslaughter rather than murder was the appropriate verdict,[77] whereas

---

69 *Galbraith* v. *HM Advocate* 2002 JC 1 [51].

70 *HM Advocate* v. *Gorrie*, High Court of Justiciary, August 2003. See *The Herald*, 15 August 2003.

71 These terms are not formally defined in Scots law, but some guidance which might be offered to juries is suggested in Judicial Studies Committee, *Jury Manual: Some Notes for the Guidance of the Judiciary* (2011) pages 14.3 and 14.4.

72 Mackay (n. 68) 297–300.

73 Somewhat surprisingly, the Scottish Law Commission did not discuss whether a causal requirement should form part of the plea and, as noted at n. 65 above, appears to have assumed in the context of intoxication and diminished responsibility that this was in fact the case.

74 See further T.B. Smith, 'Authors and Authority' (1972–1973) 12 JSPTL 3.

75 But not, however, binding on the courts. Therefore, in *S* v. *HM Advocate* 1989 SLT 469, the High Court acknowledged Hume's clear statement of the marital rape exemption but doubted whether it had ever formed part of Scots law (suggesting that Hume had borrowed the notion from Hale) and decided that even if it had formed part of Scots law this was no longer the case. This was shortly before the English courts abolished the exemption: *R* v. *R* [1992] 1 AC 599.

76 David Hume, *Commentaries on the Laws of Scotland, Respecting Crimes* (4th edn, Bell & Bradfute, 1844) by B.R. Bell i, 241. This David Hume was the nephew of the philosopher of the same name.

77 Ibid., 247.

Scots law required that the accused must have been 'in the situation of an assaulted and a grossly injured person ... constrained to strike, by the violence he was suffering at the moment'.[78] In this way, provocation as understood by Hume was close to a plea of excessive self-defence,[79] and this restrictive approach has influenced Scots law to the present day. The one anomaly, however – and Hume acknowledged that it was an anomaly[80] – was that provocation could also be pleaded where a husband killed an 'adulterer caught in the fact'.[81]

The Development of the Modern Law of Provocation

There are two aspects to the development of the modern law of provocation. The first is the intermittent reaffirmation of the requirement for a recognised provocation in the form of either violence or infidelity. Verbal provocation has been firmly rejected by the Scottish courts. Matters could have been very different, because when the bill which became the Homicide Act 1957 was passing through Parliament, consideration was given to applying the relevant section to Scotland, and so allowing provocation to be made out by 'things done or by things said or by both together'.[82] The Lord Advocate of the time, however, asserted that there was nothing in Scots law as it stood which would prevent a judge leaving provocation by words to a jury.[83] It is difficult to find any basis for that statement in the case law or textbooks as they stood at the time,[84] and the appeal court was subsequently to rule out the availability of verbal provocation in emphatic terms.[85]

The law has, however, changed more significantly with regard to provocation by adultery. Here, the plea was formerly thought to be narrowly drawn, and available only to a 'husband instantly killing the seducer of his wife, when caught in the act of adultery'.[86] In the wartime case of *HM Advocate* v. *Hill*,[87] the plea was allowed where the accused (a soldier returning home on leave) shot both his wife and her lover after they confessed to adultery in his presence. Just as the courts have permitted this plea to be based on a confession of adultery rather than cases *in flagrante delicto*, so it has also been extended to instances where the parties are not married but are in a relationship of fidelity.[88]

---

78 Ibid.
79 See Chalmers and Leverick, *Criminal Defences* (n. 17) para. 10.06.
80 Hume (n. 76) i 246.
81 Ibid., 248, and see *James Christie* (1731) Maclaurin 625.
82 Homicide Act 1957, s. 3.
83 See HC Deb., 28 January 1957, cols 769–88. The Lord Advocate's statement is at col. 784.
84 See Gordon, *Criminal Law*, 3rd edn (n. 5) vol. 2 paras 25.26–25.28; Chalmers and Leverick, *Criminal Defences* (n. 17) paras 10.13–10.14. Cf., however, T.B. Smith, 'Scotland' in G.W. Keeton (ed.), *The British Commonwealth: The Development of its Laws and Constitutions* vol. 1 (Stevens, 1955) 603 at 732.
85 *Thomson* v. *HM Advocate* 1986 SLT 281; *Cosgrove* v. *HM Advocate* 1986 SLT 281. *Berry* v. *HM Advocate* (1976) SCCR (Supp) 156 and *Stobbs* v. *HM Advocate* 1983 SCCR 190, which suggested a more liberal approach to verbal provocation, must now be disregarded. See, however, the peculiar discussion found in *Anderson* v. *HM Advocate* [2010] HCJAC 9, 2010 SCL 584 [18], which suggests that verbal provocation is available in Scots law. These comments were made without reference to the prior case law and must be regarded as an aberration.
86 John Macdonald, *A Practical Treatise on the Criminal Law of Scotland* (4th edn, 1929) 138–9.
87 1941 JC 59. See also the earlier case of *HM Advocate* v. *McWilliam*, High Court of Justiciary, November 1940 (see *The Times*, 6 November 1940) where a husband killed his wife after finding letters from another man in her handbag, and pleaded provocation successfully.
88 *McKay* v. *HM Advocate* 1991 JC 95. The relationship need not be heterosexual: *HM Advocate* v. *McKean* 1997 JC 32.

The courts have, however, stressed that in order to found the defence, a confession of infidelity must be 'clear and unequivocal' and accepted by the accused.[89] The plea has therefore failed in two cases where the provocation consisted of a statement by the deceased that the accused was not the father of their child, in one case because the accused already knew that the deceased had been seeing other men around the time of the child's conception,[90] and in another because he asserted that he had not believed the (repeatedly made) claim but had been provoked into killing her to stop her making it.[91]

The Law as it Now Stands: Two Separate Defences

Following recent case law, it may now be said that there are two different forms of provocation in Scots law.[92] The first form requires first, provocation by violence; secondly, a loss of self-control; and thirdly, a 'reasonable or proportionate relationship between the conduct amounting to the provocation and the act of the accused'.[93]

In *Drury v. HM Advocate*,[94] however, the appeal court held that the nature of provocation by infidelity was such as to make a proportionality test unworkable.[95] Accordingly, this plea now requires first, provocation in the form of a revelation of infidelity; secondly, a loss of self-control; and thirdly, a reaction such as that which might have been expected from the ordinary person.

The 'ordinary person' test – not previously a feature of Scots law – was adopted against a background of considerable difficulty and controversy over the application of that test elsewhere.[96] The Scottish courts have simply not been required to date to consider the extent to which that test may be subjectivised by reference to the accused's personal characteristics.[97] In practical terms, such a point may not be particularly likely to arise, because the appeal court has firmly rejected the suggestion that the 'ordinary person' test might, post-*Drury*, be relevant to cases of provocation by violence, which must still be determined by reference to a test of proportionality.[98] Its sphere of operation is therefore very limited.

---

89 The plea can, however, be founded on a 'substantially different' confession by a partner whom the accused already knew had been unfaithful on another occasion: *Rutherford* v. *HM Advocate* 1998 JC 34.

90 *McKay* (n. 88).

91 *McCormack* v. *HM Advocate* 1993 SLT 1158. See also *McCormack* v. *HM Advocate* 2003 JC 1; *McCormack* v. *HM Advocate* [2005] HCJAC 38.

92 Michael Christie, 'The Coherence of Scots Criminal Law: Some Aspects of *Drury* v. *HM Advocate*' 2002 Juridical Review 273, 285.

93 *Robertson* v. *HM Advocate* 1994 JC 245, 249.

94 2001 SLT 1013.

95 It might, of course, be argued that because lethal violence is never a proportionate response to infidelity, the plea should be barred entirely in such cases. The court was conscious of these arguments but took the view that such a change would be for Parliament to make (see, in particular, Lord Nimmo Smith at [9] and Lord Mackay of Drumadoon at [3]).

96 This was acknowledged by Lord Justice-General Rodger in *Drury*: see [29].

97 Cf. *Cochrane* v. *HM Advocate* 2001 SCCR 655, where it is noted that such characteristics would not normally be taken into account in applying full defences but that provocation's status as a partial defence might warrant a different approach.

98 *Gillon* v. *HM Advocate* 2007 JC 24. For discussion, see James Chalmers and Fiona Leverick, 'Murder Through the Looking Glass' (2007) 11 Edinburgh Law Review 230, where it is argued (233–4) that reliance on a proportionality test may not successfully exclude questions of the relevance of an accused's personal characteristics.

Why Has there Been No Impetus for Reform?

Given just how controversial the partial defence of provocation has proved in the academic literature and other jurisdictions – to the extent of calls being made for its abolition[99] – why has Scotland remained seemingly immune? One answer may be that provocation has simply not given rise to the same difficulties here as it has elsewhere. Alan Norrie has summarised the 'three main problems' which the Law Commission identified with the English plea of provocation prior to the 2009 Act's reforms in the following terms:

> ... provocation had become too loose so that a judge may be obliged to leave the issue to the jury where the conduct or words relied upon are trivial; the concept of loss of self-control had proved to be troublesome, giving rise to serious problems, to complaints of gender bias, and of the law having to be stretched in the "slow burn" type cases; and the objective, reasonable person test under the 1957 Act had become too subjectivised in the interpretation given to it in *Morgan Smith*, enabling a D to rely on "personal idiosyncrasies which make him or her more short tempered than other people".[100]

From the discussion above, it will be evident that these are not problems which trouble Scots law, at least to the same extent. To take the first, provocation can hardly be described as 'loose' in Scots law, although there is clearly at least room for argument as to whether the law should recognise provocation by infidelity. As it stands, however, the doctrine has given rise to little public controversy. This may simply reflect the limited number of cases that have attracted any attention. The most recent appellate decision, *Drury* v. *HM Advocate*,[101] where an appeal against conviction was allowed on the basis of misdirection by the trial judge on the plea, might have attracted some criticism given the nature of the fatal assault (at least seven blows with a claw hammer after the accused claimed to have become aware of the victim's infidelity). However, the case was sent for a retrial and – to avoid prejudicing the accused's right to a fair trial – reporting restrictions were placed on the appeal court's judgment until the conclusion of that new trial.[102] Drury was convicted of murder at the retrial,[103] thus leaving little scope for argument that the law was reaching the wrong result.

Absent empirical research, the extent to which provocation by infidelity succeeds as a plea is unclear, but in the relatively small number (three) of successful pleas of this nature which have reached the law reports recently, it is surprising that female accused (and male victims) are in the majority.[104] While there is no reason whatsoever to think that this is a representative sample, it is one potential cause for arguments that Scots law's recognition of provocation by infidelity

---

99 See, for example, Celia Wells, 'Provocation: The Case for Abolition' in Andrew Ashworth and Barry Mitchell (eds), *Rethinking English Homicide Law* (Oxford University Press, 2000) 85. The plea has been abolished in Victoria: see Victorian Law Reform Commission, *Defences to Homicide: Final Report* (2004) ch. 2 and the Crimes (Homicide) Act 2005, s. 3 (Vic).

100 Alan Norrie, 'Loss of Control' [2010] Criminal Law Review 275, 276, quoting Law Commission, *Report on Partial Defences to Murder* (Law Com. No 290, 2004) para. 3.21 and citing *R* v. *Smith (Morgan)* [2001] 1 AC 146.

101 2001 SLT 1013.

102 See 2001 SLT 1035.

103 Ibid.

104 *HM Advocate* v. *McKean* 1997 JC 32; *Rutherford* v. *HM Advocate* 1998 JC 34; *Houghton* v. *HM Advocate* 1999 GWD 17-789.

privileges male jealousy having failed to gain the traction either in academic or public discourse which might have been expected. There has simply, and perhaps by no more than chance, not been a prominent case on which to hook such an argument.

As for the second problem, it is likely that the letter of the law in Scotland gives rise (or at least would give rise) to exactly the same problems identified in England. Here, however, the exercise of prosecutorial discretion (and perhaps jury nullification) seems to have avoided substantive injustice. And as regards the third, the problem has simply not confronted the Scottish courts, may not do so for some time, and when it does the courts will have the benefit of the point having been thoroughly worked through in English law. They could (it is hoped) simply decline to follow the approach in *Morgan Smith*, instead adopting the reasoning of the majority of the Privy Council in *Attorney General for Jersey* v. *Holley*.[105] On that basis, a jury could and should be directed that they should take into account the accused's sex and age and other characteristics as affect the gravity of the provocation to him, but not characteristics bearing on his capacity for self-control.

Is the Scottish Approach to Partial Defences Sustainable?

This chapter has sought to set out the current law of partial defences in Scotland and to explain why these have been relatively uncontroversial in this jurisdiction. Uncontroversial they may be, but that is hardly a defence of the Scottish law as it stands.

As noted above, this chapter does not aim to provide a full evaluation of the existing Scottish legal rules.[106] But even if the current law is operating satisfactorily in terms of the outcomes arrived at in particular cases (something which is difficult to assess in the absence of empirical research), the law as it stands is overly reliant on the benign exercise of prosecutorial discretion. The exercise of such discretion is not of course restricted to Scotland, and in reviewing the English law of partial defences, the Law Commission discussed a case – *Maw* – where two young women who had killed their father (a drunkard and a violent bully) in circumstances which were sympathetic but as a matter of law amounted to murder. Pleas of guilty to manslaughter were, however, accepted and relatively short sentences imposed.

The Law Commission rightly noted that it was 'unsatisfactory that the case could only be treated as manslaughter by prosecutorial discretion which involved turning a blind eye to the law with the connivance of the judge' and advocated such a result being available 'on a principled and transparent basis'.[107] Quite apart from such considerations, what is to be done where the factual background to the killing is a matter of dispute? If, as appeared to be the case in *Galbraith*, the Crown do not accept the factual account put forward by the accused, the accused may be left with no means of putting the prosecution to proof – beyond hoping that the jury will

---

105 [2005] UKPC 23, [2005] 2 AC 580. See also *R* v. *James* [2006] EWCA Crim 14, [2006] QB 588. See now s. 54(3) of the Coroners and Justice Act 2009, under which a jury must, when considering whether a person in D's circumstances would have reacted in the same or a similar way to D, proceed on the basis that D's circumstances means 'all of D's circumstances other than those whose only relevance to D's conduct is that they bear on D's general capacity for tolerance or self-restraint'.

106 For such a critique in respect of provocation, see Clare McDiarmid, 'Don't Look Back in Anger: The Partial Defence of Provocation in Scots Criminal Law' in James Chalmers, Fiona Leverick and Lindsay Farmer (eds), *Essays in Criminal Law in Honour of Sir Gerald Gordon* (2010) 195. Diminished responsibility has been subject to less critical attention, but see Chalmers and Leverick, *Criminal Defences* (n. 17) ch. 11.

107 Law Com. No 290, 2004 (n. 36) para. 3.107.

exercise more mercy than the law requires – because such proof will in law have no effect on the appropriate verdict.

Historically, it has been both a strength and a weakness of Scottish criminal law that it has been left relatively untouched by the legislature,[108] something which is only gradually changing as a result of the devolution settlement.[109] The Scottish Law Commission's forthcoming review of the law of homicide will face many challenges, but it should not shirk from its responsibility to ensure that the letter of the law creates a clear, transparent and just framework for determining when a verdict of culpable homicide is to be preferred to one of murder.

---

108 See Christopher Gane, 'Criminal Law Reform in Scotland' (1998) 3 Scottish Law and Practice Quarterly 101.

109 The Sexual Offences (Scotland) Act 2009 is to date the only far-reaching reform of substantive criminal law passed by the Scottish Parliament.

Chapter 12

Anglo-American Perspectives on Partial Defences: Something Old, Something Borrowed, and Something New

Alan Reed and Nicola Wake

Introduction

'I'd kill for another glass of wine!' For most of us this statement is mere hyperbole, or verbiage, and alcohol consumption is a weekend social pleasure or a voluntary adjunct on an evening to relieve another stressful working day. Unfortunately for a very small minority their level of alcohol abuse is serious and destroys lives in multifarious fashions. Alcohol dependency is often coterminous with other mental conditions of depression, paranoia or delusions. This chapter addresses the treatment of the severely intoxicated and mentally abnormal killer in the context of the partial defences to murder. It focuses on extant law prior to the Coroners and Justice Act 2009 legislative reforms, and reflects on the novel classificatory system adopted therein as applied to this discrete category of offenders. How should we reconcile or align conditions of depression with alcohol dependency syndrome in terms of potentially explanatory behavioural patterns towards partial exculpation? Can appropriate delineations be made between chronic/harmful/acute intoxication as relevant factors in the context of diminished responsibility? In respect of individual loss of self-control how relevant are voluntary intoxication or mental frailties to 'personification' or 'characterisation' of a societal expectation standard of 'reasonable' conduct?

A comparative extirpation is briefly provided in this regard by reviewing the position adopted in traditional states in the US, set against the liberalised regime prevailing in the few states that have adopted a version of the Model Penal Code (hereinafter MPC). The latter iteration focuses on the standard template of 'extreme mental or emotional disturbance'. It is submitted that extant law ought to reflect contemporary standardisations of attitudinal behaviour. There needs to be an appraisal, in effect as a moral and social barometer, of legitimate and appropriate rectitude and culpability of the chronic alcoholic or mentally abnormal killer.

Section 2 of the Homicide Act 1957 – Something Old

The partial defence of diminished responsibility represents an anomaly in English law. Introduced as a device to enable the courts 'to take account of a special category or "mitigating" circumstances',[1] the concessionary defence reduces murder to manslaughter in situations where the defendant suffers from a mental abnormality short of insanity.[2] Previously there had been a

---
1 Law Commission, *Partial Defences to Murder* (Law Com. CP No 173, 2003) para. 6.8.
2 Ibid., paras 7.6–7.7.

'rigid dichotomy between sane or insane, responsible or not responsible, bad or mad'.[3] Diminished responsibility in this regard supplied the law with a new moral and social barometer upon which a mentally abnormal defendant's lower level of responsibility could be measured. When the plea was first introduced the mandatory sentence for murder was the death sentence.[4] By returning a verdict of manslaughter the defence gave the trial judge discretion in the sentence to be imposed.[5] Retention of the mandatory life sentence for murder remains a key factor in the preservation of the partial defence in the twenty-first century, especially in light of piecemeal government reforms to homicide rather than a more radical restructuring of hierarchical offences as the Law Commission suggested.[6] The Coroners and Justice Act 2009[7] provisions in this regard, considered below, amend the concessionary defence in a manner which is arguably reflective of 'developments in diagnostic practice'.[8] Predicated on an 'abnormality of mental functioning' arising from a 'recognised medical condition', the partial nature of the defence is retained, aligned with a burden of proof on the defendant.[9]

Under the original wording of s. 2 of the Homicide Act 1957 the defendant was required to prove an 'abnormality of mind'. Fact-finders were required to consider whether the 'abnormality of mind' arose 'from a condition of arrested or retarded development of mind or any inherent causes' or alternatively, whether the abnormality was 'induced by disease or injury'. Further, the jury were charged to determine whether the abnormality of mind 'substantially impaired' the defendant's 'mental responsibility' for the killing.

A controversial feature of the old law, subject to evaluation by the Law Commission,[10] and a fascinating array of conflicting authorities, concerned the discordant relationship between the partial defence and established intoxication doctrine.[11] This dissonance was explicit in cases involving the intoxicated defendant who killed while suffering from an abnormality of mind. Initial debate concentrated on whether voluntary intoxication should preclude the partial defence to a mentally abnormal defendant,[12] with intoxication *per se* correspondingly stigmatised as potentially introducing an inculpatory fault element.[13] More recently, deliberations have focused upon whether

---

3   Ibid., para. 6.52.
4   Ibid., para. 7.9.
5   Ibid., para. 7.7.
6   Law Commission, *Partial Defences to Murder* (Law Com. No 290, 2004) paras 5.10–5.11. See generally, Law Commission, *Murder, Manslaughter and Infanticide* (Law Com. No 304, 2006).
7   Section 52 of the Coroners and Justice Act 2009 amended s. 2 of the Homicide Act 1957 on 4 October 2010 (Coroners and Justice Act 2009 Transitional and Saving Provisions (Commencement No 4) Order 2010, SI 2010/816, Art. 5). The original wording of s. 2 of the Homicide Act 1957 continues to apply to acts committed wholly, or in part, before 4 October 2010 (Coroners and Justice Act 2009 sch. 22, para. 7).
8   Ministry of Justice, *Murder, Manslaughter and Infanticide* (MoJ CP No 19, 2008) para. 49.
9   Homicide Act 1957, s. 2 (as amended by Coroners and Justice Act 2009, s. 52). Placing the burden of proof on the defendant is not incompatible with the European Convention on Human Rights, Art. 6(2); *Lambert, Ali and Jordan* [2002] QB 1112.
10 Law Com. CP No 173, 2003 (n. 1) para. 7.71–7.92. See also Law Com. No 290, 2004 (n. 6) para. 5.85.
11 See further discussion below. See also *Majewski* [1977] AC 443; and Andrew Simester, 'Intoxication Is Never a Defence' [2009] Criminal Law Review 1, 3–14.
12 See for example, *R v. Dietschmann* [2003] UKHL 10 (HL), [2001] EWCA Crim 2052 (CA); *R v. Egan* (1992) 95 Cr App R 278 (CA); *R v. Inseal* [1992] Crim LR 35 (CA); *R v. Atkinson* [1985] Crim LR 314 (CA); *R v. Gittens* (1984) 79 Cr App R 272 (CA), [1984] QB 698 (CA), [1984] 3 WLR 327 (CA); *R v. Fenton* (1975) 61 Cr App R 261 (CA).
13 Simester (n. 11).

alcohol dependence syndrome could independently constitute an abnormality of mind, and exist as a bespoke qualifying condition.[14] Doctrinal criminal law principles have struggled, often in vain, to keep pace with ascertainable psychiatric developments *vis-à-vis* alcohol dependence syndrome and alcohol abuse in this arena. The jurisprudential landscape prior to the 2009 reforms highlighted the dilemmatic choice(s) presented to the courts in demarcation of the alcoholic killer who may also be suffering from other medical conditions.

In the context of s. 2(1) of the Homicide Act 1957, the 'abnormality of mind' requirement was not a 'legal or medical concept';[15] however, it was soon recognised that the phrase was capable of encompassing both 'volitional' and 'cognitive' disorders.[16] The seminal case of *Byrne*[17] interpreted the 'abnormality of mind' requirement as:

> [a] state of mind so different from that of ordinary human beings that the reasonable man would term it abnormal. It is wide enough to cover the mind's activities in all aspects, not only the perception of physical acts and matters, and the ability to form a rational judgement as to whether an act is right or wrong, but also *the ability to exercise will power to control physical acts* in accordance with that rational judgement.[18]

The impact of the decision in *Byrne* was to broadly introduce the concept of 'irresistible impulse' into English law as an element of the partial defence.[19] Subsequently, in *Fenton*,[20] the appellate court identified that 'cases may arise where the accused proves such a craving for drink or drugs as to prove in itself an abnormality of mind'.[21] This postulation, although implying that the diminished responsibility plea could be made available in rare situations to the chronic alcoholic, failed to specify how such a defendant would meet the 'abnormality of mind' requirement, and the level of impairment that was tangentially related to facilitate the defence.

The 'craving for drink' aphorism in *Fenton* received direct consideration in the pivotal appellate decision of *Wood*,[22] immediately prior to recent legislative enactments. It is suggested that *Wood* is central to evaluation herein in terms of the old and new law. The defendant was a chronic alcoholic, and had killed the victim who allegedly made unwanted homosexual advances. The defendant had engaged in a 36-hour drinking session prior to the fatal act. Medical experts called for the defence and the Crown were in unanimity *vis-à-vis* the import and level of the defendant's alcohol dependence syndrome. Although the defendant had not suffered brain damage as a result, he manifested at least six of the symptoms identified by the ICD-10 criteria for alcohol dependence syndrome, considered below.[23] The question was whether the defendant's alcohol dependence syndrome constituted a 'disease', capable of giving rise to an 'abnormality of mind'

---

14   See, for example, *R* v. *Stewart* [2009] EWCA Crim 593 (CA), [2009] 1 WLR 2507 (CA); *R* v. *Wood* [2008] EWCA Crim 1305 (CA), [2008] 2 Cr App R 34 (CA); *R* v. *Tandy* [1989] 1 WLR 350 (CA), (1988) 87 Cr App R 45 (CA).
15   Law Com. CP No 173, 2003 (n. 1) para. 7.22.
16   Ibid., para. 7.6.
17   [1960] 2 QB 396 (CA).
18   Ibid., 403 (Parker LJ) (emphasis added).
19   Ronnie Mackay, 'The Abnormality of Mind Factor in Diminished Responsibility' [1999] Criminal Law Review 117, 118.
20   *Fenton* (n. 12).
21   Ibid., 263 (Lord Widgery CJ).
22   *Wood* (n. 14).
23   Ibid., [9]. See generally, World Health Organization (Management of Substance Abuse: Dependence Syndrome) <http://www.who.int/substance_abuse/terminology/definition1/en/> (accessed 19 March 2011).

for the purposes of the diminished responsibility plea. In effect, should the jury be entitled to take into account the defendant's alcohol dependence syndrome when assessing the abnormality of mind requirement where that alcohol dependence syndrome had not resulted in observable brain damage? The trial judge, in light of earlier precedential authorities, struggled with the notion of an intoxicated defendant being afforded the partial defence, and provided a straitened test that the alcohol dependence syndrome would *only* be relevant if the defendant suffered brain damage as a result, or alternatively, if *every* drink consumed on the day of the killing was truly involuntary.

A prevailing judicial resistance existed, constraining the nature of the partial defence, and refusing to deviate from the established principle that voluntary intoxication did not negate the defendant's criminal liability, save in the limited context of specific intent offences and operatively as a denial of the requisite *mens rea* at the time of the relevant act.[24] Prior to *Wood*, the appellate court in *Tandy* had stipulated that 'the law simply will not allow a drug user, whether the drug be alcohol or any other, to shelter behind the toxic effects of the drug which he or she need not have used'.[25] In that context, the law rendered the question of whether the defendant 'could not resist his impulse' and whether he 'did not resist his impulse' nugatory in situations where the first drink of the day had been voluntary.[26] The effect was to 'accept the doctrine of diminished responsibility as it applies to alcoholism only in terms of black and white rather than shades of grey: either the defendant was wholly incapable of resisting the impulse to drink or [he] was responsible for [his] actions and should be convicted of murder'.[27]

The idea that *every drink* consumed by the chronic alcoholic had to be involuntary was antithetical to the 'concept of alcoholism as a disease'.[28] Even a 'true alcoholic' would stop drinking sometimes, for example to get dressed, wash and go to bed. Moreover, the concessionary defence had been introduced as a moral and social barometer upon which the defendant suffering from a mental abnormality short of insanity should be adjudged. There was no stipulation within s. 2 of the Homicide Act 1957 which required the defendant to be acting under 'some form of automatism' in order to establish the defence.[29] In essence, the courts failed to recognise that 'a world of difference' existed between cases of homicide where the defendant killed whilst voluntarily intoxicated and killings committed under the influence of alcohol dependence syndrome.[30]

The stark reality of the law's failure to understand alcohol related disorders had been made clear following the death of Linda Tandy,[31] who committed suicide in prison, shortly after the Court of Appeal upheld her conviction for murder.[32] The defendant was a chronic alcoholic, and had killed her daughter by strangulation after having consumed almost an entire bottle of vodka. The trial judge's direction, confirmed on appeal in an 'unduly artificial and restrictive'[33] fashion, was to the effect that the defendant's alcoholism would only have caused a gross impairment of her

---

24 *Majewski* (n. 11).

25 *Tandy* (n. 14) 354 (Watkins LJ, citing the trial judge's direction).

26 Andrew Ashworth, 'Diminished Responsibility: Defendant Diagnosed as Suffering from Alcohol Dependency Syndrome but Having Sustained no Brain Damage as Result' [2008] Criminal Law Review 976, 978.

27 Jonathan Goodliffe, '*R v. Tandy and the Concept of Alcoholism as a Disease*' (1990) 53 Modern Law Review 809, 809–14.

28 Ibid.

29 *Wood* (n. 14) [37] (Sir Igor Judge P).

30 Law Com. No 290, 2004 (n. 6) para. 5.45 (Dr Keith Rix).

31 *Tandy* (n. 14).

32 Nicola Padfield, *Criminal Law* (7th edn, Oxford University Press, 2010) 190.

33 Law Com. No 290, 2004 (n. 6) para. 5.85, and Law Com. CP No 173, 2003 (n. 1) para. 7.82.

judgement and emotional responses (an abnormality of mind) if she had suffered brain damage as a result, or alternatively if every drink taken on the day of the killing had been involuntary.

The impact of *Tandy* was to introduce an unreasonable test, unduly constrained in ambit, which required the defendant to 'conform to a model of alcoholism that even the most hardened alcoholic would find difficult to meet'.[34] If the chronic alcoholic was unable to conform she would be adjudged according to the normative expectations society has of the ordinary sober person, rather than as an individual suffering from a mental abnormality. The decision showed a flagrant disregard for the moral and social barometer set by s. 2 of the Homicide Act 1957, by supplanting the provision with a juridical bar which required the chronic alcoholic to have suffered brain damage or be acting, in effect, under 'some form of automatism' before she could establish the partial defence.[35] As Mackay expertly articulated, 'It is one thing to say that the accused may be suffering from an abnormal craving for drink, but quite another to require that before such a craving can be established, the first drink in the relevant series must be shown to have been consumed "involuntarily".'[36] In reality it was not the first drink, but the cumulative effect of the alcohol consumption, which resulted in the defendant's grossly impaired judgement.[37] The determination in *Tandy* fundamentally undermined the rationale underpinning the partial defence by failing to recognise that a complete destruction of the defendant's free will was not required for her liability to have been substantially impaired.[38]

The House of Lords in *Dietschmann*,[39] in light of the vituperative criticism levelled at the effects of the *Tandy* decision, had the opportunity to reassess the appropriate standardisation. Their Lordships were required to reconcile and separate coterminous issues of depression aligned with intoxication. Seizing the chance to partially reinstate the ethical barometer of responsibility afforded by the defence, the House of Lords considered that the primordial focus in such cases should be on the underlying mental abnormality distilled from the intoxication. Lord Hutton identified that the issue was not whether the defendant would have carried out the killing in the absence of intoxication, but whether, if he did kill, he killed under diminished responsibility.

The appellate court in *Wood* considered that the House of Lords decision in *Dietschmann* required 'a reassessment' of the way in which *Tandy* had been applied in the context of alcohol dependency syndrome where observable brain damage had not occurred.[40] No requirement existed for brain damage to have resulted from alcohol dependence syndrome, but fact-finders could still evaluate whether the extent and nature of the syndrome met the abnormality of mind threshold. In future cases the court would be required to 'focus exclusively on the effect of alcohol consumed by the defendant as a *direct result* of his illness or disease and ignore the effect of any alcohol consumed voluntarily'.[41] It was no longer the case that unless every drink consumed by a defendant on the fatal day was involuntary, then the syndrome was to be disregarded. Rather the posited issue for jury evaluation became whether an accused's mental responsibility for the conduct was substantially impaired as a concomitant of the alcohol, 'consumed under the baneful influence of the syndrome'.[42] Despite the ostensible difficulties associated with a test which appears to require

---

34 Julia Tolmie, 'Alcoholism and Criminal Liability' (2001) 64 Modern Law Review, 688.
35 *Wood* (n. 14) [37] (Sir Igor Judge P).
36 See generally, Ronnie Mackay, *Mental Condition Defences in Criminal Law* (Oxford University Press, 1995) 8.
37 Law Com. CP No 173, 2003 (n. 1) para. 7.82.
38 Mackay (n. 36) 197 .
39 *Dietschmann* (n. 12).
40 *Wood* (n. 14) [41] (Sir Igor Judge P).
41 Ibid., [41] (Sir Igor Judge P).
42 Ibid., [40] (Sir Igor Judge P).

the jury to 'separate out each drink of the day',[43] the decision in *Wood* represented a significant jurisprudential landmark in repudiating the artificial bar that had prevented alcohol dependent defendants from relying on the partial defence.

The revised test 'delineated more by mud than by crystal'[44] invited the jury to engage in mental gymnastics to determine 'the degree of voluntariness and involuntariness in the defendant's drinking'.[45] Unsurprisingly, the appellate court in *Stewart*,[46] immediately following *Wood*, deemed it appropriate to provide further guidance for juries, vis-à-vis the articulation of the defence in terms of appropriate specimen directions for future signposting. The consumption of vast amounts of alcohol could reduce murder to manslaughter:

> first, where the effect of the intoxication was so extreme that the prosecution had failed to prove the necessary intention to kill or cause grievous bodily harm; and, second, assuming that the necessary intention was proved notwithstanding the consumption of alcohol, on the basis of diminished responsibility.[47]

In determining whether the defendant's mental responsibility was substantially impaired, Lord Judge CJ in *Stewart* pronounced an additional list of five 'contact-counting' factors upon which the fact-finder should be invited to form their own judgement incorporating: (a) the extent and seriousness of the defendant's dependency, if any, on alcohol; (b) the extent to which his ability to control his drinking or to choose whether to drink or not, was reduced; (c) whether he was capable of abstinence from alcohol, and, if so; (d) for how long; and (e) whether he was choosing for some particular reason, such as a birthday celebration, to decide to get drunk, or to drink even more than usual.[48] These five 'contact-counting' factors ask the jury to do no more than apply their common sense in determining whether the defendant's responsibility for the killing was substantially impaired. The common sense approach advocated in *Stewart* was reaffirmed in *Ramchurn*,[49] as part of a trilogy of decisions prior to enforcement of s. 52 of the Coroners and Justice Act 2009. The appellate court in *Ramchurn* reflected that 'substantially impaired' within the purview of s. 2(1) of the Homicide Act 1957 meant something 'more than trivial but less than total'. This was in line with the earlier ruling in *Lloyd*[50] which amounted to authority that the word 'substantial' constituted a word 'for which one should not try to find a synonym. It is a word which members of the jury, with their own common sense, can tell what it means.'[51] The direction was 'a welcome departure from the current trend towards requiring the jury to be directed to do what their common sense would naturally lead them to do anyway'.[52] The decision in *Ramchurn* indicated that providing the chronic alcoholic's condition was more than trivial, the question of

---

43 *Stewart* (n. 14) [28].

44 Alan Reed, 'Alcohol Dependency Syndrome and the Ambit of Diminished Responsibility' (2009) 173 Criminal Law and Justice Weekly 263; see also Nicola Wake, 'Alcohol Dependency Syndrome and Diminished Responsibility' (2009) Journal of Criminal Law, 17.

45 Ashworth, 'Diminished Responsibility: Defendant Diagnosed as Suffering from Alcohol Dependency Syndrome but Having Sustained no Brain Damage as Result' (n. 26) 978.

46 *Stewart* (n. 14).

47 Ibid., [29] (Sir Igor Judge P).

48 Ibid., [34] (Sir Igor Judge P).

49 [2010] EWCA Crim 194 (CA).

50 (1966) 50 Cr App R, 61, 63.

51 *R v. Mitchell*, The Times, 2 December 1994; John Smith, '*R v. Mitchell*' [1995] Criminal Law Review 506 (note).

52 Ibid., 506–7.

whether his responsibility was substantially impaired should be left to the jury. Following *Stewart* it was evident that the more serious the defendant's alcohol dependence syndrome, the more likely it became that his responsibility was substantially impaired.

The pre-2009 position regarding assessments of mental abnormality and chronic intoxication, iterated in *Dietschmann* and *Wood*, reflected a significantly more liberalised and empathetically valid perspective than the restrictive deontological approach applied in *Tandy*.[53] The contemporary contextual approach to intoxication doctrine, with a predominant emphasis on 'mental abnormality', was more in keeping with developments in medical understanding of substance disorders, albeit points of confusion remained. The beguiling judicial precedents in this context highlighted that recognition of substance disorders had developed beyond the malfunctioning identified within the original plea.[54] It is significant to re-evaluate how the alcoholic killer or mentally abnormal accused will now be treated within the confines of new reforms.

Coroners and Justice Act 2009, Section 52 – Something New

Parliament made significant revisions to the original diminished responsibility plea in s. 52 of the Coroners and Justice Act 2009, and key provisions became effective in law on 4 October 2010, replacing s. 2(1) of the Homicide Act 1957. The revised formulation postulates a new test for alcohol dependency syndrome in cases akin to *Wood* and *Stewart* where diminished responsibility is adduced. It also imports principles adduced in *Dietschmann* more directly into a legislative framework. The defendant, to rely on the reformulated defence, must now be shown to have been suffering from an 'abnormality of mental functioning'.[55] Medical experts will be charged to provide evidence as to whether this abnormality of mental functioning arose from a 'recognised medical condition'.[56] Alcohol dependence syndrome must comport to this straitened test with evaluation of the International Classification of Diseases (ICD-10)[57] and the Diagnostic and Statistical Manual of Mental Disorders (DSM-IV-TR) criteria for alcohol dependence syndrome of potential significance.

It is noteworthy that the DSM-IV-TR diagnosis can only be made if three or more of the following conditions have been present simultaneously at some time during the previous year. These incorporate: (a) tolerance; (b) withdrawal; (c) taking the substance in larger amounts over a longer period than intended; (d) a persistent desire or unsuccessful efforts to cut down or control substance abuse; (e) a great deal of time spent in activities necessary to obtain the substance; (f) giving up important social, occupational and recreational activities; and (g) continuing use of the substance, notwithstanding knowledge that this had caused recurrent physical and psychological

---

53 Law Com. No 290, 2004 (n. 6) para. 5.85.
54 Law Com. No 304, 2006 (n. 6) para. 5.111.
55 Homicide Act 1957, s. 2(1), as amended by the Coroners and Justice Act 2009, s. 52.
56 Ibid., s. 2(1)(a).
57 The ICD-10 diagnosis can only be made if three or more of the following conditions have been present simultaneously at some time during the previous year: (a) a strong desire or compulsion to drink alcohol; (b) difficulty in controlling alcohol use; (c) a physiological withdrawal state; (d) evidence of tolerance; (e) progressive neglect of alternative pleasures or interests; and (f) persistent use of alcohol despite evidence of harmful consequences; World Health Organization (ICD-10: Mental and behavioural disorders due to psychoactive substance abuse, Ch. V, F10–F19) <http://apps.who.int/classifications/apps/icd/icd10online/> (accessed 28 March 2011).

problems.[58] The new provision itself does not define 'recognisable medical condition', but evidently alcohol dependence syndrome will satisfy this criterion given recognition of the syndrome by these leading classificatory systems.

Further, the fact-finders are required to consider two issues in order for the partial defence to be crystallised. First, the jury will be required to decide whether the recognised medical condition substantially impairs the defendant's ability to: (a) understand the nature of the defendant's conduct; (b) form a rational judgment; or (c) exercise self-control.[59] Secondly, the jury would have to assess whether the mental abnormality provides an explanation for the killing.[60] Moreover, it is asserted in s. 52 that an explanation will be provided if 'it causes, or is a significant contributory factor in causing the person to carry out that conduct'. This latter requirement, arguably implicit under the old law, but applied 'benevolently' in favour of a defendant, has now become explicit as part of a narrowed ambit for this defence.[61]

Pre-2009 consultation, conducted by the government and the Law Commission, revealed very disparate views on contemporary standardisation and attitudinal behaviour attached to those suffering from medical conditions brought on by long-term abuse of alcohol or drugs, and whether this category of offenders ought to be excluded from using the partial defence.[62] One consultee proposed a formulation of the defence which would be available to those suffering from 'a mental disorder as defined in s. 1 of the Mental Health Act 1983' which would specifically exclude 'any temporary alteration of mental state caused by drugs of any kind'.[63] As 'knowledge of mental illness is a developing science' the Commission considered that tying the revised plea to the 'definition contained in the Mental Health Act 1983 might be over restrictive'.[64] The 'recognised medical condition' requirement under the Coroners and Justice Act is, therefore, designed to accommodate future 'developments in diagnostic practice'.[65] It is expected that the wording of the defence will 'encourage reference within expert evidence to diagnosis in terms of one or two of the accepted international classificatory systems of mental disorders (WHO ICD10 and AMA DSM)'.[66] Interestingly, from 2013 the DSM-V Substance Use Disorder Workgroup recommends that alcohol abuse and alcohol dependence syndrome be combined into one disorder of graded clinical severity, with two criteria required to make a diagnosis. At present, a diagnosis of alcohol abuse can be made under DSM-IV-TR if one or more of the following conditions have been present at some time during the previous year: (a) recurrent substance use resulting in a failure to fulfil major role obligations at work, school, home; (b) recurrent substance use in situations in which it is physically hazardous; (c) recurrent substance-related legal problems; (d) continued substance use despite having persistent or recurrent social or interpersonal problems caused or exacerbated by the effects of the substance.[67]

---

58   American Psychiatric Association, *DSM-IV, Diagnostic and Statistical Manual of Mental Disorders* (4th edn, Washington, DC, 1994).
59   Above (n. 55) s. 2(1A)(a)–(c).
60   Ibid., s. 2(1B).
61   See, generally, Ronnie Mackay, '(2) The New Diminished Responsibility Plea' [2010] Criminal Law Review, 290, 297–300.
62   Ministry of Justice, *Murder, Manslaughter and Infanticide* (MoJ CP No 19, Response to consultation, 2008) para. 91.
63   Law Com. No 290, 2004 (n. 6) para. 5.67.
64   Ibid., para. 5.76.
65   Law Com. No 304, 2006 (n. 6) paras 1.49 and 5.107.
66   Ibid., para. 5.114 (Royal College of Psychiatrists).
67   DSM-IV (n. 58).

The rationale behind the move to a single disorder of graded clinical severity is that the current distinction between dependence and abuse renders ongoing diagnoses of alcohol abuse less reliable than ongoing diagnoses of dependence syndrome.[68] The distinction was also criticised as creating 'diagnostic orphans' who might satisfy two of the criteria for dependence but none of the conditions required for a diagnosis of abuse.[69] If the Workgroup's recommendation is accepted, alcohol dependence syndrome will no longer be recognised as an independent disorder for the purposes of the DSM. Instead the DSM-V manual will refer to 'substance use disorder' which will be diagnosed where two or more of the symptoms identified for alcohol dependence syndrome and/or alcohol abuse are present simultaneously in a 12-month period.[70] Clearly 'substance use disorder', in requiring only two symptoms, will be diagnosed more readily than current diagnoses of alcohol dependence syndrome. This renders the new defence potentially more generous to the alcoholic defendant than the original plea.

The revised plea remains silent as to levels of gradation of voluntary intoxication that may or may not constitute a 'mental abnormality' when an individual kills. It is likely that the courts will be required to consider whether states of acute intoxication (drunkenness) will satisfy the 'recognised medical condition' requirement, given that acute intoxication is regarded by the ICD-10 as a disorder of clinical significance.[71] Although acute intoxication is unlikely to satisfy the requirement, it might have been beneficial if the legislation were to include specific direction on this issue, rather than requiring the courts to distinguish, inter alia, between acute intoxication, harmful use, alcohol abuse (considered above) and alcohol dependence syndrome.[72] This problem may not arise north of the border. The newly proposed diminished responsibility plea in Scotland states 'that a person ... under the influence of alcohol, drugs, or any other substance at the time of the [killing] does not in itself – (a) constitute abnormality of mind for the purposes of [the defence],

---

68 Deborah Hasin, Andrea Paykin, Jean Endicott and Bridget Grant, 'The Validity of DSM-IV Alcohol Abuse: Drunk Drivers versus All Others', Journal of Studies on Alcohol and Drugs (1990) 60, 6.

69 Deborah Hasin and Andrea Paykin, 'Dependence Symptoms but No Diagnosis: Diagnostic "Orphans" in a 1992 National Sample' (1992) Drug and Alcohol Dependence, 53, 3, 215–22.

70 'American Psychiatric Association DSM 5 Development' (Substance Use Disorder) <http://www.dsm5.org/ProposedRevisions/Pages/proposedrevision.aspx?rid=431#> (accessed 19 March 2011).

71 'World Health Organization' (ICD-10: Mental and behavioural disorders due to psychoactive substance abuse, Ch. V, F10–F19) (n. 57).

72 Ibid. The WHO identifies several different mental and behavioural disorders arising from psychoactive substance use, as follows: acute intoxication ('A condition that follows administration of psychoactive substances resulting in disturbances in level of consciousness, cognition, perception, affect or behaviour, or other psycho-physiological functions and responses.'); harmful use ('A pattern of psychoactive substance use that is causing damage to health e.g. episodes of depressive disorder secondary to heavy consumption of alcohol.'); dependence syndrome ('A cluster of behavioural, cognitive, and physiological phenomena that develop after repeated substance use and that typically include a strong desire to take the drug, difficulties in controlling its use, persisting in its use despite harmful consequences, a higher priority given to drug use than to other activities and obligations, increased tolerance, and sometimes a physical withdrawal state.'); withdrawal state ('A group of symptoms of variable clustering and severity occurring on absolute or relative withdrawal of a psychoactive substance after persistent use of that substance.'); withdrawal state with delirium ('delirium tremens – alcohol induced'); psychotic disorder ('A syndrome associated with chronic prominent impairment of recent and remote memory. Immediate recall is usually preserved and recent memory is characteristically more disturbed than remote memory. Disturbances of time sense and ordering of events are usually evident, as are difficulties in learning new material. Confabulation may be marked but is not invariably present. Other cognitive functions are usually relatively well preserved and amnesic defects are out of proportion to other disturbances.') The DSM-IV recognises alcohol abuse, considered in the text above.

or (b) prevent such abnormality from being established'.[73] The effect will be afford the defence to the intoxicated, but mentally abnormal defendant, akin to *Dietschmann, Wood* and *Stewart,* while excluding it to the voluntarily intoxicated defendant not suffering from an underlying mental abnormality. The Scottish Law Commission deemed it necessary to exclude the latter on the basis that 'an intoxicated person is at the time of intoxication suffering from an abnormal state of mind which does affect his ability to determine or control his conduct. Accordingly, the basis of the exclusion is not the definition of the plea, but the clear policy of the criminal law ... that voluntary intoxication does not elide criminal responsibility.'[74]

Beyond the classificatory adoption of 'alcohol dependence'/'alcohol abuse' the real limitation on the defence exists in the three specified ways in which the defendant's ability can be 'substantially impaired'. It will be the role of the medical expert to offer an opinion on 'whether and in what way the abnormality had an impact on'[75] the defendant's ability to: (a) understand the nature of the defendant's conduct; (b) form a rational judgement; or (c) exercise self-control.[76] These three specified things are included[77] to 'make clear what impact on capacity the effects of an abnormality of mental functioning must have'.[78] Presumably alcohol related disorders will affect the defendant's level of 'self-control', although there may also be cases which affect the defendant's ability to form a 'rational judgement'.[79] It is likely that there will be disagreement between medical experts in this context, 'so it seems that the question of substantial impairment by the medical condition – not the alcohol voluntarily taken' will remain an onerous task for the jury.[80]

The term 'substantial impairment' is one of few remnants of the original diminished responsibility plea. In this respect, it would seem that the courts will continue to apply the 'more than trivial but less than total' approach adopted in *Ramchurn* (see above). The jury will only be entitled to return a manslaughter verdict, however, if (providing all of the other elements of the defence are satisfied) the mental abnormality provides an explanation for the killing.[81] In 2004 the Law Commission recommended that the abnormality must be a 'significant cause'[82] of the killing, but repudiated that requirement following consultation.[83] Academicians in criminal law, together with the Royal College of Psychiatrists, specifically advised against the creation of 'a situation in which experts might be called on to "demonstrate" causation on a scientific basis'.[84] Despite this, the revised plea stipulates that an explanation will only be provided if 'it causes, or is a significant

---

73   New s. 51(3)B of the Criminal Procedure (Scotland) Act 1995 as inserted by the Criminal Justice and Licensing (Scotland) Act 2010, s. 168(3). Section 168 was still to be brought into force at the time of writing.

74   Scottish Law Commission, *Report on Insanity and Diminished Responsibility* (Scottish Law Commission No 195, 2004) para. 3.40.

75   Law Com. No 304, 2006 (n. 6) para. 5.117–5.118.

76   Above (n. 55) s. 2(1A)(a)–(c).

77   The first element bears resemblance to the first limb of the M'Naghten Rules (1843) 8 ER 718; (1843) 10 CJ & F 200, 210, which require the defendant to prove that the defendant 'did not know the nature and quality of the act he was doing'. The second and third elements are modelled on the leading judgment in *Byrne* [1960] 2 QB 396 (considered above).

78   Law Com. No 304, 2006 (n. 6) para. 5.121.

79   Ashworth, 'Diminished Responsibility: Defendant Diagnosed as Suffering from Alcohol Dependency Syndrome but Having Sustained no Brain Damage as Result' (n. 26) 978.

80   Ibid.

81   Above (n. 55) s. 2(1B).

82   Law Com. No 290, 2004 (n. 6) para. 1.17.

83   Law Com. No 304, 2006 (n. 6) para. 5.112.

84   Ibid., para. 5.123. See, generally, Jo Miles, 'A "Dog's Breakfast" of Homicide Reform' (2009) Archbold News, 10, 6.

contributory factor in causing the person to carry out that conduct'. In the context of substance related disorders it appears the causal requirement is likely 'to direct attention to the interaction of the medical condition with any other causal factor, such as alcohol consumption not stemming from the condition itself'.[85] The causative effect of alcohol voluntarily consumed will not prevent the defendant's alcohol dependence syndrome from 'substantially impairing his' mental capacity providing the disorder is a significant contributory factor in the killing. The rationale for this explicit causal requirement appears to be that the abnormality of mental functioning ought to be 'some connection between the condition and the killing in order for the defence to be justified'.[86] As Yeo identifies, if this is the case, the term 'explanation', as recommended in the Law Commission's 2006 report,[87] would have been preferable to the word 'cause', because this would avoid the difficulties associated with having to demonstrate a specific causal link.[88]

Extreme Mental or Emotional Disturbance – Something Borrowed

In retaining diminished responsibility as an independent partial defence, the Law Commission had rejected recommendations of a merger between diminished responsibility and provocation predicated on the concept of extreme emotional disturbance.[89] This formulation is broadly derived from the MPC provocation proposal which requires the jury to determine whether the defendant killed 'under the influence of extreme mental or emotional disturbance for which there is reasonable explanation or excuse'.[90] The effect is to provide a wider mitigation than under the provocation doctrine applicable in 'traditional' states in the US, which is rooted in English common law antediluvian heritage, and is encapsulated by personification of a 'heat of passion' excusatory doctrine, embracing subjective and objective elements centred on the amorphous reasonable man conceptualisation.[91] This implementation of heat of passion doctrine in traditional states is subject to solipsistic implementation in respective criminal law jurisdictions, but the pre-eminent inculcated adoption reflects the intentional killing of another while under the influence of a reasonably induced 'heat of passion' causing a temporary loss of normal self-control.[92] As such, while individual characteristics of the accused are considered as part of subjective loss of self-control, they are excluded as part of the reasonable man anthropomorphism, beyond age and sex. In many respects this mirrors the English position, pre-reforms adopted in *DPP* v. *Camplin*[93] and *Attorney General for Jersey* v. *Holley*.[94] A radically different perspective, enervating current

---

85   Ashworth, 'Diminished Responsibility: Defendant Diagnosed as Suffering from Alcohol Dependency Syndrome but Having Sustained no Brain Damage as Result' (n. 26) 978.
86   MoJ CP 19, 2008 (n. 8) para. 51.
87   Law Com. No 304, 2006 (n. 6) paras 5.112 and 9.20.
88   Stanley Yeo, 'English Reform of Partial Defences to Murder: Lessons for New South Wales' (2010) 22 Current Issues in Criminal Justice 1, 6.
89   Law Com. No 173, 2003 (n. 1) paras 12.78–12.81. See also Law Com. No 290, 2004 (n. 6) paras 3.59, 3.164–3.165; and Ronnie Mackay and Barry Mitchell, 'Provoking Diminished Responsibility: Two Pleas Merging into One' [2003] Criminal Law Review 745.
90   Model Penal Code and Commentaries §210.3(1)(b) (hereinafter MPC).
91   See, generally, Douglas Brown, 'Disentangling Concessions to Human Frailty: Making Sense of Anglo-American Provocation Doctrine through Comparative Study' (2007) 39 New York University Journal of International Law & Politics 675.
92   See, generally, Wayne LaFave, *Criminal Law* (4th edn, West, 2003).
93   *DPP* v. *Camplin* [1978] AC 705.
94   *Attorney General for Jersey* v. *Holley* [2005] UKPC 23; [2005] 2 AC 580.

discussion, applies to the 'subjectivised provocation plea' within MPC jurisdictions,[95] identified herein as 'reform' states. The Code mitigates murder to manslaughter where:

> Murder is committed under the influence of extreme mental or emotional disturbance for which there is a reasonable explanation or excuse. The reasonableness of such an explanation or excuse shall be determined from the viewpoint of a person in the actor's situation under the circumstances as he believes them to be.[96]

The partial defence requires the killing to have been committed 'under the influence of extreme mental or emotional disturbance'.[97] The cause of the disturbance is not restricted to acts committed by the victim[98] and the defence is not limited by a 'cooling-off' period.[99] The drafters of the Code recognised that a lapse of time between the disturbance and the fatal act may exaggerate the effect of the disturbance.[100] The defence may even be left to the jury in the absence of a provocative event, for example, a victim's refusal to accept gifts from the defendant.[101]

The Code also requires a 'reasonable explanation or excuse' for the disturbance.[102] This is a partially subjectivised test which must be determined 'from the viewpoint of a person in the actor's situation under the circumstances as he believes them to be'.[103] Failing to offer specific guidance on this aspect of the provision, the drafters of the MPC noted:

> The term "situation" ... is designedly ambiguous and is plainly flexible enough to allow the law to grow in the direction of taking account of abnormalities that have been recognised in the developing law of diminished responsibility ... Like blindness or other physical infirmities, perhaps it should be that mental abnormality should be regarded as part of the actor's situation that is relevant to the moral assessment of his or her conduct.[104]

The drafters identified that characteristics peculiar to the defendant such as 'an exceptionally punctilious sense of personal honour or an abnormally fearful temperament' would not always be 'irrelevant to the ultimate issue of culpability'.[105] Notwithstanding the ostensible subjectivisation[106]

---

95 James Chalmers, 'Merging Provocation and Diminished Responsibility: Some Reasons for Scepticism' [2004] Criminal Law Review 198, 211.
96 MPC (n. 90) §210.3(1)(b).
97 Ibid.
98 Law Com. No 290, 2004 (n. 6) App. F, para. 3.
99 Ibid. Many states have amended the partial defence to include a 'loss of self-control' requirement. See Chalmers (n. 95) 204.
100 MPC (n. 90) §210.0–213.5, 72, 73.
101 *People v. Casassa* 404 NE2d 1310 (NY 1980). See, also, Joshua Dressler, 'Why Keep the Provocation Defense? Some Reflections on a Difficult Subject' (2002) 86 Minnesota Law Review 959, 987; Stephen Garvey, 'Passion's Puzzle' (2005) 90 Iowa Law Review 1677, 1690; and Susan Rozelle, 'Controlling Passion: Adultery and the Provocation Defense' (2005) 37 Rutgers Law Journal, 197.
102 MPC (n. 90) §210.3(1)(b).
103 Ibid.
104 Ibid., §210.0–213.5, 72, 73.
105 Ibid., §210.3, 62. See also Rozelle (n. 101) 202.
106 Joshua Dressler, 'Rethinking Heat of Passion: A Defense in Search of a Rationale' [1982] 73 Journal of Criminal Law and Criminology 421, 431 (2), notes that 'the actor's sex, sexual preference, pregnancy, physical deformities, and similar characteristics are apt to be taken into consideration in evaluating the reasonableness of the defendant's behaviour'.

of the plea, in terms of provocation Chalmers has cogently identified that the formulation 'was never designed as a "merged" provision',[107] to embrace 'diminished responsibility' within the confines of mental disturbance. The lack of an equivalent diminished responsibility defence meant that 'the drafters were prepared to accept a "substantial enlargement" of the traditional plea of provocation'.[108] This liberalisation resulted in the proposal being met with considerable resistance amongst the states, with not a single state being prepared to adopt the provision in its entirety.[109] A common variation to the formulation was the repudiation of the term 'mental'.[110] This is indicative of the bulwark prevailing against murder reductions to manslaughter predicated upon mental disorders within American jurisdictions,[111] and effectual rejection of alcohol dependence syndrome as a concessionary partial defence *per se*. Any attempt to introduce a diminished responsibility plea equivalent to that in English law occurred by sleight of hand, 'through the judicial back door'.[112] Of the five successful attempts to introduce the mitigation for murder, four were abolished upon adoption of the MPC.[113] The fifth was abolished following public rioting in response to the decision in *People* v. *White*.[114] White had assassinated Mayor Moscone and Harvey Milk in 1978. At his trial for first degree murder, White successfully pleaded diminished responsibility on grounds of a depressive condition. During the course of the trial it was suggested that a symptom of the depression was White's compulsion for junk food. Diminished responsibility subsequently became dubbed the 'Twinkie Defense'.[115] Commenting on the risks associated with the diminished responsibility defence, the Drafters of the MPC stated:

> By evaluating the abnormal individual on his own terms, [diminished responsibility] decreases the incentives for him to behave as if he were normal. It blurs the law's message that there are certain minimal standards of conduct to which every member of society should conform. By restricting the extreme condemnation of liability for murder to cases where it is warranted in a relativistic sense, diminished responsibility undercuts the social purpose of condemnation. In short, diminished responsibility brings formal guilt more closely in line with moral blameworthiness, but only at the cost of driving a wedge between dangerousness and social control. The MPC does not recognize diminished responsibility as a distinct category of mitigation.[116]

---

[107] Chalmers (n. 95) 200. For alternative views see Mackay and Mitchell, 'Provoking Diminished Responsibility: Two Pleas Merging into One?' (n. 89); Ronnie Mackay and Barry Mitchell, 'Replacing Provocation: More on a Combined Plea' [2004] Criminal Law Review 219; Dressler, 'Why Keep the Provocation Defense? Some Reflections on a Difficult Subject' (n. 101) 985.

[108] Chalmers (n. 95) 200. See also Law Com. No 290, 2004 (n. 6) para. 3.59.

[109] Law Com. No 290, 2004 (n. 6) App. F, para. 5. See also Rozelle (n. 101) 209.

[110] Law Com. No 290, 2004, ibid., App. F, paras 5–6.

[111] Stephen Morse, 'Criminal Law: Undiminished Confusion in Diminished Capacity' (1984) 75 Journal of Criminal Law & Criminology, 1, 24. See also Brown (n. 91) 701

[112] Ibid.

[113] Brown (n. 91). See also Law Com. No 290, 2004 (n. 6) para. 3.59.

[114] 172 Cal Rptr 612, 612 (Ct App 1981). See also the film, *The Times of Harvey Milk*.

[115] See, generally, Kelly Snider, 'The Infamous Twinkie Defense – Fact or Fiction?' (2006) 9 Annals of the American Psychotherapy Association 42, 43.

[116] MPC (n. 90) §210.3, 71.

A concomitant of requiring the 'reasonableness' analysis within the MPC to be conducted 'from the viewpoint of'[117] the defendant provides a heightened discretion to the jury.[118] This liberalisation has transmogrified the role of judge and jury in reform states, with primordial focus attached to the latter in a remarkably inclusionary fashion:

> Jurors are told to put themselves into the defendant's position, to adopt his or her perspective and, yet, at the same time, to be "reasonable". They are asked to exercise independent "moral judgement", and, at the same time, adopt the defendant's vantage point.[119]

The extensive role of the jury in reform states, and allowing their consideration of 'appropriate' emotional disturbance, has facilitated a liberal perspective to partial defences beyond the confines of the Coroners and Justice Act 2009 provisions.[120] The fact-finders, as moral and sympathetic arbiters of justice, have been allowed to apply their particularised 'judicial' divining rod to normative considerations.[121] The corollary, as Ramsey has suggested, is that 'allowing the broad defence in the first place, without providing any fixed standard to guide jury deliberation, erodes the criminal law's legitimacy and creates the potential for inconsistent, arbitrary results'.[122] The Drafters of the Code conceded that, 'In the end, the question is whether the actor's loss of self-control can be understood in terms that arouse sympathy in the ordinary citizen.'[123]

Although criticised for the ad hoc nature of relevant individual characterisation in provocation, and the 'unguided and undisclosed discretion'[124] presented to fact-finders in the subjectivised and empathetically intuitive nature of the MPC, nonetheless it has been asserted that the perspective advanced may be irrefragable:

> Unfortunately, while the Code purports to solve the problem of tailoring an objective standard to the defendant, the solution it offers masks an illusion. Beyond that illusion, criminal law theory has yet to find a principle that will convincingly distinguish the characteristics that ought to be included from those that ought to be excluded when individualising the reasonable person standard. In the absence of such a theory, let alone a workable provision implementing a theory, it is hard to see any approach other than uncontrolled ad hoc discretion the MPC Drafters have adopted.[125]

Arguably, a 'workable provision' for provocation enjoyed a period of gestation in English law, as set out in the following section, with the development of *control* and *response* characteristics attendant to the reasonable man. Unfortunately, this operational dichotomy was diluted by a

---

117 Ibid., §210.3(1)(b).
118 Chalmers (n. 95) 211, identifies that the MPC proposal assumes 'that there is some form of community standard on the proper borderline between murder and manslaughter which juries are capable of applying'. See, generally, Law Com. No 290, 2004 (n. 6) App. C.
119 Victoria Nourse, 'Passion's Progress: Model Law Reform and the Provocation Defense' (1997) 106 Yale Law Journal 1331.
120 Chalmers (n. 95) 211.
121 See generally, Dressler 'Why Keep the Provocation Defense? Some Reflections on a Difficult Subject' (n. 101) 959; Rozelle (n. 101) 197.
122 Carolyn Ramsey, 'Provoking Change: Comparative Insights on Feminist Homicide Law Reform' (2010) 100 Journal of Criminal Law & Criminology, 33.
123 MPC (n. 90) §210.3, 5(a), 60–61.
124 Paul Robinson, 'The Modern General Part: Three Illusions', in Stephen Shute and Andrew Simester, *Criminal Law Theory: Doctrines of the General Part* (Oxford University Press, 2002) 75, 90–91.
125 Robinson, ibid.

failure to develop a barometer of moral and social rectitude attached to ethically creditable or discreditable indicia. This tangentially prompted the need for a root and branch legislative reform of the provocation defence.

Provocation – Something Old

The defence of provocation in crimes of homicide, like diminished responsibility, has always represented an exceptional mitigatory factor in English law. In violent crimes that resulted in injury short of death, the fact that the accused committed the violent act under provocation did not affect the nature of the offence.[126] The fact that the provocation caused the accused to lose his self-control was merely a matter to be taken into consideration in determining the appropriate penalty to impose. In homicide, however, provocation effected a change in the offence, reducing it from murder, for which the penalty became imprisonment for life, to manslaughter where the penalty lay at the discretion of the judge.[127] The Coroners and Justice Act 2009 provisions in this regard, considered below, have replaced provocation with a straitened and constrained defence of loss of self-control subject to qualifying triggers,[128] but the partial nature of the defence is retained, aligned with a corresponding burden of proof on the prosecution.[129]

A controversial aspect of the old law, subject to two detailed Law Commission Reports,[130] and a potpourri of conflicting authorities,[131] focused on which of the defendant's personal characteristics could be attributed to the reasonable person as part of the objective (second limb) of the prevailing dual standard.[132] The debate concentrated on whether the jury should be required or permitted to take into account individual characteristics of an accused, liable to affect the level of self-control that he or she could be expected to show in the face of any provocation. Should lower levels of ratiocination, and correspondingly, reduced expectation levels, be ascribed to an intoxicated, or an immature or mentally impaired defendant, in that they are unable to exercise the same level of self-control, in the context of provocation generally, as a sober adult with normal mental capacities?[133]

The dilemmatic choice(s) that underpinned the above question centred on evaluations of who and how reasonable is the reasonable man. Lord Diplock, in *DPP* v. *Camplin*, expounded the best

---

126   *Camplin* (n. 93) 705 and 713 (Lord Diplock).

127   See, generally, Timothy Macklem, 'Provocation and the Ordinary Person' (1987) 11 Dalhousie Law Journal 126; and Alan Reed, 'Duress and Provocation as Excuses to Murder: Salutary Lessons from Recent Anglo-American Jurisprudence' (1996) 6 Florida State University, Journal of Transnational Law and Policy 51.

128   Coroners and Justice Act 2009, s. 55.

129   Ibid., s. 54(5) states: 'On a charge of murder if sufficient evidence is adduced to raise an issue with respect to the defence under subsection (1), the jury must assume that the defence is satisfied unless the prosecution proves beyond reasonable doubt that it is not.'

130   See Law Com. No 173, 2003 (n. 1); Law Com. No 290, 2004 (n. 6); and Law Com. No 304, 2006 (n. 6).

131   See below (nn. 147–153); and, see generally, Richard Holton and Stephen Shute, 'Self-Control in the Modern Provocation Defence' (2007) 27 Oxford Journal of Legal Studies 49; John Gardner and Timothy Macklem, 'Compassion without Respect? Nine Fallacies in *R* v. *Smith*' [2001] Criminal Law Review 623; and Dressler, 'Rethinking Heat of Passion: A Defense in Search of a Rationale' (n. 106).

132   The first limb prescribes a subjective test which relates to the defendant him or herself, and asks, was the defendant acting in a provoked manner within the legal meaning of the term?; and see *Duffy* [1949] 1 All ER 932.

133   See, generally, John Gardner, 'The Gist of Excuses' (1998) 1 Buffalo Criminal Law Review 575.

known biographical iteration of the reasonable man for the purposes of the defence of provocation. He suggested that the 'reasonable man ... is a person having the power of self-control to be expected of an ordinary person of the sex and age of the accused, but in other respects sharing such of the accused's characteristics as they think would affect the gravity of the provocation to him'.[134] Lord Diplock consequentially posited two uses for the defendant's characteristics in answering the objective question, beyond the consideration of whether the defendant exhibited the power and self-control of an ordinary person of their own sex and age. The first concerned the extent to which characteristics may affect self-control, and thus the ease with which a defendant may be provoked. Academicians have at various times labelled these issues *provocability*,[135] and those characteristics which the reasonable man may be taken to possess in the determination of his power of self-control, *control* characteristics.[136] The second use which Lord Diplock perceived for the characteristics of the defendant was in determining the gravity of the provocation to the accused. This issue has been anthropomorphised as *provocativeness*,[137] and the corresponding characteristics, *response* characteristics.[138]

The law developed, prior to the Coroners and Justice Act 2009 reforms, as it appears Lord Diplock envisaged, such that the list of characteristics, including alcoholism, immaturity and mental abnormality, with which it was possible to endow the reasonable man, differed depending on whether one was considering the issue of *control* or *response*. The problem created thereby for ethical determination by the fact-finders, as extrapolated below, was that any 'lodestar' in decision-making, attendant to a moral or social barometer of acceptable characteristics (or otherwise) for legitimate consideration, was obviated by the straitjacket of the *control/response* dichotomy. No morally acceptable standard developed of personification, operating as a barometer of social mores at a junction in time, but contrarily a distinctive hue emerged whereby fact-finders were inappropriately transmogrified to provide a normative as well as fact-finding function.

On the question of *response*, it appeared that the reasonable man shared any characteristics of the accused which affected the gravity of the provocation to him or her. The question of the gravity of provocation concerned those provoking events which were in some way directed at the relevant (*response*) characteristic.[139] Thus the reasonable man, when considering the issue of *response*, was invested with any characteristics of the accused, provided they were sufficiently permanent to meet the criterion of being a 'characteristic' within the meaning of the law, and of course, provided that it was the question of response that was being addressed. That was to say the provoking event(s) were somehow, in substance if not literally, directed at the characteristic in question.[140]

The bifurcatory independence of applicable *response* and *control* characteristics, separated between the Scylla and Charybdis, received crystallisation in the seminal case of *Morhall*.[141] In retrospect, the rejection of the morally positive pathway and social barometer indicia provided by

---

134 *Camplin* (n. 93), 718.

135 See Andrew Ashworth, 'The Doctrine of Provocation' (1976) 35 Cambridge Law Journal 292, 300, asserting: 'the proper distinction ... is that individual peculiarities which bear on the gravity of the provocation should be taken into account, whereas individual peculiarities bearing on the accused's level of self-control should not'; and see, generally, John Smith [1995] Criminal Law Review 891 (note).

136 Peter Seago and Alan Reed, 'Criminal Law' [1997] All England Law Reports Annual Review 117.

137 Ashworth, 'The Doctrine of Provocation' (n. 135).

138 Seago and Reed (n. 136).

139 See, generally, Adrian Briggs, 'Provocation Re-Assessed' (1996) 112 Law Quarterly Review 403; and Alan Norrie, 'The Structure of Provocation' (2001) 54 Current Legal Problems 307.

140 See, generally, Jeremy Horder, *Provocation and Responsibility* (Clarendon, 1991).

141 *Morhall* [1996] 1 AC 90.

the appellate court in *Morhall*[142] represented a crucially significant jurisprudential landmark, and a precursor to the need for legislative reforms. The defendant was addicted to glue-sniffing, and had killed the victim who had taunted him about his inability to kick the habit. Thus, the provocation was directed at a particular trait of the defendant. The question was whether an addition to glue-sniffing was to be taken into account in addressing the issue of how a reasonable person would have responded to the provocation. In effect, should the jury in assessing the gravity of the provocation be required to ask how a reasonable person addicted to glue-sniffing would have responded to a taunt about being addicted to glue-sniffing? Unsurprisingly, the Court of Appeal struggled with the very idea of a 'reasonable person' in this antithetical juxtaposition, and Lord Taylor CJ stated that the addiction could not be relevant because it was a characteristic repugnant to the concept of a reasonable person:

> Otherwise, some remarkable results would follow. Not only would a defendant, who habitually abuses himself by sniffing glue to the point of addiction, be entitled to have that characteristic taken into account in his favour by the jury; logic would demand similar indulgence towards an alcoholic, or a defendant who had illegally abused heroin, cocaine or crack to the point of addiction. Similarly a paedophile, upbraided for molesting children, would be entitled to have his characteristic weighed in his favour on the issue of provocation. Yet none of these addictions on propensities could sensibly be regarded as consistent with the reasonable man ... they surely cannot include characteristics repugnant to the concept of the reasonable man.[143]

The House of Lords, however, disagreed in *Morhall*, reversing the decision of the Court of Appeal, and suggesting that the 'reasonable' person, in this context, was merely a yardstick against which to measure the conduct of the defendant taking into account all the relevant circumstances.[144] That is to say, the reasonable person was not necessarily reasonable in the sense that they were absolutely morally upstanding; in fact, the obverse transpired as discreditable/creditable characteristics were to be treated alike provided a tautological link was evident – alcoholism, drug addiction, immaturity, mental abnormality were all part of the same subset provided a characteristic was 'permanent' not 'transitory' and thus potentially supererogatory if directly the subject matter of the taunt. The moral and social standardisation was rendered nugatory, an ethical barometer opportunity was obfuscated, supplanted by an excusatory template which, 'did not get to the nub of the problem'.[145]

As for *control* characteristics, if Lord Diplock was to be taken literally, the list was closed. Age and sex, and only age and sex, would be relevant to powers of self-control. Prior to *Holley*,[146] however, a remarkable development occurred whereby in a panoply of cases a concoction of liberalised judicial assessments removed boundaries of moral/ethical rectitude attached to individual defendants. This solipsistic and ad hoc development, and with predictive outcome as likely as tattooing soap bubbles, was empathetically promulgated by a desire to allow certain defendants to benefit from the defence of provocation. A sympathetic hand was extended to normative evaluation of psychological/physiological conditions: battered women syndrome and personality disorder;[147]

---

142 *Morhall* [1993] 4 All ER 888.
143 Ibid., 893.
144 *Morhall* (n. 141) 98.
145 Alan Norrie, 'The Coroners and Justice Act 2009 – Partial Defences to Murder: (1) Loss of Control' [2010] Criminal Law Review 275, 283.
146 *Holley* (n. 94).
147 *Thornton (No 2)* [1996] 2 Cr App R 108.

stress and anxiety effected by caring for a newborn baby;[148] obsessive traits;[149] emotional immaturity and attention-seeking behavioural patterns;[150] low intelligence;[151] clinical depression;[152] and even sexual jealousy and possessiveness.[153] A schism was created, viewed through different lenses as, 'an evaluative free-for-all in which anything that induces sympathy by the same token helps to excuse, and in which little more than lip service is paid to the all-important objective (impersonal) standard of the reasonable person',[154] and denigrated as 'weak excuse' theory;[155] or alternatively, 'that the criminal law ought not to expect people to behave in a manner beyond their abilities, and that this necessarily means we should reform the law in a way which is consistent with contemporary psychiatric and psychological thinking'.[156]

Post-*Holley*,[157] the 'orthodoxy' of a closed list of age and sex as *control* characteristics was restored. The defendant's alcoholism (and by parity of reasoning other personality traits of depression, strong feelings of worthlessness, avoidant personality, and anxiety) was excluded from consideration in the context of a 'uniform objective standard',[158] and no longer were fact-finders, 'free to set whatever standard they consider appropriate in the circumstances by which to judge whether the defendant's conduct is "excusable"'.[159] A lengthy tradition existed that the transitory state of intoxication *per se* was inapplicable as a relevant characteristic,[160] but similarly in *Holley* a permanent condition of chronic alcoholism was stigmatised in similar vein:

> the defendant's intoxicated state is not a matter to be taken into account by the jury when considering whether the defendant exercised ordinary self-control. The position is the same, so far as provocation is concerned, if the defendant's addiction to alcohol has reached the state that he is suffering from the disease of alcoholism.[161]

The *control* characteristics bulwark presented in *Holley* straddles the analytical and the practical, and is fundamental to the evaluation that follows of the new reforms. Our empirical and normative expectations differ, as Tadros expertly highlights,[162] in the scenario of the voluntarily/involuntarily intoxicated offender. In the former case, although intoxication may have reduced the accused's capacity for self-control, nonetheless 'societal' expectations remain unaltered. A markedly different analysis prevails in relation to the 'in'-voluntarily intoxicated killer, suffering from a disease of alcoholism (see earlier) whereby, 'we no longer expect him to show the levels

---

148 *Doughty* (1986) 83 Cr App R 319.
149 *Dryden* [1995] 4 All ER 987.
150 *Humphreys*[1995] 4 All ER 1008.
151 *Acott* [1997] 1 All ER 706.
152 *Smith (Morgan)* [2001] 1 AC 146.
153 *Weller* [2003] EWCA Crim 815; [2004] 1 Cr App R 1.
154 John Gardner and Timothy Macklem (n. 131) 635.
155 Jeremy Horder, 'Between Provocation and Diminished Responsibility' (1999) 10 Kings College Law Journal 143, 145–6; and see, generally, Jeremy Horder, *Excusing Crime* (Oxford University Press, 2004) 125.
156 Barry Mitchell, Ronnie Mackay and Warren Brookbanks, 'Pleading for Provoked Killers: In Defence of *Morgan Smith*' (2008) Law Quarterly Review 675.
157 *Holley* (n. 94).
158 Ibid., 593 (Lord Nicholls).
159 Ibid.
160 See for example, *McCarthy* [1954] 2 QB 105; and *Newell* (1980) 71 Cr App R 331.
161 *Holley* (n. 94) 594 (Lord Nicholls).
162 Victor Tadros, *Criminal Responsibility* (Oxford University Press, 2010) 365–6.

of self-control that reflect normative reasons'.[163] This demarcation is rendered nugatory in *Holley*'s objective personification. The position taken in *Holley* attempted to draw a line between provocation and diminished responsibility, despite cogent views to the contrary on coalescence of the defences,[164] and alcoholism/mental abnormalities were pigeonholed accordingly. It left open an egregious situation whereby a defendant was not *sufficiently* mentally impaired to benefit from the defence of diminished responsibility, but also could not make use of provocation, because on the issue of self-control, no characteristics other than age or sex became casuistically relevant. The position has arguably worsened post-2010 reforms for categorisation of impairment not within the purview of 'medically recognised conditions',[165] potentially embracing delusions, paranoia, variants of anxiety disorders and avoidant personalities.

The Coroners and Justice Act reforms, considered below, can helpfully be deconstructed in the evaluative context of the post-*Holley* schematic template. A bizarre iteration prevailed, extrapolated from *response* and *control* characterisations. A clear distinction operated between characteristics of the defendant which were relevant to the degree of self-control exercised by the reasonable person (age and sex only are relevant); and characteristics which affect the gravity of the provocation to the defendant (any characteristics might be relevant). The fact-finders were consequently presented with a tautologous dilemma involving opaque mental gymnastics, and it was difficult for them to understand the difference. In a scenario where a drunken defendant was taunted about his alcoholism, the jury would be instructed to ignore his intoxicated state. However, in a volte-face, they would be expected to take into account his alcoholism in so far as it affected the gravity of the provocation to him but not in so far as it might have affected his ability to control himself. The yardstick against which the jury would be expected to measure the conduct of the defendant would be the 'reasonable' (sober, non-alcoholic) person being taunted about their alcoholism. Consider, similarly, a defendant as in *Luc*[166] suffering from organic brain disease, but taunted about their mental frailty. When determining the objective question, the fact-finders would have to be asked what the *response* to such a taunt would have been from a reasonable, non-mentally impaired person of the same age and sex of the defendant taunted about a mental abnormality which he or she actually had. In many respects jurors were placed in a perfidious conundrum.

A lack of definitional certainty also existed post-*Holley* in that situations prevailed where it was unclear whether a particular characteristic was being invoked on the self-control issue or on the touchstone of the gravity of the provocation. By way of postulation, as stated,[167] it is interesting to reflect a scenario where a defendant with a pathological sensitivity to noise was provoked by the sound of loud shouting. Did the nub of this dispute focus upon the accused asserting, 'My self-control is lowered by my sensitivity to noise' (in which case a court would be required to ignore it) or 'Noise affects me in an especially grave manner because of my sensitivity (in which case it could be taken into account)'. In essence, post-*Holley* our law lacked a moral and social barometer in terms of guiding characteristics, it demanded mental gyrations of confused jurors, and lacked definitional clarity. As such, it was ripe for reform, but has change brought cathartic panacea or simply engendered fresh ills in new bottles?

---

163 Ibid., 366.
164 See Mackay and Mitchell, 'Provoking Diminished Responsibility: Two Pleas Merging into One?' (n. 89); Ronnie Mackay and Barry Mitchell, 'But Is This Provocation? Some Thoughts on the Law Commission's Report on Partial Defences to Murder' [2005] Criminal Law Review 85; and Mitchell, Mackay and Brookbanks (n. 156).
165 See, generally, Alan Reed and Ben Fitzpatrick, *Criminal Law* (4th edn, Sweet & Maxwell, 2009).
166 *Luc Thiet Thuan* [1996] 2 All ER 1033.
167 Reed and Fitzpatrick (n. 165).

The Coroners and Justice Act 2009 – Something Borrowed and Something New

The government, in setting qualifying triggers as preliminary filter devices for engagement of the new loss of self-control defence (replacing provocation), have consequently raised the discretionary bar in an exclusionary fashion. The prescribed aspiration has been to 'raise the threshold' so that words and conduct would constitute a defence 'only in exceptional circumstances'.[168] A by-product is that defendants in the types of 'provocative' situations presented in *Doughty*[169] (stressed parent of persistently crying child), or *Dryden*[170] (obsessional home owner embroiled in planning dispute), or *Baillie*[171] (affronted parent of drug-dealing son) and presumptively *Morhall*[172] (glue-sniffing addiction) are no longer within the operational purview of the defence as falling far below the threshold standard(s) of fear or justifiable anger. Maria Eagle, Parliamentary Under Secretary of State for Justice, set out the new terms in the following explicit fashion:

> What we, therefore, sought to do in respect of the change to a provocation defence is to raise the threshold generally, so that those who kill in anger can succeed in having their conviction reduced to manslaughter only in exceptional circumstances. So, we are raising the bar of the availability of that defence and extending it to cover those who kill in fear of serious violence as well as those who kill in anger.[173]

The new partial defence of loss of self-control contains a remodelled 'reasonable person' test, derived in part from *Camplin/Holley* in terms of 'control' elements, but obviates explicit reference to the taunt/characteristic linkage purveyed in *Morhall*. To the extent that *control/response* characteristics are relevant at all they have been coalesced together in a fudged merger. The ambit of permissible provocative conduct, in any event, is restrictively circumscribed as the accused's loss of self-control must be attributable to (i) a fear of serious violence[174] or (ii) circumstances of an extremely grave character which cause a justifiable sense of being seriously wronged.[175] In the latter context the law has broadly shifted away from the excusatory nature of the gravity of the provocation to the particularised defendant via the direct link of taunt and characteristic, and looks instead at partly condonable anger as a derivative of actions or words producing an insulted response.

This unchartered legislative sea change, as all key concepts are left undefined, has been expertly summarised as a shift from 'compassionate excuse' towards 'imperfect justification'[176] with a new moral and social barometer of partly appropriate anger; 'under the new ethical approach ... sympathy for human frailty is rejected in favour of a recognition of imperfectly justified anger. Anger is partially rightful ... it is the imperfectly valid moral connection between the provocation and the response that is relevant. Provocation causally links the anger felt to the deed done or

---

168 HC Deb., Tuesday 3 February 2009, 8 (Maria Eagle, Parliamentary Under Secretary of State for Justice).
169 *Doughty* (n. 148).
170 *Dryden* (n. 149).
171 *Baillie* [1995] 2 Cr App R 31.
172 *Morhall* (n. 141).
173 HC Deb. (n. 168).
174 Coroners and Justice Act 2009, s. 55(3).
175 Ibid., s. 55(4).
176 Norrie, 'The Coroners and Justice Act 2009 – Partial Defences to Murder: (1) Loss of Control' (n. 145).

words said.'[177] A marked shift towards objectification has occurred throughout the new reforms: the trial judge can unilaterally remove the defence on the premise that no properly directed jury could reasonably conclude its applicability;[178] sexual infidelity is excluded;[179] incited, directed violence is outwith the new parameters;[180] and revenge is inconsistent with the ambit of the defence.[181] Moreover, it is only personal characteristics, or rather circumstances of the defendant which *caused* them to have a sense of being seriously wronged (inculcated partially rightful anger) that are in a sense relevant.[182] It is no longer necessary to consider other potentially applicable phemenological aspects of loss of self-control such as grief, emotional distress, or sadness, but these conditions, if applicable at all, will be within the contextual ambit of diminished responsibility as redefined, and evaluated above.[183]

A new definition is purveyed of the amorphous and inherently characterless Clapham omnibus driver in the context of loss of self-control as a partial defence. By s. 54(1)(c) it refers to a person of the defendant's sex and age with a normal degree of tolerance and self-restraint who, in the same circumstances as the defendant found himself in, *might* have acted in the same way or a similar way. Further, s. 54(3) allows the jury to consider *all circumstances* except those whose only relevance to the defendant's conduct is that they have a bearing on his general capacity for tolerance and self-restraint.

The new objective standardisation within s. 54 will have important resonances in novel applications to the intoxicated or mentally impaired killer. It is significant that the identifiable and particularised relevant characteristics of the accused (sex, age, tolerance and restraint) are conjoined together with explicit reference to *the circumstances of the defendant*.[184] The corollary of this momentum shift is presumptively a departure from primordial focus on gravity of provocation and capacity for self-control within the proclivities of internalised characteristics.[185] Modern reflection will instead relate to an accused's overarching circumstances as explanatory behaviour for loss of self-control attached to fear or anger.[186] Utilisation of prevailing 'circumstances' suggests an elongated consideration by jurors of cumulative 'personal history' of the defendant, or underlying events or episodes, and consequentially embracing organic brain disease, depressive illnesses, chronic alcoholism, personality disorders, or drug addiction. Excluded will be circumstances that *only* have relevance to an accused's general capacity for tolerance and self-restraint. It is unclear at this juncture how wide the spectrum of circumstances can be drawn in the context of transitory, as opposed to permanent events, such as temporary intoxication, recreational drug use or drug-related

---

177 Ibid., 284.
178 Coroners and Justice Act 2009, s. 54(6).
179 Ibid., s. 55(6)(c).
180 Ibid., s. 55(6).
181 Ibid., s. 54(4).
182 Ibid.
183 Ibid., s. 52.
184 See, generally, Amanda Clough, 'Loss of Self-Control as a Defence: The Key to Replacing Provocation' (2010) 74 Journal of Criminal Law 127; Susan Edwards, 'Anger and Fear as Justifiable Preludes for Loss of Self-Control (2010) 74 Journal of Criminal Law 223; Miles (n. 84); and Carol Withey, 'Loss of Control' (2010) 174 Criminal Law and Justice Weekly 197.
185 For an excellent discussion of key reforms pertaining to sexual infidelity see Rudi Fortson QC, 'Homicide Reforms under the CAJA 2009' (Criminal Bar Association of England and Wales Seminar, October 2010) <http://www.rudifortson4law.co.uk/legaltexts/Homicide%20Offences_CBA_handout_for_16th Oct2010_R_Fortson_submitted_v.7.pdf> (accessed 27 March 2011).
186 See Stanley Yeo, 'English Reform of Provocation and Diminished Responsibility: Whither Singapore?' (July, 2010) Singapore Journal of Legal Studies 177.

paranoia. The benefit of allowing circumstances to be evaluated in such a fashion, and underlying events or episodes, is that it obviates deeming it, 'as a characteristic by internalising it as some kind of syndrome or character flaw'.[187] This may allow enhanced hermeneutic consideration by fact-finders in an empathetic and sympathetic[188] manner, albeit that 'legitimate' provocative conduct itself has been constrained.

The new provisions omit any reference to the position where an accused acts in mistaken belief as to prevailing circumstances, and kills in excessive self-defence. In this regard the Law Commission explicitly stated that no need existed to 'supplement the common law in these cases'.[189] Difficulties may prevail within the first qualifying trigger, that of fear of serious violence. If the fear is irrationally based as a product of mental abnormality, where for instance a defendant kills under a paranoid delusion about threatening conduct by the victim, it is submitted that diminished responsibility, not provocation, is the appropriate defence and the post-*Holley* division is applicable.

Drunken mistaken belief arising from self-induced intoxication has proved troublesome at common law.[190] Voluntary intoxication can at best afford a defence only if it negatives the *mens rea* required of the offence:[191] 'it is not the drunkenness that is supplying the exculpation ... it is the lack of *mens rea*'.[192] For murder, intoxication will *only* be a defence if it means that the accused did not form the intention to kill or cause grievous bodily harm. A divide has been made between specific/basic intent crimes following *Majewski*[193] whereby lack of *mens rea* in the former run of cases may exculpate, but arguably voluntary intoxication provides inculpation in the latter as the defendants, 'evinced the level of culpability that the *mens rea* requirement is designed to track'.[194] Indeed, there are suggestions in *Majewski*[195] that the prosecution may be entitled to lead evidence of drunkenness in basic intent crimes (such as manslaughter) in substitution for proving the required *mens rea*. If the accused is indeed so drunk that he does not form the *mens rea* of a basic intent crime, the prosecution will be unable to establish the fault element for culpability. In such circumstances the prosecution should be entitled to prove that the accused did not form the *mens rea* for the offence, but that had he not been drunk he would have done so. This would achieve the same result as the US MPC, which provides, 'When recklessness establishes an element of the offence, if the actor, due to self-induced intoxication, is unaware of a risk of which he would have been aware had he been sober, such unawareness is immaterial.'[196]

The correlation between drunken mistaken belief and self-defence has arisen in English law in *O'Grady*,[197] *O'Connor*,[198] and more recently in *Hatton*.[199] A sober defendant is to be judged

---

187 Clough (n. 184) 124.
188 See, generally, Fortson QC (n. 185).
189 See Law Com. No 290, 2004 (n. 6) para. 3.160; and see *Letenock* (1917) 12 Cr App R 221.
190 See Finbarr McAuley, 'The Intoxication Defence in Criminal Law' (1997) 32 Irish Jurist 243.
191 See, generally, Paul Robinson, 'Causing the Conditions of One's Own Defences' (1985) 73 Virginia Law Review 1.
192 Simester (n. 11) 13: 'The criminal law does contain an intoxication defence, but it is a doctrine of *inculpation*, not exculpation'; and ibid., 4.
193 *Majewski* (n. 11); and see, generally, Simon Gardner, 'The Importance of *Majewski*' (1984) 4 Oxford Journal of Legal Studies 279.
194 Simester (n. 11) 13.
195 *Majewski* (n. 11); see, generally, Jeremy Horder, 'Pleading Involuntary Lack of Capacity' (1993) 52 Cambridge Law Journal 298.
196 MPC (n. 90) §208.2.
197 [1987] QB 995.
198 [1991] Crim LR 135.
199 [2005] EWCA Crim 2951.

on the issue of justification on the facts he honestly believed to exist, however unreasonable his belief. Since murder is a crime of specific intent, may a drunken defendant plead that because he was drunk he mistakenly believed that circumstances existed requiring a need to defend himself with fatal force? A negative response has been elicited for the offences of murder (specific intent) and manslaughter (basic intent): 'where the jury are satisfied that the defendant was mistaken in his belief that any force or the force that he in fact used was necessary to defend himself and are further satisfied that the mistake was caused by voluntary induced intoxication, the defence must fail'.[200] Common law principles in this regard have been replicated by s. 76(5) of the Criminal Justice and Immigration Act 2008.[201] It is submitted, despite the finality of earlier statements, that caution needs to be exercised in this regard when drunken mistakes, excessive force in self-defence and loss of self-control are intertwined. In murder, the specific intent is the intent to kill or cause grievous bodily harm and so the accused would be able to raise intoxication to show that he did not intend to kill or seriously injure a human being, but not to show that he believed he was acting in self-defence or that he believed the victim not to be within the Queen's Peace. It is postulated that, in the context of the Coroners and Justice Act qualifying trigger relating to 'fear' of serious violence, the position remains that voluntary intoxication is relevant in crimes of specific intent, but only in so far as it relates to the requirement of intention, rather than subjectivised mistaken beliefs in circumstances of justification.

Unreasonable mistaken belief induced by voluntary intoxication has arisen infrequently at common law in the US. An interesting point of comparison arose in the court of appeals decision in *State* v. *Mauricio*.[202] The accused, severely intoxicated at the time of the fatal act, killed the victim upon mistaking him for a nightclub bouncer with whom he had engaged in conflict earlier in the night, and from whom he feared violent repercussions. The Supreme Court of New Jersey found that the superior court had erred in failing to allow jury evaluation of the heat of passion defence: a self-induced unreasonable drunken mistake did not obviate consideration by fact-finders of a provocation defence.[203] Interestingly, conflicting statements were delivered in *Howell* v. *State*,[204] reflective of a preponderance of jurisdictions, wherein the court of appeals extrapolated that the concept of 'reasonableness' is inherently inconsistent with provocation, 'the existence of serious provocation must be determined through the eyes of a reasonable (and sober) person standing in the defendant's shoes', and in qualifying terminology that sober is 'here taken to mean that the reasonableness of one's determination of provocation is to be presumed unreasonable in the case that the determiner is intoxicated'.[205]

---

200 *O'Grady* (n. 197) 999 (Lord Lane CJ).

201 Section 76(5) of the Criminal Justice and Immigration Act 2008 provides that, 'subsection 4(b) does not enable D to rely on any mistaken belief attributable to intoxication that was voluntarily induced'.

202 568 A 2d 879, 881 (NJ 1990). See, generally, Reid Griffith Fontaine, 'Adequate (Non) Provocation and Heat of Passion as Excuse Not Justification' (2009) 43 University of Michigan Journal of Law Reform 27; and Peter Western, 'How Not to Argue that Reasonable Provocation Is an Excuse' (2009) 43 University of Michigan Journal of Law Reform 175.

203 Ibid., 887.

204 917 P2d, 1207.

205 Ibid.

Conclusion

This chapter has aimed to add further grist to the mill towards facilitation of appropriate treatment of the severely intoxicated and/or mentally abnormal offender who kills. The subject matter has been enervated by the novel classificatory system provided by the Coroners and Justice Act 2009, and comparative extirpation of reform and traditional states in the US. It is submitted that whatever schematic template is purveyed to partial defences to murder, whether in the contextual ambit of diminished responsibility or loss of self-control, it is fundamental that 'objectification', 'characterisation' and 'personification' of individual defendants reflect appropriate societal expectations and legitimate beliefs of attitudinal behaviours. The defence provided is only partial not full, and consequently allows a mitigating sentencing discretion. The concomitant of this partially excusatory framework is that any moral barometer standardisation needs to be reflective of appropriate gradations of rectitude and culpability. In a number of respects, as iterated, this barometer remains either ineffective or uncertain in regard to the chronic alcoholic or mentally abnormal killer.

Chapter 13

Provoking a Range of Responses: The Provocation Defence in British Overseas Territories and Crown Dependencies

Claire de Than

Introduction

> It would seem to us to be highly undesirable that ... [a defence] should be different in the two jurisdictions [of Jersey and Guernsey]. ... it would seem highly desirable that any reform of the law should result from legislation and involve a co-ordinated law applicable in all jurisdictions in the United Kingdom and in the jurisdictions of Jersey and Guernsey.[1]

> ... it is earnestly to be hoped that it [a judicial decision clarifying the law of Jersey] will not be based either upon historic practice in Guernsey or upon statutory intervention in the United Kingdom, neither of which seems particularly relevant to what is the law of Jersey.[2]

On reading official reports and reform proposals from any of the larger Commonwealth states, including England, it would be easy to form the impression that the widest possible definition of Britain is England, Wales, Scotland and Northern Ireland and that there are five or six Commonwealth nations. In proposing what became ss. 54–6 of the Coroners and Justice Act 2009, the Law Commission of England and Wales referred to the relevant law of Australia, India, New Zealand, Canada, South Africa, Ireland and Scotland[3] and the government referred only to England and Wales.[4] There is a widespread misapprehension that British Overseas Territories have 'no real law of their own', cited by some very credible sources,[5] but this is demonstrably untrue in criminal law, where codification and the varying extents to which English law has been imported have led to a great deal of variance.[6] Such impressions may be forgivable, given the dearth of source materials and academic commentary.[7] European Union law has, in other fields, been responsible for the laws of UK and her sister islands moving apart rapidly, but that has not occurred with

---

1 *Prior* v. *Attorney General* [2002] JLR 11 (CA) (Jersey) 15 (Vaughan JA), concerning the definition of insanity.
2 Editorial Miscellany, Jersey Law Review, June 2002, referring to the above comment of the Court of Appeal in *Prior*.
3 Law Commission, *Partial Defences to Murder* (Law Com. CP No 173, 2003), Apps A–F.
4 Ministry of Justice, *Murder, Manslaughter and Infanticide: Proposals for Reform of the Law* (MoJ CP 19, 2008).
5 Who shall remain anonymous to avoid any embarrassment!
6 These issues will be discussed below.
7 See Graeme Broadbent, 'Provocation – Does *Paria* Add Anything Useful?' (2004) 68 Journal of Criminal Law 244 for a rare recent exception.

substantive criminal law. Far from simply following English common law, the more populous British Overseas Territories have largely codified criminal laws, with some notable variance in their provisions since they have been derived from different sources at a wide range of dates. Thus they are becoming increasingly divergent from English criminal law, and this will continue unless legislative developments in England are mirrored in the sister jurisdictions. Most British Overseas Territories and all Crown Dependencies are free to choose whether to adopt their own versions of English statutes.

It is also untrue that Crown Dependencies defer to English law. Thought should at least be given in the reform process to the effect which reform of English law has on other British territories and Crown Dependencies, particularly when they have been responsible for positive developments in English law. As may be seen from the two quotes which began this chapter, views differ as to the desirability of consistency[8] between English law and that of its sister jurisdictions, but until now there has been no attempt even to make basic points of comparison. Space constraints do not allow detailed consideration of the arguments for and against consistency of criminal law across British jurisdictions, but a few points may be noted on this hotly disputed issue. Lord Goff has spoken in favour of a single approach in English and Scottish criminal law, finding it astonishing and 'scarcely a satisfactory state of affairs' that 'identical killing can be murder in Gretna Green and manslaughter in Carlisle'.[9] Many factors, including the avoidance of pointless multiplication of effort, indicate that Commonwealth jurisdictions should look to each other's legal developments when considering reform. The case is stronger where the jurisdictions have such strong links as do those discussed in this chapter. As Sornarajah puts it,[10] 'Though uniformity in the reform of the law is not always desirable, it is necessary that changes that are made in each Commonwealth jurisdiction are made with an awareness of the considerations that were taken into account in the other jurisdictions. In this way, the underlying consistency of the law in the various Commonwealth jurisdictions could be preserved.' Whether or not the underlying consistency should be preserved, consideration of updating in line with moral and other standards is surely desirable.

The Privy Council long insisted on consistency in the common law: 'it is of the utmost importance that in all parts of the Empire where English law prevails, the interpretation of that law by the courts should be as nearly as possible the same'.[11] Times, constitutions and labels have moved on a great deal, but since the Privy Council remains the final court of appeal for all British jurisdictions, such arguments recur within their courts. When interpreting laws modelled upon English statutes, decisions of English courts are generally followed both by the Privy Council and the courts of the British sister jurisdictions. This can lead to slightly bizarre results, as can be seen in the discussion of Bermuda and of the Commonwealth Caribbean states in this chapter.

This chapter will consider the continuing impact of the provocation defence in the smaller sister jurisdictions and the possibilities for its future. The provocation defence is a long way from defunct: we may well continue for decades to deal with English provocation cases where the

---

8   I have examined similar arguments elsewhere in the context of consent as a defence in English criminal law: see Catherine Elliott and Claire de Than, 'The Case for a Rational Reconstruction of Consent in Criminal Law' [2007] Modern Law Review 225.

9   Lord Goff 'The Future of the Common Law'[1997] 46 International and Comparative Law Quarterly 745, 750.

10   Muthucumaraswamy Sornarajah, 'Duress and Murder in Commonwealth Law' [1981] 30 International and Comparative Law Quarterly 660, 681.

11   Trimble v. Hill (1879) 5 App Cas 342, 345.

death occurred before the Act came into force[12] and a narrower defence still exists in Scotland.[13] Further, the unreformed provocation defence continues to apply in many British territories and in the Crown Dependencies, and there are no signs yet of abandoning it. What will the effect of this be? Are British Overseas Territories and Crown Dependencies also reforming their laws? Could England learn from their experience?

British Overseas Territories and Crown Dependencies – The Constitutional Position

Before examining the relevant law of the jurisdictions in question, some explanation of their historical, constitutional, and legislative positions may be helpful. There are some similarities between the two groupings, but also important differences. Some key variances are size, legal culture, the extent to which they deviate from English law, and social factors. For example, some have many murders, others go a decade without one; those with more murders also have relatively high levels of guilty pleas to manslaughter by provocation.

British Overseas Territories are former British Dependencies, once colonies, and remain British by choice. Each has a Governor to represent the UK. Most have written constitutions and constitutional protection for human rights. While all follow English common law to some extent, they do so to differing degrees, and many have detailed codified criminal laws. Standard clauses adopt the common law and/or English statutes 'so far as local circumstances permit'.[14] English law was adopted by each territory at different dates,[15] and so the principles applied include snapshots of English legal history.[16] Resources can be a major factor in the development of local laws; the smaller territories tend to stay closer to English common law principles, and the larger have bodies of their own codified laws. Most have their own courts and legislatures. When drafting their criminal codes, British Overseas Territories looked beyond English law and adopted rules from a range of other sources. In the Caribbean territories, membership of the Eastern Caribbean Supreme Court leads to a great deal of influence from other Commonwealth and ex-Commonwealth territories with recent case law, so the common law jurisdictions outside Britain may be as influential as England and Wales in legal developments. Practical issues also influence each territory's law: for example most British Overseas Territories do not have their own law schools, so lawyers are trained at the University of the West Indies, the Cayman Islands Law School, or qualified in other Commonwealth countries. This can lead to a sharp learning curve on moving jurisdictions since there is a great deal of variance of codified law in particular, and is also likely to have led to transplantation of concepts, interpretation and precedent. There is major difficulty in researching the law of British Overseas Territories, since few have comprehensive law reporting, and there may

---

12 Since there is no limitation period on homicide offences, and the 2009 Act applies only to 'new' killings.

13 See James Chalmers' discussion in Chapter 11 of this book.

14 See Derek O'Brien, 'The Caribbean Court of Justice and Reading Down the Independence Constitutions of the Commonwealth Caribbean: The Empire Strikes Back' [2005] European Human Rights Law Review 607–27, for discussion of some of the relevant clauses.

15 Usually via a 'reception clause' which imports common law principles and statutes already in existence by a particular date; see Bruce Harvey McPherson, *The Reception of English Law Abroad* (Supreme Court Library of Queensland, 2007) for a comprehensive account of the impact of English law on overseas territories.

16 This is particularly evident in criminal law and financial law, each of which has widespread departures from the current English principles.

be significant delays in cases becoming available online even when that service is available.[17] The potential problems with precedent should be obvious.

Crown Dependencies are unfortunately named, since they are the more independent category. They are part of the British Isles, but not Great Britain. The Queen is Head of State and each has a Lieutenant-Governor to represent her. However they are not part of the UK nor of the EU,[18] are self-governing and have their own legal systems, courts, legislatures and elections. Laws require Royal Assent once passed, but Royal Assent may only be denied where the legislation threatens UK interests.[19] Very few Acts of the Westminster Parliament now extend to them. The extent to which each follows English common law differs, but the Channel Islands are 'mixed' jurisdictions, using principles drawn from both common law and civil law systems. English precedents are used when appropriate to interpret laws, and appeals to the Privy Council have led to reciprocal influences.

The Range of Provocation Defences in British Overseas Territories and Crown Dependencies[20]

We shall examine the British Overseas Territories first, with some comparison to the Commonwealth Caribbean jurisdictions, then the Crown Dependencies. As we shall see, the position is quite complex and the jurisdictions may be grouped as follows:

- some have no recent case law and a recent constitution so are currently using codified versions of the English provocation defence;
- some have no recent case law and an older constitution and so may soon have an opportunity to reform or may be bound by the 2009 Act;
- some have recent case law applying the Homicide Act 1957 as interpreted in *Holley*;[21]
- two have recent case law applying a non-UK provocation definition in their code;
- none has recent case law ignoring *Holley*, but that would be an option for the non-Privy Council Commonwealth states;
- some have codified criminal laws, from various sources; others are applying the old English law;
- some are in the process of recodifying their criminal law and one is proposing to adopt the 'loss of control' defence.

British Overseas Territories

Anguilla[22]
The Anguilla Criminal Code 2000 restated existing common law and statute, including the provocation defence;[23] no recent relevant cases have been reported.

---

17 This chapter would not have been possible without personal contacts in various jurisdictions, both lawyers and government members, to whom thanks are owed.
18 Space precludes consideration of the 'special relationship' with the EU.
19 See the section on Guernsey, below, for further detail.
20 With a little information about each jurisdiction for background and context.
21 [2005] UKPC 23.
22 Population c. 15,000, appeals to Eastern Caribbean Supreme Court, has a criminal code.
23 Section 186 definition of murder, s. 187 diminished responsibility, s. 189 provocation.

Bermuda[24]

The current definition of murder and the partial defences is to be found in the Criminal Code Act 1907, a fascinating combination of English, Australian and Canadian legal provisions, with a local twist. Unusually for a British Overseas Territory, the homicide provisions were based not on existing English law but the Queensland Criminal Code 1899.[25] Bermuda has two categories of murder: premeditated murder;[26] and simpliciter murder,[27] which has further subdivisions. Anecdotally, there have been debates amongst lawyers recently as to when intention becomes premeditation, and further clarification may be necessary. There is a partial defence of killing in excessive force in s. 296. Strikingly,[28] provocation may be a defence to assault offences as well as to murder.[29] Provocation is defined in s. 254:

Provisions of law relating to provocation

Provocation

254(1) "provocation", in relation to an offence of which an assault is an element, means, except as hereinafter provided, any wrongful act or insult of such a nature as to be likely, when done to an ordinary person, or in the presence of an ordinary person to another person who is under his immediate care, or to whom he stands in a conjugal, parental, filial, or fraternal, relation, or in the relation of master or servant, to deprive him of the power of self-control, and to induce him to assault the person by whom the act or insult is done or offered.

(2) When such an act or insult is done or offered by one person to another, or in the presence of another to a person who is under the immediate care of that other, or to whom the latter stands in any such relation as aforesaid, the former is said to give to the latter provocation for an assault.

(3) A lawful act is not provocation to any person for an assault.

(4) An act which a person does in consequence of incitement given by another person in order to induce him to do the act, and thereby to furnish an excuse for committing an assault, is not provocation to that other person for an assault.

(5) An arrest which is unlawful is not necessarily provocation for an assault, but it may be evidence of provocation to a person who knows of the illegality.

Section 255 applies the provocation defence to assault offences:

(1) A person is not criminally responsible for an assault committed upon a person who gives him provocation for the assault, if he is in fact deprived by the provocation of the power of self control, and acts upon it on the sudden and before there is time for his passion to cool:

---

24 Population c. 69,000, has own Supreme Court and Court of Appeal, has a criminal code.
25 Itself echoing the English Draft Criminal Code of 1879 and thus containing some of the same elements as s. 232 of the Canadian Criminal Code, although the latter applies to murder only.
26 Section 286A and B as amended.
27 Section 287.
28 With apologies for the pun.
29 Again, as in the Queensland Criminal Code, ss. 268 and 269.

Provided that the force used is not disproportionate to the provocation, and is not intended, and is not such as is likely, to cause death or grievous bodily harm.

Subsection (2) states that the following are questions of fact: whether an act or insult is such as to be likely to deprive the reasonable man of the power of self-control; whether the person provoked was actually deprived of self-control; the proportionality of the force used; whether death or GBH was intended or likely; and whether D acted 'on the sudden' before there was time for passion to cool.

The provocation defence to murder is in s. 295:

Subject as hereinafter provided, when a person who unlawfully kills another person under circumstances which, but for the this section, would constitute murder, does the act which causes death in the heat of passion caused by sudden provocation and before there is time for his passion to cool, he is guilty of manslaughter only:

Provided that the foregoing provisions of this section shall have no effect so as to reduce an unlawful killing to manslaughter where the force used or the mode of retaliation is not reasonably proportionate to the provocation given.

As far as the colon, this provision is based upon s. 304 of the Queensland Criminal Code 1899.[30] Reforms were proposed to that Code in 2008,[31] and are in the new Criminal Code and Other Legislation Amendment Act 2011. The Queensland Act received assent on 4th April 2011, and aims to respond to similar concerns to those which led to the new English law. In particular, Section 5 of the Act will: remove the ability to argue the defence on the basis of an insult or of sexual possessiveness or jealousy in a domestic relationship, except where the circumstances were of 'an extreme and exceptional character'; and will also reverse the burden of proof for provocation so that it would rest upon the defence. However, there are no plans in Bermuda to amend their law in line with either the English changes or the Queensland Act. The result is that a nineteenth century defence, which has never fully represented English law and is being reformed in its source jurisdiction, survives in Bermuda.[32]

Bermuda has had several recent cases concerning the applicability of and sentencing for the defence. The wording of s. 295 and the other relevant sections differs in several respects from that of the former English defence. The provocation must not be something lawful; the cooling period rule is explicit in the section; and there is an express proportionality test for both the assault and murder defences. However, the effect in cases appears to be very similar to the former English approach although the sentencing is higher. The similarity of effect is due at least in part to the use of some English cases to interpret the Code provisions: although their source may be Australian, English cases are used to interpret Bermudan laws whenever the former are relevant. If the key purposes of codifying criminal law are certainty, clarity and accessibility, to create a comprehensive Code and then interpret some of its provisions in line with the quite different common law of another jurisdiction would appear counterproductive. In fact, in Queensland a similar process has occurred

---

30 And is similar to the 1914 Criminal Code of Western Australia; both were based on English common law of the nineteenth century and some elements of the English Draft Criminal Code 1879.

31 See Queensland Law Reform Commission, *A Review of the Excuse of Accident and the Defence of Provocation* (Law Com. No 64, 2008).

32 See J.A. Iliffe, 'Provocation in Homicide and Assault Cases' (1954) 3 International and Comparative Law Quarterly 23, for more detailed discussion of the historical basis of these defences.

since English and other Commonwealth decisions have been used to interpret the relevant Code provisions; the Queensland Code does not have a full definition of provocation, so that has been added from the common law,[33] and it also lacks a 'reasonable/ordinary man' element, which has also been interpreted in by judges. Bermuda's use of English case authority has probably saved her from the difficulties seen in recent Queensland cases, where a seven-point model direction formulated by the Court of Appeal was later rejected by the High Court of Australia since it erroneously denied the defence where an ordinary person's passion would have cooled by the time of the killing.[34] Although some of the elements of ss. 254 and 255 are not repeated in s. 295, the provocation defences are interpreted in parallel, as will be seen in the case of *Burgess* below.

The most thorough recent interpretation of these defences was in an assault case, *Leroy Elmer Burgess* v. *Angela Cox (Police Constable)*,[35] where the appeal concerned the application of the defence to assault, but the court applied English authority on the homicide defence. Other recent cases have been appeals against sentencing or procedural issues. In *Burgess*, the appellant prison inmate was convicted of assaulting (and injuring) a prison officer (H) in the execution of his duty. He appealed on the basis of the definition of provocation. Earlier on the weekend of the assault, H had told B that rumours were circulating about him, and B had blamed another inmate, Damien Smith, saying 'He's lucky I don't kill him'. H warned Smith that B had made a threat against him. B's evidence was that he assaulted H after the latter said to him later that day, 'You know what you're in here for. You're in here for murder. He [Damien Smith] should know that you threatened his life.' H's statement was factually slightly incorrect: B was serving life in prison for manslaughter due to diminished responsibility! B's case was that he lost control and lunged at H because 'This made me more angry than I was. I'd not threatened Damien Smith's life. I was not in there for murder ... '.

The appeal court accepted that B had lost control and that the immediate cause was H's statement, which he regarded as an insult. B was feeling depressed and frustrated about his prison experience and in those circumstances the remark was 'particularly provocative'. The key issue was then whether an 'ordinary person'[36] was likely to lose self-control as a result of the insult, and which characteristics of B that ordinary person should possess. The magistrate had framed the question as whether an ordinary person serving prison time for an unlawful killing would be provoked when he was told that he was in prison for murder rather than manslaughter, and had answered it in the negative. The ordinary person would be one in B's situation, in prison for manslaughter after a charge of murder must have been brought against him, but already angry and upset. The ordinary man would, however have ordinary powers of self-control, not the appellant's; the appeal court agreed with the magistrate that an ordinary man would not have been provoked to violence by the insult. The appellant's general state of mind was the reason for the assault, not the specific remark. In spite of the court referring to *Smith (Morgan)*,[37] the additional use of Archbold[38] and the wording of the Code sections resulted in a narrow view being taken of that case; the 'ordinary man' had to remain part of the test in line with local law. Hence, although the present case

---

33 Since *Kaporonovski* v. *The Queen* [1973] HCA 35.
34 *R* v. *Pollock*, unreported, 20 October 2010, [2010] HCA 35; a third trial was ordered in this case, which had been the basis of the model direction.
35 *Leroy Elmer Burgess* v. *Angela Cox (Police Constable)* [2004] Bda LR 23.
36 Rather than the English 'reasonable man/person'.
37 *Smith (Morgan)* [2000] 4 All ER 289.
38 John Frederick Archbold, *Criminal Pleading, Evidence & Practice* (Sweet & Maxwell, 2003) paras 19–61 excludes 'excessive pugnacity and excitability' from the characteristics of the reasonable man, who always has reasonable self-control.

is pre-*Holley*, the effect is remarkably similar. It is very likely that *Holley* would now be followed since Bermuda still appeals to the Privy Council's jurisdiction.[39] The same result would probably be achieved under the Coroners and Justice Act 2009 in an English case; perhaps the formulation of the defence matters less than judicial and juries' attitudes to the circumstances of the killing.

The same tendency can be seen in *Andre Kirk Everett Hypolite* v. *The Queen*[40] where the appellant had been convicted of murder and unlawful wounding, receiving sentences of life and three years' imprisonment respectively. The victims were a cohabiting couple, P and D; the woman had agreed that she would exchange sex with the appellant for cocaine. The prosecution case was that the appellant, H, visited their shack with the cocaine, bringing a large knife with him, and stabbed D in the back after D refused to have anal sex with him. D survived long enough to plead for his life, but was then stabbed again repeatedly (suffering wounds and injuries in 27 different sites). P went to D's aid with a machete she found nearby and was struck with the knife on the forehead, as well as suffering defensive injuries and other stab wounds. The appellant denied that he had proposed homosexual activity with D and also that he had a weapon; he argued that he had been attacked by the others and had defended himself without a weapon, in spite of two other witnesses having seen him with knives that night. This was a difficult case since P, D, H and H's girlfriend were all habitual drug-users; P, D and H were intoxicated at the time of the killing; and P had a conviction for manslaughter using a knife. The trial judge directed the jury on the issues of self-defence and provocation, indicating that the latter could lead to a verdict of manslaughter, as well as the potential verdicts of murder or involuntary manslaughter. The jury rejected both defences; hence they took a robust approach to the evidence in ruling out provocation. An appeal based on the witnesses' credibility and on the trial judge's direction on involuntary manslaughter failed.

Juries have sometimes been kinder to defendants who kill after suffering domestic violence. In *Andrina Tamara Smith* v. *The Queen*[41] the appellant was convicted of manslaughter by provocation and sentenced to eight years' imprisonment. She killed the father of her young child, with whom she still had a relationship, by stabbing him in the neck through a door in her house. Her account was that there had been an argument, then the deceased had thrown her to the floor, put his hands around her throat and said that he felt like killing her, dragged her around by her hair then choked and punched her. The jury rejected self-defence but found provocation. An appeal against conviction failed, and the appellant also argued that the sentence was excessive. The trial judge had referred to the circumstances as being a 'passion of vengeance, a passion not tolerated by the law' after a cooling period while the appellant talked to her granny then fetched the knife, but the jury evidently disagreed enough to find that provocation had been possible. This case also demonstrates Bermuda's approach to sentencing; there is sufficient local case law to allow local sentencing precedents. The appellant's counsel argued that there was medical evidence that she had been the victim of domestic violence for a period of time, and hence that a sentence of four to six years would be indicated. The Court of Appeal found that a sentence of 10 to 12 years was appropriate for manslaughter by provocation where a knife or other offensive weapon had been used,[42] and so upheld the sentence.

---

39 See the following two cases for references to *Holley* in Bermuda courts.

40 *Andre Kirk Everett Hypolite* v. *The Queen* [2010] CA (Bda) 14 Crim, 23 November 2010; this was in fact a retrial, after the original verdict was quashed on the grounds that H had not received a fair trial.

41 *Andrina Tamara Smith* v. *The Queen* [2009] CA (Bda) 9 Crim.

42 Based on Bermudan authorities from 1996 to 2004 where sentences ranging from ten to 14 years had been upheld.

British Antarctic Territory and the British Indian Ocean Territory
Since these are military bases with no permanent population, they will be excluded from the discussion in this chapter.

British Virgin Islands[43]
The provocation defence is to be found in s. 151 of the Criminal Code 1997, which is worded identically to s. 3 of the Homicide Act 1957.[44] There have been several reported and unreported cases in recent years, with the main live issue being sentencing.

The Queen v. *Brian Walters*[45] was a high-profile case where a 15-year-old boy killed a 16-year-old during the 2007 Carnival. W pleaded not guilty to murder and was convicted by a 7:2 majority jury verdict of manslaughter by reason of provocation under s. 151. There had been fights between two groups of youths and the victim had killed W's 19-year-old uncle during the fighting. The jury must have found that W inflicted the fatal stab wounds to the victim after seeing the latter kill his uncle. In sentencing, the court applied the relevant UK sentencing guidelines and applied the process from the English case of *Attorney General's References (Nos 74, 95 and 118 of 2002)*.[46] They then looked at the sentencing practice of the Eastern Caribbean Supreme Court, referring to cases from St Lucia, Saint Vincent and the Grenadines, Antigua and Barbuda, as well as from the BVI. A benchmark of 15 years' imprisonment was seen as appropriate and, in the circumstances of W's youth and having seen the fatal attack on his uncle, a sentence of six years was imposed.

Since Commonwealth Caribbean cases are treated interchangeably with English cases and those from other British Overseas Territories, the changes to English law may make little difference in BVI. This is a noticeable tendency in British Overseas Territories, which is leading to the development of local sentencing principles, as seen recent cases: in *The Queen* v. *Shonovia Thomas*[47] T was convicted by a unanimous[48] jury of manslaughter by reason of provocation. She stabbed her partner with a tailcomb, and he survived long enough to identify her as his attacker. She argued self-defence, saying that V had pushed her around the building, onto parked vehicles and onto the ground before she stabbed him. There was a history of domestic violence and abuse. The trial judge directed the jury on provocation although T's counsel had not raised it. Defence counsel argued that cumulative provocation and the immediacy of the response should be taken into account. On sentencing, the court considered the English Sentencing Guidelines and the *AG's Reference* case[49] but again applied a higher sentence noting that 'our traditions and social matrix are so remote from England'.[50] Using decisions from Saint Lucia, Saint Vincent and the Grenadines, Barbados, Antigua and Barbuda, and BVI itself, the benchmark of 15 years' imprisonment and the 11 mitigating factors argued by the defence resulted in a 10-year sentence. Thus again, the structure of English sentencing for provocation cases was adopted, but the benchmarks raised in line with

---

43   Population c. 23,000, appeals to the Eastern Caribbean Supreme Court, has a criminal code.

44   Although the courts tend to state that 'section 3 of the Homicide Act 1957 in the United Kingdom mirrors verbatim section 151 of the Criminal Code 1997 (Virgin Islands)' – see *The Queen* v. *Brian Walters*, Case No 3 of 2008, High Court of Justice [13].

45   Eastern Caribbean Supreme Court, High Court of Justice (Criminal) Case No 3 of 2008, May 2008.

46   [2003] 2 Cr App R (S) 42.

47   Eastern Caribbean Supreme Court, High Court of Justice (Criminal), Criminal Case No 7 of 2009, July 2010.

48   And all-female.

49   *AG's Reference* case (Nos 74, 95 and 118 of 2002).

50   Ibid. [16].

Caribbean practice. (See also, *The Queen* v. *Keon Edwards*, ECSC, 1-7th April 2011, where a sentence of 20 years was imposed after a similar process.)

An older decision, *Sherwin Fahie* v. *The Queen*,[51] demonstrates both sentencing practice and the use of precedent in BVI cases. There was a fight between the 19-year-old appellant (F), the victim, and the victim's mother, involving a cutlass (waved by V's mother) and an axe (in the hands of V). The victim swung the axe twice at F's back. The fighting went on for some time and ended with F striking V repeatedly from behind with a baseball bat. F was convicted of murder, and appealed on grounds of self-defence and the trial judge's failure to leave provocation to the jury.[52] On appeal the court found that the trial judge's repeated statements that F had not raised the defence of provocation were equivalent to withdrawing that defence from the jury. Since the actions of V and his mother clearly raised the possibility of that defence, there had been a misdirection. A conviction for manslaughter and a 15-year sentence were substituted for the murder conviction. The only case cited in the appeal concerning provocation[53] was from the English Court of Appeal;[54] a perusal of the cases in this chapter will reveal that this is a common event.

The Cayman Islands[55]

Section 186 of the Penal Code (2010 Revision) is identical to s. 3 of the English Homicide Act 1957. Various appeal cases have considered aspects of the defence and the appropriate sentencing in recent years. The interpretation of the elements of the defence has stayed close to English and Privy Council authorities. Again, there are two local trends visible in the cases: sentencing is generally higher than in English cases, and reference is made to the practice of other Caribbean jurisdictions.

This jurisdiction has had the opportunity to review a wide range of issues re the provocation defence in a recent case which had convenient facts and timing for elucidation of legal principle. Key cases and principles from the English form of the defence have generally been followed, with the (happy) exception of *Smith (Morgan)*. The issue must be left to the jury if there is any evidence that the defendant may have been provoked, regardless of whether D has raised it,[56] and then the Crown must disprove the defence.[57] In *Moncrieff*, M stabbed his girlfriend four times during an argument; she had taunted him about his drinking and unemployment, then asked him to leave their home. The relationship was not a calm one and M suffered from depression, as well as addiction to alcohol and drugs. M pleaded provocation and diminished responsibility, arguing that a reasonable man with his depressive disorder would have acted similarly. The Crown argued (inter alia) that the reasonable man would not have any such characteristic, and would not have acted as M did in response to the victim's behaviour. The provocation defence failed in the Grand Court,[58] which found that the events, including 'heated and unkind arguments', were 'not sufficient provocation to make a reasonable man beat the victim with a broom handle and stab her four times';[59] a reasonable

---

51 *Sherwin Fahie* v. *The Queen* Criminal Appeal No 2 of 2000.

52 The issue of when a judge should leave provocation to the jury has arisen separately in each jurisdiction. This could have been avoided by greater cross-referencing to other British jurisdictions.

53 The only other case cited was *R* v. *Beckford* [1987] 36 WLR 300, honest belief in self-defence (Privy Council) (Jamaica).

54 *R* v. *Johnson*, 89 CAR 148, [1989] 2 All ER 839, self-induced provocation is still provocation.

55 Population c. 56,000, has appeal courts and a penal code.

56 *Ebanks*, unreported, 27 April 2006.

57 *Moncrieff* [2002] CILR 629.

58 On the basis that a reasonable man would not have been provoked by V's words and actions; however, diminished responsibility succeeded.

59 *Moncrieff* (n. 57) 27.

man would have left, not grabbed the knife. As for the issue of the reasonable man's characteristics, Sanderson J noted that the reasonable man would always have reasonable self-control, and that to attribute M's depression to the reasonable man would incorporate diminished responsibility into provocation.[60] The judge considered the treatment of *Smith (Morgan)* in Archbold[61] in order to reach that conclusion. Given that the Privy Council decision in *Holley* was still some time away,[62] this was a significant statement, since the court chose not to follow *Smith (Morgan)*, which left it bound by the Privy Council decision in *Luc Thiet Thuan*.[63] A further point worth noting about this case is that, in sentencing M, the Grand Court[64] lacked any recent local authority on diminished responsibility cases,[65] and so fell back upon reviewing the range of sentences imposed both for manslaughter by reason of provocation in Caymanian courts,[66] and in 25 English diminished responsibility cases.[67] A life sentence was imposed since M was considered a danger to the public.

Sentencing does seem to vary more than in some other British Overseas Territories, ranging from 18 months upwards, but usually in the area of 8–12 years. The start point is 15 years, then aggravating and mitigating factors are considered. Other recent cases fit the same pattern.[68]

---

60 Ibid., 22: 'In the present case this court is bound by the decision in the Privy Council. I do not consider the reasonable person to be the ordinary man who is suffering from a mental illness or disease. To do so could allow a defendant to include or incorporate the defence of diminished responsibility within the defence of provocation. I do not think the legislature intended the words 'reasonable man' to mean an ordinary man with a mental disorder.'

61 John Frederick Archbold, *Criminal Pleading, Evidence & Practice* (Sweet & Maxwell, 2002) paras 19–60, 1605.

62 Indeed the courts in Jersey were at precisely the same time applying the decision in *Smith (Morgan)*, when Jersey is technically freer to depart from a House of Lords decision since she is a Crown Dependency not a British Overseas Territory

63 [1996] 2 All ER 1033.

64 [2003] CILR 22 (Sanderson J).

65 The only previous diminished responsibility case in the Cayman Islands being *R v. Bush* (1983) where a five-year sentence was imposed since D was not considered a danger to the public.

66 *R v. Pascal*, Court of Appeal, Crim App No 7 of 1998, unreported, life; *R v. Sandoval*, Grand Court, 1997, unreported, 18 months; *R v. Connor*, Court of Appeal, Crim App No 17 of 1999, unreported, 15 years, *R v. Thomas (S.W.)* [2000] CILR N-17, ten years; *R v. Baker*, Court of Appeal, Crim App, No 19 of 2000, unreported, 13 years; *R v. Forbes*, Court of Appeal, Crim App. No 12 of 2001, unreported, ten years; *R v. Solomon*, eight years and ten years (two defendants).

67 Where sentencing ranged from three years' probation to nine years' imprisonment.

68 *Russell*, March 2006, was sentenced to 11 years after killing W; the provocation was that the previous day, W and another man, armed with an M16 assault rifle and a handgun had fired 27 shots at his house, narrowly missing R's baby granddaughter and other family members. However, R also shot at police officers after the killing. *Colin (Sheldon) Scott*, January 2008, was sentenced to 13 years on a guilty plea for stabbing his partner to death after she told him she was leaving him for another man. The judge described the evidence of provocation as 'extremely borderline'. *Rodriguez*, August 2008, was sentenced to five years after pleading guilty to manslaughter; after some confrontation between two rival groups, the victim had hit him over the head with a beer bottle and beaten and kicked him before he retaliated and stabbed V. The judge indicated that six to eight years' imprisonment would have been awarded after trial. *Gordon*, September 2009 pleaded guilty to manslaughter after killing V during a brief fight. V was the new boyfriend of G's former girlfriend. The sentence was 11 years, with the trial judge noting that the response was 'excessively out of proportion' to the provocation. *S.W. Thomas*, August 2000, pleaded guilty to manslaughter after killing his partner on discovering that she had been unfaithful. A ten-year sentence was imposed; the court noted that this was a higher sentence than would have been applied by an English court for a domestic killing, and that sentencing for manslaughter should be higher than that for non-fatal offences.

Falkland Islands
Given the population size (c. 3,200), the great rarity of murder trials (low single figures since 1900), and the lack of reported cases, there is little that can usefully be said here.

Gibraltar[69]
Section 62 of the Criminal Offences Act 1960 (Part XI) is identical to s. 3 of the former English Homicide Act 1957, and subsequent English common law applies under s. 2(1) of the English Law (Application) Act 1962, with the usual exemption for local circumstances. There has been one recent case in the Supreme Court, that of *Maria del Carmen Gomez*,[70] who pleaded guilty to manslaughter by reason of provocation after stabbing her long-term partner. There was evidence that G was the victim of domestic verbal abuse and had been accused repeatedly of infidelity.[71] A four-year sentence was given, which is broadly in line with English sentencing for domestic killings.

A Crimes Bill to update Gibraltar's criminal law, including the homicide provisions, has been in preparation and consultation for some four years, but has not yet been published or presented to the legislature and Clause 152 would replicate the effect of the new English law, abolishing the provocation defences and replacing it with loss of control. Some local barristers note uncertainty in the defence's current legal position.

Montserrat[72]
Section 152 of the Montserrat Penal Code (2008 version) has the same effect as did s. 3 of the English Homicide Act 1957. There are not many relevant cases of which details are available, unsurprisingly given the population.[73]

One case reached the Court of Appeal and is available on the Eastern Caribbean Supreme Court website: *Samuel Greenaway* v. *The Queen*.[74] G was sentenced to death for murder and appealed on the grounds that the trial judge had failed to give adequate directions as to the burden of proof in provocation cases, and the possibility of provocation arising on the evidence even where the accused denied it. These are both issues which have arisen in most of the sister islands. G stabbed V after becoming enraged that V and another man were clearing a blockage on the road adjoining G's land. The Court of Appeal found that there was no evidence on which provocation could be based, applying Lord Devlin's ruling in *Lee Chun-Chuen* v. *R*[75] that the defence should only be left to the jury if there was a 'credible narrative of events suggesting the presence of' the three elements of provocation, and hence there had been no misdirection. The appeal was dismissed. It is likely that local courts would now use the most modern English approach to these issues, and it is clear that the Privy Council would do so, as seen in the Commonwealth Caribbean case of *Bull* v. *The Queen*,[76] discussed below.

---

69   Population c. 31,000, has appeal courts and codified criminal law.
70   *Maria del Carmen Gomez*, Supreme Court, 16 January 2009.
71   Under the new English law, this could still give rise to a defence in England, since it is the reverse of the exclusion of 'sexual infidelity' as a trigger under s. 54(6).
72   Population c. 5,000, appeals to Eastern Caribbean Supreme Court, has penal code.
73   Circa 12,000 before the volcanic activity.
74   *Samuel Greenaway* v. *The Queen* October 1978, Criminal Appeal No 6 of 1978.
75   *Lee Chun-Chuen* v. *R* [1963] 1 All ER 73 at 79; the three elements being stated as 'the act of provocation, the loss of self-control, both actual and reasonable, and the retaliation proportionate to the provocation'.
76   *Bull* v. *The Queen* [1998] 1 WLR 1523.

Pitcairn
The population is c. 50 and there is no written substantive homicide law; under s. 42 of the Constitution, the jurisdiction is bound by English statutes in force as well as common law 'so far as local circumstances permit'. Thus the 2009 Act could be followed, rejected, or adapted, should a case arise. Significant and complex issues have arisen in this jurisdiction in criminal law due to its legal vacuum.[77]

St Helena/Ascension/Tristan Da Cunha[78]
It is a pivotal time for criminal law in these islands. At present, s. 3 of the Homicide Act 1957 and its interpretative cases apply, since there is no Criminal Code and English law is imported as it stood on 1 January 2006, when the English Law (Application) Ordinance came into force.[79] But St Helena is in the process of codifying criminal law, and the new draft Crimes Bill is due to enter consultation at the time of writing (spring 2011). The initial draft contains a clause headed 'Loss of self-control' which reflects the new defence under the Coroners and Justice Act 2009. Thus St Helena has a strong chance of being the first, and possibly one of only two, non-UK British territories to move to the loss of control defence. If so, this could cause a ripple effect of reform across the sister jurisdictions, although the end result might well differ from the Coroners and Justice Act 2009 since each territory could reach different conclusions as to the desirability of those provisions.

South Georgia and the South Sandwich Islands
These islands will not be discussed since they currently have no permanent inhabitants.

Turks and Caicos Islands
These islands are outside the scope of this chapter, being currently under direct rule due to political scandal.

Crown Dependencies

Guernsey[80]
Guernsey has, very recently, codified a provocation defence identical in effect to that of s. 3 of the English Homicide Act 1957. Article 3 of the Homicide and Suicide (Bailiwick of Guernsey) Law 2006[81] was given Royal Assent in 2009, and came into force in November 2009.[82] Thus the Royal Assent was granted after it became likely that the equivalent English provision, on which Article 3 was based, would be replaced. However this is not surprising: Royal Assent may only be denied to a law passed by a Crown Dependency if that law would put the United Kingdom into

---

77 See Dawn Oliver (ed.) *Justice, Legality, and the Rule of Law: Lessons from the Pitcairn Prosecutions* (Oxford University Press, 2009) for discussion of many difficult issues concerning the application of English law during the Pitcairn sexual abuse trials in *Christian and others v. The Queen* [2006] UKPC 47; [2007] 2 AC 400; see also the judgments of Lord Hope and Lord Woolf in that case.

78 Population c. 4,000, has own appeal courts, applies common law and English statutes.

79 Under ss. 2 and 3, common law, equity and statutes are imported, subject to the usual 'local conditions' exemption.

80 Population c. 63,000.

81 Which also abolishes constructive malice, creates a diminished responsibility defence, abolishes the crime of suicide, creates accomplice liability for suicide and adds a defence of suicide pact

82 Three days before the Coroners and Justice Act 2009 was passed in England, abolishing the provocation defence and replacing it with loss of control.

breach of its international obligations, infringe principles of good government, adversely affect the UK's responsibility for the defence of the Dependency, or otherwise be contrary to fundamental constitutional principles. No such threats exist or are possible from legislation which is simply moving in the opposite direction to that of England and Wales.

Before the 2006 law came into force, Guernsey was already choosing freely to apply the provocation defence as interpreted by the Privy Council in *Holley*.[83] In *Law Officers of the Crown v. Rouget*[84] the grounds of appeal were that the judge had misdirected the jurats[85] on self-defence and provocation. R was convicted of murder after stabbing V four times in a fight on a Saturday night in St Peter Port. Both R and V had been drinking, each was with a group of friends, V headbutted R and there were mutual taunts and insults. At trial for murder the Lieutenant Bailiff noted that the Homicide and Suicide (Bailiwick of Guernsey) Law 2006 had been passed but was still awaiting Royal Assent. Referring to the Jersey case on insanity, *Prior v. Attorney General*,[86] he quoted Vaughan JA,[87] who said 'It would seem to us to be highly undesirable that the effect of "insanity" should be different in the two jurisdictions [Jersey and England] since there is a need for certainty and uniformity in the criminal law.' He opined that provocation should be treated in the same way as insanity, avoiding clashes between English law and that of the Channel Islands. To do otherwise would not be in the interests of justice. Thus there is still some judicial feeling of a need for consistency between the jurisdictions, in spite of the contrary views expressed in the quotation at the beginning of this chapter. He then gave directions based on the Judicial Studies Board specimens and the majority of the Privy Council in the Jersey case of *Holley*, as applied in *James and Karimi*.[88] R was convicted unanimously of murder. The appeal was dismissed, with the court finding no misdirection and hence no reason to set aside the verdict. Of the 13 cases cited, only two, *Holley* and *Prior*, were from the Channel Islands, both Jersey cases; the others being English, Scottish or Privy Council. Hence, on this issue, Guernsey courts have been influenced greatly by those of their sister islands.

Isle of Man[89]

The Criminal Code 1872, s. 21A, as amended by the Criminal Law (Amendment) Act 1985, provides a defence of provocation in identical terms to those of s. 3 of the English Homicide Act 1957. There have been recent cases applying the defence. In *R v. Lindon*[90] the appeal was on sentencing, the Attorney General arguing that the five-year sentence imposed for manslaughter by provocation was unduly lenient. L, who had a history of self-harm, depression and a suicide attempt, killed his estranged wife after visiting her, taking with him a kitchen knife with a view to killing himself with it. L stated that his wife said 'why don't you do us all a favour' when he threatened to kill himself, and the jury found that there was provocation. The appeal court applied the list of assumptions from the (English) *Attorney General's References Nos 74, 95 and 118 of 2002*[91] and examined the

---

83 A case with which that Court of Appeal's members were extremely familiar, one of them having judged one of the trials, his brother having referred the third trial's appeal to the Privy Council and Guernsey's bailiff having heard one of the appeals.
84 *Law Officers of the Crown v. Rouget* 23 April 2008, Guernsey Court of Appeal, 2007–8 GLR 307.
85 The permanent jury, lay people who decide questions of fact in the Channel Islands.
86 *Prior v. Attorney General* [2002] JLR 11 (Vaughan JA).
87 Ibid., [15].
88 *James and Karimi* [2006] EWCA Crim 14.
89 Population c. 84,000.
90 28 October 2005, High Court of Justice of the Isle of Man.
91 *Attorney General's References Nos 74, 95 and 118 of 2002* [2003] 2 Cr App R (S) 281.

English lines of authority distinguishing 'family' manslaughter cases from other contexts. In such cases a sentencing range of five to eight years was apparent, and the Crown did not argue that Manx sentences should be longer than English. Although the Crown had argued that where an offender goes out armed with a knife to use as a weapon he should be sentenced to ten to 12 years, again in line with English authority, the relevant cases were not domestic killings. Hence the appeal court, following a previous local case,[92] expressly took the English sentencing approach and dismissed the appeal. One point to note is that the appeal court actually asked the Crown whether, given the Privy Council's then very recent decision in *Holley*, they wished to seek a reference under s. 40 of the Criminal Jurisdiction Act 1993. The Crown confirmed that they had considered the issue and did not wish to contend that there had been any misdirection.

Jersey[93]

Article 4 of the Homicide (Jersey) Law 1986 is identical to the former s. 3 of the English Homicide Act 1957. Again, as in England, the defence had arisen at common law before the 1986 law; the latter had clarified issues such as whether 'things said' could amount to provocation, the extent to which the test was objective, and the role of the judge and jury.

The decision of the Privy Council in the case of *Her Majesty's Attorney General for Jersey* v. *Holley*[94] is, of course, well known and features in other chapters of this book. Its interpretation of the provocation defence has been applied in all British Overseas Territories and Crown Dependencies which have since dealt with that defence, and has also bound courts in the Commonwealth Caribbean. But it is less well known that the case had already had three trials and two appeals in Jersey.

The first trial took place in June 2001. Both H and V, his long-term partner, were frequently drunk and violent to each other. On the day of the killing, they argued in a pub, then H went back to V's flat. H alleged that when V came home, she told him there was nothing for him to eat and that she had just had sex with another man. H picked up an axe; V said words to the effect that he did not have the courage to hit her with it,[95] but he struck her with it at least seven times. H's defence was provocation but he was convicted unanimously of murder. He appealed, inter alia,[96] on the basis that his characteristics – depression, strong feelings of worthlessness, avoidance of problems, anxiety, and dependence on women and alcohol – should have been attributed to the reasonable man in the second limb of the provocation test. The Court of Appeal[97] discussed *Luc Thiet Thuan* and *Smith (Morgan)* and decided that 'in our judgment the courts of Jersey should adopt the view which has now prevailed in England and Wales, the majority view in *Smith (Morgan)*. We consider, like that majority, like the Court of Appeal in the same case, and like Lord Steyn in *Luc Thiet Thuan*, that statutory interpretation, logic and the dictates of justice combine to make that view the appropriate one for Jersey.'[98] Both prosecution and defence had agreed at trial to follow the famous passage from Lord Hoffmann's speech in *Smith (Morgan)*:[99] 'in my opinion, therefore, judges should not be required to describe the objective element in the provocation defence by reference to a reasonable man, with or without attribution of personal characteristics. They may instead find

---

92   *Pate* v. *R* [1981–83] MLR 130 (Isle of Man Law Reports).
93   Population c. 94,000.
94   Privy Council Appeal No 3 of 2004, 15 June 2005.
95   Allegedly 'you haven't got the fucking guts'.
96   There were eight grounds of appeal.
97   *Attorney General for Jersey* v. *Holley* (Southwell, Smith and Tugendhat JJA).
98   Ibid., [12].
99   *Smith (Morgan)* [2001] 1 AC, 173.

it more helpful to explain in simple language the principles of the doctrine of provocation. First, it requires that the accused should have killed while he had lost self-control and that something should have caused him to lose self-control. ... Secondly, the fact that something caused him to lose self-control is not enough. The law expects people to exercise control over their emotions. A tendency to violent rages or childish tantrums is a defect in character rather than an excuse. The jury must think that the circumstances were such as to make the loss of self-control sufficiently excusable to reduce the gravity of the offence from murder to manslaughter ...'. However, the Bailiff varied from that speech in his summing-up to the jury. The Court of Appeal allowed the appeal,[100] finding that the Bailiff had erred by failing to make it clear to the jury that they could take H's characteristics into account as affecting the degree of control which society could expect of H. The conviction for murder was set aside as a miscarriage of justice.[101] A retrial was ordered but had to be abandoned since two jurors had connections with V. A third trial took place in the Royal Court, and the sole issue was provocation. H brought expert evidence of his alcoholism as a disease but was again convicted of murder. He appealed again to the Court of Appeal, which heard the case in January 2003.[102] The grounds were that the Deputy Bailiff: had not directed the jury to consider whether H's chronic alcoholism reduced the standard of self-control expected of him; had wrongly used the concept of the 'reasonable man' as part of the defence; had given an incomplete direction on cumulative provocation, and several other grounds. The appeal was allowed on the basis of such misdirections[103] and a conviction for manslaughter was substituted, since ordering a further retrial would not be fair.[104] In considering sentencing, the starting point was 12 years: in Jersey provocation and diminished responsibility cases[105] (which the court considered first) the range was seven to eight years for such cases, or ten years if the case was 'close to murder'; in Guernsey 12 years had been given for the one relevant case,[106] a particularly serious manslaughter; and in England the starting point was 5–15 years depending on the amount of provocation, whether a weapon was used, and cooling time. A sentence of eight years was imposed[107] after mitigation, which included H's characteristics. Thus it can be seen that Jersey's courts have sought to remain consistent with English law on this issue, albeit that the law in question has since been rejected twice.

On appeal to the Privy Council, the 'reasonable man' element was restored to the test and Lord Hoffmann's approach from *Smith (Morgan)* was disapproved as 'unduly favourable to [the defendant]',[108] along with the rest of the majority in that case. The Jersey Court of Appeal had applied *Smith (Morgan)* accurately, and could not be criticised for doing so, but this was

---

100 [2001] JLR 606, 25 October 2001.

101 Court of Appeal (Jersey) Act 1961, Art. 25.

102 [2003] JLR 22.

103 With the failure to invite the jury to consider H's chronic alcoholism as a relevant characteristic for provocation considered a particularly serious misdirection. The Court applied *obiter dicta* from the English case of *R* v. *Tandy* [1989] 1 All ER 267 on alcoholism as diminished responsibility, in the absence of English or Jersey authority on alcoholism as a relevant characteristic for provocation.

104 Since it would be impossible to find a jury who did not know that H had twice been convicted of murder and there had been substantial publicity since the killing.

105 *Attorney General* v. *Carrel*, Royal Ct (1982) 42 PC 67, 73, unreported; Attorney General v. de Azevedo [1987–88] JLR N-20; *Attorney General* v. *Marks*, 7 February 1980, Royal Ct, unreported; Attorney General v. O'Brien, [1979] JJ 187.

106 *R* v. *Tilley*, Guernsey Ct of Appeal (Criminal Division), 27 November, 1973, unreported.

107 And has now been completed, since it was to run from H's arrest on 14 April 2000.

108 At 38.

the wrong approach[109] and alcoholism should not have been taken into account re the second limb of the test. It had been agreed that the appeal would be an academic one, with no effect on H's conviction or sentence, and so the appeal was allowed[110] but the Jersey Court of Appeal's disposal of the case stood.

Jersey has had two murder cases since *Holley*, a third was pending at the time of proofreading this chapter. The first, a murder trial when the Privy Council judgment was handed down, ended with a guilty plea since provocation on the basis of characteristics could no longer be run as a defence. The second ran a diminished responsibility defence, which failed. There are no current plans to reform or replace Art. 4 of the Homicide (Jersey) Law 1986 at the time of writing of this chapter. Murder cases are few in this jurisdiction, and under the current law provocation defences are likely to remain rare. Even with the very defendant-friendly variant applied by the trial courts in *Holley*, the two juries who got as far as a decision rejected the defence on the facts, again showing a very robust approach.

The Commonwealth Caribbean – Some Points of Comparison

Given that the courts of the British Caribbean territories refer to and apply the case law of independent Caribbean courts, cross-pollination is likely to continue and will probably become stronger if the Caribbean Court of Justice expands and develops new principles.[111] The creation of the Eastern Caribbean Supreme Court has meant that sentencing practice is being standardised across both British and independent Caribbean criminal courts, and is deviating to a greater extent from the English sentencing guidelines. The use of precedent from independent Caribbean states in the Eastern Caribbean Supreme Court has had some interesting effects on homicide law, since the definitions of provocation in the independent states do vary from those of the British territories. Some examination of the provocation laws of those independent states most often cited by the ECSC is worthwhile for those reasons. Of course there are other Commonwealth states which have similar provocation defences to those in this region, but because of geography and court hierarchy they have not had such influence on the British jurisdictions and so will not be considered in this chapter.

Jamaica
Provocation is defined in s. 6 of the Offences Against the Person Act, which is identical to the former s. 3 of the English Homicide Act 1957. In *R* v. *Damion Thomas*,[112] T was convicted of murder and, after a successful appeal, a verdict of manslaughter and a sentence of 20 years' hard labour were substituted. He was in prison at the time when he stabbed another inmate to death, saying that V had called him 'a batty man'. The trial judge directed the jury in line with *Camplin*.[113] The grounds of appeal had included that the trial judge had erred in law in leaving murder to the jury, when there was clear evidence of provocation in the prosecution's case against T. The court found that the judge had no power to direct the jury to return a verdict of not guilty to murder, since this would be a usurpation of the role of the jury. But there had been a misdirection: applying the

---

109 At 37.
110 Lords Bingham, Hoffmann and Carswell dissenting.
111 See O'Brien (n. 14) 607–27, for discussion of the likely impact of the CCJ once it becomes final court of appeal for the independent Caribbean states.
112 Court of Appeal, Criminal Appeal No 192/2000, 7 April and 21 May 2003.
113 [1978] 2 All ER 168.

English approach,[114] the trial judge had wrongly failed to direct the jury that if there was any chance of provocation, they should acquit of murder. The same issue arose in *R* v. *Dwight Wright*,[115] where the Court of Appeal again substituted a manslaughter conviction and a sentence of seven years' imprisonment. W stabbed V fatally during an Independence Day celebration on 7 August 2006. A witness saw W and V arguing for about five minutes before the stabbing. The trial judge withdrew provocation from the jury, telling them that the prosecution had led evidence that there was nothing said or done to W at the time of the killing which could found that defence. The Court of Appeal confirmed that the duty on trial judges in such cases is clear: they must leave the defence to the jury.

There have been some worrying cases recently which appear out of line with the other jurisdictions discussed in this chapter, and certainly would not succeed under the Coroners and Justice Act 2009. For example, in January 2009 a man who chopped off his former girlfriend's head because of sexual jealousy was convicted of manslaughter due to provocation. He had somewhat surprisingly argued self-defence at trial. However, in general, a more robust approach is taken by the courts. In *Smalling* v. *Queen*,[116] S had been convicted of three counts of murder after killing his former girlfriend, her young son, and his own baby son. He argued provocation at trial, saying that the woman had told him that she 'had a boyfriend outside' but also that 'weed' told him to kill them all. The baby was decapitated. The Court of Appeal found that the appellant had not given any convincing argument in favour of any of the grounds of appeal he had filed, and so leave to appeal was refused. The Privy Council heard the case on the ground that the trial judge had failed to leave the defence of provocation to the jury, directing them that manslaughter was not a possible verdict. The Court of Appeal had also made no reference to provocation or manslaughter. The Privy Council stated that it is indeed the case that a judge must leave manslaughter open to the jury even where D has denied involvement in the death, if there is any evidence of provocation which is fit for a jury to consider.[117] Interpreting s. 6 of the Offences Against the Person Act 1864 in exactly the same way as in English cases, S's former girlfriend's words were capable of being provocation in relation to her death, but it did not appear that they had caused S to lose self-control; he had repeatedly said that the 'ganja' made him kill all three victims. The death of the baby was particularly horrific and it was absolutely clear from S's own account that provocation did not have any relevance to that death.[118] Thus there was no evidence on which a properly directed jury could reasonably have found that S was provoked in relation to any of the killings, and the appeal was dismissed. However the case was referred back to the Court of Appeal for diminished responsibility and intoxication defences to be considered.

Trinidad and Tobago
Section 4(B) of the Offences Against the Person (Amendment) Act 1985 is identical to the repealed English s. 3. The defence has been argued in some very weak cases, but then rejected by juries and appeal courts. The Privy Council has understandably interpreted the defence in line with its English equivalent. In *Adolphus Campbell* v. *The State*[119] C attacked several people with a cutlass, killing one, and argued defences of temporary insanity and provocation, claiming that he had seen

---

114 From *R* v. *McPherson* [1957] Cr App R 213, as applied by the Jamaican Court of Appeal in *R* v. *Lumumbo Rankine* SCCA No 61/2000, 31 May 2001, unreported.
115 Unreported, May 2010, Court of Appeal.
116 [2001] UKPC 12.
117 Citing Lord Tucker in *Bullard* v. *The Queen* [1957] AC 635, 642.
118 He claimed that he killed his son because otherwise the baby might cry.
119 Privy Council Appeal No 63 of 1998.

a sexual act in the house where the killings took place.[120] The trial judge directed the jury that there was no evidence of provocation since the alleged sexual act did not involve C's wife or common law wife, and if what he had seen was pimple-picking, that was not sufficient provocation. One of the grounds of appeal was that the trial judge had erred in failing to leave provocation to the jury. The Privy Council were satisfied that, even if the trial judge had left the issue to the jury, they would inevitably have rejected the defence because there was nothing said or done which was enough to make a reasonable man do as C did.

St Lucia

Section 91 of the Criminal Code has identical wording to the English defence, although the previous version used the 'extreme provocation' format which still applies in some other Caribbean states, as discussed below. Recent sentences again have a 15-year benchmark as the starting point, and statutory guidelines are laid down in s. 11 of the Criminal Code. The many sentencing decisions from St Lucia have been very influential, applied as precedent across the Commonwealth Caribbean, including the British Overseas Territories.

Barbados

Section 5 of the Offences Against the Person Act reproduces the former English provocation defence. Many defendants offer guilty pleas to manslaughter to avoid the death penalty for murder. This creates a danger that, unless prosecutors are rigorous in ensuring that the elements of the defence have been met, the legitimacy of the provocation defence will be undermined in public eyes. Most cases apply the correct tests and so avoid that danger, but some controversial decisions will be noted below. As in so many Commonwealth Caribbean states, the key issue has been the appropriate sentencing, and sentences are generally lengthy. In *Ricardo Deverne Griffith*[121] the prosecution accepted a guilty plea to manslaughter and the issue for the appeal was whether the 18-year sentence imposed was excessive. G shot his girlfriend, claiming that she said that she was risking her job by seeing him and that she had pulled a gun out of her handbag, saying 'I got this fuh you', whereupon they struggled for the gun and a fatal shot occurred. He drove off with the gun and threw it into the sea. Defences of provocation, accident, or self-defence could have been put to a jury. Applying the assumptions to be made by a judge on sentencing from the English case of *Attorney General's Reference (Nos 74, 95 and 118 of 2002)*[122] and taking account of the 'definitive' decision of the Privy Council in *Holley*, the Court of Appeal found that although the trial judge had not explicitly referred to those assumptions, she had not contradicted them. The sentence was appropriate, after taking into account time served on remand, since the benchmark under local authority[123] was 18–22 years for serious firearm killings with provocation, reduced to 14–18 years where there was an early guilty plea. In *Clyde Dacosta Clarke v. The Queen*,[124] the issue was again whether the sentence was excessive. Twelve years' imprisonment had been imposed; C was infatuated with V and regularly gave her money. He killed her after seeing her in bed with another man.[125] The DPP accepted a guilty plea to manslaughter since he regarded it as 'the classic case of

---

120 Although according to the evidence he may have seen a woman picking her boyfriend's pimples.

121 Criminal Appeal No 6 of 2007, unreported, 19 June 2009.

122 [2003] 2 Cr App R (S) 42, for sentencing where provocation arose out of jealousy, possessiveness or unfaithfulness.

123 *Pierre Lorde v. R*, Criminal Appeal No 11 of 2003, unreported, 24 February 2006.

124 Criminal Appeal No 20 of 2008, November 2009, Court of Appeal.

125 And so would be denied the defence under English law due to Coroners and Justice Act 2009, s. 54(6).

provocation'. The Court of Appeal applied the sentencing guidelines laid down in *Ricardo Griffith v. The Queen*,[126] where the English approach was adopted, but also quoted extensively from the Privy Council decision in *Holley*, which was not binding since Barbados no longer appeals to the Privy Council.[127] In effect, the court was issuing a reminder that *Smith (Morgan)* is no longer good law. The Court of Appeal decided not to apply sentencing criteria based on 'domestic' cases since there was no such relationship between C and V. Using a starting point of 17 years, the sentence was upheld.

Although the courts have followed *Holley*, it appears from the above case that prosecutorial practice may not always be doing so. The acceptance of a guilty plea to manslaughter in a another recent case caused some public discussion; P was a man who was enraged when a woman changed her mind about having sex with him for money for rent,[128] and the DPP was satisfied that a jury, properly directed, could have found that to be provocation. It is submitted that even if P lost self-control because of V's refusal, a reasonable man would not have done so. Such decisions are out of line with contemporary moral standards, and it would be extremely difficult to make a case for 'local conditions' requiring different standards.

The Bahamas, Belize and Grenada
These states have similar provisions in their criminal codes concerning provocation. They are all based on instances of the historical English common law defence of provocation and reflect the (English) Draft Criminal Code 1879. The defence is one of 'extreme provocation' and its interpretation has recently been modified by the Privy Council to fit more closely with the former English defence as modified by the 1957 Act. For example, the Belize Criminal Code provides:

> A person who intentionally causes the death of another person by unlawful harm shall be deemed to be guilty only of manslaughter, and not of murder, if there is such evidence as raises a reasonable doubt as to whether –
>
> (a) he was deprived of the power of self-control by such extreme provocation given by the other person as is mentioned in section 120.[129]

Section 120 lists triggers for extreme provocation: assault or battery by the other 'likely to deprive a person, being of ordinary character, and being in the circumstances in which the accused person was, of the power of self-control; an attitude showing intention to attack in a deadly manner; adultery and incest; assault, battery or sex offences committed on someone in a close relationship to D; anything said to the accused person by the other person or by a third person which were grave enough to make a reasonable man to lose his self-control'. Section 121 lists circumstances in which provocation will not be a partial defence: where D was not deprived of self-control; where D had a prior purpose to cause death or serious harm; where there is a cooling-off period or circumstances in which an ordinary person would have regained self-control; or the act was grossly disproportionate to the provocation. There are also provisions for mistaken provocation in ss. 122 and 123. Thus there is a set of tests which partly codify the former English defence, but also deviate from it, and show signs of earlier versions of the defence (for example in the references to fights and adultery). There have been some issues in each jurisdiction with the burden of proof and with

---
126 Criminal Appeal No 6 of 2007, unreported, 19 June 2009.
127 Having accepted the final jurisdiction of the Caribbean Court of Justice in 2005.
128 *Pile*, January 2011, unreported.
129 There is also a defence of killing in excessive self-defence.

the phrasing of directions to the jury. In *Cleon Smith* v. *R*[130] the ground for appeal was misdirection on provocation. There was evidence of previous resentments between S and V, and before the killing V had said 'Before the night finish I will catch you and stamp you down', then there been an angry confrontation. The jury convicted of murder after being directed to the effect that they could not consider provocation if they found the killing was intentional. The Board allowed the appeal and stated the defence as 'if he kills when provoked to lose his self-control by words or conduct if the provocation is so extreme that a reasonable man would have been provoked to act as the defendant did'. Hence the word 'extreme' is being given an objective element which is not in the code, and brought closer to both the former and new English law.

The Bahamas Penal Code has very similar provisions in ss. 299–303, accompanied by a set of explanatory examples. It then has identical wording to s. 3 of the Homicide Act 1957 in s. 304. Grenada's Criminal Code contains almost identical words in ss. 238–41, but with the burden of proof placed on the defendant; as we shall see below, this has been reversed by case law. In *R* v. *Kester Williams*[131] W killed his employer after a workplace argument. The High Court took 'ordinary' provocation into consideration as a mitigating factor for sentencing, even though the facts did not meet the threshold of extreme provocation to enable a defence. The end effect in each case is rather similar to that of the new 'loss of control' defence under ss. 54–6 of the Coroners and Justice Act, since it has a reasonableness factor within the subjective limb, applies only where there is 'extreme' provocation, and is accompanied by provisions for 'excessive self-defence'. However, decisions so far have interpreted the defence in line with English common law and the 1957 Act, treating the remainder of the test as largely surplus.

In *Vasquez* v. *The Queen*[132] the Privy Council interpreted the previous version of Belize's provisions as placing the burden of proof on the prosecution, although the code then in force and the Belize Court of Appeal had always placed the burden on the accused.[133] Judges should 'discard the outdated language of the old law and ... concentrate instead on the modern law of provocation when they are summing up'.[134] In *Bull* v. *The Queen*[135] Lord Steyn said that judges should sum up in line with the equivalent provision to s. 3 of the Homicide Act 1957, ignoring the weight of the 'old law' in their own jurisdiction. Given that the English defence no longer exists in that form, this leaves such states with a choice: whether to remain with an interpretation which does not reflect the whole of their code provisions and is no longer English law; to revert to their earlier interpretations in line with the clear words of their codes; or to codify new defences. As yet there is no clear indication as to which path will be taken. Belize replaced the Privy Council's jurisdiction with that of the Caribbean Court of Justice in 2010, and Grenada has signed the treaty but not yet submitted to the court's final jurisdiction. Such developments may have an impact on the development of criminal law, and these jurisdictions do clearly influence the law in British Overseas Territories even though British Overseas Territories all appeal to the Privy Council.

---

130 Privy Council Appeal No 59 of 2000, 24 May 2001.
131 1 June 2010, High Court of Justice (Grenada).
132 [1994] 1 WLR 1304.
133 In contrast to the courts of The Bahamas and Grenada, which had held in the 1970s that the burden of proof remained on the prosecution, regardless of the wording in their criminal codes: *Clarke* v. *The Queen* [1971–6] 1 LRB 143 (The Bahamas) and *Ambrose* v. *The Queen* (1978) 2 OESCSLR 32.
134 *Yearwood* v. *The Queen*, Privy Council Appeal No 75 of 2000, from Grenada, 26 June 2001 per Lord Hope.
135 [1998] 1 WLR 1523 at 1525A.

Conclusions

There is a great deal of similarity in the way provocation defences are being interpreted in the sister jurisdictions, but that position may very soon be replaced by a much more complex picture since the smallest British Overseas Territories will be bound by the Coroners and Justice Act provisions, only one of the remainder is planning to adopt the new English Act, and the influence of Commonwealth Caribbean developments on the British Caribbean territories is arguably stronger than that of English statutes.

Many of the problems with the former defence turn out to have been universal, and resolved by judges in each jurisdiction separately. This emphasises the need for swift, accessible law reporting and dissemination of model directions, since much time and effort could have been saved. The laws of several British Overseas Territories cannot be accessed without substantial payment, and many have no comprehensive law reports.

Most British Overseas Territories and all Crown Dependencies still have the provocation defence, either through incorporation of the common law[136] or through their own codes. The Crown Dependencies have chosen it freely. Although there is a great deal of adherence to the s. 3 version of provocation, variances have been noted in the burden of proof, prosecutorial practice, and sentencing, as well as in the core definition. This is partly due to the differing extents to which each territory must follow English statutes and common law. British Overseas Territories' constitutions tend to incorporate existing English statutes up to the date of their enactment, so have largely incorporated the 1957 Homicide Act and are bound by the common law, adapted to local customs and needs. Some territories have little relevant case law of their own and/or have not had a provocation trial in a generation, which makes future developments more uncertain. Yet other historical influences have led to a wide range of homicide offences and defences, including several distinct models of a provocation defence, one of which is a codified version of eighteenth century English common law, and several reflecting reform proposals rejected in the UK. This rich range of examples could have been examined as part of the English reform process; they are a living set of snapshots of legal history. There is a much larger, richer and more diverse British criminal law than has been recognised.

It is notable that many cases, regardless of jurisdiction, involve sexual jealousy and violent relationships, and so would have little chance of a successful defence should the loss of control defence be adopted. Some jurisdictions continue to struggle with the issues which the English reform sought, at least in part, to redress, particularly in cases where the 'trigger' is minor.[137] There remains debate as to whether the interests of justice are served by having different defences in different British jurisdictions for the same offence, when once they were the same. Of course each British Overseas Territory is free to find that 'special local factors' require a particular approach, but so far this has not been argued in any reported case – sister jurisdictions have shown a desire to follow the s. 3 approach even where their codes state otherwise.

The reliance on English textbooks in law schools and lack of written judgments or comprehensive law reports in most British Overseas Territory jurisdictions increases the likelihood of continued use of common law, on a regional basis, rather than adopting the new English statutory defence. As they have developed a local approach to sentencing, so they could have a local approach to triggers

---

136 Since the common law provocation defence has been abolished only for England, Wales and Northern Ireland by the Coroners and Justice Act 2009, s. 56.

137 See, for example, the *Pile* guilty plea, which has led to public anger.

and objectivity. Those British Overseas Territories which are in the process of modernising their constitutions or of codifying or updating criminal law are more likely to adopt 'loss of control'.

Considering *all* British jurisdictions' application of the defence when proposing reform could have led to different conclusions and proposals for English law. As Yeo notes,[138] 'Had the Australian and English lawmakers made a practice of studying the Indian law, it is likely that many ... improvements to the law would have been implemented sooner.' The various criminal codes within British jurisdictions could have been used not only as many-dated historical research tools of the common law, but also as a source of improvements of the latter. Since some are the result of enactment of English reform proposals or bills which fell by the wayside on the mainland,[139] there is the opportunity to learn from what English law could have been, as well as from what it has been.

What can the mainland UK learn from the sister jurisdictions? Judges and juries in British Overseas Territories and Crown Dependencies do tend to expect both more evidence of provocation than their English equivalents have done[140] and more severe provocation before a reasonable man would lose self-control. Those factors, together with the heavier sentencing, make for fairer labelling. Some British Overseas Territories saw the problems with *Smith (Morgan)* before English courts did, and reached the same conclusion as did the Privy Council eventually in *Holley*. Other chapters in this book examine potential problems with the new law in detail; I submit that the new defence would not be needed if its predecessor had been applied more rigorously as in these jurisdictions. Reformers could have considered whether sentencing was the real problem with the old law, perhaps additionally raising the threshold to 'extreme provocation' as a filter for undeserving cases?

There are some remaining difficulties for the future. Any provocation reform in British Overseas Territories would face difficulty with sexual jealousy cases; British Overseas Territories appear to have a greater rate of pleading provocation in such cases than England and Wales so adoption of the loss of control defence would, in some jurisdictions, lead to an increase in mandatory life sentences. In the Commonwealth Caribbean, it might well lead to an increase in the death penalty. A further issue is the amount of evidence necessary before the prosecution must disprove the defence. The former English test has now been adopted by all the jurisdictions, but this is now at variance with England and Northern Ireland.

Those British Overseas Territories bound only by the common law could ultimately conclude that the Coroners and Justice Act has not truly abolished the common law provocation defence, but merely amended it in a more extreme manner than did the Homicide Act 1957. If so, judges' greater ability to withdraw the defence from the jury and the partial objectivisation of the first limb of the test[141] would be the main changes although, as has been seen, in some cases those tests have already been applied by judges. In relation to 'justifiable sense of being seriously wronged', local and cultural factors would presumably be relevant to what is justifiable.[142] If we apply Pound's

---

138 Law Com. CP No 173, 2003, App. A, para. 2.21.

139 Such as Stephen's Indictable Offences Bill and the related Draft Criminal Code 1879, which have influenced the Criminal Codes of various British Overseas Territories and Commonwealth states.

140 Although it may of course be a factor that juries are not involved in all homicide cases in these jurisdictions.

141 'Justifiability' of the sense of being seriously wronged.

142 There might in practice be some difficult cases; there have been instances of non-violent homosexual advances being argued to be provocation in various Commonwealth and British jurisdictions, and the implications of such cases are discussed in Anthony Gray, 'Provocation and the Homosexual Advance Defense in Australia and the United States: Law Out of Step with Community Values' (2010) 3 The Crit 53. See also Muthucumaraswamy Sornarajah, 'Commonwealth Innovations on the Law of Provocation' [1975] 24

assertion[143] that criminal law codes preserve moral attitudes prevailing at the time when they were passed, then some British jurisdictions could well need an update.

This is not yet a field in which the common law speaks 'with accents appropriate to the country in which it applies',[144] except in relation to sentencing, but eventually may become so if tendencies towards local law development in the Commonwealth Caribbean continue.

International and Comparative Law Quarterly 204, for discussion of parallel developments in the provocation defence in various Commonwealth countries and also of the difficulties caused by cultural factors in local variants.

[143] R. Pound, *Jurisprudence* (vol 3) 734.

[144] Geoffrey Bartholomew, 'English Law in Partibus Orientalium', in Harding (ed.), *The Common Law in Singapore and Malaysia* (Butterworths, 1985) 39.

Chapter 14
A Comparative Analysis of English and French Defences to Demonstrate the Limitations of the Concept of Loss of Control

Catherine Elliott

Introduction

The most important change to the partial defences to murder by the Coroners and Justice Act 2009 was the introduction of fear of serious violence as a possible trigger for the defence.[1] Up until this reform, the emphasis of the defence of provocation had been on anger leading a person to lose their control because of things said or done. Now, the emotion of fear as well as anger can be the basis for the new defence of loss of control. A key reason for introducing this reform was to achieve justice for battered women who killed their abusive partners. This reformed version of the defence has similarities with self-defence[2] and the statutory public defence[3] (together referred to in this chapter as self-defence). Historically, self-defence has rarely succeeded in removing criminal liability from women who have killed their abusive partners. This chapter will compare the fear of serious violence branch of the loss of control excuse and self-defence to see where the former will succeed when the latter will not. It is only where loss of control extends beyond the scope of self-defence that the new branch of the law will have any impact, since where there is an option to rely on either defence, an accused would logically favour the complete defence of self-defence over the partial one of loss of control. This comparison will show that not only does the new defence share similar constraints to the old one of self-defence, but it also contains an additional constraint that the accused must have lost their control. The significant overlap of these defences combined with the additional constraint of loss of control renders the new extension relating to a fear of serious violence close to redundant.

The English defences will then be compared with the approach taken in French criminal law. Through this comparison it will be argued that the government was misguided in clinging on to the concept of loss of control as the basis of a defence for battered women who kill. Instead, a three-pronged approach needs to be taken to make sure that justice is done in such cases. Firstly, the law on self-defence should be developed so that it ceases to be a sexist defence that is more likely to succeed for male defendants than female defendants. This could be done by changing the burden of proof where the defendant had been subjected to physical or mental abuse by the victim. Secondly, a new partial defence of self-preservation could be created which would be available where a court concluded that excessive force had been used in an attempt at self-preservation, reducing the defendant's liability from murder to manslaughter. Finally, the sentencing arrangements could be

---
1 Coroners and Justice Act 2009, s. 55(3).
2 See, for example, *Palmer* v. *R* [1971] AC 814.
3 Criminal Law Act 1967, s. 3.

revisited to make sure that the sentence matches the gravity of the attack in the context of a fatal attack on a victim of domestic abuse.

Comparing Self-Defence and Loss of Control

The old defences of self-defence and the public defence are available where the defendant feared serious violence, as with the loss of control defence. A comparison between self-defence and the fear of serious violence branch of the loss of control defence will demonstrate that the reasons why self-defence has not succeeded for battered women who kill will also create problems for the application of the new defence. In addition, a battered woman relying on the partial defence will have to prove that she had lost control of herself. This was a logical requirement when the defence of provocation was built on the notion of defendants losing their temper, but illogical when the defence is based on a rational fear of serious violence.

There are three key elements of these defences which need to be examined in order to determine how far the defences differ: the timing of the defendant's response to the fear of serious violence, the proportionate response to the threat; and the requirement of loss of control. Each of these three issues will be considered in turn.

The Timing of the Defendant's Response to the Fear of Serious Violence

For self-defence to succeed it must have been necessary for the defendants to have taken defensive action and their response must have been proportionate. In determining whether it was necessary to take defensive action, there must have existed an imminent threat. This does not mean that defendants have to wait until they are hit, for example, before hitting back, but it does mean there must be some immediacy about the threat posed.[4]

Thus, on first impressions a factual situation where the defence of loss of control may be available and self-defence not, is where the threat of serious violence was not imminent. But while the threat of violence need not be imminent for the defence of loss of control, timing is not irrelevant to the defence. Under the new defence, there is no longer any requirement that the defendant's response must be sudden,[5] but the explanatory notes to the Act state that delay could be evidence as to whether defendants had actually lost their self-control.[6] Where there is a delay then there is a greater possibility that the defendant acted out of calculated revenge and s. 54(4) expressly states that the defence is not available if the defendant 'acted in a considered desire for revenge'. Thus the potential for defendants who were not viewed as having reacted to an imminent threat to argue that they still came within the defence of loss of control will be quite limited.

A Proportionate Response

Self-defence is only allowed if the defendant has used a reasonable amount of force. This has proved to be the most controversial issue in practice. Section 76(6) of the Criminal Justice and Immigration Act 2008 provides:

---

4 *Attorney General's Reference (No 2 of 1983)* [1984] AC 456; *Malnik v. DPP* [1989] Crim LR 451.
5 Coroners and Justice Act 2009, s. 54(2).
6 Coroners and Justice Act 2009 Explanatory Notes, para. 337.

The degree of force used by D is not to be regarded as having been reasonable in the circumstances as D believed them to be if it was disproportionate in those circumstances.

What constitutes reasonable force is a matter for the jury to decide, balancing the amount of force used against the harm the accused sought to prevent – so that, for example, force considered reasonable for protecting a person might be considered excessive if used to prevent a crime against property. Defendants are not expected to perform precise calculations in the heat of the moment as to the minimum amount of force required in the circumstances.[7] The law recognises that in the kind of situation where the defence is used, there is rarely much time to consider what should be done. As Lord Morris put it in *Palmer*: 'A person defending himself cannot weigh to a nicety the exact measure of his necessary defensive action.'[8] The law imposes an objective test, so it does not matter if defendants thought they were using a reasonable amount of force, what matters is whether objectively they actually have used a reasonable amount of force. The Criminal Justice and Immigration Act 2008 restates the requirement of reasonable force in this context,[9] confirming the case law on the point.[10]

The objective test was confirmed in the high-profile case of *R* v. *Anthony Martin*,[11] though it was watered down slightly because the Court of Appeal left open the possibility of sometimes taking into account specific characteristics of the accused when applying this test. The defence barrister submitted that in deciding the issue of reasonable force the courts ought to take the same approach as the House of Lords laid down in *Smith (Morgan)*[12] for the objective test in provocation. This would have enabled the defendant's characteristics to be considered when determining whether his or her reaction had been reasonable, which in this case would include the fact that Martin suffered from a paranoid personality disorder. The Court of Appeal accepted that the jury could take into account the physical characteristics of the defendant. They also stated that, in exceptional circumstances that rendered the evidence especially probative, judges could take into account the fact that the defendant was suffering from a psychiatric condition. But this was not such an exceptional case, and the court found on the facts that reasonable force had not been used.

Thus, self-defence is only available to women who kill their abusive partners if the force used by the women is reasonable and necessary to protect them from an imminent attack. It is, therefore, not available to an abused woman who fears violence in the future and kills her abuser when, for example, he is asleep or has his back to her. Aileen McColgan has argued that the law discriminates against women in this context:

> The relative scarcity of female killers has resulted in a paradigmatically male ideal model and this, together with the incompatibility of aggressive force with stereotypical femininity, means that the apparently gender-neutral concept of reasonableness is actually weighted against the female defendant.[13]

---

7   *Attorney General for Northern Ireland's Reference (No 1 of 1975)* [1977] AC 105.
8   *Palmer* v. *R* [1971] AC 814, 817.
9   Section 76(3), (7) and (8).
10   *Williams (Gladstone)* [1987] 3 All ER 411.
11   [2001] EWCA Crim 2245.
12   [2001] 1 AC 146.
13   Aileen McColgan, 'In Defence of Battered Women Who Kill' (1993) 13 Oxford Journal of Legal Studies, 508, 515.

In addition, Edwards has pointed to research which shows significant differences between the way men and women kill. Men who kill their female partners tend to use bodily force whilst women who kill their male partners use knives in 83 per cent of cases. Where weapons such as knives are used a conviction for murder is more likely.[14] Edwards has argued that self-defence has been:

> skewed to the detriment of women since a defendant's action is only considered "reasonable" when the killing is a proportionate response to an immediate threat of deadly force.[15]

The new loss of control defence does not specify that the defendant must not use excessive force, but it specifies that the defence is only available if a person of the defendant's sex and age with an ordinary level of tolerance and self-restraint and in the circumstances of the defendant might have acted in the same or similar way to the defendant.[16] The reference to the defendant's 'circumstances' includes all circumstances except those that are only relevant to the defendant's general level of tolerance and self-restraint.[17] The Explanatory Notes to the Act provide that a defendant's history of abuse at the hands of the victim could be taken into account when considering whether an ordinary person might have behaved as he or she did, whereas the defendant's short temper cannot.[18] Under the former defence of provocation the case law referred to the defendant's characteristics rather than their circumstances. It is not yet clear whether this change of terminology will make any real difference, though it may allow a wider range of factors to be considered than had been allowed under *Attorney General for Jersey* v. *Holley*.[19] Amanda Clough has suggested:

> "Circumstances" suggests being able to consider prior abuse as an external element rather than having to try and deem it as a characteristic by internalising it as some kind of syndrome or character flaw.[20]

Both the defence of loss of control and the defence of self-defence are therefore restricted by the application of an objective test. These objective tests have slightly different nuances but following the shift away from *Smith (Morgan)*[21] the reasonable person should be quite a consistent individual (though taking into account differences between juries). One view is that the objective test for loss of control will be less stringent than the objective test for self-defence. Thus, Withey has observed:

> When comparing the normal person against the defendant's conduct in losing self-control, the jury have to ask whether the normal person *might* have had the same or *similar* reaction. ... The new

---

[14] Susan Edwards, 'Injustice that Puts a Low Price on a Woman's Life', *The Times* (2 September 2003) Law Supplement, 5.

[15] Susan Edwards, 'Abolishing Provocation and Reframing Self Defence – The Law Commission's Options for Reform' [2004] Criminal Law Review 181, 188; See also, McColgan (n. 13). An illustration of the law in practice is *Rossiter* (1992) 95 Cr App R 326.

[16] Coroners and Justice Act 2009, s. 54(1)(c).

[17] Ibid., s. 54(3).

[18] Ibid., Explanatory Notes, para. 338.

[19] [2005] 2 AC 58.

[20] Amanda Clough, 'Loss of Self-Control as a Defence: The Key to Replacing Provocation' (2010) 74 Journal of Criminal Law 118, 125.

[21] [2001] 1 AC 146.

test could therefore make the defence available to those who fail with public and private defence because of an excessive use of force.[22]

On this logic, where excessive force has been used self-defence will not be available but the partial defence may be available because the excess amount of force might be explained by the loss of self-control. In practice, however, the amount of force that might be used for self-defence may not differ significantly from the amount of force that would be permissible for the new defence of loss of control. There are circumstances where a person will be entitled to kill in self-defence and these are circumstances where a normal person in those circumstances would have reacted in this way. A normal person will rarely use a disproportionate amount of force, whatever their circumstances, thus this limitation, which has caused controversy in the context of the defence of self-defence, may well prove problematic in the context of the loss of control defence.

Loss of Control

The new defence is only available where the defendant has lost control. The Law Commission had recommended that the requirement of loss of self-control should be dropped altogether because it is the wrongful words or conduct which provide the justification for the defence, and there was no need for a loss of control to justify providing a defence.[23] Alan Norrie has noted:

> Indeed to be out of control might take the moral edge off what has been done in righteous, but sanctionable, anger [or fear].[24]

He has also pointed out that the requirement of loss of control seems to 'work against the core logic of the new defence'.[25] The defence will often only work in practice if the meaning of loss of control is strained to include situations which on the surface might not really fit. Thus, has a woman who has suffered years of abuse and eventually killed her abusive partner really suffered from a loss of self-control at the time of the killing? The government chose to keep the concept of loss of control because it thought the concept was needed to exclude people who killed in cold blood, particularly as the requirement that the killing be sudden was being removed. However, the provision in the legislation that the killing could not be committed for revenge would probably have been sufficient.

The requirement of loss of control is an additional restriction on the availability of the new defence which is not required for self-defence. In the past it was difficult for defendants to argue both that they behaved rationally in self-defence and alternatively that they lost their self-control due to provocation, as the defences seemed to contradict each other. With this alternative form of the new loss of control defence it might be easier to argue self-defence in the alternative, though there remains the complication that the government kept the requirement for a loss of control which the Law Commission would have dropped.

---

22 Carol Withey, 'Loss of Control' (2010) 174 Criminal Law and Justice Weekly, 197, 200.
23 Law Commission, *Murder, Manslaughter and Infanticide* (Law Com. No 304, 2006) para. 5.17.
24 Alan Norrie, 'The Coroners and Justice Act 2009 – Partial Defences to Murder: (1) Loss of Control' [2010] Criminal Law Review 275, 278.
25 Ibid., 288.

Crimes of Passion in France and England

The comparison drawn between self-defence and loss of control has shown that it is far from certain whether the new defence of loss of control will make any significant impact with regard to its extension to include a fear of serious violence because it will rarely be available where the complete defence of self-defence is not available. At this point it is helpful to draw a comparison between the direction that English law has taken in this context with the approach to these defences in French criminal law. The first thing to note is that today there is no equivalent defence to provocation or loss of control in French law. Historically there had been a defence available to crimes of passion,[26] which would have included where a man found his wife in the act of being unfaithful with her lover.[27] In the 1800s, approximately 50 per cent of trials for a crime of passion would result in an acquittal.[28] The old Criminal Code was changed in 1832 so that a finding that there had been a crime of passion was no longer a complete defence, but rather a mitigating factor which could reduce the defendant's sentence. Thus the old Napoleonic Criminal Code provided:

> Article 324. Murder committed by a husband on his wife, or by the latter on her husband, is not excusable, if the life of the husband or the wife who committed the murder has not been put in danger at the very moment when the murder took place.
>
> Nevertheless, in the case of adultery, provided for by article 336, murder committed by the husband on his wife, as well as on the accomplice, at the moment when he surprised them in flagrante delicto in the conjugal home, is excusable.[29]

Article 326 of the old Criminal Code explained that the sentence imposed could be significantly reduced in such cases:

> Article 326. When the fact of an excuse is proven, if it is a question of a serious crime carrying the death penalty, or forced labour for perpetuity or deportation, the punishment will be reduced to imprisonment for one to five years. If it is a question of any other crime, it will be reduced to imprisonment from six months to two years.[30]

In the past, French juries showed misplaced compassion for defendants in such cases and were prepared to acquit defendants despite the fact that the legislation aimed to simply reduce liability

---

26 Marc Ancel, 'Le crime passionnel' (1957) 73 Law Quarterly Review 36.
27 Maurice Garçon, *Histoire de la justice sous la IIIe République* (Fayard, 1957), vol. 3, 105.
28 Annik Houel, Patricia Mercader and Helga Sobota, *Crime passionnel, crime ordinaire* (Presses Universitaires de France, 2003) 48; Eliza Earle Ferguson, 'Judicial Authority and Popular Justice: Crimes of Passion in Fin-de-Siècle Paris' (2006) Journal of Social History 40, 293. For an international perspective see Melissa Spatz, 'A Comparative Study of Legal Defenses for Men Who Kill their Wives' (1991) 24 Columbia Journal of Law and Social Problems 597.
29 'Art. 324. Le meurtre commis par l'époux sur l'épouse, ou par celle-ci sur son époux, n'est pas excusable, si la vie de l'époux ou de l'épouse qui a commis le meurtre n'a pas été mise en péril dans le moment même où le meurtre a eu lieu. Néanmoins, dans le cas d'adultère, prévu par l'article 336, le meurtre commis par l'époux sur son épouse, ainsi que sur le complice, à l'instant où il les surprend en flagrant délit dans la maison conjugale, est excusable.'
30 'Lorsque le fait d'excuse sera prouvé, s'il s'agit d'un crime emportant la peine de mort, ou celle des travaux forcés à perpetuité ou celle de la déportation, la peine sera réduite à un emprisonnement d'un an à cinq ans. S'il s'agit de tout autre crime, elle sera réduite à un emprisonnement de six moins à deux ans.'

not excuse defendants altogether. People who committed a crime of passion might be treated as if they were suffering from a brief period of mental ill-health and have a defence on this basis. Paragraph 2 of article 324 was only repealed in 1975.[31]

Similarities in the development of the English law regarding crimes of passion and the defence of provocation can be noted. During the medieval period in England, a man finding his wife in the act of adultery was entitled to kill her and be acquitted of murder.[32] Blackstone wrote that such circumstances:

> [Are] of the lowest degree of [manslaughter]; and therefore ... the court directed the burning in the hand to be gently inflicted, because there could not be a greater provocation.[33]

The defence of provocation was traditionally available when a husband discovered his wife committing adultery.[34] By the twentieth century, with effective divorce laws, the courts regarded this leniency as an anachronism and were not prepared to extend the defence to engaged or cohabiting couples.[35] However, following the passing of the Homicide Act 1957, any infidelity could potentially amount to provocation. While by 1975 French legislators considered there was no role in a civilised society for a defence or mitigation based on loss of control and loss of temper for crimes of passion, in England just before the passing of the 2009 Act, a jury found a defendant liable for manslaughter rather than murder when he killed his wife and her lover who he claimed were about to engage in sexual intercourse.[36]

The law has moved on in France and, in an effort to tackle the social problem of domestic violence, an attack on a spouse, whatever the circumstances, is, since 2006, viewed as an aggravating factor rather than a mitigating factor.[37] The amended article 132-80 of the new Criminal Code states:

> In the cases laid down by the law, the punishments incurred for a serious crime or a major crime are aggravated when the offence is committed by the spouse, the lover or the partner linked to the victim by a civil pact. The aggravating circumstance laid down in the first paragraph is equally applicable when the facts are committed by a former spouse, a former lover or the former partner linked to the victim by a civil pact.[38]

---

31 Loi du 11 juillet 1975 n° 75-617 portant réforme du divorce, JO, 7171.

32 Jeremy Horder, *Provocation and Responsibility* (Clarendon Press, 1992).

33 Manning 16761 T. Raym 212, quoted by Susan Edwards, 'Anger and Fear as Justifiable Preludes for Loss of Self-Control' (2010) 74 Journal of Criminal Law 223, 231.

34 *R v. Mawgridge* (1707) Kel J 119 at 137; 84 ER 1107, 1115. See further Susan Edwards, 'Abolishing Provocation and Reframing Self-Defence – The Law Commission's Options for Reform' [2004] Criminal Law Review 181, 186.

35 *R v. Palmer* [1913] 2 KB 29 at 31, *R v. Greening* [1913] 3 KB 846, 849, *Holmes v. DPP* [1946] AC 588 at 598, *per* Viscount Simon.

36 Susan Edwards, 'Anger and Fear as Justifiable Preludes for Loss of Self-Control' (2010) 74 Journal of Criminal Law 223, 231.

37 Loi n° 2006-399 du 4 avril 2006 renforçant la prévention et la répression des violences au sein du couple ou commises contre les mineurs, JO n° 81 du 5 avril 2006.

38 'Dans les cas prévus par la loi, les peines encourues pour un crime ou un délit sont aggravées lorsque l'infraction est commise par le conjoint, le concubin ou le partenaire lié à la victime par un pacte civil de solidarité.

Where this provision applies, and the offence committed is murder, the maximum sentence is increased from 30 years to life imprisonment. The problem with this provision is that it does not draw any distinction between abusive partners who kill and partners who are themselves the victim of domestic abuse who kill their abusers. While it seems appropriate to treat the former situation as an aggravating factor, it would seem more appropriate to treat the latter situation as a mitigating circumstance.

In England, sexual infidelity has now been expressly removed as a basis for the defence of loss of control,[39] which in some respects responds to concerns about the sexist values underpinning lenient approaches to crimes of passion. While this exclusion has been described as 'gesture politics',[40] and was subject to considerable criticism during its progress through Parliament,[41] when looked at from the context of historical attitudes in France and England to crimes of passion, its exclusion seems completely logical in a modern society. Where the issue of sexual infidelity was raised in the past, a trial risked focusing on the deceased's behaviour rather than the defendant's. Inevitably, the deceased was not able to answer these accusations and the whole process could be extremely distressing to the deceased's family and friends. An acquittal of murder on grounds of provocation could, and often did, appear to relatives of the victim to be a travesty of justice. It appeared to imply a judgment by the court that the defendant's responsibility for killing the deceased was seriously lessened by the behaviour of the victim. Thus, in a case where a defendant had killed through sexual jealousy because the victim had formed an association with someone else, a verdict of manslaughter by reason of provocation often understandably appeared to the victim's relatives to be an insult added to injury.

At the same time, the exclusion of sexual infidelity highlights the inappropriateness of basing a defence on loss of control and then excluding the one factual situation where a person might have traditionally argued that he or she had lost control. As Susan Edwards has observed:

> Of all "triggers", sexual infidelity, both done and when spoken about, has been at the very epicentre of reasons for loss of self-control accepted and validated by law.[42]

By then seeking to extend the defence to a person who has both lost control and feared serious violence highlights that the two concepts do not really fit together. The emphasis should have been on the fear of serious violence and the necessity for self-preservation and the concept of a loss of control is simply a historical distraction.

La circonstance aggravante prévue au premier alinéa est également constituée lorsque les faits sont commis par l'ancien conjoint, l'ancien concubin ou l'ancien partenaire lié à la victime par un pacte civil de solidarité.'

39 Coroners and Justice Act 2009, s. 55(6)(c).

40 Jo Miles, 'The Coroners and Justice Act 2009: A "Dog's Breakfast" of Homicide Reform' (2009) *Archbold News*, 6, 7.

41 See, for example, Lord Henley and Lord Thomas' comments in HL Deb., 11 November 2009, cols 840–41, and the comments of Claire Ward and Mr Grieve QC, HC Deb., 9 November 2009, cols 80–90.

42 Susan Edwards, 'Anger and Fear as Justifiable Preludes for Loss of Self-Control' (2010) 74 Journal of Criminal Law 223, 230.

A Comparison with the French Defences

While the law as it stands in France has no separate defence based on a loss of control, there is a defence of legitimate defence which is very similar in remit to that of self-defence and public defence. Article 122-5 of the Criminal Code lays down the parameters of the legitimate defence. This states:

> A person who, faced with an unjustified attack against themselves or another, carries out at that time an act required by the necessity of the legitimate defence of themselves or another is not criminally liable, except if there is a disproportion between the means of defence used and the gravity of the attack.
>
> A person who, in order to prevent the commission of a serious or major offence against property, carries out an act of defence, other than voluntary homicide, when this act is strictly necessary for the goal sought is not criminally liable when the means used are proportionate to the gravity of the offence.[43]

As with the English law, in order for the legitimate defence to apply there must be an actual or imminent attack. For example, if a person is threatened, but the aggressor is held back by others on the scene, the person threatened cannot lash out violently at their aggressor and then rely on their legitimate defence, as the attack was no longer actual or imminent.[44] Where the threat is not actual or imminent the defence is not available because the individual should have sought the protection of the authorities, rather than take the law into their own hands. If there is a time gap between the attack and the response, the latter amounts to a revenge attack and the defence is not available.[45]

As with the English law, the defendant is only allowed to use a proportionate amount of force against his or her aggressor. In one case, some people had just climbed over a boundary wall and the homeowner had sought to frighten them away by shooting into the darkness. One of the intruders was hit and injured. The defence was not available to the homeowner since he had carelessly used excessive force.[46] Where the accused mistakenly thinks they are about to be attacked they are entitled to rely on the defence if that mistake was reasonable.[47]

The legitimate defence is available to protect property, but tighter limitations on the defence are placed in this context.[48] This is expressly provided for in the second paragraph of article 122-5 of the new Criminal Code. Thus it is sometimes permissible to use force against a thief. Article 122-5 lays down that the violent response must have been 'strictly' necessary to prevent the attack, an

---

43 'N'est pas pénalement responsable la personne qui, devant une atteinte injustifiée envers elle-même ou autrui, accomplit dans le même temps, un acte commandé par la nécessité de la légitime défense d'elle-même ou d'autrui, sauf s'il y a disproportion entre les moyens de défense employés et la gravité de l'atteinte.

N'est pas pénalement responsable la personne qui, pour interrompre l'exécution d'un crime ou d'un délit contre un bien, accomplit un acte de défense, autre qu'un homicide volontaire, lorsque cet acte est strictement nécessaire au but poursuivi dès lors que les moyens sont proportionnés à la gravité de l'infraction.'

44 Crim. 28 mai 1937, *G.P.* 1937.2.336.

45 Crim. 4 juill. 1907, *B.*, 243; Crim. 28 mai 1937, *G.P.* 1937.2.336; Crim 16 oct. 1979, *D.*, 1980, *I.R.*, 522.

46 T. Corr. Mayenne, 6 mars 1957, *D.*, 1957.458, note Pageaud.

47 Crim. 21 fév. 1996, B., 84, obs. Bouloc, R.S.C., 1996, p. 849; Paris, 9 oct. 1979, *J.C.P.*, 1979. II.19232, note Bouzat.

48 Art. 122-5.

adverb which is not used in the context of preventing an offence against the person. As a result, the defendant should normally give the victim a warning before using violence when a property crime is involved. On the issue of proportionality, a voluntary homicide cannot be committed simply to protect property.

As well as the legitimate defence, there is also a general defence of necessity which was introduced by the New French Criminal Code in 1994.[49] The old Criminal Code did not contain a general defence of necessity, but there were certain offences which could not be committed where the person acted through necessity, such as obstructing the highway[50] or having an abortion.[51] During the nineteenth century, the courts were reluctant to recognise openly a general defence of necessity, preferring to treat these cases as falling under the defence of constraint[52] (which is similar to the English defence of duress). Alternatively, the courts would find defendants not liable on the basis that they lacked the requisite intention to commit the offence.[53] But both these approaches were artificial, since the defence of constraint implies that the defendant was unable to make a free choice, but actually when a defendant is acting under necessity he has made a positive choice. For the same reason, such individuals do actually have *mens rea*, and to suggest otherwise is to confuse *mens rea* with motive. Eventually, in the 1950s a court of first instance recognised the defence of necessity. A defendant charged with building without a permit was acquitted because he was trying to provide decent living conditions for his family who had been living in slum accommodation.[54] Soon afterwards the *Cour de cassation* formally recognised the general defence of necessity.[55] The defence is now expressly laid down in article 122-7 of the new Criminal Code which states:

> A person is not criminally liable who, faced with an existing or imminent danger which threatens themselves, another or property, carries out a necessary act to safeguard the person or property, except if there is disproportion between the means used and the gravity of the threat.[56]

This defence is available to all types of offences, but three conditions must be satisfied in order for it to be applied: there must be an existing or imminent danger, this danger must have necessitated the commission of the offence, and the offence must have been proportionate to the danger. These conditions are very similar to those for the legitimate defence because the latter is really just a special form of the former, always requiring that the danger to which the defendant was responding be a criminal offence.

The European Convention on Human Rights

There have been suggestions that the availability of self-defence and public defence where the defendant has made an honest, but unreasonable, mistake as to the necessity to take defensive

---

49   Art. 122-7.
50   Art. R. 38, old Criminal Code.
51   Act of 17 January 1975.
52   Crim. 15 nov. 1856, *B.*, no 358; 14 aôut 1863, *D.P.*, 64.I.399.
53   Amiens, 22 avr. 1898, *S.*, 1899.2.1, note Roux; Crim. 27 janv. 1933, *G.P.*, 1933.I.489.
54   Trib. Corr., Colmar, 27 avril 1956, *D.*, 1956.500.
55   Crim. 25 juin 1958, Lesage, *J.C.P.*, 1959.II.10941, note J. Larguier, *D.*, 1958.693, note M.R.M.P.
56   'N'est pas pénalement responsable la personne qui, face à un danger actuel ou imminent qui menace elle-même, autrui ou un bien, accomplit un acte nécessaire à la sauvegarde de la personne ou du bien, sauf s'il y a disproportion entre les moyens employés et la gravité de la menace.'

action may breach the European Convention of Human Rights. Fiona Leverick[57] has argued that the law on this issue may violate the right to life, protected by Art. 2 of the Convention. She considers that Art. 2 requires a criminal sanction to be applied where a person kills on the basis of an erroneous and unreasonable belief. The European Court of Human Rights has consistently stated that for exceptions to Art. 2 to be made where actions are based on a mistaken belief, that belief must be held for good reasons. A counter-argument was put forward by the late Professor J.C. Smith[58] who considered that the English law on this issue did not breach the Convention. He pointed to the case of *Re A (Children)*[59] where the Court of Appeal interpreted Art. 2 as only concerned with intentional killings and noted that intention is given a narrower meaning under the Convention than under English law. Under the Convention it is restricted to direct intention, where the killing was the defendant's purpose. Thus, Professor Smith interpreted *Re A (Children)* as deciding that Art. 2 did not apply to someone who killed when they acted honestly in self-defence. His argument is not totally convincing, since the European Court of Human Rights has ruled that Art. 2 does not only apply to intentional killing, but also places an obligation on the state to protect the individual from any unjust deprivation of life, intention or not: *LCB v. UK*.[60]

Both Professor Smith and Fiona Leverick agree that for this type of case, the most appropriate label might be manslaughter rather than murder. The defence of self-defence could be removed where an unreasonable mistake has been made. Instead, a partial defence of self-preservation could be developed which would avoid a potential breach of the European Convention because liability for manslaughter would be imposed.

Burden of Proof

With self-defence the ordinary rules regarding the burden of proof apply with the defendant having to put forward some evidence to support the defence. Once this evidence has been provided, the prosecution have to prove that the defence is not available. Before the Homicide Act 1957 judges could withdraw provocation from the jury's consideration if they thought a reasonable person would not have acted as the defendant did. Under the 1957 Act, if there was evidence that a person was provoked to lose his or her self-control, the judge was required to leave the partial defence to the jury even where no reasonable jury could conclude that a reasonable person would have reacted as the defendant did.

For the new defence of loss of control, if sufficient evidence of the partial defence is raised, the burden of disproving the defence of loss of control beyond reasonable doubt rests with the prosecution.[61] The evidence will be sufficient where a reasonable jury, properly directed, could conclude that the partial defence might apply. It will be a matter of law, and therefore for a judge to decide, whether sufficient evidence has been raised to leave the partial defence to the jury.[62] Where there is sufficient evidence for the issue to be considered by the jury, the burden will be on the

---

57 Fiona Leverick, 'Is English Self-Defence Law Incompatible with Article 2 of the ECHR?' [2002] Criminal Law Review 347.

58 Professor John Smith, 'The Use of Force in Public or Private Defence and Article 2' [2002] Criminal Law Review 958.

59 [2001] Fam 149, [2001] 2 WLR 480.

60 (1999) 27 EHRR 212. See Fiona Leverick, 'The Use of Force in Public and Private Defence and Article 2: A Reply to Professor Sir John Smith' [2002] Criminal Law Review 963.

61 Coroners and Justice Act 2009, s. 54(5).

62 Coroners and Justice Act 2009, s. 54(6).

prosecution to disprove it. This is the same burden of proof as most other defences including self-defence, but amounts to a significant departure from the previous law, as it gives the judge control over whether there is a case fit to go to the jury. As Norrie notes:

> Under the new law, the idea of a justifiable sense of being seriously wronged directs the jury to consider what is morally or politically acceptable, and, further, the judge has the power to remove cases from the jury's consideration. Interestingly it should be noted that, with regard to the power of removal, the matter is taken from the "actual" jury's consideration in the name of an "ideal" jury.[63]

Amanda Clough has observed that the 2009 Act is moving the law backwards in the direction it had been before 1957, in other words one could wonder whether the legislation in this respect is regressive rather than progressive.[64]

An interesting aspect of the French law of legitimate defence is the approach taken to the burden of proof. Normally the defendant has to prove that the conditions of the defence have been satisfied. On the issue of proportionality, where the threat was to the person, the burden of proof is on the prosecution to show that the response was disproportionate, while with threats to property it is on the defendant. More significantly, the legislator has sought to strengthen the protection of individuals in particularly dangerous situations by reversing this burden of proof. Article 122-6 of the Criminal Code lays down two categories of presumption of legitimate defence:

> Article 122-6. A person is presumed to have acted in a state of legitimate defence when they carry out the act:
>
> 1. To repel, at night, an entrance by force, violence or fraud into inhabited premises;
> 2. To defend himself against the authors of theft or looting carried out with violence.[65]

In such circumstances it would be up to the prosecution to prove that the individual was not acting in a state of legitimate defence. For a long time this presumption was thought to be irrebuttable. Thus, on several occasions an individual had entered a house for an amorous rendezvous with a woman inside. Her husband was aware of his intentions and, having armed himself for his arrival, killed or injured him with a gun. In such cases, the conditions of legitimate defence were not satisfied, but the prosecution could not rebut the presumption that the defence applied.[66] In 1959 the *Cour de cassation* reversed its position on the matter, ruling that the presumption was rebuttable.[67] This is the approach adopted by the new French Criminal Code of 1994.[68]

---

63 Alan Norrie, 'The Coroners and Justice Act 2009 – Partial Defences to Murder: (1) Loss of Control' [2010] Criminal Law Review 275, 280.
64 Amanda Clough, 'Loss of Self-Control as a Defence: The Key to Replacing Provocation' (2010) 74 Journal of Criminal Law 118.
65 'Est présumé avoir agi en état de légitime défense celui qui accomplit l'acte:
1. Pour repousser, de nuit, l'entrée par effraction, violence or ruse dans un lieu habité;
2. Pour se défendre contre les auteurs de vols ou de pillages exécutés avec violence.'
66 Crim 11 juil. 1844, S. 1844, I, 777.
67 Crim 19 fév. 1959, D., 1959.161, note M.R.M.P., JCP, 1959.II.11112, note Bouzat.
68 Crim 21 fév. 1996, bull., no 84.

Self-Preservation

Even after the Coroners and Justice Act 2009, if a woman in an abusive relationship kills her partner to protect herself from further violence in the future, she may have no defence to murder – under loss of control, diminished responsibility or self-defence. She will therefore face the mandatory sentence of life imprisonment and this sentence might be disproportionate to her personal guilt. The government ignored the Law Commission's recommendation to remove the requirement of loss of control from the definition of the reformed defence in the 2009 Act and instead put this requirement at centre stage. By doing so, the defence is clinging to its rather dubious social and moral roots which in France had long ago caused the equivalent defence to be dropped altogether. By extending the defence to include fear of serious violence, but still requiring the defendant to have lost their control, there is a real tension in the current law. In addition, by sticking to the framework of the old defence of provocation, the objective test and timing factors are still determinant of whether the defence is available. The problems with the defence of provocation/loss of control are so fundamental that a mere redefinition has still left an unsatisfactory defence. It is regrettable that with the Coroners and Justice Act 2009 the government did not take the more radical option of moving away from a defence based on loss of control altogether.

There is today a risk that battered women who kill their abusive partners will fall outside the new partial defence. The key goal of trying to provide justice for women who had suffered years of abuse at the hands of their abusive partners who subsequently reacted by killing their abuser, might be achieved more effectively by abandoning a defence based on loss of control altogether. As there has been a historical reluctance to recognise a general defence of necessity in English law,[69] unlike in France, the way forward would be to create a narrow focused form of a necessity defence: a defence of self-preservation. This new partial defence of self-preservation would not be limited to battered women who killed;[70] it could, for example, be used by victims of racial abuse or bullying who react by killing their tormentors. The new defence could move the focus onto what ought to be the central issue of the defence: the terrible and dangerous abuse suffered by the victim. Undoubtedly, the woman's reaction to this abuse – killing – was wrong, and as a result this defence would only offer a partial defence.

The defence of self-preservation could be defined to offer a defence where the offender, or another person with whom he or she is closely associated, has been repeatedly subjected to serious violence or tormenting behaviour.[71] The defence could be available where force has been used not just to protect oneself, but also to protect another. For example, a son might kill his mother's violent boyfriend to protect her from further violence.[72] The violence or torments would have had to be directed against a person, it would not be sufficient if they were directed against property. This behaviour must have caused the offender to be in a state of severe emotional disturbance[73] (a concept which incorporates both emotions of fear and anger) at the moment of the fatal attack. The accused must have honestly believed that killing was the sole way to prevent grave future violence

---

69   R v. *Dudley and Stephens* (1884) 14 QBD 273.

70   The Criminal Law Revision Committee recommended the introduction into English law of a new partial defence to murder where excessive force was used in self-defence: Criminal Law Revision Committee, Fourteenth Report, *Offences Against the Person*, Cmnd 7844 (1980) para. 288.

71   Ibid., para. 12.88.

72   Ibid., para. 10.105.

73   See the Model Penal Code, The American Law Institute, s. 210(3)(1)(b), discussed in Ronnie Mackay and Barry Mitchell, 'Provoking Diminished Responsibility: Two Pleas Merging into One?' [2003] Criminal Law Review 745, 758.

or torment to him or herself or another.[74] That belief need not have been reasonable.[75] Nor should there be any requirement that the amount of force used was reasonable. A possible definition of the new defence is:

> A person will have a defence to murder so as to reduce their liability to manslaughter if he/she (or another person to whom he/she was closely associated) had:
>
> (a) before the killing, been subjected by the victim to repeated, serious violence or tormenting behaviour; and
> (b) reacted in a state of severe emotional disturbance in the honest belief that this was the only way to protect him or herself (or the other person) from further serious violence or torments.[76]

As the defence is only a partial defence there would be no need for an imminent threat to have existed. As regards the burden of proof, where the defendant had themselves been the victim of domestic abuse there would be a presumption that the defence was available.

If the victim is a spouse, lover or civil partner of the defendant who was abused by the defendant before the final attack, then consideration could be given by the Sentencing Council as to whether this should be treated as an aggravating factor, as in France, when determining the sentencing tariff.

Self-Defence and the Burden of Proof

Politicians have been looking at reform options for the defence of self-defence. The Conservative Party's election manifesto promised greater protection for householders against intruders.[77] Conservative politicians suggested that the right of self-defence should be lost only where the householder used 'grossly disproportionate force' on the intruder.[78] But this is not a satisfactory solution for self-defence because the law of self-defence operates in a wide variety of social contexts. It is not just available to homeowners confronted by a burglar, but also to someone involved in a fight in a local pub, or to a woman suffering domestic violence or to the police who shoot a suspect. At the moment a single test of reasonable force applies in all these different contexts and a 'grossly disproportionate' standard would not be appropriate.

Instead of trying to change the boundaries of self-defence, a more effective reform would be to change the burden of proof in appropriate cases. Historically, the defence of self-defence has not succeeded for battered women who kill their abusive partners.[79] We could consider building on the example of the French law in this field and applying a rebuttable presumption that the defence is available in the context of battered women who kill.

---

74 Criminal Law Revision Committee, Fourteenth Report, *Offences Against the Person*, Cmnd 7844 (1980), para. 10.101.

75 Ibid., para. 10.102.

76 See Catherine Elliott, 'What Future for Voluntary Manslaughter?' (2004) 68 Journal of Criminal Law 253, 263.

77 *Invitation to join the Government of Britain: The Conservative Manifesto* (Pureprint Group, 2010), 56.

78 Nigel Morris, 'No Need for New Laws over Confronting Burglars', *The Independent*, 28 December 2009.

79 Aileen McColgan, 'In Defence of Battered Women Who Kill' (1993) 13 Oxford Journal of Legal Studies 508, 521.

Conclusion

In attempting to move away from its indulgent approach to crimes of passion, the French criminal law has left no defence based on the concept of a loss of control. Instead the focus is on whether the defendant had a legitimate defence or acted out of necessity. The French Parliament has used the rules on the burden of proof to try to make sure that justice is done in appropriate cases and adapted the rules on sentencing to treat domestic violence as an aggravating factor. The retention of the concept of loss of control is an irrational distraction in English law and by retaining the conceptual framework of the old defence of provocation, unnecessary obstacles are being put in the way of defendants who deserve at least a partial defence. In order to make sure that our law complies with the European Convention on Human Rights we need to reconsider the boundaries of the partial defences to murder. Justice could be achieved by developing a defence of self-preservation, changing the burden of proof for the defence of self-defence in certain specific contexts and taking into account in sentencing the existence of domestic abuse. While it is disappointing to be recommending legislative reform of the defences to homicide so soon after the passing of a parliamentary Act on the subject, the 2009 Act does not provide an adequate solution to the problems identified in the earlier defence of provocation. The proposed reforms will allow battered women who kill their abusive partners a partial defence (self-preservation), and in limited circumstances a complete defence (self-defence) in order that justice can prevail for both men and women.

Chapter 15

When the Bough Breaks – Defences and Sentencing Options Available in Battered Women and Similar Scenarios under German Criminal Law

Michael Bohlander

O, you have torn my life all to pieces ... made me be what I prayed you in pity not to make me be again! – Thomas Hardy, *Tess of the d'Urbervilles* (Chapter 56)

Introduction

German law does not know of a concept of partial defences in the meaning traditionally given to provocation, now loss of control, and diminished responsibility in English law. Diminished responsibility as a sentencing factor exists (§21 StGB[1]) and is applicable to all offences, not just to murder. Loss of control as such is not a recognised separate defence at all, but may form the basis of a number of recognised defences or sentencing options. In fact, German law would appear to put both loss of control and diminished responsibility in the same conceptual drawer as far as their defining mental characteristics are concerned and the two concepts may overlap in the individual case. The 'reasonable person' test for the second prong of the provocation defence in English law does not appear in the same form, but a similar balancing exercise is performed in some of the defences when weighing the lethal response against the sanctity of life and the availability of less intrusive alternatives (see below). Also unlike in English law, using §21 will never entail a shift in the material characterisation of an offence (e.g. from murder to manslaughter) but only impact upon the sentencing frame. Similarly, while certain provisions recognise the impact of provocation on either the sentencing frame (e.g. §213 – see below) or on the court's power under §199 to order a discharge for minor offences such as mutual insults etc., the fact that someone was provoked can under the general sentencing provision of §46 also apply in the sentencing stage of any offence:

> Imagine the case of D, whose sister S had (validly) sold – for a fraction of its value – D's valuable vase which D had loaned her as a decoration for a party, to D's arch-enemy V in order to finance her drug habit and pay her dealer. D asks V to give the vase back, if need be in exchange for the price he paid to S, but V refuses and exploits the situation by mercilessly goading D about his and S's stupidity and asking ten times the real value until D can take it no more, flies into a rage, takes the vase and runs away. D has committed theft under §242 StGB and the provocation is probably

---

 1 All sections cited are from the Criminal Code (*Strafgesetzbuch* – StGB) unless otherwise mentioned. Sections of the StGB not excerpted in the text can be found at <http://www.gesetze-im-internet.de> under the tab 'Translations'. The German custom of using the '§' character for 'section' has been retained. Subsections are indicated by their number in brackets, e.g. '(1)'. Within subsections, citation proceeds by 'sentence', 'no' and 'alternative', e.g. '§123(2) 2nd sentence, no 4, 3rd alt.'. Note that this is not hierarchical, and that 'alternatives' and 'nos' may have several 'sentences'.

not sufficient to trigger §21, but it is highly likely that the court will take the provocation into account when fixing the sentence within the sentencing frame provided by s 242 StGB.

Depending on the circumstances, the situation of a provoked person or a battered woman in particular may be covered by self-defence or excessive self-defence, duress or scenarios of mistake as well as diminished responsibility and other general or specific sentencing provisions. This chapter[2] will first provide an overview of potential defences and sentencing laws and then look at their applications with respect to the special issue of battered women who kill, at the example of homicide law, drawing largely on a study by Gropengießer from 2008.[3] This contribution can naturally only provide an overview; for more details the reader will have to refer to the German literature and case law[4] on the topics.

Justificatory Defences

Justificatory defences that might apply are self-defence and necessity. The latter can be excluded *in limine*: just as with self-defence, in principle any legal interest can be defended on the basis of necessity, yet there seems to be agreement that killing cannot be justified,[5] with the possible exception of tyrannicide.[6] We shall thus concentrate on self-defence.

Self-Defence

Self-defence is regulated in §32:

§32 Self-Defence

(1) A person who commits an act in self-defence does not act unlawfully.

(2) Self-defence means any defensive action that is necessary to avert an imminent unlawful attack on oneself or another.

The material meaning of self-defence has traditionally been considered to exist in two facets: the protection of the individual victim on the one hand and the protection and assurance of the legal order as a whole on the other.[7] Self-defence can cover virtually any private and some public legal interests, yet as a vehicle of protecting the legal order it does not go as far as to give the individual a right to act as a sort of private law enforcement agent. Section 32(2) defines the concept of self-defence as understood in German doctrine. The first requirement is that there be an attack, which

---

2 A large part of the text is a modified excerpt of the relevant passages from my *Principles of German Criminal Law* (Hart, Oxford 2009) – hereinafter POGCL.
3 Helmut Gropengießer, *Der Haustyrannenmord* (Springer, Berlin 2008).
4 See the literature listed by Gropengießer, ibid., 193–214.
5 Amtliche Sammlung der Entscheidungen des Reichsgerichts in Strafsachen (RGSt) 63, 215; 64, 101.
6 So the view of Schönke/Schröder (hereinafter Sch/Sch)-Lenckner/Perron, *Strafgesetzbuch*, 27th edn (CH Beck, Munich 2006), §34, Mn. 11.
7 See Amtliche Sammlung der Entscheidungen des Bundesgerichtshofes in Strafsachen (BGHSt) 24, 356 and the further references, also on differing points of view, in Sch/Sch-Lenckner/Perron, §32, Mn. 1–1a.

in turn is defined as an immediate threat[8] to legally protected interests through human behavior.[9] The attack must in principle be already happening or at least be imminent in the sense that the attacker is on the very verge of beginning to act. This does, however, not mean that the actual aggressive conduct as such has to have begun, but the time immediately preceding that moment can be sufficient. For example, if V is about to shoot D with a pistol, D does not have to wait until V points the gun at him, but can already defend himself when V reaches for the gun in his pocket.[10] Similarly, if V approaches D with a menacing posture and the intention of attacking D, or if a group of hooligans enter a bar in order to start a brawl with the customers present, the courts have held that this can already suffice as an imminent attack.[11]

If there is no attack at all and D is – even honestly – mistakenly assuming that there is, self-defence is excluded, unlike under English law; D may be able to rely on putative self-defence, i.e. a mistake of fact about the facts underlying a recognised defence. This under German law then becomes a question of *mens rea* and liability for negligent commission of the offence, if punishable under law, remains an option.[12] If the attack is not imminent in the manner described above, D will not be able to rely on §32 but will in principle have to have recourse to necessity under §34, although the courts have apparently recognised a special justificatory defence of so-called 'quasi-self-defence' or 'pre-emptive self-defence'.[13] This concept was developed against the background of secret recordings made by D of calls from V wherein V was insulting or blackmailing D etc. and D made the recordings in order to expose V to the police and prevent any future infringement of his rights by V.[14] However, on a strict analysis of the issues involved, the academic commentators that consider this scenario to fall squarely under necessity would appear to have the better arguments on their side.[15] An attack will remain ongoing until the aggressive conduct and the infringement of the legal interest have been *factually* completed either by abandoning the attempt, by its failure or by causing the definite violation of the protected interest with the consequence that there is no further harm that could be averted by self-defence.[16] The completion of the legal elements of an offence is not necessarily determinative: if V takes D's bag and runs away, the theft will be made out as soon as V takes the bag from D and starts running, yet the attack will be ongoing until V has secured full and safe possession of the bag, which is why pursuing D may still act in self-defence[17] and use force to regain possession.

The attack must be unlawful; however, this does not mean that it has to be a criminal offence, more to the point, the attacker need not act with full guilt.[18] Any factual aggression that is at odds with the mandates of the legal order as a whole will in principle qualify.[19] Self-defence will not lie

---

8 Impossible attempts are thus not attacks if they cannot cause any danger to the protected good, see Sch/Sch-Lenckner/Perron, §32, Mn. 12. If D does not recognise this, it may be a case of mistake under §16.

9 Sch/Sch-Lenckner/Perron, §32, Mn. 3.

10 BGH Neue Juristische Wochenschrift (NJW) 1973, 255.

11 BGHSt 25, 229; 39, 376; BGH Neue Zeitschrift für Strafrecht (NStZ) 2000, 365; BGH NJW 1995, 973.

12 See for a detailed explanation Bohlander, POGCL, 60ff.

13 Sch/Sch-Lenckner/Perron, §32, Mn. 17.

14 See Amtliche Sammlung des Bundesgerichtshofes in Zivilsachen (BGHZ) 27, 289; BGH NJW 1982, 277.

15 Sch/Sch-Lenckner/Perron, §32, Mn. 17.

16 BGHSt 27, 339.

17 RGSt 55, 84.

18 BGHSt 3, 217 and the further references at Sch/Sch-Lenckner/Perron, §32, Mn. 24.

19 Sch/Sch-Lenckner/Perron, §32, Mn. 19–20.

against behaviour by V which is in itself lawful,[20] especially if based on a justificatory defence, or if V commits a mistake of fact under §16 which negates the *Tatbestand* or is treated in an analogous manner. In such cases, where the denial of self-defence may lead to unbearable results, D may be able to rely on necessity under §34.[21] The defence[22] must be directed against the attacker; collateral damage caused by the actions of D to a third party T when defending herself against V is in principle not covered by §32.[23] The defence against the attack must be the least intrusive and serious measure that promises the immediate cessation of the attack on an *ex ante* basis;[24] that means must also be employed in the least intrusive manner possible. There is no longer a general duty to retreat[25] yet D will generally have to employ merely defensive means (*Schutzwehr*) before moving towards a counter-attack (*Trutzwehr*),[26] but he need never risk the endangerment of his own legal position in order to spare the attacker.[27] The measure for this evaluation is the actual 'combat situation' (*konkrete Kampflage*[28]) which means that the characteristics of the persons involved, their age, strength, whether they are armed, etc., can and must be considered.[29] These principles also apply to the use of firearms in defence which may be permissible in certain circumstances even if the attacker is unarmed; however, because of the extreme dangerousness of firearms and the serious consequences for the attacker's health or life, their use must, wherever possible, be threatened first, be it by the use of a warning shot or otherwise, unless such prior warning would render the defensive action futile.[30]

In principle, the question of proportionality of value between the attacked interest and the interest endangered or sacrificed in the course of the defence is neither here nor there.[31] If no less intrusive course of action is available, D may sacrifice a higher interest of V to her own defence. There are exceptions to this principle, however, which are based on the idea of abuse of rights or

---

20 If D is coming to the aid of a third person T who chooses not to defend herself against V, he will in principle not be able to rely on §32 as long as T is aware of and fully capable of consenting to the attack and as long as the attack does not endanger legal interests not under the control of T; see BGHSt 5, 248.

21 Sch/Sch-Lenckner/Perron, §32, Mn. 21.

22 D must be acting with the intention of defending himself, as was mentioned above with respect to all justificatory defences; this includes cases where D is acting in knowledge of the defence situation but has also other motives unless he merely abuses the objective situation, as, for example, in the case of intentionally provoked self-defence; see Sch/Sch-Lenckner/Perron, §32, Mn. 63.

23 RGSt 58, 29; BGHSt 5, 248.

24 BGH NJW 1969, 802; BGH Strafverteidiger (StV) 1999, 143.

25 Sch/Sch-Lenckner/Perron, §32, Mn. 40, although in the older case law, much like under the common law of self-defence in England, there was a tendency to require D to retreat if that could be done without dishonour or violating his dignity or other interests. However, even under the present law D may be required to desist from defending himself if help from third parties, especially public authorities such as the police, is readily available and as effective as his own defence: equally effective police assistance must always be accepted, see BGHSt 39, 137. Private help must only be accepted if it is offered and leads to the possibility of the use of a less intrusive means of defence: D is weaker than V and would have to use a knife to defend himself, but T who is a Taekwondo trainer offers to help and will be able to stop V's attack with a few punches; compare RGSt 66, 244.

26 BGHSt 24, 356; 26, 147.

27 BGHSt 25, 229; BGH NJW 1980, 2263; NJW 1991, 503.

28 Sch/Sch-Lenckner/Perron, §32, Mn. 36.

29 RGSt 55, 83; BGHSt 26, 256; 27, 336; BGH NStZ 1998, 508.

30 Consistent jurisprudence of the courts: RGSt 55, 83; 58, 27; BGHSt 24, 356; 25, 229; 26, 143; 27, 336 and the many further references in Sch/Sch-Lenckner/Perron, §32, Mn. 37.

31 RGSt 69, 310; 72, 58; BGH Goltdammers Archiv (GA) 1968, 183; 1969, 24; BGH Verkehrsrechtssammlung (VRS) 30, 281; BGH StV 1982, 219; 1996, 146.

general considerations of a gross discrepancy between the goods involved, the blameworthiness of the attacker or special relationships between the actors.[32] Thus the defence may be restricted:

- in cases of *de minimis* attacks, such as shining a light into someone's face[33] or touching another person in the course of an argument without the intention of physical aggression;[34]
- if there is a gross and unacceptable discrepancy as in the cases (some of which emanated from the hard times after the Second World War[35]) of protecting a peach tree by means of a lethal electric installation,[36] a shot with fatal consequences at a thief fleeing with a bottle of syrup worth 10p,[37] defending a lien on a chicken by hitting its owner over the head with an axe,[38] threatening to set dogs on cross-country walkers and to use firearms against them because they use D's private path;[39]
- if the attacker is acting without guilt, as for example in the cases of children, insane persons or those labouring under an unavoidable mistake of law, where D may be required to resort only to defensive action, or at least more so than against an average person, the reason here being that the law as such is not being disobeyed by V to the same extent as in the ordinary case;[40]
- if there is a special relationship between D and V, such as, for example, husband and wife or family members, which may at the very least require D to avoid lethal means of defence,[41] which does, however, not apply to broken down relationships and situations of long-standing abuse such as in battered women scenarios;[42]
- if D has provoked[43] the attack, which – apart from raising concerns about whether D is actually acting with the intent to defend herself if the attack was intentionally provoked[44] – may restrict D's alternatives to purely defensive action and may additionally give rise to a duty to retreat, and in the case of an intentional provocation, depending on the circumstances of the case, lead to an absolute exclusion of the right to self-defence.[45]

---

32 See for an overview Sch/Sch-Lenckner/Perron, §32, Mn. 46–47.
33 Sch/Sch-Lenckner/Perron, §32, Mn. 49.
34 BGH MDR 1956, 372.
35 Note, however, that financial and social hardship in those times has for public policy reasons been consistently held not to be sufficient grounds for a defence of necessity, see Sch/Sch-Lenckner/Perron, §34, Mn. 41d and compare the English case of the squatters in *Southwark LBC* v. *Williams* [1971] 1 Ch 734 (CA).
36 Oberlandesgericht (OLG) Braunschweig, Monatsschrift für Deutsches Recht (MDR) 1947, 205.
37 OLG Stuttgart Deutsche Richterzeitung (DriZ) 1949, 42.
38 Bayerisches Oberstes Landesgericht (BayObLG) NJW 1954, 1377.
39 BayObLG NJW 1965, 163.
40 BGHSt 3, 217; BGH GA 1965, 148; BGH MDR 1974, 722; Bundessozialgericht (BSG) NJW 1999, 2302.
41 BGH NJW 1969, 802; 1975, 62; 1984, 986; 2001, 3202.
42 BGH NJW 1984, 986; BGH NStZ 1994, 581.
43 This does not include those cases where the provocation was already an attack in itself and V's reaction is in exercise of §32, see BGH NStZ 2003, 599.
44 BGH NJW 2001, 1075.
45 BGH NJW 2001, 1075; 2003, 1958 and the references at Sch/Sch-Lenckner/Perron, §32, Mn. 54–57.

Excusatory Defences

Excessive Self-Defence

Self-defence will normally only be available to D if he uses reasonable force and is under attack at the time of his 'defensive' action. What if he (1) exceeds the degree of force necessary to repel the attack, or if he is mistaken about the fact that there (2) is an attack and/or (3) the degree of violence directed at him? These cases of excessive defence are also known as

- 'intensive excess' (first scenario),
- 'extensive excess' (second scenario) and may come in the mixed form of the
- 'putative excess' (third scenario).

These are in principle cases either of mistake of fact regarding the factual basis for a recognised defence,[46] or of a mistake of law with regard to whether D exceeded the necessary force. Section 33, however, has a partially modified answer for these problems:

> A person who exceeds the limits of self-defence out of confusion, fear or terror shall not be held criminally liable.

Section 33 is, according to the majority view and the courts, not applicable to the 'extensive excess' and the 'putative excess', which follow the general rules on mistake of fact and law.[47] Section 33 thus only covers the 'intensive excess' and is almost unanimously considered to be an excusatory defence although its mere wording does not make that conclusion cogent.[48] The purpose behind §33 is to exonerate the defendant if she has made these errors of judgement in a psychologically stressed state of mind that did seriously affect her full self-control,[49] because[50] she felt threatened.[51] If these criteria are fulfilled, recourse to the subsidiary liability principles of mistake of fact under §16 or mistake of law under §17 is precluded with the consequence that D cannot be held liable for negligent offences either (see above). In a way, it is an extension of the risk attribution that is based on the fact that D is being attacked unlawfully by V, which already led to the omission of a general proportionality requirement in §32 as opposed to §34. The scope of

---

46 Although the BGH seems to have previously disagreed with that contention by stating that §33 and §16 have nothing to do with each other, see BGH NStZ 1987, 20. This interpretation is hard to reconcile with the purpose and systematic position of §33; better therefore the view of Sch/Sch-Lenckner/Perron, §33, Mn. 6.

47 BGH NJW 1962, 309; BGH NStZ 1983, 453; 1987, 20; 2002, 141; 2003, 599; BGH Neue Zeitschrift für Strafrecht-Rechtsprechungsreport (NStZ-RR) 2002, 204.

48 RGSt 56, 33; BGHSt 3, 198; BGH NStZ 1981, 99; NStZ 1995, 77.

49 Despite this basic principle, the majority view appears to be prepared to countenance the idea of an intentional excess as being covered by §33 as well; see, for example, BGHSt 39, 139. Lenckner/Perron rightly point out that this concept is hardly imaginable if the state of mind required by §33 is reached, see Sch/Sch-Lenckner/Perron, §33, Mn. 6.

50 There must be causality between the perception of the attack, the frightened state of mind and the loss of control by D: BGH NJW 1991, 505; 2001, 3202. This does not exclude situations where other motives accompany the states of mind mentioned in §33 (motive cluster) as long as the latter are the dominant ones or at least co-causal; see for the latter standard BGHSt 3, 198; BGH NJW 2001, 3202 and for the debate in the literature Sch/Sch-Lenckner/Perron, §33, Mn. 5.

51 BGH NJW 1991, 505; 2001, 3202.

the provision is restricted to the so-called 'asthenic' states of fear, terror and confusion; it cannot be extended[52] by analogy to the so-called 'sthenic' states of rage, hate, indignation, etc., even if they reach a similar severity; D will in the latter cases have to rely on the general rules but under these the subsidiary liability may also be excluded.[53] If D provoked the attack against which she then acted in (excessive) self-defence, the application of §33, according to more recent opinion,[54] is now tied to the question of whether she nonetheless retained any right of self-defence at all; if so §33 may still apply in principle, yet a meticulous examination will be required whether D really acted out of fear etc., which may be especially problematic if there is evidence of a *deliberate* provocation by D in order to attack V.[55]

Duress

We remember that necessity under §34 in its traditional interpretation did not allow for justification in cases where the legal interests involved were of roughly equal value and where the means used were disproportionate. More to the point, § 34 does not allow attacks on the attacker's life. What if there is a danger to D's life or limb, or freedom, that cannot be otherwise averted but §34 is not available? D may be threatened by V into committing a serious offence or be pressured by circumstances to act in a manner that will expose him to criminal liability. German law regulates these questions of duress on the level of guilt[56] by the excusatory defence of §35, which reads:

(1) A person who, faced with an imminent danger to life, limb or freedom which cannot otherwise be averted, commits an unlawful act to avert the danger from himself, a relative or person close to him, acts without guilt. This shall not apply if and to the extent that the offender could be expected under the circumstances to accept the danger, in particular, because he himself had caused the danger, or was under a special legal obligation to do so; the sentence may be mitigated pursuant to §49(1) unless the offender was required to accept the danger because of a special legal obligation to do so.

(2) If at the time of the commission of the act a person mistakenly assumes that circumstances exist which would excuse him under subsection (1) above, he will only be liable if the mistake was avoidable. The sentence shall be mitigated pursuant to §49(1).

The concept of duress had previously been contemplated, for example, in cases of defendants who

- had been involved in the machinations and atrocities of the National Socialist regime,[57]
- had been spying for or against totalitarian governments,[58]
- had killed violent relatives that posed a constant serious threat,[59]

---

52 RG Juristische Wochenschrift (JW) 1932, 2432; BGH NJW 1969, 802.
53 Sch/Sch-Lenckner/Perron, §33, Mn. 4.
54 The BGH in earlier times tended to exclude §33 altogether in cases of provocation: BGH NJW 1962, 308.
55 BGHSt 39, 133; BGH NJW 1995, 973; BGH NStZ-RR 1997, 194.
56 Sch/Sch-Lenckner/Perron, §35, Mn. 1–2.
57 BGHSt 2, 251; 3, 271; 18, 311; BGH NJW 1964, 370; 72, 834.
58 BGH Recht in Ost und West (ROW) 1958, 81; BGH MDR 1956, 395.
59 RGSt 60, 318; BGH NJW 1966, 1823.

- had committed perjury to avoid bodily harm or worse,[60]
- had killed a person under threat of being killed themselves if they did not[61] or who
- had committed sexual intercourse with their mother/son under threat of force from the mother's husband.[62]

The wording of §35 makes it clear that duress only protects D if he tries to avert a danger to his life, limb and personal liberty or that of a relative or person who is close to him;[63] the prevailing opinion rejects the possibility of analogies with regard to other protected interests, such as property,[64] because the rule under §35 is an exception from the general principles laid out under necessity and its commands to abide by the law instead of deciding for oneself what is right. Section 35 indeed presupposes an unlawful act and its concession to human frailty in cases where virtually no one can be expected to deny the demands of human nature militates against an excessive interpretation.

'Life' in the context of §35 also covers that of the unborn child.[65] 'Limb' in principle covers only acts against bodily integrity, in a holistic understanding, but not mental harm. It must be of a level of seriousness comparable to a threat to life, thus merely transitory and lighter dangers may be excluded.[66] Finally, 'freedom' means physical freedom or freedom of movement as covered in §239, not the general freedom of action or personal choice under Article 2 GG.[67] This restriction is also based on the idea that the degree of seriousness required by comparison with dangers to life and limb will not normally be reached otherwise.[68] The danger and its imminence within the context of §35 are, in principle, similar if not identical to the concept as used under necessity in §34:[69] other than in §32, the danger will be 'imminent' within the meaning of §34 either if it is an

---

60 BGHSt 5, 371.
61 RGSt 64, 30.
62 BGH GA 1967, 113.
63 This encompasses the persons listed as relatives in §11(1) No 1, where the actual existence of a close personal relationship is irrelevant, as well as any person with whom D has such a close relationship as long as it is reciprocated by the other, which excludes the 'secret love' and ex-girl- or boyfriends, regardless of whether D still has feelings for them; note, however, that the ex-husband or -wife are still relatives within the meaning of §11, yet no close relationship is required for them. See Sch/Sch-Lenckner/Perron, §35, Mn. 15.
64 See Sch/Sch-Lenckner/Perron, §35, Mn. 4.
65 Sch/Sch-Lenckner/Perron, §35, Mn. 5.
66 Sch/Sch-Lenckner/Perron, §35, Mn. 6–7.
67 Sch/Sch-Lenckner/Perron, §35, Mn. 8–9.
68 There may be difficult cases that are on the borderline, though, such as, for example, 16-year-old D killing or seriously wounding her despotic Kurdish father V as the, in her view, only available remedy against a forced marriage that is meant to take place in a week's time, because she is penniless and her father keeps her passport etc. so she cannot escape by merely running away: D cannot rely on necessity and she cannot rely on §35, either, as none of the protected interests are involved; what is threatened is her freedom to choose her own husband, an essential part of her human right to privacy. Should it make a material difference that in the case of D's disobedience, V will seriously beat or even kill her, or send her back to Turkey or Iraq, thus triggering the elements required by §35? When will that danger materialise and thus become imminent in the meaning of §35?
69 However, Sch/Sch-Lenckner/Perron, §35, Mn. 11, propose to use an objectivised *ex ante* view for all elements of the evaluation, the diagnostic and prognostic ones, in contrast to what they advocate for necessity, see Sch/Sch-Lenckner/Perron, §34, Mn. 13 with references to the debate. This because §35 as opposed to §34 does not grant a right to interfere based on the *danger* itself – with the attending severe consequences for the defence of the interest infringed by the action based on necessity – but because of the *psychological stress* caused to D.

ad hoc situation that is about to move from impending to real within a short time, as, for example, a person bleeding to death after an accident, or if it is a permanent danger that can materialise at any time without prior warning, such as a dilapidated building falling down. In addition to these categories, the courts have also accepted a danger to be imminent if the damage may only arise in the future but immediate action is required to prevent the future result.[70]

As with §34, human agency is not required as a cause of the danger. Like in §34, the reaction by D must be capable of ending the danger and at the same time be the least intrusive means, as is evident from the use of the words 'which cannot otherwise be averted'. These elements of proportionality already carry in themselves connotations of '*Zumutbarkeit*' i.e. of the question of whether D can legitimately be expected to undergo the danger; it is strictly speaking not necessary to have recourse to the criteria set out in §35(1) second sentence, such as, for example, whether D caused the danger or is under an obligation to suffer it. The law expects people to take measures which the average morally guided person would take under the circumstances without asking for heroism;[71] D must not simply choose the path of least resistance[72] but must make every effort to evade the danger.[73] This may include other avenues that are fraught with risk, possibly and depending on the circumstances even to the level of endangering one's own life[74] otherwise. The courts have, for example, held that the following scenarios were *outside* what could be legitimately expected of D:

- recourse to only temporarily effective police or judicial protection in situations of a permanent danger;[75]
- continuing to live in a dilapidated house that can collapse any moment, or face homelessness;[76]
- litigating a divorce or the institutionalisation of a cruel and violent husband if during the proceedings the violence would continue;[77]
- immediately leaving the former GDR and giving up one's entire livelihood instead of serving as an informer to the state security service.[78]

Compare to this, however, the following cases where the courts required D to suffer serious danger to himself rather than actively avert it:

- An SS officer feigning the execution of a criminal order or 'going underground' instead of carrying out an order to commit murder;[79]
- insubordination by a soldier instead of aiding murder.[80]

---

70 See for detail the case law in RGSt 36, 339; 60, 318; 66, 225; BGHSt 5, 373; 39, 137; 48, 258 and the references at Sch/Sch-Lenckner/Perron, §34, Mn. 17.
71 BGH MDR 1951, 537.
72 BGH NJW 1972, 834.
73 BGHSt 18, 311.
74 BGH NJW 1952, 113 and the further references at Sch/Sch-Lenckner/Perron, §35, Mn. 14.
75 RGSt 60, 322 (killing a violent relative) and 66, 226 (perjury).
76 RGSt 59, 69 (arson).
77 BGH NJW 1966, 1825 (murdering husband).
78 BGH MDR 1956, 395.
79 Entscheidungen des Obersten Gerichtshofes der Britischen Zone in Strafsachen (OGHSt) 2, 228.
80 BGHSt 2, 257 (in the context of the so-called 'Röhm-Putsch' under the Nazi regime).

If one looks at these cases, one may be able to discern a certain pattern and that is that in the first list of cases, D in substance was faced with the danger without having previously and voluntarily associated with the potential source of the danger, whereas in the cases of the SS officer and the soldier in the context of the time (Nazi terror regime) there was a primary and a priori collaboration with the dangerous source, i.e. the Nazis, and their general political agenda, even if D may not have subscribed to the use of violence; however, because D was fundamentally and willingly a part of the 'machine' in the first place, so to speak, he was under a duty to suffer greater danger than if he had not been.[81]

As is the case with the justificatory defences, §35 requires a subjective element of finality, namely that D act *with the purpose* of averting the danger; the wording and substance of the defence exclude acting in the mere knowledge of the facts that support it as a sufficient subjective element; as with §33 it is enough if the purpose is part of a motive cluster.[82] The courts also require D to exert due diligence as to possible other avenues and the proportionality elements,[83] yet Lenckner/Perron are correct when they point out that it is hard to see how omitting this exercise of diligence should make a difference if in fact D arrives at the right conclusion; where it may make a difference is with the question about the avoidability of an error under §35(2).[84]

According to the structure of the law, if the criteria of §35(1) first sentence are met, D acts without guilt and this privilege is then excluded by the second sentence related to legitimately expected alternative options. The first alternative, that D cannot rely on duress if she caused the danger herself, is worded unfortunately because the element of 'causing' the danger would also apply in the case of witness D who makes a truthful incriminating statement in court and then is threatened by the accused to withdraw her testimony in the next hearing or face grave consequences.[85] The mere causation element must thus be augmented by an element of moral blameworthiness, i.e. whether D caused the danger knowingly or recklessly *and* without good reason in that she would have had to realise that she would not then later escape the materialising danger unless she herself caused harm or damage to others.[86] The second alternative requires D to suffer the danger if he is under a legal obligation to do so. This should not be confused with the material duty to act *vis-à-vis* a specific person as used in the context of omission offences; what is meant here are those cases where a person has taken over[87] a position or office based on which she is generally obliged by the law regulating the exercise of that office to protect individuals and the common good, such as, for example, police officers, firemen, soldiers, civil servants, doctors

---

81   This may in effect be a parallel to the English case law on duress and prior voluntary association with criminal groups, which also leads to a serious restriction on D's ability to rely on duress. See the House of Lords in *Hasan* [2005] UKHL 22, per Lord Bingham [38].

82   BGHSt 3, 275.

83   BGHSt 18, 311; BGH NStZ 1992, 487.

84   Sch/Sch-Lenckner/Perron, §35, Mn. 16–17.

85   Example used by Sch/Sch-Lenckner/Perron, §35, Mn. 20.

86   Sch/Sch-Lenckner/Perron, §35, Mn. 20.

87   The rule also applies to persons who have to suffer certain infringements of their rights on the basis of official legal acts, such as prisoners who have been convicted and sentenced, or car drivers who may be subjected to a legitimate taking of a blood sample under §81a StPO. See Sch/Sch-Lenckner/Perron, §35, Mn. 24. Section 35 remains a problem, however, for the case of D who has been imprisoned (maybe even for life) after a fully lawful and fair trial and after exhaustion of all appeals, but who is in fact innocent. German law would probably countenance giving D the benefit of duress if she tried to escape from prison and, for example, took one of the prison guards hostage for that purpose. See for references to the legislative *travaux préparatoires* Sch/Sch-Lenckner/Perron, §35, Mn. 26.

and medical personnel of hospitals, sailors, flying staff in airplanes, etc.[88] The exact scope of the obligation must be found through reference to the purpose of the respective office and the dangers typically connected with its exercise; there is no general duty identical to all of these positions.[89] In the case of third persons with whom D has a special close relationship or who are relatives of his the special obligation can have harsh consequences: if D is under one of these obligations and the dangers he is meant to accept under it also involve T who is his daughter, the duty to suffer the danger takes precedence which in effect imposes on T a burden of suffering that danger, too, or at least expecting no privileged help from D. An example will clarify this: D is a fireman and called to a fire which threatens several persons inside a house, one of whom is his ten-year-old daughter T, who he knows is visiting there. He cannot find her immediately, but there are other inhabitants that (only) he can reach easily and take to safety. D is not covered by §35 if he searches the house for T instead of rescuing the others.

D may also have to suffer the danger if it can be legitimately expected for other reasons, because the two alternatives mentioned are, as we saw, only examples and not an exhaustive list. Examples for further reasons are:

- duties to act arising from the categories explained in the context of omissions liability,
- duties to suffer an infringement of one's own rights based on another person's acting in the exercise of a justificatory defence such as self-defence or necessity,
- if the harm to another is out of proportion to that threatening D,
- the degree of the danger to D,
- if the chances of success of the rescue action are questionable and there is a high likelihood that it may cause further harm.[90]

Note the harsh sentencing rule that the possible reduction of the sentence under §49(1) does not apply if D had to suffer the danger; his difficult position may only be considered as a general sentencing factor within the regular sentencing scale. If at the time of the commission of the act D mistakenly assumes that circumstances exist which would excuse him under §35(1), i.e. he assumes that there is a danger or he does not know that he caused it himself or is under an obligation to suffer it, he will not be liable if the mistake was unavoidable. Otherwise his sentence will be mitigated pursuant to §49(1). If D otherwise exceeds the ambit of the permissible reaction under §35(1) he will not be exempt from liability; §33 does not apply by analogy. Errors by D about the fact that an emergency exists at all or its actual circumstances, for example that D wrongly thinks he may have caused it, are not regulated in §35; the same applies to a mistake about the legal boundaries of §35 (for example if D thinks that danger to property was sufficient). Their treatment is controversial: while the second sort is generally seen as irrelevant, the first category may in some cases benefit from the general principle underlying the mitigation made possible by §35(2) second sentence, second alternative.[91] If only one of several participants to an offence acts under duress, §29 states that this will not affect the liability of the others, but it may have an impact on their sentencing.

---

88 See the examples listed at Sch/Sch-Lenckner/Perron, §35, Mn. 23.
89 BGH NJW 1964, 730.
90 See on all of these with references to case law and literature Sch/Sch-Lenckner/Perron, §35, Mn. 33–35.
91 See, for these problems, the references at Sch/Sch-Lenckner/Perron, §35, Mn. 38–45.

Supra-Legal Duress?

Although not yet recognised by the courts, the prevailing opinion in the literature supports the recognition of a defence of so-called supra-legal duress (*übergesetzlicher entschuldigender Notstand*). This is meant to cover cases that are not within the remit of either §34, because the interests cannot be quantified, such as for example, human lives, or of §35, the latter because the danger is to legal interests not covered in §35 or to persons other than relatives and close friends, etc. The cases envisaged by the proponents of the supra-legal duress idea are to a large extent based on conflicts of conscience and religious freedom. The development of this concept arose partially from the post-war euthanasia trials, where, for example, doctors had been forced to decide whether to cooperate to a certain extent with the NS authorities in the concentration camps in the selection of mentally ill patients who were destined to be killed, and to save as many of them as possible, or to refuse to participate in the selection and risk that colleagues without similar scruples would take their place and apply a much harsher practice. The courts tried to acknowledge the dilemma of the doctors who participated by holding that there was a general exemption from liability (*Strafausschließungsgrund*)[92] or by arguing a mistake of law.[93] It is clear that in such cases one moves at the limits of what the administration of criminal justice is capable of doing in supporting and affirming the societal moral consensus, yet one will also understand the need of relatives or of survivors for a judicial closure to their indescribable ordeals. Especially in the case of human lives, the development of this concept is a direct consequence of the traditional refusal in German case law and literature to subscribe to the idea that lives can in extreme cases be counted.[94] Manuel Ladiges has recently argued in a very perceptive paper that it is time to reconsider this stance[95] based on the 9/11 scenario and similar cases where a choice *has* to be made in practice.

Insanity and Diminished Responsibility

D will also be acting without guilt if he can successfully plead the full defence[96] of insanity. Insanity under §20 is a different concept from the one used in England and Wales, and it is closely linked to the defence of diminished responsibility under §21, which again contrasts with the English position in that it applies to all offences across the board, but as a mere sentencing factor. It is therefore helpful to present both provisions together and merely address a few specific issues on §21 under a separate heading.

§20 Insanity

Any person who at the time of the commission of the offence is incapable of appreciating the unlawfulness of their actions or of acting in accordance with any such appreciation due to a pathological mental disorder, a profound consciousness disorder, debility or any other serious mental abnormality, shall be deemed to act without guilt.

---

92   OGHSt 1, 335; 2, 126.
93   BGH NJW 1953, 513.
94   See the arguments at Sch/Sch-Lenckner, Vorbem §§32 ff., Mn. 116.
95   See his article online at <http://www.zis-online.com/dat/artikel/2008_3_220.pdf>.
96   However, in cases of dangerous offenders, certain measures of rehabilitation and incapacitation may be ordered, see, for example § 63 on mental hospital orders and § 64 on custodial addiction treatment orders.

§21 Diminished responsibility

If the capacity of the offender to appreciate the unlawfulness of his actions or to act in accordance with any such appreciation is substantially diminished at the time of the commission of the offence due to one of the reasons indicated in §20, the sentence may be mitigated pursuant to §49(1).

Note that §20 is a provision about material guilt, whereas §21 is a mere sentencing provision: §20 thus affects the conviction, §21 only the sentence. The rule with adult offenders is that their sanity will be assumed unless there are facts that give rise to some doubt.[97] Another major difference to the English approach that needs to be pointed out again at this stage is the fact that intoxication is not a separate defence, but a sub-category of §20 and §21, and at least within the defence of §20 it is entirely irrelevant whether the intoxication was voluntary or not; as we will see under §21 the voluntariness may have a consequence for the sentencing, but not for the establishment of diminished responsibility as such. The basic structure of both defences is that the criteria set out in §20, to which we will turn presently, must lead to D's being incapable either

- of appreciating the unlawfulness of her actions or
- of acting in accordance with any such appreciation.

These two states, which are reminiscent of the M'Naghten Rule,[98] cannot occur cumulatively.[99] If D cannot appreciate the unlawfulness in the first place it is illogical to say that he cannot act in accordance with that appreciation as well. The two criteria are the actual central problems of the defence, because based on the expert evidence with regard to the mental states the court must decide, again maybe with the aid of an expert, whether these criteria are met or not; judicial experience leads to the realisation that in the majority of all cases the answer is more likely to be one of reasonable doubt than of positive affirmation, although strictly speaking the very question of whether D could appreciate the unlawfulness or act on that appreciation is considered to be a question of law based on a comparison of the normal standards of behaviour with the abnormal, which as such would exclude the use of the *in dubio pro reo* principle.[100] While it is true that one is comparing standards, it does not necessarily follow that they are normative in the sense of legal-normative standards, or whether they are not more like mere brackets of expected behaviour within an empirical framework based on an average drawn from the cases actually studied by psychological science or psychiatry. One might thus at least argue that it is a mixed question of fact and law. Section 20 lists the following categories of mental disturbances in the wider meaning that can be a basis for a claim of insanity in law:

- a pathological mental disorder (*krankhafte seelische Störung*)
- a profound consciousness disorder (*tiefgreifende Bewußtseinsstörung*)

---

97   This does not mean that D is under any burden of proof, evidential or probative, with regard to establishing his insanity or diminished responsibility. It is the task of the prosecution and more to the point, the court, under §244(2) of the Code of Criminal Procedure, to clear up the question regarding D's alleged insanity. The level needed to establish it is a balance of probabilities to the degree that the court cannot safely exclude the possibility that D was insane at the time of the offence. As in England, deciding such issues will in the majority of cases require the aid of an (in Germany mostly court-appointed) expert.
98   *M'Naghten's Case* (1843) 10 Cl & Fin 200.
99   Consistent case law of the BGH: BGHSt 21, 27; BGH NStZ 1982, 201; 1991, 529; 2000, 578.
100 Sch/Sch-Lenckner/Perron, §20, Mn. 43.

- debility (*Schwachsinn*) or
- any other serious mental abnormality (*schwere seelische Abartigkeit*).

It is generally irrelevant whether the disturbance is permanent, intermittent or temporary, as long as it affected the offender at the time of his actions that are the basis of the criminal liability.[101] In fact, some of them may only be imaginable in a temporary fashion, for example, those based on alcohol and drug abuse or extreme affect. In principle these four categories, particularly the first one, are meant as disturbances that start from a 'biological' basis, e.g. of a disease or illness (*krankhaft*), disorder or abnormality, and have their impact on the 'mental' level, yet how far this dichotomy, if there is one at all, can actually be maintained is open to question. The wording of §20, especially the last category, is wide enough to catch all the relevant mental states.[102] One has to remember that §20 is concerned with making psychological phenomena usable for the legal process; as with causation, for example, the meaning of the concepts need not and sometimes cannot be the same in both law and science. It is, for example, also recognised that medical and psychiatric research has not yet found a physical cause for many of the disturbances that are considered in the daily practice of the courts, and that even in medical science there is no consensus as to what constitutes an 'illness' within the meaning of the word *krankhaft*.[103] The topic is extremely wide and as far as the psychiatric side is concerned it would merit a book on its own. For the purpose of obtaining an impression in the context of an introduction to the general principles it may, however, be best to give examples for each of the categories:

1. Pathological mental disorder (krankhafte seelische Störung):[104]

- Exogenous psychosis: physical cerebral traumata; infection-based psychosis; genuine epilepsy; dementia; cerebral arteriosclerosis or cerebral atrophy; cerebral damage caused by excessive substance abuse.
- Endogenous psychosis: schizophrenia; manic depression.

2. Profound consciousness disorder (tiefgreifende Bewußtseinsstörung):[105]

- Affect: an explosive reaction based on an extreme emotional state where no deliberate decision-making occurs any more, for example extreme rage, hate, shock, panic or fear. Some instances of battered woman syndrome and provocation generally can be caught under this category. The question of whether affect is excluded as a defence if it had been caused by D is controversial; the prevailing opinion would appear to do so, yet the courts have recently become more reluctant in their approach.
- Intoxication:[106] as was already mentioned the question of whether D voluntarily intoxicated himself is irrelevant for insanity. As far as the concept of the *actio libera in causa* (D himself, while in a state of full mental control, causes the state of insanity to occur either in the knowledge of or with negligence with regard to a potential offence occurring in

---

[101] Sch/Sch-Lenckner/Perron, §20, Mn. 5 for the first category.
[102] See Sch/Sch-Lenckner/Perron, §20, Mn. 1 and 5.
[103] Sch/Sch-Lenckner/Perron, §20, Mn. 9–10.
[104] See the references to case law and literature at Sch/Sch-Lenckner/Perron, §20, Mn. 11–11a.
[105] See the references at Sch/Sch-Lenckner/Perron, §20, Mn. 12–17.
[106] Note that in certain circumstances D may be liable under §323a for putting himself in a drunken state, but *not* for the offence committed while drunk.

that state) is still applicable after the landmark decision of the BGH[107] in which the court doubted the constitutionality of that judge-made institution, D can still be liable even if he acted in a state of insanity.[108] The main criterion for insanity by intoxication is in practice the blood-alcohol concentration determined by an expert. If the value is 3.0 or more, the courts will as a rule accept the defence unless there are other factors that justify the assumption that despite that high level of alcohol, D was still capable of understanding what he was doing or of acting on that understanding. This may be a factor with defendants who are used to drinking large amounts of alcohol. A level of 2.0 or above will usually lead to diminished responsibility, and in between those two the circumstances of the individual case will determine the outcome of whether §20 or §21 will apply. For intoxication by drugs other than alcohol no such simple measure exists and the courts will refer to the question of whether D was on overdose or in withdrawal; during the normal saturation phase the use of drugs is generally considered to be irrelevant.

3. Debility (Schwachsinn):[109]

- This category is a special case of the fourth and covers solely the retarded development of intelligence in its different clinical stages of idiocy, imbecility and moronity.

4. Other serious mental abnormality (schwere seelische Abartigkeit):[110]

- Under this heading we find all those mental states that are not caught by the other three and especially those which do not fall under the meaning of *krankhaft* within the first category but are of a similar gravity. Examples are personality disorders, neuroses, deviations and perversions, alcoholism and drug addiction (as opposed to actual alcohol and drug use during a specific offence, which falls under the second group).

Section 21 is based on the same structure as §20 with the only difference that D's capabilities of appreciation or acting on the same are not entirely excluded, but are merely severely impaired. All of the above on the different categories within §20 applies therefore to §21 as well. It is not a material defence in the strict meaning of the word, but a sentencing provision that leads to a *facultative* shift in the sentencing scale according to §49(1) within the discretion of the judge. It applies to all offences. Compared to the English approach under *Majewski* for intoxication it is interesting to see that while the law does not require it, the courts have regularly used the fact that D was voluntarily intoxicated as a reason to deny the mitigation under §49(1),[111] especially if D had a proclivity for committing offences while intoxicated and if he was aware of that.[112] Note that none of this applies without further consideration if D suffered from chronic alcoholism or other

---

107 BGHSt 42, 235.
108 See on the discussion regarding the *actio libera in causa* the references to case law and literature at Sch/Sch-Lenckner/Perron, §20, Mn. 33–42.
109 References to case law and literature at Sch/Sch-Lenckner/Perron, §20, Mn. 18.
110 References to case law and literature at Sch/Sch-Lenckner/Perron, §20, Mn. 19–24.
111 BGHSt 43, 77.
112 BGHSt 34, 33; BGH NStZ 2004, 495; 2005, 151 and with slight modifications BGH NJW 2004, 3350.

disorders that had an impact on his freedom of choice or which combined with the use of alcohol led to the state of §21.[113] The range of available sentences after application of §21 is set out in §49:

§49 Special mitigating circumstances established by law

(1) If the law requires or allows for mitigation under this provision, the following shall apply:

1. Imprisonment of not less than three years shall be substituted for imprisonment for life.

2. In cases of imprisonment for a fixed term, no more than three quarters of the statutory maximum term may be imposed. In case of a fine the same shall apply to the maximum number of daily units.

3. Any increased minimum statutory term of imprisonment shall be reduced as follows:

a minimum term of ten or five years, to two years;
a minimum term of three or two years, to six months;
a minimum term of one year, to three months;
in all other cases to the statutory minimum.

(2) If the court may in its discretion mitigate the sentence pursuant to a law which refers to this provision, it may reduce the sentence to the statutory minimum or impose a fine instead of imprisonment.

Note that subsections (1) and (2) are separate 'provisions' within the meaning of §49 with different sentencing regimes, and that the respective law must refer to either (1) or (2).

Homicide Offences

Structural Overview

German law calls homicide offences 'offences against life', which include abortion. The main offences against life can be found in §§211–222. There are, however, many homicide offences in other sections of the Special Part in the form of result-qualified offences where D causes death by committing a non-homicide basic offence, as for example §227 on bodily harm causing death. One fundamental distinction from English law is that German law under §222 knows of a form of negligent homicide that does not require gross negligence. German law does not recognise constructive liability in homicide or any other offences, either (see §18[114]). The intentional homicide offences, §211 and §212, and the sentencing provision of §213 present a problem as far as their structural and doctrinal relationship is concerned. They read as follows:

---

113 Sch/Sch-Lenckner/Perron, §21, Mn. 20 with further references.
114 §18 Aggravated sentence based on special consequences of the offence. If the law imposes a more serious sentence based on an extended result of an offence, any principal or secondary participant is liable to the increased sentence only if they acted at least negligently with respect to that result.

§211 Murder under specific aggravating circumstances

(1) Whosoever commits murder under the conditions of this provision shall be liable to imprisonment for life.

(2) A murderer under this provision is any person who kills a person for pleasure, for sexual gratification, out of greed or otherwise base motives, by stealth or cruelly or by means that pose a danger to the public or in order to facilitate or to cover up another offence.

§212 Murder

(1) Whosoever kills a person without being a murderer under §211 shall be convicted of murder and be liable to imprisonment of not less than five years.

(2) In especially serious cases the penalty shall be imprisonment for life.

§213 Murder under mitigating circumstances

If the murderer (under §212) was provoked to rage by maltreatment inflicted on him or a relative, or was seriously insulted by the victim and immediately lost self-control and committed the offence, or in the event of an otherwise less serious case, the penalty shall be imprisonment from one to ten years.

Despite the sequence of these provisions which should normally be a strong indicator as to what is the basic norm, what is a qualification, etc., the courts and the commentators disagree as to the relationship between §212 and §211, and the ensuing consequences for the other forms of intentional homicide. The BGH has traditionally held[115] that because of the different substance of both provisions, §211 and §212 are two separate offences that are not to be considered in a relationship of basic or qualified norm. The literature, however, views them precisely thus; opinion is divided about whether §211 is the basic norm and §212 a less serious case, or §212 the basic norm and §211 an aggravated form. The literature view that treats them as basic offence and qualification is to be preferred; it has at least systematic interpretation on its side, because firstly, §211 is the first offence to be mentioned and secondly, §212 talks about a person who is not a murderer under §211. That the majority view still sees §212 as the basic norm is of secondary importance, as the only real application of the different views is in §28 on participation and complicity.[116] Section 213 – and §212(2) for that matter – are mere sentencing provisions in relation to §212(1); note that §213 does not apply to §211 as it makes clear reference only to §212. However, the fact that both §21 and §213 are sentencing provisions that can lead to different sentencing frames if applied to §212 can lead to problematic sentencing decisions because of §50 on the ban on double counting of mitigating circumstances:

---

115   And still does; see BGHSt 36, 233.
116   See Sch/Sch-Eser, Vorbem §§211 ff., Mn. 5. – under §28, the classification of §§211 and 212 has an effect on the liability of a participant who does not himself fulfil one of the personal elements of §211. Depending on the theory, he may be liable for participating in §211 or merely in §212.

§50

Multiple mitigating circumstances

> A circumstance which alone or together with other circumstances justifies the assumption of a mitigated offence under the provisions of the special part and which is also a special statutory mitigating circumstance for the purposes of section 49, may only be considered once.

Thus if a certain fact may fall under §21 and under §213, the court can use it only once; this applies especially to diminished responsibility based on a mental state caused by permanent abuse over long periods, but the courts have held that this state and an instance of provocation occurring in that state can be two separate facts for the purposes of §50 and thus lead to a greatly reduced sentencing frame.[117]

Section 211 – The Special Elements of Aggravated Murder

German law reserves the mandatory life sentence for especially heinous acts of intentional homicide, with the 'normal' murder having a scale from five to 15 years, and in especially serious cases not caught by §211, a discretionary life sentence (§212(2)). Section 211, as §212, requires intent to kill which may normally be conditional intent or *dolus eventualis* for the mere act of killing as opposed to the special elements. Note that German law allows for the mitigation of the mandatory sentence in line with general sentencing provisions such as §49, and according to the BGH also in cases of wholly exceptional situations where the harshness of the mandatory life sentence would be entirely inappropriate; the court then applies §49(1) no 1 by analogy (so-called *Rechtsfolgenlösung* – sentencing solution).[118] Let us refresh our memory what these heinous acts are according to §211(2). A murderer under this provision is any person who kills another person

1. for pleasure, sexual gratification, out of greed or otherwise base motives,
2. by stealth, cruelly or by means that pose a danger to the public, or
3. in order to facilitate or to cover up another offence.

These elements come in three distinct clusters because only the first and the third are relevant as personal characteristics because only they relate to the person and mind of the *offender*. The second group describes heinous modes of commission of the *offence*. The courts have traditionally treated the elements of all three clusters as a final and conclusive list of what makes murder into an offence under §211. They have tried to restrict their application by a narrow interpretation of their prerequisites.[119] The literature tends to comprehend these elements as mere typifications of the especially heinous nature of acts falling under §211 and consequently wants to allow the judge to reject a verdict under §211, despite the fact that one of the elements has been fulfilled, if the act is for other reasons not within the general bracket of seriousness as required by §211.[120] The elements of the two most relevant alternatives are – briefly – defined as follows:

---

117 BGHSt 27, 298; BGH StV 1994, 16.
118 BGHSt 30, 105.
119 BGHSt 30, 105.
120 Sch/Sch-Eser, §211, Mn. 9–10b.

- D is acting out of 'otherwise base motives' if compared to the previous three elements the nature of D's motivation, according to the moral views of society, is an expression of deepest moral depravity and utterly deplorable. Examples are killing V because she refused to have intercourse with D, killing V in order to become sexually aroused (as opposed to achieving gratification), killing one's spouse in order to enjoy fully an adulterous relationship with another partner, killing a daughter in order to save the family honour, discriminatory killing of V because of her affiliation with a certain ethnic or religious group, etc.[121]
- 'By stealth' – and this is the most relevant element for battered woman scenarios looked at below – requires D to act in an insidious manner, by intentionally exploiting the fact that V, at the time of the attack, is not expecting an attack (*Arglosigkeit*) and his consequent defencelessness (*Wehrlosigkeit*), and all of this with hostile intention. The classic cases are the shot in the back when V turns away from D, D lying in wait in an ambush and killing V when he passes by. It includes persons who are asleep, because they are said to take their *Arglosigkeit* with them into their sleep, but not those who are unconscious, because the victim must at the time of the attack at least be generally capable of forming a view about whether or not an attack might be imminent. Hostile intention can exclude such motivations as wanting to spare the victim shame she would otherwise be exposed to, pity for a terminally ill patient, etc.[122]

Let us now apply these general considerations to the situation of battered women.

The Law Applied – Battered Women Who Kill[123]

All of the above-mentioned legal concepts can be relevant for the case of a battered woman. As far as England is concerned, the suffering of battered women was a major driving factor for law reform. It is thus apt to use the battered women syndrome, hereinafter BWS, for the demonstration of the effects of the German approach. The in-depth study by Helmut Gropengießer from 2008 mentioned in the introduction provides a detailed declension of the BWS under German law. He uses four different, staggered case studies which were on the one hand analysed under the law as practised by the courts and on the other hand presented to a small group of legal practitioners and academics in semi-structured interviews to find out their reactions to those case scenarios. These empirical facets are of less interest for the current purpose, and they are obviously nothing more than an impressionistic snapshot. We shall thus restrict the discussion to the legal evaluation of the scenarios. They were as follows:[124]

General common background:

The marriage of V (husband) and D (wife) has been broken since V lost his job and started consuming large quantities of alcohol every day. There are constant quarrels and V repeatedly beats D seriously.

---

121 Compare Sch/Sch-Eser, §211, Mn. 18–20.
122 Sch/Sch-Eser, §211, Mn. 21–26.
123 In order to keep the length of this already extensive chapter to an absolute minimum I have mainly cited the passages of Gropengießer's study by the headings of the scenarios; the reader will find a wealth of further references, legal and criminological, in his book.
124 Ibid., 3.

- Scenario 1: D is no longer willing to bear the abuse and waits for an opportune moment to kill V. When she finds him asleep one evening, she kills him with an axe which she has kept handy for that purpose.
- Scenario 2: D is in utter despair because of the general state of affairs. One evening she is suddenly overwhelmed by her feelings when she sees V who has just fallen asleep after drinking heavily; she grabs a heavy object and beats him to death with it.
- Scenario 3: V has again seriously abused D; when she finds him asleep about 30 minutes afterwards, she stabs him to death with a knife.
- Scenario 4: V and D have another major quarrel; V walks towards D threatening to beat her up and D flees into the kitchen where she grabs a knife. V follows her into the kitchen and D kills him with the knife.

The background to the staggered narratives is obvious and very much mirrors the English debate around provocation: there are issues of loss of control versus deliberate behaviour, lapse of time between provocation and reaction, a long-standing condition that may give rise to mental problems, etc. All of these, however, have different effects under German law, given the fact that German law knows two offences of intentional killing and reserves the mandatory life sentence for the aggravated form, yet allows for a sentencing solution even then if, for example, §21 is triggered. We shall look at the outcome of the scenarios in turn.

Scenario 1[125]

The first problem which D will encounter is whether her actions are subsumed under §211 or §212: if the former, the sentence will be life unless a defence is triggered that would allow a reduction; if the latter, the sentencing frame is five to 15 years with the potential application of §213. D's problem is that the consistent jurisprudence of the Bundesgerichtshof sees the case of killing a sleeping person as the classic example of murder by stealth, one of the categories of §211, because people who go to sleep take their '*Arglosigkeit*' with them into their sleep. Some commentators have argued that the case law on blackmail victims could be applied by analogy, where the court argued that the blackmailer V is the aggressive party and must thus at any time expect a defensive act by D – it was easy to apply this to abusers as well. However, the same court held shortly after the blackmailer decision that in a case of BWS the sleeping man was '*arglos*', without mentioning the previous judgment at all. The court's generally restrictive interpretation with regard to the knowledge of D about the factors that make the killing one by stealth and her intention to exploit the situation would also seem to be of little use, because the BGH has held that in the case of sleeping persons that exploitative intent is typically present, and the threshold for accepting that D acted in a state of grave emotional stress and thus not in deliberate exploitation of the situation would have to be very high. In sum, D is highly likely to be guilty of aggravated murder under §211 unless a defence exists.

Self-defence and necessity are evidently not applicable for lack of an immediate attack by V and because necessity does not cover intentional killing. The situation is different for duress, because V is a permanent danger for D, despite the fact that he is asleep at the time: he will wake up and the ordeal will continue. Such a permanent state of threat is sufficient to trigger §35. However, D's actions must also cross the threshold that the danger or threat could not be averted by less intrusive means. The two obvious ones are either calling the police or leaving the joint residence.

---

125 For references to case law and literature see Gropengießer, ibid., 80 ff.

Despite the new instruments introduced by the so-called *Gewaltschutzgesetz* of 2001 (Protection from Violence Act 2001), which uses injunctions and ASBO-like sanctions against the abuser,[126] this will in fact hardly ever be a realistic avenue, if only for sheer logistic feasibility. Moving out of the joint home will often have a better chance of success, especially if the woman moves to a shelter for abused women. However, the question is why should the abused woman have to leave? In sum, much will depend on the facts of the individual case, yet it would appear that the general tendency is to ask that sacrifice of the woman, unless there are factors speaking against moving out, such as having to leave other threatened family members behind, especially children, financial problems, social stigmatisation, being of foreign nationality without proper command of German, etc. Section 35 is thus a problematic option. Insanity under §20, which could in theory be triggered by serious affect, has been traditionally interpreted very restrictively by the courts for 'mere' charged emotional states which have almost come to be considered to be excluded from §20 for all practical purposes.

D might be able to use §21. Much like in England and Wales, the courts are prepared to apply this provision broadly, based on similar considerations. The plea of affect itself may face the counter-argument of the deliberate behaviour as an indicator that D did have control over her actions. Still, the effects of long periods of serious abuse on the mental state in general have been likened by some psychiatric experts to those caused by a psychosis and thus capable of sustaining the application of §21. A reduction under §21, finally, is not mandatory, but general practice would suggest that unless there are grave factors to the contrary, the court will shift to the lower sentencing frame under §49. In recent times, the BGH apparently has been prepared to entertain the argument that D may have suffered under a mistake about the ambit of permissible reactions under duress (§35(2)); the court held that the threshold of the duty of diligence required in order to make that mistake a basis for escaping liability altogether is very high and will among other things depend on the severity of D's plight and the opportunity for reflection about the ways out of it. In a case such as scenario 1 this threshold would hardly ever be crossed, so that D may at best rely on the sentence reduction for avoidable errors under §35(2).

As mentioned above under homicide offences, the BGH has adopted an approach *praeter legem* to avoid the harsh mandatory life sentence if the life sentence was entirely inappropriate because of the exceptional situation D found herself in (*Rechtsfolgenlösung*). While generally advising extreme caution to trial judges about the use of this concept, it would appear that BWS cases present themselves as the typical field of application, especially if the offender (and the victim) belong to a different cultural sphere that requires different cultural and ethical allegiances from them, as was the case in the decision coining this approach.[127] This solution on the back of the case law, however, would appear to be strictly subsidiary to the aforementioned ones based on the actual legislation, i.e. if §21 is triggered successfully, the *Rechtsfolgenlösung* is no longer available.

Scenario 2[128]

Much like under scenario 1 above, the first question to be answered is the classification of the homicide under §211 or §212. Because D's decision to kill is taken on the spur of the moment, despite the absence of another recent dispute, verbal attack, beating, etc., because she is overwhelmed by the sudden realisation of her desperate situation, there is a higher likelihood that a court would

---

126 More on this in Gropengießer, ibid., 15.
127 BGHSt 30, 105.
128 Gropengießer, ibid., 129 ff.

accept a lack of the 'hostile intention' required for murder by stealth under §211. Once this hurdle is taken, §212 is triggered and with it, in principle, the mitigating sentencing alternative of §213, with its sentencing frame from one to ten years (previously six months to five years). Because there was no recent provocation leading to loss of control, only the general second alternative of §213 can be applicable. Matters such as serious previous abuse and an emotional state of affect even if not reaching the level of §21 have been used by the courts, but at the same time the BGH emphasises that the high value of the legal interest 'life' requires a very meticulous balancing exercise, which may mean that as far as §213 is concerned, scenario 2 may be a borderline case. Note that if both §213 (or any other provision about a less serious case) and §21 can be triggered by the same facts, those facts must typically first be used to establish a less serious case and may then no longer be available to reduce the sentence further within the frame of the less serious case by applying §21, because of §50, unless the gate to the less serious case is already opened by part of the facts, which may then leave the rest for the sentencing exercise within the reduced frame. What was said above with regard to §35 and the *Rechtsfolgenlösung* applies *mutatis mutandis*.

Scenario 3[129]

Even more than in scenario 2, the likelihood of the absence of 'hostile intention' under §211 increases in this case, because it is not outlandish to say that merely 30 minutes after an altercation and serious physical abuse a woman may still be under the influence of shock and thus not be making rational decisions. Much, as in any of these scenarios, will depend on psychiatric and/or psychological expertise at trial. Assuming the court will opt for the basic variant of murder under §212, the mitigated version of §213 becomes applicable, this time possibly based on the first alternative which is the equivalent of the traditional English provocation/loss of control concept. Much like in English law, the question will be whether 30 minutes' delay will rob D of the criterion of immediacy, and at least as far as the result is concerned, the courts come to similar conclusions: what matters is not the lapsed time as such, although that factor will have an indicative effect, but whether the emotional state still had an influence on D's decision-making processes when the act occurred. This has been held to be the case even after one or several hours.

If one accepts that the first alternative of §213 has been triggered, the relationship to §21 changes dramatically in relation to scenario 2: now §21 can in theory be used to reduce the frame within §213 even further, because the BGH has held that the first alternative of §213 and §21 are based on separate and distinct facts, and thus §50 does not apply because there is no double counting. This means in practice that according to §49 the sentencing frame first drops from five to 15 years under §212 to one to ten years under §213, and then to three months to seven and a half years under §21. This brings D into the safe zone of suspended sentences, which may be imposed for any sentence not exceeding two years in the actual case. D could thus in theory be convicted of murder (*Totschlag*) and receive a three-month suspended sentence, although in practice the courts will probably reach higher but possibly still well below the two-year mark. In such cases, the desired sanction often drives the decision about the length of the sentence: if the court wants to get to a suspended sentence, which it more often than not will in BWS cases, it has to stop at two years.

---

[129] Gropengießer, ibid., 145 ff.

Scenario 4[130]

This last scenario opens up many more options for D to avoid liability for murder. Section 211 now would appear to be wholly sidelined for lack of any aggravating element. It may even be questionable whether D has intent to kill under §212 or whether she just blindly stabs V merely to end the attack: remember that German law does not have constructive liability such as the English GBH rule but requires intent for the lethal result. In any event, the attack in itself would trigger §213.

However, this is obviously also a case of potential self-defence under §32 – or putative self-defence if V did not actually follow D in order to continue the attack. If V did actually intend to continue the abuse, the question turns on whether the defensive action by D was the least intrusive means of ending the attack effectively. That, in effect, is a question of fact for each individual case: did D have any other way out, how frightened was she, was V carrying a weapon, etc.? Generally, the use of lethal force must be the *ultima ratio* of any defence, but this *ultima ratio* can arrive very quickly. Note that the previous case law requiring spouses to suffer at least minor harms from each other before employing seriously dangerous means of defence has come under heavy criticism recently and the BGH has indicated that it may no longer adhere to this view; in any case this restriction had always been reserved for marriages that were as such still intact – in the typical BWS scenario this will, of course, not be the case. Should the court view this case as one of inadequate use of force, the way to §33 is opened, and – again bearing in mind the need for medical expertise at trial – the chances for D to benefit from that provision are quite good.

If D was mistaken about the attack – assuming for argument's sake that V followed her in order to apologise – and her defence would have been within the bandwidth of acceptable responses had V actually been meaning to attack her, then she will be judged according to the analogous application of §16, i.e. acquitted of the intentional offence, and if the mistake was unavoidable, also of the negligence offence under §222, for example. However, if the response was outside the hypothetical scope of reasonable force, then D cannot simply rely on §16, because she cannot be treated any better than she would have been had she really been attacked and used unreasonable force. Some commentators argue for the analogous application of §33 to this scenario, but the majority view still rejects this, which leads to the application of §17 about mistakes of law (i.e. the ambit of reasonable force) and thus to a conviction for the intentional offence if the error was avoidable, albeit under §213, possibly with a further reduction under §21, and an acquittal if it was not avoidable.[131]

---

130 Gropengießer, ibid., 158 ff.

131 The BGH in NStZ 1987, 322 had to decide the following instructive case: D had been humiliated and maltreated by her husband V over a long period of time and wanted to get a divorce. When V learned of her intention he said 'I'm going to waste everyone now!' and began looking for his pistol. D had previously taken his gun out of the drawer where he kept it. While the altercation was going on, their daughter started crying in her room upstairs. V then said words which led D to believe that he was going to kill the child, and V went to another room looking for something, which D thought was an axe. She positioned herself in front of the door and drew the loaded gun, taking off the safety. When D entered the room, V fired four shots at him from a distance of two to three metres without looking at him; in fact she had closed her eyes. V was hit by all four shots and killed by two of them. He had not been carrying an axe. The trial court argued that D was mistaken about the fact that she was under attack by V and thus acting in self-defence, she was acquitted of murder but convicted of negligent homicide by application of §16. The private prosecutor (*Nebenkläger*) appealed the verdict and the BGH quashed the trial judgment, remanding the case for re-trial. The BGH argued that even if one accepted that D was under a misapprehension regarding the attack, which would normally afford her the defence of §16, she had to be treated exactly the same as if she had really been acting

Conclusion

This tour de force through the German law on loss of control and diminished responsibility and related defences with special reference to BWS cases should have given a good first impression of how German courts deal with the issues involved. Much like in English law, there seems to exist a benign conspiracy among the players involved to try to achieve an adequate and compassionate solution for battered women and similar cases. The need for doctrinal coherence much prized in the German context does, however, present challenges for further reform efforts: Gropengießer concluded that despite some points where the law is lacking and where reform should be considered, for example within the specific structure of the homicide offences and especially §211, or the ambit of §35, the traditionally high doctrinal systemic sophistication of the German criminal law and the consequences of unprincipled tinkering on such a system should make the legislator wary of shots from the hip in order to appease understandable requests from pressure groups as part of day-to-day politics. This is certainly correct, but does not absolve the legislator from addressing the relevant issues. All too often these days, such reforms take a back seat to the problems of the day which currently seem to centre on matters of security and crime control. Yet overall, one will be able to agree with Gropengießer's judgement that while the German law is certainly not perfect it may nonetheless be one of the best of all possible criminal law systems.[132]

---

in self-defence. In that context, the (potentially and uncontrolled, because she did not take proper aim) lethal use of a firearm was normally a means of last resort and the trial court had not established clearly whether that stage had been reached (clearly it had not) and whether D could have avoided an error about her being entitled to use the gun to avert the danger of V's killing their child, because this mistake would fall squarely under §17.

132   Ibid., 192.

Chapter 16

Partial Defences to Murder in New Zealand

Warren Brookbanks

Introduction

New Zealand, like England, has been concerned in recent years to address a range of issues around partial defences to murder. Initially, the catalyst for considering these issues was the problem of domestic violence and abuse, which is a serious problem in New Zealand society. Accordingly, legislation specifically regulating domestic violence and providing measures of protection for the immediate victims of such conduct was enacted, supplemented by new victim's rights and sentencing legislation.[1] Legislation acquired a more overt focus on the participation of victims within the criminal justice system. With battered defendants as their primary focus, the New Zealand Law Commission had published a preliminary report, entitled *Some Criminal Defences with Particular Reference to Battered Defendants*[2] in which it recommended the repeal of provocation, together with the abolition of the mandatory life sentence in favour of a sentencing discretion in murder.

The mandatory sentence for murder was abolished in the Sentencing Act 2002, s. 102 of the Act providing for discretionary sentencing in murder cases, subject to a presumption of life imprisonment. The proposal to abolish provocation remained 'on the boil' while further consultation with the legal profession and other governmental agencies and interest groups continued. In September 2007 the Law Commission published a further, and more comprehensive, report,[3] in which it again recommended the repeal of the partial defence of provocation and recommended that provocation should instead be dealt with as a sentencing issue. The report was exclusively concerned with provocation and did not address other existing partial defences.

In November 2009 the defence of provocation was formally repealed.[4] At the date of writing, New Zealand now has only two partial defences to murder, namely, infanticide[5] and killing pursuant to a suicide pact.[6] New Zealand has never had a statutory defence of diminished responsibility, despite strong support in some quarters for such a defence. Nor has it ever accepted the claims of excessive self-defence. As a result of these developments New Zealand now effectively has no palliative defences capable of reducing murder to manslaughter in an appropriate case. The defence of infanticide is a closely circumscribed, gender-specific defence, that is of no assistance to male homicide offenders. It will not be considered further in this discussion. Killing pursuant to a suicide pact seldom occurs. On this basis, homicide offenders for whom other defences like self-defence, intoxication or lack of *mens rea* are unavailable, and who are ultimately convicted of murder, are forced to take their chances with sentencing judges,

---

1 See Domestic Violence Act 1995, Victims Rights Act 2002.
2 NZLC R73, 2001.
3 Law Commission, *The Partial Defence of Provocation – Report 98* (Wellington, Law Commission, 2007).
4 Section 4 Crimes (Provocation Repeal) Amendment Act 2009 (2009) No 64.
5 Crimes Act 1961, s. 178.
6 Crimes Act 1961, s. 180.

who alone have the discretion to assess relative culpability but without the ability to signal reduced culpability with a manslaughter verdict.

Further compounding the problems for homicide offenders in New Zealand is the recent enactment of a 'three strikes' sentencing regime which, inter alia, requires mandatory life imprisonment without parole for any homicide offender on a second or third 'strike'.[7] These developments in New Zealand's criminal law have placed homicide offenders in an especially difficult position as regards mitigation of their offending.

In the following discussion I propose to consider the implications of the demise of partial defences in New Zealand for the development of a coherent system for assessing criminal culpability in homicide cases. This will involve consideration of the history of and reasons for the abolition of provocation and the reasons why alternative and/or supplementary palliative defences of diminished responsibility and excessive self-defence have never found favour within the jurisdiction. The chapter will conclude with a discussion of the likely impact of the new sentencing measures, in particular the 'three strikes' law, on those defendants who might previously have benefited from the partial defence of provocation.

Review of New Zealand Law on Provocation

A provocation defence was first enacted in New Zealand in 1893. The definition contained in s. 165 of the Criminal Code Act 1893 is virtually identical in its wording to s. 176 of the draft Code of 1879, although the language and arrangement differ slightly. The inclusion of words as a sufficient source of provocation was provided in the expression 'any wrongful act *or insult*'[8] occurring in both s. 176 of the draft Code and s. 165 of the Criminal Code Act 1893. Thus an insult without a blow became sufficient to constitute provocation at law.[9]

An objective test was incorporated into s. 165 of the Criminal Code Act of 1893 and subsequently into s. 184 of the Crimes Act 1908, where, the expression 'reasonable man' was adopted. With the 1961 Crimes Act the 'reasonable man' had become the 'ordinary person'. Early formulations of the defence also required that homicide should have been committed 'in the heat of passion caused by sudden provocation' and that the offender acted on the provocation 'on the sudden' before there had been 'time for his passion to cool'.

Between 1893, when New Zealand criminal law was first codified, and 1961, there were no significant amendments to either the form or substance of the provocation rules. However, during 1956 and 1957 the then Minister of Justice instructed the preparation of a preliminary draft for a revision of the Crimes Act. A bill was prepared and introduced in the House of Representatives in 1957. The new provocation clause represented a 'radical change in the law', substituting a mixed subjective/objective standard for the 'hard' objective standard that had hitherto prevailed in both New Zealand and the UK. The new provision represented an effort to remove the hardship and injustice implicit in the *Bedder*[10] decision, but reflected the difficulty in devising a formula which would not so enlarge the area of provocation that the whole topic would become unlimited and uncertain. On this basis the new provision purported to adhere to an objective standard while attempting a sufficient qualification to meet the difficulty in *Bedder*'s case.

---

7 See Sentencing and Parole Reform Act 2010, amending the Sentencing Act 2002 by adding new sections 86A to 86I.
8 Emphasis added.
9 *R v. McGregor* [1962] NZLR 1069, 1075.
10 *Bedder* [1954] 1 WLR 1119.

The 1961 Amendment

In 1961 a new Crimes Act was enacted which consolidated and amended the Act of 1908. In respect of provocation it effected an alteration in the substance of the law. The relevant provisions state:

> 169. Provocation –
>
> (2) Anything done or said may be provocation if –
>
> > In the circumstances of the case it was sufficient to deprive a person having the power of self-control of an ordinary person, *but otherwise having the characteristics of the offender*, of the power of self-control; and
>
> > (b) It did in fact deprive the offender of the power of self-control and thereby induced him to commit the act of homicide. (emphasis added)

Section 169(2) was the critical provision. It dispensed with the common law requirements for physical violence and the exclusion of words as sufficient provocation[11] and provided for two general tests which had to be satisfied. Paragraph (a) imposed an objective condition that required an estimation of the effect of the provocation on the self-control of a hypothetical ordinary person, modified to meet the difficulty in *Bedder*, while paragraph (b) required that the provocation actually deprived the offender of the power of self-control and by that means led to the killing.

It would seem, notwithstanding the English common law position, that the drafters of the new Act did attempt the task of investing a reasonable man with the characteristics of the accused, despite the opinion that to do so would make the objective standard meaningless. But in order to make the section capable of application, while preserving the ordinary man test, it was suggested that there must be some limitation of the term 'the characteristics', despite the fact that the legislature had given no guide as to what limitations might be imposed.[12] The new phrase 'but otherwise having the characteristics of the offender' required, in effect, that the ordinary person be placed in the circumstances with which the accused was confronted and that he or she be invested with the characteristics of the accused. The jury was required to take into account both factors when assessing the reaction of the hypothetical ordinary person to provocation, essentially an amalgamation of both subjective and objective tests and involving, as North J observed in *McGregor*, the 'fusion of two discordant notions'.[13] It is enough to say, in a post-provocation era, that the attempted fusion proved extremely difficult to give practical effect to and was a significant factor in the growing calls for reform/repeal of the statutory test.

Criminal Law Reform Committee Proposal

In July 1976, the New Zealand Criminal Law Reform Committee presented a report on culpable homicide.[14] The report recommended major changes to the law on homicide, including the abolition

---

11 See *Holmes* v. *DPP* [1946] AC 588 at 600, [1946] 2 All ER 124, 128 (HL).

12 Sir Francis Boyd Adams, *Criminal Law and Practice in New Zealand* (2nd edn, Sweet & Maxwell, 1971) para. 1264.

13 *McGregor* (n. 9) 1081.

14 See *Report on Culpable Homicide*, Criminal Law Reform Committee New Zealand, July 1976. The Criminal Law Reform Committee, now disbanded, was an ad hoc law reform body under the auspices of the

of the defence of provocation and the creation of a generic offence of 'unlawful killing'. The specific proposal was that provocation should no longer be a defence to a charge of murder and should be relevant only on sentence,[15] foreshadowing the future direction that reform would take. Amongst the objections of the Committee to provocation as a defence was the fact that, because on charges less than murder courts regularly take provocation into account when imposing the penalty, provocation as a defence to murder had become an anomaly in the law. Furthermore, it was thought that amending the law on provocation might make it possible to deal justly with cases calling for special treatment but not lying within the bounds of legal insanity. It was also thought that the law on provocation was unnecessarily complex and directions on the nuances of the statutory provision were often too difficult for jury members to fully comprehend. Finally, while the then prescribed punishment for murder was a mandatory sentence of life imprisonment, the judge was unable to make any allowance for provocation unless killing under provocation was excluded from murder. Ironically, while this concern provided an important *ex ante* reason for revisiting the structure of the provocation defence, events subsequent to the repeal of provocation, in particular the introduction of the three strikes law, have effectively reinstituted the prohibition on making any allowance for provocation *in any circumstances*.

The Committee concluded that if the sentence of life imprisonment for murder ceased to be mandatory, this would eliminate the need for the legal definition of provocation, which the Committee regarded as unsatisfactory. It, therefore, recommended, under the aegis of a new single offence of 'unlawful killing', that provocation should cease to be a defence and become a matter of fact to be taken into account by a judge at the time of sentencing. That the Committee's recommendations regarding the abolition of provocation have now been incorporated into New Zealand law is a historical fact. From one perspective repeal of the defence may be seen to validate similar calls for repeal made subsequent to the Criminal Law Reform Committee's recommendations, in particular, the Labour government's introduction in 1989 of a new Crimes Bill, which would have amounted to a 'root and branch re-codification' of New Zealand criminal law,[16] including a proposal to abolish of the defence of provocation and its substitution with a provision that would have allowed it to be taken into account as a question of penalty.[17]

These proposals were later endorsed by the Crimes Consultative Committee, established by the Labour government to report to the Minister of Justice on the Crimes Bill, and appeared to reflect a growing consensus that the mandatory life sentence for murder should be abolished together with the provocation defence.

Criticism of Reform Proposals

However, there was not universal support for the abolition proposals, despite the apparently growing consensus on the need for radical reform of the provocation defence. Amongst the more outspoken critics of the Crimes Bill's proposed expansive reforms was the late Lord Cooke, then Sir Robin Cooke. While conceding that there were problems with the judicial interpretation of the statutory defence of provocation,[18] Lord Cooke was not persuaded that it was necessary to do away with the defence altogether. His Lordship contended that while there may be a perception

---

Department of Justice. Its role is now subsumed by the New Zealand Law Commission.
   15 Ibid., 3.
   16 See Robin Cooke, 'The Crimes Bill 1989: A Judge's Response' [1989] New Zealand Law Journal 235, 236.
   17 Crimes Bill 1989, cl. 128.
   18 See Cooke (n. 16) 235 –6.

that sometimes juries accept provocation defences too lightly, that is their prerogative and is, in any event, consistent with confining the stigma of murder to the worst killings. Lord Cooke also considered that the 'very gravity of murder justifies singling it out from the generality of offences, where provocation bears on penalty only'.[19] His Lordship dismissed the suggestion that judges find summing up on provocation too hard or that juries may reject the provocation defence unreasonably. It was a vigorous defence of what seemed an increasingly embattled doctrine.

Lord Cooke was in good company in his rejection of calls to abolish provocation. The late Professor Gerald Orchard also rejected the notion that provocation was anomalous. He considered that the arguments against provocation, while having some force, lacked sufficient weight to justify the removal of the accused's right to have the fact of provocation determined by the jury and reflected in the verdict. He was also not persuaded that the arguments justified the legal abandonment of the notion and name of murder[20] and held the view that plain murder should be stigmatised as such, but that killings as a result of real provocation should not be.[21] Like Lord Cooke, Professor Orchard considered 'speculative' the idea that the defence is too difficult for juries and felt that its fundamental principles were readily understood. In Orchard's view the defence also recognised in an appropriate way that in a crime of passion culpability is diminished.

Orchard concluded his commentary with observations that are eerily apt, now that provocation has gone. One argument favouring abolition of provocation and the mandatory penalty for murder was said to be that it would encourage more guilty pleas and avoid 'unnecessary trials'. In response to this claim Professor Orchard expressed doubt whether such abolition would lead to any great reduction in trials, but that any reduction that might occur would be likely offset by the need for more elaborate sentencing hearings, involving more evidence.[22] Although figures have yet to confirm any clear patterns of legal activity post-provocation, we may speculate that this will almost certainly prove to be the case. Given the non-availability of parole for second and third strike murder convictions and the real prospect of full life sentences upon conviction for murder it is inevitable that responsible defence counsel will take elaborate steps to minimise the risk of indeterminate incarceration upon conviction for murder. This may include defending more cases in which an early guilty plea might otherwise have conferred a significant penalty advantage by reducing the non-parole period, or by challenging the facts upon which the accused was convicted in disputed facts hearings. Success in this context could affect the length of any non-parole period that might otherwise be imposed.

The New Zealand Law Commission's Approach

The New Zealand Law Commission has now looked at the merits of the available partial defences in a number of different contexts, in the course of developing specific policy recommendations. Provocation was considered in the context of an investigation of legal responses to the problem of domestic violence and the particular criticism that battering relationships had not been well understood by the community or the legal profession.[23] In a preliminary discussion paper the Law

---

19   Cooke (n. 16) 239.
20   Gerald Orchard, 'Homicide' in N. Cameron and S. France (eds), *Essays on Criminal Law in New Zealand; Towards Reform?* (Wellington, Victoria University of Wellington Law Review in conjunction with the Victoria University Press 1990) 149.
21   Ibid.
22   Ibid., 150.
23   Law Commission, Preliminary Paper 41, *Battered Defendants: Victims of Domestic Violence Who Offend – A Discussion Paper* (Wellington, Law Commission, 2000) 1.

Commission identified three major problems with provocation, namely, how to take account of mental characteristics affecting the power of self-control, the use of the defence to partially excuse domestic violence and the difficulty victims of domestic violence have in accessing the defence. Although the Commission made no specific recommendation as regards provocation's future, the direction of its thinking was clear.

The Law Commission published its final report on battered defendants in May 2001.[24] The report reiterated the findings in the discussion paper. In particular, the Commission noted that the defence has been difficult for battered defendants because of the requirement for loss of self-control and the 'paradigm' requirement of a 'sudden angry retaliation following immediately upon the provocation'.[25] It noted that battered defendants who kill their violent partners tend to do so because of fear and despair, rather than anger, and although fear and despair may also affect self-control, they are 'less likely to lead to a sudden explosive reaction immediately following the provocation'.[26] The Law Commission concluded that, for these reasons, provocation may be a difficult defence for battered defendants to argue.

In finding that the weight of submitted opinion was in favour of abolition of the partial defence of provocation, the Law Commission itself recommended abolition of the partial defence, with matters of provocation being taken into account in sentencing. It was ultimately unimpressed by the 'lesser culpability' argument as a reason favouring retention of provocation and found 'compelling'[27] the submissions favouring abolition. The Law Commission concluded that the conflict between the two fundamental public interest values of the preservation of human life and allowing compassion a role in the criminal justice system is best resolved by abolishing the partial defence of provocation and replacing it with a sentencing discretion for murder.

However, there would seem to be little doubt that a major driver in the Law Commission's recommendation of abolition was its perception that the defence was gender biased and unfavourable to victims of domestic violence, while favouring its perpetrators. Indeed, given the context of a report dealing with criminal defences and battered defendants, it would have been surprising if the final report had not contained some negative findings concerning the applicability of the provocation defence to domestic violence scenarios. It is, nonetheless, a huge leap in logic to argue that because provocation does not 'work' for the victims in battering relationships it ought, for that reason, to be abolished. Yet no other scenarios were canvassed in the report in which provocation might conceivably be argued to support such a radical change, beyond the claims of battered defendants.

The 2007 Report

In 2007 the Law Commission released its most recent reflections on the provocation defence. Its report was entitled 'The Partial Defence of Provocation'.[28] This was a much more wide-ranging report. The report's terms of reference required the Law Commission to further consider whether the repeal of partial defences would unduly disadvantage persons with mental illness or disability, battered defendants and any other minority groups that may be particularly reliant on such defences.

---

24 Law Commission Report 73, *Some Criminal Defences with Particular Reference to Battered Defendants* (Wellington, Law Commission, 2001).
25 Ibid., para. 103.
26 Ibid., para. 104.
27 Ibid., para. 116.
28 Law Commission, Report 98, *The Partial Defence of Provocation* (Wellington, Law Commission, 2007).

The terms of reference also asked the Commission to undertake a 'gender analysis' of the current operation of partial defences and to consider the gender implications of the recommendation for partial defence repeal. However, given events that have transpired since the defence was repealed perhaps the most important of the terms of reference was the request for the Commission to examine whether there was risk of 'unduly harsh sentences under section 102 of the Sentencing Act as currently drafted (and should the section therefore be amended) if partial defences are repealed'.[29] The two remaining terms of reference asked about the appropriateness of the stigma of a murder conviction where persons act by reason of adverse circumstances for which society may feel some sympathy, and whether there should be a separate defence for battered defendants.

In this discussion I will focus on the Commission's recommendations concerning the risk of unduly harsh sentences under s. 102 Sentencing Act 2002 with the repeal of provocation. As I shall endeavour to show, the repeal of provocation accompanied by the introduction of the three strikes sentencing regime for serious and violent offences has created a situation in which homicide offenders are now exposed to significantly harsher sentences, such that it may be argued that the abolition of provocation has created a major distortion in sentencing for violent offences. But before examining the implications of the three strikes law for sentencing for murder and manslaughter, I wish to briefly describe the process by which provocation came to be repealed.

The Catalyst for Repeal of Provocation

The defence of provocation was abolished in New Zealand in November 2009. The immediate catalyst for its abolition was not the weight of opposition reflected in the investigations surveyed above, but rather the dramatic facts of a homicide case which, through media manipulation, empowered an unprecedented public reaction against the statutory defence of provocation. Its eventual removal was the product of an unseemly popular outcry that the defence had had its day and should go.

The Weatherston Case[30]

The defendant, Clayton Weatherston, was a 33-year-old economics tutor at Otago University. He formed an intimate relationship with a former student, Sophie Elliott, which eventually soured. On the day before Miss Elliott was due to leave Dunedin for a new job in Wellington, Weatherston visited her at her parents' home, armed with a large kitchen knife. After being admitted to the house by Miss Elliott's mother, Weatherston proceeded to Sophie Elliott's bedroom, where he embarked on a brutal attack, in which he stabbed or sliced (including deliberate mutilation of the body post-mortem) some 216 times. Weatherston had accepted that he was guilty of manslaughter, which he pleaded on arraignment, but denied the charge of murder. His only defence was provocation, which the trial judge allowed to go to the jury. In the circumstances it was difficult to see how provocation could have succeeded before a jury. The jury was evidently unimpressed with Weatherston's testimony and convicted him of murder. He was eventually sentenced to life imprisonment with a minimum non-parole period of 18 years.

The television images of the defendant, bespectacled and with shoulder length hair, giving 'self-promoting' testimony over several days in the witness box, placed the dramatic, and disturbing, facts of the case at a degree of propinquity that was hitherto largely unknown in New Zealand

---
29 Ibid., 8.
30 R v. *Weatherston*, High Court Christchurch, CRI 2008-012-137, 15 September 2009 (Potter J).

trial history. When, in the course of giving his evidence, the accused picked over the victim's life, made public the contents of her diaries and coldly (and cruelly) dissembled her character, that behaviour became the straw which was to break the (provocation) camel's back. Talk-back radio and blog sites, newspaper editorial pages and TV interviews were overwhelmed with strident voices claiming that the defence had 'run its course' and should go. This sentiment was endorsed by the Justice Minister who claimed that the law on provocation was flawed in that it 'rewards lack of self-control by enabling an intentional killing to be categorized as something other than murder and effectively provides a defence for lashing out in anger, not just any anger but violent, homicidal rage'.[31] These sentiments constituted a powerful rationale for the defence's eventual abolition.

A compelling feature of the case was the defendant's decision to give evidence. His apparent narcissism was widely commented on. Public rumours quickly began to emerge about Weatherston's personality. A veritable flood of articles and opinion pieces, around the characterisation of Weatherston as narcissistic, followed and reinforced claims that the provocation defence was abusive and promoted the possibility of people, like Weatherston, getting away with murder. His narcissism was evident from the time when he first entered the dock at arraignment,[32] and on being asked did he plead guilty or not guilty, said: 'guilty of manslaughter, but not guilty of murder', giving the appearance, as one commentator noted, of making a clever point in one of his economics lectures. Throughout his evidence he sparred with the prosecutor, to the point of asking the prosecutor on one occasion, 'Are *you* telling the truth?' and on another that the prosecution were 'scraping the barrel' in their questioning of him. To a psychiatrist who had given evidence at the trial he had acknowledged that he 'had played a part in Sophie's death', then adding that he'd thought so much about what had happened since then he was 'over it'.

Similarity to the Hinkley Case

Clearly, this chronicle of ill-conceived forensic dialogue from a defendant against whom the evidence of guilt was overwhelming fuelled the public's anger and reinforced its view that provocation was the true enemy. The parallel with the trial of John Hinkley for the attempted murder of President Ronald Reagan is striking. Writing around the time of the events of outrage against the insanity defence, which Hinkley *successfully* pleaded at his trial, Michael Perlin said:

> Separate streams of public opinion – outrage over the court's perceived "softness on crime"; ... outrage over a jurisprudential system that could even allow a defendant who shot the President in cold blood (on national television) to plead "not guilty" (by any reason); outrage at a jurisprudential system that countenanced obfuscatory and confusing testimony by competing teams of psychiatrists as to the proper characterisation of a defendant's mental illness; in short, outrage over the "abuse" of the insanity defence ... became a river of fury after the ... verdict was announced.[33]

Although no 'river of fury' surrounded the widely applauded guilty verdict in Weatherston's trial, nevertheless the outrage at the very *existence* of the provocation defence was palpable, as ill-

---

31 *New Zealand Herald*, Friday 27 November 2009.

32 A psychiatrist, who provided a pre-sentence report at the request of the defence, referred to Weatherston as having features of anxiety disorder and personality features of narcissism and obsessionality. See *R* v. *Weatherston*, High Court Christchurch CRI 2008-012-137, 15 September 2009, at para. 17.

33 See Michael Perlin, 'The Things We Do for Love: John Hinkley's Trial and the Future of the Insanity Defense in the Federal Courts' (1985) 30 New York Law School Law Review 857, 859.

informed as much of the criticism was. It was clear that many commentators and members of the public had made up their minds that the *Weatherston* case represented an abuse of the provocation defence which, although it had not succeeded at trial, should be abolished.

Similarly, following John Hinkley's acquittal on account of insanity, there was great public and official agitation and the defence was abolished in a number of American states. Building on the public desire for reform of the defence, the House of Representatives Report accompanying the House version of the Insanity Defense Reform Act acknowledged:

> Although abuses of the insanity defense are few and *have an insignificant direct impact upon the criminal justice system*, the Committee nonetheless concluded that the present defense and the procedures surrounding its use are in need of reform ... The insanity defense has an impact on the criminal justice system that goes beyond the actual cases involved. The use of the defense in highly publicized cases, and the myths surrounding its use, have undermined public faith in the criminal justice system.[34]

Similarly, while it might properly be claimed that abuses of the provocation defence in New Zealand have been few and have had little direct impact upon the criminal justice system, the effect of the media 'beat up' in the Weatherston trial, together with myths surrounding the use of provocation, was to undermine any faith the public might have had in even a limited role for the defence. As a result Clayton Weatherston became a symbol of what was bad about the provocation defence. His remorseless presentation and 'undisguised and chilling' detachment were at some level seen to personify the defence of provocation, which became the 'fall guy' for a hard case with bad facts.

On 4 August 2009 the *New Zealand Herald* announced that the government had introduced a bill to Parliament that would 'remove the partial defence of provocation *from the statute books*'. Of course, it would have been enough to have said that s. 169 of the Crimes Act would be repealed, since that is the only reference to provocation in the 'statute books'. Nevertheless, the sense of finality represented in removal 'from the statute books' demonstrated the 'vividness heuristic' which operated throughout the Weatherston trial. The heuristic was also evident in the media presentation of the dramatic facts of the case, whereby the public imagination was enflamed and the complexity of the issues for debate dumbed down. The vividness heuristic is well known to insanity defence jurisprudence. It is a cognitive-simplifying device through which a 'single, vivid, memorable case overwhelms mountains of abstract, colorless data upon which rational choices should be made'.[35] The point is that the public clamour to get rid of provocation was based largely on a media-fuelled visualisation of the defence, whereby the intense media exposure of the case has made the case for abolition 'inappropriately persuasive'.[36] Yet this was surely an occasion for *some* detached reflection. Changing a law of such long standing without adequate reflection can lead to unintended and unanticipated consequences.

In its 2007 report the Law Commission had recommended that the partial defence of provocation be abolished by repealing s. 169 of the Crimes Act. Defendants who would otherwise

---

34 See HR REP NO 577, 98th Cong., 1st Sess., 9–10 (1983), cited in Michael Perlin, *The Hidden Prejudice: Mental Disability on Trial* (Washington, DC, American Psychological Association, 2000) 239 (emphasis added).

35 See Michael Perlin, '"His Brain Has Been Mismanaged with Great Skill": How Will Jurors Respond to Neuroimaging Testimony in Insanity Defense Cases?' (2009) 42 Akron Law Review 885, 892.

36 See Neal Feigenson, 'Brain Imaging and Courtroom Evidence: On the Admissibility and Persuasiveness of MRI' (2006) 2 International Journal of Law in Context 233, 243, cited in Perlin (n. 35) 892.

have relied on the partial defence should be convicted of murder and evidence of provocation in the circumstances of their particular case should be weighed with other aggravating and mitigating factors as part of the sentencing exercise. Of course, this has all the appearance of simplicity. But now that provocation has gone in New Zealand the question arises 'what *will* happen in cases where provocation arises on the facts but is unavailable in defence?'

It is no justification for abolishing the defence of provocation to say that defences like self-defence will do the work previously done by provocation, as some have claimed.[37] Nor does it assist to say that the repeal of the partial defence of provocation will not preclude self-defence being raised in appropriate cases, or that if a person is under attack they will be able to use reasonable force to repel that threat. Such statements, as a purported justification for repealing provocation, are misleading, if not mischievous. Self-defence is a justification[38] and serves a wholly different purpose to provocation in criminal law theory. It is not based on a loss of self-control, but on the necessary use of defensive force. No other existing criminal defence in New Zealand comes anywhere near doing the work of provocation, since New Zealand has never had a statutory or common law defence of diminished responsibility.

Provocation and Disputed Facts

Nevertheless, it is unlikely, now that provocation has been abolished in New Zealand, that homicide trials will be run significantly differently. Trial lawyers are inventive. The abolition of provocation will, in all likelihood, simply lead to a change of location as to where argument on provocation is presented in a trial. In particular, the locus of argument on provocation will, in all probability, shift from the adjudicative phase to the sentencing phase of trials. New Zealand law now makes provision for 'disputed facts' hearings.[39] This means that where a fact relevant to the determination of a sentence or other disposition is asserted by one party and disputed by the other, the court is required to indicate the weight it would be likely to attach to the disputed fact if it were found to exist, and its significance to the sentence. If a party wants to rely on the fact the parties can adduce evidence as to its existence, unless the court is satisfied sufficient evidence was adduced at the hearing or trial (s. 24 (2)). However, since evidence as to provocation will be of reduced utility in the adjudicative phase, counsel, will, no doubt, endeavour to have facts in support of provocation proven at a disputed facts hearing as a mitigating fact, in order to persuade the court that the fact(s) justify a lesser penalty than might otherwise be appropriate for the offence.

Since the disputed facts hearing is an adversarial proceeding in which fresh evidence may be led as to matters of aggravation and mitigation, it is inevitable that it will be seen by defence lawyers as an opportunity to litigate facts tending to support a mitigatory claim, and to adduce expert evidence for this purpose. We can be sure that the ugly facts of homicide trials will not suddenly disappear, simply because the *defence* of provocation is no longer on the horizon. Rather, facts consistent with provocation will be canvassed in an attempt, either to persuade the court that life imprisonment would be manifestly unjust,[40] or in order to persuade the court to impose a minimum term of imprisonment below the mandatory minimum period of 17 years or more for

---

37 In public debates surrounding the abolition proposals MPs rejected arguments that provocation should remain for certain categories of defendants (e.g. battered defendants) instead asserting that it 'would be more appropriate for them to rely on self-defence, which could result in an acquittal rather than a manslaughter conviction'. *New Zealand Herald*, Tuesday, 20 October 2009.
38 See Crimes Act 1961, s. 48 (NZ).
39 See Sentencing Act 2002, s. 24.
40 See Sentencing Act 2002, s. 102 (1).

the worst kinds of murders.[41] Since much is at stake in this regard, in terms of very lengthy jail terms upon conviction for murder, we can expect that the case for mitigation of penalty will be vigorously argued in those cases where provocation might otherwise have been a defence.

Provocation as Mitigation in Sentencing

As was noted above, one of the effects of the enactment of the Sentencing Act 2002 (NZ) has been to render life imprisonment the *maximum* (rather than the mandatory) penalty for murder with a strong presumption in favour of its imposition in nearly every case, i.e., where there is at least one serious aggravating factor. It is now clear that the new sentencing regime has increased the complexity and length of sentencing hearings, although it is still too early to judge the actual impact of the abolition of the provocation defence. It is not clear the extent to which courts are allowing evidence of provocation to be taken into account in mitigating culpability, although the scope for doing so is substantially reduced. Of particular concern is the fact that with manslaughter no longer available as a fallback, in the event that provocation successfully palliates liability for murder, judges are only able to reflect differences in culpability by rebutting the presumption in favour of life imprisonment and imposing a finite term of imprisonment of less than life imprisonment, on the basis that imprisonment for life would be 'manifestly unjust'.[42] However, it is recognised that the presumption in favour of life imprisonment is strong and that there is only a limited discretion not to impose life imprisonment where offending is at the lowest end of the range of culpability for murder.[43] A lesser sentence is likely to be given only in a very small number of cases, including, for example, 'mercy killings', failed suicide pacts and where the offender is a 'battered defendant'.[44]

At the time of writing there appear to be no reported or unreported decisions of the New Zealand courts considering the status of the provocation post-abolition in relation to the Sentencing Act 2002 in a prosecution for murder. However, it is clear that in determining whether the statutory presumption of life imprisonment has been displaced, the court must take into account all mitigating and aggravating factors and may decide not to impose life imprisonment where to do so would be clearly and obviously unjust.[45] It is assumed that this approach will extend to cases where evidence of provocation was insufficient at trial to reduce murder to manslaughter but was nevertheless a relevant factor to be considered in mitigation of penalty at sentencing.

In reflecting on the impacts of sentencing for murder in a post-provocation environment, it seems appropriate to consider the various types of pathological mental states that might be implicated in an invincible loss of self-control and, therefore, having a bearing on provocation in mitigation of penalty. I have suggested[46] that there may, in fact, be many psychological precursors to homicidal loss of self-control which are, at present, poorly understood by legal professionals. Furthermore, if lawyers are to be effective in revamped homicide trials, where loss of self-control becomes a sentencing issue, they will need to understand and explore a range of unfamiliar mental state conditions. These could include narcissistic rage, psychological impotence, catathymic process, impulse control disorders and other forms of explosive aggression that might provide an explanation for the offender's behaviour and thereby reduce the risk of a harsh retributive

---

41 Sentencing Act 2002, s. 104.
42 Sentencing Act 2002, s. 102 (1) (NZ).
43 *R v. Williams and Olson* [2005] 2 NZLR 506 (CA) paras 104.1.1–104.1.3.
44 See Geoffrey Hall, *Sentencing – 2007 Reforms in Context* (Wellington, LexisNexis, 2007) 481.
45 *R v. Law* (2002) 19 CRNZ 500.
46 Warren Brookbanks, 'Provocation: Psychological Precursors for Loss of Self-Control as a Mitigatory Claim' (2009) 16 Psychiatry, Psychology and Law 196.

sentence. Indeed, failure to explore such possibilities might be regarded as professional neglect in circumstances in which a verdict of manslaughter has a much reduced prospect of success in a prosecution for murder. Counsel will be expected to explore all available possibilities in order to minimise the risk of lengthy condign sentences for homicide committed in a state of violent rage.

In any event, it is likely that the abolition of provocation as a defence will lead to a greater exploration of a range of mental state issues going beyond the narrow formulation of provocation itself. Even though diminished responsibility has never been formally accepted as part of New Zealand law, it is clear that the language of diminished responsibility is well known to New Zealand judges. The concept is frequently employed to describe what is in reality a reduction of 'mental responsibility' caused by some overwhelming psychological pressure. In one case the New Zealand Court of Appeal held that an accused's conviction for manslaughter, where there was evidence that he was mentally ill and had experienced some provocation, was 'in substance' manslaughter on the grounds of diminished responsibility.[47] In the absence of provocation we may expect that the language of diminished responsibility will continue to intrude into sentencing submissions, potentially expanding the scope for mitigatory claims based on irresistible impulse and the radical loss of self-control.

With the abolition of provocation in New Zealand and the decision (for the meantime) not to replace it with any other partial defence, there are important consequences for all citizens. Under previous law, a successful provocation defence signalled that there was a difference in culpability between a person who kills in cold blood and one who, in a frenzy of passion and impulsiveness, lashes out at another with fatal effect. Fair labelling requires that we properly describe the former as a murderer, to reflect society's utter rejection and denunciation of the conduct. The title 'manslaughterer' is properly reserved for those whose homicidal violence is the product of a disturbed and pathological impulsiveness. Since the criminal law speaks to society as well as wrongdoers when it convicts them, it ought to communicate its judgement precisely by accurately naming the crime of which they are convicted.[48] The abolition of provocation, for all its many defects, disturbs this important distinction and leaves all killers undifferentiated as murderers.

Diminished Responsibility

Status of the Doctrine in New Zealand

Diminished responsibility has never been officially part of New Zealand law. There was a proposal to introduce the defence into New Zealand in the Crimes Bill 1960. Clause 180 of the bill provided for the reduction of murder to manslaughter where the jury was 'satisfied that at the time of the offence the person charged, though not insane, was suffering from a defect, disorder, or infirmity of mind to such an extent that he should not be held fully responsible'. A successful plea of diminished responsibility would have resulted in an order for detention during Her Majesty's Pleasure.[49] However, with the abolition of the death penalty for murder in clause 182 of the bill there was little enthusiasm to retain the defence and the clause was dropped from the bill.

Diminished responsibility was later considered by the Crimes Consultative Committee set up by the then Labour government following its unsuccessful attempt to introduce a new Crimes

---

47 See *R v. Ashton* [1989] 2 NZLR 166 and *R v. McCarthy* [1992] 2 NZLR 550.
48 Andrew Simester and Warren Brookbanks, *Principles of Criminal Law* (3rd edn, Wellington, Brooker/Thomson, 2007) 29–30.
49 Crimes Bill 1960, clause 187(2).

Bill in 1989. However, because of its preference to deal with matters of impaired criminal responsibility as mitigating factors in sentencing, rather than as partial defences, the Committee did not favour the adoption of a separate diminished responsibility defence. It considered that the difficulties involved in establishing a discrete diminished responsibility provision were likely to be exacerbated by complexities in achieving sufficiently precise wording for the statutory defence.[50] However, the concept of diminished responsibility continued to engage the courts. In *McGregor*,[51] North P determined to deliberately limit the scope of available 'mental' characteristics in order to avoid giving any legitimacy to the concept of diminished responsibility which, the court noted, has never been given a statutory mandate in New Zealand. More recently, its non-availability as a defence was reaffirmed in a case in which psychological evidence had been admitted in support of a defence claim that the accused had arranged for her husband's murder while suffering from post-traumatic stress disorder, battered wife syndrome and depression.[52] In *Gordon*, the New Zealand Court of Appeal held that sympathy for the defendant could not prevail over the current statutory provisions and that it was unable to accept expert testimony that the accused 'had diminished responsibility because of her mental state at the time [of the offence]'.[53] The court did find, however, that where an accused person is suffering from an illness that might affect her responses or judgement, its consequences may be beyond the experience and knowledge of a jury, and so expert evidence may be adduced to show that those consequences may be such as to weaken or negate the inference of intent that could properly be drawn in the case of a 'normal' person.[54] In such circumstances a court might acquit, not on the grounds of diminished responsibility, but simply because it is not satisfied beyond a reasonable doubt that the accused possessed *mens rea* at the relevant time. However, despite these court-imposed strictures, which evidently sought to prevent the development of a common law doctrine of diminished responsibility in New Zealand, another line of appellate authority pointed in a different direction. It is arguable, as a result of these authorities, that a de facto form of diminished responsibility had insinuated itself into New Zealand law via the 'back door' of provocation. With the demise of the provocation defence, however, the future relevance of this body of case law is doubtful, since provocation was the vehicle through which a notion of diminished responsibility was operationalised in practice.

Ashton[55] concerned a respondent who had been convicted of arson and manslaughter following an incident in which he had shot and killed the proprietor of a service station then set fire to the service station, a museum and a private home. Using the provocation defence as a legal conduit, psychiatric evidence was led at the trial that the respondent was suffering from paranoia at the time and had been provoked into losing his self-control by suggestions from the deceased that he was homosexual. It was accepted by the trial judge that the respondent's mental illness played a significant part in the crimes. The court considered three Australian cases of manslaughter on the grounds of diminished responsibility, noting that this was 'in substance' the present case.[56] The court did not, however, suggest how the concept might be expected to operate in New Zealand or whether it constituted a palliative defence or a mitigatory device relevant to sentencing only.

---

50   Crimes Consultative Committee Crimes Bill 1989: Report of the Crimes Consultative Committee (Wellington, 1991) 45–6.
51   [1962] NZLR 1069, 1081.
52   *R v. Gordon* (1993) 10 CRNZ 430 (CA).
53   Ibid., 439.
54   Ibid., 437.
55   [1989] 2 NZLR 166, (1989) 4 CRNZ 241(CA).
56   Ibid., 245.

In *McCarthy*,[57] another case involving a homicidal response to an alleged homosexual advance, the Court of Appeal suggested that the availability of diminished responsibility, while it had never been expressly accepted by a New Zealand Parliament, might nevertheless, within the limited field of the provocation defence, be seen as the 'inevitable and deliberate effect of the statutory changes embodied in s. 169 of the Crimes Act 1961'.[58] The wider implications of this concession were never explored by the New Zealand courts, and are unlikely to be with provocation now moribund.

The Law Commission's Suggestions Concerning Diminished Responsibility

Diminished responsibility was also considered by the New Zealand Law Commission in its investigation into criminal defences available to battered partners who kill their abusers. The Commission briefly surveyed a range of models for diminished responsibility in other jurisdictions and considered arguments in favour and against the adoption of the defence.[59]

In addressing arguments against introducing diminished responsibility the Law Commission emphasised the ongoing criticism of the defence at English law and the problems associated with giving clinical meaning to the definitional elements of the defence. Furthermore it was noted that 'abnormality of mind' had been given a very broad definition, extending to personality disorders and sexual psychopathology. In particular the Commission was influenced by the research finding that 38 per cent of diminished responsibility pleas in England were wife killings, arising predominantly from 'amorous jealousy or possessiveness' rather than psychosis.[60] In the event the Commission recommended against adopting diminished responsibility. It found that it is a concept which is difficult to clearly define and was not persuaded that these difficulties had been satisfactorily resolved with the English version of the defence. It concluded that the factors giving rise to diminished responsibility were better considered at sentencing.

Regarding the particular focus of the discussion, the Commission was of the opinion that diminished responsibility is not of particular relevance for the majority of battered defendants. It referred to the opinion of some forensic psychiatrists that while domestic violence may lead to a range of psychological responses in the victim, it does not generally cause the victim to develop abnormality of mind to the degree required by the defence of diminished responsibility.

Excessive Self-Defence in New Zealand

Current Status of the Doctrine

In New Zealand the present test for self-defence is defined in s. 48 of the Crimes Act 1961. The new section was substituted by an amendment in 1980[61] which provides:

> Everyone is justified in using, in the defence of himself or another, such force as, in the circumstances as he believes them to be, it is reasonable to use.

---

57 [1992] 2 NZLR 550, (1992) 8 CRNZ 58 (CA).
58 Ibid. at 558, 66 (Cooke P).
59 NZLC PP41 at 39 et seq.
60 NZLC PP41 at 40.
61 See Crimes Amendment Act 1980 No 63, s. 2(1) as from 1 January 1981.

The amendment removed the requirement for a belief that force was necessary to have been an objectively reasonable belief, a requirement that has now been departed from at common law. However, because the moral right to use self-defence is not unlimited, the statute requires that the defence be confined to the use of reasonably necessary force. For this reason New Zealand law has never provided for the doctrine which allows for manslaughter by excessive defence. The statutory authority for this limitation is s. 62 of the Crimes Act 1961 which provides that 'everyone authorized by law to use force is criminally liable for any excess according to the nature and quality of the act that constitutes the excess'. Although the actual effect of the section is uncertain, it clearly has an important application in cases where an accused kills another by using excessive force in self-defence. The question that arises, but has never been directly judicially considered in New Zealand, is whether, if excessive force is used in self-defence, the excess is necessarily fatal to the operation of the defence in any degree. In *Godbaz*,[62] the New Zealand Court of Appeal held that excessive force used in repelling an assault was not protected by self-defence and itself constituted an assault. The view of Adams, author of the leading practitioners' criminal law text in New Zealand, is that if the defence fails on the ground that excessive force was used then s. 62 applies, and the accused is guilty of whatever offence was involved in the act of excessive force, be it murder or any other.[63]

Thus New Zealand law aligns with that of Australia, where the qualified defence of 'excessive force' in self-defence has now been abandoned. In *Zecevic* v. *DPP*,[64] a majority of the High Court of Australia held that there should no longer be any rule whereby, if a plea of self-defence to murder fails by reason only that disproportionate force was used by the accused person, the verdict should be not guilty of murder but guilty of manslaughter.[65] This development is consistent with the approach taken by the Privy Council in *Palmer* v. *The Queen*.[66] Their Lordships, while allowing for a generous degree of latitude in determining the necessary measure of self-defensive force to repel a grave assault, concluded that if ultimately the prosecution has shown that what was done was not done in self-defence then the issue is eliminated from the case. In such an event the issue of manslaughter does not arise unless there is also a question as to whether there was provocation which may reduce murder to manslaughter.

The position in Canada is similar. There the rule is that where an accused, acting in self-defence in terms of s. 34 of the Criminal Code, causes death by the use of an excess of force, then a verdict of manslaughter is not available, unless he lacks the requisite intent for murder. In *Reilly* v. *The Queen*,[67] Ritchie J, delivering the judgment of the Supreme Court, cited with approval the unanimous judgment in *Faid*[68] in which Dickson J said:

> The position of the Alberta Court of Appeal that there is a "half-way" house outside section 34 of the Code is, in my view inapplicable to the Canadian codified system of criminal law. It lacks any recognizable basis in principle, would require prolix and complicated jury charges and would encourage juries to reach compromise verdicts to the prejudice of either the accused or the Crown. Where a killing has resulted from the excessive use of force in self-defence the accused loses the justification provided under s. 34. There is no partial justification open under

---

62 (1909) 28 NZLR 977.
63 Adams (n. 12) para. 548.
64 (1987) 61 ALJR 375.
65 In this respect the legal position in Australia is now the same for both Code and common law states.
66 [1971] AC 814.
67 (1984) 15 CCC (3d) 1 (SCC).
68 (1983) 2 CCC (3d) 513, 517 ff (SCC).

the section. Once the jury reaches the conclusion that excessive force has been used the defence of self-defence has failed.

As regards the current New Zealand position it might be claimed that the law gives conflicting signals concerning the degree of force which is permissible in self-defence. On the one hand it is clear that the defence must fail if the force used by the accused is excessive. On the other hand, the courts, following English jurisprudence, have said they will not 'weigh to a nicety' what is reasonable defensive force.[69] This has generally meant that the courts have been generous in allowing a degree of latitude to defendants who, faced with a grave threat, are forced to determine for themselves the measure of force necessary to repel the threatened attack.[70] However, it is also clear that lawful self-defence is a threshold question and that once the threshold of acceptable (reasonable) force has been passed, the offender is at risk of being branded as an aggressor and disentitled to claim self-defence at all. The difficulty with having such an open-ended and ill-defined threshold is that an offender can never be sure whether he or she has exceeded what is reasonable self-defensive force. This problem has not been considered directly by New Zealand courts.

The Law Commission's Proposals on Excessive Self-Defence

The New Zealand Law Commission has considered the claims of excessive self-defence but has recommended against the creation of a new partial defence for New Zealand. In a discussion paper published in 2000[71] and a report published in 2001[72] the Commission investigated excessive self-defence in the context of a broad review of the legal defences available to those who commit criminal offences as a reaction to domestic violence. In the discussion paper the Commission suggested a form of words for a possible excessive self-defence provision, modelled around the words of the statutory self-defence rule in s. 48 Crimes Act 1961 (NZ). The rule would have provided:

> It is a partial defence to a charge of murder reducing the offence to manslaughter if, in the defence of himself or herself or another, a person uses more force than it is reasonable to use in the circumstances as he or she believes them to be.

Although the Commission conceded what it considered the strength of arguments in support of excessive self-defence as a partial defence, and nominated it as the partial defence it would be most in favour of introducing into New Zealand law, it was, in the final analysis, disinclined to recommend its adoption.[73] The Commission recognised that such a defence was more morally favourable than either provocation or diminished responsibility, in that with excessive self-defence the defendant intends to do something that is lawful within limits.[74] It also considered

---

69 *Palmer v. R* [1971] AC 814, 832.
70 Andrew Simester and Warren Brookbanks, *Principles of Criminal Law* (3rd edn, Wellington, Thomson/Brookers 2007) 473.
71 See Law Commission, Preliminary Paper 41, *Battered Defendants Victims of Domestic Violence Who Offend – A Discussion Paper* (Wellington, 2000).
72 Law Commission, Report 73, *Some Criminal Defences with Particular Reference to Battered Defendants* (Wellington, 2000)
73 NZLC R 73 [25]–[26].
74 Ibid., [25].

that the link between excessive self-defence and self-defence meant that it was more appropriate to the circumstances typical of cases involving battered defendants than the other aforementioned defences. However, the Commission ultimately rejected the defence because its adoption would have been inconsistent with its preference not to retain or introduce partial defences, but rather to rely on a sentencing discretion for murder to accommodate the diverse situations when lesser degrees of culpability should be recognised in intentional homicide.[75]

The Three Strikes Law in New Zealand

With the abolition of provocation as a substantive partial defence to murder in New Zealand law the legal protections available to offenders charged with murder were considerably diminished. As the preceding discussion has indicated, New Zealand law reformers and policy makers have long been averse to partial defences to murder generally and disinclined to further expand their scope. Because such defences have only ever been of assistance to those offenders charged with the gravest of all offences, their further diminution in favour of enhanced sentencing discretion is of major concern to law practitioners concerned with the development of a fair and just criminal justice system. Just as New Zealand criminal lawyers were beginning to think that things could not get much worse as regards the erosion of protections for murder accused, they have been forced to confront the enactment of one of the harshest criminal laws ever enacted in New Zealand in the now notorious Sentencing and Parole Reform Act 2010, which amends the Sentencing Act 2002. Following so closely on the heels of the demise of provocation, the 2010 Act tightens the screws on offenders convicted of murder even further by radically enhancing the penalty for murder, for which there can be no mitigation at all. I shall briefly describe the scheme of the 'three strikes' law before commenting on its likely consequences, in particular its impact on offenders convicted of murder and manslaughter.

The 'Three Strikes Scheme'

The 'three strikes' regime applies to a range of 40 qualifying offences. The regime depends on a system of warnings by sentencing judges as to the consequence of a 'strike' offence and imposes a graduated scale of harsher penalties as repeat offenders acquire convictions for 'strike' offences. An offender receives a normal sentence and a warning for strike one, the full sentence imposed by the court without parole for strike two and the maximum sentence for the offence, without parole, for strike three, unless ineligibility for parole would be 'manifestly unjust'. The Act came into force on 1 June 2010, and as at 6 December 2010, 132 offenders had been convicted of a strike offence and given a first strike warning. At the time of writing no second or third strikes had been issued. However, the total number of strike offences was 274 – some offenders had been issued warnings relating to multiple offences in the same incident. Undoubtedly, the harshest impact of the new law will be upon offenders convicted of murder or manslaughter, for whom the prospect of a whole life sentence without any chance of parole is now a real likelihood.

---

75   Ibid., [26].

Manslaughter

Upon a third strike conviction for manslaughter the court must impose a life sentence but need not order that the sentence be served without parole. Rather, the court must impose a minimum period of imprisonment (i.e. a non-parole period) of at least 20 years unless that is manifestly unjust, in which case the period must be at least ten years.[76] An example may assist in demonstrating how the legislation works. A is convicted of an indecent act on a child.[77] He receives a first warning and is sentenced to, say, nine months' imprisonment. This becomes strike one. The offender may some years later commit the offence of indecent assault and is sentenced to 18 months' imprisonment. That is strike two. He must serve the whole of the sentence imposed by the court and is ineligible for parole. Eight years later, while in regular employment as a car mechanic and supporting a young family, A is working on a motor vehicle and negligently fails to connect a tie-end on the car's suspension. The car is delivered to its owner who loses control because of the defect in the steering, crashes the car and is killed.

A is then charged with manslaughter based on his negligence. Since it is his third strike he must be sentenced to life imprisonment, but the court must order that the offender serve a minimum period of imprisonment of not less than 20 years. If that term is considered to be manifestly unjust the court must order that A serve a minimum period of imprisonment of not less than ten years.[78] That is to say upon *any* conviction for manslaughter, regardless of the nature of the offence and the offender's culpability, he or she can never serve less than ten years on a third strike. Mitigating factors which might, in other circumstances, have significantly affected the length of sentence are wholly irrelevant in this case.

Murder

The rules governing murder are different. The normal law is that murder is punishable by life imprisonment unless that is manifestly unjust.[79] Where the court imposes a life sentence it must impose a minimum period of imprisonment of at least ten years,[80] or where the murder has some special aggravating feature, at least 17 years, unless that sentence would be manifestly unjust.[81] Where an offender commits murder after a first or a final warning (strike two or strike three), the normal law no longer applies. Instead, where the offence is a second strike, the court must impose life without parole, unless manifestly unjust. If parole ineligibility is manifestly unjust then the court must instead impose life with at least ten years without parole, or 17 years in particularly serious cases. Where murder is a third strike conviction, the judge must impose life without parole, again, unless that is manifestly unjust. If it is manifestly unjust the court must impose life and a minimum non-parole period of at least 20 years, unless that also is manifestly unjust. In those circumstances, as with a second strike murder, the minimum sentence is ten years, or 17 years in really serious cases.

What is especially disturbing about this regime as it applies to homicide offences is that there is absolutely no scope for mitigation once a second or third strike has been triggered. So whether the killing is the mercy killing by an elderly man of his aged, dementing wife, the killing by a woman

---

76 Sentencing Act 2002, s. 86D (4).
77 Crimes Act 1961, s. 132 (3).
78 Sentencing Act 2002, s. 86D (4).
79 Ibid., s. 102.
80 Ibid., s. 103.
81 Ibid., s. 104(1).

of her bullying and abusive partner, a killing in excessive self-defence or the cold-blooded slaying of a police officer by a hardened criminal, it will make no difference in terms of the sentence the court is mandated to impose. Evidence of gross provocation, diminished responsibility or serious impulse control disorder will have no bearing whatsoever on the penalty that must be imposed by the court. What is more, the three strikes scheme makes it likely that a second or third strike murder (e.g. killing in bar room brawl) will be sentenced more severely than a more serious type of murder on a first strike (e.g. the rape and murder of a child).

In effect, the scheme authorises the imposition of arbitrary and disproportionate sentences simply because an offender has a previous (albeit not necessarily serious) qualifying conviction. Although provocation, while no longer a defence, may be taken into account in sentencing to determine whether or not it would be manifestly unjust to sentence the offender to life imprisonment for murder,[82] it is necessarily excluded from consideration in the three strikes regime. This is simply because the legislative regime does not invite consideration by the courts of any mitigating factors going to an offender's culpability where a second or third strike murder has occurred. The expression 'manifestly unjust' in this context relates exclusively to whether an offender ought to be eligible for parole. It is not intended, as with the expression when used in s. 102 Sentencing Act 2002, to engage consideration of the purposes or principles of sentencing in ss. 7 and 8 of the Sentencing Act 2002 or the aggravating and mitigating factors under s. 9,[83] which are wholly irrelevant to the three strikes regime.

Consequences

As this discussion shows, the three strikes regime has seriously distorted the protections previously available for offenders charged with homicide. In terms of the minimum penalty that must be imposed upon a second or third strike conviction for either murder or manslaughter, both offences are now an undifferentiated category. Given the abolition of the provocation defence, an offender who commits murder under gross provocation on a second or third strike offence will necessarily be labelled as a murderer, regardless of the mitigating factor which might otherwise have applied. Equally a second or third strike offender who commits manslaughter, for example, through hapless, albeit serious, negligence, will be treated as though he were a murderer, given the penalty that must be imposed in such cases.

For these and other reasons it has been argued that a court should have discretion not to impose a life sentence for murder if doing so would be manifestly unjust.[84] Such an extension would be intended to cover cases of 'mercy killing', provocation, excessive self-defence or killing by a battered defendant. The legislation could be amended to provide for murder and manslaughter. Such an amendment would also be consistent with the approach of the New Zealand Law Commission which argued that abolition of the defence of provocation made sense in part because it could always be taken into account at sentencing.[85] However, it is fair to say that when the Law Commission made this recommendation it had no inkling that a three strikes law would be enacted in three short years and, in particular, that it would have the effect of rendering provocation wholly irrelevant in some cases of murder.

---

82   Ibid., s. 102 (1). Evidence of provocation might be one of the 'circumstances of the offence or the offender' relevant to manifest injustice.

83   *R v. Rapira* [2003] 3 NZLR 794; (2003) 20 CRNZ 396 (CA).

84   Warren Brookbanks and Richard Ekins, 'The Case Against the 'Three Strikes' Sentencing Regime' [2011] New Zealand Law Review (forthcoming).

85   Law Commission, *The Partial Defence of Provocation* (New Zealand Law Com. R98, 2007) 7.

Conclusion

Partial defences to murder seem to be in terminal decline in New Zealand, if not effectively moribund. Provocation has gone and with it the prospect, at least for the immediate future, of diminished responsibility taking its place. Excessive self-defence has never been part of New Zealand law and with the current official antipathy towards partial defences is unlikely to be officially supported. The partial defence of infanticide is a historical anomaly and gender bound and has always had a very limited role within a broader framework of partial defences to murder. Killing by a suicide pact occurs so infrequently as to barely justify a mention. The recent enactment of a three strikes sentencing regime has significantly altered the legal landscape as regards sentencing for murder and manslaughter and has effectively rendered all mitigatory devices that might otherwise have influenced a reduction in culpability for murder at the sentencing stage wholly irrelevant. Not only can provocation no longer be pleaded to reduce murder to manslaughter, but such factors as an early guilty plea, significant remorse, the offender's mental state and the offender's age can no longer have any bearing on the length of sentence upon conviction for murder. It is, indeed, a bleak and featureless landscape where mitigation of penalty has no currency.

The defence of diminished responsibility is still officially not part of New Zealand law. However, *dicta* in recent case law suggest that the concept is alive as a paradigm for construing mental characteristics in provocation law. But what this means in practical terms is less than clear. Although New Zealand courts have inclined towards accepting the reality of diminished responsibility as a descriptive paradigm for mental characteristics, it has never been available as a palliative defence. Furthermore, while New Zealand courts continue to distinguish between susceptibility and self-control as a basis for limiting the scope of 'characteristics', any nascent notion of diminished responsibility will always be denied the power to affect a central ground of inquiry in the defence, namely, whether the accused possessed the capacity to exercise willpower to control physical acts with rational judgement.[86] To this extent it is my judgement that it will continue to be of very limited usefulness in the context of battering relationships. Finally, the 'defence' of excessive self-defence has never been part of New Zealand law. Although there seems to be some theoretical support for the concept, the prevailing preference for a broader sentencing discretion in murder over the availability of partial defences would suggest that it is unlikely to be further pursued, at least for the foreseeable future.

---

86 *R v. Byrne* [1960] 2 QB 396, 403 (Lord Parker CJ).

Chapter 17

Abnormal Mental State Mitigations of Murder: The US Perspective

Paul H. Robinson

Introduction

Homicide grading statutes in the United States typically operate according to a single paradigm: grading corresponds to the offender's state of mind at the time that he causes the death of his victim. In particular, statutes typically require the fact-finder to look to the offender's state of mind *as to causing the victim's death*. An actor who purposefully or knowingly causes death typically commits murder, while one who recklessly causes death commits the lesser offence of manslaughter (and one who negligently causes death commits the still-lesser offence of negligent homicide).[1] These four culpability terms – purposeful, knowing, reckless, and negligent – are the central features of homicide grading and are defined with some detail in most American criminal codes.[2]

Two doctrines that mitigate intentional (purposeful or knowing) killing from murder to manslaughter arise from the actor having some abnormal mental state, either transient or long term. They are the subject of this chapter. In the modern view, the first doctrine, typically referred to as the doctrine of 'extreme emotional disturbance', mitigates murder to manslaughter when an intentional killing 'is committed under the influence of extreme mental or emotional disturbance for which there is reasonable explanation or excuse'.[3] The second doctrine, most accurately described as 'mental illness negating an offense element' but sometimes misleadingly referred to by the terms 'diminished capacity' or 'partial responsibility', allows a mitigation from murder if the actor is suffering from a mental disease or defect that has such an effect as to make it impossible for him to have the purpose or knowledge as to causing death that is required for murder.[4] The actor may have liability for a lesser offence, such as manslaughter, but only if the effect of his mental illness is such that he has the reckless culpability required for that lesser offence. Some mental illness may have the effect of negating even the recklessness required for manslaughter.

A different kind of mitigation based upon mental illness – one that functions as a partial insanity defence (and thereby properly deserves the labels 'diminished capacity' or 'partial responsibility') – mitigates liability upon presentation of evidence that mental illness influenced the killing (rather than completely excused it). This form of homicide mitigation is generally no longer recognised in the United States. This chapter reviews the existence and several variations of these mitigations under current US law, how they came to their present form, and what rationales one can offer in support of such mitigations.

---

1 In most jurisdictions, this broad scheme was drawn from Model Penal Code Art. 210.
2 The definitions typically track those of Model Penal Code §2.02(2).
3 See, for example, Model Penal Code §210.3(1)(b).
4 See, for example, Model Penal Code §4.02(1).

The Model Penal Code Reform of Common Law Rules

Most of current American homicide law is based in significant part on the American Law Institute's Model Penal Code.[5] Starting even before its formal adoption in 1962, the Model Code has served as a basis for wholesale replacement of existing criminal law in almost three-quarters of the states.[6] Some states have adopted the Code with only minor revision, while others have kept much of their existing doctrine but codified it in the style, structure, and language of the Model Code. A full understanding of current American homicide law requires an appreciation of how and why the Model Code drafters changed the previously existing common law rules.

Provocation and Extreme Emotional Disturbance

The American common law doctrine of provocation mitigated intentional killings from murder to manslaughter – specifically, to what was commonly termed 'voluntary manslaughter' – if the killer was 'provoked' into committing the crime. The mitigation reflected the view that passion frequently obscures reason and in some limited way renders the provoked intentional killer less blameworthy than the unprovoked intentional killer. At the time of the Model Penal Code, few jurisdictions had codified doctrines of provocation. Most relied upon common law. The few statutory formulations that existed simply codified the common law rules.[7] The American common law mitigation had demanding standards. Typically, the provocation had to be 'reasonable', in the sense that a reasonable person would have been similarly provoked. An early twentieth-century court described the doctrine this way, and this was a common formulation confronting the Model Penal Code drafters:

> The doctrine of mitigation is briefly this: That if the act of killing, though intentional, be committed under the influence of sudden, intense anger, or heat of blood, obscuring the reason, produced by an adequate or reasonable provocation, and before sufficient time has elapsed for the blood to cool and reason to reassert itself, so that the killing is the result of temporary excitement rather than of wickedness of heart or innate recklessness of disposition, then the law, recognizing the standard of human conduct as that of the ordinary or average man, regards the offense so committed as of less heinous character than premeditated or deliberate murder. Measured as it must be by the conduct of the average man, what constitutes adequate cause is incapable of exact definition ...[8]

---

5   The American Law Institute, which drafted the Code, is a non-governmental, broad-based, highly regarded group of lawyers, judges, professors and others who undertake research and drafting projects designed to make American law more rational, sensible and effective. After nine years of work and a series of tentative drafts, the American Law Institute approved an Official Draft in 1962. The original commentary, which was contained in the various tentative drafts, was consolidated, revised, and republished with the 1962 text in 1980 and 1985 as a seven-volume set. Three volumes containing Part II of the Model Penal Code, Definition of Specific Crimes, with revised comments, were published in 1980. Three additional volumes containing Part I of the Code, General Provisions, with revised comments, were published in 1985. An official version of the completed text of the Model Penal Code was published in 1985.
6   Model Penal Code Commentaries Part I foreword at xi.
7   Model Penal Code Official Comment to §210.3 at 45 (1985).
8   *State v. Gounagias*, 88 Wash 304, 311–12, 53 P 9, 11–12 (1915).

One significant aspect of the rule was the requirement that the actor must not have had time to 'cool off'; he lost the mitigation if sufficient time passed for 'the blood to cool and reason to reassert itself'. The manslaughter mitigation was thus often described as covering killings that occur in the 'heat of passion'.

The American common law doctrine had several additional specific limitations. For one, the person killed must be the person who created the provocation. Early forms of the mitigation also required the provoking incident to have occurred in the presence of the defendant. Finally, only certain common types of provoking situations would typically make the mitigation available: 'extreme assault or battery upon the defendant; mutual combat; defendant's illegal arrest; injury or serious abuse of a close relative of the defendant's; on the sudden discovery of a spouse's adultery'.[9] Even where the mitigation was not explicitly limited to specific types of provoking situations, certain events were often held inadequate, as a matter of law, to support the mitigation.[10] For example, it was common to hold that 'mere words' were insufficient to support a mitigation,[11] even if the words described an incident (such as adultery, or harm to a relative) that would itself count as sufficient provocation if the defendant had witnessed it personally.[12]

It may seem unrealistic or even inappropriate for the provocation mitigation to apply a purely objective test, at least if the test asks whether a reasonable person would have acted in the same way as the defendant did. If the defendant's killing satisfies such a test – if a reasonable person would have acted in the same way in the same situation – then one could argue that the defendant ought to be held to be entirely without blame. It is likely more accurate to say that the American common law mitigation meant to assess whether the actor's conduct was *reasonable* only in the sense that it was *understandable*. In other words, the mitigation was meant to cover cases where the killing remained condemnable, but the conditions of the killing suggested that the actor was *noticeably less blameworthy* than one who killed without such provocation. However, the common law restrictions failed to make a full assessment of the actor's blameworthiness and by their rigidity made the mitigation unavailable to many actors whose killings would seem considerably less blameworthy than the paradigmatic intentional murder.

Modern American codes that follow the Model Penal Code typically give a broader mitigation than the common law provocation doctrine. The Code's manslaughter mitigation applies where:

---

9 *Girouard v. State*, 321 Md 532, 583 A 2d 718 (Md Ct App 1991). Indeed, sometimes cases falling within these categories have been treated as if they provided adequate provocation as a matter of law. See, for example, *State v. Thornton*, 730 SW 2d 309 (Tenn 1987) (previously well-behaved husband discovers wife committing adultery in bedroom of their home, shoots other man, who dies from wounds; appellate court reverses murder conviction, calling it 'a classic case of voluntary manslaughter', explaining that in 'our opinion the passions of any reasonable person would have been inflamed and intensely aroused by this sort of discovery').

10 See, for example, *State v. Hockett*, 70 Iowa 442, 30 NW 742 (1886) (sexual relations between the victim and the defendant's sister is insufficient provocation); *State v. Kotovsky*, 74 Mo 247 (1881) (a woman's refusal to go to St Louis fairgrounds is inadequate provocation); *State v. Hoyt*, 13 Minn 132 (1868) (driving of defendant's cattle off the road by victim is not sufficient provocation).

11 See, for example, *People v. Murback*, 64 Cal 369, 30 P 608 (1883) ('words of reproach' are not sufficient provocation regardless of their grievousness).

12 See Corpus Juris Secundum, Homicide §122. These rules hint that, notwithstanding its asserted focus on the actor's state of mind, the common law mitigation may have approached provocation as a partial justification of sorts, where the objective circumstances of the killing are such as to reduce its overall harmfulness or wrongfulness.

murder is committed under the influence of extreme mental or emotional disturbance for which there is reasonable explanation or excuse. The reasonableness of such explanation or excuse shall be determined from the viewpoint of a person in the actor's situation under the circumstances as he believes them to be.[13]

This formulation of the mitigation has two components. First, the killing must have been committed 'under the influence of extreme mental or emotional disturbance'. A defendant will not be eligible for the mitigation if he did not personally suffer such a disturbance or if the disturbance did not drive or dictate his act, even if the circumstances would have created such a disturbance in most other people and would have driven them to violence. Second, there must be a 'reasonable explanation or excuse' for the disturbance. No mitigation is available if the disturbance has no reasonable basis or is peculiar to the actor.[14]

The Model Code broadens the American common law mitigation in several important respects. Unlike the common law rules, it does not explicitly require, or exclude, particular situations; there are no conditions that are inadequate as a matter of law to provide a mitigation. It also drops the common law rule barring the mitigation if the killing occurs some period of time after the provoking event. In other words, the Code postulates that an actor's emotional disturbance does not necessarily decrease with time; indeed, it might increase.[15] Further, nothing in the Code's mitigation limits it to cases where the actor kills the source of the provocation, as the common law does. The Code's position is that if the actor's killing is less blameworthy by virtue of the influencing conditions, then such reduced blameworthiness exists no matter who is killed. Indeed, the Code does not even require a provocation as such; the relevant 'disturbance' may arise from any source so long as it satisfies the rule's requirements.

The Model Penal Code's mitigation doctrine has also altered – however slightly – the allocation of the burden of persuasion between the prosecution and the defendant. At common law, if there is any evidence presented by either party that the defendant acted in the heat of passion, the state must prove the absence of heat of passion beyond a reasonable doubt.[16] Since the doctrine makes provocation an element of manslaughter, any alternative formulation that places the burden on the defendant to prove provocation is not constitutionally permitted.[17] Similarly, the Model Penal Code shifts the burden from the defendant to the prosecution once evidence of an extreme emotional or mental disturbance is introduced.[18] Some states following the Model Penal Code (hereinafter MPC) have nevertheless departed from its burden-shifting framework and decided to keep the burden of persuasion on the defendant to establish the extreme emotional or mental disturbance. States are

---

13 Model Penal Code §210.3(1)(b). For the Code drafters' discussion of their formulation and how it changed then-existing common law, see Model Penal Code §210.3 comment at 53–65.

14 See, for example, *People* v. *Casassa*, 49 NY 2d 668, 404 NE 2d 1310 (NY 1980) (trial court found defendant acted under required disturbance but no reasonable explanation or excuse for it, thus denied mitigation; affirmed on appeal).

15 Model Penal Code §210.3 cmt, 48 (Tent Draft No 9, 1959).

16 See Corpus Juris Secundum, Homicide §279 (collecting cases and describing the burden of proof for manslaughter at common law).

17 See *Mullaney* v. *Wilbur*, 421 US 684, 703 (1975) ('We ... hold that the Due Process Clause requires the prosecution to prove beyond a reasonable doubt the absence of the heat of passion on sudden provocation when the issue is properly presented in a homicide case.').

18 Model Penal Code §1.12(2).

constitutionally permitted to do so because the MPC's extreme emotional or mental disturbance doctrine is an independent basis for mitigation and not an element of the offence.[19]

Finally, the Model Penal Code mitigation uses a 'reasonableness' standard, as the common law doctrine does, but instead of adopting a purely objective understanding of reasonableness, the modern rules allow a partial individualisation of the standard by requiring that the reasonableness of the explanation or excuse be determined 'under the circumstances as [the actor] believes them to be' and 'from the viewpoint of a person in the actor's situation'. These two phrases provide significant opportunities for a court, or jury, to take account of the particular characteristics of the defendant and the specific conditions in which the defendant acted. (The same two phrases are used in the Code's definitions of recklessness and negligence to achieve the same partial individualisation of the reasonable person standard.[20]) The Code's drafters intended the second phrase – in particular 'in the actor's *situation*' – to permit a trial judge great leeway in this partial individualisation.[21]

The most difficult aspect in applying this component of the modern 'extreme emotional disturbance' mitigation is in determining which characteristics of the defendant should be used in judging the reasonableness of the defendant's conduct. Clearly such things as an actor's age may be relevant in assessing the reasonableness of his disturbance. But, presumably, a defendant's certifiably bad temper would not be a basis for lowering our expectations of him with respect to engaging in violent behaviour. He is not to be judged against the standard of the 'reasonable bad-tempered person', for having an improperly short fuse might be exactly what makes his behaviour seem unreasonable and blameworthy. To fully individualise the objective standard would turn it into a purely subjective standard, which would give mitigations where the community would see no reduced blameworthiness. More difficult to deal with are factors like a claim of a genetic predisposition to a violent reaction when provoked. If true, should it alter the standard by which the actor is judged? We are inclined to believe that people can, and must, control their tempers, but the claim of genetic predisposition clouds the issue by making it seem that the actor may lack such an ability through no fault of his own.[22] Unfortunately, criminal law theory has yet to develop a clear principle that will distinguish those characteristics that are properly included from those that are properly excluded when individualising the reasonable person standard. The Model Penal Code leaves the issue to the ad hoc determination of the trial judge.[23] (The analogous problem

---

19 See *Patterson* v. *New York*, 432 US 197, 207 (1977) ('To recognize at all a mitigating circumstance does not require the State to prove its nonexistence in each case in which the fact is put in issue, if in its judgment this would be too cumbersome, too expensive, and too inaccurate.').

20 Model Penal Code §2.02(2)(c) and (d). For further discussion of these phrases in the context of culpability definitions, see Paul Robinson, *Criminal Law* (Aspen 1997) §4.3.

21 As the Model Penal Code commentary explains, 'There is an inevitable ambiguity in "situation." If the actor were blind or if he had just suffered a blow or experienced a heart attack, these would certainly be facts to be considered in a judgment involving criminal liability, as they would be under traditional law. But the heredity, intelligence or temperament of the actor would not be held material in judging negligence, and could not be without depriving the criterion of all its objectivity. The code is not intended to displace discriminations of this kind, but rather to leave the issue to the courts.' Model Penal Code §2.02 cmt 4, 242 (1985). See also n. 27 (noting that a similar problem exists with recklessness, and that discriminations similar to those required by the negligence standard must be made).

22 If genetics create only a *predisposition* toward violence, it would seem that the actor retains the ability to control his conduct. If genetics are to be relevant, the actor must show that the influence of genetics on his conduct is sufficiently strong that we should see him as less blameworthy. For a related discussion in the context of the requirements of excuse defences, see Robinson (n. 20) *Criminal Law* §§9.1, 9.4.

23 See Model Penal Code §210.3 cmt, 63 (1980).

arises when the same partial individualisation device is used in the definitions of negligence and recklessness.[24])

Mental Illness Negating an Offence Element

The second doctrine that can mitigate murder is based upon the mental illness of the actor at the time of the offence. The mitigation can come in two forms. First, the actor's mental illness may negate (make it impossible to prove that the actor had) a culpable state of mind required by the offence definition, in this instance the purpose or knowledge as to causing death required for murder. As noted, the labels *diminished capacity* or *partial responsibility* are sometimes applied to this mitigation, but such use is misleading because it suggests a kind of partial insanity defence, as if a mitigation is given because the actor suffers some degree of mental illness short of that required for a full insanity defence. That is not an accurate description of the doctrine. The doctrine applies when an actor's mental illness *negates a culpable state of mind* required for the offence charged. It looks not to the actor's general capacity to function or to his degree of responsibility for his conduct in some general sense, but only to the specific issue of whether he has the carefully defined culpable state of mind contained in the offence definition for murder: purpose or knowing as to causing death.

Indeed, mental illness negating an element is not a doctrine of mitigation at all, but rather a claim that the defendant plainly does not satisfy the elements of murder. It is simply an absent element defence, like an actor's mistake negating a required offence culpability element.[25] Depending on whether the offence charged has lesser included offences with lower culpability requirements, and depending on the actual effect of an actor's mental illness in negating the culpability elements of the lesser offences, the doctrine may provide only a slight mitigation or it may provide a complete defence. Model Penal Code section 4.02(1) states the modern form of the doctrine:

> Evidence that the defendant suffered from a mental disease or defect is admissible whenever it is relevant to prove that the defendant did or did not have a state of mind which is an element of the offense.

Unlike the insanity defence, the actor's general mental capacity or incapacity is not the issue.[26] Impaired ability to control one's conduct, in particular, is not relevant here, because only cognitive dysfunctions can negate a culpable state of mind element. Such is the nature of the requirements of purpose, knowing, recklessness and negligence.[27] Mental illness that impairs an actor's ability to control his or her conduct is unlikely to negate offence culpability requirements, which typically concern specific cognitive functioning (e.g., being aware of facts or consequences) rather than matters of control. Typically, only cognitive dysfunction will cause an actor not to know the nature, circumstances, or potential consequences of his or her conduct, and therefore not satisfy a culpability element. (Where an actor's mental illness does not negate a required element, the actor nonetheless may have a general defence if he or she satisfies the conditions of a general insanity excuse.[28])

---

24   For a discussion, see Robinson (n. 20) *Criminal Law* §4.3.
25   For further discussion of the concept of an absent element defence and its distinction from 'true' general defences, see Robinson (n. 20) *Criminal Law* §8.0.
26   Compare Model Penal Code §4.02(1) to §4.01(1).
27   See Model Penal Code §2.02(2).
28   See Robinson (n. 20) *Criminal Law* §9.3.

While this is the Model Code's approach, the original doctrine in American common law was to *prevent* an actor from using evidence of mental illness to negate a required culpable state of mind.[29] The earlier law treated mental illness negating an offence element as analogous to the doctrine of voluntary intoxication, according to which the required but absent culpability is imputed to the actor if the actor voluntarily intoxicated himself. The analogy to mental illness is flawed, obviously. The imputation of culpability may well be justified in the context of voluntary intoxication; the actor culpably caused his own intoxication and that culpability ought to be taken into account.[30] While one may question some aspects of this rationale for imputing culpability,[31] it provides at least the semblance of a rational reason. No similar claim can be made in the context of mental illness negating an offence element. An actor is rarely accountable for causing his own mental disease or defect. What, then, is the rationale for treating the mentally ill actor as if he has a required culpability when he does not? As with all doctrines of imputation – treating an actor as if he has a culpable state of mind that he in fact does not have – imputation itself is not objectionable, but may become so if not adequately justified.[32]

The Model Penal Code approach obviates constitutional concerns about placing the burden of proving an offence on the defendant. In *In re Winship*, the Supreme Court held that the prosecution must prove beyond a reasonable doubt 'every fact necessary to constitute the crime with which [the defendant] is charged'.[33] But, since the common law approach has the effect of barring the introduction of mental illness evidence, the defendant may be prohibited from even raising a reasonable doubt on certain culpability elements. The Model Penal Code, by requiring every element to be proved beyond a reasonable doubt, better tracks the *Winship* court's concerns.[34]

The MPC approach has been consistently attacked, however. During the debates on the issue, one form of attack on the use of mental illness evidence to negate an offence element was to claim incompatibility between behavioural science and criminal law. It was argued, for example, that behavioural science admits of gradations of responsibility while the criminal law does not; it must decide whether to impose liability.[35] But this argument rests upon a mistaken view of the diminished capacity defence as somehow assessing partial liability for partial responsibility. As noted above, the actor's mental illness either negates an offence element or it does not; it does not ask the criminal law to admit of gradations. More importantly, this argument seems out of place when discussing a grading doctrine, such as murder mitigations to manslaughter, rather than a liability doctrine. The function of murder mitigations is not one of determining whether there will be liability but rather whether there should be a lower grade of liability than there is for the paradigm intentional killing.

Another argument was that the behavioural sciences were not yet sophisticated enough for the criminal law to rely upon them. A similar argument stressed the tendency of the diminished

---

29 Robinson (n. 20) *Criminal Law* §4.5, 'Limiting the culpability that may be negated'.

30 See, for example, Model Penal Code §2.08(2).

31 For a discussion of how and why the justification is not entirely accurate, see Robinson (n. 20) *Criminal Law* §5.3, 'Common law vs. Model Penal Code rule'.

32 See Robinson (n. 20) *Criminal Law* §III.1 (Principles of Imputation: Introduction).

33 397 US 358, 364 (1970).

34 In *Clark v. Arizona*, 548 U.S. 735 (2006), the court nevertheless found that the common law approach was constitutional. See, *infra*, n. 65 and accompanying text.

35 See *Bethea v. United States*, 365 A2d 64, 68 (DC 1976). Following an argument with his estranged wife, defendant shot her five times at close range; at trial defendant claimed at the time of the shooting his mental condition was such as to preclude a finding of 'sound memory and discretion' and 'deliberate and premeditated malice' as required for the offence.

capacity doctrine to take 'full decision-making authority' from the jury and shift it to the expert witness.[36] But what is asked by the modern doctrine is not to have criminal law rely on behavioural science; what is asked is that juries be given access to such evidence along with all other relevant evidence, so that the *jury* can decide whether the required offence mental element is present. The jury has full authority to reject or give little weight to any or all psychiatric evidence (and is particularly likely to do so where psychiatrists disagree, as frequently occurs).[37]

Another challenge to allowing mental illness to negate culpability focused on the nature of culpability. Culpability is a legal concept, not a scientific one. Thus, it was argued, it must necessarily be decided on an objective standard. And, application of an objective standard means that personal abnormalities cannot be taken into account.[38] While this view of culpability might have been true at early common law, it does not accurately describe the nature of current doctrine. It is true that an actor's state of mind cannot be known directly, and it is true that a culpable state of mind must be proven by objective evidence. This does not imply an objective standard for culpability, however. Current law rejects such common law rules as the presumption that 'an actor intends the natural and probable consequences of his conduct'.[39] It requires instead a finding by the jury that, based on all the evidence, the jury believes that the actor actually had the culpable state of mind required by the offence definition. The members of the jury may call upon their own life experiences in reaching their factual conclusions, including judgements about how people normally function. Still, the issue they are asked to decide is not whether the ordinary person would have had the required culpable state of mind, but rather whether this defendant actually did have it.

One final argument, perhaps the most persuasive argument against permitting mental illness to negate an element, focuses on the need to protect society from the mentally ill people who commit crimes. We must bar the defence of diminished capacity because such dangerous people must be convicted of something in order to provide authority for incarceration or treatment or whatever else is necessary to prevent them from causing further harm. Further, the danger to the public in permitting such a defence is particularly high because everyone who commits a brutal offence is, to some extent, mentally abnormal, so allowing the defence would frustrate the needed criminal law authority over just the people from whom we most need to protect ourselves. But, even if it were true that those who commit brutal offences are mentally abnormal, it does not follow that all such persons would get a defence under the Model Code formulation. Only those who are mentally ill and, as a result, do not have a *required offence element*, get a defence for mental illness negating an element. Further, 'mental illness' typically is defined expressly to exclude abnormality manifested only by anti-social conduct.[40]

---

36   Ibid., 89.

37   In *United States* v. *Brawner*, 471 F 2d 969, 983 (DC 1972), the court addressed these concerns about expert testimony, albeit in the context of formulating the District of Columbia's insanity defence rather than its diminished capacity doctrine: 'The experts have meaningful information to impart, not only on the existence of mental illness or not, but also on its relationship to the incident charged as an offence. In the interest of justice this valued information should be available, and should not be lost or blocked by the requirements that unnaturally restrict communication between the experts and the jury.'

38   Ibid., 1002.

39   See, for example, *Regina* v. *Wallett* [1968] All ER 296 (Criminal Justice Act of 1967 excluded common law presumption; jury instruction on ordinary person standard for determining intent in murder case was in violation of Act; murder conviction reduced to manslaughter); *Sandstrom* v. *Montana*, 442 US 510, 99 S Ct 2450, 61 L Ed 2d 39 (1979) (jury instruction in accordance with common law presumption had effect of either conclusive presumption of intent or shift of burden of persuasion, and therefore unconstitutional because violates Fourteenth Amendment requirement that state prove every offence element beyond reasonable doubt).

40   See Model Penal Code §4.01(2).

Most importantly, the proper way to protect ourselves from the dangerously mentally ill is not through distortion of the criminal law system by having it convict blameless offenders, but rather through providing an effective system for civil commitment of the dangerously mentally ill. As social science has recently shown, punishing people who are seen as morally blameless undermines the criminal law's moral credibility with the community it governs, and thereby undermines its crime-control effectiveness in harnessing the powerful forces of social influence and internalised norms.[41] (Note that this 'protection of the public' line of argument would call for abolition not only of the use of mental illness negating an element, but also of the insanity defence.)

'Diminished Capacity' or 'Partial Responsibility'

There have been attempts by some American courts – but no legislatures – to create a true 'diminished capacity' or 'partial responsibility' mitigation, one that would mitigate an intentional killing to manslaughter based upon reduced responsibility because of an actor's reduced capacity due to mental illness. While the actor would not qualify for a complete insanity defence, it is argued that he ought to get at least a partial insanity mitigation if his mental illness is such that his capacity to fully appreciate or control his conduct is diminished to an extent that makes him noticeably less blameworthy than an intentional killer not suffering similar mental illness. The Model Penal Code rejected such a mitigation.[42]

The attempts to create such a mitigation occurred in older cases in which courts were interpreting the common law 'malice aforethought' requirement for murder, and saw themselves as having the authority, or at least the flexibility in interpretation, to define malice aforethought so as to exclude such cases of 'diminished capacity'. Manslaughter liability would result because, at common law, that offence commonly was defined as a catch-all comprised of 'all other killings' that were not murder and not justified or excused.[43] Such an approach is no longer possible in a Model Penal Code jurisdiction because manslaughter is a defined offence, with specific requirements.

The five cases that sought to create such a mitigation were all pre-codification.[44] Four of the five – Hawaii, Ohio, Oregon and Utah – are all now Model Penal Code jurisdictions in which the common law typically has been abolished by statute,[45] and therefore provide no diminished capacity mitigation – or any other – unless it is explicitly included in their codified homicide scheme.[46] The fifth, a 1966 California case, *People* v. *Conley*, was repudiated by statute in 1981 when the California legislature abolished the state's diminished capacity defence.[47]

A form of the 'diminished capacity' mitigation still exists in Model Penal Code jurisdictions, at least in a sense. Recall the previous discussion of the modern mitigation of extreme emotional

---

41 See Paul Robinson, 'Punishing Dangerousness: Cloaking Preventive Detention as Criminal Justice' (2001) 114 Harvard Law Review 1429; Paul Robinson, Geoff Goodwin and Michael Reisig, 'The Disutility of Injustice' (2010) 85 New York University Law Review 1940; Paul Robinson, *Distributive Principles of Criminal Law: Who Should Be Punished How Much?* (Oxford 2008) chs 6 and 8.

42 See Model Penal Code comment §210.3, 67–73.

43 See Model Penal Code comment §210.3, 44–48.

44 *People* v. *Conley*, 64 Cal 2d 310, 411 P 2d 911, 49 Cal Rptr 815 (1966); *State* v. *Santiago*, 55 Haw 162, 516 P2d 1256 (1973); *State* v. *Nichols*, 3 Ohio App 2d 182, 209 NE 2d 750, 32 OO 2d 271 (1965); *State* v. *Scheigh*, 210 Ore 155, 310 P 2d 341 (1947); *State* v. *Green*, 78 Utah 580, 6 p2d 177 (1931).

45 Model Penal Code, §1.05(1).

46 See Haw Rev Stat Ann §701-102 (Michie 2002); Ohio Rev Code Ann §2901.03 (LexisNexis 2005); Or Rev Stat §161.035 (2001); Utah Code Ann §76-1-105 (2008).

47 See Cal. Penal Code §188 (West 2003); *People* v. *Bobo*, 271 Cal Rptr 277, 290 (1990) (noting that the *Conley*'s diminished capacity mitigation of murder to manslaughter is no longer available).

disturbance, which reduces murder to manslaughter. By its terms it applies to 'extreme *mental or* emotional disturbance', which, thus, applies to an actor who suffers a disturbance due to mental illness. Recall also that the Model Code's formulation allows the judge to partially individualise the reasonable person standard against which the actor's conduct is compared. Thus, the judge might have the jury assess the conduct of a mentally ill offender by comparing it against that of a reasonable person suffering a mental illness similar to that of the actor. The Model Code drafters explicitly note this possibility in their official commentary.[48]

Current United States Rules

It is commonly difficult to state 'the American rule' on an issue because there are 52 American jurisdictions.[49] (Federal criminal law applies only to special federal offences, which typically concern only areas in which there is a special federal interest, such as organised crime involving several states. Under the US Constitution, the police power is among the powers traditionally reserved to the states,[50] and state criminal codes govern the vast bulk of homicide prosecutions.[51]) While more than three-quarters of the state criminal codes are based upon the Model Penal Code, their provisions sometimes vary from those of the Model Code and the two homicide mitigations at issue here are examples of where such variance is common.

Provocation and Extreme Emotional Disturbance

It is no surprise that the seven states that never seriously considered enacting a modern comprehensive criminal code all adhere to some variation of the common law provocation mitigation: Idaho, Louisiana, Maryland, Mississippi, Nevada, North Carolina and Wisconsin.[52] Nor is it a surprise

---

48   Model Penal Code §210.3 comment [72]–[73].

49   The 50 states, the District of Columbia, and the federal system each have their own criminal code.

50   US Const amend X ('The powers not delegated to the United States by the Constitution, nor prohibited by it to the States, are reserved to the States respectively, or to the people.'). See also *Panhandle Eastern Pipe Line Co* v. *State Highway Commission for Kansas*, 294 US 613, 622 (1935) (state's police power 'springs from the obligation of the state to protect its citizens and provide for the safety and good order of society').

51   For instance, in 2004, state courts convicted nearly 40 times as many homicide defendants as did federal district courts (8,400 defendants were convicted of homicide in state courts, compared to 220 in federal court). Kathleen McGuire, ed., *Sourcebook of Criminal Justice Statistics Online*, tbls. 5.44.2004 and 5.17.2004.

52   Idaho Code Ann §18-4006 (Michie 2002) ('Manslaughter is the unlawful killing of a human being', including 'upon a sudden quarrel or heat of passion'.); La Rev Stat Ann §14:31 (2007) ('Manslaughter is ... [a] homicide which would be murder... but the offense is committed in sudden passion or heat of blood immediately caused by provocation sufficient to deprive an average person of his self-control and cool reflection.'); *Cox* v. *State*, 534 A 2d 1333, 1335 (Md 1988) ('We define voluntary manslaughter as an intentional homicide, done in a sudden heat of passion, caused by adequate provocation, before there has been a reasonable opportunity for the passion to cool.'); Miss Code Ann §97-3-35 (West 2008) ('The killing of a human being, without malice, in the heat of passion, but in a cruel or unusual manner, or by the use of a dangerous weapon ... shall be manslaughter.'); Nev Rev Stat §200.040 (2007) ('Manslaughter must be ... caused by a provocation apparently sufficient to make the passion irresistible, or involuntary, in the commission of an unlawful act ...'); *State* v. *Ligon*, 420 SE 2d 136, 146 (NC 1992) (holding that mitigation to voluntary manslaughter available only when there is evidence that '(1) defendant [killed victim] in the heat of passion; (2) this passion was provoked by acts of the victim which the law regards as adequate provocation; and (3) the [killing] took place immediately after the provocation'); *State* v. *Williford*, 307 NW 2d 277, 283

that the 11 jurisdictions that contemplated comprehensive modern codification but never carried it out, similarly all rely upon some variation of the common law provocation mitigation: California, District of Columbia, Massachusetts, Michigan, Oklahoma, Rhode Island, South Carolina, Tennessee, Vermont, West Virginia and the federal system.[53] Many of the codification proposals in these jurisdictions proposed adopting the Model Penal Code 'extreme emotional disturbance' formulation of the mitigation.[54]

(Wis 1981) ('The heat of passion which will reduce what would otherwise be murder to manslaughter is such mental disturbance, caused by a reasonable, adequate provocation as would ordinarily so overcome and dominate or suspend the exercise of the judgment of an ordinary man as to render his mind for the time being deaf to the voice of reason.') (internal citations omitted).

53   Cal Penal Code §192 (West 2003) ('Manslaughter is the unlawful killing of a human being without malice', including 'upon a sudden quarrel or heat of passion'.); *High* v. *United States*, 972 A2d 829, 833 (DC 2009) ('Voluntary manslaughter is an unlawful, intentional killing that would be second-degree murder but for the presence of mitigating circumstances, which exist where [the] person acts in the heat of passion caused by adequate provocation.') (internal citations omitted); *Commonwealth* v. *Burgess*, 879 NE 2d 63, 78 (Mass 2008) ('The jury must be able to infer that a reasonable person would have become sufficiently provoked and that, in fact, the defendant was provoked. Furthermore, a verdict of voluntary manslaughter requires the trier of fact to conclude that there is a causal connection between the provocation, the heat of passion, and the killing.') (internal citations omitted); *People* v. *Townes*, 218 NW 2d 136, 143 (Mich 1974) ('A defendant properly convicted of voluntary manslaughter is a person who has acted out of a temporary excitement induced by an adequate provocation and not from the deliberation and reflection that marks the crime of murder.'); Okla Stat Ann tit 21, §711 (West 2002) (defining homicide as murder when 'perpetrated without a design to effect death, and in a heat of passion, but in a cruel and unusual manner ...'); *State* v. *McGuy*, 841 A2d 1109, 1113 (RI 2003) ('voluntary manslaughter exists when (1) the provocation is so gross as to cause the ordinary reasonable man to lose his [or her] self control and to use violence with fatal results, and (2) the defendant is deprived of his self control under the stress of such provocation and committed the crime while so deprived') (internal citations omitted); *State* v. *Knoten*, 555 SE 2d 391, 394–5 (SC 2001) ('Voluntary manslaughter is the unlawful killing of a human being in sudden heat of passion upon sufficient legal provocation. ... The sudden heat of passion, upon sufficient legal provocation, which mitigates a felonious killing to manslaughter ... must be such as would naturally disturb the sway of reason ... and produce ... an uncontrollable impulse to do violence.') (internal citations omitted); Tenn Code Ann §39-13-211 (2009) ('Voluntary manslaughter is the intentional or knowing killing of another in a state of passion produced by adequate provocation sufficient to lead a reasonable person to act in an irrational manner.'); *State* v. *King*, 897 A2d 543, 548 (Vt 2006) ('Heat-of-passion manslaughter, at issue here, requires: adequate provocation; inadequate time to regain self-control ("cool off"); actual provocation; and actual failure to cool off.') (internal citations omitted); *State* v. *Morris*, 95 SE 2d 401, 408 (W Va 1956) ('A sudden intentional killing with a deadly weapon, by one who is not in any way at fault, in immediate resentment of a gross provocation, is *prima facie* a killing in heat of blood, and therefore, an offense of no higher degree than voluntary manslaughter.'); 18 USC §1112 (2006) ('Manslaughter is the unlawful killing of a human being without malice', including '[u]pon a sudden quarrel or heat of passion').

54   See, for example, Ark Criminal Code Revision Commission, Arkansas Criminal Code: Proposed Official Draft §1504(1)(a) (1974); Fla Comm on Criminal Justice, Revision of the Florida Criminal Code: Second Tentative Draft §1001.07 (1972); State of Maryland Commission on Criminal Law, Proposed Criminal Code §125.20(1)(d) (1972); Mass Criminal Law Revision Commission, Proposed Criminal Code of Massachusetts ch. 265 §3(a)(2) (1972); Special Comm. of the Mich State Bar for the Revision of the Criminal Code, Michigan Revised Criminal Code: Final Draft §2010(1)(d) (1967); Neb Commission on Law Enforcement and Criminal Justice, Proposed Revision of the Nebraska Criminal Code §3-104(b) (1972); 1 NJ Criminal Law Revision Commission, Final Report §2C:11-4(a)(2) (1971); State of N.Y. Temp. Comm'n on Revision of the Penal Law and Criminal Code, Proposed New York Penal Law §130.20(2) (1964); H.R. 1338, 1983 Sess. §14A-2103(b) (NC 1985); HR 419, S 250, 62nd Sess tit 5 §19.03 (Tex 1971).

On the other hand, it is a bit surprising that, given the enormous influence of the Model Penal Code in most areas, in this area its influence has been quite limited. Of the 34 states that adopted modern comprehensive criminal codes inspired by the Model Penal Code,[55] only 11 of those codes adopt the Model Penal Code's 'extreme emotional disturbance' formulation: Arkansas, Connecticut, Delaware, New York, Hawaii, Kentucky, Maine, Montana, North Dakota, Oregon and Utah.[56] The remaining 23 Model Penal Code jurisdictions retain their previously existing common law provocation formulations or some variation on it: Alabama, Alaska, Arizona, Colorado, Florida, Georgia, Illinois, Indiana, Iowa, Kansas, Minnesota, Missouri, Nebraska, New Hampshire, New Jersey, New Mexico, Ohio, Pennsylvania, South Dakota, Texas, Virginia, Washington and Wyoming.[57]

Mental Illness Negating an Offence Element

American jurisdictions take a variety of positions on the admission of mental disease or defect evidence offered to negate a required culpability element. The most common position is that of the Model Penal Code. About 40 per cent of jurisdictions follow the Code in admitting any evidence of mental disease or defect that is relevant to negate any culpable state of mind offence element. These include Alaska, Arkansas, Connecticut, Colorado, Hawaii, Idaho, Kentucky, Maine, Maryland, Missouri, Montana, Nevada, New Hampshire, New Jersey, Oregon, Tennessee, Utah and Vermont.[58] Another 30 per cent allow such evidence to be admitted but purport to limit such

---

55   See Model Penal Code and Commentaries (Official Draft and Revised Comments), Part I §§1.01 to 2.13, Foreword at xi (1985).

56   Ark Code Ann §5-10-104 (Michie 2002); Conn Gen Stat Ann §53a-55 (West); Del Code Ann tit 11, §641 (West); NY Penal Law §125.22 (McKinney 2009); Haw Rev Stat Ann §707-702 (Michie 2002); Ky Rev Stat Ann §507.030 (West); Me Rev Stat Ann tit 17-A, §203; Mont Code Ann 45-5-103; ND Cent Code §12.1-16-01(2); Or Rev Stat §163.118 (2001); Utah Code Ann §76-5-205.5(1)(b) (2008).

57   Ala. Code §13A-6-3; Alaska Stat §11.41.115 (Michie 2002); Ariz Rev Stat. Ann. §13-1103; Colo Rev Stat Ann §18-3-103; Fla Stat Ann §782.03; Ga Code Ann §16-5-2; 720 ILCS 5/9-2; Ind Code Ann §35-42-1-3; Iowa Code Ann §707.4; 2010 Kansas Laws Ch. 136 (HB 2668) New Sec. 39; Minn. Stat. Ann. §609.20; Mo. Rev. Stat. §565.023; Neb. Rev. St. §28-305; NH Rev Stat Ann §630:2; NJ Stat Ann §2C:11-4; NM Stat Ann §30-2-3; Ohio Rev Code Ann §2903.03 (LexisNexis 2005); 18 Pa Cons Stat Ann §2503; SD Codified Laws §22-16-15; Tex Penal Code Ann §19.02(d); *Barrett* v. *Commonwealth*, 341 SE2d 190, 192 (Va 1986) ('To reduce a homicide from murder to voluntary manslaughter, the killing must have been done in the heat of passion and upon reasonable provocation.'); *State* v. *Frederick*, 579 P2d 390, 394 (Wash Ct App 1978) ('The rule of provocation has four requirements: (1) There must have been adequate or reasonable provocation. (2) The defendant must have been in fact provoked, and, if provoked, did not in fact cool off. (3) The circumstances are such that a reasonable person would not have cooled off. (4) There must have been a causal connection between the provocation, the heated passion, and the fatal act.'); Wyo Stat Ann §6-2-105.

58   See Alaska Stat §12.47.020 (Michie 2002); Ark Code Ann §5-2-303 (Michie 2002); *State* v. *Burge*, 487 A2d 532 (Conn 1985); Colo Rev Stat Ann §18-1-803 (West 2003); Haw Rev Stat Ann §704-401 (Michie 2002); Idaho Code §18-207 (Michie 2002); *Robinson* v. *Commonwealth*, 569 SW 2d 183 (Ky Ct App 1978); Me Rev Stat Ann tit 17-A, §38 (West 2003); *Hoey* v. *State*, 536 A2d 622 (Md 1988); Mo Ann Stat §552.030 (West 2002); Mont Code Ann §46-14-102 (2002); *Finger* v. *State*, 27 P3d 66 (Nev 2001) (finding abolition of insanity defence unconstitutional and holding that evidence not meeting legal insanity standard may be admitted at trial to negate an offence element); *Novosel* v. *Helgemoe*, 384 A2d 124 (NH 1978) (applying only in bifurcated trials); NJ Stat Ann §2C:4-2 (West 2002); Or Rev Stat §161-300 (2001); *State* v. *Perry*, 13 SW 3d 724 (Tenn Crim App 1999); 2003 Utah Laws Ch. 11 (making minor revisions to Utah Code Ann §76-2-305 (2002)); *State* v. *Smith*, 396 A2d 126 (Vt 1978); *United States* v. *Pohlot*, 827 F2d 889 (3d Cir 1987) (holding that in codifying an insanity excuse, 18 USCA §17 (West 2003), Congress abolished defences of 'diminished

admission to negating only a 'specific intent' or, even more restrictively, to negate only the 'malice' or 'premeditation' requirements in murder prosecutions – concepts that have little meaning under the Model Penal Code's scheme. The 'specific intent' jurisdictions include California, Iowa, Kansas, Michigan, New York, Pennsylvania, Rhode Island, South Dakota and Washington.[59] The even more restrictive 'premeditation' jurisdictions include Illinois, Massachusetts, Nebraska, New Mexico, North Carolina and Virginia.[60] The final 30 per cent purport to exclude the admission of mental illness evidence to negate any offence element. These most restrictive jurisdictions include Alabama, Arizona, Delaware, the District of Columbia, Florida, Georgia, Indiana, Louisiana, Minnesota, Mississippi, Ohio, Oklahoma, South Carolina, Texas, West Virginia and Wyoming.[61]

Some courts have concluded that barring the use of mental illness evidence to show the absence of a required offence element is unconstitutional.[62] This is said to follow from the cases holding that the state is constitutionally required to prove all elements of an offence beyond a reasonable doubt. Such a constitutional rule may be broader than is appropriate; it would seem to bar all forms of imputation of required offence elements. Many doctrines of imputation – such as the doctrine of complicity, which imputes the conduct of another – are well justified and universally accepted. If there is to be a constitutional rule, it ought to focus instead upon the adequacy of the justification for the imputation.[63] Given the difficulty of showing a basis of blameworthiness of an actor whose mental illness negates a culpability element, imputation of the negated element seems unwise. Whether the rejection of such bad policy ought to be enshrined as a constitutional rule is another

---

capacity' and 'partial responsibility' but did not intend to preclude admission of psychiatric evidence relevant to negate an element of the offence).

59   Cal Penal Code §28 (West 2003); *Veverka* v. *Cash*, 318 NW 2d 447 (Iowa 1982); *State* v. *Dargatz*, 614 P2d 430 (Kan 1980); *People* v. *Atkins*, 325 NW 2d 38 (Mich Ct App 1982); *People* v. *Segal*, 444 NY S 2d 588 (NY 1981); *Commonwealth* v. *Walzack*, 360 A2d 914 (Pa 1976); *State* v. *Correra*, 430 A2d 1251 (RI 1981); *State* v. *Huber*, 356 NW 2d 468 (SD 1984); *State* v. *Bottrell*, 14 P3d 164 (Wash App 2000).

60   *People* v. *Leppert*, 434 NE 2d 21 (Ill App Ct 1982) (considering defendant's claim that, due to mental defect, he lacked the requisite intent to attempt murder); *Commonwealth* v. *Baldwin*, 686 NE2d 1001 (Mass 1997); *Washington* v. *State*, 85 NW2d 509 (Neb 1957); *State* v. *Beach*, 699 P2d115 (NM 1985); *State* v. *Shank*, 367 SE2d 639 (NC 1988); *LeVasseur* v. *Commonwealth*, 304 SE2d 202 (Va 1979).

61   *Barnett* v. *State*, 540 So 2d 810 (Ala Crim App 1988); *State* v. *Schantz*, 403 P2d 521 (Ariz 1965); *Bates* v. *State*, 386 A2d 1139 (Del 1978); *Bethea* v. *United States*, 365 A2d 64 (DC 1976); *Zamora* v. *State*, 361 So 2d 776 (Fla Dist Ct App 1978); *Hudson* v. *State*, 319 SE2d 28 (Ga Ct App 1984); *Brown* v. *State*, 448 NE 2d 10 (Ind 1983); *State* v. *Murray*, 375 So 2d 80 (La 1979); *State* v. *Bouwman*, 328 NW 2d 703 (Minn 1982); *Garcia* v. *State*, 828 So 2d 1279 (Miss Ct App 2002); *State* v. *Wilcox*, 438 NE 2d 523 (Ohio 1982); *Gresham* v. *State*, 489 P 2d 1355 (Okla Crim App 1971); *Gill* v. *State*, 552 SE 2d 26 (S C 2001); *Warner* v. *State*, 944 SW 2d 812 (Tex App 1997); *State* v. *Flint*, 96 SE 2d 677 (W Va 1957) (providing statement against diminished capacity defence which has since been questioned but not overruled, in *State* v. *Simmon*, 309 S E2d 89 (W Va 1983); *Muench* v. *Israel*, 715 F 2d 1124 (7th Cir 1983) (finding that Wisconsin may constitutionally reject the diminished capacity defence and refuse to admit evidence proving defendant's inability to form requisite intent); *Price* v. *State*, 807 P 2d 909 (Wyo 1991). To date, North Dakota courts have not explicitly spoken to this issue – their position remains unclear.

62   See, for example, *Hendershott* v. *People*, 653 P 2d 385 (Colo 1982) (denial of defendant's request to present mental impairment evidence to negate requisite culpability held violation of due process; exclusion of mental impairment evidence rendered prosecution's *mens rea* evidence uncontestable as matter of law and lessened prosecution's burden to something less than mandated by due process).

63   For a general discussion of the value and propriety of doctrines of imputation, see Robinson (n. 20) *Criminal Law* §III.1.

matter.[64] In any case, the Supreme Court's 2006 decision in *Clark v. Arizona* holds that states are not required to allow admission of evidence of mental illness.[65]

The Special Resistance to the Reform of Homicide Requirements

The state of current law described in the subsections above presents something of a puzzle. Why would the Model Penal Code be so enormously influential in so many areas yet see such resistance to its homicide mitigations? There are few other areas where its model has not been followed. One might be inclined to simply mark this off as an area of policy and theoretical dispute, but, interestingly, there is not large disagreement among scholars about the Model Code's homicide reforms. It seems that the resistance is primarily a legislative animal. Yet if legislatures were willing to defer to the Model Code in most other areas, why resist in this one?

The resistance to the Model Code was in one direction – insisting on keeping the more narrow common law mitigations. One explanation for the resistance may be that homicide, especially intentional homicide, as the most serious offence in American criminal law, has special status in the politics of crime. And proposals for homicide *mitigations*, in particular, may draw special attention. What could be worse than supporting the 'coddling of killers'? In the US at least, crime politics has a special dynamic all of its own. The charge of being 'soft on crime' can be politically lethal and, thus, can heavily influence the public positions of even liberal politicians. It is not necessarily the case that politically popular crime legislation reflects community views about just deserts. The distorting effect of crime politics can be seen in a recent study that showed that the most politically popular crime-control doctrines of today – such as 'three strikes' and other habitual offender statutes, abolition or serious narrowing of the insanity defence, adult prosecution of juveniles, the felony murder rule, strict liability for statutory rape, and high penalties for drug offences – regularly and predictably produce sentences that conflict with the community's intuitions of justice.[66] In the context of homicide specifically, other research has shown that the lay intuitions of justice do not support a felony murder rule and, indeed, do support the Model Code's partial individualisation of the reasonable person standard.[67]

While many of these doctrines have rational crime-control underpinnings, it is nonetheless interesting, if not odd, that they could be so readily and widely enacted despite their tendency to predictably and regularly produce what the community apparently sees as injustice. How can a democratic process produce liability rules that the community sees as unjust? As has been argued elsewhere,[68] one can point to a number of factors that work together to cause such results. The influence of the media in shaping public opinion often causes people to profess opinions that they

---

64 Recall the troublesome inflexibility created by the constitutionalisation of the rule that the state ought to bear the burden of proof on offence elements, as in encouraging strict liability rather than a rebuttable presumption of negligence. See Robinson (n. 20) *Criminal Law* §2.7, 'Mandatory presumptions'.

65 *Clark v. Arizona*, 126 S Ct 2709 (2006). The *Clark* opinion appears to admit that lay and expert 'observational' evidence of mental abnormality may be admissible on the *mens rea* issue and seems to imply that it cannot be excluded. It seems to uphold the permissibility of excluding only 'disease' and 'capacity' evidence to negate *mens rea*. The latter types of evidence must be 'channelled' into the insanity defence. Thus, it seems at least an open question whether a state could exclude purely observational evidence of mental abnormality proffered to cast a reasonable doubt on whether the prosecution had proven the *mens rea* required by the definition of the crime.

66 For a fuller account of the study, see Robinson, Goodwin and Reisig, 'Disutility' (n. 41).

67 Paul Robinson and John Darley, *Justice, Liability and Blame: Community Views and the Criminal Law* (Westview Press 1995) 116–22; 169–80.

68 For a fuller discussion of the issue, see Robinson, Goodwin and Reisig, 'Disutility' (n. 41), Part IV.

would not hold if given all of the information in any particular case. People's generalisation of crime opinions, and their construction of crime archetypes upon which they base their sentencing judgements, often simplify their thinking to the point that because only the worst crimes are reported and come to mind, they, when polled, often want to impose only the worst punishments. As such, any particular legislator can look to this flawed public opinion and conclude that the majority support harsher crime laws, when in fact they do not. Moreover, the democratic process on the whole tends to invite harsh punishment laws. The media's crime reporting is often based on information provided by the government – and it has been shown that public concern about crime often *follows* legislative consideration of crime issues, rather than being the cause of said action. Additionally, legislators' self-preservation interest dictates that they do not put themselves in a position that could be vulnerable to attack by a rival – a situation that is often brought about by advocating sentencing reduction or opposing harsher penalties, even if such reforms would be in accord with lay intuitions of justice (empirical desert). It may well be that these same dynamics help explain why the Model Penal Code's intentional homicide mitigations stand out as having faced surprising resistance to reform among the states, even those states heavily influenced by the Model Code in most other areas.

Underlying Rationales and their Implications for Reform

The previous sections describe current American law regarding the murder mitigations and how they came to be as they are. What can one say about whether and how the mitigations should be formulated? The following section considers which distributive principles of criminal liability and punishment would support each of the two mitigations and which would not. It concludes that only a desert distributive principle seems to offer support. This desert basis for the mitigations has implications for how they should be formulated, as discussed above.

The Mitigations under Alternative Distributive Principles: A Desert Foundation

As with any criminal law rule, the proper formulation of the two mitigation doctrines, or even their existence, depends in large part on the system's distributive criteria for criminal liability and punishment. Different distributive principles produce quite different liability and punishment rules, and those different rules commonly conflict with one another. To advance one distributive principle by adopting the rule supported by that principle, it is commonly necessary to undermine the effective operation of an alternative distributive purpose.[69]

If one were to rely upon efficient deterrence as one's distributive principle, either special or general deterrence, it would seem unwise to give a mitigation in the circumstances in which these two doctrines do. Where an event provokes an actor to commit an offence, the law's deterrent threat must, if anything, increase, not decrease – yet the existence of the mitigations promises the possibility of reduced (or no) liability. Where the circumstances of the mitigation involve a cognitive failure and irrational thinking by the actor, a distributive principle of special deterrence might tolerate the mitigation, but not one of general deterrence. Potential offenders need to be told beforehand that when things get difficult they nonetheless must remain law-abiding, that there is no hope for them to avoid liability or to gain a mitigation because of provoking or challenging

---

69 For a general discussion, see Paul Robinson, *Distributive Principles of Criminal Law: Who Should Be Punished How Much?* (Oxford 2008) ch. 2.

circumstances, and thus they must struggle to remain law-abiding even if they are highly tempted to break the law.

Similarly, if one were to rely upon a distributive principle of either rehabilitation or incapacitation of the dangerous, it would be counterproductive to provide either of these mitigations. To the extent that provoking circumstances, the defendant's emotional reaction to them, or the defendant's longer-term mental disease or defect played a role in bringing about his offence conduct, either a rehabilitative or an incapacitation distributive principle would want to take control of the offender to assure its authority to rehabilitate or incapacitate. This is especially true where the circumstances or characteristics are long term or predictably recurring.

Contrast these conclusions with an analysis of the two mitigations under a distributive principle of desert. The conditions of the mitigations seem well designed to identify those cases where the actor has noticeably less moral blameworthiness for the killing than the paradigm case of an intentional killing without the mitigation. This is particularly true of the struggles to formulate a proper reasonable person test. The point of the exercise – and the terms of the debate – commonly focus around what formulation best captures the offender's true blameworthiness, given his obligation to abide by society's norms.

Implications for Reform

What implications for reform follow from the unsurprising conclusion that the two mitigations are desert based? That conclusion focuses the reform inquiry on this question: what formulation of the doctrines best (most reliably and most accurately) sorts offenders into two groups of distinguishable blameworthiness? An ideal formulation would be one that marks out for mitigation those cases where the offenders getting the mitigation are all less blameworthy than all those offenders who do not qualify for it.

The model code mitigations should be preferred because they better
track offender blameworthiness than do the common law formulations
What decisional criteria for the mitigations would be most accurate and reliable in assessing relative blameworthiness? Ideally all of the cases that remain in the unmitigated group should be more blameworthy than all of the cases in the mitigated group. In that respect, the Model Penal Code drafters would certainly argue that the common law provocation mitigation is unreliable and that the Code's extreme emotional disturbance mitigation should be preferred. In particular, the Code drafters would argue that many of the offenders who would be excluded from the common law mitigation by virtue of its many limitations (yet who would be included in the extreme emotional disturbance mitigation) are offenders of importantly less blameworthiness. For example, the Model Code drafters seemed particularly disapproving of cases like *People* v. *Gounagias*,[70] in which the deceased committed sodomy on the unconscious defendant and subsequently spread the news of his accomplishment. Those who learned of the event taunted and ridiculed the defendant until he finally lost control and shot his assailant some two weeks after the forcible sodomy.[71] It would seem hard to dispute that Gounagias was meaningfully less blameworthy than the paradigm case

---

70   88 Wash 304, 153 P 9 (1915). The drafters discuss the case at Model Penal Code §210.3 comment 59–60 (1980).

71   The court rejected the defendant's theory that the cumulative effect of reminders of former wrongs could support a sudden passion and allow mitigation and held that the passage of time precluded the original act of forcible sodomy from being a basis for mitigation.

of an intentional killing, yet the common law formulation would fail to distinguish the two, while the Model Code formulation would.

Similarly problematic is the fact that the common law provocation doctrine may give a mitigation in cases where there is some doubt that the actor's blameworthiness is markedly reduced. For example, several courts have submitted manslaughter charges to juries on the theory that a victim's 'non-violent homosexual advance' may mitigate murder to manslaughter since such an advance constitutes a battery.[72] Thus, one defendant who stomped his victim to death after the victim took off his pants and reached for the defendant's penis was able to successfully argue for a voluntary manslaughter jury charge.[73] Another defendant who shot his victim after the victim attempted to perform oral sex on him was able to secure a voluntary manslaughter mitigation.[74] While the Model Penal Code's requirement that a claimed extreme mental or emotional disturbance be one 'for which there is reasonable explanation or excuse' is subject to judicial interpretation, it nonetheless leaves room for a judge to reject a mitigation in non-violent homosexual advance cases if the community would find such objectionable,[75] and juries under the Model Code's formulation may commonly reject such a mitigation.

The partial insanity mitigation should be reconsidered
Another implication of the desert basis for the mitigations concerns the partial insanity mitigation that was rejected by the Model Penal Code drafters.[76] The drafters concede in their official commentary that such a partial insanity mitigation – in this form, the mitigation is accurately described by the labels 'diminished capacity' or 'partial responsibility' – would be appropriate on purely desert grounds. They reject it because they see it as undermining the goal of incapacitating dangerous offenders.[77] However, if one were willing to promote incapacitation of the dangerous at the expense of desert, then there would be little reason to recognise any such provocation mitigation, as noted above, and certainly not the Model Code's broad extreme emotional disturbance mitigation. The

---

72 See Robert Mison, 'Homophobia in Manslaughter: The Homosexual Advance as Insufficient Provocation' (1992) 80 California Law Review 133 (listing instances in which courts have allowed the mitigation and arguing that the mitigation should not be permitted).

73 *Schick v. State*, 570 NE 2d 918 (Ind Ct App 1991).

74 *Broome v. State*, 687 NE 2d 590 (Ind Ct App 1997).

75 Several courts have rejected the non-violent homosexual advance mitigation. See, for example, *Commonwealth v. Martin*, 1 A3d 868, 2010 WL 3222018, *8 (Pa 2010) (rejecting defendant's argument that victim's advance, coupled with defendant's history of sexual abuse as a child, should provide adequate provocation); *Davis v. State*, 928 So.2d 1089, 1120 (Fla. 2005) (finding 'unpersuasive' defendant's contention that victim's non-violent sexual advance should mitigate murder to manslaughter); *People v. Page*, 193 Ill 2d 120, 139, 737 NE 2d 264, 275 (Ill 2000) (distinguishing earlier cases' acceptance of the defence by emphasising that they relied on 'mutual combat' rationale).

76 See discussion above under heading *'Diminished Capacity' or 'Partial Responsibility'*.

77 Model Penal Code §210.3 comment at 71–2. The drafters explain: '[Diminished responsibility] looks into the actor's mind to see whether he should be judged by a lesser standard than that applicable to ordinary men. It recognizes the defendant's own mental disorder or emotional instability as a basis for partially excusing his conduct. This position undoubtedly achieves a closer relation between criminal liability and moral guilt. Moral condemnation must be founded, at least in part, on some perception of the capacities and limitations of the individual actor. To the extent that the abnormal individual is judged as if he were normal, … to the extent, in short, that the defective person is judged as if he were someone else, the moral judgment underlying criminal conviction is undermined. … But this approach has its costs. [The] factors that call for mitigation under this doctrine are the very aspects of [an] individual's personality that make us most fearful of his future conduct. In short, diminished responsibility brings formal guilt more closely into line with moral blameworthiness, but only at the cost of driving a wedge between dangerousness and social control.' Ibid., 71.

Model Code drafters seem to be somewhat internally inconsistent here when they reject the partial insanity mitigation on incapacitation grounds.

Perhaps more importantly, the American Law Institute recently amended the Model Penal Code for the first time since its promulgation in 1962, and the primary thrust of that amendment is to reject the Code's earlier distributive principles for criminal punishment. The Code's original Section 1.02(2) purported to allow some sort of balancing of competing distributive principles. The new Section 1.02(2) sets desert as the dominant principle and prohibits reliance upon the other distributive principles to the extent that such would violate the demands of desert.[78] If this had been the Code's distributive principle at the time of its initial promulgation, the drafters presumably would not have so clearly rejected a partial insanity mitigation. Commentators have in fact urged just such a defence.[79]

The mitigations should be made available beyond murder, if practicable
A final reform question asks whether the mitigations at issue should be applied beyond the homicide offence. First, note that the mitigation that arises from mental illness negating an element, under Model Penal Code Section 4.02(2), already applies to all offences, not just homicide. The jurisdictions that deviate from the Code and attempt to limit the admissibility of evidence of mental illness to negate an offence element most commonly allow it to negate the culpability required for murder or first-degree murder. Thus, the arguments summarised above suggesting that this is an indefensible position and that the Model Penal Code position should be much preferred,[80] are essentially arguments for why this form of 'mitigation' should indeed be available for all offences, not just homicide.

Should the extreme emotional disturbance mitigation (and the partial insanity 'diminished capacity' mitigation, if one were recognised) be applied beyond homicide offences? It seems hard to think of principled reasons for why they should not be. To the extent that they rely upon general criteria that reliably distinguish less blameworthy offenders from more blameworthy offenders, all other things being equal, any system that cared about tracking moral blameworthiness would want to take this criteria into account. On the other hand, there may be practical limitations to broader application. In its current terms, the extreme emotional disturbance mitigation can operate only if there exists some lesser-included offence to which the greater offence can be mitigated. Homicide, as the criminal law's most serious offence, has such lesser offences, such as manslaughter, readily available. Unfortunately, even modern criminal codes commonly lack such different grades within the same offence. But, one could imagine efforts to construct non-homicide mitigations that would work in an analogous fashion. Property destruction, for instance, might operate across several grades, each perhaps designed to take into account the value of the property destroyed; one of those lesser grades could serve as a mitigation grade.

However, a cleaner approach might be to simply adopt a general principle that grants a one-grade reduction if the conditions of the mitigation are satisfied. (A decrease in one grade typically approximately halves the maximum punishment. If some lesser adjustment were desired, it could be specified.) Such an approach is already used in a variety of modern codes in the context of inchoate liability. An attempt to commit an offence is commonly graded as one grade less than

---

78 For a general discussion of the amendment, see Paul Robinson, 'The A.L.I.'s Proposed Distributive Principle of "Limiting Retributivism": Does It Mean in Practice Pure Desert?' (2004) 7 Buffalo Criminal Law Review 3.

79 See, for example, Stephen Morse, 'Diminished Rationality, Diminished Responsibility' (2003) 1 Ohio State Journal of Criminal Law 289.

80 See discussion above under heading *Mental Illness Negating an Offence Element*.

the substantive offence attempted.[81] Of course, this approach assumes that the code is built upon a system of fixed offence grades. This is true of all modern American criminal codes, but is not necessarily true in non-Model Penal Code jurisdictions.

If such a general principle of mitigation were not adopted in the criminal code, it could be adopted as a 'general adjustment' within a sentencing guideline system. That is, a general principle would authorise a lower guideline sentence or a downward departure from the guideline sentence whenever the conditions of the mitigation are satisfied.[82]

To summarise, a criminal justice system that cares about matching the degree of liability and punishment to the degree of an offender's blameworthiness would want to recognise all three of the mitigations discussed here and would want those mitigations available in all cases and for all offences in which the mitigating circumstances could arise. Certainly, their recognition is most important in the most serious offence, murder. While such mitigation might best be done through grading provisions of substantive criminal law, they could alternatively be applied by a general adjustment within sentencing guidelines.

Conclusion

It is worth noting that the issues discussed here might, or might not, be of great importance. The extent of their importance depends upon the nature of a jurisdiction's sentencing system and the practical effects that follow from the determination of offence grade. First, notice the limits of the exercise. These mitigations do not involve the critical assessment of determining whether there shall be liability or not. Nor do they typically determine the actual amount of punishment that will be imposed. They represent an intermediate – and often less critical – stage in which the offence grade is determined. At issue here commonly is only which of two alternative offence grades is to apply – such as murder versus manslaughter – and the practical effect is simply to mark out one set of cases (the mitigated) in which the sentencing judge will have a limit on punishment that she will not have in the other set (the unmitigated). That admittedly can be an important effect, but it is not as critical as many other punishment decisions.

Also, notice that there is probably no magical point on the continuum of blameworthiness that marks off cases that should be given the mitigation from those that should not. If one imagines a continuum of blameworthiness from 1 to 100 on which all cases will fit, the definition of a mitigation doctrine merely sets the point on that continuum that divides the range of cases into the mitigated and the unmitigated. It may be that there is no great reason to prefer a formulation that sets that point at 40 rather than at 60.[83] (More important is adopting a formulation that reliably distinguishes cases of greater and lesser blameworthiness – that avoids denying a mitigation to cases at points 38 and 35 yet granting it to cases at points 42 and 45.)

---

81 See, for example, NY Penal Law §110.05 (discounting attempts one grade unless crime attempted is particularly serious, as in first-degree murder or first-degree possession of a controlled substance); Ga. Code. Ann. §16-4-6 (providing that an attempt to commit a felony should be punished for no more than half the maximum sentence or fine); Mo Rev Stat §564.011 (reducing felony grade by one degree when actor only attempts to commit an offence)

82 Compare this to the USSC Guidelines §5H1.3, which expressly rejects 'mental or emotional conditions' as relevant in determining whether a departure is warranted.

83 If one had a sufficiently sophisticated system, of course, it would be ideal to have the line drawn at that point where the deserved punishment of the mitigated killer matches the punishment that would be imposed upon a non-homicide offender of similar blameworthiness.

Ultimately, the practical effect of the grading categorisation is highly dependent upon the nature of the sentencing system in a given jurisdiction. If the system has mandatory minimum sentences that attach to the offence grade, and if those mandatory minimums are high enough to be significant, then the grading assessment can be quite important. Indeed, if the higher grade offence, such as murder, carries a mandatory death sentence, then the grading decision is all-important. In the US, at least, a mandatory death sentence is essentially unconstitutional.[84] (And relatively undemanding forms of the mitigation conditions at issue here are commonly included as mitigation factors in the formal death penalty decision process so as to preclude imposition of that penalty.[85])

On the other hand, if the only effect of the grade is to set a maximum sentence beyond which the sentencing judge may not go, as is commonly the case, then the distinction may have limited importance. This is especially true if the maximum sentence for the lower grade is sufficiently high that even many unmitigated cases would in practice be given sentences less than the lower grade's maximum. Further, if broad sentencing discretion is available, as it commonly is, the sentencing judge is likely to note and give deference to the mitigating circumstances even if the offender does not qualify for a formal mitigation of offence grade. On the other hand, even in cases where the sentencing implications are limited, there may be other non-sentencing values in getting the offence grade right.[86] For example, a criminal justice system that wants to build moral credibility with the community, and thereby harness the powerful forces of social and normative influence,[87] would want to show that it perceives the important blameworthiness difference between cases of the unmitigated and mitigated case of intentional killings that the community perceives.

---

84 In *Woodson* v. *North Carolina*, 428 U.S. 280, 96 S. Ct. 2978, 49 L. Ed. 2d 944 (1976), the Supreme Court rejected the argument that mandatory death penalty statutes satisfy constitutional requirements for reducing arbitrary and wanton jury discretion. While the court has not yet ruled that mandatory death penalty statutes are never appropriate, it has rejected a statute that mandated death for the killing of a law enforcement officer, *Roberts* v. *Louisiana*, 431 U.S. 633, 97 S. Ct. 1993, 52 L. Ed. 2d 637 (1977), as well as a statute that automatically imposed death for a defendant convicted of a serious offence while serving a life sentence without the possibility of parole, *Summer* v. *Shuman*, 483 U.S. 66, 107 S. Ct. 2716, 97 L. Ed. 2d 56 (1987).

85 See, e.g., Model Penal Code §210.6(4)(b) and (g) ('The murder was committed while the defendant was *under the influence of extreme mental or emotional disturbance*' or 'At the time of the murder, the capacity of the defendant to appreciate the criminality [wrongfulness] of his conduct or to conform his conduct to the requirements of law was *impaired as a result of mental disease or defect or intoxication*').

86 There exist a range of reasons, even beyond sentencing implications, for getting offence grades right. See Paul H. Robinson et al., 'The Modern Irrationalities of American Criminal Codes: An Empirical Study of Offense Grading' (2010) 100 Journal of Criminal Law & Criminology 709, 710–17.

87 Paul Robinson and John Darley, 'Intuitions of Justice: Implications for Criminal Law and Justice Policy' (2007) 81 South California Law Review 1; Robinson, *Distributive Principles* (n. 41) ch. 8; Robinson, Goodwin and Reisig, 'Disutility' (n. 41).

Chapter 18

The Conflation of Provocation and Justification: An Analysis of Partial Defences to Murder in Islamic Law

Mohammad M. Hedayati-Kakhki

Introduction

When comparing Islamic criminal law and the law of England and Wales, one rarely encounters commonalities in offences or defences. This is largely due to the differences between the secular origins of the latter and the religious underpinning of the former. Nonetheless, a surprising similarity existed until the recent passage of the Coroners and Justice Act 2009 (hereafter the 'Act') with regard to defences to charges of homicide. The partial defence of provocation in English law has been criticised for its discriminatory effects toward women, in that it was open to unmeritorious use by men when alleging that the female victim had provoked the violence by, for instance, being unfaithful. By targeting the partial defence of provocation, the Act pushes the law of homicide into the era of legislated equality. The Act implements the vast changes in Western views on social equality and gender roles that have occurred in the 50 years since the last review of the defences to murder had occurred. This belated reform of domestic law poses the question: are other jurisdictions far behind? Islamic law is a particularly interesting subject for the study of provocation and diminished responsibility defences as its conception of the offence itself is grounded in religious principles. On the issue of provocation in particular, it is of interest to examine whether the vastly different treatment of women in society affects the application of the provocation defence to cases of murder – and whether the provocation defence in that context had similarly discriminatory effects as in English practice prior to the Act.

The purpose of this chapter is therefore to set out the Islamic law's position on the defences of provocation and diminished responsibility, including reference to some instances of its application. A principal jurisdiction to be examined is Iran, which has codified some of the principles relating to provocation in the very controversial form of, for instance, allowing the killing of an adulterous wife (and her lover) by her husband without any judicial process. Iran is an invaluable case study through which the Islamic law's defences to murder can be examined in practice. This requires a brief review of the law on homicide in Islamic jurisprudence to set the context for the analysis of defences. The chapter will also consider whether women are disadvantaged by the law and the extent to which the type of changes introduced by the Act might be ripe for integration into Islamic law – and if so, whether this is viable from a religious and legal perspective. The question of whether abstract perceptions of 'family honour', which currently permit a degree of justification for murder in Islamic law, can constitute a qualifying trigger for purposes of provocation defences needs to be addressed. The chapter will also consider the test of 'diminished responsibility' in Islamic law and the criteria which dictate its application. However, the focus will be on the issue of provocation as this is the legal doctrine within which the starkest differences appear between

Islamic and English law. Diminished responsibility, on the other hand, follows the same principles in both Western and Islamic jurisdictions, save for largely technical variations.

Overview of Homicide in Islamic Law

In addition to providing a context for the subsequent analysis of defences to homicide, an overview of this category of offences is important in order to understand that Islamic criminal law is far more focused on victims' (or their families') actions and opinions than is the case in English law. Furthermore, there is a profound difference in the purposes of the criminal law – whereas Western systems discount the interest in retribution, Islamic law emphasises this purpose, particularly where murder is concerned.

Unlike in most other systems where offences are classified in accordance with the crime, Islam follows a structure where the type of punishment determines the type of offence. This is because punishment types vary not only on basis of extent of penalty or type (execution, lashing, prison sentences) but also on basis of the discretion available to a judge in a given case. There are four types of punishment-based categorisation, but for purposes of this chapter the most relevant categories are those involved in homicide cases – *qisas* (retaliation) and *diyya* (blood money).

Revenge-Centred Punishment in Homicide Cases and its Impact on Provocation

Killing or wounding a person will only entail punishment or financial liability if it is done unlawfully. The Islamic law of homicide is governed by three principles:

a. the principle of private prosecution;
b. the principle that redress consists in retaliation or financial compensation;
c. the principle of equivalence, meaning that the punishment is only allowed if the monetary value of the victim is the same as or higher than that of perpetrator.[1]

It is apparent from these three categories that there is a profound divergence from English law in terms of the interests that punishment should serve. Revenge/retaliation is openly recognised as the priority in murder cases, thus shifting the focus to the victim and his family, as well as the subjective circumstances of the homicide. *Qisas* is the term used if the victim or her family chooses retaliation over compensation and is entitled (through the state) to have the offender put to death. The closest equivalent to this concept is 'an eye for an eye' – the victim's next of kin can, for example, demand retaliation in the form of execution for the killer of their loved one.

To elaborate on the rationale for this revenge emphasis, the claims of the victim or the next of kin are regarded as 'claims of men' and not 'claims of God'. This means that the private prosecutor is the *dominus litis* and that the prosecution, the continuation of the trial and the execution of the sentence are conditional upon his will. Prior to the execution of the sentence, the prosecutors may forgive the defendant or accept a financial settlement. In this situation, the judge cannot interfere and acts merely as an arbiter who supervises the procedure, assesses the admissibility of evidence and finally pronounces judgment on the bases of the victim's claim. The state only plays a

---

1 Rudolph Peters, *Crime and Punishment in Islamic Law* (Cambridge University Press, Cambridge, 2006) 38–9.

subsidiary role in cases of homicide, and the principles of family/relatives' grievances are brought to the fore in a way similar to many cases of provocation, which are based on a perceived slight between victim and offender. If there are no terms for retaliation, state authorities or the court may inflict punishment by way of *ta'zir* (a discretionary form of punishment, usually short of death).

For purposes of analysing the family-to-state involvement in a homicide case, it is significant that the maximum that the state can prescribe as punishment for a murderer who has compensated/been forgiven by the victim's family, is ten years' imprisonment (using Iran's Penal Code as an example.) This is a relatively short term compared to an individual's lifespan (as in life imprisonment) and to the death sentence – signifying that the revenge interest far exceeds the public interest. Victims' families play the decisive role in determining the punishment for the homicide – deciding literally between life and death. If there is no next of kin, the head of state, or his representative, acts as a prosecutor. As discussed above, this creates a greater acceptability and rationality for a provocation defence as it portrays revenge as a valid and legally protected interest. Consequently, acting on the basis of emotions and grievances, even if leading to murder, can be a form of justice in certain cases of provocation – bypassing the state, but nonetheless not completely culpable.

Divisions of Homicide and General Comparison to English Homicide Law

There are three main categories of homicide which ought to be understood before moving on to considering provocation. The availability and success of provocation defences can vary with the type of homicide involved, as deploying provocation in cases of premeditated rather that impulsive murder is more difficult. Homicide is divided into three groups by most schools (the Hanafi have five):

1. 'Wilful homicide' results in death with no legal excuse, having the intention to wound or kill, and by means of an 'inherently lethal' method. The penalty entailed is retaliation or the heavier amount of compensation.
2. 'Manslaughter' is a death stemming from an assault with a tool or weapon that is not inherently lethal. If death occurs, the punishment is the more extensive *diyya*, acts of penitence, and loss of inheritance rights.
3. 'Accidental homicide' is where the offender did not intend to kill a person or thought he was legally justified in doing so. A classical case is missing an animal while hunting, killing a person – the penalty is then the payment of lower compensation.[2]

According to most schools, retaliation for homicide or bodily harm is only allowed if the victim's blood price is the same as or higher than the offender's. Therefore, a person cannot be sentenced to retaliation if he has killed a person with a lower blood price; in archaic terms, a free man cannot be executed for having killed a slave, nor a Muslim for having killed a *dhimmi* (protected non-Muslim resident). The only exception is that a man may be executed for having killed a woman, although her blood price is only half that of a man. In Shiite law, if a woman is killed by a man the latter may be sentenced to death if the woman's heirs demand it, but they must pay one half of the blood price of a free man to the heirs of the perpetrator by way of compensation,

---

2   Ibid.

since the blood price of a woman is half that of a man.[3] In subsequent consideration of potential gender bias in provocation defences, this gender-based discrimination in homicide law generally is an important piece of circumstantial evidence that shows the existence of precedent for unequal treatment of women in the context of homicide. Further evidence of discrimination against women in homicide law relevant to the analysis of provocation's gender bias, is the issue of compensatory payment needed to avoid retribution. A woman who killed a man would not only have to pay twice the amount of *diyya* (blood money) compared to how much the man would have had to pay for killing her, but she is also less likely to afford this compensation.

Before proceeding to an analysis of the defences including provocation, it is important to distil several key differences between Islamic and English homicide law, generally. The first is that Islamic law, unlike English law, fully accepts that revenge and retribution are valid interests of justice, leading to a cultural and legal acceptance of defences such as provocation, based on similar considerations of revenge and personal justice. The second conclusion is that homicide law in Islam is more centred on private prosecution and interests of victims' families, which implicitly authorises private action rather than full deference to the law in homicide disputes. This too implicitly supports provocation, in that it is a privately initiated action to punish conduct that may otherwise have been prosecuted by the state (especially in cases of infidelity). Lastly, there is a consistent bias against women in homicide law which manifests itself in their lives' lower value and greater risk of retaliation rather than compensation when involved in homicide proceedings. It can be concluded that Islamic homicide law would certainly fall foul of the European Convention on Human Rights (to which English homicide law conforms) – not only because of the cruel and unusual punishment involved in retaliation, but also because of the gender discrimination in criminal proceedings.

The Law on Defences to Murder in Islamic Law Generally

As a basis for the comparative analysis of Islamic and English provocation defences, the topic now to be considered is the nature of defences to murder, in particular provocation, in the law of Islamic states. The analysis will first consider general Islamic law (which is the basis for all Islamic states' individual statutes) and a subsequent section will focus on particular applications in individual states.

Capacity and Diminished Responsibility

The starting point in analysing defences in Islamic law is the law's perception of individuals in relation to criminal law, namely whether an individual is meant to be the subject of the law or whether the law is meant to serve an individual. The general principle, unsurprisingly, is that individuals are only responsible for acts which are their own decision, meaning that murder committed in an abnormal state of mind does not lead to liability. The criminal law generally only applies to those who are qualified to be subject to Islamic law, and are referred to as *mahkum 'alayh*. These persons are so qualified if they understand the imposed legal injunction (*fahm*) and

---

3 Ibid., 47 – As an example of such differences, Article 209 of the Iranian Penal Law states that if a Muslim man commits first-degree murder against a Muslim woman, the penalty of retribution shall apply. The victim's next of kin, however, shall pay to the offender half of his blood money before the act of retribution is carried out.

have the competency/ability to fulfil this obligation (*ahliyya*). The issue of competency is integral to diminished responsibility rather than provocation, but it does show that at a certain basic level, Islamic and English law are in agreement as regards the minimum characteristics necessary for criminal liability to arise. The Islamic position is supported by the statements of the Prophet Mohammad, known as Hadith, who said that there would be no responsibility in relation to a '*sleeping person until he wakes, a child until puberty is reached and a deranged person until sanity is regained*'.[4] It is of note that mental incapacity or young age does not have the same extensive effect of creating a shield against liability as in other jurisdictions. While children/people without mental competency are protected against criminal liability in murder, they are still responsible for paying maintenance (*zakah*) and liability on a civil level (*nafaqa*).

Diminished responsibility in English law, as distinct from lack of capacity, does not operate to absolve the defendant of all criminal liability but rather only transform a murder conviction to one of manslaughter. In turn, it does not require complete impairment of mental responsibility but only substantial impairment, which renders it applicable to more cases. In Islamic law, the effect of a determination of diminished responsibility is similar in that it falls short of complete exculpation. Rather, when an individual is convicted of deliberate murder but was in a state of substantial impairment at the time, the sentence will be commuted to payment of *diyya* instead of retribution (death penalty).[5] The factors that influence the state of diminished responsibility in Islamic law do not differ substantially from those in English law – medical evidence would still form a substantial part in making out the defence and an 'abnormality' of some description (such as a mental ailment) would be required. The burden of proof is on the party raising the diminished responsibility issue (if in the form of the defence, on the defendant), which is set in English law at 'on the balance of probabilities' rather than the higher standard of 'beyond reasonable doubt'. In Islamic law, the burden of proof is also on the defence when raising diminished responsibility, and to a similarly lower standard.

A significant distinction arises, however, in relation to the effects of alcohol consumption on the diminished responsibility defence. Drunkenness *per se* is not an 'abnormality' that can activate the defence in English law as it is not an 'inherent cause' within the meaning of s. 2 of the Homicide Act 1957. Nonetheless, in principle chronic alcoholism can result in diminished responsibility if it becomes an overwhelming craving that contributed to the offence by being the 'abnormality' of mind.[6] As drinking alcohol is illegal in Islamic countries (with a potential death penalty for third-time offenders), there is naturally more of a nuanced approach with regard to alcohol-craving-based diminished responsibility defences.

Provocation Defence in Homicide

The basic position on defences based not on the characteristics of the murderer (as in diminished responsibility and incapacity) but on the attributes of the act itself and the surrounding circumstances is stated in the Quran:

---

4 Mawil Izzi Dien, *Islamic law: From Historical Foundations to Contemporary Practice* (Edinburgh University Press, Edinburgh, 2004) 102.

5 Roelof Haveman and Olaoluwa Olusanya (eds), *Punishing Mentally Incapable Offenders under Supranational Criminal Law, Sentencing and Sanctioning* (Intersentia, Antwerp, 2006) 5.

6 *R v. Tandy* (1989) 1 All ER 267.

You shall not kill any person – for GOD has made life sacred – except in the course of justice. If one is killed unjustly, then we give his heir authority to enforce justice. Thus, he shall not exceed the limits in avenging the murder; he will be helped. (17:33)

The key exception to liability for murder based on features of the act itself is therefore the concept of 'justice' or in other words, the acts being 'justified' by some circumstances, usually the characteristics of the victim as someone against whom justice must be enforced. Islamic law does not set out, in the primary sources, the scope of the act-based defences but does make clear that such defences are to be applied with reference to morality (that is, the concept of 'justice'). The question therefore arises: what type of interests does the 'justice' exception to murder liability strive to protect in Islamic law? By identifying the interests whose protection is seen as an act of 'justice' even if conducted through homicide, giving rise to the provocation defence, the scope of the defence can be better analysed. Provocation in Islamic law can be applied in fairly pedestrian circumstances of the type that frequently arise in provocation defences in English law – for instance, with the homicide occurring following a slur or insult by one individual to another, without any particular connection or larger dispute between them. However, the more interesting two categories to examine – which are largely peculiar to Islamic law – are justification based on the concept of 'family honour' and justification based on enforcing Islamic morality against an 'immoral' victim.

'Family Honour' and Provocation

The reason why 'honour' can form the substance of a provocation defence to homicide is that family is extremely important in Islamic states and there is particular emphasis on the idea of 'honour' attached to family within certain communities, particularly those of a tribal nature. The practice of 'honour killing' is so controversial and topical precisely because Islamic law as applied in certain countries does not create a substantial deterrent to those contemplating such killings, thus allowing them the use of a very broad provocation defence. The act of provocation is considered to be the act that defies family honour – quite frequently a relationship by a woman with an individual from a hostile clan. Most honour killings occur in countries where the concept of women as a vessel of the family reputation predominates. The practice of honour killing is defined by Human Rights Watch as: 'Acts of violence, usually murder, committed by male family members against female family members, who are perceived to have brought dishonour upon the family … The mere perception that a woman has behaved in a specific way to "dishonor" her family is sufficient to trigger an attack.'[7]

The rationale for the implicit condoning of honour killings in Islamic states is not that the victim's behaviour undermines Islam (although quite often this can be an alternative interpretation) but rather that the victim's action was an attack on the perpetrator that compelled a lethal response. In a rather tenuous way, it is therefore a semblance to self-defence, except the act to which the defendant responds with violence is not physical but rather one against the more metaphysical concept of honour.

---

7 Human Rights Watch, 5 April 2001, 'Item 12 – Integration of the Human Rights of Women and the Gender Perspective: Violence Against Women and "Honor" Crimes Human Rights Watch Oral Intervention at the 57th Session of the UN Commission on Human Rights', Human Rights Watch Online. <http://www.hrw.org/en/news/2001/04/05/item-12-integration-human-rights-women-and-gender-perspective-violence-against-women> (accessed 16 October 2010).

It is important to draw certain distinctions between 'crimes of passion', which form a recognised category in the United States' criminal law, for instance, and 'crimes of honour' as applied in Islamic law. 'Crime of passion' is a classification for an offence meeting certain requirements regarding the immediate circumstances leading up to the killing, rather than the general state of affairs within the family environment, as is the case with honour killings. The notion of honour acts as a justification, stressing the act's nature rather than that of the actor (i.e. the murderer).[8] On the other hand, crimes of passion are a type of 'excuse' rather than a justification – with the actors being excused and not the act. Thus, the act can be illegal and wrong, yet it does not reflect on the merits of the murderer – the person being judged.

There are some very practical distinctions between honour crimes and crimes of passion. There is, for instance, no requirement for a crime of honour to have occurred on the spur of the moment, for example, when someone is caught in flagrante delicto;[9] the focus is not on the circumstances of the murderous act itself but the scale of the 'dishonour' brought on by the victim. On the other hand, 'crimes of passion' require a fit of fury, or a loss of control which arises upon the sudden discovery of some fact. Another important difference is the number of persons who can take advantage of a provocation defence based on honour as opposed to leniency based on a 'crime of passion'. While it would usually be the one person who discovers the traumatising situation and is sexually connected to the victim (e.g. a husband walking in on a wife with another man) that would be eligible to claim 'a fit of fury', the pool of potentially justifiable murderers is far greater in honour killing – it could literally be anyone within a (usually) large extended Muslim family.

Needless to say, the Islamic law position of sometimes regarding a breach of 'honour' as grounds for a provocation defence to succeed is wholly alien to English law, where the act that provokes the defendant must be far more tangible and direct. The practice of honour killing, bypassing all judicial protections or mechanisms of civilised society, cannot be condoned by permitting a defendant to use the idea of 'honour' to put forward a provocation defence successfully.[10] Not only does this encourage violence rather than serving the deterrent purpose of Islamic law, but it also perpetuates gender inequality and strips women of protection by making them 'fair game' for unmerited killings. The idea of 'honour' itself is so expansive and ill-defined, that the judicial practice of basing a defence on breach of that honour is tantamount to issuing a blank cheque to potential murderers.

Provocation Based on Immorality of Victim

The second ground for a provocation defence peculiar to Islamic law is the concept of a 'good Muslim' choosing to enforce Islamic law against someone who had committed a severe immoral act contrary to sharia, including by committing murder. Whereas in English law this would be considered vigilantism and punishable to the full extent of the law, in Islamic law and the Islamic states which choose to incorporate this principle into their domestic law, it can become a carte blanche for individuals to dispense justice at their own discretion, and in many cases avoid

---

8   Joshua Dressler, 'Rethinking Heat of Passion: A Defense in Search of a Rationale' (1982) 73 Journal of Criminal Law & Criminology 421.

9   Lama Abu-Odeh, 'Comparatively Speaking: The "Honor" of the "East" and the "Passion" of the "West"' (1997) 2 Utah Law Review 293i. ers,dd 19 November 2010 421, ople known as mn the boundaries of the above Ariclessmuggling.view Record), he may incur an addi.

10 Suad Joseph and Afsaneh Najmabadi, *Encyclopaedia of Women & Islamic Cultures: Family, Law, and Politics* (Koninklijke Brill NV, Leiden, 2005) 400.

punishment by pleading provocation/justification. The rationale for Islamic law allowing for 'justified killings' to become part of provocation defence is that certain crimes are punishable by *hadd* punishment (crimes the punishment for which is immutable as the sentence is set in Islamic law) – most importantly, through the *hadd* penalty of execution. The vigilante thus simply 'bypasses' or takes a shortcut through the judicial process that would follow the detection of such a crime, and simply carries out the killing as he was 'provoked' by the outrageous breach of Islamic law and, as a good Muslim, had to act.

Islamic scholars are split on the issue of scope of the provocation defence when arising in these circumstances (private punishment of an immorality). Some jurists suggest that the ability to kill the offending individual, often a woman (the most frequent case scenario being that of a woman engaging in relations outside marriage while married), is limited to defendants who are relatives of that woman rather than just any bystander/Muslim who becomes aware of the offence. However, most jurists justify such a killing on the basis of a 'duty to fend off sin' which is seen as universal to all Muslims witnessing such a sin, rather than just to relatives of the woman. They thus distinguish clearly the scenario of an 'honour killing' (where a relationship of blood is required) and a general 'Islamic duty to fend off sin' killing which requires no such relationship.

The most common example of a 'justified killing' defence arises in the context of alleged adulterous relationship by a woman. The rationale for this conclusion is that the *hadd* punishment for intercourse outside marriage, while married, is death. Therefore, the adulteress makes her blood *halal* by engaging in these illicit activities and she becomes subject to private execution. The logic of 'immorality as provocation' is less sound, however, when considering that Islamic law also appears to allow the 'provoked' murder of individuals who are not married but are caught having intercourse. The maximum possible sentence for such an offence (which is also *hadd*) is 100 lashes, yet an individual may execute the unmarried person and still escape punishment. The logical question that arises is how can the defendant's actions be defended on basis of provocation if he had enforced a punishment which radically exceeds the maximum penalty under Islamic law? No clear answer appears to this question, although it can be supposed that Islamic law may draw such wide boundaries with the purpose of encouraging private vigilantism/combating immorality, so that the defendant need not excessively worry about just which Islamic offence the victim was committing.

A justification advanced for the use of 'immorality' as the basis of provocation defences is that if the defendant had killed someone in the belief they were committing adultery, but then subsequent proceedings determined that they were not, in fact, guilty of that offence, the defendant himself will be liable for the death penalty and the defence will fail.[11] However, this argument has serious flaws. First of all, it does not explain *why* an individual should be given the right to act as a vigilante rather than performing his duty as a 'good Muslim' by reporting the matter to the police, or detaining the immoral persons. Secondly, it assumes that trials, to determine if adultery (or any other offence meriting a killing) had taken place, will occur fairly and in each case when a killing had occurred. In practice, there may well be little interest in conducting any sort of trial if the alleged perpetrator (i.e. the 'immoral' person) is already dead – it may seem like a waste of public resources, particularly if the victim was a person without a family prepared to pursue the matter. Furthermore, the courts may enforce a 'reasonable belief' standard when it comes to the defendant's actions – which can result in absurd situations where the victim is found not to have been immoral, yet the defendant escapes liability on the basis that he did have reasonable belief

---

11 Ibid., 221.

to conclude that he/she was indeed deserving of death. Such a conclusion would fly in the face of logic and justice.

Some criticisms arise in relation to the practice of allowing de facto vigilantes to enforce Islamic justice and then benefit from a provocation defence. The lack of checks and balances in relation to the use of 'moral' provocation is staggering – for instance, there is no requirement that the murder can only be committed with the subsequent use of a provocation defence where there is no alternative viable means of alerting the authorities to the infidelity (or other moral outrage) instead, or detaining the subjects. Nor is there a clearly defined test to determine what extent of belief is needed to enable the aggrieved party to take lethal action. That which amounts to a 'moral outrage' for one 'good Muslim' may be a mere infraction for another – where would the line be drawn? Another issue which is left unclear in general Islamic law is whether provocation can be used as a defence in 'moral' killings, if the killing was premeditated rather than a crime of passion upon discovery of the act. For instance, if a 'good Muslim' named Ibrahim notices that his female married neighbour, Fatima, is visited by a young man, Mohammad, when her husband is out of town, would Ibrahim be entitled to use 'provocation' as a defence if he decided to burst into the house and kill Fatima and Mohammad in the act of intercourse – in spite of having no personal interest or 'stake' in the situation? Additionally, there seem to be few checks to prevent the 'murderer' from resorting to the provocation defence in order to cover up a murder for alternative reasons, for instance, for financial reasons. Abu-Odeh suggests that even if it is inevitable that some form of 'just killing' provocation defence exists, it should at least be limited to 'crimes of passion', thus excluding any deliberation by the defendant.[12] He points out that a number of countries have already taken steps to codify the 'just deserts' provocation defence in a manner that limits it to crimes of passion; this also minimises the prospect of judicial activism to extend the provocation defence to genuine crimes of honour, where a family member knowingly plans and executes the killing of (usually) a female relative.[13]

Application of Defences in Islamic States

Having set out the Islamic law on defences, which is quite vague in its general form, it is important to particularise the analysis by focusing on specific countries applying these defences in its criminal law, most notably Iran. Due to the potential for abuse of honour/'justice'-based provocation defences highlighted in the previous section, a comprehensive analysis must look not only at the statutory provisions within these countries but also on how the judiciary had treated cases where the defences have been deployed – did the outcome always conform to the ideals of Islamic justice which is the premise of these defences?

Iran

Iran is seen as a jurisdiction which faithfully yet controversially adopts Islamic criminal law, in pursuance to its constitutional obligation to do so. It is a Shi'ite country and its system of criminal law is mostly codified within the Islamic Penal Code, which covers both substantive offences and

---

12 Lama Abu-Odeh, 'Comparatively Speaking: The "Honor" of the "East" and the "Passion" of the "West"' (1997) 2 Utah Law Review 287–308,
13 Ibid., 290.

defences; however, some residual uncodified Islamic offences remain, which can be enforced with reference to the Islamic law generally.

Statutory Basis of Law on General Provocation

The Penal Code contains a general article which governs provocation, albeit that this provision is somewhat conflated with the defence of self-defence, which can introduce some confusion. The provision in question, article 61, pertains to criminal offences generally and thus also encompasses murder offences. This article states that:

> Any defendant whose crime was the result of an attempt to defend his safety, life, property or honour [*namous*] or that of another, will not bear responsibility for the said offence.

As can be seen from this provision, the traditional elements of self-defence or defence of another (life, property, etc.) are expanded by the addition of the concept of 'honour' (not limited to the defendant's honour but including the honour of another). This concept of *namous* is not defined within the article and certainly diverges from Western interpretations of self-defence, because there is no immediate threat to life, limb or property but rather a fairly vague 'honour' threat. The 'honour' portion of the article extends to cover situations which would traditionally be seen as 'provocation' in English criminal law (for instance, highly offensive statements that lead to a lethal fight – as 'honour' would be infringed) but also extend far beyond its limits, into retributive killings to protect 'honour' of family members etc.

A key contrast to English law emerges from consideration of the effects of a successful provocation defence. Whereas manslaughter will be substituted for murder in an English trial should the defence succeed, Iranian law waives all liability – meaning that a 'provoked' murderer can walk completely free if he fulfils, inter alia, the requirements of the above article. It is submitted that this consequence is unacceptable and stems from the conflation of self-defence and provocation into a single provision. While a person defending his own life or the life of another clearly has a full defence, having had the right to kill, by allowing the defence to waive all liability in the wider and ill-defined 'honour' provocation cases means that those who have potentially planned and executed a murder in cold blood can enjoy the same benefits of the defence. It is suggested that the superior solution would have been to impose some degree of punishment, but of a lower degree, on a defendant pleading provocation successfully. A potential example could include a prison sentence and compensation to the victim's family, but with the option for retaliation (i.e. death penalty) being taken out of the equation. Most importantly, provocation should be separated from self-defence provisions by the *Majiles* (Iranian Parliament).

As has been intimated, the provocation defence is not contained wholly in the article analysed above. In fact, there are other variations of what amounts to a 'provocation' defence in other provisions of the Penal Code, including with regard to 'justified' killing. However, before proceeding to that controversial category, there remains one residual area to consider where provocation applies outside the scope of the article above. In certain cases, the requirement of 'defence of honour' in the above provision will not be made out, yet provocation will be used, with procedural rather than substantive effect, in order to assist the defendant deploying the defence. These cases are of the type where the defendant can point to a 'provocation' which does, however, neither attack honour nor fulfil the 'justified killing' provisions of the Penal Code – but the stimulus to which the defendant reacts nonetheless constitutes provocation in the wider sense. In such cases, the judge will ordinarily specifically direct that the investigation not be concluded and a verdict not be issued until the defendant has had ample opportunity to negotiate compensation with the victim's family, so as to avoid death in the form of retribution. By holding off on the issuance of the verdict (which is a process that is usually rather more expedited than in the English system, due to lower fair trial standards), the judge effectively increases the chances of a compromise being reached and the average defendant with the wider defence will be more likely to be spared the maximum sentence. If a compromise is reached, the Penal Code will still require a sentence of up to ten years' imprisonment for the 'public interest' component of the sentence.

The pattern of discriminatory law as regards murder is continued with a recent Iranian case illustrating gender bias. It was reported in Iranian media that an Iranian man cut off his seven-year-old daughter's head after suspecting she had been raped by her uncle; the allegation turned out to be false as a post mortem showed she was a virgin. The killing took place on the (false) belief that the family's honour was tarnished, and the man was arrested after the falsity of the allegation became clear. The provocation defence itself would be unlikely to succeed in these circumstances (since no honour was tarnished in actuality) but under Iran's Islamic law only the father of the victim (and not the mother) has the right to demand the death sentence, which means that by virtue of being male rather than female, the man will escape the death sentence.[14] This therefore shows the additional layer of protection offered by Islamic law to men, which impacts on the analysis of provocation.

The breadth and power of these two variations on a provocation defence are quite peculiar when viewed in light of the strictness that describes Iranian murder law, generally. For instance, the defence of duress is so limited as to be non-existent where murder is concerned – so that, for instance, an individual forced to pull a trigger because there is a gun held to his head with the threat of death if he fails to do so, would still be liable for that murder in full. Yet, provocation appears to offer multiple generous methods of partly or fully escaping liability if deployed successfully. It is suggested that this inconsistency is unacceptable.

Provocation Based on the 'Immorality' of the Victim

The analysis of the Islamic law's provocation defence has established the role of 'vigilantism' as a valid provocation defence. There is substantial replication and even particularisation of these principles in the Penal Code, which wholeheartedly adopts the concept that an individual should be fully exempt from criminal liability for murder where the victim 'deserved to be killed' according to Islamic principles. This defence is contained in several articles of the Penal Code, some of which pertain to very specific situations, but it is important to distinguish it from the article analysed in the previous section, as an 'attack on the honour' of the defendant or another person is not a prerequisite for provocation defences in these assorted situations.

A representative example of situation-specific provocation defences to murder arises in the context of adultery. In Iran, a Muslim may be sentenced to death under sharia for the crime of adultery if he is found guilty on the basis of the Islamic standards of proof, although extensive penalties also apply for single men who have relations outside marriage. The penalty of death for adultery (while married) is prescribed by article 83 of the Iranian Penal Code, with the sentence taking the particularly cruel form of stoning. The above are all state-enforced penalties, but the law

---

14 Charles Johnson, 'Honor killing in Iran' (Reuters, 9 September 2002) <http://littlegreenfootballs.com/weblog/?entry=4046> (accessed 19 November 2010).

does not stop there and actually authorises the murder of a wife by her husband if she is adulterous. According to article 630 of the above Code:

> If a man finds his wife in an adulterous situation with a strange man and has knowledge that the woman is willing he can kill both of them in that situation. If the woman is resisting, he can only kill the man. The same rules apply to beating and injury as it does to killing.

There is therefore a double risk for women involved or suspected of involvement in an adulterous relationship – both from the state and from their husband, with the latter having clear legal authority to execute both the wife and her lover on the spot. Notably, there is no converse power for women to do the same if they discover their husband in an adulterous position. The Iranian Parliament did set up certain restrictions on this right which are not found in wider Islamic law – for instance, the words 'finds his wife in an adulterous situation' clearly limit the provocation defence to flagrante delicto situations where actual intercourse is occurring.

In the analysis of general Islamic law on provocation based on 'justified' killing, one logical inconsistency that was flagged up was the permissibility of killing someone involved in a sexual relationship while single, while in fact that person could not be killed (only flogged 100 times) if he were to be prosecuted. As such, it was unclear how the individual could 'deserve to die' (as per the substance of the provocation defence) if, in fact, he/she did not so deserve even according to sharia. A careful reading of article 630 shows that this serious flaw has been transposed into Iranian law – the husband is permitted to kill both the wife (which is in line with the stoning sentence in such cases) and her lover, yet there is no requirement that the latter be married (and thus liable to execution). In fact, an unmarried man engaging in sexual intercourse according to article 88 shall be punished by 100 lashes, not stoning/execution. The question must therefore be: from where does the husband derive the authority to kill the unmarried man, and how can the extent of his authority exceed that of the state if the lover were to be prosecuted? It is suggested that this is illogical and forms yet another flaw in the Iranian interpretation of provocation.

As mentioned, in addition to Penal Code provisions allowing provocation defences to murder in specific circumstances (as article 630 above) there is also a general authority in article 226 of the Penal Code which excuses the killing of any person who 'deserves to be killed'.[15] The article imposes no further requirements as to the relationship between victim and defendant (thus not limiting it to 'family' honour scenarios), nor does it specify what the victim must do to deserve being killed. The availability of this provision has resulted in some genuine injustices being done in the name of enforcing Islamic morality against those who allegedly 'deserve to be killed', with a consistent attitude of judicial apathy/inaction in response to these killings. In a prominent case that had reached the Iranian Supreme Court in 2007, a vigilante killing was carried out by members of a hard-line Islamic organisation, the Basij, against two individuals they did not previously know. The two victims, a male and a female (who were engaged to be married), were drowned in a pool based on the incorrect belief that they were engaged in an illicit relationship. There was no intercourse occurring, which meant that the death penalty would not have been possible based on the behaviour witnessed by the vigilantes, meaning that the execution exceeded the legal penalties available. The vigilantes were convicted on numerous occasions by first instance courts, but each time the case was appealed to the Supreme Court, which overturned the death sentence against them and sent

---

15 Article 226: Murder is subject to retaliation when the murdered person is not, according to sharia law, one who deserves to be killed. If the person deserves to be killed, the murderer must demonstrate the necessity of the murder, according to sharia principles, in a court of law.

the case for retrial – with the implication that the provocation defence should succeed and thus allow them to escape liability altogether. This law can be abused by organisations with the power to defend their members in any resulting court proceedings, as occurred here (with alleged pressure being placed on victims' families to accept compensation in lieu of death penalties). The case also makes clear the potential for erroneous vigilante executions – with the victims in this case not, in fact, being guilty of the crime the vigilantes suspected. It is suggested that as long as Iranian law, in the form of the above article, continues to grant such a wide provocation defence without any checks and balances, such abuses of justice will inevitably continue.

Conclusion: Islamic/Iranian Provocation Defences Compare Unfavourably to the Revised Defence in the 2009 Act

While analysis of the 2009 Act lies outside the scope of this chapter, it is helpful to provide a basic overview of the reforms to provocation within the Act, to reach the culmination of the analysis of its Islamic equivalents. The 2009 Act reformed the Homicide Act 1957's regime on provocation by rebranding provocation as 'loss of control'. Section 54 of the Act introduces the requirement for a 'qualifying trigger', clarified in s. 55 as largely relating to fear of serious violence and/or 'circumstances of an extremely grave character, giving rise to a justifiable sense of being seriously wronged'. Section 54 explicitly bars 'loss of control' defences in cases of revenge (i.e. honour killing) and s. 55(6)(c) clearly regards sexual infidelity as having no special status as a reason for 'loss of control'. By contrast to Islamic equivalents, the 2009 Act is essentially the exact opposition as it explicitly bars reliance on adulterous behaviour/immorality that is so favoured by Islamic/Iranian law, when considering whether the trigger is 'qualifying'. Its effect appears to address the criticism that it was used excessively against women as 'provokers' and was not sufficiently available to women being abused.

There is considerable gender bias in the use of the provocation defence, with women in Iran, for instance, being potential murder victims in cases of the discovery of infidelity but without a corresponding defence of their own if they were to kill the husband in similar circumstances. It is suggested that the 2009 Act's specific insistence on addressing gender inequalities in 'loss of control' situations benefits from clearer focus on the type of defendants that merit leniency, while barring the honour and 'morality' killing provocation defences so common to Islamic countries. It is likely to send a clear message that honour killings within Islamic communities will neither be tolerated nor justified through a provocation defence.

Due to the overwhelmingly different goals of the Islamic provocation law (to enforce 'morality' and discourage infidelity) and the 2009 Act, there appears to be little purpose in making comparative judgements – they are, in essence, opposites. It is apparent that the Islamic position, which permits arbitrary and vigilante killings without the benefit of due process, is hopelessly outdated and is further flawed due to its gender bias. However, there is no chance at this time that the position in Iran, for instance, will be reformed in line with the English 'loss of control' defence as the law is so firmly ingrained in religious tradition and outdated views on women's role in society. It is apparent that even in Pakistan, the struggle to legislatively address the use of provocation defences in honour killings is a difficult one and is far from over. For the time being, the most optimistic prediction as regards the Iranian Penal Code's provocation defence is that it may be clarified, narrowed and reduced to a partial defence. This will still leave the legal position wholly unsatisfactory, but may be an improvement for Muslim women nonetheless.

Chapter 19

Provocation and Diminished Responsibility in Dutch Homicide Law

Hein D. Wolswijk

Introduction

In English law, provocation (now 'loss of control') and diminished responsibility are 'partial defences' to the criminal offence of murder. A successfully pleaded defence of provocation or diminished responsibility has the effect of reducing the offence of murder, carrying a mandatory life sentence, to that of manslaughter which has a discretionary sentencing range. In Dutch law, neither provocation nor diminished responsibility plays such a role. In fact, Dutch law recognises neither provocation nor diminished responsibility as independent legal concepts (statutory or otherwise), although the second term is recognised by courts to a certain extent. Consequently, neither concept has been developed doctrinally; there are no criteria, let alone exact criteria, indicating when and whether provocation or diminished responsibility exists. The literature has paid little or no attention to these concepts, particularly to provocation. Still, a 'Dutch perpetrator' can be provoked, and his responsibility diminished, that is, his degree of culpability may vary. Has Dutch law consciously chosen not to give statutory recognition to these ideas, and, if so, why? Are there perhaps defences or mitigation grounds which are in fact similar to these ideas? These issues will be addressed below. First, some general characteristics of Dutch substantive criminal law will be briefly discussed. Dutch homicide law will then be explained. After several general remarks about defences and mitigation grounds have been made, the notions of provocation and diminished responsibility will be examined at length.

General Characteristics of the Dutch Criminal Code

The Dutch Criminal Code dates from 1886. It replaced the French Code Pénal, which applied in the Netherlands, too, and was also a reaction to this French code. The new Dutch code was presented as a genuinely 'national' criminal code, characterised by such aspects as simplicity, practicality and faith in the judiciary. These characteristics, which the criminal code has retained despite countless amendments, are specifically relevant to the subject matter of this article.

In particular, the discretion which the law affords courts is apparent in numerous areas, first and foremost in the area of criminalisation of conduct. At first glance, courts seem to be strictly bound by the law as a result of the principle of legality: 'No act or omission is punishable which did not constitute a criminal offence under the law at the time it was committed' (art. 1.1).[1] 'Law'

---

[1] All articles refer to the Dutch Criminal Code. Translations of articles are taken from: *The Dutch Penal Code* (The American Series of Foreign Penal Codes), translated by Louise Rayar and Stafford Wadsworth, Colorado 1997.

in this connection means 'statutory law'. However, many basic general concepts, such as terms denoting forms of culpability (for example, intention), are not statutorily defined. In fact, most general defences, such as duress or insanity, are hardly defined at all (see below). The Dutch legislator has always disliked creating doctrinal distinctions and definitions, and has thought it best to let certain matters – often rather important ones – be worked out by the courts on a case-by-case basis. The courts, it has reasoned, should be as free as possible to develop the law. The faith in the judiciary is even more evident with regard to sentencing: there are no specific minimum terms of imprisonment. Dutch criminal law merely establishes specific *maximum* punishments for each offence, but no specific *minimum* punishments. A general minimum punishment applies to all offences: one day of imprisonment (art. 10.2). This is the case for even the most serious crimes subject to the maximum punishment (life imprisonment) such as murder, with judges being allowed to take extenuating circumstances into account. Finally, it should be noted that the law has placed sole confidence in a professional judiciary, in that Dutch criminal law does not allow for adjudication by laymen (juries). Only professional judges are allowed to assess the relevant questions, including those concerning evidence.

Homicide Offences

Intention to Kill

Dutch law recognises several homicide offences (arts 287–95). The basic offence is voluntary manslaughter:[2]

> Art 287. A person who intentionally takes the life of another is guilty of manslaughter and liable to a term of imprisonment of not more than fifteen years …

A few specific forms of manslaughter have been regulated. Some of these constitute aggravated forms of manslaughter, for example, murder, which is manslaughter committed with premeditation:

> Art. 289. A person who intentionally and with premeditation takes the life of another is guilty of murder and liable to life imprisonment or a term of imprisonment of not more than thirty years …

Several less serious forms exist as well, for instance, euthanasia:

> Art. 293.1. A person who intentionally takes the life of another person at that other person's express and earnest request is liable to a term of imprisonment of not more than twelve years …

A constituent element of all homicide offences is that the perpetrator 'intentionally takes the life of another'. This *mens rea* element distinguishes homicide offences from other offences which involve 'causing the death of another person'. Firstly, there is the offence of involuntary manslaughter, i.e. death through criminal negligence (*culpa*):

---

2 This is different from English law, where intentional killing is murder, unless there is a partial defence. Under Dutch law, murder is voluntary manslaughter committed with premeditation.

Art. 307.1. A person who through negligence is responsible for the death of another is liable to a term of imprisonment of not more than two years ...

Secondly, the homicide offences differ from offences in which death is an 'objectified consequence' of the conduct, also known as 'result-qualified offences'. This means that neither intent nor negligence is required with respect to the death; a causal connection between the conduct and the death is enough in principle. An example is aggravated physical abuse resulting in the victim's death:

Art. 302.1. A person who intentionally inflicts serious bodily harm on another person is guilty of aggravated physical abuse and is liable to a term of imprisonment of not more than eight years ...

Art. 302.2. Where death ensues as a result of the act, the offender is liable to a term of imprisonment of not more than ten years ...

The existence of these result-qualified offences particularly shows that Dutch criminal law draws a sharp distinction between offences, based on whether or not the intention was to kill. Specifically, unlike under English law, the perpetrator cannot be guilty of voluntary manslaughter (or murder) if, although he caused another person's death, he 'merely' intended to cause serious bodily harm.

Meaning of 'Intention'

The term 'intention' is not defined under the law. While the legislative history provides several clues, the legislator wanted this concept to be developed further in practice and through academic discussion. Today, Dutch criminal law recognises several gradations of intent, comprising not only 'wilful intent' (*dolus directus*) and 'awareness of a high degree of probability' (*dolus indirectus*), but also 'conditional intent' (*dolus eventualis*, 'bedingter Vorsatz'), which is considered the 'lower limit' of intent. 'Conditional intent' means that the perpetrator is aware of the considerable possibility that a certain result will occur, yet nevertheless accepts that possibility.[3] Under this definition, 'intent' includes not only a cognitive element (awareness of the possibility), but also an element, albeit slight, of volition (accepting the possibility). As regards the latter point, intention is distinguished from *culpa* in the form of 'conscious negligence'. With conscious negligence, the perpetrator is likewise aware of the considerable possibility that the result will take place, but instead of accepting this possibility, wrongfully trusts that the result will not occur. In this way, Dutch law contains, on the one hand, a limited idea of intention, in that the intention must be to kill another person; intention to cause serious bodily harm is insufficient. On the other hand, the Dutch idea of intention is broad, for it encompasses conditional intent as well.

Emotions, Motives, Mental Disorders and Intention

The term 'intention' has a cognitive and a volitive element but is otherwise a rather elementary, neutral concept. Specific emotions or evil motives are irrelevant to intention. In general, such factors hardly play any role under Dutch criminal law in terms of the definitional elements of an

---

3   See, for example, HR (Hoge Raad, the Supreme Court) 25 March 2003, *NJ* (Nederlandse Jurisprudentie, the Dutch Law Reports) 2003, 552.

offence. An important consideration for the legislator was that emotions are difficult to prove (and he was seeking to design a 'practical' code). Very rarely, the presence of a certain emotion may end up *reducing* the punishment – for instance, as will be discussed further below, if a mother kills her newly born child 'under the influence of the fear that she will be discovered to have given birth to a child' (art. 290). Otherwise, emotions and motives are mainly important with regard to defences (see below) and sentencing.

Just as intention does not presume the presence of certain emotions or motives, certain emotions or motives likewise do not preclude the existence of intention. The fact that the perpetrator acted impulsively in a fit of rage does not mean that he did not do so with intention. As a rule, 'out of control' conduct – a jealous man, for example, who, in a high state of passion, strangles his girlfriend out of anger, and once he has regained his senses, tries to bring her back to life – is 'ordinary' intentional conduct. Although there is no wilful action steered by reason in this instance – indeed, the perpetrator's faculties of reason controlling his behaviour have vanished – intention is still present. All in all, the legal concept of 'intention' does not have much 'psychological depth'.

This is also shown by the fact that it is irrelevant in principle that a perpetrator has a mental disorder. A mental disorder only precludes an assumption of intentional conduct if the defendant because of the disorder 'lacks any insight into the scope of his actions and the potential consequences thereof'.[4] In practice, at least a minimal level of awareness or understanding is typically assumed. The same applies to disorders of a temporary nature which the perpetrator himself has caused, such as offences committed while the perpetrator was drunk. While it is not impossible for the drunkenness to be of such a degree that intention can no longer exist, courts will generally assume that insight on the part of the perpetrator into the implications of his conduct was not entirely lacking.

In short, disorders and emotional states seldom pose an obstacle to proving intention. The following should also be noted in this regard. If the perpetrator has satisfied the definitional elements of an offence by killing someone with intent, he still may not be punished in the end, because of a mental disorder; 'insanity' is a defence, an excusatory ground excluding liability (see below). In such a situation, the criminal court must not impose punishment on the perpetrator (no punishment without guilt, see below), though it can impose a non-punitive measure (placement in a (mental) hospital, arts 37, 37a). On the other hand, if the definitional elements, including intention, cannot be proved, an acquittal must follow, and the court cannot impose any punishment or measures. Thus Dutch courts are reluctant to acquit criminal defendants because of mental disorders.[5]

Murder; Premeditation

Murder (art. 289, above) is voluntary manslaughter (the intentional killing of another person) committed with premeditation. Premeditation is a statutory ground for increasing the punishment beyond that for the basic offence of voluntary manslaughter. A perpetrator acting with premeditation may be sentenced to life imprisonment, and the maximum non-life sentence (30 years) will be higher than for voluntary manslaughter (15 years). Again, there is no specific minimum punishment for murder; rather, the general minimum punishment of one day imprisonment applies to it as well.

Premeditation is not a form of intention. Indeed, it precedes intentional conduct. Premeditation may also be coupled with any gradation of intention, including conditional intent. The law does

---

4 HR 22 July 1963, *NJ* 1968, 217. (All quotations in this chapter are translations into English by the author.)

5 See G. Knigge, *Strafuitsluitingsgronden en de structuur van het strafbare feit*, Preadvies voor de vergelijkende studie van het recht van België en Nederland, Den Haag 1993, 21.

not provide any definition of premeditation. According to the legislative history, a moment of calm deliberation or quiet reflection must precede the commission of the crime; premeditation is the opposite of a spontaneous surge of emotion.[6] This alone makes it clear that, like the general concept of intention, premeditation has a fairly 'flat', neutral meaning. Bad motives in particular are irrelevant (unlike, for example, with 'Mord' under German law). The case law has ascribed an even more limited significance to the term: for premeditation to be present, it is enough 'that the defendant had time to contemplate the decision to be taken or the decision taken, so that there was an opportunity for him to think about and be conscious of the significance and consequences of his intended actions'.[7] In other words, the requirements for premeditation are not very stringent. The perpetrator need not act 'in cold blood', as this was called in the legislative history, and does not even have to actually think about the decision to kill the other person. It is sufficient that the perpetrator had the time or opportunity to do this.

As shown earlier, the existence of a mental disorder usually does not preclude intentional conduct. Given the limited significance of the term, premeditation can likewise easily be accompanied by a mental disorder. For instance, it is very possible for murder to be found to have been proved, even though the defendant can ultimately only be held accountable for that murder to a diminished degree (see below). Murder can even be deemed to have been proved, notwithstanding that the defendant cannot be held accountable at all because of the mental disorder, and the defendant is therefore not criminally liable in the end.[8] Punishment may not be imposed in that instance, but a non-punitive measure, such as placement in a mental hospital, is an option. Thus, a simple, objective criterion is used to determine premeditation, with emotions and motives not being part of the equation. It is a very manageable concept for courts, generating few evidentiary problems. This limited interpretation, though, gives rise to the question whether premeditation is a justifiable ground for increasing punishment. If someone had the opportunity to deliberate on his actions, is he *per se* more worthy of punishment than someone who acts without having had this opportunity?[9]

Defences and Mitigation Grounds Generally

Dutch law includes several 'full defences', grounds that exclude liability. The relevant statutory grounds in this context are insanity (art. 39), duress (art. 40), self-defence (art. 41.1) and excessive self-defence (art. 41.2). These are general defences applicable to all offences. A distinction is commonly made between justificatory defences and excusatory defences. Justifications concern the lawfulness of the act, while excuses pertain to the absence of guilt (culpability). Self-defence provides for justification, because the perpetrator did not act unlawfully. In contrast, insanity is an excuse: the perpetrator acted unlawfully, but cannot be blamed for this. Apart from the statutory excusatory grounds, the case law has recognised non-codified excusatory grounds. The defence of 'absence of all guilt' is relevant in this context. A principle of Dutch law is that there is no punishment without guilt. 'Absence of all guilt' serves as a kind of safety net: this defence offers a way out in those cases in which guilt is lacking, while a statutory defence does not apply. One example is 'excusable ignorance of the law'.

---

6   H.J. Smidt, *Geschiedenis van het Wetboek van Strafrecht*, Part II, 2nd edn, revised by J.W. Smidt, Haarlem 1891, 460.
7   HR 27 June 2000, *NJ* 2000, 605.
8   See, for example, HR 5 February 2008, *NJ* 2008, 94.
9   J. de Hullu, *Materieel strafrecht – Over algemene leerstukken van strafrechtelijke aansprakelijkheid naar Nederlands recht*, 4th edn, Deventer 2009, 252.

The notion of 'partial defences', with the result that a certain mandatory punishment, such as life imprisonment, need not in fact be imposed, is not a feature of Dutch criminal law. After all, Dutch criminal law contains no specific minimum punishments (and, thus, no 'mandatory punishments', either), but merely maximum punishments. Dutch law does, however, provide for mitigation grounds, that is, grounds which reduce the maximum punishment imposed for a certain offence. Yet, these grounds are exceedingly rare under Dutch law. Due once again to the lack of specific minimum punishments, there is also less of a need for this, with courts always having the discretion to reduce punishments if extraordinary circumstances furnish cause to do so.

How do provocation and diminished responsibility fit into this system? As mentioned in the introduction, Dutch law recognises neither provocation nor diminished responsibility as independent legal concepts (statutory or otherwise). Provocation and diminished responsibility are thus neither (full) defences nor mitigation grounds. Why is that so? Has Dutch law consciously chosen not to give statutory recognition to these concepts, and, if so, based on which reasoning? And are there perhaps defences or mitigation grounds which are in fact similar to these ideas?

Provocation

Provocation is Not a Statutory Mitigation Ground

The Dutch Criminal Code does not include any *general* statutory mitigation ground (that is, one which is applicable to all offences). And it only recognises one pure *specific* statutory mitigation ground, namely for the offence of abandoning a person in need:

> Art. 256. A person who abandons a child under the age of seven ... is liable to a term of imprisonment of not more than four years and six months ...

> Art. 259. Where a mother, under the influence of the fear that she will be discovered to have given birth to a child, abandons the child ... the maximum terms of imprisonment mentioned in Art. 256 ... shall be reduced by half ...

In addition, a few other offences falling in fact under the category of homicide offences and referred to as 'privileged offences' basically contain mitigation grounds. Child manslaughter, in which the same circumstances for reducing punishment as in art. 259 come into play, is particularly relevant here:

> Art. 290. A mother who, under the influence of the fear that she will be discovered to have given birth to a child, intentionally takes the life of the child at birth or shortly afterwards is guilty of child manslaughter and liable to a term of imprisonment of not more than six years ...

Although child manslaughter is formulated as if it were a separate offence, this provision serves in effect as a ground for reducing the maximum punishment for the basic offence of manslaughter. Given the relationship between this mitigation ground and the concept of provocation, the legislative history behind the ground merits a brief discussion.

Firstly, it should be noted that this ground – both for article 259 and for article 290 – was controversial. A minority in the Dutch House of Representatives felt it was superfluous, in view of the absence of minimum punishments and the ensuing latitude for courts. The Minister of

Justice, however, thought it was important for this 'specific excuse' which reduces the degree of guilt instead of excluding it to be expressly mentioned in the law.[10] Secondly, the *ground* for the reduction of punishment with both offences – the special state of mind in which the mother acts 'under the influence of the fear that she will be discovered to have given birth to a child' – has explicitly been included *as such* in the law. In this way, as the explanatory notes to the law make clear, the dangers of casuistic reasoning will be avoided, and the provision can be applied each time in accordance with the legislator's intention.[11]

As already noted, provocation is *not* a statutory mitigation ground for homicide offences (nor for other offences). It *was*, however, such a ground in the original draft of the Dutch Criminal Code. The proposed provision, which had its roots in the French Code Pénal, read:[12]

> Art. 311. If the manslaughter is committed under the direct influence of a furious rage which the victim himself provoked through deliberate hostile acts, insults or challenge, either towards the perpetrator or towards third parties, the maximum terms of imprisonment mentioned in Article 310 shall be reduced by half.

This proposed provision, which was left out in the end, was explained as follows:

> It is based on the principle that a person can and must always control his will, can exercise free will even under the influence of the most intense emotions, and thus remains criminally liable for actions committed under the influence of such emotions, but that there is a state of mind in which control over his will becomes extremely difficult, an emotion, which more so than other ones, gives rise to acts of violence against people. Where this emotion, rage, is, as it were, merely the exaggeration of a noble feeling, *indignation about injustice*, this exaggeration is too much a natural consequence of the imperfect moral nature of human beings to not take this emotion specifically into account for those crimes in which a distinction based on the extent to which the perpetrator acts with cool deliberation or not already results in a substantial difference in the punishment applied.[13]

Provocation makes manslaughter to a certain extent 'excusable', reducing the degree of guilt. Just as with the mitigation ground under arts 259/290 discussed above, the perpetrator's special state of mind, resulting in his not being able to exercise complete free will, excuses his actions. The special reasons giving rise to this state of mind, however, are critical. After all, not every fit of temper should lead to a reduction in punishment. The special reason has to do with the fact that the perpetrator is faced with injustice. To this extent, there is a similarity to self-defence (see below), in which the perpetrator defends himself against injustice. The major difference is that self-defence involves injustice against which the perpetrator is *entitled* to defend himself. This is not so with provocation. An insult may be unfair, but defending oneself against it by committing a criminal offence (even manslaughter) is not justifiable. Unlike with self-defence, limited recognition of the notion of 'taking the law into one's own hands' is *not* the basis for the excuse of provocation.

---

10 Smidt (n. 6), 386.
11 Ibid. (n. 6), 461.
12 Ibid. (n. 6), 450.
13 Ibid. (n. 6), 452. The last sentence is a reference to the distinction between manslaughter and murder. Murder is the intentional killing of a person with premeditation. The reasoning was that premeditation and provocation are mutually exclusive, and, thus, provocation did not have to be a ground for reducing the punishment for murder.

In the debate about this provision, the same issues apparently were relevant as with the mitigation ground under arts 259/290. As with the mitigation ground under arts 259/290, opponents of the provocation provision saw no reason to include provocation, by way of exception, as an extenuating circumstance in the law. The Minister of Justice nonetheless pointed out that the proposed provision did not contain an extenuating circumstance (*circonstance atténuante*), but rather, an 'excuse' reducing the degree of guilt. And, he added: 'the elimination of *minima* should not cause differences to be ignored which demand differences in *maxima*'.[14] A provoked perpetrator of manslaughter bears less guilt, so that the manslaughter is less worthy of punishment, which must be expressed in the maximum punishment. For this reason, a statutory mitigation ground was to be opted for. On further examination, however, the Minister also favoured deletion of the provision, 'Because the right line cannot be drawn *a priori* between provocation which *can* and *cannot* serve as an excuse.'[15] Obviously, not every form of provocation diminishes culpability. The forms of provocation which *do* reduce culpability should actually be recognised as a statutory mitigation ground. But the law must then indicate when provocation will have the effect of reducing punishment. The legislator was apparently unable to formulate a general rule in this regard. And the legislator, who generally had little inclination to support casuistic approaches, did not find a way to specify the instances in which provocation would justify reduced punishment.

Although the legislator did not indicate a *general* vision concerning the idea of statutory mitigation grounds, the following may be inferred from the foregoing. Firstly, the absence of specific minimum punishments means that there is generally less need for statutory mitigation grounds; courts can always make allowance for this in the sentencing process. Nevertheless, the legislator – and this is the second point which must be made – did not oppose statutory mitigation grounds as a matter of principle, specifically not excuses lessening culpability. It only used them very sporadically, which leads to the third point: an appropriate statutory description must be found for each ground for excuse. The legislator thought that this was possible for the excuses under arts 259/290, but not for provocation. This conclusion was probably based in part on the following: as shown above, for arts 259/290, the mitigating circumstance – the special state of mind in which the mother acts 'under the influence of the fear that she will be discovered to have given birth to a child' – also constitutes the *ground* for the excuse. By including the *ground* for the excuse – hence, the rationale – explicitly in the law, the legislator did not itself need to set forth under which circumstances this ground would arise. That was left to the court's judgement (and the legislator does not generally object to this). In this respect, the ground for excuse under arts 259/290 is 'manageable' and easily specified. The situation with provocation is different. Provocation is not automatically a ground for excuse. The law would therefore have to indicate when provocation would have the effect of reducing punishment, something the legislator did not feel it was capable of doing.

Provocation and (Full) Defences

Provocation as such is not a ground that excludes liability but may be a factor that plays into several other defences, in particular self-defence, excessive self-defence and duress.

---

14   Ibid. (n. 6), 456.
15   Ibid. (n. 6), 457.

Self-Defence

The justificatory ground of self-defence can be invoked for every offence, including homicide offences. In the case of self-defence, an individual exercises the right to avert injustice. It is an exception to the prohibition on 'taking the law into one's own hands' and is therefore only permissible under strict conditions. Compared to other defences, self-defence has thus been rather precisely described:

> Art. 41.1. A person who commits an offence where this is necessary to defend his person or the person of another, or his or another person's integrity or property, against an immediate, unlawful attack is not criminally liable.

First of all, self-defence can only come into the picture when a person defends certain interests against attack. There must be an 'attack against his person or the person of another, or his or another person's integrity or property'. 'Integrity' refers to sexual integrity in the physical sense. Consequently, the term 'integrity' does not add much to 'attack against a person'. Another important condition is that the attack must be 'immediate'. This does not mean that the interest already needs to have 'actually been attacked'. A person does not have to wait to receive the first blow before he starts defending himself. An 'imminent danger' of attack is enough, whereas the mere fear of being attacked is not. On the other hand, the 'immediate attack' requirement suggests that the attack is not finished yet. Hence, self-defence cannot be successfully invoked if the attack is already over. Besides these requirements related to the 'attack', the defence against the attack must, of course, also satisfy certain conditions. First, the defensive actions must have been 'necessary': could and should the person attacked have got away from the attack (for example, could this person have easily escaped)? Further, the person must have intended to defend himself (the person must not have regarded the attack as an invitation to participate in a fight). Finally, a person can only claim self-defence if the manner in which he defended himself satisfies the requirements of proportionality and subsidiarity; briefly stated, the actions taken in self-defence must have been reasonable.

In view of these conditions, particularly those pertaining to the 'attack', the invocation of self-defence will, in many instances of provocation, fail. Unlike in some other cultures, for example, a provocative insult does not justify the commission of a criminal offence, because, in such a situation, no interest is impaired which is entitled to protection through self-defence. Threats of physical violence which are merely uttered verbally will usually not be sufficient, because of the requirement that the attack be 'immediate': a threat need not constitute an actual attack yet, nor an imminent danger thereof. This issue comes up, for example, in 'battered woman syndrome' cases. At the time the victim decides to 'defend' herself, there will not typically be an attack or imminent danger thereof going on (for instance, her husband may be in bed sleeping). Justification of retaliatory actions will generally be thwarted by this requirement, too. Moreover, such actions are typically not motivated by the *intention* to defend oneself.

Self-defence presumes an attack, and provocative conduct by another person can likewise represent an attack. Self-defence and provocation can therefore go hand in hand, but that does not have to be the case. There is a fundamental difference. Because self-defence involves the right to avert injustice (a form of law enforcement), it is deemed a justificatory defence. Persons acting in self-defence go unpunished because they were entitled to act as they did. In contrast, as shown earlier, provocation has to do with whether the conduct is 'excusable'. The perpetrator acts while in a special state of mind, which deprives him of complete free will. His conduct is therefore less blameworthy. The special state of mind may ensue from a confrontation with injustice, but, unlike with self-defence, this is not injustice against which he is *allowed* to defend himself. In sum, self-defence changes the nature of the criminal offence (the offence is justifiable), while provocation does not change the nature of the offence, but may reduce the perpetrator's guilt.

Excessive Self-Defence

Unlike many other countries, the Netherlands recognises, in addition to self-defence, a defence for situations in which the person attacked 'exceeds the limits of necessary defence':

> Art. 41.2. A person exceeding the limits of necessary defence is not criminally liable, where such excess directly resulted from a strong emotion brought about by the attack.

This defence also applies to all offences. In a certain sense, it builds on self-defence. Excessive self-defence will only be successful if defensive action was necessary, that is, there was an immediate, unlawful attack against which the person attacked was *entitled* to defend himself. If the manner of defence then does not satisfy the requirements of proportionality and subsidiarity – the person attacked exceeded the limits of necessary defence by, say, hitting back harder or longer than strictly necessary – self-defence cannot be invoked, but excessive self-defence can, 'where such excess directly resulted from a strong emotion brought about by the attack'. The underlying rationale is that, if someone must defend himself against an immediate, unlawful attack, it is conceivable that the limits of necessary self-defence will be exceeded. The excitement caused by the attack causes the person to lose the right sense of proportion and to grasp at means which carry the conduct beyond the limits of necessary self-defence.

As the statutory wording makes clear, 'double causation' is required. The exceeding of the limits of necessary defence must have had its direct cause in a strong emotion, and said strong emotion must in turn have been caused by the attack. This severely limits the applicability of this defence. The strong emotion, for instance, may not primarily spring from emotions already existing previously (caused by an earlier incident) or from a mental defect of the perpetrator. Moreover, it must relate to a more or less spontaneous reaction to the attack by the other person. Ultimately, the assessment of 'double causality' revolves around a normative question: what could reasonably have been expected of the perpetrator and which type of excessive reaction is acceptable?

The nature of this defence is controversial.[16] Some authors see it as an excusatory ground. The focus is then on the fact that the perpetrator acted under the influence of a 'strong emotion', a fact excusing that the limits of necessary defence were exceeded. The question which arises, however, is why a 'strong emotion' in this context causes liability to disappear *completely*, while the 'strong emotion' under arts 259/290 – the special state of mind in which the mother acts 'under the influence of the fear that she will be discovered to have given birth to a child' – merely results in reduced punishment. According to other commentators, excessive self-defence cannot therefore be regarded as a true ground for exemption from guilt. 'Strong emotion' does not mean that guilt is completely absent. Rather, as with arts 259/290, it merely reduces the degree of guilt. That the perpetrator goes unpunished thus has to do with other factors.[17] 'Utility' plays a role, in the sense that it is desirable that a person who is forced to defend himself against an unlawful act should not feel too inhibited. Similarly, it is relevant that the person exceeding the limits of necessary defence

---

16 De Hullu (n. 9) 319.
17 See A.J.M. Machielse, *Noodweer in het strafrecht*, Amsterdam 1986, 674–6.

nonetheless partly stayed within those limits. The degree of wrongfulness in acting in excessive self-defence is thus less in comparison to the situation in which the same behaviour occurs without any connection to an unlawful attack.

The foregoing suggests that there are both similarities and differences between excessive self-defence and provocation. With both excessive self-defence and provocation, the perpetrator is seized by a 'strong emotion'. In both cases, guilt only exists to a diminished degree. The difference is also clear, though, which explains why excessive self-defence completely excludes liability. As mentioned earlier, excessive self-defence builds on self-defence. For excessive self-defence to be invoked successfully, some of the conditions for successful invocation of self-defence must be met. There must have been an immediate, unlawful attack against which the person attacked was entitled to defend himself. And, as was apparent from the discussion of self-defence, this is not or need not be so with many instances of provocation. Provocative conduct may be unlawful, but people are not entitled to defend themselves by use of force against every injustice.

Duress

Finally, provocation may come into play in connection with the excusatory ground of 'duress'.

> Art. 40. A person who commits an offence as a result of a force he could not have been expected to resist is not criminally liable.

This, too, is a general defence, which may apply to any offence. Article 40 is an example of a defence which has been formulated in a very 'open' manner. The Explanatory Memorandum described the ground as 'any force, any coercion or any pressure which a person is unable to resist'.[18] The legislator deemed the term 'irresistible force' so clear that a statutory description would have been superfluous and, moreover, dangerous, because it would have limited the court's discretion. Article 40 now includes two separate defences, 'necessity' and 'duress'. With 'necessity', the perpetrator is faced with a choice between complying with a certain criminal norm on the one hand and serving another social or other legal interest on the other. In this conflict of interest, the perpetrator has, by opting for the other interest and thereby violating the criminal law, made an objectively reasonable choice. 'Necessity' is therefore a justificatory ground. In the assessment of the correctness of the choice, the principles of subsidiarity and proportionality are essential. This defence is irrelevant to our subject.

With 'duress', an external pressure is exerted on the perpetrator such that his freedom of choice is impaired, while he cannot reasonably be expected to resist this pressure. The external force may be a threat (unlawful or otherwise) emanating from another person or a natural force, i.e. the pressure of circumstances, which causes the perpetrator to make a wrong choice but for which he cannot be blamed. The assessment of duress requires both a psychological test (*could* the perpetrator have resisted?) as well as a normative one (*should* he have resisted?). The principles of proportionality and subsidiarity play a role in the normative test, albeit somewhat differently than with necessity. The test applied to these requirements is less objective here. Instead, it is more geared towards the perpetrator's person: what could reasonably have been expected from this person?

Provocative conduct may constitute the required external pressure which impairs the perpetrator's freedom of choice. Although raised rather frequently, duress is rarely accepted in

---

18   H.J. Smidt, *Geschiedenis van het Wetboek van Strafrecht*, Part I, 2nd edn, revised by J.W. Smidt, Haarlem 1891, 404.

practice by the courts. This is certainly true with homicide offences. With very serious offences, a court will not be quick to find that different behaviour could not reasonably have been expected. This is seen in 'battered woman syndrome' cases, for example. If a woman kills a man at a moment when she is not in immediate danger, a claim of duress will probably fail for that reason. The woman should have avoided the situation in some other way. Duress is often invoked, too, for 'cultural offences'. This almost always pertains to homicides or violent offences ensuing from an insult to the perpetrator's own or his family honour ('honour killing'). This insult supposedly then constitutes the external pressure limiting the perpetrator's freedom of choice. Although courts typically acknowledge that the perpetrator was subjected to certain pressure, they ultimately deem it implausible that the perpetrator was not reasonably capable of refraining from the criminal conduct. With serious offences, courts are reluctant to accept that cultural influences can have such an impact on freedom of choice that a perpetrator could not reasonably have been expected to refrain from the conduct. Undoubtedly, this conclusion is prompted in part by the fact that, in honour killing cases, the provocative conduct is often not unlawful at all. To the contrary, an individual has every right – under Dutch law – to engage in the conduct (example: sexual contact between a Muslim woman and a non-Muslim), so that the perpetrator's 'taking the law into his own hands' is all the more grievous.

Diminished Responsibility

Insanity

Before the concept of 'diminished responsibility' is looked at, some remarks must be made regarding 'insanity' as providing a *full* exemption from criminal liability:

> Art. 39. A person who commits an offence for which he cannot be held responsible by reason of a mental defect or mental disease is not criminally liable.

This provision does not in itself mean much, for it goes without saying that a perpetrator cannot be punished for an offence if he is not 'responsible' for that offence. The words 'cannot be held responsible' refer to the fact that the perpetrator bears no blame. It is a complete and full excusatory ground. The perpetrator's conduct was unlawful, but he is not criminally liable, since he acted without guilt and thus cannot be blamed for the unlawful act. A non-punitive measure (placement in a (mental) hospital, arts 37, 37a) may be imposed, however.

Some aspects of the insanity provision require explanation. Application of art. 39 presupposes a *normative* test. Under the former French Code Pénal, a perpetrator was not liable if he acted in a state of *démence*. If a doctor found that the perpetrator had been in a state of *démence*, the court had to rule that the perpetrator could not be punished. In this way, a statutory, mandatory legal decision was linked to a statutorily described mental state. The Dutch legislator backed away from such a static approach, with a clear connection between illness and legal consequence being assumed. Because the term 'responsible' has been made the focus of art. 39, it is obvious that, as with all defences, liability ultimately turns on a normative test.

Strangely enough, the law does not indicate when a disorder removes responsibility. Which criterion will apply? Article 39 does not mention any characteristics which point to any specific mental state concerning free will, intellect, emotionality, understanding of good and evil, and so forth. The literature has not given much attention to this, and the Dutch Supreme Court has not developed any criteria, either. The law does indicate, however, which disorders may be relevant, with art. 39 mentioning two mental abnormalities: by 'mental defect', the legislator had congenital abnormalities in mind; 'mental disease' was a reference to non-congenital abnormalities. In practice the distinction is not significant. Usually the general term 'mental disorder' is used. The scope of art. 39 is thus limited in that a *mental* abnormality must be at issue. This does not encompass affect or intense emotion such as anxiety, desperation or rage. Such emotions may be factors with other excusatory grounds (including excessive self-defence and duress). Furthermore, the provision must be interpreted broadly, consistent with the legislator's intention: 'Specification is not likely to be beneficial. Instead, a formula must be adopted which is *so* broad that it does not constrict either experts or courts.'[19] The assumption is therefore that no mental abnormalities are excluded from the reach of art. 39.

Alcoholic intoxication deserves a special mention in this regard. Nowadays it is assumed (when the Criminal Code was drafted, there was a lot of discussion about this) that this state can also fall under the scope of art. 39, because drunkenness may be related to a serious addiction problem which can be labelled 'mental'. Yet, whether voluntary intoxication ultimately renders the perpetrator not 'responsible' under art. 39 is a different question. The extent to which the perpetrator himself is to blame for the intoxication (*culpa in causa*) is particularly relevant here. In deciding whether a perpetrator can be held responsible, courts generally must rely on opinions from behavioural experts: did the perpetrator exhibit a mental disorder when he committed the offence, and, if so, was there a causal connection between the disorder and the offence? However, the question of whether the perpetrator should not be held accountable is a pre-eminently normative question. It is perhaps not all that relevant to a behavioural expert that the intoxication was the perpetrator's own fault. Courts will rarely accept invocation of art. 39 in cases of intoxication and certainly not if the perpetrator knew about the intoxicant's effects.[20]

In sum, lack of accountability has been formulated in a broad, open manner. This deliberate choice by the legislator is generally endorsed in the literature: 'Our legislator deserves a big compliment for having designed a provision on accountability in 1881 which has made it possible to utilize new insights from psychiatry without limitation.'[21]

Diminished Responsibility

A state of insanity is a fairly exceptional situation. More often, when the perpetrator cannot bear full responsibility because of a mental abnormality, he cannot be said to be entirely blameless, either. This is referred to as 'diminished responsibility'. This concept is unknown to Dutch law. The law (art. 37a) does give courts the power to impose both a punishment and a non-punitive measure (hospital order, art. 37a) on a perpetrator with a mental disorder who can be deemed blameworthy (art. 39 does not apply). This combination permits the courts to give consideration to the fact that the perpetrator is not fully accountable, by ordering a lesser punishment than normal, while at the same time protecting society from the perpetrator through a hospital order. The court can also decide merely to impose this non-punitive measure.

Diminished responsibility is not a statutory mitigation ground under Dutch criminal law. The legislator expressly wanted to avoid this concept:

---

19 Smidt (n. 18), 373.
20 See, for example, HR 12 February 2008, *NJ* 2008, 262.
21 J.M. van Bemmelen/Th.W. van Veen, *Het materiële strafrecht, Algemeen deel*, 14th edn in the revision by D.H. de Jong and G. Knigge, Deventer 2003, 148.

Under the criminal law, a defendant is either accountable for his conduct or not. Certainly, there are various degrees of guilt, depending on the extent to which the defendant's mental faculties are developed or not, but "partial accountability" does not exist. If it is clear that the defendant did what he could not refrain from doing ... he is not accountable for the offence. In contrast, if his state of mind did not exclude free will, he is accountable for the offence, however excusable it was. *Tertium non datur*.[22]

Indeed, at the end of the day, a defendant is either accountable for an offence or not. Yet, that does not change the fact that if he is accountable, his degree of culpability may vary, which, as is apparent from the quote, the legislator recognised ('degrees of guilt'). In practice, diminished responsibility usually results in a lesser punishment. But why did the Dutch legislator not recognise diminished responsibility as a statutory mitigation ground? Undoubtedly, this had something to do with the fact that, in a system without specific minimum punishments, there is generally less of a need for statutory mitigation grounds. Still, as shown earlier (see arts 259/290), lawmakers *did* statutorily recognise a mitigation ground a few times. Why not here? Presumably, the reason was that diminished responsibility can arise in all sorts of gradations. Not only may there be 'very diminished' responsibility, but also 'somewhat diminished' responsibility, or something in between. On the one hand, within the Dutch context of the absence of specific minimum punishments it does not make much sense to link a mandatory reduction of punishment to just one particular gradation of diminished responsibility. On the other hand, a framework which tried to do justice to the reality that diminished responsibility can arise in different gradations and which would therefore attempt to indicate by how many years the maximum punishment would be reduced for each particular gradation of diminished responsibility would surely be extremely complex. The situation is different in a legal system which, unlike the Dutch, includes specific minimum punishments. If, as in England, diminished responsibility has the effect of reducing the offence of murder, carrying a mandatory life sentence, to that of manslaughter, it does not in principle matter much that diminished responsibility can manifest itself in all sorts of gradations. The sole question is: when is the responsibility so diminished that a mandatory life sentence is not justifiable? That such responsibility can be diminished to an even much greater degree is irrelevant.

It would have been conceivable for the legislator to lay down in the law that, with diminished responsibility, the punishment must be reduced *proportionately* to the causal impact of the mental disorder on the offence.[23] Yet the legislator did not do this either. Nor has this idea been recognised in the case law; on the contrary, it has been explicitly rejected. Under the Dutch Supreme Court's consistent jurisprudence the principle 'no punishment without guilt' is an element of Dutch law, but *not* the principle 'no punishment more serious than required by guilt' (punishment in accordance with the measure of guilt). The degree of culpability is a factor – indeed, a very important factor – which courts consider when sentencing, but it is not the only one. The need to protect society against the danger posed by the defendant may, for instance, be a factor as well. The result is that the maximum punishment for an offence – for murder, life imprisonment – can also be imposed on a perpetrator who actually bears only diminished responsibility for the crime. This turns out to be the case in practice, too.[24]

---

22 Smidt (n. 18), 389.
23 G.A.M. Strijards, *Strafuitsluitingsgronden*, Zwolle 1987, 88.
24 See, for example, HR 4 December 2007, *NJ* 2008, 19.

Conclusion

This chapter dealt with the question of how Dutch criminal law deals with the phenomena of provocation and diminished responsibility. Dutch criminal law recognises neither provocation nor diminished responsibility as independent legal concepts, with the consequence that neither concept has been developed doctrinally. This situation – a conscious choice of the legislator – can be largely explained by general characteristics of the Dutch Criminal Code, such as practicality and faith in the professional judiciary, which excludes lay judges. These characteristics are also evident from the absence of specific minimum sentences and of definitions of many important concepts, leaving the development of criminal law doctrine in general to the courts. These characteristics and their elaborations can, of course, be criticised. They offer merely an explanation, not a justification for the Dutch position.

Chapter 20

Partial Defences Due to Loss of Control and Diminished Responsibility under Spanish Criminal Law

Manuel Cancio Meliá

Introduction

Spanish criminal law[1] is one of the criminal justice systems oriented towards the *principle of legality*. This implies that there is no customary definition of the various infringements, but these must be fixed in the text of the statutory law. The codification of criminal law in Spain dates from the early nineteenth century (the first Criminal Code[2] was passed in 1822) and has also evolved, as in other countries with the civil law model, so that there are two distinct parts of criminal law: on the one hand, the specific descriptions of the criminal offences; on the other, the general rules applicable to all offences. These general rules have been extracted especially from intentional result-based crimes and, within these, especially from the law of homicide and offences against the person,[3] because at the time of codification, negligence still played a subordinate role, and violations of law that involved the causation of a mere risk were virtually unknown and, where appropriate, were integrated into administrative law. These general rules of criminal responsibility present a separate field of study, called the 'General Part' of criminal law, also a separate part in the Penal Code: the first book (arts 10 to 137), dedicated to 'General provisions on crimes and faults, persons responsible, penalties, security measures and other consequences of the offence'. Rules on individual responsibility (*culpabilidad* or culpability) are also regulated in the General Part. However, although the general rules are subject to the principle of legality, and therefore also codified, their operation is very different, in comparison to the standard of interpretation of the various infractions under the Special Part containing the offences: the interpretation is much more flexible and based on axiomatic starting points, general principles that guide the application of these rules.

---

[1] An excellent summary in English can be found in Luis Chiesa and Carlos Gómez-Jara, 'Spanish Criminal Law', in Kevin Jon Heller and Markus Dirk Dubber (eds), *The Handbook of Comparative Criminal Law* (Stanford University Press 2009). Available at SSRN: <http://ssrn.com/abstract=1317689> (accessed 1 January 2011). See also the wider exposition made by Lorena Bachmaier and Antonio del Moral García, *Criminal Law in Spain* (Wolters Kluwer 2010) 59, 63, 72, 80ff.

[2] Código penal, Spanish Penal Code (hereinafter CP), last amended by Organic Law 5/2010 (entry into force: 23 December 2010).

[3] Therefore, a continental criminal law scholar can, in a manual of English criminal law, find the most important issues pertaining to the 'General Part' (for example, those relating to causation or intention) in the chapter on murder or manslaughter.

Spanish criminal law is heavily influenced by German legal theory.[4] The technique of resolution of cases and the principles that inform the Spanish criminal law have been determined since the 1920s and, especially after the end of the dictatorship of General Franco in 1975, by the importation of the German theoretical and constitutional doctrine. This influence is manifested in the existence of a general theory of crime under which the concept of crime is defined as (a) a human act which falls (b) under an offence description, and is (c) unlawful (which means that there are no causes of justification), (d) culpable and (e) punishable (including various reasons beyond the wrongful act and the offender's conditions that exclude punishment).

Among those dogmatic categories and fundamental principles stand two in particular: firstly, the definition of the harm principle by the so-called 'legal interests' concept which must underlie any criminal infringement (material element, wrongfulness) and, secondly, the so-called principle of culpability (or subjective guilt) as the basis for personal blameworthiness and individual responsibility, i.e. guilt, and the ensuing subjection to criminal liability (culpability).[5]

The *concept of culpability* generally accepted in doctrine and court rulings is not based on the existence of a particular mode of behaviour (intent or negligence[6]), but on the so-called *normative concept of culpability*, pursuant to which subjective guilt is based on legal blame directed in a particular form against the person who carried out the wrongful conduct. The vast majority of commentators take as a point of reference of that blame – regardless of the position to be adopted in each case on the question of free will – the assumption that the offender was able, firstly, to understand the wrongfulness of the act and, secondly, to act according to that understanding. Therefore, one commonly speaks of a mixed concept of culpability: the (normative) blame is based on a (factual) individual condition.

In the last decades, there are new theoretical approaches in Spain to the concept of culpability which base their understanding on social needs of general prevention rather than on an a priori concept of being able to act in another way (theory of positive general prevention, especially as developed by the German scholar Günther Jakobs[7]). They are gaining ground, as in Germany, in the theoretical discussion. But the truth is that the applicable provisions are still based on the common definition of culpability: the offender, understanding what the rules demand, could act according to that understanding. In other words, according to the dominant position, the assessment of culpability takes as a starting point (the reconstruction of) a factual situation, while according to the theory of positive general prevention (and the 'functional concept of culpability' emanating

---

4   See Markus Dirk Dubber, 'Theories of Crime and Punishment in German Criminal Law' (2005) 53 American Journal of Comparative Law 679.

5   Chiesa and Gómez-Jara (n. 1) 5; Bachmaier and del Moral García (n. 1) 80.

6   In fact, most authors feel today, according to the prevailing view in Germany, that these forms of conduct are not elements of culpability, but of the material element of the infringement (wrongfulness), the fact prohibited by law, taking into account that the conduct which the legislature prohibits is always defined either as intentional or negligent. Moreover, it is assumed that there can be no infringement that does not incorporate such subjective elements; a crime of strict liability would be considered unconstitutional, as it violates the principle of culpability. In any case, in this context, the consideration of whether a specific question belongs to the material definition of intent or negligence, as a subjective reality, or rather to evidential rules, changes the perspective on the continental ban on strict liability. See Manuel Cancio Meliá, 'Crisis del lado subjetivo del hecho?' (2005) 10 Derecho Penal Contemporáneo 43; Ramon Ragués i Vallès, *La ignorancia deliberada en Derecho penal* (Atelier 2007); Matthias Hörster, *Die strict liability des englischen Strafrechts. Zugleich eine Gegenüberstellung mit dem deutschen Straf- und Ordnungswidrigkeitenrecht* (Duncker and Humblot 2009).

7   See Manuel Cancio Meliá and Bernardo Feijoo Sánchez, 'Prevenir riesgos o confirmar normas? La teoría funcional de la pena de Günther Jakobs', in Günther Jakobs (ed.), *La pena estatal: significado y finalidad* (Civitas 2006) 15ff, with further references.

from it), this is actually a purely normative concept, in which biological-factual elements are a mere social reconstruction of the operating conditions of the system of imputation, i.e. a completely *normative* concept. This theoretical discussion on the definition of culpability does not affect the judicial practice in the field; rather the theoretical approaches try to explain what the practical operation of the legal system of imputation is.

The category of culpability, as a filter of analysis in a general theory of crime, starts from the common concept of culpability, with three elements:

- Firstly, *accountability* (*imputabilidad*),[8] sometimes called capacity of culpability, i.e. the set of psychic conditions that allow a person to motivate himself normally.[9] It is the basis for the personal blame of culpability.
- Secondly, the *(potential) conscience of wrongfulness*, i.e. the person's knowledge (or, in the context of negligence, the possibility of knowing) the demands underlying the criminal standard.
- Finally, *lack of extenuating circumstances* (*exigibilidad*):[10] the absence of an exceptional situation – like situations of necessity or duress which do not justify, but may excuse: cases such as Table of Carneades or the *Mignonette* case. While the law cannot justify these it can affirm the existence of a situation in which there are extenuating circumstances, and it therefore cannot be the basis of culpability (even if the behaviour is materially wrongful).

When considering the influence a special situation of motivation or emotional excitement can have on leading to a loss of control by the agent, we should note, firstly, the existence of *two levels of intensity* in which the category of culpability can be affected when there is no accountability and/ or there are extenuating circumstances, or when these elements exist only to a diminished degree: The culpability can be completely *excluded*, leaving the subject exempt of any responsibility (*exemption grounds*). Or the culpability can be *attenuated*, when the responsibility can also be reduced in two different ways: on the one hand, by stating a partial existence of grounds of complete exemption of responsibility (*incomplete exemption*); on the other, through the application of one of the general grounds of attenuation of responsibility (*mitigation grounds*).

Due to the regulatory design derived from the principle of legality (legal determination of the grounds of exemption), what could constitute a single partial defence or a single point of analysis in the common law model is fragmented in Spanish law into various locations within the structure of the theory of crime:

- Firstly, the situation of violent emotion may reach such intensity that it completely excludes culpability,[11] as a full exemption ground classified as a *temporary mental disorder* (art. 20.1

---

8 The leading monograph is Lucía Martínez Garay, *La imputabilidad penal. Concepto, fundamento, naturaleza jurídica y elementos* (Tirant lo Blanch 2005).

9 Defined as 'that state of normal mental capacity of the perpetrator of the offence that allows him or her to understand the wrongfulness of the conduct performed, and govern his or her behaviour according to that understanding' (Lucía Martínez Garay, 'Imputabilidad y causas de inimputabilidad', in Fernando Molina Fernández (ed.), *Memento penal 2011* (Lefebvre 2010) no 2195).

10 See María Martín Lorenzo, *La exculpación penal. Bases para una atribución legítima de responsabilidad penal* (Tirant lo Blanch 2009).

11 It should be noted that the CP in art. 20 merely speaks of exemption from 'criminal liability', without mentioning which systematic level is affected (justification or excuse). In some cases, their nature of defences of justification is obvious, such as self-defence (art. 20.4 CP) or the legitimate exercise of a right (art. 20.7

CP[12]), in a situation of *full intoxication* by ingestion of alcohol or other drugs (art. 20.2 CP[13]) or by being a case of *insurmountable fear* (art. 20.6 CP[14]).[15]
- Secondly, these three grounds of complete exemption of responsibility may arise – which is a peculiarity of the Spanish system – in a merely partial manner, as cases of *incomplete exemption*, reducing in a very significant manner the penalty by lowering the sentencing frame for the offence in the Special Part (arts 21.1[16] and 68 CP[17]).
- Thirdly, there might be a case of a general mitigation ground: 'serious addiction' to toxic substances (art. 21.2 CP[18]) or 'fury or blindness to reason' (art. 21.3 CP[19]). Furthermore, there could be a situation analogous to these causes of attenuation, but not identical to them (art. 21.7 CP[20]). These causes of attenuation lead either to the application of the lower half of the penalty for the offence or, if they appear as 'highly qualified', may even reduce the punishment below the minimum sentence (art. 66.1, first and second rules CP[21]).

CP), as it is also clear that the defence in art. 20.1 CP (mental disorder) contains a ground of excuse. However, in other cases it is left to the interpretation of the commentators and the courts to determine which systematic level is affected. Similarly, the general causes of mitigation or aggravation of responsibility (arts 21 and 22 CP) do not mention the systematic level – wrongfulness or culpability – on which they are based.

12   Art. 20 CP: 'A person is exempt from criminal liability: 1. who at the time of the commission of the offence, because of any mental defect or mental impairment, cannot understand the wrongfulness of the act or act on that understanding. Temporary mental disorder does not exempt from punishment if it has been caused by the person with the aim of committing the crime or if he expected or should have expected its commission.'

13   Art. 20 CP: 'A person is exempt from criminal liability: ... 2. who at the time of committing the criminal offence is in a state of full intoxication through the consumption of alcohol, toxic drugs, narcotics, psychotropic or other substances with similar effect, provided he has not sought [this state] for the purpose of committing the offence or expected or should have expected its commission, or who is under the influence of withdrawal syndrome, because of his addiction to such substances, which prevents him from understanding the unlawfulness of the act or to act on that understanding.'

14   Art. 20 CP: 'A person is exempt from criminal liability: ... 6. who acts out of insurmountable fear.'

15   We leave out of consideration the state of necessity in art. 20.5 CP, which, according to the majority view (called, much as in Germany, the theory of differentiation), contains both a justification (for cases in which there is great disparity between the good saved and the good sacrificed) and an excuse (exemption for lack of enforceability in cases in which the saved goods belong to the agent or to persons near to him), since in any case, even in the latter situation, there exists a situation of need, rather than its impact on the ability to control/culpability of the agent.

16   Art. 21 CP: 'Mitigating circumstances shall be: 1. the grounds described in the previous chapter, when they do not concur with all elements necessary to exempt from responsibility in their respective provisions.'

17   Art. 68 CP: 'In the cases provided by the first alternative of art. 21, the court shall impose a penalty lower by one or two degrees than the one prescribed by law, depending on the number and extent of missing requirements, and to the personal circumstances of the offender, notwithstanding article 66 of this Code.'

18   Art. 21 CP: '... 2. if the offender acted because of his serious addiction to the substances mentioned in no 2 of the previous article'.

19   Art. 21 CP: '... 3. Acting on causes or stimuli so powerful that they produce fury, blind rage or another passionate state of similar importance'.

20   Art. 21 CP: '... 7. any other circumstance of importance comparable to the ones set out above'.

21   Art. 66 CP: '1. In sentencing intentional crimes, the court or tribunal shall observe, depending on whether or not mitigating or aggravating circumstances concur, the following rules:

Unlike other continental systems, as, for example, in German criminal law,[22] Spanish law does not have a specific provision in the Special Part in cases in which a state of emotional excitement leads to a crime of homicide. Consequently, the peculiarities that characterise these cases are treated within the general framework outlined above, as conditions of the exemption or reduction of liability in doctrine and case law. In particular, rules have been established in the case law for the appreciation of the specific elements of murder (aggravating circumstances established in the Special Part, in particular, art. 139 CP[23]), which in Spanish criminal law, as in other continental systems, is defined as an aggravated alternative of intentional homicide by three alternative circumstances (treachery, damage, cruelty), and reaches the peak of the Spanish punitive system by allowing the imposition of imprisonment for up to 25 years if two of the circumstances that make the homicide a murder concur.[24]

It should now be clear how to approach the treatment which Spanish criminal law gives the cases of decrease in liability for loss of control situations or diminished culpability (partial defence): firstly and very briefly, we shall treat the cases of complete defences, including also the characteristics of those same defences when they are incomplete. Secondly, we shall explain the mitigating circumstances which are relevant and the focus of cases of partial responsibility for intense emotion. Based on this, the characteristics of the combination required to decrease responsibility, which have been established primarily through case law, will be addressed. The chapter ends with some general conclusions about the characteristics of the Spanish system with regard to violent emotion and partial responsibility and its relationship with the general understanding of culpability.

Complete and Incomplete Exemptions

As was indicated, Spanish law starts (art. 20.1 CP) from the paradigm of the offender's ability to act according to the law. This starting point has constitutional rank and is the main element of the principle of culpability.

The analysis for the cases on which we are going to focus – cases of diminished responsibility – is to be referred to the rules for complete exemption, where there is a total disability of the person to behave in another way, i.e. to act according to the law. The three exemptions relevant here are temporary mental disorder (art. 20.1 CP), full intoxication and withdrawal symptoms (art. 20.2 CP)

---

1. When only one mitigating circumstance exists, the penalty will be applied in the lower half of the penalty established by law for the offence.

2. When two or more mitigating circumstances concur, or one or more highly qualified mitigating circumstances, and no aggravating circumstances, they shall apply the penalty lower by one or two degrees than that required by law, taking into account the number and extent of such mitigating circumstances.'

22 Namely, § 213 Strafgesetzbuch. See Bernd Müssig, *Mord und Totschlag. Vorüberlegungen zu einem Differenzierungsansatz im Bereich des Tötungsunrechts* (Carl Heymanns Verlag 2005) 315 with further references.

23 Art. 139 CP: 'A penalty of imprisonment of fifteen to twenty years is to be suffered by a murderer who kills another under any of the following circumstances:

(1) with treachery;
(2) for payment, reward or promise;
(3) with cruelty, deliberately and inhumanly increasing the pain of the victim.'

24 Art. 140 CP.

and insurmountable fear (art. 20.6 CP). There is a common view related to the first two exemptions, considering them to contain a reduction in the accountability. The exemption of insurmountable fear is hardly ever used in practice and does not clearly have any systematic standing, although it is understood by the majority of the doctrine and the case law as a cause of exemption which excludes the third element of culpability, i.e. there are extenuating circumstances.

Using any of these exemptions as complete ones excludes any criminal responsibility, and the incomplete exemption reduces it, as it has been pointed out. Nevertheless, a measure of rehabilitation and incapacitation, i.e. a sanction geared towards the danger presented by the offender to the public rather than a penalty for his past misconduct, can be imposed if the offender is held to be not responsible, either completely or partially.

Unaccountability Due to Temporary Mental Disorder (Article 20.1 CP)

Apart from those situations of 'mental disorder' in where a permanent condition exists, art. 20.1 CP includes situations called 'temporary mental disorder'. This cause of exoneration, introduced for the first time in 1932, is a temporary state of exactly the same intensity as the permanent 'mental abnormalities or disturbances' which exclude culpability. It is a part of what it is called a *mixed system* which defines the accountability: on the one hand, there are the biological-individual factors, and on the other hand, their psychological effects. The case law views the requirement of a sudden situation as a necessary criterion to trigger the exemption, affecting the intellectual and/or voluntary capacities of the person to the point of extinguishing them, for a short duration and absent an *actio libera in causa*, that is, the individual did not create in a culpable manner the situation in which she loses control.[25]

The most important cases are:

- delirium or psychotic disorders, understood as states of disturbance due to different causes: cranial traumas, cerebral strokes, intense metabolic disorders or due to any illness, and
- cases of very deep emotional disturbances, i.e. a state of passion. According to the Spanish Supreme Court (Tribunal Supremo – TS), it must be an abnormal reaction, so overwhelming for the individual's mind that it deprives him of all capacity to reason, eliminating his capacity to make decisions and his free will, always created by an external factor, regardless of its source. The consciousness must be extinguished completely, prohibiting the individual from knowing how unlawful his conduct is, dispossessing him of the free will which should prevail in any responsible human conduct.[26]

Exemption is considered incomplete (art. 21.1 CP) or as merely mitigating ground (art. 21.7 CP), if the intensity of the situation does not completely extinguish the accountability of the individual. So, for example, recently an incomplete exemption was considered to exist in a case in which a mother with a mixed adaptive disturbance, due to the fact that her under-age daughter had been raped, set fire to the rapist after sprinkling him with gasoline when she encountered him by

---

25 See Lucía Martínez Garay and Eliseu Frígols Brines, 'Anomalía o alteración psíquica y transtorno mental transitorio', in Fernando Molina Fernández (ed.), *Memento penal 2011* (Lefebvre 2010) no 2334ff.

26 STS (Spanish Supreme Court ruling, *Sentencia del Tribunal Supremo*) of 6 July 2001 (Second (Criminal) Chamber) (there is currently no official collection for courts' rulings – with the exception of the Constitutional Court which publishes its own rulings; therefore it is necessary to rely on commercial databases. The most common collection might be that of Westlaw/Aranzadi. As there are few rulings for every chamber and day, rulings are usually classified by the legal concept used).

surprise, and so killing him;[27] and an analogous mitigating ground was applied to a young mother who was a foreign citizen from Latin America, and who left her newborn baby[28] to die because of the emotional stress she felt and the fear of losing her job and being expelled from Spain.[29]

Total Intoxication and Withdrawal Symptoms (Article 20.2 CP)

The adjective 'total' refers to the effect produced on the individual: his accountability is completely excluded. Since the coming into force of the 1995 CP, other substances are expressly mentioned beside the most common legal drug, alcohol. The decisive element of the consumption is not its legal or illegal nature (for example, also entirely legal medicine may be considered) but its effects. The origin of the intoxication is the consumption, no matter how, of a toxin which produces the effect of extinguishing the capacity to understand the unlawfulness of his act or to act in accordance with that understanding.

According to the TS, the exemption is regulated in the current Penal Code in a so-called mixed system, which has a twofold requirement when a criminal offence is committed: firstly, a pathological-biological cause consisting of either a state of intoxication ... or withdrawal symptoms; and secondly, the psychological effect, due to any pathological-biological cause, of the lack of capacity of the individual to understand the unlawfulness of the act, the ability to act according to that understanding (complete exemption) or that this capacity is substantially reduced or otherwise affected (incomplete exemption).[30] The variety of individual cases, depending on the toxic substance in particular, its dose, its mixture with other elements, as well as the personal characteristics of each consumer, obviously make it extremely difficult to formulate general principles.

In the case law we find the following main points:[31] it is not necessary for a complete exemption that all the mental capacities of the individual to be 'completely extinguished',[32] in spite of the courts occasionally using this term. Complete exemption is not commonly accepted and is more likely when there is a mixture of different substances. It is much more common to consider the exemption as incomplete or to affirm a mitigating circumstance.

Apart from the cases of intoxication, in order to establish the exemption due to the existence of withdrawal symptoms, the courts usually ask for an occurrence of a situation in which the individual is subject to impulses beyond his control due to the withdrawal.[33] Cases of withdrawal symptoms are not usually considered as an incomplete or complete exemption by the courts; the majority of cases are placed in the specific mitigation ground under art. 21.2 CP.

---

27 STS of 2 June 2010.
28 In the new Criminal Code of 1995, there is no mitigation for the crime of infanticide because of the need 'to hide the shame of the mother', as it had traditionally been in previous legislation, oriented on patriarchal-Catholic morality (art. 410 CP revised 1973).
29 Ruling of the Audiencia Provincial (Superior Court) of Madrid, Section 1, of 13 November 2002.
30 STS 22 January 1999; see also STS 20 October 2002; 22 March 2002; 27 March 2000.
31 See Martínez Garay (n. 9), nos 2355ff.
32 This situation of 'lethargic inebriation' can in the continental systems negate an element conceptually prior to wrongfulness and culpability, namely the existence of a 'human act'.
33 See Martínez Garay (n. 9), nos 2363ff.

Insurmountable Fear (Article 20.6 CP)

A reader trained in the common law may be especially interested in the exemption ground – close to duress – of 'insurmountable fear'. Nevertheless, judicial practice in this context will probably lead to disappointment: this exemption ground,[34] with a very ancient tradition in Spanish criminal law, its origins rooted in the Middle Ages, has no more than a symbolic presence in the practice of Spanish criminal law – with exceptions in some cases, that are very limited, and which are judged by a jury. There is widespread confusion about the systematic foundation for this case of liability exemption. It seems that the majority of commentators and a few courts start from the concept of extenuating circumstances. The problem is that it seems impossible to distinguish its ambit from those of other exemptions such as excessive self-defence, necessity or temporary mental disorder.[35]

Mitigation Grounds

The mitigation grounds provided by statutory law (*circunstancias*) are part of a sentencing system that is closely linked to the legalistic tradition introduced by the French Revolution and its distrust in the court's discretion as a source of unequal application of the law not supported by democratic legitimacy which resides only in the legislator.

The general catalogue of mitigating and aggravating circumstances provided in art. 21 CP is a sentencing instrument complementing the specific regulation of the different offences in the Special Part; that is why art. 67 CP specifies what it is called the 'principle of inherence', namely that general causes of mitigation or aggravation are not to be applied if their content has already been taken into account by the law when describing the offence, sometimes also called the ban on 'double counting'.

The mitigating or aggravating circumstances are elements which are related to the nucleus of the offence but do not belong to its definitional elements, yet they acquire relevance in the determination of the concrete penalty; consequently it has become a common view that they should be proved in the same manner as the elements of the criminal offence itself.[36] There are different approaches to the material foundation of the concept: the most far-reaching point of view affirms that it is a quantitative matter, i.e. that these are cases in which the two basic elements of crimes, wrongfulness and culpability, are increased or reduced.[37]

As was indicated, the problem of loss of control is treated in two specific mitigation grounds: serious addiction to toxic substances under art. 20.2 CP and fury or blindness to reason or another similar state of passion under art. 20.3 CP.

Serious Addiction (Article 21.2 CP)

As with the cases of complete or incomplete exemptions, the emphasis here lies on the effect of the substance on the offender, and not on its origin. Since 1995 the mitigation ground includes all kinds of substances.

---

34 See the leading monograph by Daniel Varona Gómez, *El miedo insuperable: una reconstrucción de la eximente desde una teoría de la justicia* (Comares 2000); Martín Lorenzo (n. 10), 460ff.

35 See Fernando Molina Fernández in *Memento* (n. 9), nos 2595ff, 2598, 2605ff.

36 See STS 19 September 2007.

37 See Muñoz Conde and García Arán, *Derecho penal. Parte General* (8th edn, Tirant lo Blanch 2010) 477–8.

Nevertheless, it should be borne in mind that unlike in the field of exemption, this mitigating factor does not refer to the effects of intoxication or of withdrawal symptoms, but to the addiction itself, as a state in which the individual is 'trapped'.[38] The addiction has to be serious, which the courts interpret as a deep and long-term dependence, a circumstance which must be proved.[39] The mitigation ground concurs, according to the general comprehension, in two ways: on the one hand, the situation of dependence may *directly* affect the accountability of the person, thereby reducing it. On the other hand, it may have a *functional* effect, that is, the addiction as a permanent state bears on the motivation of the person while making a decision to commit the offence, as is clear in the context of property offences mostly, to obtain a substance on which she depends. Consequently, it is far more difficult to affirm this mitigating ground in relation to offences committed to obtain alcohol,[40] a legal substance, which is easily accessed and mostly inexpensive. This focus on the consequences of the dependency on the motivation to commit an offence allows – through the analogous mitigating circumstance in art. 21.7 CP – the consideration also of cases of addiction that do not derive from substance abuse, such as, for example, in the case of compulsive gambling.[41]

To sum up, it is not enough according to the prevailing judicial practice to be a drug addict; the condition must affect the culpability.[42] Beyond these general lines, it has to be stated that judicial practice is limited to a casuistic approach, and therefore generates a very unpredictable ambit for this mitigation ground.[43]

Violent Emotion (Article 21.3 CP)

This mitigation ground, directly related to cases of violent emotion, mentions fury (*arrebato*), blindness to reason (*obcecación*), and a catch-all clause which includes any violent emotion ('state of passion') of the same importance. There is a general consensus which views this mitigation ground as a clear case of reduction of accountability.[44] The differences between this ground and temporary mental disorder are only quantitative aspects; this mitigating ground is placed between the cases of complete exemption and the typical state of excitement during the commission of serious violent crimes and does not affect culpability.

Starting from the ancient distinction between emotions and passions, fury is defined as a *sudden* emotion, as a momentary loss of self-control, whereas blindness to reason means a *lasting* state which affects the person.[45] The clause of 'other state of passion' has to be considered in connection with these two elements.

As the TS held in a ruling which represents its common position and in which it refused the application of this mitigation ground:

> [it is] obviously not meant to privilege angry reactions, [and] operates based on the importance of certain stimulations for persons with certain character traits ... causing an evident temporary reduction of their ability to appreciate that they are acting wrongly. This mitigating ground has, therefore, as its upper limit the temporary mental disorder and at its lower end the emotional state

---

38 See Martínez Garay (n. 9), no 4062.
39 See, amongst others, STS 27 January 2009.
40 See STS 27 April 2000.
41 See STS 9 May 2003; 12 November 2002.
42 Amongst many others, STS 8 July 2009; 16 February 2007; 30 October 2002.
43 Martínez Garay (n. 9), nos 4067ff.
44 Santiago Mir Puig, *Derecho penal. Parte General* (8th edn, Reppertor 2008) no 25/27.
45 Martínez Garay (n. 9), no 4102.

that typically accompanies so-called crimes of blood ... it is quite clear that in a situation of violent reaction against the deception produced by the unfolding of events, in which the accused has been seen the drug stolen from him, the heat that such an event will create leads to an absolutely passionate, stressful situation, to obfuscation and even to a certain lack of mental control. But it must have had a sufficient passionate intensity to break the inhibitory mechanisms; so that the person is immersed in an emotional situation that the law calls "fury" or "blindness to reason".[46]

The specific elements in the interpretation of this mitigation ground are the following: first, the fury or blindness to reason must have been caused by a serious stimulus unrelated to the person. Typically, these causal factors come from the victim, as the courts continue to underline, echoing the historical regulation before 1995, which contained two mitigation grounds, replaced by the current art. 20.3 CP, which referred exclusively to reactive cases,[47] and therefore, according to case law, the affirmation of the attenuation is not possible when it comes to a mutually instigated brawl.[48] The basis of the emotion is described as a situation of anger or rage that affects the intellect or the will of the individual. There must be a causal relationship between the stimulus, the state of passion and the commission of the offence. There must be a relevant connection in time between stimulus and response:[49] for example, this connection will not exist if the person goes home to find a weapon with which to commit the crime.[50] Finally, the situation of emotional excitement should not violate the ethical rules governing the rules of cohabitation in society. In this way, in cases of so-called 'gender violence' (male violence against women) which have achieved great social impact and attention from the mass media,[51] fury is not recognised as a mitigating circumstance regardless of the specific intensity of excitement of the aggressor, precisely because of the intense social stigma attributed to anger in the context of the domination of men over women.[52]

These general points show an image of a considerable legal uncertainty,[53] in which it is not at all clear what role corresponds to the internal state of the person, as becomes evident at the problem of persons of a particularly irascible character. In this manner, it is affirmed that this mitigating ground is bound not 'to privilege angry reactions'[54] and it is very unclear – as is the case for the complete exemption in art. 20.1 CP, which refers to permanent mental disorders – which role, for instance, psychopathy[55] may have under this mitigation ground.[56]

---

46 STS 4 November 2002.
47 The previous art. 9.5 CP (revised 1973), which included that the offence was 'immediately preceded by adequate provocation or threat by the victim' and art. 9.6 CP (1973), 'having performed the act in vindication of a grave offence close in time'.
48 STS 22 January 2010.
49 STS 19 January 2006.
50 STS 23 February 2010.
51 In addition to several amendments both in the policing context (specific police units) and procedural law (special courts and injunctions restraining and forbidding any contact), new provisions were created which establish new penalties (adding a prohibition on the offender's communicating with the victim) and which also modify a number of offences, creating specific crimes and aggravating other pre-existing offences when committed by men against women in a relationship/gender abuse context.
52 STS 27 April 2010.
53 Martínez Garay (n. 9), no 4104.
54 STS 18 April 2001.
55 See the recent ruling STS 16 April 2010.
56 Although it must be borne in mind that the term 'psychopathy' is used in Spanish case law in a way inconsistent with the essential elements of the latest advances in its treatment in psychology and neuroscience,

Some Conclusions

A first impression that a common-law trained reader may have is this: the answer to the simple question posed (how does the Spanish criminal law react to situations of violent emotion, for the purpose of total or partial excuse?) is a systematic nonsense of institutions, categories and differing opinions that confirms Anglo-Saxon prejudice that the civil law obsession with the principle of legality does not generate the superior level of legal security of which their protagonists say they are so proud. The lack of predictability of the criminal law at this point is much higher than usual in the institutions of the General Part. This is especially astonishing taking into account that the phenomenon of loss of control has always been known and processed through legal forms of long tradition.

To explain this particularly high level of imprecision of the system two hypotheses may be adduced: firstly, it seems clear that a possible part of the explanation lies in the fast progress of scientific-biological knowledge regarding mental processes that we describe as violent emotion. As the intense and profound discussion within the field of criminal law generated by recent advances in neuroscience shows,[57] the increase of knowledge about the human mind generates multiple uncertainties in legal discourse, and what for centuries remained stable in terms of legal analysis, must now be under revision. Secondly, from the point of view assumed here, there are also theoretical problems within the legal system that contribute to the insecurity just described: it seems that the paradigm that is at the heart of the concept of culpability – the idea that the offender is able to act in another way, which is understood on many occasions as merely factual – does not explain adequately the reality in this field. On the contrary, there are many *normative* filters that overlap the individual-factual reality which is intended to be the basis of exemption and mitigation grounds. To use an extreme example: the disappearance during the national-Catholic dictatorship in 1963 of the (asymmetric) mitigation ground for the man whose honour was insulted by his wife who committed adultery does not indicate that the emotional excitement that this situation may generate has changed significantly, but shows that what has changed is the patriarchal social structure that assigned the wife to the property of the male, and therefore also the normative superstructure which justifies the man who *defends* with violence what *belongs* to him. This overlapping of normative structures with the factual-biological elements shows that progress towards a clearer definition of the involved culpability categories implies taking into account the normative character of the concept of culpability, which means moving towards a *functional* concept of culpability.

In any case, it can be noted that Spanish criminal law knows a wide range of options to mitigate or exclude culpability of someone who is in a situation of loss of control due to an intense emotion. The necessary future clarification of the legal institutions involved may certainly benefit from the efforts now being made in England and Wales and from the contributions to this collection from other countries. The mutual knowledge of an essential element of every legal system such as the criminal law is a prerequisite to building a common Europe governed by the *Estado de Derecho*, the rule of law.

---

and should be seen more as a reference to sociopathy. See, on this issue, from a modern point of view, Stephen Morse, 'Psychopathy and Criminal Responsibility' (2008) 1 Neuroethics 205.

57 See Grischa Merkel and Gerhard Roth, 'Bestrafung oder Therapie? Möglichkeiten und Grenzen staatlicher Sanktion unter Berücksichtigung der Hirnforschung', in Rechtswissenschaftliche Fakultät der Universität Zürich (ed.) *Hirnforschung – Chancen und Risiken für das Recht* (Schulthess 2008) 21, with further references.

Chapter 21
Between Lack of Responsibility and Dangerousness: Determinism and the Specificity of the French Criminal Law on Lack of Intellectual Insight and Loss of Control

Caroline Fournet

Introduction

Similarly to the great majority of domestic criminal law systems, French criminal law – as embodied in the Code Pénal – recognises a series of specific grounds for modifying, by way of mitigation or aggravation, and sometimes altogether excluding, individual criminal responsibility. Rather predictably, the causes for modifying or excluding individual criminal responsibility under French criminal law may be either objective or subjective. While objective causes relate to the offence itself and act as a retroactive eraser of the offence, an *ex post facto* neutraliser of the prohibited character of the act(s) perpetrated, subjective causes are in contrast directly linked to the personality of the offender. They may cover such cases as coercion, duress, *force majeure* as well as psychological and/or neuropsychological disorders entailing lack of intellectual insight and/or loss of control. Where French criminal law seems to stand out from other domestic systems, however, is precisely in its specific understanding of this last category of potential grounds for modifying or excluding individual criminal responsibility.

The French legislation on psychological and/or neuropsychological disorders entailing lack of intellectual insight and/or loss of control as grounds for modifying or excluding individual responsibility in criminal matters has evolved and a close look at the legal developments rapidly reveals the politicisation of the debates and considerations. On the one hand, the detractors of such grounds for mitigating or excluding criminal responsibility rely on the utmost seriousness of the acts prohibited under criminal law to reject any suggestion that a mental disorder could ever diminish, let alone exclude, the responsibility of the authors of such acts. In their views, such a diminution or exclusion would not only render the law far too lenient, it would also make a mockery of justice by allowing for far too easy a way out for criminals and by ultimately insulting all the individuals who suffer from such conditions but who would never engage in any form of criminal conduct. On the other hand, the proponents of the grounds for mitigating or excluding criminal responsibility argue that in a democratic system based on the rule of law, the legislation and its application must remain fair and there can only be responsibility where there are responsible individuals.[1] As Mayaud puts

---

1 See, for example, debates in the Sénat in 'Proposition de loi relative à l'atténuation de responsabilité pénale applicable aux personnes atteintes d'un trouble mental ayant altéré leur discernement au moment des faits', Examen en commission, Sénat, 26 January 2011. <http://www.senat.fr.> (accessed 10 February 2011).

it, 'criminal law is a reaction to human behaviour, and *there can only be punishment where there is responsibility*'.[2]

Not only have these confrontational perspectives to a certain extent flawed the legislative discussion with political – and possibly electoral – considerations,[3] but the inherently medical and psychiatric aspects of the notions of psychological and neuropsychological disorders seem to have further plagued their legal characterisation by generating a certain degree of confusion and misunderstanding. With this in mind, it is unsurprising therefore that the legal acknowledgement and judicial recognition of psychological and/or neuropsychological disorders entailing lack of intellectual insight and/or loss of control as grounds for modifying or excluding individual criminal responsibility under French criminal law have generated serious controversies and legal debates, prompting the legislator and the judiciary to act, react and interact in a manner which appears to be very specific to the French domestic legal system.

The Legislative Evolution:
From Dementia to Psychological and Neuropsychological Disorders

Interestingly, the criminal lack of responsibility of the individual suffering from a mental condition impairing intellectual insight and/or control is far from a new principle under French criminal law. Already at the end of the eighteenth century, the criminal lack of responsibility of the 'person of unsound mind' (*'insensé'*) had been recognised and subsequently codified in article 64 of the 1810 Code Pénal, which referred to 'dementia' ('état de démence') as a ground for altogether excluding criminal responsibility. Subsequently, reacting to the developments in psychiatry and the medical findings on a possible gradation of mental diseases, both the Law of 25 June 1824 followed by the Law of 28 April 1932 gave the judge the possibility of taking into account the mental condition of the perpetrator of an offence so as to *mitigate* punishment. Adopting a new terminology, the Nouveau Code Pénal, which entered into force in 1994, now refers to 'psychological or neuropsychological disorder'(*'trouble psychique ou neuropsychique'*) in its article 122-1:

> A person is not criminally liable who, when the act was committed, was suffering from a psychological or neuropsychological disorder which destroyed his intellectual insight or his ability to control his actions.
>
> A person who, at the time he acted, was suffering from a psychological or neuropsychological disorder which reduced his intellectual insight or impeded his ability to control his actions, remains punishable; however, the court shall take this into account when it decides the penalty and determines its regime.[4]

---

2   Yves Mayaud, *Droit pénal général* (3rd edn, Presses Universitaires de France, 2010) 469. Translation by the author, the original version reads :'Le droit pénal est une réaction à des conduites humaines, et *il n'est de désordre punissable que sous couvert de personnes imputables*' (emphasis added).

3   See, for instance, 'Proposition de loi relative à l'atténuation de responsabilité pénale applicable aux personnes atteintes d'un trouble mental ayant altéré leur discernement au moment des faits', Examen en commission, Sénat, 26 January 2011 <http://www.senat.fr.> (accessed 10 February 2011).

4   Article 122-1 of the Code Pénal. Official translation <http://www.legifrance.gouv.fr> accessed 1 April 2011. For clarity purposes, this translation has been slightly altered and the term 'discernment' used in the original has been replaced with 'intellectual insight'.

Through its use of a broader – yet scientifically more precise and accurate – terminology covering a wider array of possible mental disorders rather than exclusively dementia, in itself a particular medical condition, article 122-1 has seemingly extended the scope of grounds for modifying or excluding individual criminal responsibility. This disposition however remains rather ambiguous. As noted by Rousseau, the question arises as to whether criminal responsibility – or lack of – here relates to the cause, namely the psychological and/or neuropsychological disorder, or to the consequences, namely the destruction of intellectual insight and/or the loss of control.[5]

An analysis of the evolution of the law and case law would seem to indicate that criminal responsibility here attaches to the lack of intellectual insight and/or control rather than to the psychological and/or neuropsychological disorder – an admittedly reasonable approach in so far as it does avoid, at least to a certain extent, a *judicial* appreciation of a *medical* condition which would not only be misplaced but which would also carry the risk of serious error.

In this respect, academic scholars tend to view article 122-1 as covering a very wide range of psychological and neuropsychological disorders, the trigger for its application being not the disorder itself but the alteration of intellectual insight and/or loss of control.[6] In other words, what matters in terms of individual criminal responsibility is not the disorder itself or its medical qualification but the alteration of intellectual insight and/or loss of control generated by the disorder. According to doctrine, these disorders include severe psychiatric conditions as well as a variety of other psychological states such as sleepwalking, epilepsy, hypnosis, amnesia or drunkenness.[7] This theoretically wide understanding of the law seems to be in line with its judicial interpretation: even when applying article 64 of the Code Pénal, the Cour de cassation[8] has been able to interpret dementia – a restrictive medical condition – as including epilepsy.[9]

Further confirming the proposition that criminal responsibility here attaches to the lack of intellectual insight and/or control rather than to the psychological and/or neuropsychological disorder are the role, powers and attitude of the judiciary. And indeed, the judge may only assess and qualify the psychological or neuropsychological disorder by reference to its impact and consequences on mental capacity and ability. In other words, under French criminal law, there exist no psychological or neuropsychological disorders which are by and of themselves generators of lack of responsibility, no mental condition which is inherently a factor of non-responsibility.[10] Regardless of the scientific qualification, medical categorisation and psychiatric characterisation

---

5   François Rousseau, *L'imputation dans la responsabilité pénale* (Dalloz, Paris 2009) 45.

6   See, for example, Bernard Bouloc, *Droit pénal général* (20th edition, Dalloz, Paris 2007) 364.365; Jean Pradel, *Droit pénal général* (16th edition, Cujas, Paris 2006) 477; Jacques-Henri Robert, *Droit pénal général* (6th edition, Presses Universitaires de France, Paris 2005) 290.

7   Ibid. These disorders, to be taken into account as grounds for impacting or excluding criminal responsibility under article 122-1, must, however, be attached to the person of the defendant: French criminal law does not recognise any theory of 'provocation' as entailing total loss of control in response to another person's provocative attitude and behaviour. Total loss of control may thus not be invoked in cases of domestic violence and rapes, for example. French criminal law, nonetheless, includes self-defence as a valid ground for mitigating or excluding individual criminal responsibility and article 122-1 could also probably be invoked if an aggression had generated a psychological and/or neuropsychological disorder entailing loss of intellectual insight and/or loss of control. Yet, this seems theoretical and purely hypothetical in so far as self-defence is already covered by articles 122-5 and 122-6 of the Code Pénal.

8   The Cour de cassation is the highest court in the French judiciary. It is not a court of a third instance: it only reviews the application of the law and does not rule on the merits.

9   Cour de cassation, chambre criminelle (Cass. Crim.), 14 December 1982, *Gazette du Palais* 1983, 1, 178.

10 Mayaud (n. 2) 478.

of the mental disorder, the judge must only use established certainties exclusively linked to the offence and the personality of its author. There are no presumptions of lack of responsibility.[11] Despite the fact that medical expertise is to be taken into account by the court and undoubtedly plays a crucial role in the determination of the mental disorder entailing the lack of intellectual insight and/or loss of control, it never replaces the judicial appreciation of the impact of the disorder on mental capacity. In this context therefore, the judge will not restrict his appreciation to the medical certificates and psychological or psychiatric assessments. He will take into account all the circumstances of the case so as to decide whether or not the impairment of mental capacity is established in a particular instance and whether it generated a total destruction or merely an alteration of intellectual insight and/or control. As unequivocally held by the Cour de cassation, under French criminal law, the judge remains sovereign in his appreciation of the psychological state of a defendant.[12]

The Judicial Evolution: From Enhanced Powers to an Increasing Severity

Whether in cases of declared total lack of responsibility (paragraph 1 of article 122-1) or in cases where the intellectual insight and/or ability to control oneself were only altered (paragraph 2 of article 122-1), the French legislation on the matter has evolved, thereby paving the way for increased judicial activism and arguably reinforced severity on the matter.

From Declaring Lack of Responsibility to Assessing Dangerousness

The first paragraph of article 122-1 is labelled in clear and unequivocal terms: if the perpetrator of the offence was, at the time when the offence was committed, suffering from a psychological and/or neuropsychological disorder which destroyed his intellectual insight and/or his ability to control his actions, he will be considered not responsible for his actions under French criminal law.

Once the destruction of intellectual insight and/or the total loss of control have been recognised therefore, there seemingly remains very little leeway for further judicial action and the role of the judge admittedly becomes less significant. The perpetrator of the offence will be considered not criminally responsible and the ruling will automatically be a declaration of lack of responsibility.

Yet, since the Law of 25 February 2008, the powers of the judge on the matter have dramatically increased.[13] With this legislative change, the judge has been empowered not only to declare the lack of responsibility of the perpetrator but also to order his institutionalisation in a specialised medical environment (*rétention de sûreté*). This 'protective custody' in a socio-medico-legal centre must be justified and must follow the conclusions of a psychiatric expertise according to which the mental condition of the individual constitutes a *potential danger* to his own safety as well as to public safety and indeed requires specific care.[14] This resort to the concept of dangerousness (*dangerosité*), has been heavily criticised because it relates to the potential criminality of acts which have yet to be committed rather than to acts which have already been perpetrated and which do constitute criminal offences. Furthermore, it is precisely this concept of dangerousness which may be invoked by the judge as a justification to indefinitely renew the protective custody, thereby

---

11   Ibid.
12   See Cass. Crim., 8 June 1955, *Bulletin criminel* (*Bull. crim.*) n° 286.
13   See loi n° 2008-174 of 25 February 2008, 'loi relative à la rétention de sûreté et à la déclaration d'irresponsabilité pénale pour cause de trouble mental', Journal Officiel, 26 February 2008, 3266.
14   See article 706-135 of the Code de Procédure Pénale. On this point, see generally Mayaud (n. 2) 477.

indirectly condemning the individual to a form of life imprisonment. If this aspect of the legislation is undoubtedly questionable,[15] it must, however, be noted that protective custody may only apply to murder, torture or barbaric acts, rape, abduction and illegal detention perpetrated against minors or with aggravating circumstances,[16] or – in other words – to some of the most serious crimes under French criminal law.

Notwithstanding this judicial placement in a hospitalised environment, the judge may also order further preventive measures (*mesures de sûreté*) so as to ensure that no further criminal acts will be perpetrated.[17] Among these measures are the prohibition from approaching the victims or other individuals, the prohibition from entering specifically designated areas, the prohibition from keeping a weapon, and the prohibition from certain professional activities as well as the suspension or annulment of the driving licence.

If the French legislation does therefore recognise lack of intellectual insight and/or loss of control as grounds for excluding individual criminal responsibility, this does not, however, mean that the victims of the offence are completely neglected and left out of the proceedings. In an attempt to ensure the fairness of the proceedings while taking into account the sufferings of the victims, the latter remain – under the French category of *parties civiles* – associated with the judicial debate on the issuing of a declaration of lack of responsibility.[18] Furthermore, and even if this might seem a meagre consolation, the declaration of lack of responsibility does not erase or neutralise the unlawfulness of the acts perpetrated and must still be accompanied by a judicial description of the facts. Not only does this allow for civil proceedings to take place, it also constitutes a judicial acknowledgement of the seriousness of the acts perpetrated against the victims and of the losses they have unduly incurred.

From Mitigating Circumstances to Aggravating Factors

The second paragraph of article 122-1 arguably leaves more scope for judicial interpretation and action as, if the principle here remains that of individual criminal responsibility, the judge may nonetheless moderate its effect in terms of the penalty and sentencing regime. This disposition is arguably less controversial than the previous one: it appears to be legally coherent to consider that the mere alteration of intellectual insight and/or impairment of control do not erase individual criminal responsibility as they may remain consistent with a conscious or controlled action. As for the cases when the psychological and/or neuropsychological disorder reduce or impede – rather than destroy as in the first paragraph – one's intellectual insight and/or ability to control one's actions, paragraph 2 of article 122-1 rejects the exclusion of individual criminal responsibility but recognises that it may be considered as a factor which impacts on sentencing. The wording of this disposition is interesting as it does not refer to mitigating or aggravating circumstances but merely to the fact that 'the court shall take this [the reduced intellectual insight and/or impaired control] into account when it decides the penalty and determines its regime'.[19] Unlike the above-mentioned laws of 25 June 1824 and 28 April 1932, which gave the judge the power to take into account the mental condition of the perpetrator of an offence so as to *mitigate* punishment,[20] article

---

15 See infra on the '*rétention de sûreté*'.
16 Article 706-53-13 of the Code de Procédure Pénale.
17 Note that the Conseil constitutionnel acknowledged the constitutionality of this piece of legislation. See Cons. Const. 21 February 2008, n° 2008-562 DC, Journal Officiel, 26 February 2008, 3272.
18 See article 706-119 ff. of the Code de Procédure Pénale.
19 The word 'regime' here refers to the different enforcement measures implementing the penalty.
20 In this sense, see Cass. Crim., 1885, *Bull. crim.* 1885, 285.

122-1 makes no specific and explicit mention of mitigation. This legislative choice of terminology appears to have had an important impact in practice: once criminal responsibility is judicially recognised, mere alterations of intellectual insight and/or of control have more often than not been interpreted as aggravating circumstances, notably in cases where the perpetrator of the offences was aware of the psychological and/or neuropsychological disorder causing such alterations and failed to take precautionary measures.[21]

In itself, the wording of the second paragraph of article 122-1 is not an oddity in the French criminal legislative landscape and the reference it contains to the power of the court to 'take this [the reduced intellectual insight and/or impaired control] into account when it decides the penalty and determines its regime' perfectly mirrors the well-established principle of the individualisation of sentencing (*personnalisation des peines*) as explicitly formulated in article 132-24 of the Code Pénal:

> Within the limits fixed by Statute, the court imposes penalties and determines their regime according to the circumstances and the personality of the offender. When the court imposes a fine, it determines its amount taking into account the income and expenses of the perpetrator of the offence.[22]

In this sense, what some commentators have rightly labelled the 'expression of a complementary logic' ('*l'expression d'une logique complémentaire*')[23] in article 122-1 might also appear to be an unnecessary – and somewhat redundant – repetition of article 132-24. Yet, in so far as the matter is one of crucial importance in the determination of individual criminal responsibility, it seems reasonable to assert that the French legislator proved adequately cautious and inserted within article 122-1 a realistic safety net against any form of judicial abuse and a useful guide for judicial interpretation and assessment. In line with the general principles of French criminal law, the alteration of intellectual insight and/or impairment of control therefore require penalties to be adapted to the circumstances of the case and the personality of the author of the offence.

This individualisation of sentencing inevitably entails a judicial appreciation of the facts and, similarly to the case contemplated in the first paragraph of article 122-1, the court is not bound by the findings of the medical expert. Here also, criminal responsibility seems to relate to the lack of intellectual insight and/or control rather than to the psychological and/or neuropsychological disorder. While medical assessments and certificates understandably play an important role and are to be taken into account by the judge, the judicial determination of individual criminal responsibility also rests on a consideration of all the circumstances of the case and notably on the moment of occurrence of the psychological and/or neuropsychological disorder.

The Sovereignty of the Judicial Interpretation

As previously mentioned, under French criminal law the judge is the sovereign authority appreciating and evaluating the psychological state of the individual perpetrating the offence.[24]

---

21 See below on the pre-existing fault.
22 Article 132-24 of the Code Pénal. Official translation <http://www.legifrance.gouv.fr> (accessed 1 April 2011). For clarity, this translation has been slightly altered and the term 'size' used in the original has been replaced with 'amount'.
23 Mayaud (n. 2) 476 (translation by the author).
24 See Cass. Crim., 8 Jun 1955, *Bull. crim.* n° 286.

Practically speaking, this means that he may accordingly use all circumstantial evidence not only to *take into account* the moment of occurrence of the psychological and/or neuropsychological disorder altering intellectual insight and/or impairing control or altogether destroying them but also to decide *when* this disorder actually occurred.[25]

Indeed, whether impeding or totally destroying intellectual insight or control, the psychological and/or neuropsychological disorder can, in principle, only be judicially considered at the time the offence was perpetrated. Practically speaking, this means that the judge will only take into account the disorder at the exact moment of the action or omission constituting the offence and will, in principle, consequently ignore any disorder that could have occurred prior to the criminal act or after its perpetration. Applying this principle, the Cour de cassation was able to find that the mental deficiency or disturbance prior to the perpetration of an offence is not in itself sufficient to act as a ground excluding individual criminal responsibility.[26] According to consistent case law, it also follows that a psychological and/or neuropsychological disorder appearing after the perpetration of the criminal act does not exclude individual criminal responsibility for such acts.[27] The only – although far from minimal – legal consequence this *ex post facto* occurrence might bear is the suspension of the proceedings so as not to deprive the individual from the fundamental right to a fair trial and to guarantee the rights of the defence. According to consistent case law, and admittedly in line with the requirements of article 6 of the European Convention on Human Rights on the right to a fair trial, individuals charged with criminal offences have the twofold right to understand the language used in court and to communicate with their lawyers and with the court. For example, in the case of an accused suffering from a paralysis which impeded him from communicating with his defence lawyer, the Cour de cassation suspended the proceedings before it until the state of health of the accused allowed him to communicate with his lawyer and with the court.[28] Again, proceedings are here merely suspended – not abandoned – and individual criminal responsibility remains unaltered.

Yet, as with many principles, the French criminal law premise that the mental state of the offender can only be assessed at the time the offence was committed recognises two major exceptions; one judicially self-created and one legislatively granted.

The Judicial Discretion to Consider the Prior Fault

The above-mentioned principle according to which the psychological and/or neuropsychological disorder must be qualified at the time the offence was perpetrated to either exclude responsibility or impact on sentencing recognises one significant exception, namely, the consideration of a prior fault by the author of the offence (*faute antérieure*). As previously stated, the judge is sovereign in his appreciation of the psychological and/or neuropsychological disorder of the perpetrator and in some cases may take into account the existence of a fault prior to the perpetration of the offence in question. Such prior fault will notably be characterised in cases of wilful blindness. For example, the epilepsy of the author of a fatal car accident, who used his vehicle while being fully aware of his condition and of the fact that it could make him lose control of his vehicle at any moment, not only does not diminish his responsibility but his awareness of his disorder will be judicially considered as a punishable fault.[29] The offence here is thus not constituted by the car accident

---

25 Mayaud (n. 2) 479.
26 Cass. Crim., 27 March 1924, *Bull. crim.* n° 141.
27 Cass. Crim., 10 June 1985, *Bull. crim.* n° 221.
28 Cass. Crim., 5 June 1997, *Bull. crim.* n° 228. Cited in Mayaud (n. 2) 479–80.
29 Paris, 27 May 1970, *Gaz. Pal.* 1972. 2. *Somm.* 37.

but by the complacency and self-indulgence of this individual who chose to ignore the potential dangerousness of his condition and failed to take all necessary steps to prevent the car accident.

The prior fault will also be characterised in cases of voluntary intoxication. To paraphrase Eser in his analysis of international criminal law, French criminal law here follows 'the principle of *actio libera in causa* by presupposing that the person was aware of the risk and likelihood of getting involved in criminal conduct at the point of becoming intoxicated'.[30] This finds a perfect illustration in the case law relative to violence perpetrated under the influence of drugs or alcohol, where individual criminal responsibility will be qualified if the person knowingly and consciously used drugs or alcohol. As famously explained by the Tribunal correctionnel of Nevers in 1976:

> The predominant case law refuses to qualify drunkenness as a legal ground for excluding punishment, a logical and satisfactory solution: there would indeed be an obvious contradiction in doing so at a time when drunkenness is increasingly repressed as such by recent legislation. Therefore, when the individual is fully aware of the intoxicating powers of excessive drinking, an awareness which indicates his intention of reaching a particular and dangerous level of inebriation and which makes the lack of control unavoidable and criminal behaviour possible, the responsibility of the individual must be considered as full and uncompromised in so far as he has voluntarily created the only pathology revealed by the psychiatric expertise namely, intoxication.[31]

The Law of 12 June 2003 confirmed this judicial refusal to consider alcohol abuse as a legal ground for excluding individual criminal responsibility and punishment and, while addressing the issue of drink-driving, explicitly considers as a punishable fault the fact of drinking or using drugs knowingly and consciously prior to driving and causing a car accident. In such cases, the fact that drinking or using drugs may have altered or destroyed the intellectual insight and/or control is not only rejected as a ground for excluding individual criminal responsibility or mitigating punishment but is in fact considered as an aggravating factor,[32] which the judge will take into account when imposing penalties.[33] This scenario of course differs from medically diagnosed alcoholism: unlike alcoholism, alcohol abuse is a voluntary intoxication not a disease. Yet, surprisingly, case law and legal commentary on the qualification of alcoholism both seem to be unavailable and, so far, it appears that inebriation has been judicially equated to intoxication due to alcohol abuse – an aggravating factor – and that alcoholism, which supposedly could trigger a lack of individual

---

30 Albin Eser, 'Article 31: Grounds for Excluding Criminal Responsibility', in Otto Triffterer (ed.), *Commentary on the Rome Statute of the International Criminal Court: Observers' Notes, Article by Article* (Nomos Verlagsgesellschaft, Baden Baden, 1999) 547.

31 Trib. Corr. Nevers, 30 January 1976, *Gaz. Pal.* 1976, *Somm.* 227. Translation by the author, the original version reads: 'La jurisprudence dominante se refuse à voir dans l'ivresse une cause légale d'exemption de peine, solution satisfaisante sur le plan logique: il y aurait en effet une contradiction évidente, alors que l'ivresse est de plus en plus souvent réprimée en tant que telle par la législation récente, de la retenir comme une cause d'atténuation ou d'exemption de responsabilité dans les hypothèses non visées par le législateur. Ainsi, lorsque le sujet connait bien les propriétés enivrantes des multiples boissons par lui consommées, ce qui est significatif de son intention de parvenir graduellement à un point de non-retour dans l'état d'ivresse et à une excitation particulièrement dangereuse pour un buveur d'habitude, rendant inévitable l'absence de contrôle de lui-même et possible un comportement délictuel en tous domaines, il échet de considérer la responsabilité du prévenu comme entière dans la mesure où il a été volontairement l'auteur de la seule pathologie révélée par l'expertise psychiatrique, soit l'ivresse excitomotrice.'

32 Ibid.

33 See loi n° 2003-495, Journal Officiel, 13 June 2003, 9943 and articles 221-6-1, 222-19-1 and 222-20-1 of the Code de Procédure Pénale.

criminal responsibility, has been disregarded. This nonetheless seems to contravene the formulation used in article 122-1 itself which refers to the individual's 'intellectual insight or his ability to control his actions', a formulation which, far from being redundant, explicitly covers psychological and/or neuropsychological disorders affecting both the individual's conscience as well as his will power. Legal scholars are, however, divided on this particular point and if some are inclined to include within the definitional scope of article 122-1 the 'diseases of will power' (*maladies de la volonté*), such as alcoholism, kleptomania, pyromania or even eating disorders, others, however, tend to consider them as a form of psychological coercion.[34]

This issue notwithstanding, it still remains that resort to the prior fault seems reasonable and, to a certain extent, does respond to the quasi-moral objections that might be raised against the consideration of lack of intellectual insight and/or loss of control as grounds for mitigating or even excluding individual criminal responsibility. As explained at the very beginning of this chapter, such consideration might indeed hold the risk of a far too lenient law and practice. Here also, the remarks made by Eser in relation to intoxication as grounds for excluding individual criminal responsibility under international criminal law can be transposed to the French penal system:

> By excluding exculpation if the person concerned became voluntarily intoxicated, [French law] attempts to prevent a *mala fide* procured state of incapacity, as would be the case if penal law were to tolerate that a person puts himself into a state of non-responsibility by means of intoxication with the objective of committing a crime and later to invoke his lack of capacity as a ground for excluding responsibility.[35]

Yet, this judicial consideration of the prior fault also means that the judge will be able to consider not only the existence of the psychological and/or neuropsychological disorder at the time of the offence but also prior to its perpetration, a self-empowerment which reveals the increasing severity of the judicial attitude, based on a willingness to conscientiously assess the existence of the disorder and a simultaneous reluctance to issue declarations of lack of responsibility or to mitigate punishment lightly.

From a practical viewpoint, and contrary to the general principles of French criminal law, this means that in such instances individual criminal responsibility will be judicially qualified as such, not so much in its direct relation to the event causing the damage, but rather in its anteriority to this particular event. According to consistent case law, any psychological and/or neuropsychological weakness known to the individual who suffers from it requires that this individual pays particular regard to his condition: wilful blindness and a lack of prevention on his part may indeed be judicially considered as a punishable omission.[36] In this respect, Rousseau notes that '[t]he majority of legal commentators compare the "intellectual insight" of an individual with his "ability to understand" namely, the ability to interpret the impact of his actions.'[37] Put differently, if the perpetrator of the offence had the ability to understand that his actions could indeed generate this offence, not only would he be considered criminally responsible, but his understanding might constitute an aggravating factor.

---

34 For a very interesting discussion on this point, see Rousseau (n. 5) 46–7.
35 Eser (n. 30).
36 See Mayaud (n. 2) 481–2. See, for example, Paris, 27 May 1970, *Gaz. Pal.* 1972. 2. *Somm.* 37.
37 Rousseau (n. 5) 51. Translation by the author, the original version reads: 'La majorité de la doctrine compare le discernement d'une personne à sa "capacité de comprendre", c'est-à-dire la faculté d'interpréter la portée de ses actes' (footnotes omitted).

The Legislative Authorisation to Anticipate Potential Future Offences

Not only may the judge choose to review the individual's past conduct but he may also pre-emptively assess future events. Arguably increasing the potential severity of the judicial appreciation of the facts, it must be recalled here that the dispositions of the aforementioned Law of 25 February 2008[38] also apply in the case contemplated in paragraph 2 of article 122-1 when the individual has perpetrated one of the following acts: murder, torture or barbaric acts, rape, abduction and illegal detention of minors or with aggravating circumstances.[39] In such extremely serious cases, not only may the judge take preventive measures to avoid a reoccurrence of criminal acts but, more importantly, he may also decide to place the individual in ' protective custody' ('*rétention de sûreté*') in a socio-medico-legal centre once the offender has finished serving his prison sentence and if he represents a danger to himself or to society.

If this judicial assessment of dangerousness did raise some eyebrows in relation to the cases of lack of responsibility under the first paragraph of article 122-1, affirming that such an assessment in relation to the second paragraph of this provision was controversial is an understatement. What is certain is that the Law of 25 February 2008 was a legislative reaction to the tragic murders of a nurse and a nursing assistant in a psychiatric hospital. The French media were understandably keen to make headline news of this event and thereby generated a very strong emotional reaction among the public at large and in the political sphere, the President of the French Republic himself asking for legislative action. This societal reaction interestingly prompted some commentators to qualify modern criminal law and criminal procedure as a 'means of political communication' ('*un mode de communication politique*').[40]

There is no argument about the fact that this law is extremely repressive. The enforcement of protective custody does offer certain guarantees of fairness in so far as it must be judicially decided, lawfully justified and limited in time. Yet, protective custody may also be renewed indefinitely and may de facto amount to a life sentence; a form of life imprisonment in instances where individuals have already served their sentence. Furthermore, as previously emphasised, the judicial decision to place an individual under protective custody is based on a *pre-emptive* assessment of this individual's *potential* dangerousness – a situation which is alarmingly reminiscent of those fictionally described in Orwell's *Nineteen Eighty-Four*[41] or Spielberg's film *Minority Report*.

This law could lead to extremely severe abuses and to violations of the fundamental right to liberty and security, as protected by article 5 of the European Convention on Human Rights.[42] Yet, it must also be accepted that should an application be made to the Strasbourg Court on the basis of article 5(1) which guarantees to 'everyone' 'the right to liberty and security of person', it is doubtful that the Court would accede to such a claim and find a violation in so far as the French legislation seems to be Convention-compliant. As the Strasbourg Court stated:

> The deprivation of liberty must be in conformity with domestic law, *and* the domestic law must itself be in conformity with the Convention, including the general principles expressed or implied

---

38 See loi n° 2008-174 of 25 February 2008, 'loi relative à la rétention de sûreté et à la déclaration d'irresponsabilité pénale pour cause de trouble mental', Journal Officiel, 26 February 2008, 3266.

39 Article 706-53-13 of the Code de Procédure Pénale.

40 Magalie Nord-Wagner, 'L'irresponsabilité pénale pour cause de trouble mental' (translation by the author). Available at <http://www-cdpf.u-strasbg.fr> (accessed 14 March 2011).

41 George Orwell, *Nineteen Eighty-Four* (Penguin Books, London 1990; original: 1949).

42 See European Convention for the Protection of Human Rights and Fundamental Freedoms (ECHR), Council of Europe, 1950.

therein. ... The notion underlying the term in question is one of fair and proper procedure, namely that any measure depriving a person of his liberty should issue from and be executed by an appropriate authority and should not be arbitrary.[43]

As recalled by the Strasbourg Court in *M. v. Germany*, 'Compliance with national law is not, however, sufficient: Article 5(1) requires in addition that any deprivation of liberty should be in keeping with the purpose of protecting the individual from arbitrariness.'[44] Reviewing the German legislation on preventive detention[45] and finding a violation of article 5(1) of the ECHR where it was unable to find 'a sufficient causal connection between the applicant's conviction by the sentencing court in 1986 and his continued deprivation of liberty beyond the period of ten years in preventive detention',[46] the Strasbourg Court interestingly proceeded to a comparative analysis with the French legislation on the matter, suggesting its compatibility with the Convention; a finding which is worth reproducing here:

> the Act of 25 February 2008 on post-sentence preventive detention and diminished criminal responsibility due to mental deficiency (*Loi relative à la rétention de sûreté et à la déclaration d'irresponsabilité pénale pour cause de trouble mental*) has introduced preventive detention into French law. Under Article 706-53-13 of the French Code of Criminal Procedure, this measure may be ordered against particularly dangerous offenders who pose a high risk of recidivism because they suffer from a serious personality disorder. The French Constitutional Council, in its decision of 21 February 2008 (no 2008-562 DC, Official Gazette (*Journal officiel*) of 26 February 2008, p. 3272), found that such preventive detention, which was not based on the guilt of the person convicted but was designed to prevent persons from re-offending, could not be qualified as a penalty (§9 of the decision). To that extent, it thus took the same view as the German Federal Constitutional Court in respect of preventive detention under German law ... Nevertheless, in view of its custodial nature, the time it may last, the fact that it is indefinitely renewable and the fact that it is ordered after conviction by a court, the French Constitutional Council considered that post-sentence preventive detention could not be ordered retrospectively against persons convicted of offences committed prior to the publication of the Act (§10 of the decision). In this respect, it came to a different conclusion than the German Federal Constitutional Court ...[47]

In other words, the compatibility of protective custody with the ECHR would rest on the detention being decided by an appropriate authority following a fair and proper procedure as well as on the existence of available proceedings enabling the individual to regularly challenge the lawfulness of his detention, which is exactly what is specified in the French legislation.[48] According to article 5(4) of the ECHR, 'the lawfulness of [the] detention shall be decided speedily' and, as noted by White and Ovey, 'There are two aspects to this requirement: first, the opportunity for legal review must be provided soon after the person is taken into detention (and thereafter ...

---

43 *Winterwerp* v. *The Netherlands* (App no 6301/73) ECHR 24 October 1979, para. 45.
44 *M.* v. *Germany* (App no 19359/04), ECHR 17 December 2009, para. 91.
45 See also *Haidn* v. *Germany* (App no 6587/04), ECHR 13 January 2011; *Schummer* v. *Germany* (App nos 27360/04 and 42225/07), ECHR 13 January 2011; *Mautes* v. *Germany* (App no 20008/07), ECHR 13 January 2011; *Kallweit* v. *Germany* (App no 17792/07), ECHR 13 January 2011.
46 *M.* v. *Germany* (n. 44) para. 100.
47 *M.* v. *Germany* (n. 44) [75].
48 See articles 706-53-13 ff. of the Code de Procédure Pénale. In this sense, see *Schiesser* v. *Switzerland* (App no 7710/76) ECHR 4 December 1979, [31].

at reasonable intervals [as] is necessary); secondly, the review proceedings must be conducted with due diligence.'[49] While the Strasbourg Court will proceed to a case-by-case assessment of the rapidity of the review and while it might accept as lawful longer periods in complex cases where medical reports are necessary, it will also verify that, in all the instances, proceedings were conducted with due diligence.[50] Even more relevant to the French legislation on protective custody is the Strasbourg finding that article 5(4) also requires that the continued legality of prolonged periods of detention be judicially reviewed at regular intervals. According to Strasbourg's case law, such detention would include indefinite detention under mental health legislation as well as cases of continuing detention justified by the dangerousness of the individual.[51]

Furthermore, it is worth recalling here that article 5(1)(e) of the ECHR explicitly lists among the lawful cases of deprivation of liberty, 'the lawful detention of persons for the prevention of the spreading of infectious diseases, of *persons of unsound mind, alcoholics* or *drug addicts*, or vagrants'.[52] The Strasbourg Court, however, specified the scope of article 5(1)(e):

> For the purposes of sub-paragraph (e) of Article 5 §1, an individual cannot be deprived of his liberty as being of "unsound mind" unless the following three minimum conditions are satisfied: firstly, he must reliably be shown to be of unsound mind, that is, a true mental disorder must be established before a competent authority on the basis of objective medical expertise; secondly, the mental disorder must be of a kind or degree warranting compulsory confinement; thirdly, the validity of continued confinement depends upon the persistence of such a disorder (see *Winterwerp* v. *the Netherlands*, 24 October 1979, § 39, Series A no 33; *Varbanov* v. *Bulgaria*, no 31365/96, §§45 and 47, ECHR 2000-X; *Hutchison Reid* v. *the United Kingdom*, no 50272/99, §48, ECHR 2003-IV; and *Shtukaturov* v. *Russia*, no 44009/05, §114, 27 March 2008).[53]

It further added that:

> there must be some relationship between the ground of permitted deprivation of liberty relied on and the place and conditions of detention. In principle, the "detention" of a person as a mental health patient will only be "lawful" for the purposes of sub-paragraph (e) of paragraph 1 if effected in a hospital, clinic or other appropriate institution (see *Ashingdane* v. *The United Kingdom*, 28 May 1985, §44, Series A no 93; *Aerts* v. *Belgium*, 30 July 1998, §46, *Reports of Judgments and Decisions* 1998-V; *Hutchison Reid*, cited above, §49; and *Brand* v. *The Netherlands*, no 49902/99, §62, 11 May 2004).[54]

The compatibility of domestic legislation on preventive detention with the ECHR is thus not automatic and, due to the inherent risks posed by such legislation to human rights, the Strasbourg Court will systematically proceed to a careful case-by-case assessment of such detention. If in itself the French legislation seems to be Convention-compliant, its application in practice will nonetheless not escape Strasbourg's meticulous scrutiny.

---

49   Robin White and Clare Ovey, *Jacobs, White & Ovey The European Convention on Human Rights* (5th edition, Oxford University Press, 2010) 238–9.
50   See *Baranowski* v. *Poland* (App no 28358/95) ECHR 28 March 2000.
51   *X* v. *UK* (App no 9088/80) ECHR 24 October 1981.
52   Emphasis added.
53   *Kallweit* v. *Germany* (n. 45) [45].
54   Ibid. [46].

The Political-Legal Reaction: A Misguided Proposal?

Even if seemingly in conformity with human rights law, the 2008 law nonetheless remains very much on the French political-legal agenda and has been the focus of recent debates before the Sénat[55] as, in January 2011, a draft law was discussed regarding an amendment to article 122-1 which would limit the judicial discretionary power in terms of imposing penalties and sentencing. According to this draft law, when it is judicially recognised that a psychological and/or neuropsychological disorder has indeed altered intellectual insight and/or impaired control, the penalty should be automatically reduced by a third. Proponents of this amendment argue that such a measure will not in reality restrict judicial discretion but will simply reduce the maximum duration of the penalty. Practically speaking, this means that if the perpetrator incurs a maximum penalty of 30 years' imprisonment, the judicial recognition of a psychological and/or neuropsychological disorder altering intellectual insight and/or impairing control will bring this maximum down to 20 years.

Rather strangely therefore, this draft law does not directly challenge the 2008 law on its most controversial aspect, namely, the understanding of dangerousness as a legal concept.[56] It thus appears to be more a political and opportunistic proposal conveniently appearing at a time of electoral debates and discussions than a legally coherent step forward that would be based on acute consideration for human rights and fundamental freedoms. What this proposal is more concerned about is the heavy-handedness of the judiciary in tending to consider the existence of a psychological and/or neuropsychological disorder altering intellectual insight and/or impairing control as an aggravating rather than a mitigating circumstance. In this respect, this law proposal might be seen as a missed opportunity to address the real issue, namely, the consideration of dangerousness as a legal concept that can be judicially assessed.

Conclusion

French criminal law thus finds itself at a crossroads, torn between two admittedly undesirable options: lack of responsibility and dangerousness. On the one hand, the law has to ensure that responsibility remains the rule and lack of responsibility the exception. Responsibility is inherent to the condition of being human and any reform of the criminal law based on the premise of lack of responsibility would open the door to abuses and undeserved leniency. On the other hand, considering dangerousness as a legal concept driving judicial reasoning and decision-making could equally lead to abuses and to an infringement of human rights and fundamental freedoms. Between these two heads of Scylla and Charybdis, both of which consider the individual as deprived of free will, either due to his inherent lack of responsibility or to his intrinsic dangerousness and criminality, the French legislature and judiciary have so far managed to maintain a delicate and fragile balance … but for how long?

---

55 See 'Proposition de loi relative à l'atténuation de responsabilité pénale applicable aux personnes atteintes d'un trouble mental ayant altéré leur discernement au moment des faits', Examen en commission, Sénat, 26 January 2011 <http://www.senat.fr.> (accessed 10 February 2011).

56 See here the excellent analysis by Jean Danet, 'La dangerosité, une notion criminologique, séculaire et mutante' (2008) 5 *Champ pénal/penal field, nouvelle revue internationale de criminologie* <http://champpenal.revues.org/6013> (accessed 14 March 2011).

Chapter 22

Diminished Responsibility and Loss of Control: The Perspective of International Criminal Law

John Cubbon[1]

Introduction

Diminished responsibility and loss of control in English law stand in stark contrast with the corresponding notions in international criminal law. While English law concepts of diminished responsibility and loss of control or, as it used to be called, provocation have developed in tandem over decades spawning a fair amount of case law and critical and scholarly comment, there has been little jurisprudence on, or discussion of, their counterparts in international criminal law.

In English law diminished responsibility and loss of control provide a basis for a finding of manslaughter. This brings out the fundamentally different framework from the one in international criminal law, where there is no distinction between murder and manslaughter. However, there is at least a solid basis for the application of the English law concept of diminished responsibility in the wording of Rule 67 of the Rules of Procedure and Evidence of the International Criminal Tribunal for the former Yugoslavia and the International Criminal Tribunal for Rwanda.

The purpose of this chapter is to identify the law and jurisprudence in international criminal law, such as it is, that relates to diminished responsibility and loss of control and to determine how these concepts have been understood in international criminal law, what their legal implications are and what factors and considerations govern their application. Throughout, English law will be the point of reference. It will be used as an example of the many common law jurisdictions which have a crime of manslaughter on the grounds of diminished responsibility[2] and the many common law and civil law jurisdictions in which there is a crime of homicide related to provocation.[3] The unifying thread running through all this domestic legislation is mental condition or provocation as the basis for a finding of a lesser crime of homicide. Inevitably the position taken in English law is not identical to that in other jurisdictions, but the similarity is such that many of its features are replicated elsewhere.

---

[1] The views expressed herein are those of the author alone and do not necessarily reflect the views of the International Tribunal or the United Nations in general. The author wishes to thank Brian Cubbon, Laura Marschner and Gabrielle McIntyre for their comments on drafts of this chapter.

[2] Examples from common law jurisdictions of legislation approximating to the model of a partial defence of diminished responsibility as provided in the Homicide Act 1957 are given in footnote 983 of the Čelebići case, Case No IT-96-21-A, Judgment, 20 February 2001.

[3] For example, Criminal Offences Act 1960, as amended, s. 62 (Gibraltar); Penal Code Act, ss. 205, 206 (Zambia); German Criminal Code (*Strafgesetzbuch*), s. 213; Criminal Code of the Republic of Slovenia (*Kazenski zakonik*), Art. 128; Criminal Code of the Republic of Albania (*Kodi Penal i Republikës së Shqipërisë*), Art. 82.

Diminished Responsibility and Loss of Control in English Law

The partial defences of diminished responsibility and loss of control concern respectively an abnormal mental state which reduces criminal responsibility and exceptional conditions which provide a partial excuse for criminal action.[4] Both before and after the entry into force of the relevant sections of the Coroners and Justice Act 2009,[5] killings in these circumstances have been classified as manslaughter – a criminal offence distinct from murder and lacking its stigma – for which there is a less severe punishment. When the Homicide Act 1957 entered into force, there was a mandatory sentence of death or life imprisonment for murder.[6] Since the death penalty has ceased to be available, there has been a mandatory life sentence. As is widely acknowledged, the inflexibility of this mandatory sentence justifies the separate offence of manslaughter on grounds of diminished responsibility or loss of control.[7] This applies also after the amendments introduced by the Coroners and Justice Act 2009.

The partial defences to murder set out in the Homicide Act 1957 are not available for criminal offences other than murder, for which there is generally no mandatory sentencing.[8] In these cases the factors that provide the basis for diminished responsibility and loss of control constitute grounds for mitigation.[9]

Homicide in International Criminal Law

Murder is referred to directly and indirectly in the definition of crimes under international criminal law. It is a constituent crime in the definition of Crimes Against Humanity in the Statutes of the International Criminal Court (ICC), the International Criminal Tribunal for the former Yugoslavia and the International Criminal Tribunal for Rwanda.[10] Common Article 3 of the Geneva Conventions identifies 'murder of all kinds' as prohibited with respect to certain categories of protected persons. Customary international law imposes criminal liability for serious violations of Common Article 3;[11] and on this basis murder in violation of Common Article 3 of the 1949 Geneva Conventions has been held to be a violation of the laws or customs of war.[12] In addition, the Geneva Conventions list 'wilful killing' as one of the categories of acts which constitute grave breaches of the Conventions

---

4 Jeremy Horder, 'Between Provocation and Diminished Responsibility' (1999) 10 Kings College Law Journal 143.

5 Coroners and Justice Act 2009, ss. 53–6.

6 Homicide Act 1957, ss. 5–9.

7 Peter Krug, 'The Emerging Mental Incapacity Defense in International Criminal Law: Some Initial Questions of Implementation' (2000) 94 American Journal of International Law 317, 330; See also, Law Commission, 'Murder, Manslaughter and Infanticide' (Law Com. No 304, 2006) para. 5.8.

8 Krug (n. 7) 330, [n. 87].

9 See Criminal Justice Act 2003, s. 166(5); Sentencing Guidelines Council, 'Overarching Principles: Seriousness' (Sentencing Guidelines Secretariat 2004), para. 1.25; *R v. Morris* (1974), *Current Sentencing Practice*, para. C3-2A (R 54 January 2005).

10 ICC Statute, Art. 7(1)(a); Statute of the International Criminal Tribunal for the former Yugoslavia, Art. 5(a); Statute of the International Criminal Tribunal for Rwanda, Art. 3(a). Cf. Nuremberg Charter, Art. 6(c); Tokyo Charter, Art. 5(c); Control Council Law No 10, Art. II(1)(c).

11 *Prosecutor v. Duško Tadić*, Case No IT-94-1-AR-72, Decision on Defence Motion for Interlocutory Appeal on Jurisdiction, 2 October 1995, para. 134.

12 *Prosecutor v. Pavle Strugar*, Case No IT-02-1-T, Judgment, 31 January 2005, para. 219.

to be criminalised by the High Contracting Parties[13] and 'killing members of the group' is one of the underlying acts of genocide.[14] Both 'wilful killing'[15] and 'killing members of the group'[16] have been identified with murder under international criminal law.

Murder is, so to speak, an important building block in the construction of crimes under international criminal law. It is not, however, accompanied by any lesser crime corresponding to manslaughter on grounds of diminished responsibility or loss of control. There are a number of reasons for this. In international criminal law there are no mandatory sentences,[17] which might provide a justification for lesser crimes for which more flexibility in sentencing would be possible. Also, it has been suggested that the absence of a distinction between murder and manslaughter reflects the early stage of development of international criminal law[18] and the fact that the task of identifying elements of international crimes is far from complete.[19] These factors have certainly prevented the distinction from appearing so far, but there are further reasons why any distinction resembling that between murder and manslaughter that might emerge in international criminal law would not be as determinative of the sentence to be imposed as the corresponding distinctions in national jurisdictions. Firstly, typically only an upper limit is set for the penalties that may be imposed for crimes in international criminal law.[20] The absence of a lower limit for the sentence for murder makes it unnecessary to have a separate crime of manslaughter for which lower penalties may be imposed. Moreover, it is highly unlikely that distinct tariffs will emerge in international tribunals for the different constituent crimes within Crimes Against Humanity or War Crimes, in part because of the variations in the sentencing practices between national jurisdictions.

Diminished Responsibility

Section 52(1) of the Coroners and Justice Act 2009 provides, inter alia, that a person who kills or is a party to the killing of another is not to be convicted of murder if that person was suffering from an abnormality of mental functioning which –

---

13 Geneva Convention I, Arts 50, 51; Geneva Convention II, Arts 50, 51; Geneva Convention III, Arts 129, 130; Geneva Convention IV, Arts 146, 147. Wilful killing as a grave breach of the Geneva Conventions is reflected in Article 8(2)(a)(i) of the ICC Statute and Article 2(a) of the Statute of the International Criminal Tribunal for the former Yugoslavia.

14 Convention on the Prevention and Punishment of the Crime of Genocide, Art. II(a).

15 *Prosecutor v. Radoslav Brđanin*, Case No IT-99-36-T, Judgment, 1 September 2004, para. 380; Čelebići case, Case No IT-96-21-T, Judgment, 16 November 1998, paras 420–3.

16 *Prosecutor v. Vidoje Blagojević and Dragan Jokić*, Case No IT-02-60-T, Judgment, 17 January 2005, para. 642.

17 Cf. Krug (n. 7) [331]–[332] (citing Article 78(1) of the ICC Statute and referring to Article 24(2) of the Statute of the International Criminal Tribunal for the former Yugoslavia and Article 23(2) of the Statute of the International Criminal Tribunal for Rwanda).

18 Antonio Cassese, 'The Proper Limits of Individual Responsibility under the Doctrine of Joint Criminal Enterprise' (2007) 5 Journal of International Criminal Justice 109, 120.

19 Krug (n. 7) [331].

20 Statute of the International Criminal Tribunal for the former Yugoslavia, Art. 24; Statute of the International Criminal Tribunal for Rwanda, Art. 23; ICC Statute, Arts 77–8.

a. arose from a recognised medical condition,
b. substantially impaired his/her ability to understand the nature of his/her conduct, to form a rational judgement and/or exercise self-control, and
c. provides an explanation for his/her acts and omissions in doing or being a party to the killing.

The requirement of *substantial impairment* of basic cognitive/volitional abilities, so to speak, sets the hurdle high, but in this respect it is like the definition of 'diminished responsibility' in a number of other common law jurisdictions.[21]

Expressions very similar to 'diminished responsibility' appear in Rule 67(B)(i)(b) of the Rules of Procedure and Evidence of the International Criminal Tribunal for the former Yugoslavia, Rule 67(A)(ii)(b) of the Rules of Procedure and Evidence of the International Criminal Tribunal for Rwanda and in Rule 145(2)(a) of the ICC Rules of Procedure and Evidence.

Rule 67(B) of the Rules of Procedure and Evidence of the International Criminal Tribunal for the former Yugoslavia provides in relevant part:

> Within the time-limit prescribed by the Trial Chamber or by the pre-trial Judge appointed pursuant to Rule 65 ter:
>
> (i) the defence shall notify the Prosecutor of its intent to offer
>
> ...
>
> (b) Any special defence, including that of diminished or lack of mental responsibility; in which case the notification shall specify the names and addresses of witnesses and any other evidence upon which the accused intends to rely to establish the special defence ...[22]

The Trial Chamber and the Appeals Chamber in the Čelebići case considered the nature of the 'special defence' of diminished mental responsibility referred to in this Rule. At that time Rule 67(A)(ii)(b) corresponded in relevant respects to what is now Rule 67(B)(i)(b). Both the Trial Chamber and the Appeals Chamber commented on the wording of the Rule. The Trial Chamber points out that the phrase 'special defence' is not defined[23] and observes that the requirement of Rule 67(A)(ii)(b) is 'terse'.[24] Similarly, according to the Appeals Chamber, Rule 67(A)(ii) is 'not happily phrased'.[25] That lack of mental responsibility can provide a defence to a charge is almost tautological; but the reference in Rule 67 to *diminished* mental responsibility is at first sight puzzling. It is evidently distinct from lack of mental responsibility. It also seems to constitute a

---

21 Crimes Act 1900 (NSW), s. 23A; Criminal Code 1995 (Qld), ss. 103–4. Many civil law jurisdictions contain provisions that permit lower penalties for any crime committed by a perpetrator whose cognitive or volitional capacities are substantially impaired, see German Criminal Code (*Strafgesetzbuch*), s. 21; Criminal Code of Bosnia and Herzegovina (*Krivični Zakon Bosne i Hercegovine*), Art. 34(2).

22 There are almost identical provisions in Rule 67(A) of the Rules of Procedure and Evidence of the International Criminal Tribunal for Rwanda, Rule 67(A) of the Rules of Procedure and Evidence of the Special Court for Sierra Leone and Rule 112(B) of the Rules of Procedure and Evidence of the Special Tribunal for Lebanon.

23 Čelebići Trial Judgment (n. 15), [1157].

24 Ibid., [1164].

25 Čelebići Appeal Judgment (n. 2) [580].

defence and the wording of the Rule can be taken to imply that the defence it provides is complete; but, if so, this Rule allows a broader defence arising from diminished responsibility than is the norm in domestic jurisdictions.

In the Čelebići case, the accused, Esad Landžo, advanced a plea of diminished responsibility.[26] Landžo was charged on various counts under Articles 2 and 3 of the International Criminal Tribunal for the former Yugoslavia Statute in connection with his actions as a guard at the Čelebići prison camp.[27]

The Čelebići Trial Chamber takes s. 2 of the Homicide Act 1957 as a source of guidance in the interpretation of Rule 67(A)(ii)(b).[28] It points out that the expressions 'abnormality of mind' and 'substantially impaired mental responsibility' occupy a central place in the definition of 'diminished responsibility' under the English law. It then cites the following passage from the judgment of Lord Parker CJ in *R v. Byrne* as the first attempt to define the phrase 'abnormality of mind' within the meaning of s. 2: 'it means a state of mind so different from that of ordinary human beings that the reasonable man would term it abnormal'.[29] The Trial Chamber comments: 'This simplistic definition is one of common sense. It avoids fastening the condition to any particular kind of mental abnormality.'[30]

The Trial Chamber held that it was 'an essential requirement of the defence of diminished responsibility that the accused's abnormality of mind should substantially impair his ability to control his actions'.[31] It also stated that the test to be applied was whether Landžo suffered from an abnormality of mind that made him incapable of controlling his actions.[32] It then went on to apply this test of volitional impairment to determine whether the special defence of diminished responsibility applied to Landžo.[33]

The interpretation of the notion of diminished responsibility by the English courts is broader than the one given here and covers cognitive as well as volitional deficiencies. In *R v. Byrne*, Lord Parker CJ held:

> "Abnormality of mind" appears to us to be wide enough to cover the mind's activities in all its aspects, not only the perception of physical acts and matters and the ability to form a rational judgment as to whether an act is right or wrong, but also the ability to exercise will power to control physical acts in accordance with that rational judgment.[34]

It is not clear why the Trial Chamber did not consider this definition. Perhaps the reason was that in Landžo's case the focus of the expert reports was on his ability to control his actions.

Landžo called three forensic psychiatrists as expert witnesses: Dr Van Leeuwen from the Netherlands, Dr Laggazi from Italy and Dr Gripon from the USA. The Trial Chamber also heard testimony from Dr Verde, a forensic psychiatrist from Italy, and Dr Sparr, a psychiatrist from the

---

26　Čelebići Trial Judgment (n. 15), [1156].
27　Ibid., [6]–[10].
28　Ibid., [1163]–[1168].
29　Ibid., [1167] (citing *R v. Byrne* [1960] 2 QB 396 (CA)).
30　Ibid., [1168].
31　Ibid., [1169]. See also ibid., [1156] (where the Trial Chamber stated that 'the plea of diminished responsibility is based on the premise that, despite recognizing the wrongful nature of his actions, the accused, on account of his abnormality of mind, is unable to control his actions').
32　Ibid., [1181].
33　Ibid., [1181]–[1186].
34　*Byrne* (n. 29) 403.

USA who was called by the prosecution in rebuttal.[35] All three defence expert witnesses were of the opinion that Landžo suffered from a personality disorder.[36] Dr Verde also attributed to him a personality disorder and was of the opinion that it influenced his ability to control his behaviour in his position as a guard.[37] Dr Sparr, however, was of the view that the abnormality of personality exhibited by Landžo 'had no pathological component, but merely reflected his personality traits'.[38] The Trial Chamber noted that the experts had little or no opportunity to verify from other sources the information that Landžo provided,[39] which it found to be unreliable.[40] The Trial Chamber was not convinced that the criminal acts attributed to Landžo were not the product of his own free will.[41] For these reasons it was not persuaded by his defence of diminished responsibility.[42] As to his mental condition, the Trial Chamber's assessment was that it appeared from the testimony of the experts that Landžo suffered from a personality disorder, but that the evidence relating to his inability to control his physical acts on account of abnormality of mind was not at all satisfactory.[43]

The Trial Chamber was, therefore, not required to take a definitive position on the implications of a finding of diminished mental responsibility, though it did state that the relevant provision in Rule 67 'would appear to suggest a complete defence since the words are without qualification or limitation'.[44] This tentative inference was subsequently rejected by the Appeals Chamber of the International Criminal Tribunal for the former Yugoslavia.[45] In response to Landžo's submission that Rule 67(A)(ii) made, or had perhaps recognised, diminished mental responsibility as a complete defence to any charge,[46] the Appeals Chamber indicated that the rule-making power of the judges of the International Criminal Tribunal for the former Yugoslavia did not extend to the adoption of rules constituting new *defences*.[47] It further held: 'If there is a "special defence" of diminished responsibility known to international law, it must be found in the usual sources of international law – in this case, in the absence of reference to such a defence in established customary or conventional law, in the general principles of law recognised by all nations.'[48] The Appeals Chamber stated that in many countries in which the defendant's total mental incapacity to control his actions or to understand that they are wrong constitutes a complete defence, diminished mental responsibility was neither a complete nor a partial defence but was relevant in mitigation of sentence.[49]

The Appeals Chamber held that the rationale for the partial defences provided by the English Homicide Act 1957 is inapplicable before the International Criminal Tribunal for the former Yugoslavia because there are no mandatory sentences and there are no appropriate lesser criminal offences available under the Statute of the International Criminal Tribunal for the former Yugoslavia for which the sentence would be lower and which could be substituted for any of the

---

35 Čelebići Trial Judgment (n. 15) [1173].
36 Ibid., [1174].
37 Ibid., [1176]–[1177].
38 Ibid., [1180].
39 Ibid., [1181].
40 Ibid., [1182].
41 Ibid., [1185].
42 Ibid., [1186].
43 Ibid., [1186].
44 Ibid., [1164].
45 Čelebići Appeal Judgment (n. 2), [590].
46 Ibid., [582].
47 Ibid., [583].
48 Ibid., [583].
49 Ibid., [588].

criminal offences it had to try.[50] It inferred that the appropriate general legal principle representing international law to be applied by the International Criminal Tribunal for the former Yugoslavia was that 'the defendant's diminished mental responsibility is relevant to the sentence to be imposed and is not a defence leading to an acquittal in the true sense'.[51] The Appeals Chamber concluded that where a defendant raised diminished mental responsibility in Rule 67(A)(ii)(b) it was to be interpreted as relevant to the mitigation of sentence.[52]

Since the Čelebići Appeal Judgment the defence has argued in a few other cases at the International Criminal Tribunal for the former Yugoslavia that the accused had diminished mental responsibility, but never successfully. In the *Todorović* Sentencing Judgment the Trial Chamber reviewed the medical examinations of the accused by two experts following notice of his intent to raise the question of diminished responsibility.[53] One expert concluded that there was no evidence of a major mental disorder or any other psychiatric disorder for the relevant period and that there was no evidence of diminished capacity or responsibility; and the other concluded that the accused had no personality disorder as such, but that he had post-traumatic stress disorder and abused alcohol during the war.[54] While both experts concluded that the accused was not suffering from a personality disorder during the relevant period, they differed in their conclusions with regard to post-traumatic stress disorder.[55] The Trial Chamber found that the accused's condition 'at the time the crimes were committed was not one which would give rise to mitigation of sentence'.[56] In the case of Damir Došen, the Trial Chamber did not consider that diminished mental capacity was a mitigating factor in the circumstances of the case.[57] One expert witness found evidence of acute stress reactions that later became a post-traumatic stress disorder; and another considered that Došen was 'suffering from vulnerability, "depressiveness" and insecurity'.[58] The Trial Chamber concluded in almost identical terms to those of the *Todorović* Trial Chamber that Došen's condition 'at the time his crimes were committed was not one which could give rise to mitigation of sentence'.[59] In the *Erdemović* Sentencing Judgment of 5 March 1998, the Trial Chamber simply states that there is nothing to substantiate the submission that the accused 'lacked mental responsibility because he suffered a temporary mental disorder or, at best, his mental responsibility was significantly diminished also'.[60]

Apart from the Čelebići case, the most detailed consideration of alleged diminished mental responsibility is given in *Prosecutor v. Mitar Vasiljević*.[61] The *Vasiljević* Trial Chamber held that 'an accused suffers from a diminished responsibility where there is an impairment to his capacity to appreciate the unlawfulness of or the nature of his conduct or to control his conduct so as to conform to the requirements of the law'.[62] It pointed out that this principle had been adopted in Article 31(1)(a) of the ICC Statute.[63] This is broader than the definition of diminished mental

---

50   Ibid., [590].
51   Ibid., [590].
52   Ibid., [590].
53   *Prosecutor v. Savo Todorović*, Case No IT-95-9/1-S, Judgment, 31 July 2001 [93]–[95].
54   Ibid., [94].
55   Ibid., [95].
56   Ibid., [95].
57   *Prosecutor v. Duško Sikirica et al.*, Case No IT-95-8-S, Judgment, 13 November 2001 [196].
58   Ibid., [198].
59   Ibid., [199].
60   *Prosecutor v. Dražen Erdemović*, Case No IT-96-22-Tbis, Judgment, 5 March 1998, [16].
61   *Prosecutor v. Mitar Vasiljević*, Case No IT-98-32-T, Judgment, 29 November 2002, [280]–[295].
62   Ibid., [283].
63   Ibid., [n. 677].

responsibility in the Čelebići Trial Judgment.[64] No explanation is given for this change in the notion. It demonstrates the persuasive force that Article 31(1)(a) of the ICC Statute can be expected to have and the degree to which the law in this field is still unsettled. The *Vasiljević* Trial Chamber rejected evidence that at relevant times the accused was suffering from psychosis.[65] It accepted the evidence of prosecution witness, Dr Folnegović-Smalc, who said that the only defects which she could find from which the accused had suffered were delirium or alcoholic psychosis.[66] Her conclusion was that at relevant times, according to the standards applied in former Yugoslavia, the accused would have been found to be fully accountable or to have an insignificant diminishment of accountability for his actions.[67]

The Trial Chamber was not satisfied that the accused had established on a balance of probabilities that at the time of the incident for which he was found guilty he was suffering from diminished responsibility.[68] The Trial Chamber did not then consider whether the accused had any mental condition which, although not reaching the threshold of diminished responsibility, nevertheless was mitigatory.

The uncertainty generated by Rule 67 of the Rules of Procedure and Evidence of the International Criminal Tribunal for the former Yugoslavia / International Criminal Tribunal for Rwanda is not present in the ICC Statute and Rules of Procedure and Evidence. Article 31(1)(a) of the ICC Statute provides that 'a person shall not be criminally responsible if, at the time of that person's conduct ... the person suffers from a mental disease or defect that destroys that person's capacity to appreciate the unlawfulness or nature of his or her conduct, or capacity to control his or her conduct to conform to the requirements of the law'. The requirement here of a mental disease or disorder that 'destroys' a person's cognitive or volitional faculties would appear not to include cases in which an abnormality of a person's mental functioning has only *substantially impaired* his or her ability to understand the nature of his or her conduct, form a rational judgement or exercise self-control. In other words, Article 31(1)(a) of the ICC Statute would appear not to incorporate cases of diminished responsibility, as defined in English law or indeed the law of many other countries with a similar notion. This is supported by Rule 145(2)(a) of the ICC Rules of Procedure and Evidence, which provides that in determining sentence 'the Court shall take into account, as appropriate ... the circumstances falling short of constituting grounds for exclusion of criminal responsibility, such as substantially diminished mental capacity or duress'. Rule 145(2)(a) of the ICC Rules of Procedure and Evidence implies that 'substantially diminished mental capacity', as a mitigating circumstance, falls short of constituting a ground for the exclusion of criminal responsibility pursuant to Article 31(1)(a) of the ICC Statute. Rule 79 of the ICC Rules of Procedure and Evidence, which corresponds to Rule 67 of the Rules of Procedure and Evidence of the International Criminal Tribunal for the former Yugoslavia / International Criminal Tribunal for Rwanda, significantly limits the defence disclosure obligations to the intent to raise the existence of an alibi or a ground for excluding criminal responsibility provided for in Article 31(1) of the ICC Statute, but, unlike Rule 67 of the Rules of Procedure and Evidence of the International Criminal Tribunal for the former Yugoslavia / International Criminal Tribunal for Rwanda, it does not refer to diminished mental responsibility or anything resembling it. It is evident from this brief overview that the ICC can be expected to treat diminished responsibility solely as mitigation and not as a defence.

---

64 Čelebići Trial Judgment (n. 15) [1169]. See also Ibid., [1156].
65 *Vasiljević* (n. 61), [284]–[287].
66 Ibid., [289]–[291].
67 Ibid., [293].
68 Ibid., [295].

There has been no jurisprudence at the ICC establishing the threshold for 'substantially diminished mental capacity', as set forth in Rule 145(2)(a) of the ICC Rules of Procedure and Evidence. The precise range of circumstances falling under it cannot be easily predicted, in part because of the inherent difficulty of the mental health concepts involved, but the jurisprudence of the International Criminal Tribunal for the former Yugoslavia and comparisons with domestic legislation suggest that the ICC will give attention to provisions in common law jurisdictions on manslaughter on the grounds of diminished responsibility and provisions in civil law jurisdictions on mitigation where a person's cognitive or volitional powers are substantially diminished.[69]

The upper limit of the space that is, so to speak, covered by diminished responsibility in international criminal law is set by lack of criminal responsibility owing to mental condition. Again, locating that notion in international criminal law is hampered by the absence of jurisprudence. Nevertheless, apart from being widely present in domestic criminal legislation, it is referred to in Rule 67 of the Rules of Procedure and Evidence of the International Criminal Tribunal for the former Yugoslavia / International Criminal Tribunal for Rwanda, a report by the UN Secretary-General outlining the manner in which the International Criminal Tribunal for the former Yugoslavia was to be established[70] and Article 31(1)(a) of the ICC Statute. Pursuant to Article 31(1)(a) of the ICC Statute, the accused is not criminally responsible if a 'mental disease or defect ... destroys' his or her cognitive or volitional capacity. Commentators have considered that the use of the word 'destroys' limits cases in which a person suffering from a mental disease or defect is not criminally responsible to the most extreme ones.[71] The requirement of destruction rather than impairment, while setting a very high standard, is nonetheless consistent with the approach that is in effect taken in most domestic jurisdictions.[72] Whenever anyone is charged with a serious crime, whether in international criminal law or otherwise, there is a reluctance to allow the perpetrator to avoid punishment altogether.[73] For these reasons it is to be expected that the ICC will very rarely make a finding that someone suffering from a mental disease or defect lacks criminal responsibility and consequently it will designate as diminished responsibility whatever just falls short of this condition. As a consequence diminished responsibility will cover persons with highly impaired cognitive or volitional faculties.

The concept of diminished responsibility, as it is found in English law and elsewhere, has certainly been recognised in international criminal law. The international criminal law jurisprudence has almost entirely come from the judgments of the International Criminal Tribunal for the former Yugoslavia. It is too slight for any confident assertions to be made as to its content. In 2006 the UK Law Commission reported that diminished responsibility 'does not play a central role in murder cases, being successful in fewer than 20 cases annually'.[74] This nevertheless is decidedly more than the total number of cases in which it has even been considered in international criminal law.

---

69 See above, n. 21.

70 Report of the Secretary-General Pursuant to Paragraph 2 of Security Council Resolution 807 (1993) UN Doc S/25704, para. 58.

71 John Tobin, 'The Psychiatric Defence and International Criminal Law' (2007) 23 Medicine, Conflict and Survival 111, 116–17, 121; Albin Eser, 'Article 31: Grounds for Excluding Criminal Responsibility' in Otto Triffterer (ed.), *Commentary on the Rome Statute of the International Criminal Court. Observers' Notes Article by Article* (2nd edn, CH Beck 2008); Sander Janssen, 'Mental Condition Defences in Supranational Criminal Law' (2005) 4 International Criminal Law Review 83, 85.

72 Robert Cryer, Håkan Friman, Darryl Robinson and Elizabeth Wilmshurst, *An Introduction to International Criminal Law and Procedure* (Cambridge University Press, 2007) 334.

73 Tobin (n. 71) 112, 121. See also Janssen (n. 71) 85.

74 Law Com. No 304, 2006 (n. 7) para. 5.84.

The state of the law on diminished responsibility in international criminal law is undeveloped and unsettled and it would plainly be premature to address the issues which have been the subject of debate over the years in England and Wales on what should fall under diminished responsibility, such as whether a 'recognised medical condition' should be required[75] or whether developmental immaturity should be included.[76] The central unifying characteristic of diminished responsibility in international criminal law is as stated by the Appeals Chamber of the International Criminal Tribunal for the former Yugoslavia in the Čelebići case, namely that it is a general principle of law that a defendant's diminished mental responsibility is relevant to the sentence to be imposed and not a defence leading to acquittal.

Diminished Responsibility as Part of a Spectrum of Mitigation in International Criminal Law

It is evident from the position of the Trial and Appeals Chambers of the International Criminal Tribunal for the former Yugoslavia on the sentencing of Landžo in the Čelebići case that diminished responsibility is not the only category of mental condition that gives rise to mitigation. In determining Landžo's sentence the Trial Chamber took account of his 'immature and fragile personality at the time, which is undisputed between the parties and has been testified to by several witnesses'.[77] It held that while the special defence of diminished responsibility had been rejected, it 'may nonetheless take note of the evidence presented by the numerous mental health experts, which collectively reveals a picture of Mr. Landžo's personality traits that contributes to our consideration of appropriate sentence'.[78] The Trial Chamber does not specify what particular expert evidence it took account of in determining Landžo's sentence or how much weight it gave to it, but the Appeals Chamber did not find fault with this approach.[79]

In the Čelebići case the Appeals Chamber has implicitly endorsed a two-level approach to mental condition as mitigation: diminished mental responsibility as referred to in Rule 67, which the Appeals Chamber found not to be a complete defence but a matter to be raised in mitigation of sentence;[80] and the 'personality traits' which did not amount to diminished responsibility, but which

---

75 Under s. 2(1)(a) of the Homicide Act 1957, as amended by s. 52(1) of the Coroners and Justice Act 2009, the presence of a recognised medical condition is now a requirement for diminished responsibility. See Ronnie Mackay, 'The Coroners and Justice Act 2009 – Partial Defences to Murder: (2) – The New Diminished Responsibility Plea' [2010] Criminal Law Review 290, 294.

76 In its report of 2006 the Law Commission recommended that it should be possible to bring in a verdict of diminished responsibility on the grounds of developmental immaturity of an offender who was under 18 at the relevant time. Law Com. No 304, 2006 (n. 7) paras 5.125–5.137. This recommendation was not followed in the Coroners and Justice Act 2009.

77 Čelebići Trial Judgment (n. 15) [1283].

78 Ibid., [1283]. This was confirmed by the Appeals Chamber. Čelebići Appeal Judgment (n. 2) [839]–[841].

79 Čelebići Appeal Judgment (n. 2) [841]. As the Appeals Chamber of the International Criminal Tribunal for the former Yugoslavia acknowledged, the mental condition of an accused was considered to be a mitigatory factor in a trial conducted in the aftermath of the Second World War. Ibid., [839] [n. 1439]. In the judgment delivered on 28 April 1948 the First Chamber of the Special Court in Amsterdam found Wilhelm Gerbsch guilty of a crime against humanity but it recognised as a mitigatory circumstance the fact that the accused's 'mental faculties were defective and undeveloped at the time of the crimes as well as at that of the trial'. Trial of Wilhelm Gerbsch (1949) 13 LRTWC 131, 132.

80 Čelebići Appeal Judgment (n. 2) [590].

nevertheless were correctly taken into account as mitigation.[81] Both levels concern mitigation, not guilt. Yet there is a major procedural difference between them: pursuant to Rule 67, the defence is obliged at the pre-trial phase to give notification of its intent to assert diminished mental responsibility and also to specify the names and addresses of witnesses and any other evidence upon which it intends to rely to establish this degree of responsibility; whereas in the case of evidence from mental health experts which also constitutes mitigation, albeit of a lesser degree, there is no such obligation.

For both diminished mental responsibility and lack of mental responsibility to constitute complete defences would have been a strange result and the Appeals Chamber in the Čelebići case has rightly avoided it. In doing so, it has left a further question: why should the defence give notification of its intent to argue diminished mental responsibility pursuant to Rule 67, if it is relevant only to sentencing, especially since other mental characteristics for which pre-trial disclosure is not required also have a bearing on sentencing? Defence pre-trial disclosure is ordinarily justified for three general sets of reasons: to ensure that disclosure is a 'two-way street'; to prevent so-called 'ambush defences'; and to promote trial efficiency and better case management.[82] Where diminished mental responsibility does not reduce murder to the lesser crime of manslaughter, the prevention of an 'ambush defence' can plainly no longer be a justification; and pre-trial disclosure of an intent to argue diminished mental responsibility will not make much of a contribution to ensuring that disclosure is a 'two-way street' or to promotion of trial efficiency and better case management, if its relevance is limited to the sentencing phase.[83] It is significant that where an accused submitted that his mental responsibility was diminished at the relevant time without giving notice pursuant to Rule 67 of the Rules of Procedure and Evidence of the International Criminal Tribunal for the former Yugoslavia the Trial Chamber nevertheless considered the submission.[84] The effect of the inclusion of diminished responsibility in Rule 67 has been reduced to the minimum. The treatment by the Chambers of the International Criminal Tribunal for the former Yugoslavia of the provision on diminished mental responsibility in Rule 67 is a classic case of a court neutralising the awkward implications of a legislative provision.

The International Criminal Tribunal for the former Yugoslavia has indicated elsewhere that mental condition may be relevant in the determination of sentence. In the first Sentencing Judgment in *Prosecutor* v. *Erdemović*, the Trial Chamber held that the individual circumstances of the convicted person which pursuant to Article 24(2) of the Statute should be taken into account in imposing sentences were characterised or affected by, inter alia, 'physical and mental condition'.[85] In the second *Erdemović* Sentencing Judgment the Trial Chamber noted a finding of emotional immaturity while dismissing a submission of lack of, or significant diminution of, mental responsibility.[86]

The defence has argued unsuccessfully in other cases before the International Criminal Tribunal for the former Yugoslavia that the mental condition of the accused, which it did not

---

81 Ibid., [841].

82 Kevin Dawkins, 'Defence Disclosure in Criminal Cases' (2001) New Zealand Law Review 35, 37–42.

83 It is noteworthy that in Rule 12.2(b) of the US Federal Rules of Criminal Procedure notice of the intention to introduce expert evidence relating to a mental disease or defect or any other mental condition of the defendant is required if it bears upon 'either (1) the issue of guilt or (2) the issue of punishment in a capital case'.

84 *Vasiljević* (n. 61) [281].

85 *Prosecutor* v. *Dražen Erdemović*, Case No IT-96-22-T, Judgment, 29 November 1996, [44].

86 *Erdemović*, Second Sentencing Judgment (n. 60), [16].

classify as 'diminished mental responsibility', was a mitigating factor. In the trial of Predrag Banović the Chamber considered a report of Dr Mikloš Biro, a professor of clinical psychology.[87] It noted that in advancing Dr Biro's evidence, the defence was not raising 'a defence of diminished mental responsibility in mitigation'.[88] The Trial Chamber rejected Dr Biro's assessment that the accused may have been unable to appreciate the unlawfulness of his conduct.[89] Dr Biro described the accused as a person of normal, below-average intelligence who showed signs of emotional immaturity, especially characterised by 'bad impulse control';[90] but the Trial Chamber did not consider it appropriate to mitigate his sentence.[91] The defence for Ranko Češić argued that at the time he committed crimes '[his] behaviour was affected by an acute stress reaction to the war'.[92] This submission was rejected by the Trial Chamber which found that the defence had failed to prove that he suffered more than the mental anguish that is to be expected in armed conflict.[93]

The extension of mitigation in international criminal law to mental conditions that fall short of diminished responsibility is paralleled in English law: even in the case of murder, where the partial defence of diminished responsibility has not been established, mental disorder or disability may nevertheless give rise to mitigation in the sense of being taken account of in the determination of the minimum term in relation to the mandatory life sentence.[94]

It is submitted that the ICC Rules of Procedure and Evidence allow for mental condition to be mitigatory, even if it does not qualify as 'substantially diminished mental capacity', as referred to in Rule 145(2)(a)(i). Rule 145(1)(b) provides that in determining the sentence the Court shall 'Balance all the relevant factors, including any mitigating and aggravating factors and consider the circumstances both of the convicted person and the crime'. This is broad enough to incorporate mental conditions that do not amount to 'substantially diminished mental capacity'. Also, 'substantially diminished mental capacity' is referred to in Rule 145(2)(a)(i) as an example of mitigating circumstances that lie outside the open-ended delineation of mitigating circumstances in Rule 145(1).[95] In any event, 'substantially diminished mental capacity' sets

---

87 *Prosecutor* v. *Predrag Banović*, Case No IT-02-65/1-S, Judgment, 28 October 2003, [76]–[80].
88 Ibid., [78].
89 Ibid., [78].
90 Ibid., [76].
91 Ibid., [80].
92 *Prosecutor* v. *Ranko Češić*, Case No IT-95-10/1-S, Judgment, 11 March 2004, para. 88(v).
93 Ibid., [93].
94 Criminal Justice Act 2003, sch. 21, para. 11(c) (which provides: 'Mitigating factors that may be relevant to the offence of murder include … (c) the fact that the offender suffered from any mental disorder or disability which (although not falling within section 2(1) of the Homicide Act 1957 (c.11)) lowered his degree of culpability.'). In German law the position is similar: where the perpetrator's cognitive or volitional capacities are diminished, but not 'substantially diminished' so as to qualify for a reduction of punishment under ss. 21 and 49 of the German Criminal Code, there may nevertheless be mitigation within the general sentencing margins. Theodor Lenckner and Walter Perron in Adolf Schönke and Horst Schröder, *Strafgesetzbuch Kommentar* (28th edn, CH Beck 2010), s. 21, mn. 25. The author is grateful to Jan Nemitz for pointing this out to him.
95 Rule 145(2)(a) of the ICC Rules of Procedure and Evidence provides that in addition to the factors mentioned in Rule 145(1) the Court shall take into account, as appropriate, mitigating circumstances such as 'the circumstances falling short of constituting grounds for exclusion of criminal responsibility, such as substantially diminished mental capacity'. The phrase 'circumstances falling short of constituting grounds for exclusion of criminal responsibility' is to be understood as covering, so to speak, a narrow space not quite reaching the limiting position of exclusion of criminal responsibility.

a relatively high threshold and it would seem unreasonable to exclude from mitigation mental conditions that do not reach it.

If the procedural requirements of Rule 67 of the Rules of Procedure and Evidence of the International Criminal Tribunal for the former Yugoslavia / International Criminal Tribunal for Rwanda relating to diminished mental responsibility are regarded as anomalous, its main significance for international criminal law is as a basis for mitigation and it should be viewed as part of a broader category of mitigation arising from a mental condition.

Loss of Control

The English law partial defence to murder of loss of control is specified in ss. 54, 55 and 56(1) of the Coroners and Justice Act 2009. Section 54(1) provides:

> Where a person ("D") kills or is a party to the killing of another ("V"), D is not to be convicted of murder if –
>
> (a) D's acts and omissions in doing so or in being a party to the killing resulted from D's loss of self-control,
> (b) the loss of self-control had a qualifying trigger, and
> (c) a person of D's sex and age with a normal degree of tolerance and self-respect and in the circumstances of D, might have reacted in the same or in a similar way to D.

Section 55(2)–(5) provides that the qualifying triggers for a loss of self-control arise if it was attributable to a fear of serious violence, to certain things done or said (or both) or to a combination of these. Pursuant to s. 54(7), a person who but for s. 54 would be liable to be convicted of murder is liable instead to be convicted of manslaughter. Section 56 of the Coroners and Justice Act 2009 repealed s. 3 of the Homicide Act 1957 which gave a similar basis for a finding of manslaughter which it termed 'provocation'. As has been pointed out, there are many common law and civil law jurisdictions which resemble English law in having a lesser offence than murder in which the perpetrator kills someone following provocation.[96]

There has been a dearth of cases in which a person accused under international criminal law has claimed to have provocation or loss of self-control as a partial excuse.[97] Provocation was argued in the case of Yamamoto Chusaburo, who was charged before a British Military Court in 1946 with having committed a war crime by killing a civilian.[98] Interestingly, the prosecutor distinguished this charge from murder under English law.[99] In the trial the accused argued that when guided by sudden impulse and obsessed by the thought of grave danger to life and property he momentarily lost control over himself and killed the victim in a rage.[100] The reasoning by which the court arrived

---

96   See above, n. 3.
97   It is noteworthy that research in England and Wales recently showed that, either on its own or in combination with another defence, provocation was the second most popular plea in the sample of murder cases examined (22.3 per cent of cases) after denial of intent (39.4 per cent). Law Com. No 304, 2006 (n. 7) para. 5.5.
98   Trial of Yamamoto Chusaburo (1948) 3 LRTWC 76.
99   Ibid.
100 Ibid., [77].

at its verdict and sentence are unknown.[101] The court found Chusaburo guilty and sentenced him to death by hanging but with a recommendation for mercy. The sentence was, however, confirmed and put into effect.[102] The defence of provocation was evidently rejected and it is not known whether the circumstances on which it rested were the basis for the recommendation for mercy.[103] In relation to provocation or loss of control in armed conflict there is a sharp contrast between international criminal law and popular perceptions.[104] Anecdotal evidence suggests that there are frequent instances of killings which might be classified in English law as manslaughter on grounds of loss of control. In his moral history of the twentieth century, Jonathan Glover cites examples of explosions of violence being triggered in combat by the experience of seeing comrades-in-arms wounded or killed.[105] This raises the question why such actions have apparently not led to charges. There are several reasons for this. Perhaps the most obvious is that these actions are often unknown beyond small circles of military personnel and are looked upon sympathetically by the chain of command.[106] The phenomenon of 'closing of ranks' protects possible perpetrators of war crimes in these circumstances.[107] Also, in the prosecution of international crimes there is a tendency to give priority to those responsible for alleged large-scale crimes.[108] Persons subject to explosions of violence in combat triggered by hostile actions would tend not to come into this category.

Just as diminished responsibility occupies, so to speak, the upper part of the field of mitigating mental conditions, so the partial defence of loss of control, as defined in English law, is only part of the range of mitigating circumstances in which a person commits a criminal offence in the heat of the moment or having lost self-control following a provocation of some type. As is the case with mental disorder or disability, provocation may in English law be taken account of in determining the minimum term for a mandatory life sentence for murder, where the perpetrator has by definition not committed manslaughter on grounds of loss of control.[109] There is certainly no legal impediment to regarding provocation as mitigatory in international criminal law. Statutes of tribunals and courts operating in the international sphere define the considerations that may be

---

101 Ibid., [78].

102 Ibid., [76].

103 One of the judges on a US Military Tribunal in the trial of Erhard Milch in 1946–47 implied that uncontrollable temper on the part of the accused may be taken into account in assessing his actions. Trial of Erhard Milch (1948) 7 LRTWC 27, 47; Antonio Cassese, *International Criminal Law* (2nd edn, Oxford University Press 2008) 266. The matter is discussed so briefly that it is difficult to draw conclusions. The judge may have been giving attention to the accused's disposition and there may have been no incident resembling loss of control under English law.

104 Greenwood writes that there is a widespread belief that war crimes consist only of acts performed in the heat of battle or in furtherance of a military objective. Christopher Greenwood, 'The International Tribunal for the Former Yugoslavia' (1993) 69 International Affairs 641, 645.

105 Jonathan Glover, *Humanity* (Pimlico 2001) 54.

106 See Paul Warnke et al., 'Implementing the Rules of War: Training, Command and Enforcement' (1972) 66 American Society of International Law Proceedings 183, 194.

107 See Nathan Rasiah, 'The Court-Martial of Corporal Payne and Others and the Future Landscape of International Criminal Justice' (2009) 7 Journal of International Criminal Justice 177, 187.

108 See ICC Statute, Art. 1; Statute of the International Criminal Tribunal for the former Yugoslavia, Art. 1; Statute of the International Criminal Tribunal for Rwanda, Art. 1; Statute of the Special Court for Sierra Leone, Art. 1(1); Law on the Establishment of Extraordinary Chambers in the Courts of Cambodia for the Prosecution of Crimes Committed during the period of Democratic Kampuchea, Art. 1.

109 Criminal Justice Act 2003, sch. 21, para. 11(d), as amended by Coroners and Justice Act 2009, sch. 1, para. 52(a) (which provides: 'Mitigating factors that may be relevant to the offence of murder include ... (d) the fact that the offender was provoked (for example, by prolonged stress)').

taken into account in determining sentence so broadly as to include it.[110] Again, there is a lack of cases in international criminal law in which loss of self-control following provocation has been a mitigating factor in the determination of sentence. The reasons for this are essentially the same as the reasons for the absence of charges in cases which would be classified in English law as manslaughter on grounds of loss of control.

By contrast with diminished responsibility, the introduction to international criminal law of something resembling the English law concept of manslaughter on grounds of loss of control is not facilitated by the specific wording of any legal instrument. Whether loss of self-control following provocation, understood more broadly than as justifying a finding of manslaughter pursuant to ss. 54, 55 and 56(1) of the Coroners and Justice Act 2009, emerges as a recognised ground for mitigation in international criminal law depends to some extent on whether there will be prosecutions of 'footsoldiers' for actions performed in the heat of the moment. There is a 'Catch-22' situation here in that the likelihood of such prosecutions will be enhanced once loss of self-control is well established as a ground for mitigation and it can only be well established if there have already been a substantial number of prosecutions.

Conditions of Armed Conflict as a Cause of Mental Disorder and Loss of Control Following Provocation

It takes little reflection, experience or expertise to arrive at the conclusion that exposure to armed conflict will often give rise to mental trauma. In many of the cases in which the International Criminal Tribunal for the former Yugoslavia has considered mental condition as a possible mitigatory factor, it has been related to the armed conflict.[111] Of particular importance in this regard is the finding of the Čelebići Trial Chamber that the interaction of the harsh environment of the armed conflict with the accused's impressionable and immature state of mind was mitigatory.[112] This is to be contrasted with the Češić Sentencing Judgment in which the Trial Chamber found that the defence failed to prove that the accused suffered from more than the mental anguish that was to be expected in an armed conflict and held that it would be inconsistent with the concept of the crimes under Articles 3 and 5 of the Statute of the International Criminal Tribunal for the former Yugoslavia to accept anguish experienced in any armed conflict as a mitigating factor.[113] There are two conflicting motivations here: an inclination to find that the experience of the particular circumstances of armed conflict related to a mental condition may constitute mitigation as in the case of Landžo; and an unwillingness to reduce the punishment of persons who have committed serious crimes on the grounds that they have an illness that is invisible and can be fabricated.

While there is almost no trace of loss of self-control being held to mitigate crimes in international criminal law, circumstances which under English law would afford a partial defence of loss of control can be expected to arise in the heat of battle. Such circumstances overlap with the

---

110   ICC Statute, Art. 78(1); Statute of the International Criminal Tribunal for the former Yugoslavia, Art. 24(2); Statute of the International Criminal Tribunal for Rwanda, Art. 23(2); Statute of the Special Court for Sierra Leone, Art. 19(2) (all of which provide that in deciding on sentences, account should be taken of 'such factors as' the gravity of the offence and the individual circumstances of the convicted person).

111   *Banović* (n. 87), [77]; Čelebići Trial Judgment (n. 15), [1283]–[1284]; *Češić* (n. 92), [93]; *Sikirica* (n. 57), [198]; *Todorović* (n. 53), [94]; *Vasiljević* (n. 61), [287].

112   Čelebići Trial Judgment (n. 15), [1283]–[1284].

113   *Češić* (n. 92), [93].

category of mitigatory abnormal circumstances arising in armed conflict which may be adduced as explaining the commission of egregious criminal acts by apparently otherwise ordinary people.

The International Criminal Tribunal for the former Yugoslavia has occasionally regarded the conditions brought about by armed conflict as mitigatory.[114] In determining the sentence for Zdravko Mucić the Čelebići Trial Chamber took into account the social pressures and the hostile environment within which he operated;[115] and when sentencing Naser Orić the Trial Chamber gave weight to 'the abysmal conditions prevailing in Srebrenica town and in the surrounding area where the accused operated during the relevant time in 1992 and 1993'.[116] The future development of mental condition and loss of self-control as mitigation in international criminal law can be expected to be linked with this rarely found inclination to treat exposure to the circumstances arising in armed conflict as mitigatory. In the context of international criminal law all three grounds for mitigation are a recognition of the tendency of the abnormal conditions of armed conflict to lead some people to take actions that they would not otherwise take.

Conclusions

The main source of jurisprudence on diminished responsibility is a handful of judgments in the International Criminal Tribunal for the former Yugoslavia. Following the Appeal Judgment in the Čelebići case, it can be stated with some confidence that diminished responsibility is not a complete defence in international criminal law.[117] The jurisprudence is too sparse for it to be possible to say much else about the conditions that qualify as diminished responsibility. Rule 67 of Rules of Procedure and Evidence of the International Criminal Tribunal for the former Yugoslavia / International Criminal Tribunal for Rwanda gives the concept a minor procedural importance, but its main significance is as a basis for mitigation and, as such, it forms the upper end of a continuum of mental conditions that constitute mitigation. There is almost no instance in which loss of self-control resulting from provocation has been treated as mitigation in international criminal law, but there is a sufficient legal basis for doing so.

The relative paucity of cases in international criminal law is partly to be attributed to the early stage of its development; and there are certainly special factors related to armed conflict that tend to prevent instances of loss of self-control from coming under the scrutiny of judicial systems.

Diminished responsibility and loss of control have been conceived of as closely related in English law not just because both constitute partial defences to murder, but also because their application has been such that they have been hard to separate on occasion, even though they correspond to distinct ethical intuitions.[118] These bases for associating diminished responsibility

---

114 See Olaoluwa Olusanya, 'Excuse and Mitigation Under International Criminal Law: Redrawing Conceptual Boundaries' (2010) 13 New Criminal Law Review 23 (Olusanya argues for giving greater weight in mitigation in international criminal law to the social context of armed conflict, in particular to propaganda which might contribute to the creation of an environment in which crimes under international criminal law are committed); John M. Doris and Dominic Murphy, 'From My Lai to Abu Ghraib: The Moral Psychology of Atrocity' (2007) 31 Midwest Studies in Philosophy 25 (According to Doris and Murphy, individuals in combat are typically cognitively degraded and therefore not morally responsible for their behaviour, but they seem uncertain about the implications that this has for punishment of war criminals).

115 Čelebići Trial Judgment (n. 15), [1248].

116 *Prosecutor v. Naser Orić*, Case No IT-03-68-T, Judgment, 30 June 2006, [766]–[771].

117 Čelebići Appeal Judgment (n. 2), [590].

118 See Horder (n. 4) 143.

and loss of control are lacking in international criminal law: 'partial defences' do not exist; and diminished responsibility and loss of control have been applied too infrequently for any inferences to be drawn as to the relationship between them. It might then seem that all that diminished responsibility and loss of control have in common in international criminal law is that they belong to the vast and amorphous range of circumstances that amount to mitigation; but there is a link between them in international criminal law which in fact is not present in domestic law – namely that, in practice, both will tend to be closely intertwined with exposure to the conditions of armed conflict, which may itself be mitigatory.[119] The development of all three will depend on the interplay between two powerful, but opposing pressures: on the one hand, acknowledgement of the brutal and dehumanising nature of armed conflict and of the mental conditions and loss of self-control that may result from it; and, on the other hand, the inclination to impose the most severe penalties on those who have committed the gravest of crimes.

---

119 Olusanya (n. 114) [23] (Olusanya advocates a redrawing of the conceptual boundaries of diminished responsibility and provocation in international criminal law; but he is using 'provocation' in a broader sense than it has been given in this chapter).

Index

Italic entries indicate cases/publications.

ability requirements 17
ability to exercise self-control 34
ability to form rational judgement 34
abnormality of mental functioning
    and armed conflict 381–2
    and causal requirements 35–7
    and chronic intoxication 184–9, 189–93
    diminished responsibility/loss of self control overlap 29, 48
    under Homicide Act 1957 184
    recognised medical condition 29–30, 189–90
    sexual infidelity killings 149
    See also diminished responsibility; insanity
abnormality requirement 16–17
Abu-Odeh, Lama 319
abusive relationships. *See* domestic violence/abuse
Acott 132
Adams, Francis Boyd 285
addiction 348–9
    See also intoxication
adultery
    crimes of passion in France and England 236–8
    Islamic law 318, 321–3
    provocation by 177–8
AG for Jersey v. *Holley* 44
AG v. *O'Shea* 156
Ahluwalia 42, 84, 86
alcohol dependency/abuse
    Coroners and Justice Act 2009 189–93, 202–5
    and diminished responsibility 184–9
    Dutch law 337
    establishing/distinguishing between 189–91, 191n72
    extreme mental or emotional disturbance in the US 193–7
    France 360–1
    Germany 259, 261–2
    Islamic law 315
    mistaken beliefs due to 204–5
    response/control characteristics 197–201
    Spain 347, 348–9
    substantial impairment 192

American Law Institute's Model Penal Code 49, 123, 143, 194, 293–5, 296–7, 302, 304
Andre Kirk Everett Hypolite v. *The Queen* 214
Andrina Tamara Smith v. *The Queen* 214
anger 88–9
Anguilla 210
anticipation of violence 92–3, 95
armed conflict and mental disorder 381–2
arrested and retarded development 30
Ashton 283
Ashworth, Andrew 43, 45, 81, 89
attempted murder, sentencing for 8
Attorney General v. *O'Brien* 154
Australia 285
Australian Capital Territory 12n13

Bahamas, Belize and Grenada 226–7
Baillie 43
Banović 378
Barbados 225–6
Baron, Marcia 143–4
battered women who kill
    Germany 265–9
    See also domestic violence/abuse
belief in likely violence 93–4
Belize 227
'benign conspiracy' 26–7
Bermuda 211–14
Boyle, Christine 138
breach of trust, domestic violence as 73–5
British Antarctic Territory 215
British Indian Ocean Territory 215
British Overseas Territories
    Anguilla 210
    Bermuda 211–14
    British Antarctic Territory 215
    British Indian Ocean Territory 215
    British Virgin Islands 215–16
    constitutional position 209–10
    divergence from English law 207–8
    Falklands Islands 218
    future difficulties 229–30
    Gibraltar 218

lessons for UK from 229
Monserrat 218
Pitcairn 219
provocation 228–9
    Anguilla 210
    Bermuda 211–14
    British Virgin Islands 215–16
    Cayman Islands 216–17
    Falklands Islands 218
    Gibraltar 218
    Monserrat 218
    Pitcairn 219
    St Helena/Acension/Tristan Da Cunha 219
    St Helena/Acension/Tristan Da Cunha 219
British Virgin Islands 215–16
'brooder cases' 49–50
broodings, jealous 89
Brookbanks, William 87
Bull v. *The Queen* 227
burden of persuasion in the US 294–5
burden of proof 241–2, 244
Burgess 213–14
Byrne 32–3, 34, 185, 371

Cahn, Naomi 104
Camplin/Holley test 43, 55, 56, 57, 60, 83, 84–5, 103n56, 197–8, 200–1
Canada
    excessive self-defence 285–6
    sexual infidelity killings 146
capacity for self-control 109
capacity requirements 17, 83–5
Card, Richard 66
Caribbean territories
    Bahamas, Belize and Grenada 226–7
    Barbados 225–6
    Jamaica 223–4
    provocation 223–7
    St Lucia 225
    Trinidad and Tobago 224–5
Carline, Anna 103, 108
causal requirements 17–19, 35–7
Cayman Islands 216–17
Čelebići case 370–2, 376, 381
Chalmers, James 195
child manslaughter 330–1
children and domestic violence 75
chronic intoxication
    Coroners and Justice Act 2009 189–93, 202–5
    and diminished responsibility 184–9
    extreme mental or emotional disturbance in the US 193–7
    mistaken beliefs due to 204–5
    response/control characteristics 197–201
    substantial impairment 192
'circumstances of an extremely grave character' 59
    background to reforms 136
    in Coroners and Justice Act 2009 135
    and diminished responsibility defence 148–9
    juries, factors to take into account by 136–40
    mistaken belief in wrongdoing 142–4
    philosophy underpinning reforms 137, 141, 143, 147–8
    sexual infidelity killings 144–9
    wrongdoing directed against D/other 140–2
Clark v. *Arizona* 304n65
Cleon Smith v. *R* 227
Clough, Amanda 234, 242
Clyde Dacosta Clarke v. *The Queen* 225–6
Cobbe, Francis Power 81
Cocker 41
coercive control, domestic violence as 69–73
Commonwealth, need for consistency in 208
community standards in New South Wales 15–16
Consultation Paper on Partial Defences to Murder (Law Commission) 17
control, role of in domestic violence 70–2
control/response characteristics 197–201
Coroners and Justice Act 2009
    alcohol dependency/abuse 189–93
    'circumstances of an extremely grave character' 135
    compared to Islamic law 323
    diminished responsibility plea
        compared to old plea 9–10
    intoxication 202–5
    in Ireland, criticisms of 164–5
    loss of self-control under 45, 82
        limitations of 50
    malecentric law, concern with 81–2
    Northern Ireland 163
Crimes Amendment (Diminished Responsibility) Act 1997 (NSW) 14
crimes of passion in France and England 236–8
Criminal Justice Act (NI) 1966 161–3
Criminal Justice and Immigration Act 2009 94
Criminal Justice and Licensing (Scotland) Act 2010 175, 176
    new diminished responsibility plea 10
Criminal Law (Insanity) Act 2005 155, 157
Criminal Law Reform Committee, New Zealand 273–4
Crown Dependencies
    constitutional position 210

divergence from English law 208
future difficulties 229–30
Guernsey 219–20
Isle of Man 220–1
Jersey 221–3
lessons for UK from 229
provocation 228–9
    Guernsey 219–20
    Isle of Man 220–1
    Jersey 221–3
culpability 298, 342–3, 342n6
culpable homicide in Scotland 167–8

dangerousness concept 356–7, 362–4, 365
de Than, Claire 136
Dempsey, Michelle Madden 69, 75–6
desert distributive principle 305–9
developmental immaturity
    compared to arrested and retarded development 30
    under new s.2 Homicide Act 1957 31
    reform proposals 30–1
Diagnostic and Statistical Manual of Mental Disorders (DSM-IV-TR) 189–90
Dietschmann 36, 187, 189
Digest of Criminal Law (Stephen) 155
diminished responsibility
    ability to exercise self-control 34–5
    abnormality requirement 16–17
    Australian Capital Territory 12n13
    bases for establishing 32–4
    and the 'benign conspiracy' 27–8
    capacity requirements 17
    causal requirements 17–19, 35–7
    and chronic intoxication 184–9
    and 'circumstances of an extremely grave character' 148–9
    Coroners and Justice Act 2009 9–10
    Criminal Justice and Licensing (Scotland) Act 2010 10
    Dutch law 336–8
    experts' role 37, 37n138, 49, 50
    Germany 247, 258–62
    history of 21–2
    international criminal law 369–79, 382–3
    introduction of 183–4
    Islamic law 314–15
    moral question 25–6
    New South Wales
        ability requirements 17
        causal requirements 17–19
        comparison to UK 16–19

        development of in 12–15
        motivation for reform 15
        operation of new plea 15–16
    New Zealand 282–4
    Northern Territory 12n14
    overlap with loss of self control 28
    and provocation 48
    Queensland 12n12
    rational judgement, D's ability to form 34
    Republic of Ireland 156–8
    revised definition of 24–5
    Scotland 21–2, 168, 172–7
    understanding of nature of conduct, D's 32–4
    United States 193–7, 299–300
discretion
    judges' 27, 145
    and partial defences in Scotland 171–2
    prosecutorial, in Scotland 170–1, 180–1
'disputed facts' hearings in New Zealand 280
Dixon v. *State* 124
Dobash, Rebecca 77–8
Dobash, Russell 77–8
domestic violence/abuse
    anger as loss of self-control 88–9
    anticipation of violence 92–3, 95
    assessment of likely violence 93–4
    background to reform 66–8
    as breach of trust 73–5
    burden of proof 244
    capacity issue, two approaches to 83–5
    and children 75
    as coercive control 69–73
    control, role of in 70–2
    definition of 68–9
    discretion and partial defences in Scotland 171–2
    evaluative standard 99–102
    extent of 76–7
    'extremely grave' circumstances 89–90, 91
    fear as new grounds for loss of self-control 79
    fear of serious violence 90–4
    gender bias in law 77–8, 233–4, 276–7
    homicide, extent of 80
    impact of 74
    malecentric law, concern with 81–2, 94–5
    New Zealand 271, 276–7
    and patriarchy 75–6
    and self-identity 74
    self-preservation as new defence 243–4
    serious wrong trigger 66–7
    sexed evaluative standard
        abandonment of 106–7

    de-sexing of 107
    feminist interest in 98–9
    justification for 101–2
    problems with 104–6
    sex and gender, role of in 102–6
    solutions to problems with 106–8
  state of mind and time 87
  suddenness requirement, removal of 45, 67–8, 86
  use of intimate information in 74–5
  women on men violence 77–8
  wrongs of 69–77
Došen, Damir 373
Doughty 131, 137
Doyle v. Wicklow County Council 154–5
DPP v. Holmes 130–1, 132
Dressler, Joshua 120, 123n67
drunkenness. *See* alcohol dependency/abuse
Drury v. HM Advocate 126, 168, 178, 179
Dryden 44
Duff, Anthony 143
Duffy 40, 45, 86
duress
  Dutch law 335–6
  Germany 253–8
  supra-legal duress in Germany 258
duress defence 141
Dutch law
  child manslaughter 330–1
  defences and mitigation grounds 329–30
  diminished responsibility 336–8
  duress 335–6
  emotions 327–8
  excessive self-defence 334–5
  general characteristics of 325–6
  homicide offences 326–9
  insanity 336–7
  intention to kill 326–9
  intoxication 337
  mental disorder 328, 329
  premeditation 328–9
  provocation 330–2, 335
  self-defence 331, 333–5
Dutton, Mary Ann 70

Eagle, Maria 202
Edwards, Susan 66, 100, 103, 103n56, 234, 238
equality 139–40
Erdemović 373, 377
Eser, Albin 360, 361
European Convention on Human Rights 240–1, 362–5

evaluative standard
  for loss of control 99–102
  sexed
    abandonment of 106–7
    capacity for self-control 109
    dangers of 110–11
    de-sexing of 107
    feminist interest in 98–9
    justification for 101–2
    over-emphasis on sex 109–10
    problems with 104–6
    sex and gender, role of in 102–6
    solutions to problems with 106–8, 111–12
excessive self-defence
  Australia 285
  Canada 285–6
  Dutch law 334–5
  Ireland 160–1
experts, role of 37, 37n138, 49, 50, 298n37
'extreme emotional disturbance' in the US 291, 292–6, 300–2
extreme mental or emotional disturbance 49–50, 193–7
'extremely grave' circumstances 89–90, 91

Faid 285–6
Falklands Islands 218
'family honour' and provocation 316–17
fear
  insurmountable, in Spain 348
  limitations of in new law 94–5
  as new grounds for loss of self-control 79
  of serious violence 90–4
    cases 59–60, 61–2
    timing of response to 232
feminism
  criticism of reasonable man test 98
  sexed evaluative standard
    dangers of 110–11
    interest in 98–9
    problems with 104–6
    role of sex and gender in 102–6
    solutions to problems with 106–8, 111–12
Fenton 185
Fisher, Philip 87
fitness to plead 33
Fox, Marie 104
France
  crimes of passion compared to England 236–8
  judiciary
    amendment to limit power 365
    evolution of powers in 356–8

legitimate defence 239–40, 242
necessity as defence 240
psychological/neuropsychologicl disorders
    amendment to limit judicial power 365
    anticipation of future events 362–4
    dangerousness concept 356–7, 362–4, 365
    evolution of judiciary powers 356–8
    exact moment of occurrence 359
    individualisation of sentencing 357–8
    intoxication 360–1
    judiciary role, powers and attitude 355–6
    legislative evolution 354–6
    politicisation of debate over 353–4
    prior fault by author of offence 359–61
    protective custody, enforcement of 362–4
    sovereignty of judicial interpretation 358–65
    victims of the offence 357

Galbraith v. *HM Advocate* 21, 22, 33n102, 172, 173–4
gender
    domestic violence and bias in law 77–8, 233–4, 276–7
    in Islamic homicide law 313–14, 321, 323
    loss of self-control requirement under provocation 42
    role of in sexed evaluative standard 102–6
    See also sexed evaluative standard
Germany
    battered women who kill 265–9
    diminished responsibility 247, 258–62
    duress 253–8
    excessive self-defence 252–3
    excusatory defences 252–62
    homicide offences 262–5
    insanity 258–62
    intoxication 259, 261–2
    justificatory defences 248–51
    loss of self-control 247
    provocation 247–8
    self-defence 248–52
    supra-legal duress 258
Giboin 81
Gibraltar 218
Glover, Jonathan 380
Godbas 285
Goodman, Lisa 70
Gordon 283
government
    life sentence, reluctance to remove as mandatory 8, 23, 24

New South Wales, changes to Law Commission proposals 14
grading of homicides in US 291
Grenada 227
Griew, Edward 26
Guernsey 219–20

Harman, Harriet 147
Hasan 141
Hatton 204
Hayward 40, 87
Heaton, Russell 136
Henchy Committee 156
Her Majesty's Attorney General for Jersey v. *Holley*. *See Holley*
Hester, Marianne 75
Hickey 95
Hilberman, E. 92
Hilberman, M. 92
Hinkley case 278–9
HM Advocate v. *Greig* 172
HM Advocate v. *Hill* 126, 177
HM Advocate v. *Kerr* 21n3
HM Advocate v. *Savage* 173
Holland. *See* Dutch law
Holley 84–5, 100, 180, 197–8, 200–1, 221–3, 226
Holmes v. *DPP* 130–1, 132
Holton, Richard 68, 91
Homicide Act 1957 22, 174, 184, 371, 372
Homicide and Criminal Responsibility Bill 1963 161
homicide offences, revised structure of 23
'honour killings' 316–17
Horder, Jeremy 81, 117, 118
Howe 160
human rights 139–40, 362–5
Humphreys 44

ICC Statute and Rules of Procedure and Evidence 374–5, 378–9
immediacy requirement, removal of 45, 67–8, 86
immorality of victim and provocation 317–19, 321–3
imperfect justification 137, 141–2, 143
In re Winship 297
'in the Circumstances of D' test 55–6, 57, 60–1, 62
infanticide
    Ireland 159–60
    New Zealand 271
    Scotland 170
infidelity. *See* sexual infidelity killings
insanity

abolition of as defence in US states 279
Dutch law 336–7
Germany 258–62
Ireland 154–6
Northern Ireland 162
See also abnormality of mental functioning
insurmountable fear 348
international criminal law
   armed conflict and mental disorder 381–2
   Čelebići case 370–2, 376, 381
   diminished responsibility 369–79, 382–3
   homicide in 368–9
   ICC Statute and Rules of Procedure and Evidence 374–5, 378–9
   loss of self-control 379–81, 382–3
   provocation 379–81
   Rules of Procedure and Evidence of the International Criminal Tribunal for the former Yugoslavia 370–4, 376–8
   sentencing 376–9
intimate terrorism. *See* domestic violence/abuse
intoxication
   chronic
      Coroners and Justice Act 2009 189–93, 202–5
      and diminished responsibility 184–9
      extreme mental or emotional disturbance in the US 193–7
      mistaken beliefs due to 204–5
      response/control characteristics 197–201
      Spain 348–9
      substantial impairment 192
   Dutch law 337
   France 360–1
   Germany 259, 261–2
   Islamic law 315
   Spain 347
Iran 319–23
Ireland
   constitutional background 151–3
   Coroners and Justice Act 2009 164–5
   Northern
      Coroners and Justice Act 2009 163
      Criminal Justice Act (NI) 1966 161–2
      as following English lead 161
      Homicide and Criminal Responsibility Bill 1963 161
      insanity 162
      provocation 163
      suicide pacts 163
      temporary mental abnormality 163
   Republic of

      diminished responsibility 156–8
      excessive defence 160–1
      infanticide 159–60
      insanity 154–6
      provocation 158–9
irresistible impulse 185
Islamic law
   capacity 314–15
   categories of homicide 313
   compared to Coroners and Justice Act 2009 323
   compared to English 314–15
   diminished responsibility 314–15
   'family honour' and provocation 316–17
   gender bias 313–14, 321, 323
   immorality of victim and provocation 317–19, 321–3
   intoxication 315
   Iran 319–23
   overview 312
   provocation 315–16, 320–3
   revenge-centred punishment for homicide 312–13
   as supporting provocation 314
Isle of Man 220–1

Jamaica 223–4
Jersey 221–3
Johnson, Michael 70, 77
judges
   discretion 27, 145
   France
      evolution of powers in 356–8
      role, power and attitude in 355–6
   proposal to limit power in France 365
   in sexual infidelity killings 129–33
   sovereignty of interpretation in France 358–65
jury involvement
   'circumstances of an extremely grave character' 136–40
   moral question in diminished responsibility 25
   New South Wales 15–16
   in sexual infidelity killings 129–33
   US reform states 196
'justifiable sense of being seriously wronged' 58–9, 61
   domestic abuse victims 66–7

Kaganas, Felicity 107

Ladiges, Manuel 258
Landžo, Esad 371–2, 376, 381
Lavallee v. *The Queen* 95, 102–3

Law Commission
   'benign conspiracy' 27
   causal requirements 17–18
   Consultation Paper on Partial Defences to Murder 17
   developmental immaturity 30–1
   first suggestion for reform 14
   'justifiable sense of being seriously wronged' 58
   Murder, Manslaughter and Infanticide report 24, 56
   provocation replaced by loss of self-control 39
   Report on Partial Defences 52, 55
   revised structure of homicide offences 23
   role of 11–12
   Scotland, review by 174–5
   and sexed evaluative standard 101
   wrongdoing directed against D/other 140
legitimate defence in France 239–40, 242
Leroy Elmer Burgess v. *Angela Cox (Police Constable)* 213–14
Leverick, Fiona 241
life sentence as mandatory, government reluctance to remove 8, 23, 24
Lloyd 188–9
loss of self-control
   anger as 88–9
   burden of proof 241–2
   capacity for self-control 109
   capacity issue 83–5
   under Coroners and Justice Act 2009 45, 82
      limitations of 50
   crimes of passion in France and England 236–8
   domestic abuse cases 66–8
   emotional reactions other than anger 47, 68
   evaluative standard 99–102
   evidence of as subjective test 86–9
   extreme mental or emotional disturbance 49–50
   fear as new grounds for 79
   Germany 247
   international criminal law 379–81, 382–3
   overlap with diminished responsibility 28
   rationale for, uncertainty of 47–8
   reasonable force used 232–5
   reasons for keeping 235
   replacement of provocation by 39–40
   requirement under provocation
      as controversial 40
      criticism of 41
      gender bias 42
      lack of legal definition 41
      mixed motives 43
      objective test 43–4

      'slow-burn cases' 42–3
   and self-defence, comparison of 232–5
   suddenness requirement, removal of 45, 67–8

M v. *Germany* 363
Mackay, Ronnie 87, 149, 175, 187
Madden Dempsey, Michelle 69, 75–6
Majewski 204
malecentric law, concern with 81–2, 94–5
Maria del Carmen Gomez 218
Masciantonio v. *The Queen* 137–8
Matheson 37n138
Mayaud, Yves 353–4
McCarthy 284
McColgan, Aileen 233
McGregor 283
McInnes, John 138
McNaghten Rules 154
mental abnormality
   and armed conflict 381–2
   Dutch law 336–7
   temporary
      Northern Ireland 163
      Spain 346–7
   See also abnormality of mental functioning; insanity; psychological disorders in France
'mental illness negating an offense element' in the US 291, 296–9, 302–4
Ministry of Justice and sexed evaluative standard 101
mistaken beliefs
   in adultery and Islamic law 318–19
   due to intoxication 204–5
   European Convention on Human Rights 240–1
   in victim's wrongdoing 142–4
Mitchell, Barry 87
Model Penal Code 49, 123, 143, 194, 293–5, 296–7, 302, 304
Mohammad (Faqir) 139–40
Moncrieff 216–17
Monserrat 218
moral question of diminished responsibility 25–6
Morgan (Smith) 44, 51, 52–3, 82, 83–4, 90, 100, 118, 145, 180
Morhall 44, 198–9
multicultural society 138
Murder, Manslaughter and Infanticide (Law Commission) 24, 56
mutual violence. *See* domestic violence/abuse

nature of conduct, understanding of 32–4
necessity as defence in France 240

Netherlands. *See* Dutch law
neuropsychological disorders in France
    anticipation of future events 362–4
    dangerousness concept 356–7, 362–4, 365
    evolution of judiciary powers 356–8
    exact moment of occurrence 359
    individualisation of sentencing 357–8
    intoxication 360–1
    judiciary role, powers and attitude 355–6
    legislative evolution 354–6
    politicisation of debate over 353–4
    prior fault by author of offence 359–61
    protective custody, enforcement of 362–4
    sovereignty of judicial interpretation 358–65
    victims of the offence 357
New South Wales
    Crimes Amendment (Diminished Responsibility) Act 1997 14
    diminished responsibility
        ability requirements 17
        abnormality requirement 16–17
        capacity requirements 17
        causal requirements 17–19
        comparison to UK 16–19
        development of in 12–15
    government changes to Law Commission proposals 14
    jury involvement 15–16
    Law Reform Commission
        reformulated test recommendation 13
        role of 11–12
    R v. *Chayna* 13
New Zealand
    battered defendants 276
    Criminal Law Reform Committee 273–4
    diminished responsibility 282–4
    'disputed facts' hearings 280
    domestic violence/abuse 271
    excessive self-defence 284–7
    infanticide 271
    Law Commission's approach 275–7, 284, 286–7
    limited partial defences in 271–2
    provocation, repeal of law on 271–82
    reasonable man test 272, 273
    sentencing 281–2
    Sentencing and Parole Reform Act 2010 287
    suicide pacts, killing pursuant to 271
    three strikes law 287–9
    Weatherston case 277–9
Nicolson, Paula 72
Norrie, Alan 45, 109, 137, 139, 141–2, 147–8, 179, 235, 242

Northern Ireland
    constitutional background 153
    Coroners and Justice Act 2009 163
    Criminal Justice Act (NI) 1966 161–3
    as following English lead 161
    Homicide and Criminal Responsibility Bill 1963 161
    insanity 162
    provocation 163
    suicide pacts 163
    temporary mental abnormality 163
Northern Territory 12n14
Nourse, Victoria 120, 124

objective test 43–4
    background 51
    'circumstances of an extremely grave character' 59
    compared to *Camplin/Holley* test 60
    'fear of serious violence' cases 59–60, 61–2
    'in the Circumstances of D' 55–6, 57, 60–1, 62
    'justifiable sense of being seriously wronged' 58–9, 61
    reasonable force used 233–5
    as replacement for 'reasonable man' test 52–3, 202–3
    Republic of Ireland 158
    response/control characteristics 198–9
    self-control references as omitted 53
    'things done or said' 57–9, 62–3
    tolerance and self-restraint test 52–4, 57, 61–2, 83–5
    United States 293
O'Connor 204
O'Grady 204
ordinary person test. *See* reasonable man test
Osland, Heather 93
Ovey, Clare 363–4

Palmer 233
partner/ex-partner homicide. *See* domestic violence/abuse
patriarchal terrorism. *See* domestic violence/abuse
patriarchy and domestic violence 75–6
Pearson 141
People (Attorney General) v. *Dwyer* 160
People (Attorney General) v. *Hayes* 154
People (DPP) v. *O'Mahoney* 156–7
People v. *Gounagias* 306–7
People v. *MacEoin* 158
People v. *White* 195
Perlin, Michael 278

philosophy underpinning reforms 137, 141–2, 143, 147–8
Pitcairn 219
Prosecutor v. *Erdemović* 373, 377
Prosecutor v. *Mitar Vasiljević* 373–4
Prosecutor v. *Predrag Banović* 378
prosecutorial discretion in Scotland 170–1, 180–1
protective custody, enforcement of 362–4
provocation
    by adultery 177–8
    Anguilla 210
    Bahamas, Belize and Grenada 226–7
    Barbados 225–6
    Bermuda 211–14
    British Overseas Territories 228–9
        Anguilla 210
        Bermuda 211–14
        British Virgin Islands 215–16
        Cayman Islands 216–17
        Monserrat 218
        Pitcairn 219
        St Helena/Acension/Tristan Da Cunha 219
    British Virgin Islands 215–16
    'brooder cases' 49–50
    Caribbean territories 223–7
    Cayman Islands 216–17
    Crown Dependencies 228–9
        Guernsey 219–20
        Isle of Man 220–1
        Jersey 221–3
    definition 40
    and diminished responsibility 48
    Dutch law 330–2, 335
    emotional reactions other than anger 47, 68
    extreme mental or emotional disturbance 49–50
    Falklands Islands 218
    and 'family honour' 316–17
    Germany 247–8
    Gibraltar 218
    Guernsey 219–20
    immorality of victim 317–19, 321–3
    impact on people 46–7
    international criminal law 379–81
    Islamic law 315–16, 320–3
    Islamic law as supporting 314
    Isle of Man 220–1
    Jamaica 223–4
    Jersey 221–3
    loss of self-control requirement
        as controversial 40
        criticism of 41
        gender bias 42
        lack of legal definition 41
        mixed motives 43
        objective test 43–4
        'slow-burn cases' 42–3
    Monserrat 218
    New Zealand 271
    Northern Ireland 163
    Pitcairn 219
    as privileging male angered states 79
    rationale for, uncertainty of 47–8
    replacement of by loss of self control 39–40
    Republic of Ireland 158–9
    response/control characteristics 197–201
    Scotland 168, 176–80
    source of 46
    St Helena/Acension/Tristan Da Cunha 219
    St Lucia 225
    Trinidad and Tobago 224–5
    United States 193–7
psychological disorders in France
    anticipation of future events 362–4
    dangerousness concept 356–7, 362–4, 365
    evolution of judiciary powers 356–8
    exact moment of occurrence 359
    individualisation of sentencing 357–8
    intoxication 360–1
    judiciary role, powers and attitude 355–6
    legislative evolution 354–6
    politicisation of debate over 353–4
    prior fault by author of offence 359–61
    protective custody, enforcement of 362–4
    sovereignty of judicial interpretation 358–65
    victims of the offence 357

qisas (retaliation) 312–13
Queensland 12n12
Queensland Criminal Code 1899 211–13

R v. *Anthony Martin* 233
R v. *Byrne* 32–3, 34, 185, 371
R v. *Chayna* 13
R v. *Damion Thomas* 223–4
R v. *Dwight Wright* 224
R v. *Entwistle* 82
R v. *Garrie Matthew Light* 90
R v. *Kester Williams* 227
R v. *Lavallee* 95, 102–3
R v. *Lindon* 220–1
R v. *Mohammad (Faqir)* 139–40
R v. *Tran* 138–9, 146
Ramchurn 82, 188–9
Ramsey, Carolyn 196

Ratcliffe 81
rational judgement, D's ability to form 34
Re A (Children) 241
Reagan, Ronald, attempted murder of 278–9
reasonable man test 52–3, 83
    background 51
    feminist criticism of 98
    New Zealand 272, 273
    objective test as replacement for 52–3, 202–3
    Republic of Ireland 158
    response/control characteristics 198–9
    Scotland 178
    United States 293, 295–6
recognised medical condition 16–17, 28–9, 189–90
Reilly, Alan 116
Reilly v. *The Queen* 285
'Report on Partial Defences' (Law Commission) 52, 55
Republic of Ireland
    constitutional background 152–3
    diminished responsibility 156–8
    excessive defence 160–1
    infanticide 159–60
    insanity 154–6
    provocation 158–9
'Response to Ministry of Justice Consultation Paper "Murder, Manslaughter and Infanticide": Proposals for Reform' (Spencer) 31
response/control characteristics 197–201
revenge killings 89
revenge-centred punishment for homicide 312–13
Ricardo Deverne Griffith v. *The Queen* 225, 226
Richens 41
Rossiter 131

Samuel Greenaway v. *The Queen* 218
Savage 173
Schneider, Elizabeth M. 93
Scotland
    alcohol dependency/abuse 191–2
    Criminal Justice and Licensing (Scotland) Act 2010
        new 10
    culpable homicide 167–8
    diminished responsibility 168, 172–7
        history of in 21–2
    discretion and partial defences 171–2
    homicide law 167–9
    lack of impetus for reform 179–80
    Law Commission, review by 174–5
    prosecutorial discretion 170–1, 180–1
    provocation 168, 176–80

sexual infidelity killings 125–9, 146
unofficial categories 169–70
self-control, ability to exercise 34
    See also loss of self-control
self-defence
    burden of proof 241–2, 244
    Dutch law 331, 333–5
    and European Convention on Human Rights 240–1
    excessive
        Australia 285
        Canada 285–6
        Germany 252–3
        New Zealand 284–7
    fear of serious violence, timing of response to 232
    Germany 248–52
    Ireland 160–1
    and loss of self-control, comparison of 232–5
    reasonable force used for 232–5
self-identity and domestic violence 74
self-preservation as new defence 243–4
self-restraint, tolerance and, test 52–4, 57, 58–9, 61–2, 83–5
sentencing
    individualisation of 357–8
    international criminal law 376–9
    New Zealand 281–2
Sentencing and Parole Reform Act 2010, New Zealand 287
serious wrong trigger and domestic abuse 66–7
sexed evaluative standard
    abandonment of 106–7
    capacity for self-control 109
    dangers of 110–11
    de-sexing of 107
    feminist interest in 98–9
    interpretation following exclusion of 117–18
    justification for 101–2
    over-emphasis on sex 109–10
    problems with 104–6
    sex and gender, role of in 102–6
    solutions to problems with 106–8, 111–12
sexual infidelity killings
    Anglo-Scottish law compared 125
    'circumstances of an extremely grave character' 144–9
    contemporary standard and mores 115–17, 126–9
    continuum of severity 129
    crimes of passion in France and England 236–8
    exclusion of 90

Islamic law 318, 321–3
judge and jury in 129–33
justificatory/excuse defences 119–21
provocation 177–8
Scottish law 125–9, 146
US traditional/liberal approaches 118–25
via media 129–33
sexual jealousy 82
Shane 122–3
Sherwin Fahie v. *The Queen* 216
Shute, Stephen 68, 91
Simester, Andrew 66
situational couple violence. *See* domestic violence/abuse
'slow-burn cases' 42–3, 45
Smalling v. *The Queen* 224
Smith, J.C. 241
Smith (Morgan) 44, 51, 52–3, 82, 83–4, 90, 100, 118, 145, 180, 226
Spain
 complete/incomplete exemptions 345–8
 criminal law 341–5
 culpability 342–3, 342n6
 fragmentation of partial defences 343–4
 insurmountable fear 348
 intoxication and withdrawal 347
 mitigation grounds 348–50
 serious addiction 348–9
 temporary mental disorder 346–7
 violent emotion 349–50, 351
Spencer, John 31
St Helena/Acension/Tristan Da Cunha 219
St Lucia 225
Stark, Evan 70, 74
state of mind and time in domestic violence 87
State of Washington v. *Yvonne L. Wanrow* 95
State v. *Shane* 122–3
Stephen, J.F. 155
Stewart 188
Stingel 85, 116
subjective test
 evidence of 86–9
 Republic of Ireland 158–9
subjectivised provocation plea 194
substance use disorder 191
 See also intoxication
suddenness requirement, removal of 45, 67–8, 86
suicide pacts 163, 271
Sullivan, Bob 66
supra-legal duress in Germany 258

Tadros, Victor 200

Tandy 186–7, 189
temporary mental abnormality
 Northern Ireland 163
 Spain 346–7
 See also abnormality of mental functioning
The Queen v. *Brian Walters* 215
The Queen v. *Shonovia Thomas* 215
'things done or said' and new objective test 57–9
three strikes law of New Zealand 287–9
Todorović 373
tolerance and self-restraint test 52–4, 57, 58–9, 61–2, 83–5
Tran 138–9, 146
triggering conduct 62–3
 'extremely grave' circumstances 89–90
 and new objective test 57–9
Trinidad and Tobago 224–5
trust, breach of, domestic violence as 73–5

understanding of nature of conduct, D's 32–4
unfitness to plead 33
United States
 availability of mitigations beyond murder 308–9
 burden of persuasion 294–5
 current rules 300–5
 desert distributive principle 305–9
 diminished responsibility 193–7, 299–300
 'extreme mental or emotional disturbance' 193–7, 291, 292–6, 300–2
 grading of homicides 291
 insanity mitigation 307–8
 judging reasonableness 295–6
 jury involvement 196
 'mental illness negating an offense element' 291, 296–9, 302–4
 mistaken beliefs due to intoxication 205
 Model Penal Code 49, 123, 143, 194, 293–5, 296–7, 302, 304
 protection from mentally ill people 298–9
 rationales for mitigations 305–9
 reasonable man test 293
 resistance to reform 304–5
 sexual infidelity killings 118–25
 subjectivised provocation plea 194
United States v. *Brawner* 298n37
unofficial categories in Scotland 169–70

Vasquez v. *The Queen* 227
Vehement Passions, The (Fisher) 87
via media and sexual infidelity killings 129–33
volitional test of insanity 154–5

Walton v. *The Queen* 36
warfare and mental disorder 381–2
Weatherston case 277–9
Weiss, Paul 92
White, Robin 363–4
Withey, Carol 136, 234–5
women
    discrimination against in law 233–4
    fear as new grounds for loss of self-control 79
    loss of self-control requirement under provocation 42
    See also domestic violence/abuse; gender; sexed evaluative standard
Wood 185, 187–8, 189
World Health Organisation 191n72

Yeo, Stanley 109

Printed in Great Britain
by Amazon